DISINFORMATION AND DIGITAL MEDIA AS A CHALLENGE FOR DEMOCRACY

DISINFORMATION AND DIGITAL MEDIA AS A CHALLENGE FOR DEMOCRACY

Edited by
Georgios TERZIS
Dariusz KLOZA
Elżbieta KUŻELEWSKA
Daniel TROTTIER

Managing Editor
Ioulia KONSTANTINOU

INTERSENTIA
Cambridge – Antwerp – Chicago

Intersentia Ltd
8 Wellington Mews
Wellington Street | Cambridge
CB1 1HW | United Kingdom
Tel: +44 1223 736 170
Email: mail@intersentia.co.uk
www.intersentia.com | www.intersentia.co.uk

Distribution for the UK and
Rest of the World (incl. Eastern Europe)
NBN International
1 Deltic Avenue, Rooksley
Milton Keynes MK13 8LD
United Kingdom
Tel: +44 1752 202 301 | Fax: +44 1752 202 331
Email: orders@nbninternational.com

Distribution for Europe
Intersentia Publishing nv
Groenstraat 31
2640 Mortsel
Belgium
Tel: +32 3 680 15 50
Email: mail@intersentia.be

Distribution for the USA and Canada
Independent Publishers Group
Order Department
814 North Franklin Street
Chicago, IL 60610
USA
Tel: +1 800 888 4741 (toll free) | Fax: +1 312 337 5985
Email: orders@ipgbook.com

Disinformation and Digital Media as a Challenge for Democracy

ISBN 978-1-78068-975-3
D/2020/7849/49
NUR 820

British Library Cataloguing in Publication Data. A catalogue record for this book is available from the British Library.

FOREWORD

Fooling All of the People All of the Time: Democracy in the Age of Fake News

Jamie SHEA*

George Orwell's statue stands outside BBC Broadcasting House in central London. His presence serves to remind this news organisation to have no fear of government or seek any favour in reporting accurately and fairly on the news of the day. Orwell's *Nineteen Eighty-Four* is the classic text on the role of propaganda and the distortion of language in reshaping reality. He famously said: 'if liberty means anything at all, it means the right to tell people what they do not want to hear'.[1] Yet Orwell associated the world of 'two and two made five'[2] with the totalitarian powers of the 1930s and 1940s. They had the Big Brother dictators who could control all the instruments of public messaging and the ability to screen out alternative sources of information that made an alternative reality possible. The first step towards taking away individual freedom and the capacity for independent action is to deprive people of their access to factual information. This was the hallmark of the communist states that sprang up in Eastern Europe during the Cold War years. As the Czech playwright, dissident and later president Vaclav Havel put it, largely echoing Orwell: 'if the main pillar of the system is living a lie, then it is not surprising that the fundamental threat to it is living in truth'.[3]

When the Berlin Wall came down 30 years ago, the change was largely attributed not to Western military pressure on the Soviet Union and its satellite states, but to the ultimate ability of the West to penetrate the Eastern firewall with its own news and information. The Germans from the East watched West German television and broadcasters such as the BBC World Service, Voice of

---

* Brussels School of Governance (BSG) (an alliance between the Institute for European Studies and Vesalius College), Vrije Universiteit Brussel (VUB), Belgium. Email: dr.jamiepshea@gmail.com.

1 G. ORWELL, 'The Freedom of the Press', *The Times Literary Supplement*, 15 September 1972, p. 1.

2 G. ORWELL, *Nineteen Eighty-Four*, Secker & Warburg, London 1949, p. 69.

3 V. HAVEL, *The Power of the Powerless: Citizens against the State in Central Eastern Europe*, translated by J. KEANE, Sharpe, Armonk, NY 1985, p. 40.

America and Radio Free Europe managed to reach large audiences despite the best efforts of the local regimes to jam them. The leader of Solidarity in Poland, Lech Wałęsa, attributed the success of this movement to the Catholic Church and Radio Free Europe. It is worth recalling this time 30 years later because it underlines, along with Orwell and Havel, that the best instrument of democracies in their quest to build a more cooperative and peaceful international order is their ability to be governed by the truth. This stems from open public debates that allow citizens to come to their judgements based on free debate and a lively, unconstrained news media that is willing and able to hold public figures to account. As former US Senator Daniel Patrick Moynihan famously put it: 'you are entitled to your own opinion, but you are not entitled to your own facts'.[4]

In order for democracy to function properly, there has to be a shared and agreed baseline of truth. If people divide into ideological bubbles and virtual reality ghettoes, believing only what they want to believe or are intellectually capable of believing, politics ceases to be an exercise of mutual persuasion and tolerance, and descends into a process of endless partisan manipulation and polarisation. It can reach a stage where information warfare prevents communities and countries from taking rational decisions and moving forward. At a time of mounting complexity, people retreat into simplistic and all-embracing conspiracy theories that remove the need for compromise or serious intellectual effort. Rather than inconvenient facts and intractable realities, the non-believer becomes the enemy to be denigrated. Society splits up into hostile tribes glaring at each other across their information firewalls. As every fact or version of events is instantly contested and every event is surrounded by scores of different explanations, society distances itself further from what Voltaire is believed to have defined as the essence of democracy when he said that he disagreed profoundly with someone, but would be willing to die to defend their right to say it.[5]

Instead, we now have the motto of the Russian state RT channel which calls on us to 'Question More' and accept that every official version of events put out by our own governments hides more truth than it reveals. If, as RT proclaims, it is being unfairly victimised because there is 'always another side of the story',[6] which it undertakes to reveal, then the view of the other person is not something to be respected and taken seriously, as Voltaire would have wished, but to be mistrusted and discounted. As Putin's numerous explanations for the shooting

---

4 Quoted in T.J. Penny, 'Facts are Facts', *National Review*, 4 September 2003, https://www.nationalreview.com/2003/09/facts-are-facts-timothy-j-penny.

5 Quoted in E.B. Hall, *The Friends of Voltaire*, Smith, London 1906, p. 199.

6 E. Peltier, 'Is France the Latest Front in Russia's Information War?', *New York Times*, 20 December 2017, https://www.nytimes.com/2017/12/19/world/europe/rt-france-television.html, p. 8.

down of the Malaysian Airlines flight over Ukraine in July 2014 demonstrate, multiple versions of the 'truth' do not establish a credible alternative version, but cast enough doubt on the most likely interpretation as to give free rein to all sorts of conspiracy theories – and allow Russia to hide behind the cloak of endless deniability. This is facilitated by a social media culture that enables the rapid and widespread distribution of these alternative realities, something we have come to call fake news. Like most fakes, fake news has a glitz and a drama that prosaic reality finds difficult to emulate. It does not have to be true to be newsworthy and shareable. According to recent research by the Massachusetts Institute of Technology, fake news stories move around the Internet and social media at six times the speed of accurate reporting.[7] As governments and media in democracies need to spend more and more time debunking conspiracy theories, they have less time to promote their own version of events. If truth is always relative or politically biased in favour of one side over another, why undertake the effort to discover it in the first place? Truth is what I want it to be.

How have the Western democracies squandered in the space of just a few decades since the end of the Cold War their most important asset in winning it: the capacity to identify and to set policy by the truth? How is it that the tables have been turned and the autocracies and authoritarians of this world now exploit information and human connectivity to undermine our system rather than us undermining theirs? If they are successful, it is not because they are the masters of spin and disinformation, but because they are able to exploit the weaknesses in our own way of receiving and handling information, and our own waning interest and commitment to truth in our politics and individual behaviour.

In the first place, the Internet and social media have made the act of communicating more important than the content of communication. Descartes once said 'I think, therefore I am',[8] but today this might be better rendered as 'I communicate, therefore I am'. The Internet and social media isolate us from our fellow human beings, as we spend hours looking at screens, but also force us to be in constant contact with more and more of them. Expressing opinions and sharing tweets and posts is the price of joining the global conversation and having a sense of self-worth, even identity. The pressure to conform to the prevailing trend is intense if we are not to be left behind. So, paradoxically, the Internet and social media, which were designed to allow the expression of individual views and preferences, end up shaping a conformist mass opinion. At the same time, the Internet has allowed everyone to communicate and be

---

7 S. Vosoughi, D. Roy and S. Aral, 'The Spread of True and False News Online' (2018) 259(6380) *Science* 1146–1151, doi: 10.1126/science.aap9559.

8 R. Descartes, *Discours de la méthode*, Paris 1637.

an influencer without needing to become famous and prominent, or gaining a voice through the traditional media. The American sociologist Clay Shirkey has expressed this well in the title of his book *Here Comes Everybody.*[9] Some may see this mass participation in social and political communication as a liberating act of direct democracy and individual empowerment. Yet it also brings to the fore the darker side of humanity in the form of hatred, vitriol, bigotry and the ability to say outrageous things without the constraint of attribution and accountability. Bigots seeing their own views expressed by others believe that they are now legitimate and lose their own inhibitions about speaking out. In this way, the Internet, which began in the 1980s as the exemplar of free speech beyond government control and censorship, has become the massive purveyor of fake news. State propaganda and disinformation, radicalisation and indoctrination and state monitoring and control – so much so that recently *Foreign Affairs* magazine published an article by Richard Clarke and Rob Knake, former senior US officials, calling on democracies to set up a new Internet with stringent participation standards, because they believe the current global Internet has become irredeemably contaminated with trolls, automated bots, misinformation and disinformation, made-up hashtag campaigns and proxies pretending to be someone else.[10]

If the Internet and social media were merely being used to spread messages of peace and cooperation or to make money from the ubiquitous advertisements based on 'hit' statistics, perhaps we could live with this. Yet, the evidence of recent years with deliberate interference in elections and disinformation campaigns designed to sow divisions and undermine trust in governments points to something darker. Governments have sponsored trolling campaigns to discredit opposition activities and intimidate journalists, suppress dissent, spread lies and manipulate public opinion. Researchers at the University of Oxford found evidence in 2019 of social media manipulation campaigns by governments or political parties in 70 countries, up from 28 in 2017.[11] According to the report, Facebook was the major platform where disinformation was disseminated. Although Russia is often pointed to as the major source of these campaigns, with its Internet Research Agency in St Petersburg and Advanced Persistent Threat cyber teams in the military intelligence service having received a lot of media attention, China has also become a major player. In August 2019,

9 C. Shirkey, *Here Comes Everybody: The Power of Organizing Without Organizations*, Penguin, London 2008.

10 R.A. Clarke and R. Knake, 'The Internet Freedom League. How to Push Back against the Authoritarian Assault on the Web' (2019) 98(5) *Foreign Affairs* 184–192, https://www.foreignaffairs.com/articles/2019-08-12/internet-freedom-league.

11 P. Howard and S. Bradshaw, 'The Global Disinformation Order: 2019 Global Inventory of Organised Social Media Manipulation', https://comprop.oii.ox.ac.uk/wp-content/uploads/sites/93/2019/09/CyberTroop-Report19.pdf.

Twitter and Facebook revealed a Chinese state-supported information operation launched globally to de-legitimise the pro-democracy movement in Hong Kong. Twitter announced that it had taken down 936 accounts that were 'deliberately and specifically attempting to sow political discord in Hong Kong'.[12] Facebook said that it had undertaken a similar operation, deleting fake accounts because it does not want its services 'to be used to manipulate people'.[13] The Oxford researchers also found that Russia and China are not alone in weaponising information to gain influence and intimidate opponents. India, Iran, Pakistan, Saudi Arabia and Venezuela were also cited in their report.

As we recognise the dangers that fake news poses – not just in undermining our democracies from within, but also encouraging our adversaries to conduct low-cost/high-gain hybrid warfare against us – the question becomes: what can we do to counter this trend and make ourselves more resilient? In recent times a number of response options have been identified.

First, there are calls for better regulation of the big tech and social media companies, particularly at a time when 'deep fakes' (video or audio clips that literally put words into somebody's mouth) are becoming more widespread and sophisticated. We can debate at length whether giving people the tools to disseminate free speech to a wide audience outweighs the downside of hate speech and over-reliance on a few dominant and centralised information platforms (Google, Facebook, Amazon, etc.). Yet, we cannot dispute the fact that words have consequences and that the tech platforms cannot abdicate their responsibility with simplistic invocations of the right to free speech or that they are mere transmitters of messages with no responsibility for their content and impact, especially at a time when the majority of users are getting their news from social rather than traditional media. There must be a middle way between accepting the benefits of mass access to high-tech communication and hate speech as a regrettable but unavoidable consequence. Public policy needs to find that middle ground, for as Martin Luther King once said: 'Rarely do we find men who willingly engage in hard, solid thinking. There is an almost universal quest for easy answers and half-baked solutions. Nothing pains some people more than having to think.'[14] Admittedly, social media companies have started to face up to the problem of fake news and misuse of their platforms. In response to public concerns about their enormous power to shape the public psyche, they have introduced more stringent algorithms to weed out fakes and hate speech, and to employ more fact-checkers and to be more sensitive to privacy issues. The question is: can they and should they do more? Should regulation be voluntary

12 https://blog.twitter.com/en_us/topics/company/2019/information_operations_directed_at_Hong_Kong.html.

13 https://newsroom.fb.com/news/2019/08/removing-cib-china.

14 M.L. King, *Strength to Love*, Fortress, Philadelphia 1963, p. 2.

or imposed? Is the EU model of data protection and fines for abuse better than the US model of a voluntary public/private sector dialogue?

Next, there is the question of the traditional media. It has suffered at the hands of the Internet and the social media that have accustomed consumers to free content and the expectation that quality journalism can be provided free of charge. Lacking advertising revenue and subscribers, many great newspapers have folded or been forced entirely online. Budgets for foreign news coverage or muck-raking and investigative journalism have dwindled. In an age of fake news, some newspapers have benefited, like *The New York Times*, which has seen its readership increase as people hanker after reliable, quality journalism. This is not to say that traditional journalism can be restored to its former position and format; it has to adapt to the digital age just like the rest of us. Yet democracy depends on the Fourth Estate and having a broad spectrum of real journalism, which is independent of monopoly business ownership and political influence and control. The question is: without the state owning or subsidising newspapers, TV and radio or online traditional media, what can public policy do to make it easier for traditional quality media to survive and even thrive in the fake news environment? How can it be made more financially viable and safeguarded from political bullying and interference in an age when fake news is increasingly news that politicians do not like and any news is true if it works in their favour?

Another issue concerns political culture. Democracies do themselves no favours when they allow their leaders to demonise TV channels and newspapers as 'enemies of the people' and call on their supporters to forcibly eject journalists from political rallies. Nor do they help themselves when they hold votes, like the Brexit referendum in the UK in 2016, with the public being uninformed, misinformed and generally confused about the issue at hand and with lies and distortions dominating the media debate. Yet this referendum was the most consequential decision in British politics since the end of the Second World War. In an age when political leaders are successful because of their celebrity status rather than the breadth and depth of their intellects, the public is becoming far too forgiving of lies and exaggerations as if these are now a normal part of the political game (and the opposition does it too, right?). *The Washington Post* regularly publishes a survey of the lies and falsehoods spoken by US politicians and these extend well beyond the current White House.[15] Yet few political careers are ended by these fabrications, which are inexcusable in an age when everything can be fact-checked instantaneously on Google. Churchill once said that 'in wartime, truth is so precious that she should always be attended by a bodyguard of lies',[16] but we are not in wartime. Fake news and disinformation

15 Cf. https://www.washingtonpost.com/graphics/politics/trump-claims-database.

16 W. Churchill, *The Second World War, Volume V: Closing the Ring*, Houghton Mifflin, Boston 1952, p. 338.

will never be countered if democratically elected leaders are their main purveyors and beneficiaries. The good example has to come from the top and the notorious liars and deceivers must be punished at the ballot box. Yet this not only requires a free and vibrant press but also the engagement of civil society more generally. Politicians will pay more respect to the truth when they understand that it is in their interests to do so. Again, what measures and instruments are available to us to combat post-truth politics?

Finally, there is the question of the weaponisation of information as a tactic of hybrid warfare. Because it is below the level of a classical armed attack, provoking a robust, even military response, hybrid warfare is an attractive method for adversaries to test and undermine the resilience of democracies. The Russian interference in the 2016 US presidential election has sounded the alarm bell. Democracies are improving their intelligence gathering and situational awareness, strengthening their cyber-defences and learning from each other's experiences. Gaps and vulnerabilities are being plugged. RT, Sputnik and other purveyors of false reporting are being fined and the Baltic States are even setting up a Russian-language TV station as an alternative to the pervasive presence of Russian stations in the region. Both NATO and the EU have established units to spot and counter fake news campaigns,[17] and centres of excellence, such as that of NATO in Riga[18] and the joint EU-NATO centre in Helsinki,[19] are bringing these two institutions together with the academic and non-governmental organisation (NGO) communities to analyse the trends and identify the best practices. NGOs like the Digital Forensics Lab at the US Atlantic Council[20] and Bellingcat[21] in the UK have performed sterling service in unmasking the organisations and individuals behind the disinformation campaigns. Again, the question is: are these efforts sufficient and commensurate to the challenge of state interference? What more should governments, NATO and the EU do to make such campaigns less attractive and no longer a relatively cost-free instrument of great power competition?

A famous saying from 19th-century American politics, which is often attributed to Abraham Lincoln, states that 'you can fool all of the people some of the time and some of the people all of the time. But you cannot fool all of

---

17 The EU's European External Action Service (EEAS) has established task forces to deal with fake news and disinformation campaigns, e.g. StratCom East and StratCom South. In turn, NATO has something similar in its Press and Media Service devoted to – in NATO parlance – 'myth busting and setting the record straight'.

18 NATO Strategic Communications Centre of Excellence, Riga, Latvia, https://www.stratcomcoe.org.

19 European Centre of Excellence for Countering Hybrid Threats, Helsinki, Finland, https://www.hybridcoe.fi.

20 https://www.atlanticcouncil.org/programs/digital-forensic-research-lab.

21 https://www.bellingcat.com.

the people all of the time'.[22] It would be pleasant to think that democracies will always wake up to their threats – internal and external – and heal themselves in good time before it is too late. Yet today the virtual gulag that China is placing around its Uighur population or the use of information technology and big data to impose a social credit and control system on its citizens, laws in Russia to disconnect itself from the Internet and India's recent total isolation of Kashmir from the outside world by severing all communication links underscore the power of the information weapon to crush the open society and reduce individuals to the status of mere subjects. This is not what the empowerment of humanity via the Internet and social media promised us. Yet, it is not too late to find public policy solutions which can restore information technologies to their original role of facilitators of democracy rather than their undertakers. But the timeframe is closing and we need these solutions sooner rather than later.

This is why the present volume of expert analyses bringing together many academics arrives at just the right time. It aspires to deepen our understanding of the dangers of fake news and disinformation, but also charts well-informed and realistic ways ahead. To my mind, it is certainly one of the most comprehensive and useful studies of this topic to date and I recommend it to the general reader as much as to the policy-maker as a reliable guide and mentor.

Brussels
October 2019

[22] Although this saying has been more reliably attributed to a number of other 19th-century US politicians and the earliest reference is to a Frenchman, Jacques Abbadie, who lived in the 17th century.

INTRODUCTION

'They All Hear "Ping" at the Same Time'*

Georgios TERZIS, Dariusz KLOZA, Elżbieta KUŻELEWSKA
and Daniel TROTTIER**

Most people, in fact, will not take trouble in finding out the truth, but are much more inclined to accept the first story they hear.

– Thucydides,
History of the Peloponnesian War (5th century BC)

I.

This book is motivated, to a large extent, by some recent troubling developments in public discourse, namely the developments in information and disinformation practices. From the beginning of history, various and diverse means or channels of communication have been used to inform, misinform (unintentionally) and disinform (deliberately). However, in recent decades, the emergence and development of new information and communications technologies (ICT), combined with the ever-increasing digitalisation and globalisation of almost every aspect of modern life, among others, have opened up new and uncharted avenues to that end. This book therefore focuses on disinformation practices occurring with the help of digital media as these

* Kellyanne Conway, quoted in M.D. SHEAR, M. HABERMAN, N. CONFESSORE, K. YOURISH, L. BUCHANAN and K. COLLINS, 'The Power of Presidential Tweets', *New York Times*, 13 November 2019, pp. 6–7, https://www.nytimes.com/interactive/2019/11/02/us/politics/trump-twitter-presidency.html. All links in this Introduction are valid and accurate as of 28 November 2019.

** Georgios TERZIS: Brussels School of Governance (BSG) (an alliance between the Institute for European Studies and Vesalius College), Vrije Universiteit Brussel (VUB), Belgium. Email: Georgios.Terzis@vub.be; Dariusz KLOZA: Research Group on Law, Science, Technology and Society (LSTS), Vrije Universiteit Brussel (VUB), Belgium. Email: Dariusz.Kloza@vub.be; Elżbieta KUŻELEWSKA: Centre for Direct Democracy Studies (CDDS), Faculty of Law, University of Białystok, Poland. Email: ekuzelewska@gmail.com; Daniel TROTTIER: Erasmus School of History, Culture and Communication; Department of Media and Communication; Erasmus Universiteit Rotterdam (EUR), the Netherlands. Email: trottier@eshcc.eur.nl.

practices bring to the fore profound negative ramifications for the functioning of a democratic polity.

In particular, disinformation – nowadays frequently yet not uncontroversially labelled 'fake news',[1] 'alternative facts' or 'post-truth' in English (and imported therefrom to many other languages), 'nepnieuws' in Dutch or 'infox' in French – affects the values and principles on which many democratic polities, including the European integration project,[2] have been built, namely democracy *sensu largo*, the rule of law (*Rechtsstaat*) and the respect for fundamental rights. (This classical 'constellation of ideals that dominate our political morality' will be referred to, in this Introduction, simply as 'democracy'.)[3] Disinformation further affects many other aspects of public life, e.g. political and journalistic practices, all over the world – a development that appears to transcend cultural and political contexts.[4]

From a cursory look at recent history, the 2016 referendum on the departure of the United Kingdom (UK) from the European Union (EU)

---

1 E.C. Tandoc Jr., Z. Wei Lim and R. Ling, 'Defining "FakeNews". A typology of scholarly definitions', (2018) 6(2) *Digital Journalism* 137–153.

2 We understand Europe *sensu largo* – it is a patchwork of supranational arrangements of economic and political nature occurring on the European continent, of individual countries that partake in these arrangements as well as of their inhabitants, regardless of whether they are citizens or not. In geographical terms, this polity comprises the EU with the non-EU members of the European Economic Area (EEA), Switzerland and four microstates – Monaco, Andorra, San Marino and the Vatican City/Holy See – that partake with a varying degree in these policies. All of them but the Vatican City/Holy See are members of the Council of Europe (CoE). The Council of Europe, in turn, which is tasked with safeguarding and promoting democracy, the rule of law (*Rechtsstaat*), fundamental rights and social development, currently comprises – at the time of writing – 47 Member States, i.e. virtually all countries on European soil, with the notable exception of Belarus. Eventually, the EU is a much more closely integrated economic and political union of – at the time of writing – 28 Member States. Its main economic component – the internal market – has been open to four other countries – Norway, Iceland and Liechtenstein (linked thereto via the EEA Agreement) as well as Switzerland (linked through bilateral agreements). In parallel, at the regional level, there also exist a few politico-economic unions, such as the Benelux (Belgium, the Netherlands and Luxembourg) and a few loose, political alliances, such as the Visegrád Group (Poland, Hungary, the Czech Republic and Slovakia) or the Weimar Triangle (France, Germany and Poland). Let us borrow a commonly used phrase 'European integration project' to refer, for our purposes, to this patchwork of arrangements.

3 J. Waldron, 'The Rule of Law and the Importance of Procedure', in J. Fleming (ed.), *Getting to the Rule of Law*, New York University Press, New York 2011, p. 3. For the sake of clarity, it suffices to explain that both the rule of law and *Rechtsstaat* doctrines serve multiple purposes in a democratic polity and one of them is to channel the exercise of 'public power through law'. They achieve their goals in different manners and hence function differently, while sharing some common characteristics. The rule of law doctrine dominates on the British Isles, while the *Rechtsstaat* is dominant on continental Europe. Cf. e.g. G. Lautenbach, *The Concept of the Rule of Law and the European Court of Human Rights*, Oxford University Press, Oxford 2013, p. 18.

4 M. Moore, *Democracy Hacked*, Oneworld Publications, London 2018, pp. 246–272.

(the so-called 'Brexit') and the presidential elections that took place the same year in the United States (US) – and related alleged disinformation practices – have been perhaps the strongest reminder of the importance and the power of disinformation in society, sparking debates in academic, political and artistic circles, and beyond.[5] In the aftermath, 'post-truth' was declared the word of the year 2016 by, among others, Oxford Dictionaries.[6] Since then, 'fake news' has been attributed to, *inter alia*, fuelling the mob killings of five men in the Indian village of Rainpada. Real footage of a chemical attack in Syria was in this case falsely attributed to a nomadic tribe of alleged child abusers.[7] Nowadays, such stories are plentiful. Eventually, the *lapsus linguae* of Rudy Giuliani, lawyer to the incumbent US President, such as 'it's somebody's version of the truth, not the truth' or 'truth isn't truth' might be said to 'sum up the spirit' of the contemporary disinformation practices.[8] However, democratic polities are only at an early stage of understanding the implications of disinformation and digital media.

Consistent with the foregoing, the relations between democracy, on the one hand, and disinformation practices procured with the help of digital media, on the other hand, merit critical analysis and academic attention.

II.

1. Setting the Scene: Basic Concepts. This book focuses on a number of contested concepts, and first and foremost on 'disinformation', that is, following the *Oxford Dictionary of English*, 'false information which is intended to mislead, especially propaganda issued by a government organization to a rival power or the media',[9] for political, personal or financial reasons. The term 'disinformation' might be taken as a synonym for 'misinformation', the latter being 'false or inaccurate information,

5 A number of lengthy books have been written in the aftermath to better understand these developments. Besides the literature cited in this Introduction, cf. e.g. M. d'Ancona, *Post-truth: The New War on Truth and How to Fight Back*, Penguin, London 2017; J.W. Werner, *What is Populism?*, Penguin, London 2017; R. Eatwell and M. Goodwin, *National Populism: The Revolt against Liberal Democracy*, Pelican, London 2018; P. Pomerantsev, *This Is Not Propaganda: Adventures in the War Against Reality*, Faber & Faber, London 2019.

6 A. Flood, '"Post-truth" Named Word of the Year by Oxford Dictionaries', *The Guardian*, 15 November 2016, https://www.theguardian.com/books/2016/nov/15/post-truth-named-word-of-the-year-by-oxford-dictionaries.

7 T. McLaughlin. 'How WhatsApp Fuels Fake News and Violence in India', *Wired.com*, 12 December 2018, https://www.wired.com/story/how-whatsapp-fuels-fake-news-and-violence-in-india.

8 E. Pilkington, '"Truth isn't Truth": Giuliani Trumps "Alternative Facts" with New Orwellian Outburst', *The Guardian*, 19 August 2018, https://www.theguardian.com/us-news/2018/aug/19/truth-isnt-truth-rudy-giuliani-trump-alternative-facts-orwellian.

9 *Oxford Dictionary of English*, https://www.lexico.com/.

especially that which is deliberately intended to deceive'.[10] However, as many other commentators, we 'distinguish between misinformation as accidental falsehood and disinformation as deliberate falsehood'.[11] Both concepts stand in opposition to that of 'information', that is, 'facts provided or learned about something or someone'.[12] (Yet, 'information' is only one element of the 'knowledge pyramid', in which, hierarchically arranged, 'data precedes information, which precedes knowledge, which precedes understanding and wisdom'.[13] Nevertheless, there exist limits as to what might be known, to the certainty or quality of knowledge, etc.)[14]

The distinction between misinformation and disinformation, on the one hand, and information, on the other hand, is based on the concept of truth. 'Truth' is a foundational characteristic feature of 'facts' – i.e. things 'that [are] known or proved to be true', 'true' signifies 'in accordance with fact or reality', 'accurate or exact', or 'loyal or faithful'.[15] A 'lie', by contrast, is 'an intentionally false statement' and 'fiction' – 'something that is invented or untrue'.[16] 'Truth' has classically been defined as 'adaequatio rei et intellectus';[17] however, the very definition of truth carries multiple meanings.[18] Historians, anthropologists and philosophers have long established that what is true is not only geographically and timely bound, but also depends on the different types thereof. For example, Baggini distinguishes between religious/eternal, esoteric, authoritative, reasoned, empirical, creative, relative, powerful, moral and holistic truths.[19] Different institutions – such as the state, religious organisations, educational and scientific institutions or family – compete with each other and they will have different

10 *Ibid.*

11 B.C. Stahl, 'On the Difference or Equality of Information, Misinformation, and Disinformation: A Critical Research Perspective' (2006) 9 *Informing Science* 86.

12 *Oxford Dictionary of English.*

13 R. Kitchin, *The Data Revolution: Big Data, Open Data, Data Infrastructures and Their Consequences*, SAGE, London 2014, p. 10; cf. also H. Cleveland, 'Information as a Resource', *The Futurist*, December 1982, pp. 34–39.

14 Cf. e.g. S. Funtowicz and J. Ravetz, 'Science for the post-normal age' (1993) 25 *Futures* 739–755; A. Stirling, 'Precautionary Appraisal as a Response to Risk, Uncertainty, Ambiguity and Ignorance' in C.L. Spash (ed.), *Routledge Handbook of Ecological Economics*, Routledge, London 2017, pp. 267–277.

15 *Oxford Dictionary of English.*

16 *Ibid.*

17 Latin for 'adequacy of things and thoughts'.

18 As a digression, the Greek word for 'truth' is 'ἀλήθεια' (a-lethe-ia), meaning 'un-forgetfulness'. Already in 700 BC, Hesiod composed his monumental poem *Theogony*, in which he explained the genealogy of gods and the origins of the world, and reflected on the sense of importance of truth for the good functioning of organised society. According to him, the goddess Lethe, which is translated as oblivion or forgetfulness, has a very interesting etymology and relatives. Lethe's mother was Eris (Strife). Her brothers and sisters were Algeia (Pain), Machai (Battles), Limos (Famine), Phonoi (Murders) and Dysnomia (Disorder). Lethe's aunt was Apati (Deceit) and her grandfather was Chaos. See G. Antoniou, 'The Lost Atlantis of Objectivity' (2007) 46 *History and Theory* 92.

19 J. Baggini, *A Short History of Truth: Consolations for a Post-truth World*, Quercus, London 2017, pp. 11–105.

levels of power to establish the truth, depending on the issue (faith, health, the environment, defence, the economy, etc.). 'Post-truth', eventually, is an adjective 'relating to or denoting circumstances in which objective facts are less influential in shaping public opinion than appeals to emotion and personal belief'.[20]

This book is concerned with disinformation procured with the aid of 'digital media'. These media, defined most generally, refer to a set of technologies that individuals and other social actors use to communicate and coordinate with each other.[21] We understand this term to include both hardware, such as mobile devices, alongside software, such as applications and platforms. Although it is technically possible to consider television and radio as media that are digital, in practice the term 'digital media' is invoked in contradistinction to such forms of broadcasting. In other words, the scholarly and societal importance of 'digital media' lies in their ability to empower atypical media actors, such as those involved in media production who may lack formal credentials, training, skills, etc. – for example, laymen – to engage in activities previously restricted to media professionals, such as credentialed journalists.

Eventually, as a subset of 'digital media', we can identify 'social media platforms' as digitally mediated locations where a user base is compelled to submit information about themselves (including news items they may have read and opinions thereof) as well as consume information about others.[22] As digital environments, they may be understood as distinct from any given culture or jurisdiction. Yet, in practice, they can become deeply embedded and consequential for the diffuse contexts that they bring together. These platforms nowadays constitute perhaps the key environment in which disinformation practices take place.

2. Research and policy perspectives. What is important then is by whom and how disinformation is established in different societies, how and when it is consumed, and what kind of an impact it has on democracy. First, these new digital media alter the dynamics of disinformation by the three actors of political communication, namely politicians, media and even – these days – the public (citizen journalism). Politicians, for example, might tweet 'fake news' directly to their audience, then journalists working on 24/7 news circles reproduce them instantly and sometimes without the time to verify them, and the public forwards them to millions more of their online 'friends' on social media platforms. Similarly, a number of pieces of 'fake news' might be initiated by the media and

20 *Oxford Dictionary of English.*

21 W.L. Bennett and A. Segerberg, 'Digital Media and the Personalization of Collective Action: Social Technology and the Organization of Protests against the Global Economic Crisis' (2011) 14(6) *Information, Communication & Society* 770.

22 D. Trottier, *Social Media as Surveillance: Rethinking Visibility in a Converging World*, Ashgate, Farnham 2012.

even by citizens, and then have an impact on the media and even political agendas. Obviously, the credibility of those sources of disinformation varies widely,[23] depending on their institutional role, the mediatisation level of politics,[24] the specificities of the political system (majoritarian, proportional, etc.)[25] and the levels of media proliferation and audience fragmentation of different countries, among others.

Second, the nature and the timing of disinformation procured through digital media play a vital role. Communication and political science literature indicate that different types of disinformation practices pose different types and levels of challenges. More obtrusive stories pose different challenges compared to non-obtrusive stories, as well as sensational vs. non-sensational, more negative vs. less negative, widely covered vs. less covered stories, and stories about new issues vs. stories that have been in the public arena for some time. Moreover, research indicates that disinformation poses different challenges during different periods (e.g. election campaigns, emergencies).[26]

Finally, the impact of disinformation is to be distinguished between the three levels on the three different actors (political organisations, the media and the public). The impact might be on a 'purely' informational level, on an attitudinal level or – further – on a behavioural level. All these impacts are equally important and related, but are still different when these are considered as challenges to democracy. Thus, the relationship between disinformation and its effects on democracy is not straightforward. Given the debate in media and communication science on media effects for the past 70 years, during which the society moved from strong to minimal, to medium to conditional[27] and transactional effects (i.e. uses and gratification),[28] disinformation in certain cases might be an existential threat while in others – just a nuisance.

3. *The importance of facts and truth for the functioning of democracy, and the change of dynamics.* That the truth is essential for both private and public life has been known for centuries. Baggini, for example, observed that 'we all have a

---

23 W.L. Bennett and S. Iyengar, 'A New Era of Minimal Effects? The Changing Foundations of Political Communication' (2008) 58 *Journal of Communication* 707.

24 J. Strömbäck, 'Four Phases of Mediatization: An Analysis of the Mediatization of Politics' (2008) 13(3) *International Journal of Press/Politics* 228.

25 A. van Dalen and P. van Aelst, 'The Media as Political Agenda-Setters: Journalists' Perceptions of Media Power in Eight West European Countries' (2014) 37(1) *West European Politics* 42.

26 S. Walgrave and P. van Aelst, 'The Contingency of the Mass Media's Political Agenda Setting Power. Towards a Preliminary Theory' (2006) 56(1) *Journal of Communication* 88.

27 D.M. McLeod and G.M. Kosicki, *Media Effects: Advances in Theory and Research*, Routledge, New York 2009, pp. 228–251.

28 J.G. Webster, 'The Role of Structure in Media Choice: A Theoretical and Empirical Overview' in T. Hartmann (ed.), *Media Choice: A Theoretical and Empirical Overview*, Routledge, London 2009, pp. 221–233.

sense that truth is not merely an abstract property of propositions but somehow essential to living well. If your life turns out to have been built on nothing but lies, it is as though it has not been real'.[29]

In public life, one of the key ideas behind democracy is that – rationally speaking – free, equal and engaged citizens of a polity debate peacefully in order to convince their opponents and adversaries to their own viewpoint, with a view to eventually reaching a consensus and deciding on public affairs, for example, in the electoral process. Ideally, their decision should be rational and based on the best available information. It follows that this debate has to be based on facts and hence on truth. This debate is continuous and therefore democracy can be viewed as a process.[30] Many commentators discussed these building blocks of democracy and, for example, Popper recognised objective knowledge as a foundation of the proper functioning of democratic society.[31] Downs, in turn, favoured the rationalisation of social life,[32] where the decision-making process should rely precisely on the best available information. Finding the truth, according to Dahl, constitutes one of the basic conditions for democracy.[33] To that end, the media constitute an essential means to disseminate information for the purposes of such a democratic debate. Already in the 19th century, for example, while analysing the political and social system of the US, de Tocqueville argued for the local media to facilitate access to knowledge and to tell the truth instead of manipulating the facts.[34]

However, this debate has *not* always been based on facts and truth; instead, it has been frequently based on lies. Although not all lies are equal, lying has formed part of public – and private – life since the beginning of humanity. Furthermore, as Rosenfeld explains, the democratic idea of truth never quite lived up to its promise of influence by persuasion rather than force.[35] Nowadays, the 'post-truth' and related phenomena function as a new weapon of political manipulation. Trust in expertise and in institutions has declined, cynicism has risen and citizens are becoming their own information curators.[36]

---

29 J. Baggini, 'Is This Really a Post-truth World?', *The Guardian*, 17 September 2017, https://www.theguardian.com/lifeandstyle/2017/sep/17/is-this-really-a-post-truth-world.

30 Many commentators dealt with the concept of democracy. Cf. e.g. C. Tilly, *Democracy*, Cambridge University Press, Cambridge 2007.

31 K.R. Popper, *Conjectures and Refutations: The Growth of Scientific Knowledge*, Routledge, London 1963, p. 292ff; cf. also K.R. Popper, *Objective Knowledge: An Evolutionary Approach*, Clarendon Press, Oxford 1979.

32 A. Downs, *An Economic Theory of Democracy*, Harper, New York, 1957, p. 28.

33 R.A. Dahl, *On Democracy*, Yale University Press, New Haven 2008, pp. 27–28.

34 A. de Tocqueville, *Democracy in America*, Cambridge University Press, Cambridge 1862, pp. 212ff.

35 S. Rosenfeld, *Democracy and Truth: A Short History*, University of Pennsylvania Press, Philadelphia 2019, pp. 12–14.

36 Ch. Ireton and J. Posetti, *Journalism, fake news & disinformation: handbook for journalism education and training*, UNESCO, Paris 2018, p. 19, https://unesdoc.unesco.org/ark:/48223/pf0000265552.

To add to this complication, new phenomena and new means of disinformation, such as 'filter bubbles' – i.e. 'personal ecosystem[s] of information … catered by … algorithms to who they think you are'[37] – have emerged. In this example, 'filter bubbles' are driven by both a demand side and a supply side. On the demand side is the human predisposition to seek ideologically satisfying news that reinforces existing worldviews.[38] This results in the 'pleonastic excommunication' created by the plethora of the new media that cannibalise on the time devoted to traditional media consumption that is more likely to include fewer partisan views.[39] On the supply side is a new media business model that is based on an attention-seeking-and-maintaining digital advertising economy that is successful by maximising the servicing of that demand.[40] These supply and demand forces that constantly reinforce each other, in combination with the existing and even more extreme ideological segregation of friends and neighbours in most societies (those same friends and neighbours who have also replaced traditional editors of one's newsfeed),[41] create a vicious circle of polarisation. This makes a compromise – one of the basic premises of democracy – nearly impossible since the population does not share the same facts.

III.

This book is split into three parts. Part I is entitled 'Theoretical approaches to and the conceptualisation of disinformation'. This begins by providing an overview of various conceptual approaches to disinformation and its redefinition. It further examines their potentially threatening impact on the media, and – more broadly – on democracy. A recurring question is whether the fight against disinformation is one of the greatest challenges modern democracies face or whether it is merely an old phenomenon with 'new clothes'.

In Chapter 1, *Papakonstantinou* opines that the term 'fake news' is inherently wrong because 'news' are facts and facts either are (in which case they cannot be fake) or are not (in which case they are simply lies). However, the

---

37 L. Parramore, 'Eli Pariser on the Future of the Internet', *Salon*, 8 October 2010, https://www.salon.com/2010/10/08/lynn_parramore_eli_pariser.

38 W.L. Bennett and S. Iyengar, 'A New Era of Minimal Effects? The Changing Foundations of Political Communication' (2008) 58 *Journal of Communication* 707.

39 G. Terzis and K. Sarikakis, 'Pleonastic Excommunication in the European Information Society' (2000) 17(1–2) *Telematics and Informatics* 105.

40 E. Pariser, *The Filter Bubble: What the Internet is Hiding from You*, Penguin, London 2011, pp. 1–20.

41 M. Gentzkow and J.M. Shapiro, 'Ideological Segregation Online and Offline' (2011) 126(4) *Quarterly Journal of Economics* 1799.

streamlined use of the term shows that it is used mostly as an accusation against news (i.e. facts) that we either do not like *per se* or do not like the way they are presented. The only thing different from similar phenomena in the past is the Internet and its social media platforms that provide a suitable environment for the deployment of such 'fake news'. However, if we are to find any meaningful way of fighting against them, we need to understand them for what they are and fight against each case separately. *Papakonstantinou* concludes that 'fake news' deserves no special treatment and should not be the cause of any regulatory intervention.

Daubs demonstrates in Chapter 2 how the term 'fake news' has been redefined by the political right in order to de-legitimise the press. Whereas the press was once seen as the defender of the people and the mediator between the state and its populace, it now needs the populace to defend it at a time when public confidence in the press is at an all-time low. The combination of the deployment of 'fake news' as a combative term to marginalise journalists and the lack of confidence in the press represent a threat to press freedom, the ability for people to be informed and engaged citizens, and – hence – to democracy itself. However, the increasingly frequent attacks on the press and journalists work not only towards limiting the freedom of the press, but are also creating conditions in which journalists themselves are under threat. Through a discourse analysis of comments and online content from the incumbent US President and other government officials, combined with a comparative historical analysis, it is illustrated how the term 'fake news' has been reconfigured into the modern evocation of *Lügenpresse*, the German propaganda term meaning 'press of lies' used by the Third Reich.

In Chapter 3, *Klepka* analyses the problem of disinformation and its growing scale, with particular emphasis on 'fake news' as a new communication phenomenon. He indicates the threats to modern democracy posed by new phenomena in the area of mass communication. The main motive of the outlined concept is the presentation of successive sequences of information processing methods, which, together with technological progress, are increasingly distant from neutrality and the idea of reflecting reality. Over time, political bias, which has always been present in the media, began to use human natural predispositions and technical possibilities to create 'echo chambers' and 'filter bubbles'. The latest step in the development of the analysed trend is 'fake news', which, however, seems to be only the next stage in the discussed process and not its final stage. It seems that only adequate preparation to be an aware citizen and responsible consumer of media content can be an attempt to fight the ubiquitous tendency towards disinformation. The pursuit of opposition to disinformation is undoubtedly one of the greatest challenges facing modern democracies.

On the contrary, in Chapter 4, *Stocchetti* argues that (dis)information is not a threat to democracy, because the political regimes inspired by democratic values are based on epistemic and political grounds that neutralise the effects of involuntary or deliberate disinformation in both the social construction of reality and in the competition for control over the use of legitimate power. The main problem with the current debate about (dis)information and democracy is the possibility that undemocratic efforts to control the subversive effects of communicative freedom in the digital age may instrumentalise the genuine concern about the future of democracy. To disambiguate this element of ambivalence, four points are proposed. Amongst these, on the strength of democracy, he concludes that it primarily depends not on the quality of circulating information, but on the quality of its citizens or, more precisely, on the quality of their critical or hermeneutic competences and their resolve to use these competences to think and act on behalf of a shared notion of the public good. Without these competences and determination, there is no imaginable quality of information that can do the trick in their absence.

Chapter 5 investigates the legitimacy of representative democracy in relation to the communicative landscape staged by the digital revolution. *Lukkassen* concludes that it is not possible to have an honest and sincere representative democracy based on the precondition of communicating with the electorate using modern media. Political and ideological sincerity is no longer indisputable, since for his or her success, a politician depends mainly on factors which transform a people's representative into a media personality. The nature of the medium itself can also influence a discussion or even change its content through the dynamics between the media, velocity and space of communication. However, this does not imply that democracy cannot survive at all under these conditions. 'Democracy of the 19th century is urgently in need of an overhaul in order to be sincere and representative in the 21st century'.

In Chapter 6, *Farkas and Schou* systematically unpack and critically discuss contemporary 'post-truth' discourses and their democratic underpinnings. Instead of asking whether democracy really is suffering from a 'post-truth' crisis, they examine the discourses presenting this claim with a higher aim of interrogating the very real democratic struggles they contain and foreclose. Democracy is perceived as a truth-telling and rational project concerned with using facts as the foundation for consensus-based political decision-making. This widespread tendency – to take notions like truth, democracy and 'fake news' for granted – is criticised, as these terms are deeply politically and socially charged and constructed, instead of mere descriptions of the world. Instead of seeking to find supposedly 'real' or 'neutral' definitions of 'fake news' and 'post-truth', we need to investigate how they are mobilised as part of political conflicts. In the end, democracy is not just about truth alone; it is about the voice of the people and what they, collectively, deem appropriate.

Barnhizer and Candeub claim in Chapter 7 that 'fake news' undermines the rule of law as it derives its strength from appetitive and emotional responses in a manner that threatens both the rule of law and the willingness of a political culture to trust in democratic institutions. The phenomenon of 'fake news' furthermore creates an atmosphere in which political, media and cultural elites can exploit fear about 'fake news' in order to forward their own agenda and undermine democratic institutions in favour of political control by a dominant oligarchic elite. The authors place the 'fake news' concern in the context of media regulation in the US. Looking to the 'elite theory', i.e. a generalisation that nearly all political power is held by a relatively small and wealthy group of people sharing similar values and interests, and mostly coming from relatively similar privileged backgrounds, they suggest that the 'fake news' cause may simply be an elite power grab that US media regulation would allow. The authors eventually suggest that the best response is 'dynamically prophylactic', including active training of individuals to recognise fake news, encouraging greater freedom of expression and resorting to state-based structural responses (e.g. antitrust enforcement).

Part II is entitled 'Experience of dealing with disinformation'. Moving from theory to practice, in this section the authors report insights from dealing with 'fake news', including case studies from the EU and the US. In particular, the authors share experience and their aftermath on why 'fake news' thrives during financial and political crises, whether disinformation was a tool for implementing a security policy and a method for fact-checking.

In Chapter 8, *Terzis* shares the phenomenon of non-coverage of certain 'truths' using Greece as a case study: during the financial crisis (2009–2018), in its coverage, some of the most important 'true stories' failed to be covered substantially and consistently by the media. The lesson from the Greek financial crisis non-coverage only confirms that in today's globalised economy and political world, liberal democracies cannot afford to neglect having an independent press that oversees at governments' and businesses' possible abuses. A discredited economy and democracy would be restored only through an independent and critical press that reports the 'true stories' that matter, raising the above issues high in its media agenda and thus the public agenda, and forcing politicians to act on these and, by doing so, safeguarding democratic systems.

Experiences from Greece continue in Chapter 9, where *Sitistas* examines how and why 'fake news' has thrived in Greece, especially during the financial crisis, what it is based upon and what is its impact on the Greek society. Greece was already poorly equipped to battle 'fake news' even before 2009. The economic crisis that started 10 years ago managed to make things even worse. Greeks already had a poor understanding of what caused the economic downfall and would rather attribute it to 'foreign powers' than accept even the slightest responsibility. From that point on, it was rather easy for 'fake news' and conspiracy theories to thrive, along with populist politicians who took advantage of Greeks' insufficiency of media literacy and populistic journalism. As Greece is emerging from 10 years of harsh austerity, the challenges remain the same.

In Chapter 10, *Reilly* discusses the impact of digitally manufactured 'fake news' upon political institutions in Northern Ireland. He does so by first presenting an in-depth study of digital disinformation in 'post-conflict' Northern Ireland through the development of a historical understanding of the role of propaganda in a deeply divided society. Next, he provides an overview of the emergent literature on information disorders, as well as efforts to mitigate their impact on democratic processes, such as elections and referenda. In the absence of a political consensus on how to address complex conflict-legacy issues, digital disinformation looks likely to persist and possibly thrive in this deeply divided society. In this regard, the current genre of information disorders may have much more in common with the 'propaganda war' than was previously thought. A holistic approach towards addressing the causes of information disorder in deeply divided societies such as Northern Ireland is finally proposed.

In Chapter 11, *Waśko-Owsiejczuk* stresses the use of disinformation and appeal to fear as a tool for implementing US security policy during the presidency of George W. Bush. The terrorist attacks carried out on 11 September 2001 in the US created a convenient situation for the introduction of controversial policy pursued by the White House in the months following the attacks, which in other circumstances would not gain acceptance from either US society or the wider international community. As it turned out, the Bush administration presented false information, thus disinforming the public. The author examines the purpose of the use of disinformation and appeal to fear by the Bush administration and the impact that these tools had on public opinion. The analysis demonstrates how disinformation and propaganda are equally common in democratic polities and not only in authoritarian regimes.

In Chapter 12, *Pavleska, Školkay, Zankova, Ribeiro and Bechmann* present a study that for the first time integrates theory and practice directly from the 'battlefield' of fact-checking and combating 'fake news' into a novel method for the performance analysis of fact-checking organisations. This method includes the development of a scheme of performance indicators and the definition of a taxonomy of fact-checking systems, supported by an already-existing conceptual framework. The results from the study reveal huge space for improvements in the workflows and the functionality of fact-checkers, and lead to the extraction of a set of recommendations in this regard. The authors make a proposal for a general research and assessment framework for the performance of fact-checking organisations, including the successful 'marriage' between technology, and human efforts and public involvement. In addition to its practical value, this study also contributes to the development of pressing and crucial societal issues and the improvement of democratic and governance processes.

Part III is entitled 'Solutions to deal with disinformation and their critique' and moves the focus of the book to various proposed measures to deal with disinformation.

Chapter 13 maps the current approach of the European Court of Human Rights (ECtHR) towards disinformation through the inductive analysis of its case law thus far. *Hanych and Pivoda* identify the Court's approach to various aspects connected with 'fake news', especially those related to the freedom of expression, and the right to respect for private and family life. Even though the ECtHR has not yet had the chance to decide on a case directly concerning the issue of the proliferation of 'fake news', the Court has already commented on several substantial aspects of such a phenomenon. However, the examination of a procedural side of judicial protection indicates some potential drawbacks, such as the identification of a probable perpetrator, which in the cases of the creation or spread of false information online can be *per se* impossible. Furthermore, even if national legal systems provided for certain kind of appropriate remedies, taking legal action might still be unpredictable and be a rather financially and time-consuming means.

In Chapter 14, *Pauner Chulvi* discusses the influence of 'fake news' that is placed online and is spread quickly through social media on the freedom of expression and information in the context of the US presidential election, the Brexit referendum and the Colombian referendum (2016). The rise of 'fake news' is becoming a threat to democracy as it constitutes an assault on the right to information, pluralism and the right of citizens to freely form an opinion. Whereas 'fake news' has always existed, what is new now is its proliferation on social media and the lack of any quality control. The challenge posed by 'fake news' requires a paradigm shift in terms of the tools used to combat it and the entities involved in the battle. Fact-checking, the cornerstone of journalistic practice, needs to be the main tool employed in this endeavour. In terms of which parties should be involved in combating 'fake news', calls have been made for the state, the media, technology firms and civil society to participate.

In Chapter 15, *Kuczerawy* examines the European Commission's *Code of Practice on Disinformation*, published in September 2018, from the perspective of the right to freedom of expression. Enlisting private sector organisations to regulate the speech of their users may seem to be a practical and efficient approach, as it places the burden directly on the platforms who have the technical means to address the problem. However, it could also be seen as the passing of a 'hot potato' instead of approaching the problem responsibly and in accordance with the rule of law. Thus, it should be accompanied by safeguards that could introduce balance and elements of due process: an addition of a notification, counter-notification or an appeal mechanism, which may slow down the process of handling disinformation. However, a strive for efficiency should not trump the respect for fundamental rights. Disinformation is a highly complex problem that requires a proportionate and evidence-based response. Imprudent solutions that do not sufficiently safeguard fundamental rights may lead to unintended consequences on legitimate public debate and – more broadly – democracy.

In Chapter 16, *Meyer, Marsden and Brown* review policy initiatives relevant to illegal content and disinformation online with the aim of understanding how they recommend the use of technology as a solution to curb certain types of content online and what they identify as the necessary safeguards to limit the impact on the freedom of expression. In particular, they analyse commitments and recommendations made towards transparency in technical interventions aimed at decreasing the prevalence of disinformation. All these policy developments and EU initiatives fit into a context where social media platforms and search engines are increasingly scrutinised on competition grounds and are called upon to take their share of responsibility in the online ecosystem. This chapter thus identifies the limits of technology in regulating content online and makes policy recommendations aimed at ensuring independent, transparent and effective appeal and oversight mechanisms in the use of technology for online content moderation.

In Chapter 17, *Archontis* takes into consideration the implications that arise from spreading disinformation online and examines not only the factors that led to that problem but also what tools are available to ascertain the accuracy of any given claim encountered online or in the print media. Such tools are available online, and their presentation can help every aspiring fact-checker in developing his or her own skills and improving his or her experience through practice. While writing an original news story may be already a laborious task, fact-checking a published article may sometimes be even more demanding. The purpose of this chapter is not to provide a full documentation of the tools used by every fact-checker, but to help the reader fully grasp the extent of the problem faced regarding 'fake news'.

In Chapter 18, *Bentzen* builds on the Cambridge Analytica scandal to highlight the lack of definition of 'scientific research' in the General Data Protection Regulation (GDPR) – in the context of personal data processing – as a potential threat to democracy. By not defining 'scientific research', the GDPR may extend the privilege such research affords to an unintentionally broad range of actors and activities; for example, data and research based thereon might be used to manipulate. As an utmost consequence, this could endanger the research participants' legitimate expectations, trust and fundamental rights, and could even endanger democracy as such. Unless the 'scientific research' term is clarified, it cannot function as a safeguard against misuse. There are three main potential assessment criteria to be derived from ECtHR and Court of Justice of the European Union (CJEU) jurisprudence for the assessment of 'scientific research', although these do not provide sufficient safeguards by themselves: the role of the legal entity, the role of the persons carrying out the activity, and quality standards, including the scientific method applied. Adding an additional criterion – an ethical assessment including respect for context, inspired by Nissenbaum's theory on contextual integrity – will make the definition of 'scientific research' more robust against cases such as Cambridge Analytica, protecting both individuals and democracy.

Finally, in Chapter 19, an invited contribution, *Kritikos* comments on the COVID-19 pandemic and a related 'infodemic', ongoing at the time of writing, and analyses, from the lens of democracy, the early efforts to combat mis- and disinformation in the context of scientific uncertainty. *Kritikos* first overviews the development of the problem, sketching its political, cybersecurity and (public) health dimensions, as well as its consequences for democracy. He presents and evaluates the relevant initiatives to tackle mis- and disinformation at both international and EU levels. He continues by examining some of the informational challenges associated with the spread of falsehood surrounding the pandemic, such as its novelty, and scarcity and the (still) unverified nature of much of the available information. Finally, *Kritikos* offers a few preliminary suggestions as how to deal with the 'infodemic' while maintaining the democracy standards to which Europe has always adhered to. In particular, he argues that, with regard to fact-checking, *inter alia*, a strive for efficiency should not trump the respect for fundamental rights and freedoms, and for scientific and ethical plurality. In parallel, open-science and data-sharing initiatives should complement the existing efforts to combat the pandemic and the 'infodemic'.

IV.

Taking into account the topics discussed in the chapters in this volume, we cannot help but offer a few points of reflection on the past, present and future of disinformation, digital media and democracy in the European integration project.

First, disinformation in public life is nothing new, as for example *Papakonstantinou* and *Daubs* also argue in this volume. Misinformation (unintentional) and disinformation (intentional), deception, manipulation, populism, bigotry, conspiracy theories, censorship, propaganda, indoctrination and other distortions of the truth have all been part of democracy since its conception in Athens. (In fact, of any political system.) Already in Plato's *Republic*, Socrates proposes the 'noble lie', i.e. a fundamental myth of identity and belonging, and of a social structure, that those who govern disseminate to their subjects to organise them, maintain harmony and sustain a political system, e.g. a democracy.[42] (Speaking even more broadly, civilisations have been

42 BAGGINI, *supra* note 19, p. 35. Cf. also M. SCHOFIELD, 'The Noble Lie' in G.R.F. FERRARI (ed.), *The Cambridge Companion to Plato's Republic*, Cambridge University Press, Cambridge 2007, pp. 138–164.

built on the humane ability to 'create and spread fictions'.)[43] In ancient Rome, in the same vein, it was observed that 'populus vult decipi, ergo decipiatur'.[44] The 20th century alone witnessed, *inter alia*, the ascent of the Soviet propaganda machine, including the daily newspaper *Pravda* (Russian for 'truth'),[45] alongside the Third Reich's *Lügenpresse* (German for 'press of lies') and even a mantra of propaganda to 'repeat a lie often enough and it becomes the truth', frequently attributed to the Nazi Joseph Goebbels. Development of technology magnified the effects. At the time, thanks to the 'rapidly evolving medium of radio', never before 'had such an efficient tool of manipulating the human mind been available'.[46] At the dawn of 21st century, disinformation and propaganda are still used to implement controversial security policy, for example in the post-9/11 US, as *Waśko-Owsiejczuk* explained, and the 'infodemic' challenges decision-making not only in (public) health matters, as *Kritikos* observed. In addition to altering the present, rewriting the past took place not only in Orwell's *Nineteen Eighty-Four*, but in reality too – for example, Leon Trotsky, Nikolai Yezhov and perhaps many more communists were erased from Soviet history, having turned from allies into enemies of the state.[47] The contemporary functioning of the media, even in (still) democratic polities in Europe (e.g. Hungary and Poland),[48] manipulation and the (rhetorical) attacks on media freedom, even in the US,[49] are cases in point.

It might require further investigation, but it seems that the term 'fake news' appeared, in the context of the media, for the first time in a 1894 issue of American humour magazine *Puck*, which published Opper's cartoon 'The Fin de Siècle Newspaper Proprietor'.[50] The drawing shows a 'newspaper owner, possibly meant to be Joseph Pulitzer, sitting in a chair in his office next to an open safe where "Profits" are spilling out onto the floor; outside this scene are many newspaper reporters … rushing to the office to toss their stories onto the printing press'.[51] In the picture, one of these stories bears the label 'fake news'.

---

43 Y.N. Harari, *21 Lessons for the 21st Century*, Jonathan Cape, London 2018, pp. 233–234.

44 Latin for 'people want to be deceived, so let them be deceived'.

45 P. Groenendijk, 'An Analysis of the Bolshevik Propaganda and its Effectiveness' in I.S. Grat (ed.), *Człowiek przeciwko człowiekowi. Filozofia, polityka i prawo a systemy totalitarne*, Prymat, Białystok 2008, pp. 75–90.

46 M.K. Albright, *Fascism: A Warning*, Harper Perennial, New York 2018, pp. 40–41.

47 M. Gessen, 'The Photo Book That Captured How the Soviet Regime Made the Truth Disappear', *The New Yorker*, 15 July 2018, https://www.newyorker.com/culture/photo-booth/the-photo-book-that-captured-how-the-soviet-regime-made-the-truth-disappear; D. King, *The Commissar Vanishes: The Falsification of Photographs and Art in Stalin's Russia*, Metropolitan Books, New York 1997.

48 Cf. e.g. Council of Europe, 'Platform to Promote the Protection of Journalism and Safety of Journalists', (2015–), https://www.coe.int/en/web/media-freedom.

49 Cf. e.g. Reporters without Borders, 'World Press Freedom Index' (2017–), https://rsf.org/en/united-states.

50 F.B. Opper, 'The Fin de Siècle Newspaper Proprietor' (1894), Library of Congress, Washington DC, https://www.loc.gov/resource/ppmsca.29087.

51 *Ibid.*

Since this illustrates that disinformation and similar practices are 'nihil novi sub sole',[52] and in line with the tradition that the *European Integration and Democracy* book series has established, this very detail has been reproduced on the front cover of this book. Furthermore, the colour of the cover – yellow – alludes to the so-called 'yellow press', i.e. the 'use of lurid features and sensationalized news';[53] this also emerged in the late 19th century, alongside the term 'fake news'.[54]

Second, disinformation and similar practices only seem new due to their form, dynamics and – as we discussed in the opening paragraph – their (frequently controversial) label: these have changed over time, as observed in this volume by *Klepka*. The essence nonetheless has remained. Each era brings new tools of communications, from word of mouth, to the written word, to the invention of the telegraph, the computer and the Internet. The characteristics of the latter means of communication, such as speed, cost and the overcoming of the constraints of distance, brought completely unprecedented dimensions of disinformation. One of the paradoxes of these new technologies, and of digital media that run thereon, is that of a possibility of their use for both licit and illicit ends. These technologies might be at the same time fostering and suppressing democracy, as illustrated in this book by *Lukkassen, Farkas and Schou*, and *Barnhizer and Candeub*. For example, while digital media make it possible to express oneself more freely, e.g. during an electoral campaign, they also allow for direct contact between politicians and the citizenry. As a case in point, Twitter has become the prime communication tool of the incumbent US President. Kellyanne Conway, Donald Trump's advisor, once commentated that it was 'the democratisation of information' as '[t]hey all hear "ping" at the same time'.[55] Yet, this is only one side of the coin. At times, this direct contact – which is quite a novelty – comes at the expense of democracy, for example the integrity of the electoral process, due to manipulation, as this does not help the citizenry making an informed choice,[56] as *Pauner Chulvi*, *Bentzen* and *Reilly* highlighted.

Third, 'fake news' is often characterised as a tension between traditional media and new actors on social media platforms, while we contend that we

52 Latin for 'nothing new under the sun'.

53 Cf. B. Duignan, 'Yellow Journalism', *Encyclopaedia Britannica*, 2019, https://www.britannica.com/topic/yellow-journalism.

54 W.J. Campbell, *Yellow Journalism: Puncturing the Myths, Defining the Legacies*, Praeger, Westport 2001.

55 Cf. *supra*, first asterisked note.

56 Cf. e.g. C.J. Bennett, 'Voter Databases, Micro-targeting, and Data Protection Law: Can Political Parties Campaign in Europe as They Do in North America?' (2016) 6(4) *International Data Privacy Law* 261; C.J. Bennett and S. Oduro-Marfo, *Privacy, Voter Surveillance and Democratic Engagement: Challenges for Data Protection Authorities*, Office of the Information Commissioner, Wilmslow 2019, https://privacyconference2019.info/wp-content/uploads/2019/11/Privacy-and-International-Democratic-Engagement_finalv2.pdf.

are in fact not witnessing a radical displacement of 'the usual suspects' behind disinformation campaigns. Although it is tempting to position conventional journalism and related practices like fact-checking as endangered by the growth of digital platforms, in practice there is a more symbiotic relationship between these entities, a factor also observed by *Archontis*. Journalists do not work against social media platforms, but rather within and through these.[57] We may speculate that both conventional press and digital platforms are beholden to a business model that privileges attention-seeking and audience engagement, which in turn redirects traditional news values and selection criteria, and consequentially journalism and media ethics. Moreover, even when the so-called political or journalistic 'nobodies' are responsible for prominent 'fake news' incidents, as in the cases presented by *Terzis* and *Sitistas*, their efforts are more likely to inform existing press or political activity rather than simply disrupt it.[58]

Fourth, this book has probably proven the obvious that the efforts thus far to combat disinformation and similar practices have been rather insufficient, as, for example, *Pavleska et al.*, *Meyer et al.* and *Kritikos* have argued. (Some commentators, however, question the very need for any reaction to 'fake news', e.g. *Papakonstantinou*, or argue that the problem lies elsewhere, e.g. *Stocchetti*, or suggest to first use the existing avenues, e.g. *Hanych and Pivoda*.) While many other commentators have lamented that, in the public sphere, 'falsehoods are mostly left unchallenged',[59] reactions to the new dimensions of disinformation, if undertaken, can range from some organisational and technological measures to regulatory ones. While the former include fact-checking (human-led, technology-led, or both) and journalism education,[60] the latter can vary from mild self-regulation (e.g. codes of practice) to even outright imposition of (criminal) liability (e.g. laws against defamation, unfair commercial practices, competition or against Holocaust denial). However, as *Stocchetti* observes, a high level of education of the citizenry – in addition to (digital) media literacy, their awareness, critical hermeneutic competences, resilience, vigilance and some common sense – is frequently proposed as one of the remedies.[61] At times, journalists and media outlets are reminded that truthfulness is one of the basic principles of any code of ethics of their profession and that members of a democratic polity would normally expect them to observe these codes

57 A. Chadwick, *The Hybrid Media System: Politics and Power*, Oxford University Press, Oxford 2017, p. 4.

58 D. Trottier, 'Scandal Mining: Political Nobodies and Remediated Visibility' (2017) 40(6) *Media, Culture & Society* 903.

59 P. Oborne, 'It's not just Boris Johnson's lying. It's that the media let him get away with it', *The Guardian*, 18 November 2019, https://www.theguardian.com/commentisfree/2019/nov/18/boris-johnson-lying-media.

60 Cf. Ireton and Posetti, *supra* note 36.

61 Cf. e.g. H. Davies, 'Why Education is the Only Antidote to Fake News', *The New Statesman*, 19 February 2018, https://tech.newstatesman.com/guest-opinion/education-antidote-fake-news.

of conduct.[62] In addition, many media outlets have a reputation to uphold. Most scholars and policy-makers seem to agree. Nevertheless, more is needed. Some commentators argue further that more time and effort should be invested in combating disinformation by, for example, diversifying sources of information and their comparison, and be willing to pay credible media outlets for reliable information.[63] However utopian the suggestion that all the citizenry should be informed about all public affairs, that an individual has sufficient means to verify what is true and what is not, and that total transparency is feasible or even desirable, the fight against disinformation should be perceived as a shared competence among various actors and a combined use of different tools (cf. *Pauner Chulvi*).

Fifth, some of the efforts to fight disinformation might conflict with the values and principles on which a democratic polity has been built, as many commentators have stressed, and – in this volume – *Stocchetti*, *Kuczerawy*, *Bentzen*, and *Hanych and Pivoda* have struck the same chord. As the most mundane examples, the proposed 'ministries of truth' would challenge due process (fair trial) or, simply, falsehood might be afforded protection set by the freedom of expression (free speech),[64] hence largely limiting the intellectual and legal 'arsenal' to fight disinformation. Yet, human rights law – at least in theory – already has known the solution to how two or more seemingly conflicting human rights, freedoms or – broadly – individual and collective interests can walk together. To a large degree, the answer lies in the principle of proportionality. Proportionality 'was originally used by Euclid as a mathematical term relating to relationships between shapes' and was subsequently transposed to other domains, such as aesthetics and ethics.[65] In law, its contents have been formulated in different terms by commentators and courts alike.[66] Typically,

---

62 S.R. Stroud, 'Pragmatist Media Ethics and the Challenges of Fake News' (2019) 34(4) *Journal of Media Ethics* 178–192. Cf. also e.g. P.L. Plaisance, *Media Ethics: Key Principles for Responsible Practice*, SAGE, London 2013; Society of Professional Journalists, *SPJ Code of Ethics*, 2014, https://www.spj.org/ethicscode.asp; Accountable Journalism, *Codes of Ethics: International*, n.d., https://accountablejournalism.org/ethics-codes/international; The New York Times, *Ethical Journalism. A Handbook of Values and Practices for the News and Editorial Departments*, n.d., https://www.nytimes.com/editorial-standards/ethical-journalism.html.

63 Harari, *supra* note 43, pp. 243–244.

64 Cf. e.g. D. Voorhoof, *Freedom of expression, the media and journalists: case-law of the European Court of Human Rights*, Council of Europe, Strasbourg 2015; D. Voorhoof, 'Same standards, different tools? The ECtHR and the protection and limitations of freedom of expression in the digital environment', in M. O'Boyle, *Human Rights Challenges in the Digital Age: Judicial Perspectives*, Council of Europe, Strasbourg 2020, pp. 11–46.

65 K. Macnish, 'An Eye for an Eye: Proportionality and Surveillance' (2015) 18(3) *Ethical Theory and Moral Practice* 529, 534.

66 D. Lindsay, 'The Role of Proportionality in Assessing Trans-Atlantic Flows of Personal Data' in D. Svantesson and D. Kloza (eds.), *Trans-Atlantic Data Privacy Relations as a Challenge for Democracy*, Intersentia, Cambridge 2017, p. 53.

proportionality could involve up to four components: legitimacy (i.e. whether a measure intended to intrude on the enjoyment of a human right has an 'objective of sufficient importance');[67] suitability (i.e. whether it is 'capable of achieving' this legitimate objective);[68] necessity (i.e. 'whether the measure is necessary to achieve that aim, namely, whether there are other less restrictive means capable of producing the same result'); and proportionality *stricto sensu* (i.e. 'even if there are no less restrictive means, it must be established that the measure does not have an excessive effect' on one's interests).[69] If found disproportionate on any of these ground, the measure would be – at minimum – illegal.

Sixth and finally, as Huxley once observed, 'life is short and information endless'.[70] Fighting disinformation and related practices is a strenuous exercise, particularity due to an abundance of information and, in parallel, a scarcity of resources to address the problem. The COVID-19 'infodemic' is a case in point, which has further highlighted the difficulties in decision-making in both public and private life. The dilemma is precisely how to act in situations in which 'facts are uncertain, stakes high, values in dispute and decisions urgent'.[71] Traditionally, science is meant to offer a solid base, largely quantitative predictions, for informed decision-making and the abundance of falsehoods stands in opposition thereto. But in a situation like a pandemic, such predictions are limited and unreliable (as e.g. information is novel, out of context, incomplete and, frequently, unverified), and, in the 'infodemic', furthermore, truth is difficult to distinguish from falsehood or e.g. sensationalism, while decisions must be taken immediately. This recalls Funtowicz and Ravetz's 'post-normal' approach to science, and more concretely using it for decision-making processes.[72] Post-normal science joins the chorus of appeals to democratise science and resort to an 'extended peer community', i.e. 'the knowledge base should be pluralized and diversified to include the widest possible range of high-quality potentially usable knowledges and sources of relevant wisdom, without enforcing the demand for science to speak with one voice'.[73] Admitting the uncertainty of information, post-normal science emphasises not only the gathering of information (i.e. public participation), but also its quality assurance through multiple channels.

---

67 F. Urbina, 'A Critique of Proportionality' (2012) 57(1) *American Journal of Jurisprudence* 49.

68 M. Klatt and M. Meister, 'The Structure of the Proportionality Test' in *The Constitutional Structure of Proportionality*, Oxford University Press, Oxford 2012, p. 8.

69 T. Tridimas, *The General Principles of EU Law*, Oxford University Press, Oxford 2013, p. 139.

70 A. Huxley, *Brave New World Revisited*, Random House, London 1958, p. ix.

71 S.O. Funtowicz and J.R. Ravetz, 'Science for the Post-Normal Age' (1993) 25(7) *Futures* 744.

72 *Ibid.*, 739–755.

73 D. Waltner-Toews, A. Biggeri, B. De Marchi, S.O. Funtowicz, M. Giampietro, M. O'Connor, J.R. Ravetz, A. Saltelli and J.P. Van Der Sluijs, 'Postnormal pandemics: Why COVID-19 requires a new approach to science', *STEPS*, 25 March 2020, https://steps-centre.org/blog/postnormal-pandemics-why-covid-19-requires-a-new-approach-to-science/.

Hence, it is not surprising that *Kritikos* argues, *inter alia*, for a coordinated opening up of the repositories of non-personal data (open data) and more robust fact-checking by media outlets, governed by a dedicated ethical code of conduct.

To conclude, in order for a democratic polity – in which we see intrinsic value – to exist and flourish, it is indispensable that it is based on facts and, hence, truth, to the extent that these are attainable. There are instances in which fiction, satire and fantasy are desirable, such as an artistic recounting of events that may exaggerate or even fabricate certain details. Disinformation and comparable practices, in contrast, negatively affect the very building blocks of democracy. As undesirable as this may be, misinformation (unintentional) and disinformation (intentional) may always feature in democratic debate, within the boundaries of the freedom of expression (free speech) and decency, yet falsehood must be clearly designated as such each time. In other words, the citizenry has to be able to distinguish fact from fabrication and – to paraphrase the epigraph – not to 'to accept the first story they hear', suggesting the need for a capacity to draw distinctions (e.g. true vs. false, fact vs. interpretation) as well as for media literacy that extends beyond being technologically savvy. Having heard 'ping', the choice of what to do with clearly labelled 'fake news' nonetheless rightly remains in their hands.

Democracy is a process and it would be naïve to conclude it was a given. Already in 1939, Dewey argued against the belief that 'democratic conditions automatically maintain themselves, or that they can be identified with fulfilment of prescriptions laid down in a constitution'.[74] In his Foreword to this volume, *Shea* too observes that 'it would be pleasant to think that democracies will always wake up to their threats – internal and external – and heal themselves in good time before it is too late'.[75] Instead, as Voltaire's Candid said, 'il faut cultiver notre jardin'[76] and this 'cultivation' would *also* mean a 'commitment to culture, to civility, to civilization itself'[77] so that 'a piece of the world' is improved.[78] All in all, democracy is an Aristotelian habit to be practised and upheld equally by those who govern and by those who are governed.[79]

---

74 J. Dewey, *Freedom and Culture*, G.P.Putnam's Sons, New York 1939, p. 34.

75 J. Shea, 'Foreword' in this volume.

76 French for 'We must cultivate our garden'. Voltaire, *Candide*, Le Livre de Poche, Paris 1997 [Geneva 1759], p. 167.

77 R. Darnton, 'To Deal With Trump, Look to Voltaire', *The New York Times*, 27 December 2018, p. 19, https://www.nytimes.com/2018/12/27/opinion/trump-voltaire-enlightenment.html.

78 W. Berry, *Think Little: Essays*, Conterpoint, Berkley 1972.

79 Cf. 'For by acting as we do in our dealings with other men, some of us become just, others unjust; and by acting as we do in the face of danger, and by becoming habituated to feeling fear or confidence, some of us become courageous, others cowardly […] So it is not unimportant how we are habituated from our early days; indeed it makes a huge difference or rather all the difference'. Aristotle, *Nicomachean Ethics*, tr. R. Crisp, Cambridge University Press, Cambridge 2000, 1103b.

In this process, for such a democratic polity to face disinformation practices procured with the aid of digital media, there exists many responses, and e.g. hermeneutic competences and the principle of proportionality – of course – are not the sole ones. In the previous volume in this book series, devoted to irregular migration as a challenge for democracy,[80] its editors have argued, *inter alia*, for the adherence to the foundational values and principles on which the European integration project – and any other democratic polity – was founded, for an ethical reflection, and for greater decency and moderation of public debate in dealing with irregular migrants.[81] It is not surprising that these postulates recall a 'commitment to […] civilization' and are equally valid for dealing with disinformation and digital media.

V.

The book constitutes the sixth volume in the *European Integration and Democracy* series. The Series was launched in 2011 and is edited at the Centre for Direct Democracy Studies (CDDS) at the Faculty of Law of the University of Białystok, Poland. Since 2014, Belgo-British Intersentia publishes our series. Each volume in the series tackles a pressing issue that is of utmost importance for the European integration project and – at the same time – that poses a challenge to the values and principles on which Europe has been built. Thus far, our books have discussed, through that lens, the elections to the European Parliament, transatlantic data privacy relations or – as already mentioned – irregular migration.[82]

Like all volumes published thus far in this series, this book originated from a call for papers, which was issued in May 2018. Yet again, the response received was indicative of the topicality of the chosen subject matter and the variety of interest from academic scholarship. Authors originate from academia, government institutions and non-governmental organisations, among others.

---

80 Cf. *infra*, section V.

81 E. Kużelewska, A. Weatherburn and D. Kloza, 'Introduction: Asking Big Questions: Migrants *Ante Portas* and What to Do with Them?' in E. Kużelewska, A. Weatherburn and D. Kloza (eds.), *Irregular Migration as a Challenge for Democracy*, Intersentia, Cambridge 2018, pp. xiii–xlvii.

82 The previous volumes are: E. Kużelewska and D. Kloza (eds.), *The Challenges of Modern Democracy and European Integration*, Aspra-JR, Warsaw 2012; E. Kużelewska and D. Kloza (eds.), *Elections to the European Parliament as a Challenge for Democracy*, Aspra-JR, Warsaw 2013; E. Kużelewska, D. Kloza, I. Kraśnicka and F. Strzyczkowski (eds.), *European Judicial Systems as a Challenge for Democracy*, Intersentia, Cambridge 2015; D.J.B. Svantesson and D. Kloza (eds.), *Trans Atlantic Data Privacy Relations as a Challenge for Democracy*, Intersentia, Cambridge 2017; E. Kużelewska, A. Weatherburn and D. Kloza (eds.), *Irregular Migration as a Challenge for Democracy*, Intersentia, Cambridge 2018.

All submissions underwent a double-blind peer-review process in accordance with the Guaranteed Peer-Review Content (GPRC) scheme, a standard used by Intersentia.[83] As a result of this careful selection process, 18 submissions were accepted. In addition, given the impact of the COVID-19 pandemic on the functioning of a democracy, in April 2020 we welcomed an invited contribution that reflects on the on-going developments and their relations to mis- and disinformation, which resulted in an essay included in this book as the 19th chapter.

This book does not aspire to be a monograph on disinformation, digital media and democracy in Europe; rather, it is an anthology compiling diverse yet rich academic and professional comments on a wide range of pressing issues within a broad topic. It is meant to contribute to a debate and a reflection on the condition of our democracy at the dawn of the third decade of the 21st century. We have been exceptionally careful in allowing the authors to express their ideas as they wish to, with only minimal editorial intervention. Our intention is that this book will act as both a commentary and reference work, and will reach not only our fellow academics in Europe and beyond, but also policy-makers, civil society organisations and journalists concerned with disinformation, digital media and democracy in Europe and beyond.

VI.

Every book is a product of a team. We thank the authors and congratulate them for their contributions, which have been further bolstered by the apt and thought-provoking Foreword. For that, our gratitude and thanks go to Jamie Shea, former official of the North Atlantic Treaty Organization (NATO), where he held the posts of spokesperson (1993–2000) and Deputy Assistant Secretary General for Emerging Security Challenge (2010–2018), among others. We particularly thank Ioulia Konstantinou, Managing Editor of the series. We thank the peer-reviewers who have all contributed to ensuring the scientific quality and integrity of this volume. We have received with gratitude further help from Rocco Bellanova, Simone Casiraghi, Laura Drechsler and Mihalis Kritikos. Once again, we thank Intersentia, and our publisher Tom Scheirs and editor Rebecca Moffat. Finally, we gratefully acknowledge the financial support received for this book from the Vrije Universiteit Brussel (VUB) and the Faculty of Law of the University of Białystok.

Brussels – Białystok – Rotterdam
November 2019–April 2020

[83] Cf. http://www.gprc.be/en/content/what-gprc.

CONTENTS

LIST OF ABBREVIATIONS

AfD	Alternative für Deutschland (Germany)
AFP	Agence France-Presse
ANEL	Ανεξάρτητοι Έλληνες – Independent Greeks (Greece)
BBC	British Broadcasting Corporation
CCTV	Closed Circuit Television
CDC	Centre for Disease Control and Prevention (US)
CFREU	Charter of Fundamental Rights of the European Union
CIA	Central Intelligence Agency (US)
CJEU	Court of Justice of the European Union
CNN	Cable News Network (US)
COVID-19	Coronavirus disease 2019
DUP	Northern Ireland's Democratic Unionist Party
EBU	European Broadcasting Union
EC	European Commission
ECB	European Central Bank
ECDC	European Centre for Disease Prevention and Control
ECFR	European Council of Foreign Relations
ECHR	European Convention on Human Rights
ECtHR	European Court of Human Rights
EDPB	European Data Protection Board
EDPS	European Data Protection Supervisor
EEAS	European External Action Service
EP	European Parliament
EPI-WIN	Information Network for Epidemics
ERT	Ελληνική Ραδιοφωνία Τηλεόραση – Hellenic Broadcasting Coorporation (Greece)
EU	European Union
FCC	Federal Communications Commissions
FM	Frequency Modulation
FT	Financial Times
FYROM	Former Yugoslav Republic of Macedonia (North Macedonia)
GDPR	General Data Protection Regulation
HLEG	High-Level Expert Group on Fake News and Online Disinformation

HR	High Representative of the Union for Foreign Affairs and Security Policy
ICT	Information and Communications Technologies
IFCN	International Fact Checking Network
IMF	International Monetary Fund
IRA	Internet Research Agency (Russia)
ISIS	Islamic State of Iraq and Syria
ISSPs	Information Society Service Providers
IT	Information Technology
KGB	Komitet Gossoudarstvennoï Bezopasnosti – State Security Committee (Russia)
LPPU	Loyalist Peaceful Protest Updater
MLA	Member of the Legislative Assembly
MP	Member of the Parliament
MSM	Mainstream Media
NATO	North Atlantic Treaty Organization
NGO	Non-Governmental Organisation
NHS	National Health Service
NIO	Northern Ireland Office
NPI	National Policy Institute
OECD	Organisation for Economic Co-operation and Development
Pegida	Patriotische Europäer gegen die Islamisierung des Abendlandes – Patriotic Europeans against the Islamisation of the West
PHEIC	Public Health Emergency of International Concern
PIRA	Provisional Irish Republican Army
PISA	Program for International Student Assessment
PNAS	*Proceedings of the National Academy of Sciences of the USA*
PSNI	Police Service of Northern Ireland
RCCE	Risk Communication and Community Engagement
SABAM	Société d'Auteurs Belge – Belgische Auteurs Maatschappij – Belgian Association of Authors, Composers and Publishers
SAS	Special Air Services
SDLP	Socialist Democratic and Labour Party (Northern Ireland)
SEEBRIG	South-Eastern Europe Brigade
SEME	Search Engine Manipulation Effect
SGP	Staatkundig Gereformeerde Partij – Christian Reform Political Party (the Netherlands)
SOMA	Social Observatory for Disinformation and Social Media Analysis
SYRIZA	Συνασπισμός Ριζοσπαστικής Αριστεράς – Coalition of the Radical Left (Greece)
TEU	Treaty on European Union
TFEU	Treaty on the Functioning of the European Union

UK	United Kingdom
UN	United Nations
UNESCO	United Nations Educational, Scientific, and Cultural Organization
US	United States
UUP	Ulster Unionist Party
UVF	Ulster Volunteer Force
VVD	Volkspartij voor Vrijheid en Democratie – Liberal Political Party (the Netherlands)
WDF	Wardle and Derakhshan Framework
WHO	World Health Organization

LIST OF CONTRIBUTORS

Stamos Archontis
Ellinika Hoaxes, Greece

Daniel Barnhizer
College of Law, Michigan State University, United States

Anja Bechmann
School of Communication and Culture – Media Studies, Aarhus University, Denmark

Heidi Beate Bentzen
Centre for Medical Ethics and Norwegian Research Center for Computers and Law, University of Oslo, Norway

Ian Brown
Research ICT Africa, South Africa

Adam Candeub
College of Law, Michigan State University, United States

Michael S. Daubs
School of English, Film, Theatre and Media Studies, Victoria University of Wellington, New Zealand

Johan Farkas
School of Arts and Communication, Malmö University, Sweden

Monika Hanych
Faculty of Law, Masaryk University, Czech Republic

Rafał Klepka
Faculty of Social Sciences, Pedagogical University of Cracow, Poland

Dariusz Kloza
Research Group on Law, Science, Technology and Society (LSTS), Vrije Universiteit Brussel (VUB), Belgium

Ioulia Konstantinou
Research Group on Law, Science, Technology and Society (LSTS), Vrije Universiteit Brussel (VUB), Belgium

Mihalis Kritikos
Scientific Foresight Unit (STOA), Directorate-General for Parliamentary Research Services (EPRS), European Parliament, Belgium

Aleksandra Kuczerawy
Centre for IT and IP Law (CiTiP), KU Leuven, Belgium

Elżbieta Kużelewska
Centre for Direct Democracy Studies (CDDS), Faculty of Law, University of Białystok, Poland

Sid Lukkassen
Dr. Sid Consultancy, the Netherlands

Christopher T. Marsden
@SussCIGR Sussex Centre for Information Governance Research, University of Sussex, United Kingdom

Trisha Meyer
Brussels School of Governance (BSG) (an alliance between the Institute for European Studies and Vesalius College), Vrije Universiteit Brussel (VUB), Belgium

Vagelis Papakonstantinou
Research Group on Law, Science, Technology and Society (LSTS), Vrije Universiteit Brussel (VUB), Belgium

Cristina Pauner Chulvi
Faculty of Legal and Economic Sciences, University Jaume I, Castellon, Spain

Tanja Pavleska
Laboratory for Open Systems and Networks, Jozef Stefan Institute (JSI), Slovenia

Marek Pivoda
Faculty of Law, Masaryk University, Czech Republic

Paul Reilly
Information School, University of Sheffield, United Kingdom

Nelson Ribeiro
School of Human Sciences, Universidade Católica Portuguesa (UCP), Portugal

Jannick Schou
Independent researcher, Denmark

Jamie Shea
Brussels School of Governance (BSG) (an alliance between the Institute for European Studies and Vesalius College), Vrije Universiteit Brussel (VUB), Belgium

Thanos Sitistas
Ellinika Hoaxes, Greece

Andrej Školkay
School of Communication and Media (SCM), Slovakia

Matteo Stocchetti
Department of Culture and Media, Arcada University of Applied Sciences, Finland

Georgios Terzis
Brussels School of Governance (BSG) (an alliance between the Institute for European Studies and Vesalius College), Vrije Universiteit Brussel (VUB), Belgium

Daniel Trottier
Erasmus School of History, Culture and Communication; Department of Media and Communication, Erasmus Universiteit Rotterdam (EUR), the Netherlands

Ewelina Waśko-Owsiejczuk
Department of History and International Relations, University of Białystok, Poland

Bissera Zankova
Media 21 Foundation, Bulgaria

PART I

THEORETICAL APPROACHES TO AND THE CONCEPTUALISATION OF DISINFORMATION

1. SHOULD WE BE AFRAID OF *FAKE NEWS*?

Vagelis Papakonstantinou*

1. INTRODUCTION

Over the past few years, 'fake news' has dominated public discourse, being blamed for anything from affecting electoral results to manipulating consumers, ultimately giving online social media and Internet platforms a bad name. However, I believe that there is no such thing as 'fake news'. For the reasons explained below, I think that 'fake news', a contradiction in terms, is merely a neologism, a clever catchphrase used today by politicians in order to swiftly discredit opponents and at the same time wink at their voters. The only thing different from similar phenomena in the past is the Internet and its champions, online social media platforms, that provided a suitable environment for the deployment of such 'fake news'. However, this to me being merely an early-adoption problem that will be addressed once these new technological phenomena have been properly assimilated by society and social sciences, I believe that legislators, no matter how concerned they are in the short term, should sit this one out.

2. WHAT IS 'FAKE NEWS' EXACTLY?

According to the *Cambridge Dictionary*, 'fake news' is 'false stories that appear to be news, spread on the Internet or using other media, usually created to influence political views or as a joke'[1] – in short, therefore, false stories. 'False', in turn, means 'not real, but made to look or seem real'.[2] Thus, ultimately, 'fake news' seems to be unreal but plausible made-up stories.

* Research Group on Law, Science, Technology and Society (LSTS), Vrije Universiteit Brussel (VUB), Belgium. Email: evangelos.papakonstantinou@vub.be.

1 Definition of 'fake news' from the *Cambridge Advanced Learner's Dictionary & Thesaurus*: https://dictionary.cambridge.org/dictionary/english. All links in this chapter are valid and accurate as of 8 January 2020.

2 *Ibid.*

If only things were so simple. In the UK, the Digital, Culture, Media and Sport Committee of the House of Commons identified the following types of 'fake news' in its relevant report: fabricated content, manipulated content, imposter content, misleading content, false context of connection, satire and parody. It also added 'micro-targeted messaging', before finally recommending that the term be completely abandoned and either 'misinformation' or 'disinformation' used instead.[3] The futility of suggesting new terms to replace a globally used term aside, this is useful to demonstrate that, in fact, when we are talking about 'fake news', we do not really know what we are talking about.

The difficulty of actually defining the term 'fake news' is identified by another prominent lexicographer, Merriam-Webster. 'Fake news' has entered its watchlist, but the entry in its actual dictionary has been rejected: 'The reason fake news is unlikely to be entered in our dictionary anytime soon is that it is a self-explanatory compound noun – a combination of two distinct words, both well known, which when used in combination yield an easily understood meaning. Fake news is, quite simply, news ("material reported in a newspaper or news periodical or on a newscast") that is fake ("false, counterfeit").'[4]

I think that the cause for confusion is that 'fake news' is a contradiction in terms. News refers to facts, i.e. something that really happened.[5] Facts cannot be fake – fake facts are simply lies. As such, 'fake news' refers either to facts or lies.

2.1. 'FAKE NEWS' AS LIES

Lies are easy to deal with; in fact, there is not much to discuss about them, because all the relevant issues have been resolved by law. In broad terms, if one lies, then one is potentially committing a crime for which one can be called to answer in court.

So, if I post on the Internet that 'Martians have invaded earth'[6] or that 'politician X received a trillion euros by businessman Y',[7] then in all likelihood

---

3 House of Commons. Digital, Culture, Media and Sport Committee, *Disinformation and 'Fake News': Interim Report*, 24 July 2018.

4 'Word We're Watching: The Real Story of Fake News', https://www.merriam-webster.com/words-at-play/the-real-story-of-fake-news.

5 '"News" usually refers to novel information about relatively recent affairs.' M. Schudson, 'News' in T.P. Vos, F. Hanusch, D. Dimitrakopoulou, M. Geertsema-Sligh and A. Sehl (eds.), *The International Encyclopedia of Journalism Studies*, John Wiley & Sons, New York 2018.

6 As was done, apparently inadvertently, by Orson Welles in 1938 (see 'Welles Scares Nation', *History.com*, 21 August 2018, https://www.history.com/this-day-in-history/welles-scares-nation). It should be noted that the Federal Communications Commission did investigate the programme, but found that no law was broken.

7 Confirmed 'fake news' stories during the 2016 US presidential election, all unfavourable to Hillary Clinton, included 'Clinton was in "very poor health" due to a serious illness'; 'Pope Francis endorsed Trump'; 'Clinton approved weapons sales to Islamic jihadists,

I am committing a crime. Politician X or the public prosecutor can sue me. If they choose not to do so for whatever reason,[8] the fact remains that my lies are assessable under a criminal law procedure. On the other hand, if my lies are not assessable under a criminal law procedure, then in all likelihood they should be accepted as facts – unless one wishes to enter the field of morality where, however, practical answers are rarely to be found. Consequently, it is distracting to name such stories 'fake news'. They are simply lies.

2.2. 'FAKE NEWS' AS (NUANCED) FACTS

Facts are far more difficult to deal with. Instead of endlessly theorising, let's work with a well-known fact: the Greeks won the 10-year Trojan War. There must be a million ways of reporting this news item, even if one does not wish to go to the lengths that Homer did in his *Iliad.* The simplest way would be to say exactly that, and in fact that was indeed the case back then, when Agamemnon had arranged for *phryctoriae* to immediately transmit the news to Mycenae. However, the simplest of additions in the above sentence immediately colours its meaning: the *brave* Greeks won the 10-year Trojan War, or the Greeks won the *brutal* 10-year Trojan War, or the Greeks won the 10-year war against the *brave* Trojans.

What would be 'fake news' in the above formulations? If we follow the Select Committee's line of thinking, potentially each and every news report that added even a single word to the above sentence. The truthfulness of each resulting sentence could be challenged. However, this is exactly what adjectives do; they 'clarify' a noun, but not everyone is obliged to agree with them.

Is this really a problem? Who would be interested, and pay for, a simple transmission of the information that the Greeks won the Trojan War? There may be some merit (or even huge financial value)[9] in the single-line transmission of pure facts, for example, in stock exchange markets or when experts make exchanges within their closed circles; however, this is not how most humans function. We want explanation, we want an analysis, even gossip, if it is available. In short, we want a story. A mere transmission of the fact is not interesting.

---

including ISIS' (M. Martin, 'Fake News Stories May Have Cost Hillary Clinton This Many Obama Voters', *Metro USA*, 4 April 2018).

8 'Fake news' on social media may have originated in the town of Veles in North Macedonia (M. Wendling, 'The (Almost) Complete History of "Fake News"', *BBC Trending*, 22 January 2018).

9 According to popular legend, 'Nathan Mayer Rothschild made "a million" or "millions" out of his early information about the Battle of Waterloo', apparently another 'fake news' (under the nuanced facts context) story (see https://en.wikipedia.org/wiki/Nathan_Mayer_Rothschild#Waterloo_legend).

A newspaper or a news agency offering a fact-only type of service to the public would quickly go out of business.

However, because they use adjectives and other literary tools, stories, ever since Homer invented them, are inevitably subjective. Even if the author has no hidden agenda or aims to cause no particular effect, his or her ideas, personality and views will still inevitably find a way to infiltrate the text. Readers, on their part, will also apply their own understanding on what they read or hear – very rarely do two people understand the exact same meaning from the same text.

At any event, what is important here is that these stories are based on a fact, i.e. something that really happened. They are, consequently, facts – nuanced facts perhaps, as will always inevitably be the case, but still facts.

3. WHY THE FUSS THEN?

If 'fake news' merely denotes lies or facts and is in any case referring to a usual, ancient human trait, why then today's witch-hunt against 'fake news'? To me the most plausible explanation is its use in modern politics. The prominent example of course is set by President Trump (not my choice – the Select Committee referred expressly to his case).[10] President Trump has become famous by calling all news items that he does not like 'fake news'. His example has been imitated by countless politicians, admittedly of the populist stream, across the globe.[11]

However, if 'fake news' were simply lies, politicians would have sued and won in court. If they don't, it is only because this 'fake news' is 'fake news' of the second type: that of nuanced facts. In democracies, these do not give rise to claims in court, but politicians do need to fight them in any case, hence the made-up term 'fake news'.

Therefore, 'fake news' in today's politics is nothing more than a made-up term used to denote facts that politicians do not like but can do nothing about. It is the same as 'bullshit' or 'horseshit' cried on the streets; however, it has the immense benefit of being usable on camera. Its ingenuity lies in the fact that it is double-edged, being able both to discredit swiftly on-camera and at the same time pander to populist voters' basic instincts against established news agencies and journalism.

After all, 'fake news' usage in politics in order to smear opponents is as old as humanity: Athenians were the first faced with it when all of their Hermai were vandalised prior to the Sicilian expedition. The process has never stopped since, whenever people's opinions needed influencing. During the last century,

10 *Supra* note 3, p. 7.

11 See P. Gerbaudo, 'Social Media and Populism: An Elective Affinity?' (2018) 40(5) *Media, Culture & Society* 745; R.R. Barr, 'Populists, Outsiders and Anti-Establishment Politics' (2009) 15(1) *Party Politics* 29.

this was made scientific through the advent of propaganda.[12] Propaganda was a term mostly used during the tumultuous 20th century and the preferred communication tool of its wizards was radio, cinema and all other new means of mass communication.[13] A lot of time has passed since then, and now people treat what they hear on the radio or TV critically. Admittedly, regulation has intervened too, with broadcasting regulatory authorities operating in practically all countries. However, it has been a long process and one should bear in mind that Facebook just celebrated its 15th anniversary.[14]

4. THE INTERNET EFFECT

So how is today's 'fake news' any different than what Cleon, or other demagogues, did since the days of Athenian democracy?[15] I believe that the Internet makes all the difference. This is clear when one reads, for example, the Select Committee's report: a few pages on the problem definition followed by dozens of analyses on micro-targeting of people over the Internet. So, 'fake news' is not actually the problem; the Internet is.

Given that the Internet is relatively new (no more than 30 years old), it has not yet been assimilated as a social phenomenon either by individuals or by social sciences – in the EU, for example, only recently has legislation taken account of it.[16] Online platforms, despite being an even more recent addition to it, have come to account for most of the Internet's daily use by individuals: out of 4.39 billion Internet users in 2019, 3.48 billion are also social media users.[17] These numbers corroborate what each of us knows empirically, namely that

12 G. Jowett and V. O'Donnell, *Propaganda & Persuasion*, 7th ed., SAGE, London 2019, p. 1: 'Propaganda is a form of communication that attempts to achieve a response that furthers the desired intent of the propagandist' – a definition that is also suitable for 'fake news'.

13 See S. Macdonald, *Propaganda and Information Warfare in the Twenty-First Century: Altered Images and Deception Operations*, Routledge, Abingdon 2006.

14 I. Manokha, 'Facebook's Anniversary: Fifteen Years since User Data Became Commodity', *The Globe Post*, 12 March 2019.

15 On the tricks and traits of the then newly emerged type of politician, see, for example, M.I. Finley, '6 Athenian Demagogues' in P.J. Rhodes (ed.), *Athenian Democracy*, Oxford University Press, Oxford 2004; or J.T. Roberts, 'Athens' So-Called Unofficial Politicians' (1982) 110 *Hermes* 3.

16 The EU's General Data Protection Regulation that was released in 2016 (Regulation EU 2016/679) takes account of the Internet, replacing Directive 95/46/EC, which did not. In the same context, only in 2018 did Internet Services Providers come under the scope of the EU's ePrivacy legislation through the application of the EU Electronic Communications Code (Directive 2018/1972). Of course, the information society has been regulated in EU law since 2001 (in Directive 2001/29) and electronic commerce since 2000 (in Directive 2000/31), although in both cases from a functional (copyright and business) rather than a social point of view.

17 Data from the Digital 2019 Report, https://datareportal.com/reports/digital-2019-global-digital-overview.

almost everyone keeps and checks one or more Internet social accounts many times a day. However, it is two main characteristics of online platforms that are of particular interest here: first, their ability to reach people individually despite the fact that billions are using their service; and, second, their business model of being 'free'.

As far as the former is concerned, online platforms have the technical ability to process the data of billions of users and still provide each of them with a feeling of personalised contact. This is achieved through awarding individuals with personal space to upload whatever content they wish and allowing them to form groups according to common interests, beliefs, location, or other formal or informal relationships in order to exchange this content. At the end of the day, online platforms are large communities that transcend local or volume restrictions to deliver a personalised service to groups of people organised on the basis of a common attribute.[18]

The second, not yet fully assimilated, attribute of the Internet and its champions – online platforms – is the business model of being free. Unlike any other service (or product) known to humanity so far, the main service of online platforms is provided to users for free.[19] In essence, companies with a global reach and having a multi-billion market value are not making money selling their basic service or product. Nevertheless, the main service being offered for free, the product for sale in online platforms is essentially its users, whose personal data are ruthlessly processed in order to extract meaningful, and indeed valuable, information to marketing companies. All this being completely new to unsuspecting humans, the system is open to exploitation by unscrupulous marketeers offering their services to businesses and politicians alike.

Billions of users making personal exchanges in closed groups unaware that they are prone to exploitation by professionals who are given privileged access to their information is an explosive mix that can even shape electoral results, as has been by now evidenced in practice.[20] A point to be noted here is that the Internet's multiplying effect has been found court-assessable on both sides of the Atlantic, in the *Grokster*[21] and *Google Spain*[22] cases, where supreme courts found that the impact of otherwise lawful actions is augmented to such an extent over the Internet that they are ultimately rendered unlawful. However, in spite of case law and news reports, there is only so much that laws, judges and journalists can

---

18 See N. Christakis and J. Fowler, *Connected: The Surprising Power of Networks and How They Shape Our Lives*, Little, Brown and Company, New York/Boston/London 2011 (in particular Chapter 8, 'Hyperconnected').

19 See C. Anderson, *Free: The Future of a Radical Price*, Hachette, London 2009.

20 See, for example, 'Revealed: 50 Million Facebook Profiles Harvested for Cambridge Analytica in Major Data Breach', *The Guardian*, 17 March 2018.

21 Supreme Court of the United States, *MGM Studios, Inc. v. Grokster, Ltd.*, 545 U.S. 913.

22 CJEU, *Google Spain SL, Google Inc. v Agencia Española de Protección de Datos, Mario Costeja González*.

do: if people choose to believe that Martians have invaded earth, no 'fake news' regulation can fight that. If people choose to trust what they hear in pubs and coffee shops (the equivalent of online social networks in the real world), this does not mean that beer or coffee drinking needs regulation.

5. CONCLUSION: KEEP CALM AND CARRY ON

Brought down to its constituting parts, therefore, 'fake news' is either criminal content (lies) or nuanced transmission of facts or propaganda disseminated over the Internet. This is not a new phenomenon and has been dealt with before: lies through recourse to courts, opinions through democracy, and propaganda through education. The Internet and online platforms may yet be lacking in social assimilation, but humanity is quickly closing the gap. Consequently, I believe that 'fake news' deserves no special treatment and should not be the cause of any regulatory intervention, on account of a much greater danger lurking in the dark: the inadvertent establishment of 'ministries of truth'.[23]

If we turn to regulation and fact-checking algorithms in order to fight 'fake news', who is to say that these will do their job well? Who can authoritatively say what is true and what is false in a transmission of a news item or even a simple fact? Who can definitely tell the difference between news transmission and propaganda? Unless kept at a minimal level whereby only blatant lies are refuted (and even in this case experience has shown that even the selection of which lie to refute first can cause friction), such tools will have to remain, at best, arbitrary. At the end of the day, they are bound to do more harm than good: by challenging nuanced facts, they will make enemies of all users who feel fine with the original transmission, and by being provided by supreme (legal or platform owner) power to silence whatever fails their test of truth, they risk being (seen or actually) found to be dangerously close to authoritarianism.

To my mind, a far preferable approach would be to let things take their normal course. Given that the Internet and online platforms are relatively new, they have been originally assigned a high level of public trust. Recent cases and indeed the global discussion on 'fake news' have dealt a huge blow to their credibility. If we were to track the trust trajectory of online media against traditional media, radio and television dominated and formulated public opinion for decades before finally losing public trust; online platforms have followed the same path in less than 20 years.[24] If this is the case, there is apparently no need for the legislator to intervene, at least not if the goal is to protect unsuspecting individuals.

---

[23] G. Orwell, *Nineteen Eighty-Four*, Secker & Warburg, London 1949.

[24] See 'Social Media Companies are Losing Public Trust as "Traditional" Media Regains it, Report Finds', *The Independent*, 22 January 2018 (with reference to the 2018 Edelman Trust Barometer, the UK report providing these findings).

Empirically speaking, today we are living the intermediate period whereby individuals, who were once grateful to have received free entertainment (their films and music) or information (their books and news feed) services over the Internet have once again started to pay for content (music, images, text and video). New online platforms that are based on a subscription rather than an advertisement business model are beginning to bring some balance back in the content market.[25] In other words, the 'free' model is in retreat. It is only a matter of time until individuals start paying for their news feed as well. While in no way suggesting that 'paid-for' news is more objective than 'free' news, it is a fact that accountability is easier to establish under a publisher-reader model rather than a publisher-advertisement agency-reader model. Also, accountability is to me the only critical factor that at the end of the day distinguishes 'news' from 'fake news'.

25 See, for example, 'How Streaming Saved the Music Industry', *Financial Times*, 16 January 2017.

2. FROM MISINFORMATION TO MODERN *LÜGENPRESSE*

The Redefinition of Fake News

Michael S. DAUBS*

1. INTRODUCTION

Despite its relatively recent popularity, the term 'fake news' has been deployed in a number of ways in recent history, problematising our understanding of this seemingly simple term.[1] Some refer to fabricated stories and disinformation on the Internet as 'fake news', while others, as will be discussed in detail below, cry 'fake news' when they hear something in the news with which they personally disagree. The various understandings of fake news demonstrate how the term has, in the words of Johan Farkas and Jannick Schou, become a 'floating signifier' that is now 'used by fundamentally different and in many ways deeply opposing political projects as a means of constructing political identities, conflicts and antagonisms'.[2]

A concept often associated with fake news is the term 'post-truth'. In a book published in 2017, journalist Matthew d'Ancona wrote:

> To everything there is a season: 1968 marked the revolution in personal freedom and the yearning for social progress; 1989 will be remembered for the collapse of totalitarianism; and 2016 was the year that definitively launched the era of 'Post-Truth'.[3]

---

* School of English, Film, Theatre and Media Studies, Victoria University of Wellington, New Zealand. Email: michael.daubs@vuw.ac.nz.

1 N.W. JANKOWSKI, 'Researching Fake News: A Selective Examination of Empirical Studies' (2018) 25(1–2) *Javnost – The Public* 248; E.C. TANDOC JR., Z.W. LIM and R. LING, 'Defining "Fake News": A Typology of Scholarly Definitions' (2018) 6(2) *Digital Journalism* 137.

2 J. FARKAS and J. SCHOU, 'Fake News as a Floating Signifier: Hegemony, Antagonism and the Politics of Falsehood' (2018) 25(3) *Javnost – The Public* 300.

3 M. D'ANCONA, *Post-truth: The New War on Truth and How to Fight Back*, Ebury Press, London 2017, p. 7.

Lee McIntyre argues that 'post-truth amounts to a form of ideological supremacy, whereby its practitioners are trying to compel someone to believe in something whether there [is] good evidence for it or not'.[4] Noting the rapid emergence of the phrase 'post-truth politics', which itself emerged in response to untruths, lies or 'bullshit'[5] in political discourse, to borrow Princeton University philosopher Harry Frankfurt's more colourful term, Oxford Dictionaries selected the phrase 'post-truth' as its 2016 word of the year, defining it as 'circumstances in which objective facts are less influential in shaping public opinion than appeals to emotion and personal belief'.[6] The purposeful provocation of strong emotional responses is central to the concept of post-truth. For an increasing number of people, including politicians, only 'facts' that are in line with their own sense of the truth and political worldview are actually true. In other words, there is a persistent belief that facts are open to interpretation.[7]

It is in this politically charged, fact-resistant 'post-truth era' that the issue of fake news began to receive international attention. An emerging refrain in the academic literature is that the post-truth era is made possible by theories from leftist thinkers, namely, postmodernism and poststructuralism.[8] Albrech Koschorke, for example, attributes the emergence of the post-truth era to the 'Philosophie des französischen Poststrukturalismus' ('philosophy of French poststructuralism') associated with Jacques Derrida, Michel Foucault, Gilles Deleuze and Bruno Latour.[9] Such arguments, which situate the origins of 'post-truth' and thus the phenomenon of fake news in the mid-20th century, implicitly suggest that 'post-truth' is a new and unparalleled historical development.

The current political and media environment arguably contributes to and accelerates a rejection of objective fact and the emergence of a world in which people somehow 'know' what they want and 'believe' to be true.[10] However, the evolution of the meaning of fake news from a descriptive term (i.e. a fabricated

---

4 L. McIntyre, *Post-truth*, MIT Press, Cambridge, MA 2018, p. 13.

5 H.G. Frankfurt, *On Bullshit*, Princeton University Press, Princeton 2005.

6 Quoted in d'Ancona, *supra* note 3, p. 9. It should be noted that concepts such as 'truth' and 'fact' have been subject to a long history of philosophical debates, which quotations such as the one cited here over-simplify or elide. Revisiting these discussions is unfortunately beyond the scope of this chapter.

7 P. Sarasin, 'Fakten und Wissen in der Postmoderne', *Bundeszentrale für politische Bildung*, 28 March 2017, https://www.bpb.de/politik/extremismus/rechtspopulismus/245449/fakten-und-wissen-in-der-postmoderne.

8 See, for example, McIntyre, *supra* note 4, p. 123.

9 A. Koschorke, 'Die akademische Linke hat sich selbst dekonstruiert. Es ist Zeit, die Begriffe neu zu justieren', *Neue Zürcher Zeitung*, 18 April 2018, https://www.nzz.ch/feuilleton/die-akademische-linke-hat-sich-selbst-dekonstruiert-es-ist-zeit-die-begriffe-neu-zu-justieren-ld.1376724.

10 M. Binswanger, 'Was die Wissenschaft weiss und was sie glaubt', *Neue Zürcher Zeitung*, 15 September 2016, https://www.nzz.ch/feuilleton/zeitgeschehen/wissenschaftskritik-was-die-wissenschaft-weiss-und-was-sie-glaubt-ld.116772.

story) to a *Kampfbegriff* (i.e. a combative term) is hardly a unique development, which this chapter demonstrates through a comparative historical analysis of fake news to the word *Lügenpresse*, the German term meaning 'lying press' used by the Nazi regime to incite hatred against groups such as the Jews and the communists and to discredit Hitler's critics.[11] The Nazis' claims that critical reports were *Lügenpresse* did not foment distrust of foreign powers, those with alternative political ideologies (e.g. communists) and the Jews as much as prey upon existing biases in ways that served the authoritarian regime, a dynamic that is visible in contemporary accusations of 'fake news'. The goal of this historical comparison between 'fake news' and *Lügenpresse* is not to suggest that politicians that use 'fake news' as a *Kampfbegriff* are aiming to become the next Hitler or establish a Nazi-like regime; rather, this comparison acts as a warning, demonstrating how the transformation of the phrase 'fake news' into a *Kampfbegriff* is indicative of authoritarian tendencies which represent a significant threat to the freedom of the press and democracy itself.

The first section of this chapter provides a brief account of the history of the term *Lügenpresse*, including its evolution from a descriptive term to a Nazi *Kampfbegriff*. This discussion not only establishes the democratic threats of rhetorical attacks against the press, but also provides the foundations for a comparison to the more recent emergence and evolution of fake news. The following examination of fake news as a *Kampfbegriff* demonstrates how claims that certain stories are fake news and personal opinion – or, more precisely, personal feelings and beliefs – are closely linked. The final section of this chapter links past attacks against the press using the term *Lügenpresse* to comments and online posts from contemporary international politicians and government officials in order to demonstrate how the use of 'fake news' as a *Kampfbegriff* represents a recurring and determined attempt by those in power to silence their critics, intimidate journalists and threaten the freedom of the press.

2. THE EVOLUTION OF *LÜGENPRESSE*

The term *Lügenpresse* is best known for its use by the Nazis, but the word actually originated in Germany in the 19th century.[12] It featured prominently in the fourth edition of a 1914 book called *Der Lügenfeldzug unserer Feinde*

---

11 W. Hagemann, *Publizistik im Dritten Reich: Ein Beitrag zur Methodik der Massenführung*, Hansischer Gildenverlag, Hamburg 1948, p. 226; R. Noack, 'The Ugly History of "Lügenpresse", a Nazi Slur Shouted at a Trump Rally', *Washington Post*, 24 October 2016, https://www.washingtonpost.com/news/worldviews/wp/2016/10/24/the-ugly-history-of-luegenpresse-a-nazi-slur-shouted-at-a-trump-rally/?utm_term=.661ff1e5c066.

12 P. Denk, *Lügenpresse*, J. K. Fischer Verlag, Gelnhausen 2015, p. 14.

(*Our Enemies' Campaign of Lies*) by an author named Reinhold Anton,[13] which compared German, British, French and Russian news in the lead-up to and during the early years of the First World War. Although there were five editions of this book, the word *Lügenpresse* only appears in the fourth edition, which includes it in the title, i.e. *Lügenpresse: Der Lügenfeldzug unserer Feinde*. Anton used the word to describe the proliferation of misinformation that exacerbated tensions between these nations, particularly what he viewed as false news stories by journalists from countries that were Germany's enemies. The 'Pariser Lügenpresse'[14] (Parisian lying press) was one of his favourite targets, as was the British press. The following excerpt demonstrates how Anton viewed and framed foreign reports.

> German Torture
>
> Under this headline, the 'Daily Mail' printed the following report from its Saint Petersburg special correspondent Hamilton Fyfe in its 10 April issue:
>
> 'Details have come to light about how German officers tortured a young Russian corporal, who was captured inside of the German positions close to the East Prussian border ... In Andreieff, a village near Memel that was occupied by the Germans for a few hours on Wednesday, the Russians discovered, upon their return, several wounded Cossacks who had fallen into German hands. The enemy had treated them cruelly and beaten them. One of the unlucky men was skinned with a knife or sabre. Even those who defend the Germans at every opportunity are incensed and horrified by these terrible atrocities.'[15]

---

13 R. Blasius, 'Von der Journaille zur Lügenpresse', *Frankfurter Allgemeine Zeitung* 13 January 2015, http://www.faz.net/aktuell/gesellschaft/unwort-des-jahres-eine-kleine-geschichte-der-luegenpresse-13367848.html.

14 R. Anton, *Der Lügenfeldzug Unserer Feinde*, 4th ed., Verlag von Otto Gustav Zehrfeld, Leipzig 1916, p. 19.

15 *Ibid.*, pp. 10–11. The original German reads:

> Deutsche Folter.
>
> Unter dieser Spitzmarke druckt die „Daily Mail" in ihrer Ausgabe vom 10. April den folgenden Bericht ihres Petersburgers Sonderberichterstatters Hamilton Fyfe ab:
>
> 'Es ist jetzt Näheres darüber bekannt geworden, wie deutsche Offiziere einen jungen russischen Unteroffizier, der innerhalb der deutschen Stellungen dicht an der ostpreußischen Grenze gefangen genommen wurde, gefoltert haben ... In Andreieff, einem Dorfe in der Nähe von Memel, das am Mittwoch auf einige Stunden von den Deutschen besetzt war, fanden die Russen bei ihrer Rückkehr mehrere verwundete Kosaken vor, die in die Hände der Deutschen gefallen waren. Der Feind hatte sie grausam behandelt und durch Schläge übel zugerichtet. Einer der Unglücklichen war mit einem Messer oder Säbel zerfleischt worden. Sogar die, die die Deutschen bei jeder Gelegenheit in Schutz nehmen, sind über diese schrecklichen Greueltaten empört, und entsetzt.'

Translated by the author.

At the end of the excerpt, Anton adds the Latin phrase 'Audacteur calumniara [*sic*], semper aliquid haeret!' ('Slander boldly, something always sticks!'). The insinuation of this ending commentary is clear: the reports of German torture are lies spread by enemy journalists.

This example, like many of the examples in his book, demonstrates Anton's pro-Germany bias; he offers no evidence that these claims from the British press are false, nor does he even really contradict these claims. At the same time, the word *Lügenpresse*, at this point, was akin to what we might today call 'propaganda' rather than used as a direct attack against the press. However, the Nazis frequently used the word to insult and marginalise the news organisations. Newspapers were an early and frequent target of Hitler himself. For example, in *Mein Kampf*, he referred to social democratic newspapers in Austria as a 'konzentrierte Lügenlösung' ('concentrated solution of lies') and spoke of 'marxistischen Lügenblättern' ('Marxist lying newspapers').[16] During the Nazi regime, the Reich Minister of Propaganda Joseph Goebbels made liberal use of the term, often in ways that simultaneously linked the mass media to other frequent critics and targets of the Nazi regime. For example, the *Aufklärungs- und Redner-Informationsmaterial der Reichspropagandaleitung der NSDAP* (Educational and Speaker Information Material of the Reich Propaganda Directorate of the Nazi Party), a collection of official policy declarations from 1938 and 1939, included a section entitled 'Die "armen" Juden' ('The "Poor" Jews), which decried both the *Lügenpresse* in foreign countries for their *Verleumdungsfeldzug* (slander) against the Nazi regime and national (i.e. Nazi) comrades who demonstrated that they were 'unaware of what is at stake in carrying out measures against Judaism'.[17]

This example in particular demonstrates the way in which the Nazis used *Lügenpresse* to simultaneously downplay and justify their racist acts against the Jews. It also demonstrates how Goebbels and other Nazis used claims of *Lügenpresse* as a form of control over media discourse and the propagation of the Nazi *Weltanschauung* (worldview) was integral to the Nazis rise to and maintenance of power in Germany. One method they used to control news

---

16 A. Hitler, *Mein Kampf*, Franz Eher, Munich 1943, pp. 43, 265. For more discussion, see M. Beiler and J. Kiesler, '"Lügenpresse! Lying Press!" Is the Press Lying?' in K. Otto and A. Köhler (eds.), *Trust in Media and Journalism*, Springer, Wiesbaden 2018, p. 159.

17 Reichspropagandaleitung der N.S.D.A.P., 'Juden', *Aufklärungs- und Redner-Informationsmaterial der Reichspropagandaleitung der NSDAP und des Reichspropagandaamtes der Deutschen Arbeitsfront*, January 1939. The original German reads: 'Die Antwort, welche Deutschland auf das feige Attentat von Paris gegeben hat, war für eine gewisse Hetz- und Lügenpresse des Auslandes Veranlassung zu einem neuen Verleumdungsfeldzug gegen das Reich, der alles bisher auf diesem Gebiete Dagewesene weit hinter sich ließ. Ebenso muß aber auch festgestellt werden, daß es im Inlande eine Reihe von Volksgenossen gibt, die erkennen lassen, daß sie bei der Durchdührung der Maßahmen gegen das Judentum nicht wissen, worum es geht.' Of note is the use of the word *Volksgenossen* (from *Volksgenosse*), which was a word used particularly during the Nazi era to refer to fellow German countrymen or comrades. Translated by the author.

production was to establish the Deutsche Nachrichtenbüro (German news office), a 'domestic news agency to propagate their ideological and cultural goals'.[18] Other news agencies continued to operate, but while some publishers operating under the Nazi regime, such as the news agency Telegraph Union (which was nonetheless a right-wing institution), were not 'fully compliant', most learned rather quickly that '[a]nything less than adulation was insufficient'.[19] Those that did not toe the Nazi party line were decried as *Lügenpresse*, which the Nazis used as an excuse to curtail their business activities and limit access to their reporting via official Nazi policies. Most German citizens thus only had access to news that glorified the Nazi regime, which further cemented Hitler's authoritarian hold over the country. Only after the Nazis repeatedly used *Lügenpresse* in this manner did it take on a connotation as a threat to the freedom of the press.

After the Second World War, the word *Lügenpresse* became somewhat unpopular, perhaps not surprising considering its connotation as a pro-Nazi term (though it was still frequently used in East Germany to refer to Western news outlets).[20] However, members of the modern anti-immigrant group Pegida (Patriotische Europäer gegen die Islamisierung des Abendlandes – Patriotic Europeans against the Islamisation of the West) resurrected the term during protests against Muslim refugees in 2014, leading linguists in Germany to call the word the *Unwort des Jahres* (worst word of the year).[21] Trump supporters and members of the so-called 'alt-right' (many of whom are affiliated with white nationalist groups) further reinserted the term into public consciousness thanks to a video showing supporters referring to journalists covering the Trump campaign as *Lügenpresse* during a Trump rally in October 2016 and also because of a video of a lecture from Richard Spencer, the President of the National Policy Institute (NPI), a white nationalist think tank. During the NPI's annual conference in 2016, Spencer said: 'The mainstream media, or perhaps we should refer to them in the original German, *Lügenpresse* … It's not just that they are leftists and cucks. It's not just that many are genuinely stupid. Indeed, one wonders if these people are people at all.'[22] While his denigration of the press is nothing new, the issue many had with his speech was how it ended;

---

18 H. Tworek, *News from Germany: The Competition to Control World Communications, 1900–1945*, Harvard University Press, Cambridge, MA 2019, p. 183.

19 *Ibid.*, p. 185.

20 C. Buggisch, 'Die "Lügenpresse" – ein Begriff und seine Geschichte', *Publikative*, 1 January 2015, https://publikative.org/2015/01/01/die-luegenpresse-ein-begriff-und-seine-geschichte; Noack, *supra* note 11.

21 A. Chandler, 'The "Worst" German Word of the Year', *The Atlantic*, 14 January 2015, https://www.theatlantic.com/international/archive/2015/01/the-worst-german-word-of-the-year/384493.

22 Video excerpts of the speech were posted to YouTube by the magazine *The Atlantic*. See https://www.youtube.com/watch?v=1o6-bi3jlxk.

Spencer shouted 'Hail Trump! Hail our people! Hail victory!', to which members of the audience responded with the Roman or Nazi salute.

3. FAKE NEWS FROM SATIRE TO DISINFORMATION

According to German journalist Peter Denk, the history of the word *Lügenpresse* is interesting precisely because it provides a clear look at what the future might bring.[23] Denk's words could very well act as a warning when considered in relation to the evolution of the term 'fake news', which exhibits several similarities to the development of the term *Lügenpresse* over the past century and a half. In the early 2010s, it was common to refer to satire, particularly television shows such as *The Daily Show* and *The Colbert Report*, as 'fake news'. Oxford Dictionaries in fact referenced comedian Stephen Colbert, who popularised the word 'truthiness' in 2005, as one of the inspirations for the term 'post-truth'.[24] Truthiness is the idea that something '*feels* true, even if it is not necessarily backed up by the facts'.[25] During this time, CNN referred to *Daily Show* host Jon Stewart as the 'most trusted name in fake news'.[26] To be clear, satire is not neutral, but has always been political. As Laurie Ouellette and Sarah Banet-Weiser note, 'satirical news programs exemplified by *The Daily Show* and, more recently, *Full Frontal with Samantha Bee* is [*sic*] recognized as providing a more critical and active approach to political culture than traditional news and public affairs'.[27] Satire is therefore dependent on facts; satirists like Stewart, Colbert, Bee and John Oliver need to base their jokes on facts to express their political criticisms. Sophia McClennen argues that people once loved fake news when it referenced satire; it often 'saved us from a declining news media'.[28]

As *Chicago Tribune* reporter Jeff Wisser elaborates, '"fake news" meant comics playing anchormen and reporters on TV, and (almost) everybody being in on the joke, rather than the online chicanery that that phrase has come to connote'.[29] The 'online chicanery' to which Wisser refers is the spate of false

23 Denk, *supra* note 12, p. 13.

24 Oxford Dictionaries, 'Word of the Year 2016 is …', 2016, https://en.oxforddictionaries.com/word-of-the-year/word-of-the-year-2016.

25 McIntyre, *supra* note 4, p. 5, italics in original.

26 CNN, 'Jon Stewart's America', *CNN.com*, 15 October 2004, http://transcripts.cnn.com/TRANSCRIPTS/0410/15/cf.01.html.

27 L. Ouellette and S. Banet-Weiser, 'Special Issue: Media and the Extreme Right: Editor's Introduction' (2018) 11(1) *Communication, Culture and Critique* 3.

28 S.A. McClennen, 'All "Fake News" is Not Equal – But Smart or Dumb, it All Grows from the Same Root', *Salon*, 12 December 2016, http://www.salon.com/2016/12/11/all-fake-news-is-not-equal-but-smart-or-dumb-it-all-grows-from-the-same-root.

29 J. Wisser, '"The Daily Show (the Book)" Offers Candid History of Jon Stewart's Fake Newscast', *Chicago Tribune*, 8 December 2016, http://www.chicagotribune.com/lifestyles/books/ct-books-1211-daily-show-the-book-chris-smith-20161206-story.html.

news stories that were propagated online, particularly in the lead-up to the 2016 'Brexit' referendum in the UK and the 2016 presidential election in the US. One famous example is a widely spread meme that supposedly quoted a 1998 *People* magazine interview with Donald Trump, in which he said that he would run as a Republican if he were to run for President because Republicans are 'the dumbest group of voters in the country'. However, the popularity of this meme overlooks the fact that Trump never said these words.[30] This meme is just one example of the many of 'fake news' stories posted, tweeted, shared, liked and favourited on social networking sites such as Facebook and Twitter during the election campaign.

Rather than employing satire to critique governments and media, this iteration of fake news was simply comprised of factually incorrect stories and conspiracy stories presented as truth, i.e. a form of propaganda. James Ball cites several 'classics' of the fake news genre that were spread during the 2016 US presidential election, including stories that claimed that the US government had stockpiled 30,000 guillotines in order to 'wipe out Second Amendment supporters at a rate of three million an hour' and that 'Trump supporters at a New York victory rally chanted, "We hate Muslims, we hate blacks, we want our great country back"'.[31] While this particular example was used to discredit Trump, the majority of this iteration of 'fake news' was pro-Trump or anti-Hillary Clinton. Craig Silverman reports that: 'Of the 20 top-performing false election stories identified in the analysis, all but three were overtly pro-Donald Trump or anti-Hillary Clinton.'[32] One widely shared story claimed that Hillary Clinton ran a paedophilia sex ring in the basement of Washington DC pizza parlour called Comet Ping Pong. This false story inspired one man to travel to Washington DC to 'self-investigate' the claims. During his 'investigation', he discharged an assault rifle inside the restaurant, an act for which he was later arrested; luckily no one in the restaurant was injured.[33] This example is admittedly anecdotal, but demonstrates that fake news can influence beliefs and actions, and therefore has significant real-life consequences.

One impetus for the influx of misinformation is arguably financial. Fake news tends to have sensationalised, 'click-bait'-style headlines designed to attract readers (and therefore increase a website's advertising revenue).

30 R. Farley, 'Bogus Meme Targets Trump', *FactCheck.org*, 28 September 2016, http://www.factcheck.org/2015/11/bogus-meme-targets-trump.

31 J. Ball, *Post-truth: How Bullshit Conquered the World*, Biteback Publishing, London 2017, p. 1.

32 C. Silverman, 'This Analysis Shows How Viral Fake Election News Stories Outperformed Real News on Facebook', *Buzzfeed*, 17 November 2016, https://www.buzzfeed.com/craigsilverman/viral-fake-election-news-outperformed-real-news-on-facebook?utm_term=.ak4A2mxQ7z#.aiAW8xwVmM.

33 A. Unterberger, *Zwischen Lügenpresse und Fake News*, Frank & Frei, Vienna 2017, p. 42.

To further increase readership, fake news sites also tend to generate a steady stream of content. Thus, the proliferation of fake news stems from what Victor Pickard calls the 'extreme commercialism' of the news media dedicated to the accumulation of profit.[34] This sensationalising of the news for commercial purposes has a history that long pre-dates social media. At the turn of the 20th century, newspapers (e.g. the 'yellow press') and, more recently, the 24-hour news stations Pickard refers to such as CNN and Fox News, have long relied on producing short, 'exciting' stories in order to maintain or increase audiences. However, online tools and platforms, including social media, make the process of distributing these stories faster and more efficient.

The only reason why fabricated news stories are financially viable is because they are appealing to audiences. One explanation for this appeal is the emotional or affective responses that fake news stories can engender. Megan Boler and Elizabeth Davis argue that the believability of mass media in a 'post-fact era' has an aesthetic (tonal) and affective element; content that 'sounds' true and evokes a strong reaction is more believable.[35] Affect is therefore political in nature. As Boler and Davis explain: 'Affect may be understood as emotions that are collectively or intersubjectively manifested, experienced, and mobilized, out of the "private", individual realm and into shared, even public spaces, which may then be channelled into movement(s).'[36] They cite Arlie Hochschild, who describes affect as a 'deep story' or a '*feels-as-if* story'. According to Hochschild, a deep story shapes or informs 'feeling rules' that describe the relationship between various social contexts, demographic characteristics and expected emotional responses.[37] In short, something must 'sound' true and be related to the 'deep story' of a person in order to be believed and considered 'true'.

The prevalence of fake news means that people are more likely to base their beliefs, opinions and decisions on factually incorrect stories crafted to incite strong emotional reactions. Jonathan Albright stresses that, as a result, 'fact-based evidence is not relevant to a growing segment of the populace'.[38] Instead, every fact is open to interpretation, measured against opinion or belief. In addition, people tend to read *and* share stories that reinforce their existing political beliefs, which not only contributes to a lack of deliberation but also intensifies political polarisation, an outcome sometimes referred to as an 'echo chamber' or 'filter

---

34 V. Pickard, 'Media Failures in the Age of Trump' (2017) 4(2) *Political Economy of Communication* 118.

35 M. Boler and E. Davis, 'The Affective Politics of the "Post-truth" Era: Feeling Rules and Networked Subjectivity' (2018) 27 *Emotion, Space and Society* 78.

36 *Ibid.*, p. 81.

37 *Ibid.*, p. 78; A.R. Hochschild, *Strangers in Their Own Land: Anger and Mourning on the American Right*, New Press, New York 2016, p. 135.

38 J. Albright, 'Welcome to the Era of Fake News' (2017) 5(2) *Media and Communication* 87.

bubble' effect, terms that describe a limiting of cultural experiences and social connections resulting from algorithmic sorting processes.[39]

Algorithms can also 'nudge' people into certain opinions and beliefs. As Zynep Tufecki notes: 'Facebook demonstrated that it could alter the US electoral turnout by hundreds of thousands of votes, merely by nudging people to vote through slightly different, experimentally manipulated, get-out-the-vote messages.'[40] The idea of nudging is tightly tied to things like affect and emotion, specifically emotional manipulation and 'contagion' in order to get people think or act in a particular way. For example, Tufecki details an article in *Ad Weekly*, which argues that 'women are more likely to buy cosmetics when they feel "fat, ugly, lonely" or when they are feeling depressed, colorfully displayed on an informatic chart highlighting the times of the week when women are more likely to feel such emotions'.[41] Similarly, researchers at Facebook were able to demonstrate '"experimental evidence for massive-scale contagion via social networks" by reducing the number of positive or negative posts shown to Facebook users by experimentally manipulating users' algorithmically curated "News Feed"'.[42] This emotional manipulation would change the tone of users' later posts, leading many academics and activists to wonder if Facebook could algorithmically alter election outcomes.

These examples demonstrate that the power of algorithms operates as a form of what Cheney-Lippold calls 'modulation', in which 'discipline has often become more or less unnecessary if control can be enacted through a series of guiding, determining, and persuasive mechanisms of power'.[43] According to Ouellette and Banet-Weiser, '"the media!" has given way to a fragmented, niche-oriented, interactive, digitalized and increasingly polarized mediascape'.[44] 'Blue Feed, Red Feed', a website maintained by the *Wall Street Journal*, claims to demonstrate how Facebook exacerbates this fragmentation by showing how the social networks display different stories in a user's Facebook News Feed depending on their individual activities on the site, such as pages liked, links followed and stories read/shared.[45] False news stories that reinforce already-held political beliefs are supposedly much more likely to be displayed and read. Because they resonate more strongly with already-held opinions, fake

---

39 Ball, *supra* note 31, p. 8; D.G. Beer, 'The Social Power of Algorithms' (2017) *Information, Communication and Society* 7.

40 Z. Tufecki, 'Algorithmic Harms beyond Facebook and Google: Emergent Challenges of Computational Agency' (2015) 13 *Colorado Technology Law Journal* 203, 215.

41 *Ibid.*, p. 212.

42 *Ibid.*, p. 203.

43 J. Cheney-Lippold, 'A New Algorithmic Identity: Soft Biopolitics and the Modulation of Control' (2011) 28(6) *Theory, Culture & Society* 168–69.

44 L. Ouellette and S. Banet-Weiser, 'Special Issue: Media and the Extreme Right: Editor's Introduction' (2018) 11(1) *Communication, Culture and Critique* 2.

45 See http://graphics.wsj.com/blue-feed-red-feed.

news stories, which tend towards the shocking or sensational, are shared more frequently than real news stories.[46] As CNN's Brian Stelter argues, they are popular because they 'prey on people who want to believe the worst about the opposition'.[47] Denk explains:

> As a consequence, many people who do not wish to engage intensively with facts, quickly come to the opinion that this loud and frequently expressed version must really be the right one.[48]

However, although it seems as if fake news is the source of many current political and social issues, James Ball argues that it is more a symptom than a cause, linking it to other international trends such as populism, nationalism, hyper-partisanship and anti-intellectualism.[49] Compounding the power of fake news is that it is extraordinarily difficult and time-consuming to debunk, and efforts to do so often bring additional attention to fake news stories.[50]

Although the 2016 US presidential election is often the focus of discussions about fake news, it has played a role in other elections in the past year as well, particularly in Europe. During the 2017 French elections, eventual winner Emmanuel Macron blamed an 'internet army' made up of supporters of his far-right rival Marine Le Pen for spreading a forgery that claimed he was avoiding taxes by keeping money in an offshore bank account in the Bahamas.[51] Macron eventually filed a defamation case against Le Pen. In Germany, the Atlantic Council's Digital Forensic Research Lab has discovered automatic accounts or 'bots' and 'genuine' accounts from pro-Russia networks, anti-immigrant groups and backers of the far-right party Alternative für Deutschland (AfD) that were spreading anti-immigrant or pro-Russia news stories.[52] Fake news is such a concern there that the government 'unveiled a hate speech bill that would fine

---

46 Silverman, *supra* note 32.

47 C. Stelter, 'The Plague of Fake News is Getting Worse – Here's How to Protect Yourself', *CNN*, 1 November 2016, http://money.cnn.com/2016/10/30/media/facebook-fake-news-plague.

48 Denk, *supra* note 12, p. 35. In the original German: 'Sie hören eine bestimmte Meinung besonders oft and von bekannten Protagonisten, die Gegenmeinung nur vereinzelt am Rande. Somit kommen viele Menschen, die sich nicht intensiv mit Fakten auseinandersetzen möchten, schnell zu der Meinung, dass diese laute und häufig verbreitete Variante wohl die richtige sein muss.' Translated by the author.

49 Ball, *supra* note 31, p. 13.

50 *Ibid.*, pp. 1–13.

51 H. Samuel, 'Emmanuel Macron Files Defamation Complaint against Marine Le Pen over Bahamas Account Allegation', *The Telegraph*, 4 May 2017, http://www.telegraph.co.uk/news/2017/05/04/emmanuel-macron-files-defamation-complaint-marine-le-pen-offshore.

52 J. Lowe, 'European Democracy: Angela Merkel Faces Far-Right and Pro-Russia Activists Allying to Spread German Election Propaganda', *Newsweek*, 23 June 2017, http://www.newsweek.com/german-election-far-right-russia-trolls-pro-kremlin-628524.

social media companies like Twitter and Facebook up to 50 million euros … for failing to remove intentionally fake news stories or stories that incite hate'.[53] James Ball documents how the Brexit debate in the UK was 'littered' with false claims meant to influence voters. He lists stories claiming that £350 million per week going to the EU would instead go to the National Health Service (NHS) or that the Chancellor would raise income taxes if the UK voted to leave, or another story claiming the UK would be subject to 12 million Turkish immigrants if the UK voted to stay as examples.[54]

Two revelations raised public awareness of the problem of fake news. The first was that Macedonian teenagers were responsible for the crafting many of these false news stories, primarily to generate profit through online advertising programmes such as Google AdSense.[55] The second was that paid Russian 'trolls' associated with Russia's Internet Research Agency (IRA) were spreading them in comments on social media and news websites as a part of Russia's disinformation campaigns.[56] These campaigns are designed, according to one retired KGB general, to 'drive wedges in the Western community alliances of all sorts, particularly NATO, to sow discord among allies, to weaken the United States in the eyes of the people in Europe, Asia, Africa, Latin America, and thus to prepare ground in case [a] war really occurs'.[57] Once posted, these stories were then shared again by supporters of a particular candidate or party within their personal networks. The Social Media and Democracy Research Group at the University of Wisconsin in the US estimates that 'American exposure to IRA content numbered in the hundreds of millions of impressions' and also discovered that 32 American news outlets together featured a total of 116 news stories that embedded social media content from Russian IRA accounts.[58] This content was intended to 'magnify existing partisan divisions in the American political discourse environment'.[59]

Social networking sites, particularly Facebook, were often chastised for their lackadaisical approach to the dissemination of factually incorrect 'news'. While

---

53 R. Warren, 'Fake News, the Frankfurt "Sex Mob" and Why Germany Has Taken an Aggressive Stance against False News Stories', *Newsweek*, 30 May 2017, http://www.newsweek.com/2017/06/09/germany-cracking-fake-news-frankfurt-sex-mob-617536.html.

54 Ball, *supra* note 31, p. 2.

55 C. Silverman and L. Alexander, 'How Teens in the Balkans are Duping Trump Supporters with Fake News', *Buzzfeed*, 4 November 2016, https://www.buzzfeed.com/craigsilverman/how-macedonia-became-a-global-hub-for-pro-trump-misinfo?utm_term=.cul62xJWMe#.boPMjZnJgY.

56 J. Lukito et al., *The Twitter Exploit: How Russian Propaganda Infiltrated U.S. News*, University of Wisconsin Press, Madison, Wisconsin 2018, p. 3.

57 N. Bertrand, 'Before the DNC Hack, Russian Internet Trolls were Being Hired to Pose as Pro-Trump Americans', *Business Insider Australia*, 27 July 2016, https://www.businessinsider.com.au/russia-internet-trolls-and-donald-trump-2016-7.

58 Lukito et al., *supra* note 56, p. 2.

59 *Ibid.*

fake news stories in France did not prevent Macron's victory, many supporters of Hillary Clinton blamed the spread of fake news for her loss. Facebook founder Mark Zuckerberg denied that the site significantly influenced the election results[60] and a study from Stanford and New York Universities[61] supports that claim. However, another report from the cybersecurity firm Trend Micro reports that, for about US$400,000, a political campaign can generate and spread fake news through social media and fake news sites effectively enough to influence election outcomes or, for about US$200,000, instigate street protests based on false news.[62] As Ball summarises: 'It would be a gross oversimplification to claim that either electorate [in the US or the UK] was tricked into their vote, but nor can we rule out that bullshit swings votes.'[63]

4. FAKE NEWS AS *KAMPFBEGRIFF*

All of these examples cemented 'fake news' as an issue of significant public concern, and many researchers, politicians and activists are rightly focused on the algorithmic manipulation of voters via Facebook and other social media. Since the election, however, the phrase has been redefined yet again, this time by the extreme right in the US and President Trump himself. One early example is an exchange between CNN's James Acosta and then-President-Elect Trump at the latter's first post-election press conference. At one point in the press conference, Trump refused to let Acosta ask a question, calling CNN 'terrible' and 'fake news'.[64] The goal was clear: Trump believed that CNN was too critical of him during the election and wanted to silence the news organisation's reporter. In this example, Trump was appropriating the term 'fake news' and reconfiguring it into a modern evocation of the Nazi propaganda term 'Lügenpresse'.

Since his inauguration, Trump has accused everyone from individual journalists to the US intelligence community[65] and entire news organisations,

60 M. Isaac, 'Facebook, in Cross Hairs after Election, is Said to Question its Influence', *New York Times*, 12 November 2016, https://www.nytimes.com/2016/11/14/technology/facebook-is-said-to-question-its-influence-in-election.html.

61 H. Allcott and M. Gentzkow, 'Social Media and Fake News in the 2016 Election' (2017) 31(2) *Journal of Economic Perspectives* 211.

62 L. Gu, V. Kropotov and F. Yarochkin, 'The Fake News Machine: How Propagandists Abuse the Internet and Manipulate the Public' *Trend Micro*, 2017, https://documents.trendmicro.com/assets/white_papers/wp-fake-news-machine-how-propagandists-abuse-the-internet.pdf, pp. 58–62.

63 Ball, *supra* note 31, p. 4.

64 Video of this exchange is available on YouTube: https://www.youtube.com/watch?v=Vqpzk-qGxMU.

65 M. Papenfuss, 'Trump Accuses Cia Director of Leaking "Fake News" about Russian Dossier', *Huffington Post*, 16 January 2017, http://www.huffingtonpost.com/entry/trump-john-brennan_us_587c368ae4b09281d0eb87a7.

including CNN,[66] of being 'fake news' in an effort to de-legitimise them – just as Hitler and the Nazis appropriated the word *Lügenpresse* to silence and marginalise their own critics. Over 1,000 of Trump's tweets in the first three years since declaring his candidacy in June 2015 have been critical of the press.[67] More specifically, he tweeted the term 'fake news' nearly 200 times in the first 18 months of his presidency, from both his personal @realDonaldTrump and the official @POTUS accounts.[68] These tweets serve a variety of purposes, from downplaying negative reports coming from inside the Trump White House to distancing his administration from reports that he and his staff conspired with Russia to influence the 2016 US presidential election.[69] Many of these tweets also denigrate individual journalists and news organisations. For example, a tweet from @realDonaldTrump on 7 February 2017 reads: 'Any negative polls are fake news, just like the CNN, ABC, NBC polls in the election. Sorry, people want border security and extreme vetting.'[70] The phrasing here serves three purposes: first, it dismisses negative polls as 'fake news' to suggest that Trump's popularity is actually much greater than the news organisations listed are reporting; second, it implicitly suggests that any future reports about negative poll numbers are also fake, the result of slanted news reporting from biased journalistic institutions; and, finally, it explicitly frames these channels as 'fake news', thereby casting doubt on any future reporting from these organisations.

Other tweets work to expressly position the press as the 'enemy of the American people'. Many of these tweets again denigrate specific news outlets, with CNN and the 'failing' *New York Times* his favourite targets. For example, the @realDonaldTrump account tweeted the following on 18 February 2017: 'The FAKE NEWS media (failing @nytimes, @NBCNews, @ABC, @CBS, @CNN) is not my enemy, it is the enemy of the American People!'[71] Unlike the previous example, which frames Trump as the victim of a biased press, this tweet positions 'fake news' as 'a symptom of a fundamental, democratic problem, namely that mainstream media companies are biased and deliberately attempting to promote liberal agendas instead of representing "The People"'.[72] In other words, it frames

---

66 M. Snider, 'Trump Invokes "Fake News" at Press Conference', *USA Today*, 11 January 2017, http://www.usatoday.com/story/money/2017/01/11/trump-tackles-fake-news-press-conference/96438764.

67 J. Peters, 'Trump Twitter Spreadsheet Tracks "a Perpetual Campaign against the Press"', *Columbia Journalism Review*, 21 December 2017, https://www.cjr.org/united_states_project/trump-twitter-spreadsheet-press-attacks.php.

68 https://twitter.com/realDonaldTrump; https://twitter.com/POTUS.

69 For examples, see https://twitter.com/realDonaldTrump/status/984017894240604161; https://twitter.com/realDonaldTrump/status/949616329463615489; and https://twitter.com/realDonaldTrump/status/1119572078175367168.

70 https://twitter.com/realDonaldTrump/status/828574430800539648.

71 https://twitter.com/realDonaldTrump/status/832708293516632065.

72 J. Farkas and J. Schou, 'Fake News as a Floating Signifier: Hegemony, Antagonism and the Politics of Falsehood' (2018) 25(3) *Javnost-The Public* 306.

journalists as being in opposition to American citizens and therefore bad for the country. Trump returns to this theme often, such as in a tweet of 17 August 2018 that states: 'THE FAKE NEWS MEDIA IS THE OPPOSITION PARTY. It is very bad for our Great Country .... BUT WE ARE WINNING!'[73] Once again, the press is framed as a destructive adversary to citizens.

Like the Nazis' use of *Lügenpresse*, the term 'fake news' is sometimes even used to downplay and justify what many see as racist policies and initiatives.[74] One initiative which became a cornerstone of Trump's 2016 presidential campaign and his first term as President is a proposed wall on the US southern border. Trump made immigration and asylum seekers from South America an issue during his initial campaign announcement when he stated that Mexican immigrants were 'bringing drugs, they're bringing crime, they're rapists, and some I assume are good people'.[75] Many, including journalists and political pundits, saw these comments as racist and xenophobic, and link other Trump administration policies, such as the decision to detain asylum seekers at the border and to separate refugee children from their parents, to that racism and xenophobia.[76] While Trump's policies concerning immigrants and asylum seekers have not reached the extreme of the Nazis' mistreatment of the Jews, Trump (and others in his administration) use claims of 'fake news' to both justify, and dismiss critiques of, their arguably racist treatment of asylum seekers from South America, much like the Nazis used the word *Lügenpresse* in response to critiques of their treatment of Jews. For example, shortly after declaring an official national emergency on the southern US border in February 2019, Trump tweeted:

> There is far more ENERGY on the Right than there is on the Left. That's why we just won the Senate and why we will win big in 2020. The Fake News just doesn't want to report the facts. Border Security is a big factor. The under construction Wall will stop Gangs, Drugs and Crime![77]

In short, Trump resurrected his oft-debunked claims that those crossing the southern border of the US were predominantly criminals and justified the declaration of a national emergency by claiming the 'fake news' was under-reporting both the 'crisis' and public support for the border wall.

---

73 https://twitter.com/realDonaldTrump/status/1030074380397752320.

74 See, for example, S. Kohn, 'Trump's Outrageous Mexico Remarks', *CNN*, 18 June 2015, https://edition.cnn.com/2015/06/17/opinions/kohn-donald-trump-announcement/index.html.

75 R. Neate, 'Donald Trump Announces US Presidential Run with Eccentric Speech', *The Guardian*, 16 June 2015, https://www.theguardian.com/us-news/2015/jun/16/donald-trump-announces-run-president.

76 See, for example, G. Lopez, 'The Research on Race That Helps Explain Trump's Use of Family Separation at the Border', *Vox*, 19 June 2018, https://www.vox.com/identities/2018/6/19/17478970/trump-family-separation-immigration-policy-racism.

77 https://twitter.com/realDonaldTrump/status/1099366469010366464.

Trump is a prolific Twitter user and, as the statistics above suggest, provides ample material for analysis. Indeed, a complete discursive analysis of his tweets that are critical of the press could be the basis for an entire chapter on its own and, unfortunately, is outside the scope of this particular chapter. Trump is not the only politician worthy of such an analysis either; members of the White House senior staff have also taken to deploying the term 'fake news' to deflect criticism. Former White House Press Secretary Sean Spicer, for example, referred to the *New York Times* as 'literally the epitome of fake news' after the newspaper quoted a number of Trump's top advisors by name in a story about dysfunction in the White House.[78] Republican US Senator John Cornyn dismissed a report from the non-partisan Congressional Budget Office, which reported that the American Health Care Act of 2017 or 'Trumpcare' would result in spikes in premiums and lost coverage for millions of Americans, as 'fake news' on Twitter.[79] Furthermore, politicians and government staffers show no signs of deviating from this tactic. Sebastian Gorka, former deputy assistant to Trump, for example, said during an interview with CNN that 'the administration will continue using the term "fake news" until the media understands that their "monumental desire" to attack the President is wrong'.[80] Indeed, use of the term 'fake news' to de-legitimise the press is increasing and taking hold 'among politicians at all levels'[81] from local politicians in rural Idaho to heads of state around the world.

In New Zealand, for example, MP Sir Winston Peters called an April 2017 report in the *New Zealand Herald* about immigration 'fake news', accusing the *Herald* of 'peddling "alternative facts"' after it reported that a recent increase in the number of work visas, resulting in record immigration numbers, were due to people arriving from the UK, Germany, Australia, South Africa and the US rather than Asian countries.[82] In a press release, Peters argued that: '[This] *New Zealand Herald* propaganda written by two Asian immigrant reporters stating the top five source nations for work visas are not Asian is completely wrong and based on flawed data.'[83] Peters is not the only person to question

---

78 E. Stokols and N.D. McCaskill 'Trump Leans on "Fake News" Line to Combat Reports of West Wing Dysfunction', *Politico*, 6 February 2017, http://www.politico.com/story/2017/02/trump-responds-fake-news-white-house-dysfunction-234693.

79 See https://twitter.com/JohnCornyn/status/868541526976090112.

80 C. Massie, 'WH Official: We'll Say "Fake News" until Media Realizes Attitude of Attacking the President is Wrong', *CNN*, 7 February 2017, http://edition.cnn.com/2017/02/07/politics/kfile-gorka-on-fake-news.

81 R.J. Foley, '"Fake News" Smear Takes Hold among Politicians at All Levels', *Associated Press*, 11 March 2018, https://www.apnews.com/4fd6d212e9a3432d9af05574774f7206.

82 C. Peacock, 'Winston Peters Aims a Low Blow at the Herald', *Radio New Zealand*, 30 April 2017, http://www.radionz.co.nz/national/programmes/mediawatch/audio/201841790/winston-peters-aims-a-low-blow-at-the-herald.

83 W. Peters, 'NZ Herald "Alternative Facts" Misleading over Immigration', *Scoop*, 26 April 2017, http://www.scoop.co.nz/stories/PA1704/S00315/nz-herald-alternative-facts-misleading-over-immigration.htm.

the veracity of the statistics. Vernon Small of Fairfax News points out that the analysis was based on the 'stated intention' of arriving immigrants, which can change once landed.[84] However, reporter Colin Peacock also notes that by calling Lincoln Tan and Harkanwal Singh, the two reporters responsible for the story, 'two Asian immigrant reporters ... who seek justify their existence and that of mass immigration coming mainly from Asia coming into the country', Peters sought to personally attack the reporters, singling them out for their ethnicity and accusing them of being 'biased as well as bad, with no basis'.[85]

These are admittedly selective examples, but they demonstrate how use of the phrase 'fake news' allows politicians to dismiss negative news, deflect criticism and de-legitimise the popular press, just as the use of the German word *Lügenpresse* has in the past. However, these claims of 'fake news' are themselves misinformation, a rhetorical mechanism meant to problematise concepts such as 'truth', 'fact' and 'real'. Nevertheless, facts have little to do with claims of fake news. Conor Lynch asks: 'If there are really no facts and only interpretations ... then why bother adhering to a rigid line that separates fact from fiction?'[86] Only personal views and personal understanding are important.

And yet, these personal views can have far-reaching consequences. For example, Trump's team used fake news as an excuse to exclude several press organisations from a press conference in late February 2017,[87] an echo of Nazi policies that limited the activities of critical news agencies during their rule in Germany. In May 2018, Trump even proposed stripping the press credentials of reporters critical of him, tweeting: 'The Fake News is working overtime. Just reported that, despite the tremendous success we are having with the economy & all things else, 91% of the Network News about me is negative (Fake). Why do we work so hard in working with the media when it is corrupt? Take away credentials?'[88] In this tweet, he even directly equates negative coverage with fake news, suggesting that any critique of him is inherently false. Although he frames the cancellation of press credentials as a question, the implication is clear: he is actively considering banning reporters who report negative news about him from the White House.

---

84 V. Small, 'The Immigration Debate: Please Leave Your Logic at the Border', *Stuff*, 27 April 2017, http://www.stuff.co.nz/national/politics/opinion/91921613/the-immigration-debate-please-leave-your-logic-at-the-border.

85 Peacock, *supra* note 82.

86 C. Lynch, 'Trump's War on Environment and Science are Rooted in His Post-truth Politics – and Maybe in Postmodern Philosophy', *Salon.com*, 1 April 2017, https://www.salon.com/2017/04/01/trumps-war-on-environment-and-science-are-rooted-in-his-post-truth-politics-and-maybe-in-postmodern-philosophy.

87 J. Fabian, 'White House Hand-Picks Select Media Outlets for Briefing', *The Hill*, 24 February 2017, http://thehill.com/homenews/administration/321049-white-house-hand-picks-select-media-for-briefing.

88 See https://twitter.com/realdonaldtrump/status/994179864436596736.

Some see Trump's attacks against the press as evidence of his authoritarian tendencies,[89] echoing the way in which the Nazis' use of the term *Lügenpresse* served authoritarianism by intimidating and legitimising the press. The decline of press freedom in places like the US has been noted by organisations such as Reporters Without Borders, which states in its 2018 report:

> In 2017, the 45th President of the United States helped sink the country to 45th place by labelling the press an 'enemy of the American people' in a series of verbal attacks toward journalists, attempts to block White House access to multiple media outlets, routine use of the term 'fake news' in retaliation for critical reporting, and calling for media outlets' broadcasting licenses to be revoked. President Trump has routinely singled out news outlets and individual journalists for their coverage of him, and retweeted several violent memes targeting CNN.[90]

News organisations are also, of course, well aware of the attacks on their credibility and have started fighting back to some extent. For example, in 2018, CNN International aired a commercial during its daily news broadcasts that directly addressed the importance of facts. One of these ads showed a banana peel accompanied by a voiceover which stated: 'Some people might try to tell you that this is an apple. It might even start as a joke. But when they say it over, and over, and over again, and people start to believe it, it's only a matter of time until someone gets hurt.' At the end of the ad, the slogan 'Facts First' appeared.[91] This commercial seems to be written as a direct response to Trump's repeated attacks on the network, highlighted by the closing tag of 'Facts First'. Yet, despite all of this awareness, Trump and other politicians repeatedly refer to news organisations as 'fake news' on an almost daily basis, and others, including their supporters and other citizens, happily, enthusiastically and unquestioningly echo these claims. In short, they have adopted Trump's worldview.

Even more concerning is the June 2018 murder of five journalists at the offices of the newspaper the *Capital Gazette* in Annapolis, Maryland, who were apparently targeted by the perpetrator for accurately reporting his criminal record,[92] and the October 2018 mailing of pipe bombs to several targets in the US, including both prominent Democrats and the New York offices of CNN,

---

89 S. Levitsky and D. Ziblatt, *How Democracies Die*, Crown, New York 2018, p. 2; E.A. Posner, 'The Dictator's Handbook, US Edition' in C. Sunstein (ed.), *Can it Happen Here?: Authoritarianism in America*, HarperCollins, New York 2018, pp. 3–5.

90 Reporters Without Borders, 'RSF Index 2018: U.S. Falls as Canada Rises', *Reporters Without Borders*, 25 April 2018, https://rsf.org/en/rsf-index-2018-us-falls-canada-rises.

91 This ad is available on YouTube: https://www.youtube.com/watch?v=v9izUt_oe00.

92 W. Strobel, 'Gunman Angry at Maryland Newspaper Kills Five in Targeted Attack', *Reuters*, 29 June 2018, https://www.reuters.com/article/us-maryland-shooting/gunman-angry-at-maryland-newspaper-kills-five-in-targeted-attack-idUSKBN1JO2Z1.

all whom had been targets of Trump's vitriol in the past.[93] The suspect arrested in this latter example attended Trump rallies, frequently posted missives on Facebook against Muslims, Democrats including former US President Barack Obama Hillary Clinton and the press, and lived in a van decorated with pro-Trump material and stickers reading 'CNN sucks'.[94] These events suggest that CNN International's advertisement was more prophetic than even it might have realised; it was not long before someone, namely journalists, were indeed hurt – and killed. This trend is not limited to the US. Internationally, threats against journalists are increasing, as exemplified by the October 2018 murder of Saudi-born journalist and American-resident Jamal Khashoggi, a frequent critic of the Saudi government, at the Saudi consulate in Turkey.[95]

5. CONCLUDING REMARKS

There seems to be no stopping the claims that journalists and news organisations are simply fake news. In some ways, the press itself is responsible for the lack of public action against politicians' denigration of journalists. Because of the 'extreme commercialisation' of the news detailed by Victor Pickard, audiences in general discuss and act less, and instead wait for the next bit of news, the next spectacle, the next controversy. However, the increasingly frequent attacks on the press and journalists not only work to limit the freedom of the press, but are also creating conditions in which journalists themselves are under threat. The result is the weakening of the role of the press as the 'Fourth Estate'. While early newspapers were often politically biased and even established by political parties, the idea of the press as a defender of the public emerged during the 'civic populism' movement in the late Victorian era. During this movement, the press became considered as a 'public utility' that could act as a watchdog against corruption, guarantee honesty in government, and educate and defend the public. This idea is reflected in Jürgen Habermas' conceptualisation of the public sphere, in which the press acts as an institution of the public.[96]

---

93 K. de Vries, E. Perez, and S. Prokupecz, '"Act of Terror": Bombs Sent to CNN, Clintons, Obamas, Holder', *CNN*, 25 October 2018, https://www.reuters.com/article/us-maryland-shooting/gunman-angry-at-maryland-newspaper-kills-five-in-targeted-attack-idUSKBN1JO2Z1.

94 N. Chavez, 'Cesar Sayoc was a DJ, Bodybuilder and Pizza Delivery Man before He Became a Bomb Suspect', *CNN*, 28 October 2018, https://edition.cnn.com/2018/10/27/politics/cesar-sayoc-mail-bomb-suspect/index.html.

95 M. Chulov and B. McKernan, 'Jamal Khashoggi: Details of Alleged Saudi Hit Squad Emerge', *The Guardian*, 10 October 2018, https://www.theguardian.com/world/2018/oct/10/alleged-saudi-hit-squad-linked-to-jamal-khashoggi-disappearance.

96 J. Habermas, *Strukturwandel der Öffentlichkeit*, Suhrkamp, Frankfurt am Main 1990.

Rhetorical attacks against the press, as the comparison between *Lügenpresse* and fake news above demonstrates, serve to weaken public trust in the press and undermine its watchdog role. As NPR reporter Danielle Kurtzleben summarises, calling the media fake news 'implies that the news isn't serving its basic purposes: It means that the story is intended to serve something other than the public good, and that the author *intended to falsify the story*'.[97] Jonathan Albright similarly stresses that: 'The use of the "fake news" label to denote organizational untrustworthiness ... portrays media watchdogs as entities that operate to deliberately misinform.'[98] Thus, calling journalists and news networks 'fake news' cements the idea that the press is the enemy of the people and undermines the authority of journalists at a time when people's trust in the media is already at an all-time low.

In short, the use of the term 'fake news' represents a purposeful attempt by those in power to silence their detractors, intimidate journalists and shut down rather than encourage debate. These actions represent a threat to press freedom and our ability to remain informed, engaged citizens. In such an environment, democracy can quickly give way to authoritarianism. As more politicians in more countries adopt Trump's language and tactics, the threats to democracy worldwide will become increasingly significant.

---

97 D. Kurtzleben, 'With "Fake News", Trump Moves from Alternative Facts to Alternative Language', *NPR*, 17 February 2017, http://www.npr.org/2017/02/17/515630467/with-fake-news-trump-moves-from-alternative-facts-to-alternative-language. Emphasis added.

98 Albright, *supra* note 38.

3. INFORMATION AND DISINFORMATION AND THE TRANSFORMATION OF MODERN DEMOCRACY

From Media Bias through the 'Echo Chamber' and the 'Filter Bubble' to Fake News

Rafał KLEPKA*

1. INTRODUCTION

Changes in modern democracies take place in many directions determined by institutional factors, historical processes and economic, social, religious and cultural conditions. In these changes it is often difficult to find many common features, conditions or regularities. The issue and threat that all democratic states without exception have to deal with is the problem of reliably informing citizens about political processes. The classics of modern democracy, to mention only Robert Dahl, Joseph Schumpeter and Giovanni Sartori, emphasised that a citizen is needed for the functioning of this political system, especially in the face of political elections and referendums, who has reliable and if possible full information about the political offer and activities and decisions of political actors.[1] There is currently no dispute in relation to the fact that information is the basis for making decisions in democracy.[2] However, both for the rulers and contenders for government, as well as state and non-state players in the international arena, impact in the area of information becomes the most

* Faculty of Social Sciences, Pedagogical University of Cracow, Poland. Email: rafal.klepka@up.krakow.pl.

1 R. A. DAHL, *On Democracy*, Yale University Press, New Haven 2015; J. A. SCHUMPETER, *Capitalism, Socialism and Democracy*, Routledge, New York 2013; G. SARTORI, *The Theory of Democracy Revisited. Part One: The Contemporary Debate*, Chatham House Publishers, Chatham 1987.

2 C. HAPPER and G. PHILO, 'The Role of the Media in the Construction of Public Belief and Social Change' (2013) 1 *Journal of Social and Political Psychology* 321.

important, not to say the key imperative of action.[3] We have no doubt at present that it is in the area of information creation that the greatest efforts to achieve political and economic goals have been located in recent decades that affect all processes in modern democracies and democratic systems as a whole.

It seems that the fastest-growing information industry, which also has the greatest impact on the knowledge and orientation of citizens, is the media sector. Although only in the opinion of extreme idealists has the media ever remained fully objective and independent of owners, rulers and economic influences, nowadays the processes of informing citizens are increasingly deliberately isolated from the truth based on facts, aiming at simplifications and interpretations adapted to the intentions of broadcasters. This process is progressing more dynamically. It is influenced by economic, political and technological conditions. Disinformation processes no longer rely only on the biased presentation of political processes, but tend to lock the citizen in an information bubble and address completely manipulated messages towards them so that the concept of truth loses any value.

The purpose of this chapter is to analyse the problem of disinformation and, in particular, the growing scale of the phenomenon, with particular emphasis on fake news as a new communication phenomenon. This analysis aims to indicate what threats to modern democracies are posed by new phenomena in the field of mass communication. The main motive of the above-outlined phenomena is the presentation of successive sequences of information processing methods, which, together with technological progress, are increasingly distant from neutrality and the idea of reflecting reality. Over time, political bias, which has always been present in the media, began to use human natural predispositions and technical possibilities to create echo chambers and information bubbles. The latest step in the development of the analysed trend is fake news, which, however, seems to be only the next stage in the discussed process and not its final stage.

2. MEDIA BIAS

The first widely known step towards disinformation remains political media bias. We deal with it in a situation where some reasons, views, political parties, ideologies, value systems, religions, nations and professions are favoured and presented in a good light, while others are criticised, discriminated and presented in a negative way. Therefore, bias may apply not only to politics, but also to religion, attitudes, nationalities and advertised products. Bias is often defined as the opposite of objectivity. It should be pointed out here that there is a far-reaching difficulty in assessing whether the content and reception of the

[3] H. Batorowska, R. Klepka and O. Wasiuta, *Media jako instrument wpływu informacyjnego i manipulacji społeczeństwem*, Wydawnictwo Libron, Kraków 2019.

message meets this criterion. The choice of events or words for presentation, the shortness of media forms and cultural diversity are factors that make it difficult to assess whether the material presents political reality objectively. There is no doubt that the comprehensive selection of sources and their comparison with each other favours a multilateral view on a given issue. Most often, the definition of media bias is accompanied by an indication that the media should be balanced. This claim can be understood in many ways: on the one hand, as equilibrium and, on the other hand, as equality in access and presentation of specific parties, candidates or political motivations. The difficulty of clearly defining political media bias results in some researchers treating it as an imperfection resulting from a shortage of journalistic standards or a lack of compliance with these standards by media employees. They point to the lack of journalistic ethics or precision in journalistic codes. Often, bias is also seen as a departure from journalistic professionalism. In normative concepts, there are often presumptions that bias is a consequence of the fact that media employees are in too close relationships with and place too much reliance on political actors, and the claim that political journalism should be purely informative, so separating facts from values and assessments should be of key importance.

Researchers of political communication, bearing in mind the expectations formulated for the media, agree on the specificity of media coverage of political phenomena. Brian McNair emphasises that, of course, the media do not give neutral and impartial information about what is happening in the political arena. As he indicates, despite protests from some journalists emphasising their steadfast objectivity, there is enough media analysis in the communications literature to prove that their accounts of political events, like any other category of reality, are burdened with value judgements, subjectivity and prejudice.[4] Richard M. Perloff argues that the media are not a mirror of political reality, which he explains, by saying that news is not a transcript and is not synonymous with court transcriptions, conscientiously transcribed by a judicial stenographer; rather, news should be treated as a series of judgements about important events of the day and issues that citizens in democracy should know about.[5]

Media political bias is usually defined as the opposite of balance and objectivity in the presentation of politics, e.g. rewarding selected political views, showing a particular political party in a better light or quoting opinions more frequently for one reason.[6] Two forms of media bias, which are often difficult to distinguish, can be identified. The first of them, which should be described as unintended political bias, remains largely independent of the creators of media

---

4 B. McNair, *An Introduction to Political Communication*, Routledge, New York 2011, p. 11.

5 R. M. Perloff, *The Dynamics of Political Communication: Media and Politics in a Digital Age*, Routledge, New York 2014, p. 183.

6 R. Klepka, *Medialna walka o dobrą zmianę: obraz wyborów parlamentarnych w 2015 roku w wybranych mediach*, Wydawnictwo Libron, Kraków 2018.

coverage. It is a consequence of the fact that the media image of the phenomenon always remains a slice, fragment or abbreviation. Each journalist or editorial team, regardless of their intentions, will choose a different fragment of the speech or will illustrate their statement with a different picture of the politician; due to the limited duration of the material or the volume of the article, they will skip the selected fragment. To some extent, this kind of bias can be considered a natural consequence of the media coverage of reality.[7]

The intended political bias should be treated differently. It consists in presenting political phenomena in such a way as to favour a selected party to a political conflict, a political party or supporters of a specific solution, while either negatively assessing the opposing party or ignoring information about its existence.[8] David N. Hopmann, Peter van Aelst and Guido Legnante point to three major dimensions of intentional political bias.[9] The first relates to the visibility of political actors, who can be given more or less attention, and thus rewarding or eliminating their points of view. The second dimension is the tone of the materials presented in the media. Using a countless range of resources, it is possible to evaluate a particular political actor in a clearly favourable or critical way. The role of journalistic commentary, narration, confrontation with the past or another political actor will play a huge role here.[10] Finally, the third dimension concerns the selection of problems to be undertaken. Deliberate selection can lead to the elimination of selected points of view or over-representation of materials devoted to a particular issue.

The impartiality of the media, which is an unattainable dream and is constantly present in the concepts of perfect democracies, is rarely realised in practice. In turn, the constant increase in the importance of the media and the fact that they not only complement but often replace knowledge flowing from other sources lead to far-reaching consequences. At a time when information about the surrounding world, including politics, economy, health and fashion, is mainly drawn from the media, favouring specific trends, ideas or people, this may have a huge influence on the economic, political, social and cultural dimensions. This significance is increased in particular by the fact that media bias is not the only reason for the disinformation distortion of the image of the world that reaches us. A great role is also played by the echo chamber, filter bubble and the occurrence of fake news.

---

7 B. Łódzki, 'Medialny obraz rzeczywistości' (2017) 9 *Studia Socialia Cracoviensia* 123.

8 T. Groseclose and J. Milyo, 'A Social-Science Perspective on Media Bias' (2005) 17 *Critical Review* 308.

9 D. N. Hopmann, P. van Aelst and G. Legnante, 'Political Balance in the News: A Review of Concepts, Operationalizations and Key Findings' (2012) 13 *Journalism* 247.

10 W. Donsbach and T. E. Patterson, 'Political News Journalists: Partisanship, Professionalism, and Political Roles in Five Countries' in F. Esser and B. Pfetsch (eds.), *Comparing Political Communication: Theories, Cases, and Challenges*, Cambridge University Press, Cambridge 2004, p. 251.

3. THE 'ECHO CHAMBER' AND THE 'FILTER BUBBLE'

A step further from the biased presentation of facts remains the phenomena known as the 'echo chamber' and the 'filter bubble'. These explain that due to various reasons, both on the side of the media recipients and the media infrastructure, readers and viewers receive material that confirms their knowledge, beliefs, attitudes and opinions about the world of politics. The recipients of the media are primarily looking for material that would prove that their assessments are correct, which as a consequence may lead to the fact that the individual is in a metaphorical room with an echo and therefore does not have access to views, assessments and opinions that are critical of his or her position. The choice of newspaper, TV programme or website for most media users is not an expression of chance or curiosity about the world, but an implementation that is consistent with a psychological confirmation strategy, i.e. a tendency to prefer those sources of information and opinions that confirm already-held expectations or hypotheses. The media recipient who once spoke on a particular side of a political dispute has little chance to change his or her mind; in the echo chamber he does not hear any arguments that could help him change his mind or even feel doubt.[11]

The 'filter bubble' concept proves that the trend of searching for media confirming recipient beliefs is also employed by algorithms used on the Internet. Using known search engines, such as Google, users of social networking sites Facebook and Twitter have little chance of encountering entries, materials and opinions contrary to their own. Search engines and social media using knowledge about what was liked by a given recipient, and in particular what topics and opinions he or she followed for the greatest amount of time, quickly create a filter bubble. As a result, the user is always in a group of subjects and points of view similar to his own and will never be directed to other values that are incompatible with this. In this way, the recipients of modern media are convinced that they remain in the majority because all the sources they deal with not only confirm but also deepen their way of thinking, which strongly shapes political views and promotes their polarisation.[12]

The first of these phenomena to a greater extent relates to our human tendencies, while the second relates to the impact of media infrastructure. 'Echo chamber' is a concept that appeared as a result of the increase in the amount of opinion-forming and biased media content. In relation to political content, the

---

11 R. Klepka and J. Idzik, 'Polish Weeklies in Local Government Election Campaign in Light of "Echo Chamber" Theory' (2019) 280 *Annales Universitatis Paedagogicae Cracoviensis Studia de Securitate* 58.

12 R. Klepka and J. Idzik, 'Voters in The Filter Bubble: Local Government Election Campaign in Polish Opinion Weeklies in the Light of the "Echo Chamber" Concept' (2019) 4 *International Relations Review* 121.

phenomenon of the echo chamber most often refers to the flow of information on the Web and the information behaviour of Internet users. The huge number of biased websites and the multitude of politically one-sided voices on social media create a huge space where media users repeat what others have said. This phenomenon is not an intentional side-effect of contemporary journalism practice, but a consequence of the creation of a closed communication space that can potentially generate new messages with similar content and isolate them from any form of criticism.[13]

The echo chamber phenomenon was used to explain the production and dissemination of information published by information media. At a time when journalists of such media are expected to publish content 24 hours a day, seven days a week, the information is constantly processed and reused, because the same stories and opinions appear in many places at the same time. Large and recognised media companies, as well as smaller, alternative media and online dailies, are appealing to each other to promote their materials. By answering each other's messages and opinions, each of them legitimises the other.

The presumption of the existence of the echo chamber phenomenon in a closed media space was used by Kathleen Hill Jamieson and Joseph N. Cappella in 2008 in their study of conservative media and their recipients.[14] Enclosed media space has the potential to both magnify the messages delivered within it and insulate them from rebuttal, and creates a common frame of reference and positive feedback loops for those who listen to, read and watch these media outlets. They have proven that, in particular, three media products – Rush Limbaugh's radio talk show, Fox News and the editorial side of the *Wall Street Journal* – are an echo chamber that effectively promotes and defends the conservative principles and the Republican Party. These three separate media entities not only cite each other, but also create positive feedback loops for recipients, sharing links to content on each other's websites. Jamieson and Cappella concluded that the consistency and repetition of their conservative message creates an ideological space for a conservative audience because media opinions resonate from their existing beliefs.

As a consequence of the existence of a closed communication space, contemporary media recipients increasingly feel that almost all people around them think similarly, that they are in the majority and that views in opposition to those they hold are extremely rare. Often in such a situation, the results of elections and referendums or even the results of public opinion polls are surprising because it turns out that, contrary to expectations, the individual is

---

13 S. E. Bor, 'Echo Chamber Phenomenon' in K. Harvey (ed.), *Encyclopedia of Social Media and Politics*, SAGE, Los Angeles 2014, pp. 427–428.

14 K. H. Jamieson and J. N. Cappella, *Echo Chamber: Rush Limbaugh and the Conservative Media Establishment*, Oxford University Press, Oxford 2010, pp. 75–90.

in a minority and his or her views are not as popular as expected. Numerous studies prove that such feelings, as well as the broadly understood formation of our beliefs and opinions (not only in relation to our political decisions or views, but also to how others think) are created or at least co-created by the media. Interesting evidence confirming this thesis is provided by media coverage of events such as Brexit, the 2016 presidential election in the US won by Donald Trump, the hybrid war between Russia and Ukraine, waves of refugees coming to Europe after the Syrian crisis or increasingly popular fake news. They clearly prove that the very selection of information sources we use, whether made by us or by Internet search engines and social media, as well as our existing knowledge and beliefs have a strong impact on our perception and assessment of phenomena relating to politics and security.[15]

According to some of these concepts, the individual using the media is exposed to self-censorship and has contact only with filtered information, which means that one actually learns only attitudes and views similar to one's own. In this way, the citizen is placed in the chamber with a ubiquitous echo. One has many channels and sources of information at one's disposal, but on the one hand, one reaches for content which satisfies one's expectations and, on the other hand, technological solutions facilitate one's access to those sources that make it possible to confirm the judgements and feelings to which one is accustomed.

Self-censorship means that conservative people who have religious values use Catholic media, and viewers and readers with liberal views use media that present their own ideas of the world. Similarly, on the Internet, search engines and social media using knowledge about what has been liked by a given recipient, and in particular, what topics and opinions have been followed for the greatest amount of time, cause that user to always be in a group of topics of interest to him or her and points of view similar to his or her own, and will never be directed to other values that are incompatible with this.

The above example describes the audience as a passive consumer of information in a media-dominated echo chamber. However, viewers can also play a more active role when they participate in creating content in interactive digital forums. By using social networking sites, personal Internet journals and other online platforms that encourage interaction with recipients, units enhance the echo chamber effect by sending multimedia content and expressing additional feedback. In particular, scientists and critics have recognised the ability of social networks to enhance echo effects as a result of their technical structure and design. On social networking sites, users search for and maintain contact with other people with whom they share similar beliefs. Friends and connections

---

15 R. Klepka, 'Obrazy polityki w mediach: podstawowe uwarunkowania' in R. Klepka (ed.), *Medialne obrazy świata. Wybrane problemy społeczno-polityczne w mediach*, Wydawnictwo Uniwersytetu Pedagogicznego, Kraków 2018, pp. 9–25.

overlap in most networks, and so users still hear the same information. Research suggests that people who are repeatedly exposed to the same information provided by different sources eventually accept this information as true.

Fragmentation of the audience and its polarisation and creation of a false illusion of reality is only one of the negative consequences of the echo chamber phenomenon. Research in the field of communication and social sciences suggests that the audience learns about policy information, starting their reception with existing attitudes and preferences that they want to strengthen by choosing compatible media. Internet technology enables users to selectively expose themselves to certain content and opinions that resonate with their beliefs. Through this process of seeking information, viewers defend themselves against information that undermines their beliefs, and ultimately their commitment to a biased and far from objective echo leads them to adopt more extreme attitudes that increase the polarisation of political attitudes.[16]

Some researchers suggest that the echo chamber phenomenon and its polarising effects continue to increase as a result of the technical and cultural characteristics of the Internet. For example, information organisations and political campaigns are increasingly encouraging their online audience to form social groups and discussion forums around topics of common interest. Researchers say this activity creates social enclaves of like-minded people that ultimately prevent citizens from accessing different points of view and sharing common experiences. Online social groups isolate themselves and their opinions from new challenges, which widens the gap between extreme parties in public issues.

The second phenomenon – the filter bubble – is also a term referring to intellectual isolation, but which arises as a result of algorithmic personalisation. The concept was popularised by Internet activist Eli Pariser thanks to his work entitled *The Filter Bubble: What the Internet is Hiding from You* published in 2011.[17] In it, Pariser argued that due to search engines such as Google and algorithms used by Facebook, recipients only access data that they will like because of compliance with their expectations, views, tastes and opinions. This state of affairs makes Internet users feel that everyone thinks like them, which leads to strong polarisation and may have negative consequences in public, especially in terms of political discourse.

Initially, the Internet was an anonymous medium and the search results were independent of users, offering them the freedom and transparency they expected. This utopian vision soon faded. The availability of huge computing power and the ability to generate large amounts of data have impacted the transparency of search engines through the use of individualised algorithms.

---

16 C. R. Sunstein, 'The Law of Group Polarization' (2002) 10 *Journal of Political Philosophy* 175.

17 E. Pariser, *The Filter Bubble: What the Internet is Hiding from You*, Penguin, New York 2011.

A global network can increase the degree of individual autonomy. Initially, it seemed that pluralism and a variety of points of view were necessary to make well-thought-out decisions about what we identify with the most. The amount of information available online offered the opportunity to choose from a wide range of options, but over time it turned out that making decisions would not be possible without some degree of filtering. In order to be effective, dynamic decision-making becomes necessary, which would be impossible in the huge flood of information provided. Therefore, people remain limited in terms of making decisions because their brains are not able to process all the available information. Without filtering, an individual can have a high degree of autonomy, but have difficulty making decisions.

The human need for filtering has led to algorithmic personalisation. Personalised algorithms filter the content and structure of Web content to tailor it to the specific needs, goals, interests and preferences of each user. It all starts with a user model created on the basis of all user behaviours, such as click history, location and personal data. By unifying different messages under one identity, the system can predict which information will be relevant to a given user and filter out data that does not fit with the user's model, making it easier for the user to find a way forward in the flood of online information.

However, algorithmic personalisation is not without its risks because it can seriously undermine the necessary conditions for personal autonomy. In this context, it should be noted that the individual's ability to self-assess is significantly impaired. In order to determine his or her needs, he or she must be able to assess who he or she is and who he or she wants to be, but it becomes difficult, if not impossible, when personalised filtering limits his or her knowledge of the world and himself or herself. Personalisation filters are a kind of invisible self-propaganda, indoctrinating us with our own ideas, strengthening our desire for things that are familiar and leaving us unaware of any contrary information. As a result, filtering bubbles prevent users from realising that their beliefs and desires may need to be rethought, thus seriously weakening their ability to self-assess.[18]

Critics argue that filtering bubbles do not have many disadvantages, since it is natural that people actively search for reliable information and ask if their beliefs are really justified.[19] However, attention is drawn by a phenomenon known as 'affirmative bias' or the human tendency to believe in things that reinforce existing beliefs. Affirmative bias does not work in the same way as information bubbles, because affirmation error is a feature of the human mind and filtering bubbles are not. Personalised algorithms are imposed more than

---

18 D. Geschke, J. Lorenz and P. Holtz, 'The Triple-Filter Bubble: Using Agent-Based Modelling to Test a Meta-theoretical Framework for the Emergence of Filter Bubbles and Echo Chambers' (2019) 58 *British Journal of Social Psychology* 129.

19 F. J. Z. Borgesius, D. Trilling, J. Möller, B. Bodó, C. H. de Vreese and N. Helberger, 'Should We Worry about Filter Bubbles?' (2016) 5(1) *Internet Policy Review* 1.

the psychological determinants of human activities. In addition, information bubbles are a relatively new phenomenon that many people are still not aware of, especially because the information is filtered before reaching the user, which happens in isolation from his or her consciousness. Even a person aware of algorithmic personalisation can do little to combat it. The information-filtering criterion is neither transparent nor configurable. Moreover, it seems obvious that in order for users to control the services they use, they need to know what information is used for personalisation and how their data is used. However, achieving this is unlikely, especially considering that even programmers are no longer able to fully explain all the output due to the complexity of algorithmic personalisation. Therefore, perhaps the only real way to protect our autonomy and ability to self-assess would be to give up trying to self-assess, which is also an unrealistic scenario, because the human brain is not able to independently process the flood of information online.

Another consequence of the filter bubble is also noticeable – namely, it leads to the disappearance of critical reflection. In order to rationally support one specific solution rather than another, there must be the ability to question opinions. This becomes difficult without external signals that would encourage the use of this ability. After all, in order to critically reflect on one's aspirations, some kind of contradiction must occur to initiate this process. Personalised algorithms offer a vision of a world adapted to individual needs, each of which suits us perfectly. We are never bored or nervous. Our media are a perfect reflection of our interests and desires. Because of this intellectual isolation and especially because we are unaware of the essence of the filtering process, we never feel the need to look beyond our personal preferences, let alone critically reflect on them. The obliviousness of users, combined with the lack of control and transparency of personalised algorithms, completely disables the ability for critical analysis.

In the world of echo chambers and filtering bubbles, thanks to the constant provision of information consistent with the user's interests, but also confirming the assumptions and beliefs, the individual has a high degree of consistency in terms of what he or she believes – for example, a vegetarian who constantly receives information confirming his or her life choice.

4. FAKE NEWS

The development of modern means of communication, in particular the Internet, has greatly contributed to the deepening of recipients' disinformation processes. In recent years, this phenomenon has become the large-scale creation and distribution of fake news.[20] The creation and dissemination of fake messages has

[20] J. Albright, 'Welcome to the Era of Fake News' (2017) 5 *Media and Communication* 87.

a long tradition that dates back to distant times. One of the best-known examples is the 'Great Lunar Deception' of 1835, when the *New York Sun* published a series of articles about the discovery of life on the moon. At the beginning of the 20th century, *The Protocols of the Elders of Zion* was published, which described alleged Jewish plans for world domination and remains one of the best-known uses of a false text for propaganda purposes.[21] The most spectacular among the latest examples of fake news is the 'Flemish Art Nouveau' of 2006. At that time, Belgian public television reported that the Flemish Parliament declared independence and secession from Belgium, which many viewers mistakenly took to be a real message rather than a provocative joke.

Despite the long history of fake news, there are several reasons to believe that fake news is increasingly important. First of all, barriers to entry in the media industry have fallen sharply, both due to the ease of setting up websites and the ease of making money on online content through advertising platforms. Because the fear of losing reputation discourages the media from knowingly reporting false news, usually even finding a mistake or a simple error does not lead to announcing this and withdrawing from the given fake news. Second, social media is well adapted to false messaging and the use of social media has increased rapidly: in 2016, the number of active Facebook users per month reached 1.8 billion and Twitter over 400 million.[22] Third, there is a clear decline in confidence in the mass media as a source of fully accurate and reliable news. Losing trust in mainstream media can be both a cause and a consequence of the growth of fake news.

It is possible to adopt a narrow and broad definition of fake news.[23] From a narrow perspective, the sender's intentions remain the key criterion. According to this concept, fake news is material created for propaganda purposes to cause an emotional reaction of recipients and thus create or strengthen existing prejudices against a specific group or person and obtain political benefits from this. An example of fake news understood in this way may be the numerous news broadcast by the Pierwyj channel, the main public television broadcasting channel in the Russian Federation, which during the hybrid war with Ukraine presented news presenting fictional events in order to shape Russian and to some extent Ukrainian public opinion in relation to the nature and specificity of the ongoing conflict.

Adopting a broader definition of fake news means recognising as their main criterion for extracting such messages their incompatibility with the facts.

---

21 D. Welch, 'Fakes' in N. J. Cull, D. H. Culbert and D. Welch (eds.), *Propaganda and Mass Persuasion: A Historical Encyclopedia, 1500 to the Present*, ABC-CLIO, Santa Barbara 2003, pp. 123–124.

22 N. W. Jankowski, 'Researching Fake News: A Selective Examination of Empirical Studies' (2018) 25 *Javnost – The Public* 248.

23 E. C. Tandoc Jr., Z. W. Lim and R. Ling, 'Defining "Fake News"' (2018) 6 *Digital Journalism* 137.

In this approach, the fake news group will include unintentional errors in media coverage, such as an incorrect report that Donald Trump removed the bust of Martin Luther King Jr. from the Oval Office in the White House, media rumours, conspiracy theories that are by definition difficult to verify as true or false and usually come from people who consider them to be true, satirical material that may be considered unlikely to be misinterpreted as true, and extremely biased and misleading media material that mislead but are not completely false.

Fake press articles played a large role in important political events, such as the 2016 presidential election in the US, voting on the UK leaving the EU or Russia's hybrid war in Ukraine. Researchers have found that fake news comes from several types of websites. For example, some websites are created solely to generate intentionally fabricated and misleading articles, such as denverguardian.com. The names of these pages are often chosen to resemble those of legitimate news sites. Other satirical sites contain articles that can be interpreted as real when they are taken out of context, such as wtoe5news.com. Yet other sites, such as endingthefed.com, publish a mix of real, often biased articles along with some fake content. Sites that provide fake news tend to be short-lived and many of them were important in the run-up to the 2016 US presidential election. Separate investigations by BuzzFeed and *The Guardian* revealed that more than 100 sites publishing fake news were run by teenagers in the small town of Veles in North Macedonia. Endingthefed.com, the site that was responsible for four of the top ten fake messages on Facebook, was run by a 24-year old Romanian man. An American company called Disinfomedia has many fake news sites, including NationalReport.net, USAToday.com.co and WashingtonPost.com.co, and its owner claimed to employ between 20 and 25 authors. Another US fake news site owner, Paul Horner, ran a fake news report called National Report many years before the 2016 presidential election. Among his most widespread fake news stories was 2013 material that claimed that President Barack Obama used his own money to maintain a Muslim museum. During the election, Horner produced a lot of fake news, mainly about stories supporting Trump's candidacy.[24]

It has been pointed out that there are two main motivations for delivering fake news. The first is financial: news articles that are becoming popular on social media can attract significant advertising revenue when users click on the original page. It seems that this was the main motivation for most producers whose identity was revealed. For example, teenagers in Veles created stories that favoured both Trump and Hillary Clinton, earning tens of thousands of dollars from them. Paul Horner made pro-Trump stories for profit, despite claims that he was personally against Trump. The second level of motivation is ideological.

---

[24] H. Allcott and M. Gentzkow, 'Social Media and Fake News in the 2016 Election' (2017) 31 *Journal of Economic Perspectives* 211.

Some fake news providers try to express support for the candidates they support. The creator of fake news from Romania who ran the endingthefed.com portal claimed that he created the site mainly to help Trump.

Trump has been at war with the media since the beginning of his presidential campaign.[25] The media fight and Trump's daily attacks on the media through his Twitter campaigns and insights given in favour of him were significant features of both Trump's presidential campaign and the beginnings of his presidency. When the media criticised his statements or actions, Trump continued his attack. When he made dubious or evidently false statements and encountered opposite evidence, he and his supporters rejected all critical claims about him as fake news and 'alternative facts'. Referring to Mao and Stalin, Trump called the mainstream media the 'enemy of the people', and rarely a day went by without protests against the media being posted on Trump's Twitter account. The scale and scope of application by the presidential candidate, and then the US head of state, of fake news and accusations directed against all opponents of using fake news have led to a difficult situation for average citizens in losing orientation in terms of what is true, what may be true and what is erroneous.

The attention of fake news researchers is drawn to mechanisms that can influence the attention of recipients. There are applications that make it possible to quickly empower emotionally marked messages on platforms such as Twitter. These are strategic attention control tools that can accelerate the spread of disinformation and create alternative facts. When a Facebook user writes specific words, the application affects the words selected later by their friends. Sentiment-based sharing tools work similarly, such as the 'reaction' emotions on Facebook, which further complicate the problem of social distortions because they codify and aggregate feelings related to messages. This means that even if the controversial fake news can be properly verified in terms of its factual accuracy, it can cause outrage or confusion at the target audience even earlier. The main problem regarding fake news and social networking is the functioning of an entire industry traditionally focused on creating audiences. By gathering detailed knowledge about human (often the most intimate) desires and likes, platforms develop tools to create and manage specific needs. The core activities of technology companies include the design of identity-based data collection and profiling systems. This means both the potential possibility of addressing fake news to a specific group of recipients for whom the content is emotionally, or for other reasons, important, but also the ability to create the expectations of users of social networking sites to receive false content.

In many environments, there is a question about the possibility of fighting fake news. One of these methods is used in Ukraine. The crisis in this country

25 D. Kellner, 'Trump's War against the Media, Fake News, and (A)Social Media' in C. Happer, A. Hoskins and W. Merrin (eds.), *Trump's Media War*, Palgrave Macmillan, Cham 2019, pp. 47–67.

has proven the strong position of Russian television as the strongest asset of the Russian government in its information war. However, the Internet has allowed other users to question the Kremlin's narrative, creating fake news responses and refuting distorted information and false images. These assumptions are implemented by StopFake.org, which was launched in March 2014 in Kiev as a project to combat disinformation mainly from Russian media and the Internet. The initiators of the activities were initially students of journalism, but soon they were joined by other professionals and computer-savvy Internet users from Ukraine and other countries. The community mobilises ordinary Internet users to engage in detecting and revealing fake news, fabricated stories and images about the crisis in Ukraine using the 'report fake news' button.[26]

5. CONCLUSION

As indicated above, political media bias, the emergence of the echo chamber and filter bubbles, and the creation of fake news are forms of evolution in the scale, scope and manner of using disinformation. As we have proved, each of these phenomena has been present in the public space in democratic countries for a long time. However, the scale, scope and frequency of their occurrence is unprecedented. The role of each of them grew gradually. Political media bias is the first step in creating of disinformation. Information provided in a biased manner is only slightly deformed or only subject to appropriate interpretation. Echo chambers and filter bubbles are more sophisticated phenomena that use our mind technologies and Internet algorithms to influence our views and promote their perpetuation. The popularity and scale of using fake news in recent years shows that information is entering a new era in which it is not the interpretation of information or access to it, but the content itself that is manipulated in a purposeful and planned manner.

The modern functioning of democracy seems to be exposed to numerous difficulties as a result of changes in access to information and the media. Paradoxically, these changes are not about reducing this access, but about increasing it, creating the problem of the need to make a choice between what is true and what is not amongst the flood of information, selected for us by the media themselves or our predispositions from those we came across ourselves. The struggle is between recipients and their psychological predispositions, media and information infrastructure, and media institutions that seek to shape our knowledge of the world. In this fight between truth and falsehood, information and disinformation, reality and imagination, there is an increasingly thinner and

[26] I. Khaldarova and M. Pantti, 'Fake News: The Narrative Battle over the Ukrainian Conflict' (2016) 10 *Journalism Practice* 891.

harder to grasp border. What will democracy become in the face of post-truth? How will disinformation in high doses affect electoral processes, decisions taken by voters, consumers societies and politicians? Even the greatest scientific visionaries in the fields of media and politics have not yet been able to answer these questions.

It seems that the biggest problem related to the new information reality is the growing scope and extent of the use of lies, falsehood and fraud, which should also be associated with universal access to such applications as FakeApp or Deepfake.[27] These programs allow not only specialists and experts, but basically every Internet user (even those with average skills) to generate for any purpose a specific fake news equipped with a movie, image or sound recording created using special software. As a consequence of the widespread use of such tools, not only politics and business but also everyday interpersonal relationships can become an element of post-truth built from difficult-to-separate facts mixed with elements generated by competitors, enemies or other countries. Media reports about war, death and revolution can be both a fact to which a citizen should react and a fiction whose only purpose is to cause a reaction.

It is possible to present a series of advice or proposals for actions in relation to the increasing role of disinformation in modern democracy. Undoubtedly, it would be worth conducting separate, multi-faceted research on this topic. However, there is no doubt that civic education and social and political commitment remain the most effective remedies for misinformation in a democratic society. It seems that only adequate preparation to be an aware citizen and a responsible consumer of media content can be an attempt to fight the ubiquitous tendency towards misinformation. The pursuit of opposition to misinformation is undoubtedly one of the greatest challenges facing modern democracies.

---

27 O. Wasiuta and S. Wasiuta, 'Deepfake jako skomplikowana i głęboko fałszywa rzeczywistość' (2019) 289 9(3) *Annales Universitatis Paedagogicae Cracoviensis Studia de Securitate* 19; O. Wasiuta and S. Wasiuta, 'FakeApp jako nowe zagrożenie bezpieczeństwa politycznego i informacyjnego' (2019) 9(3) *Annales Universitatis Paedagogicae Cracoviensis Studia de Securitate* 129.

4. (DIS)INFORMATION, NEOLIBERALISM AND THE STRENGTH OF DEMOCRACY IN THE DIGITAL AGE

Matteo STOCCHETTI*

1. INTRODUCTION: (DIS)INFORMATION, POWER AND IDEOLOGY

Before we can discuss solutions, we need to agree on the problem or, at least, the nature of our concerns. In the discussion about (dis)information and democracy, I think there are at least two fundamental and fundamentally different sources of concern: the future of democracy and the control of information. From the viewpoint of democratic ideals and values, the question of control in general, and of control of information in particular, is always a very problematic one. From the viewpoint of control, or rather of the elites and groups that seek control, democracy may also be a problematic condition. Different sets of problems but also different and in many respects competing sets of concerns feed into the relevance of the current debate about disinformation and democracy in the digital age.

Here, I would like to engage with these problems and concerns from a perspective that would allow the reader to appreciate the roots and the implications of both. To this end, I suggest that the differences and competitive aspects can be better appreciated if we look at each viewpoint as constituted by an ideological and an epistemic dimension or, in other words, by a particular vision of the future of society and the nature of knowledge that may, or may not, bring it about.

Consequently, the approach of what follows is explicitly normative and, from this perspective, the debate about the problems of (dis)information and the concerns about the future of democracy is one particular (albeit fundamental) articulation of the broader theme concerning the 'remaking of truth' in the digital age. In this discussion, and from the viewpoint of democratic ideals, epistemic and political problems (or the problems of knowledge and the competition for

* Department of Culture and Media, Arcada University of Applied Sciences, Finland. Email: matteo.stocchetti@arcada.fi.

the control over the distribution of power in society) are interwoven because the practical possibility of a democratic regime depends on the problematisation of truth.

The role of (dis)information is thus a key one, but is also both complex and ambivalent. It is complex because, as Michel Foucault famously argued in his lectures on 'parrhesia' and the problematisation of truth, it has deep and wide ramifications that cannot be ignored. In fact, his description of the crisis of democracy in Athens at the end of the 5th century BCE is strikingly similar to the crisis of democracy in our 'digital age'. In his words:

> The problem, very roughly put, was the following. Democracy is founded by a politeia, a constitution, where the demos, the people, exercise power, and where everyone is equal in front of the law. Such a constitution, however, is condemned to give equal place to all forms of parrhesia, even the worst. Because parrhesia is given even to the worst citizens, the overwhelming influence of bad, immoral, or ignorant speakers may lead the citizenry into tyranny, or may otherwise endanger the city. Hence parrhesia may be dangerous for democracy itself. Thus this problem seems coherent and familiar, but for the Greeks the discovery of this problem, of a necessary antinomy between parrhesia – freedom of speech – and democracy, inaugurated a long impassioned debate concerning the precise nature of the dangerous relations which seemed to exist between democracy, logos, freedom, and truth.[1]

The fundamental dilemma associated with the political functions of moral truths is that of identifying the conditions in which its expression or 'freedom of speech' can strengthen or weaken the 'polis'. This dilemma has important implications for the social construction of reality, for the 'remaking of truth' in the digital age and, in particular, for the role of education in this process.[2]

To approach the same problem from the premise of (dis)information offers an opportunity to engage more directly with the epistemic and the ideological dimensions of this relationship, thus going perhaps one step further in the 'interrogation about truth and democracy' and the problematisation of 'relations between freedom, power, democracy, education, and truth'[3] in our digital age. The practical reason for this interrogation is the widespread feeling that the crisis of democracy may be brought about by an excess or misuse of (dis)information and the risk that, in the conditions of the 21st century, the end of democracy may come about because of, rather than despite, the efforts to save it.

---

1 M. Foucault, 'Discourse and Truth: The Problematization of Parrhesia: 6 lectures given by Michel Foucault at the University of California at Berkeley, Oct–Nov. 1983', 10 February 2020, p. 30, http://foucault.info/documents/parrhesia/.

2 M. Stocchetti, 'Re-making the Truth in the Digital Age. Parrhesia and Human Interest' (2017) 3 *Comunicazioni sociali* 405–414.

3 Foucault, *supra* note 1, p. 31.

In addition to being complex, the role of (dis)information is also ambivalent because 'information' is a concept with at least two and rather different functions depending on the epistemic discourse or, simply put, on the interpretation of its relationship with knowledge.

Two metaphors may help to illustrate this point: (a) information is to knowledge what a piece of a jigsaw puzzle is to the image created when all pieces are correctly placed; (b) information is to knowledge what inspiration is to an artist – a clue that is neither true nor false, but useful or useless in a creative process that is, by definition, open-ended.

These two metaphors illustrate different functions of information but also different meanings of truth. In the puzzle, truth is the relationship between the placing of the right piece and a pre-established order/image. In creative work, truth is the relationship between the artist and an elusive idea that bits and pieces of information may, or may not, help to concretise (technical skills are perhaps necessary but not sufficient to this purpose). In both metaphors, information and truth are indeed connected, but the difference resides in the way in which information and truth relate to the freedom of the agent – the puzzle fan or the artist.

Like all metaphors, these two reveal something and hide something else. In our case, what these metaphors hide is the role of power or, more precisely, the role of power relations which, in the social context, are very often unequal relations of power. This shortcoming is especially objectionable since the whole point of democratic ideals and the political regimes they inspire is precisely about the legitimisation of the use of political power. And it is because (dis)information has to do with power and knowledge that I begin my discussion by arguing that the relationship between (dis)information and democracy is constituted by an epistemic and a political dimension. In other words, it is a problem that has to do with the nature of knowledge and the nature of political power.

'Disinformation' is the word for a problem that is gaining increasing attention from both scholars and practitioners. Roughly summarised, the main points of the mainstream debate are: (a) that disinformation is a threat to democracy; and (b) that in order to protect the political stability of democratic regimes against the threat of populism at home and undemocratic states abroad, we need to deploy countermeasures that would allow the control of communication flow.

In the following pages, I argue that both these points are flawed because they misconstrue the nature of (dis)information and the problems afflicting democratic ideals and regimes in the digital age. Furthermore, I argue that the intellectual defence of these flawed points is vulnerable to ideological manipulation, as it seeks to preserve the influence of political actors against the changes and the challenges associated with the digitalisation of the social construction of reality or the disruptive effects of 'communicative freedom'.

On epistemic grounds, I would also like to disprove the claim or allegation concerning the role of social constructionism and postmodernism in the 'relativisation' of truth, the establishment of a post-truth regime, fostering disinformation and ultimately the crisis of democracy. Despite its intellectual poverty, this claim has gained a certain influence in misleading, distorting and ultimately manipulating public debates, and it has done so to such an extent that it is difficult not to suspect the influence of efforts designed to inhibit the risks of radical change in the domestic and international dimensions of the political process associated with the combination of these epistemologies with the emancipative affordances of digitalisation. Some of these changes surely imply serious risks for democratic ideals. However, the magnitude of these risks is accentuated by the failure of political elites to deliver the promises associated with these ideals and, as I will shortly argue, by the subordination of democratic ideals to the prescriptions of capitalist ideology and the interests of the elites that benefit from them.

My interpretation of disinformation is based on the epistemic grounds of social constructionism and the critical theory of knowledge, and, on more political grounds, on the notion of radical democracy. Against the naïve realism implicit in the argument that disinformation is a threat to democracy, social constructionism and the critical theory of knowledge can be combined to advance the idea that relevant social truths are associated not with empirical control, but with value-led interpretation. The notion of radical democracy is useful to remind those concerned about the power of (dis)information that true democratic regimes have distinctive elements of strength that make them far less vulnerable to subversion than other regimes. The growing concern about the impact of disinformation on Western political regimes and the arguments for enforcing control or censorship, especially as these are voiced in the US and the EU, are signs indicating the weakness of these regimes and not of the democratic ideals they claim to adhere to.

In the rest of this chapter, I will make four main points. First, disinformation is not an exceptional or 'pathological condition' of human communication, but a normal or 'physiological' one, closely associated with politics or competition for the control over the distribution of values in society. To neglect this aspect and construe (dis)information otherwise is a move compatible with the efforts of effacing politics and establishing the discursive grounds for the administrative ruling of society – something already foreseen by Marcuse, which he described as the 'closing of the political universe'[4] and which is currently referred to as the regime of post-politics.

---

4 H. Marcuse, *One-Dimensional Man: Studies in the Ideology of Advanced Industrial Society*, Routledge, London 2002 [1964], p. 21.

Second, and on epistemic grounds, these efforts are also reinstating an implicit positivist notion of reality to counter the 'subversive' effects of the constructionist 'revolution' and postmodernism, the epistemic 'relativism' of which allegedly undermines democracy by paving the way for the notorious 'post-truth' regime. Despite being intellectually 'lightweight', some of the arguments against social constructionism and postmodernism must be taken seriously as expressions of the same philistine tendencies that feed the populist and elitist aggression against democratic ideals. By challenging positivistic notions of truth and objectivistic representation of reality, the constructionist 'revolution' and postmodernism in social sciences and humanities did not bring about the intellectual conditions to undermine democracy; rather, the first brought about the repoliticisation of the social construction of reality. The latter revealed the mutual interdependence between meanings and relations of power or, in the terms of our discussion, the political role and effects of interpretation or hermeneutics. In doing so, I argue that both these intellectual traditions pave the way for the epistemic of radical democracy: the problematisation of truth within the terms of the democratic legitimisation of relations of power.

Third, I argue that the real threat to democratic ideals comes not from (dis)information *per se*, but from the effects of neoliberalism and the growing incompatibility between this permutation of capitalism and democratic ideals in the digital age. For the purposes of this discussion, I interpret this incompatibility in relation to the different roles of information in the ideal representations of capitalist and democratic social orders.

Finally, in the concluding section, I will discuss the strength of democracy: the constitutive elements of democratic ideals and regimes that make these ideals and regimes superior on both political and epistemic grounds. As I will argue, these are the elements we should look at in the digital age if the problem is to defend democracy rather than enforce control.

2. (DIS)INFORMATION SOCIETY

The main point of the argument presented in this section can be summarised as follows. First, in human communication, disinformation is normal in both connotations of the concept: deliberate or non-deliberate. Second, in contemporary 'information society', disinformation results from distortions associated with some distinctive features of capitalism. Third, intervention on distortions interferes with the working of capitalism or is itself an effort to forcefully efface what is distinctive in human communication and in political communication, i.e. to enforce a regime of post-politics.

Disinformation is usually defined in terms of information that is more or less deliberately misleading, because, for example, it is inaccurate or, more frequently, because of a manipulative effort.[5] While most of the current debate focuses on the risks associated with the advent of the Internet,[6] other scholars consider disinformation, in both its connotations, as a structural feature of human communication in general that is exacerbated by the conditions of the 'information society'.

In human communication, disinformation is a normal or 'endemic' state of affairs because, put simply, accuracy is often subordinated to 'sense making'. In other words, human communication is not only a way of sharing information, but is also a practice that establishes identities and group bonding and a ritual that, as James W. Carey put it, 'invites our participation [to the world] on the basis of our assuming often vicariously, social roles within it'.[7] To the extent that human communication involves subjectivities instead of computational systems, 'communication and information are entangled with noise, misunderstanding, degrees of inaccuracy and deception'.[8] The idea that disinformation can be eliminated and social communication fed with pure and certified truths seems based on a metaphorical confusion between social and computer 'systems', and is germane to the idea of post-politics: ruling society like administrators rule computer systems.

Presenting his case for a 'cosmopolitan society' and the need for good communication, Jonathan P. Marshal argued that human communication is characterised by 'normal patterns of distortions' that include 'complexity, categorisation, framing, power relations, standardised lying, information groups, hierarchy, and siloing'.[9] These problems are common in complex societies, but are 'extended and intensified' by information capitalism and 'relatively easily manipulated by those who find hostility, separation and miscommunication useful'.[10] In '(dis)information societies', normal patterns of distortion are intensified by 'data smog, orders of doubt, markets, precarious information work and distributed governance'.[11]

In the conditions of 'data smog', for example, 'accuracy of information can be undermined by strategies to cope with quantity' as the 'ease of information

---

5 D. Fallis, 'What is Disinformation?' (2015) 63 *Library Trends* 401–426; L. Floridi, *The Philosophy of Information*, Oxford University Press, New York 2011; J.H. Fetzer, 'Disinformation: The Use of False Information' (2004) 14 *Minds and Machines* 231–240; P.S. Piper, 'Web Hoaxes, Counterfeit Sites, and Other Spurious Information on the Internet' in A.P. Mintz (ed.), *Web of Deception*, Information Today, Medford, NJ 2002, pp. 1–22.

6 See e.g. L. Floridi, 'Brave.net.world: The Internet as a Disinformation Superhighway?' (1996) 14 *Electronic Library* 509–514.

7 J.W. Carey, *Communication as Culture: Essays on Media and Society*, Unwin Hyman, Boston 1988, pp. 20–21.

8 J.P. Marshall, 'Disinformation Society' (2017) 9(2) *Cosmopolitan Civil Societies Journal*, 1–24, at p. 4.

9 *Ibid.*, pp. 4–10.

10 *Ibid.*, p. 10.

11 *Ibid.*, p. 2.

production' makes available 'data and arguments supporting almost any position' and 'self-confirmation is easy'.[12]

'Data smog', in turn, increases the biases associated with social categorisation:

> In data smog, as reinforced by group separation, it appears that people in information outgroups *are* hopelessly biased, or deliberately trying to deceive ... Their news is easily labelled 'fake news' because it does not agree with the groups' existing information, and its accuracy does not have to be checked ... Pronouncements that other groups are lying, save time, protect group allegiances and remove any need to put energy into interpreting the messages of outgroups. However, this ongoing process of doubt leads to 'information paranoia'; the suspicion that counter-information is likely wrong or deceitful.

Furthermore, in the conditions of capitalist information societies:

> [C]ommunication becomes primarily strategic and identity based. People invest heavily in information groups around identities and meaning, and develop 'information paranoia', embracing an ordering of doubt or suspicion. They tend to become automatically suspicious of other groups, and even of their own 'side', although the suspicion of their own side largely allows them to continue to support the views and alliances they already have.[13]

'Data smog', 'group separation' and 'information paranoia' play a significant role in the widespread crisis of truth seemingly affecting contemporary social institutions. This crisis, however, is aggravated 'by neoliberal support for corporately dominated "free markets" in which the only thing to be trusted is people's monetary self-interest conditions'.[14]

In capitalism, information is 'produced and validated by economic, or political, criteria alone ... Misdirecting others with inaccurate information increases the benefit of any accurate information possessed' and 'advertising (or producing a front) becomes the model for communication'.[15] The distortions associated with the social role of information in capitalist information societies have detrimental effects on decision-making since 'by filtering and framing all information by its contribution to profit or power, capitalists limit their perception of the problems they face'.[16] Ultimately, for Marshall:

> By making artificial boundaries, commodifying information, disrupting accurate information flow, building hierarchies, issuing strategic business enhancing information, and focusing on price, capitalism becomes embedded in disinformation.[17]

---

12 *Ibid.*, pp. 10–11.
13 *Ibid.*, p. 19.
14 *Ibid.*, p. 13.
15 *Ibid.*, pp. 13–14.
16 *Ibid.*, p. 14.
17 *Ibid.*

3. THE CONSTRUCTIONIST 'REVOLUTION' AND POSTMODERNISM

In some discussions about disinformation and democracy in the digital age, disinformation, fake news and post-truth are notions used to describe a state of affairs allegedly associated with postmodernism.[18]

This interpretation of some of the most important and critical intellectual traditions of our times is interesting because it shows how the epistemic dimension of the relationship between (dis)information and democracy is itself not immune from distortions when communication shifts from scientific debate to political debate.

Those familiar with the relevant debates may have no problem in admitting that postmodernism in particular can indeed be interpreted as an epistemic expression of dissatisfaction and frustration with the resiliency of capitalism. As a matter of fact, postmodernism has been the target of important criticisms[19] that have questioned not only its epistemological grounds and analysis, but also its practical implications or, in other words, the impact that the postmodernist subversion of truth has had – and still has – on politics. The question if and to what extent the tenets of these traditions have actually contributed to the perceived increase of manipulative communication is quite a different one.

Since one of the problems with more superficial criticisms is to confuse the tenets of postmodernism with those of social constructionism, I will treat these separately in order to provide a short explanation about the value and implications of these criticisms.

3.1. THE CONSTRUCTIONIST 'REVOLUTION'

The constructionist 'revolution' was an epistemic revolution to the extent that it popularised a way of thinking about reality which has fundamental consequences on the way we act upon reality at times when many people on both sides of

18 See e.g. C. Cadwalladr, 'Daniel Dennett: "I Begrudge Every Hour I Have to Spend Worrying about Politics"', *The Guardian*, 12 February 2017, https://www.theguardian.com/science/2017/feb/12/daniel-dennett-politics-bacteria-bach-back-dawkins-trump-interview; K. Houston, 'The Necessity of Postmodernism in the Post-truth Age', *Aereomagazine*, 15 April 2018, https://areomagazine.com/2018/04/15/the-necessity-of-postmodernism-in-the-post-truth-age; P. Salmon, 'Have Postmodernist Thinkers Deconstructed Truth?', *New Humanist*, 12 March 2018, https://newhumanist.org.uk/articles/5296/have-postmodernist-thinkers-deconstructed-truth.

19 A. Callinicos, *Against Postmodernism: A Marxist Critique*, Polity, Cambridge 1989; C. Norris, *What's Wrong with Postmodernism?*, Johns Hopkins University Press, Baltimore 1990; J. Lopez and G. Potter (eds.), *After Postmodernism: An Introduction to Critical Realism*, Athlon, London 2001; B. Latour, 'Why Has Critique Run out of Steam? From Matters of Fact to Matters of Concern' (2004) 30(2) *Critical Inquiry* 225–248.

the Iron Curtain believed it was about time for a political revolution. In the West, the end of the 1960s and the beginning of the 1970s were the years of the so-called end of the 'post-war consensus'. This consensus was in essence a political compromise designed to avoid the resurgence of fascism and neutralise communist propaganda by blending capitalism with welfare – in practice, the 'free market' with state intervention. The works of Karl Polanyi and especially John Maynard Keynes were influential in the consolidation of this 'consensus' as the former warned about the risks of authoritarian reaction to the effects of the free-market economy on society and the latter showed how state intervention could avoid economic crises of the kind that brought Hitler to power in Germany. The political context of the constructionist 'revolution' was therefore one of compromise between competing visions of the social world brought together by shared apprehensions fed by the memory of a recent past, the political circumstances of the Cold War and the 'communist threat'.

As for its actual intellectual contribution, the core idea at the time was that reality is socially constructed through communicative practices and processes (e.g. institutionalisation, socialisation, externalisation, objectification and internalisation)[20] that make people forget that ultimately 'reality is what we make of it'. This idea challenges determinism, but does not necessarily support radical relativism. Social constructionism does not claim that 'anything goes', but rather that: (a) the existence of the social world does not need a transcendental explanation; and (b) the resulting immanence of the social world implies epistemological and moral responsibilities – the need to know how it works and the need to problematise the moral nature or quality of social change. The social construction of reality is therefore an emancipative epistemic to the extent that it formulates the problem of social change and continuity, removing unnecessary constraints to the scope and direction of social change that human action can achieve.

From this perspective, there are at least two major limits to the possibility of emancipative social change. At the micro-level, individuals usually engage with reality as if this was an objective 'given' whose fundamental features are beyond their reach. These beliefs are reinforced by oppressive ideologies that enforce on people deterministic ideas concerning human nature, the world and the possibility of social change. At the collective level, power relations place objective limits on the idea that reality is what we make of it. As power is usually unequally distributed in society, so is the capacity to change reality itself. In practice, this means that 'reality is what the most powerful among us are willing and able to make of it'.

---

20 The classical reference here is P. Berger and T. Luckmann, *The Social Construction of Reality: A Treatise in the Sociology of Knowledge*, Penguin, London 1966; however, see A. Lock and T. Strong, *Social Constructionism: Sources and Stirrings in Theory and Practice*, Cambridge University Press, Cambridge 2010 for a broader view of the articulations and implications of this tradition.

Social constructionism provided the intellectual tools for an important epistemic move: the reappropriation of reality by the people against deterministic representation of the future and in support of the possibility of emancipative social change. However, by doing so, this 'move' transformed reality itself from a common background on which information could support the competition among different opinions and the control of competing truth claims into a major stake of the political competition itself: the competition for the social construction of reality. In this condition, the difference between information and disinformation became inconsistent because reality itself, the common background for this distinction, is experienced by the parties involved as a self-fulfilling or self-defeating prophecy.

If this is correct, social constructionism cannot be blamed for the regime of 'post-truth', but only, perhaps, for having anticipated the situation in which the social construction of reality would become involved in a competition between incompatible visions of the world, which in our case, as I shall argue in a moment, are embodied by capitalism and democracy.

3.2. POSTMODERNISM: THE CULTURE OF LATE CAPITALISM AND ITS RADICAL CRITIQUE

Postmodernism is a term used to describe two different things. In one meaning, *postmodernism* is a particular state of affairs associated with the state of 'disenchantment' about modernity and crisis in the legitimisation of knowledge,[21] a cultural expression of late capitalism[22] or a 'regime of simulation' in which reality itself is effaced by its representations.[23] In another meaning, *postmodernism* is an intellectual tradition or perhaps more appropriately an analytical attitude and a form of radical critique of the conditions of late capitalist societies inspired by a fundamental frustration with the resiliency of capitalism and its cultural expressions.

Jean-Françoise Lyotard was influential in interpreting postmodernism as the 'condition of knowledge in the most highly developed societies' which 'designates the state of our culture following the transformations which, since the end of the nineteenth century, have altered the game rules for science, literature, and the arts'.[24] At the heart of these conditions and transformations is the

21 J-F. Lyotard, *The Postmodern Condition: A Report on Knowledge*, University of Minnesota Press, Minneapolis 1982.

22 F. Jameson, *Postmodernism or the Cultural Logic of Late Capitalism*, Duke University Press, Durham, NC 1991.

23 J. Baudrillard, *Simulacra and Simulation*, University of Michigan Press, Ann Arbor 1994. Translation by S.F. Glaser; J. Baudrillard, *The Perfect Crime*, Verso, New York 2007.

24 Lyotard, *supra* note 21, p. xxiii.

'incredulity toward metanarratives' constituting the apparatus of legitimisation for knowledge.[25]

Whereas for Lyotard postmodernism is a notion that describes a crisis of knowledge, for Fredric Jameson there is little doubt that postmodernism is a global phenomenon with identifiable ideological origins:

> [T]his whole global, yet American, postmodern culture is the internal and superstructural expression of a whole new wave of American military and economic domination throughout the world: in this sense, as throughout class history, the underside of culture is blood, torture, death, and terror.[26]

Even more than Jameson, Jean Baudrillard's critique targets phenomena and processes that are rooted in US culture and politics. The claim that 'the Gulf War did not take place',[27] for example, was not a denial of that war and its atrocities as 'post-truth' propagandist would have it, but, more radically, a provocation that meant to oppose the mainstream media interpretation of the first Iraqi invasion as a legitimate act of international politics, or 'war', and to show its deeper meaning in terms of 'deterrence' or exemplary execution. In this interpretation, the information available through media coverage was not evidence of democratic openess, but was instrumental to the hegemonic project of the US and its allies: to suppress resistance even before it materialises.

The concept of 'regime of simulation'[28] even more radically suggests the fundamental involution in Western societies:

> Such is the last stage of the social relation, ours, which is no longer one of persuasion (the classical age of propaganda, of ideology, of publicity, etc.) but one of deterrence: 'YOU are information, you are the social, you are the event, you are involved, you have the word, etc.' … No more subject, no more focal point, no more center or periphery: pure flexion or circular inflexion. No more violence or surveillance: only 'information,' secret virulence, chain reaction, slow implosion, and simulacra of spaces in which the effect of the real again comes into play.[29]

In a regime of simulation, power is no longer something one can oppose because, as Zygmunt Bauman suggested, in our days domination rests 'in the uncertainty of the ruled as to what move, if any, their rulers may make next'.[30]

In line with Lyotard's idea that in the postmodern condition the practices of knowledge are not inspired by the search for truth but by power, Baudrillard

---

25 *Ibid.*

26 Jameson, *supra* note 22, p. 5.

27 J. Baudrillard, *The Gulf War Did Not Take Place*, Indiana University Press, Bloomington 1991. Translation by P. Patton.

28 Baudrillard, *Simulacra and Simulation*, *supra* note 23.

29 *Ibid.*, pp. 29–30.

30 Z. Bauman, *Community*, Polity, London 2004.

wrote: 'Theoretical violence, not truth, is the only resource left to us.'[31] In an eerie expression of clairvoyance, Baudrillard anticipated the symbolic function of 'real catastrophe' against the 'eternal simulation of catastrophe' or:

> [W]hat terrorism is occupied with as well: making real, palpable violence surface in opposition to the invisible violence of security. Besides, therein lies terrorism ambiguity.[32]

And when the catastrophe finally arrived, in the form of the attack on New York, Baudrillard's interpretation was indeed scandalous and 'intellectually terroristic' in the sense of subverting mainstream interpretations at their very 'roots', in order to oppose its 'branches' or the political actions justified on their grounds:

> At a pinch, we can say that they *did it*, but we *wished for* it. If this is not taken into account, the event loses any symbolic dimension ... This goes far beyond hatred for the dominant world power among the disinherited and the exploited, among those who have ended up on the wrong side of the global order. Even those who share in the advantages of that order have this malicious desire in their hearts. Allergy to any definitive order, to any definitive power, is – happily – universal, and the two towers of the World Trade Center were perfect embodiments, in their very twinness, of that order.[33]

The point of this interpretation was not only provocation, but also intellectual 'terrorism' or subversion against a system that manages to preserve itself through simulation, the effacement of reality and the transfiguration of traditional power into the 'code'. In our terms, this is the effect of the hegemonic ideological influence in the social construction of the real: a condition in which resistance within the same reality is made impossible by the impossibility of alternative meanings to mobilise alternative powers and produce alternative actions.

However, using the same line of reasoning, one could argue for the limits of this kind of radical interventions. Unequal relations of power are based on meanings that information alone cannot subvert from within the ideological universe that legitimise the same relations of power. In that ideological universe, subversive information or discourse appears as noise, while information compatible with it simply cannot subvert those relations and bring emancipation.

Postmodernism is criticised from within the critical tradition because it lacks a 'pars construens': it is so effective in showing what is wrong with the culture and politics of late capitalism and, for our purposes, the futility of relying on media information to bring about significant changes in this condition

---

31 Baudrillard, *Simulacra and Simulation*, *supra* note 23, p. 163.

32 *Ibid.*, p. 57.

33 J. Baudrillard, *The Spirit of Terrorism and Other Essays*, Verso, London 2003. Translation by C. Turner 2002, pp. 5–6.

(the regime of simulation and rule of the 'code', in Baudrillard terms) that it leaves no grounds for resistance or hope for change. In short, it is a critique that for some is 'best seen as a symptom'[34] because of a fundamental epistemic problem that Jameson formulated most clearly:

> What happens is that the more powerful the vision of some increasingly total system or logic – the Foucault of the prison book is the obvious example – the more powerless the reader comes to feel. Insofar as the theorist wins, therefore, by constructing an increasingly closed and terrifying machine, to that very degree he loses, since the critical capacity of his work is thereby paralyzed, and the impulses of negation and revolt, not to speak of those of social transformation, are increasingly perceived as vain and trivial in the face of the model itself.[35]

The confusion between the critique and its object, or postmodernism and the culture of late capitalism, originates in the way in which both deal with the problem of meaning and its relationship with power and, more precisely, disrupting the former to subvert the latter:

> Now reference and reality disappear altogether, and even meaning – the signified – is problematized. We are left with that pure and random play of signifiers that we call postmodernism.[36]

And the 'disappearance' of reality makes action upon reality itself impossible.[37]

As with social constructionism, blaming postmodernism for the conditions it criticises is like blaming the terminal state of a patient on the doctor who diagnoses it. The important contribution for this discussion is that *the political role of information depends on its interpretation, and interpretation depends on the competition between antagonistic hierarchies of values and the influence of ideologies.* Constructionist and postmodernist hermeneutics (interpretation of texts and meaning in line with the postmodernist conceptual coordinate and its subversive ambitions) are both revealing and empowering. Different outcomes depend on knowledge as much as on power, and on epistemics as much as on politics.

What happened is not that postmodernism paved the way to neoliberalism, but that the hegemonic position of capitalism, and its neoliberal permutation, found more explicit expressions in the forms that postmodernism anticipated.

It may also be argued that neoliberal and populist discourses appropriated some notions of the postmodernist critique (e.g. Lyotard's 'legitimation by power'

---

34 A. Callinicos, *Against Postmodernism. A Marxist Critique*, Polity, Cambridge 1989, p. 6.

35 Jameson, *supra* note 22, pp. 5–6.

36 *Ibid.*, p. 96.

37 M. Stocchetti, 'Invisibility, Inequality and the Dialectics of the Real in the Digital Age' (2018) 34 *Interações: Sociedade e as Novas Modernidades* 23–46.

and the substitution of reality with its representation or Baudrillard's 'perfect crime') as a deliberate discursive strategy to enhance their influence in domestic and foreign political processes. The ideological appropriation of epistemic innovation motivated by the effort to control the emancipative potential of critical knowledge is a most interesting phenomenon and is foundational in the social representation theory of Serge Moscovici.[38]

The possibility to draw meaningful distinctions between information (good) and disinformation (bad) depends on the representation of reality – what we think is real. However, this representation is the fundamental stake of ideological competition, one dimension of what I would like to call 'the dialectics of the real'. From this perspective, the main function of ideology is the control of the 'production of the real', a function that, for example, Louis Althusser described in the terms of 'interpellation'.[39] Once reality is constructed within the symbolic universe of capitalism and populism, we may experience what Guy Debord wrote about the society of spectacle: 'Dans le monde *réellement renversé*, le vrai est un moment du faux'.[40]

To summarise, the lesson we learn if we combine social constructionism and postmodernism is that reality is only in principle what we make it. In practice, what we can actually do depends on interpretation, knowledge and power. Each of these alone cannot bring about deliberate emancipative action on the social construction of reality. However, the strength of capitalism is also its weakness: it is an ideology based on a performative epistemic in which social change is legitimised through power, not truth (Lyotard's 'legitimation by power').[41] In capitalist reality, the strong can oppress the weak simply because it can, and can successfully justify the winner's actions and motives. The problem with this form of legitimisation is that it generates compliance by force and, as Baudrillard noted, resistance by 'terrorism'.

4. INFORMATION, CAPITALISM AND DEMOCRACY

The real threat to democratic ideals comes not from (dis)information *per se*, but from the crisis of capitalism and the growing incompatibility between capitalism and democratic ideals and values in the digital age. In this light, disinformation is information that threatens the existing social order and, if this is plausible, two further points may follow: first, we cannot take the legitimacy

38 S. Moscovici, *Psychoanalysis: Its Image and its Public*. Polity, Cambridge 2008 [1961].

39 L. Althusser, *On Ideology*, Verso, London 2008 [1971].

40 Thesis N. 9: 'In a world that has really been turned upside down, the true is a moment of the false'. G. Debord, *The Society of The Spectacle*, Bureau of Public Secrets, Berkeley, CA 2014, p. 4. Translation by K. Knabb.

41 Lyotard, *supra* note 21, p. 47.

of the existing social order for granted; and, second, not all expressions of dissidence or disinformation are inspired by democratic ideals, and the problem for democracy is what Karl Polanyi called the 'double movement' of the 'free market' utopia feeds undemocratic response.[42] This will be discussed in more detail below.

The conceptual ambivalence of the term 'information', as it applies in social and technological discourses, reflects a broader ambivalence in the ideological roots or dimensions of the Western socio-political order of the last two centuries or so. Even before it was associated with the automatic processing of data, the meaning of information had had different connotations in capitalist and democratic discourse. In the former, information is a key resource in the individualist pursuit of profit and a condition for the regulatory functions of the 'market'. Without enough reliable information, the 'market' would not even exist because, unknown to each other, 'offer' and 'demand' would simply not have the possibility to ever 'meet'. In democratic discourse, information is also a key resource, but for a fundamentally different purpose: not the competition for profit, but for the formulation of opinions, the construction of democratic consensus and the discursive construction of the public interest from the plurality of private interests. In short, whereas in capitalism information serves the individual purpose of transforming available resources into personal profit, in democracy information is necessary for the transformation of opinions and interests into policies as well as to constitute the grounds on which competing opinions, interests and policies can be assessed in relation to their foreseeable impact on the 'public good'.

I would thus like to suggest that the problem of disinformation in the digital age should be interpreted against fundamental differences in the social role of information as these are construed in capitalist and democratic discourse. These differences construe the problem of disinformation in very different ways, providing grounds for the argument that the historic alliance between capitalism and democracy has come to an end.[43] The main implications of this state of affairs are that: (a) disinformation is a far greater risk for the former than the latter; and (b) the way in which the notions of information and disinformation are construed within the discourse of global capitalism is a far greater challenge to democratic ideals and practices.

Until the mid-20th century and the so-called 'democratic crisis of capitalism', the fundamental differences between capitalist ideology and democratic ideals have been obscured by at least two conditions. First, and more broadly, because they both contributed to establishing and legitimising the power of the state in

---

42 K. Polanyi, *The Great Transformation: The Political and Economic Origins of Our Time*, Beacon Press, Boston 2001 [1944], p. 136.

43 See e.g. E. Meikins Wood, *Democracy Against Capitalism. Renewing Historic Materialism*, Verso, London 2016 [1995].

its 'modern' format. Charles Tilly, for example, discussed the role of capital in the formation of the modern state and in securing the economic and financial basis for its military power. As he put it:

> The story concerns capital and coercion. It recounts the ways that wielders of coercion, who played the major part in the creation of national states, drew for their own purposes on manipulators of capital ... Although states strongly reflect the organization of coercion, they actually show the effects of capital as well.[44]

On the other hand, ideas and values associated with democratic ideals provided the intellectual background for the development of modern science and scientific knowledge that, in addition to supporting industrialisation and the material basis of state power, also undermined the authority of traditional and religious knowledge, and the influence of the social forces associated with them. On more political grounds, and at least since the French Revolution, combining notions of equality, participation, popular sovereignty, freedom etc., democratic ideals also provided the symbolic grounds for the mobilisation of the entire population in support of the power of the state, and for the legitimation of democratic policies and its human and material costs. The same ideals are also combined in nationalism, an ideology that, while today is often mentioned in debates about the challenges facing democracy in the digital age, 'has been closely related historically to the very rise of public life that has helped make modern democracy possible'.[45]

Second, and in relation to information, both capitalist ideology and democratic ideals provided effective arguments in support of freedom of speech and, more broadly, of policies designed to facilitate the production, improvement and circulation of knowledge against the political influence of tradition and the social forces associated with it.

However, despite the fact that capitalism and democracy both contributed in unique ways to the consolidation of the modern state, there are at least two important differences that establish the grounds for the incompatibilities of our digital age: the moral project that originates from the two and the role of information.

For Earl Gammon, the moral project of capitalism was originally inspired by the crisis of natural theology in Victorian England and the crisis of legitimisation of the social order associated with it. According to Gammon:

> [C]rucial to the ascent of the market civilization was the reconception of the market as a mechanism for the deliverance of secular retribution, replacing beliefs in a

44 C. Tilly, *Coercion, Capital and European States*, Blackwell, Cambridge 1992, pp. 16–17.

45 C. Calhoun, *Critical Social Theory. Culture, History and the challenge of Difference*, Blackwell, London 1995, p. 240.

> supernatural agency at work in the social economy. The market as a redistributive mechanism ... was more than just the negative sanctioning of productive inefficiency. It was an expression of a desire to punish and objectify those who resisted or stood in the way of the creation of a new technological utopia that was supplanting conceptions of a natural moral economy. This aggressive pursuit of the market in Victorian England ... was directly related to the anxiety stemming from the failure of the long-standing project of natural theology.[46]

The moral function of retribution was fundamental in the origins of the 'market civilisation' to legitimise social inequalities and for the protection of social hierarchies and relations of power associated with them. Instead, inherent in the moral grounds of democratic ideals is the idea of justice interpreted not in terms of retribution, but in those of inclusion, participation and entitlements which are ultimately necessary to constitute the 'public' as both the subject (the people) and the object (the *res publica*) of democracy.[47]

In relation to information, capitalism and democracy are probably something rather close to what Foucault called 'regimes of truth': different ways of organising the normative relations between information and knowledge for the social construction of truth and reality.

In capitalism, the functioning of the market as a regulatory principle is subordinated to the circulation of information. But information is also a resource that is commodified by the same market so that, for example, differential access to information quantity and quality determines the greater or lesser success of economic actors. In democracy, information is a pre-condition for essential political process, such as political participation, aggregation and articulation of interests and decision-making, and as such it is a public commodity: a commodity available to the public and not one that the citizens or democratic institutions need to compete for. Democratic competition is not in the access to but in the interpretation of available information. Interpretation is the activity that, in democracy, transforms information into knowledge, opinions and, eventually, political action. The same information, available as a public resource, also constitutes the common grounds on which, for example, the truth claims associated with different opinions and interests can be assessed in relation to the public as the object of democracy or *res publica*. As I will argue later on, this difference between capitalism and democracy becomes crucial in understanding the problem of disinformation in the digital age as a sign of the crisis of capitalist democracy.

---

46 E. Gammon, 'Affect and the Rise of the Self-Regulating Market' (2008) *Millennium: Journal of International Studies* 37, 2 251–278, p. 255.

47 C. Calhoun, *Critical Social Theory. Culture, History and the challenge of Difference*, Blackwell, London 1995, p. 241.

4.1. THE 'DEMOCRATIC CRISIS OF CAPITALISM'

The historical alliance between capitalism and democracy was the alliance between two ideologies based on different moral projects, but having in common the ambition of founding a socio-political order whose legitimacy depended upon the distinctive interpretation of the relationship between the individual and society. For capitalism, the market is the conceptual tool for the argument that the collective interest is better served by leaving people free to pursue their individual interests. For democracy, the same function is performed by the notion of (democratic) citizenship as the condition (established by law and supported by the state monopoly of legitimate violence) in which the participation of the individual to the political process is construed as both a right and a duty of the citizen.

The advantages that this alliance implied for the modern Western state contributed to the obscuration of the fundamental differences between these two ideologies and especially the dangers associated with the effects of capitalism for society. Karl Polanyi famously discussed these dangers and warned against the effects of what he called the 'double movement': the expansion of the market to every aspect of society and the 'countermovement' designed to protect society from the effects of this expansion:

> For a century the dynamics of modern society was governed by a double movement: the market expanded continuously but this movement was met by a countermovement checking the expansion in definite directions. Vital though such a countermovement was for the protection of society, in the last analysis it was incompatible with the self-regulation of the market, and thus with the market system itself.[48]

For the purposes of this discussion, I think this notion is useful for at least three reasons. The first is that if applied to the regime of information as affected by capitalism, it suggests that (dis)information in the digital age is the 'countermovement' of the expansion of the logic of the 'free market' into the communicative environment. The second is that, in line with Polanyi's original usage, it also explains why the nature of the social forces and ideologies that feed this countermovement commonly construed as disinformation are often undemocratic. Now, as then, 'at the root of the dilemma there is the meaning of freedom itself' since 'liberal economy gave a false direction to our ideals' as 'this was the result of a market view of society which equated economics with contractual relationships, and contractual relations with freedom'.[49] Nowadays, in the age of digital globalisation, the role of fascism and socialism in Polanyi's 'countermovement' is performed by a range of radical political and religious

---

48 Polanyi, *supra* note 42, p. 136.

49 *Ibid.*, p. 266.

movements that can compensate for the lack of ideological coherence by the effective usage of social media.

Thirdly, Polanyi's analysis is useful because it points to the importance of the 'meaning of freedom' at the root of the dilemma generated by the 'double movement'. This meaning and its implications on the politics of information (or, to paraphrase Harold D. Lasswell, the competition for the control over who can say what, when and how) are both part of the problem and part of the solution: the main challenge to, but also the main strength of, democratic ideals and regimes. I will address this aspect shortly, through the concept of 'communicative freedom'.

For Polanyi, this double movement had fundamental effects on the way early forms of capitalism and representation combined in the modern states of the 19th century:

> Nineteenth-century civilization was not destroyed by the external or internal attack of barbarians; its vitality was not sapped by the devastations of World War I nor by the revolt of a socialist proletariat or a fascist lower middle class. Its failure was not the outcome of some alleged laws of economics such as that of the falling rate of profit or of underconsumption or overproduction. It disintegrated as the result of an entirely different set of causes: the measures which society adopted in order not to be, in its turn, annihilated by the action of the self-regulating market. Apart from exceptional circumstances such as existed in North America in the age of the open frontier, the conflict between the market and the elementary requirements of an organized social life provided the century with its dynamics and produced the typical strains and stresses which ultimately destroyed that society. External wars merely hastened its destruction.[50]

These apprehensions associated with the disintegrative effects of the 'free regulating market' inspired the political forces that, after the Second World War, supported the post-war consensus and the Keynesian economic policies designed to address the authoritarian risks that the unrestrained functioning of the 'self-regulating market' implies for democracy. The influence of these forces lasted until the 1970s. In that decade, a sequence of events (the oil crisis, the fall of the Bretton Woods system, a prolonged recession, etc.) brought the post-war consensus to an end and signalled the beginning of the end for capitalism-cum-democracy combined.

The text that perhaps demonstrates better than any other the historical moment in which capitalism and democracy ceased to be travel companions is *The Crisis of Democracy*.[51] The paradoxical conclusion of that report is that

---

50 Polanyi, *supra* note 42, p. 257.

51 M. Crozier, S.P. Huntington and J. Watanuki, *The Crisis of Democracy: Report on the Governability of Democracies to the Trilateral Commission*, New York University Press, New York 1975.

democracy brings about its own demise since the challenges to democracy spring precisely from the effects and even the success of democratic principles:

> The successful operation of democratic governments has given rise to tendencies which impede them from functioning.
>
> (1) The pursuit of the democratic virtues of equality and individualism has led to the de-legitimation of authority generally and the loss of trust in leadership.
> (2) The democratic expansion of political participation and involvement has created an 'overload' on government and the imbalanced expansion of governmental activities, exacerbating inflationary tendencies in the economy.
> (3) The political competition essential to democracy has intensified, leading to a disaggregation of interests and the decline and fragmentation of political parties.
> (4) The responsiveness of democratic government to the electorate and to social pressures encourages nationalistic parochialism in the way in which democratic societies conduct their foreign relations.[52]

Another element that I think is important to an understanding of the significance of this crisis is the so-called 'Habermas/Luhmann debate' which, at around the same time, addresses the crisis of legitimisation through a criticism of the ethical grounds of system theory and the distortions that this approach introduced into the analysis of the social and political worlds. Habermas interpreted the crisis as one of the legitimisation of mature capitalism that could be effectively addressed only by qualitative and quantitative improvements in political participation. For Luhmann, the crisis was one of complexity or, more precisely, one produced by the complexity gap between the 'system' and its environment. Since the systemic approach postulates that the system cannot keep up with the complexity of the environment, the only way for the system to adapt is through systemic 'reduction of complexity'. Roughly put, this consists of the (political) system's capacity to distinguish which political demands are legitimate or illegitimate and, thus, which ones it can or cannot afford to ignore.

If one keeps in mind the warning of Polanyi and the interpretations of the crisis by Habermas and Luhmann, there are at least two significant interpretations of the democratic crisis of capitalism in the 1970s. In one, this crisis is construed as a 'crisis of complexity' of democratic forms of government that requires governments to engage with the problem of legitimisation by increased participation (e.g. Habermas) or 'reduction of complexity' (e.g. Luhmann). In the other, the crisis reflects the incapacity of capitalist democracy to address the challenges, the discontents and ultimately the effects of capitalism on society. While both interpretations point to the

52 *Ibid.*, p. 161.

incompatibility of democracy and capitalism, the former looks at the limits inherent in democracy, while the second is more aware of the detrimental effects of capitalism on society. Implicit in these interpretations are also different roles of information. In the first, information is mostly a problem that is experienced by governments in terms of 'overload' or an excessive quantity and diversity of demands. This overload forces governments to establish mechanisms of selective reduction of complexity or, in other words, to establish and legitimise adequate criteria to decide which demands can or cannot be ignored. In the second, the crisis of democracy is brought about by the effects of capitalism which democratic information contributes to unveil and oppose. But if one follows Polanyi, the end of the post-war consensus was also the end of interventions which helped in preserving the political viability of 'free market' ideology and which, at the same time, inhibited the resurgence of authoritarian 'countermovements'.

As the 'democratic crisis of capitalism' marked the end of the political viability of the 'capitalism-cum-democracy' formula, the rise of neoliberalism highlighted the ideological appropriation of a 'systemic' interpretation of the crisis of legitimisation in support of exclusionary practices and, ultimately, the predominance of capitalist ideology over democratic ideals. However, neoliberalism was the result of a fundamental crisis of capitalism itself or, as Terry put it:

> What drove this reorganization above all was the sudden fade-out of the post-war boom. Intensified international competition was forcing down rates of profit, drying up sources of investment and slowing the rate of growth. Even social democracy was now too radical and expensive a political option … the displacement of investment from manufacture to the service, financial and communication industries was a reaction to a protracted economic crisis, not a leap out of a bad old world into a brave new one.[53]

In the terms of our discussion, neoliberalism was thus the ideological response to the democratic crisis of capitalism on both the epistemic and the political dimensions of this crisis. By enforcing the 'reduction of complexity' through exclusion, neoliberalism adopted what Lyotard described as the epistemic of 'performative truth' and the politics of 'legitimation by power'. The fundamental implication of this response was that:

> Whenever efficiency (that is, obtaining the desired effect) is derived from a 'Say or do this, or else you'll never speak again', then we are in the realm of terror, and the social bond is destroyed.[54]

---

53 T. Eagleton, *Why Marx was Right*, Yale University Press, New Haven 2001, p. 5.

54 Lyotard, *supra* note 21, p. 46.

According to Pierre Bourdieu, the 'methodical destruction of collectives' is precisely the aim of neoliberalism that he discussed in terms of a 'strong discourse … to create the conditions under which the "theory" can be realised and can function: a program of the methodical destruction of collectives'.[55]

This 'social bond' and these 'collectives' that neoliberalism seeks to efface on epistemic and political grounds are communicatively constructed and constitutive of democratic ideals and democratic regimes. If our concern is the future of democracy, our interest is to strenghten rather than weaken it. For efforts in this direction, as I will shortly argue, (dis)information may actually be part of the solution rather than the problem.

4.2. THE NEW INTERNATIONAL INFORMATION AND ECONOMIC ORDER

In the decade that preceded the end of the Cold War, 'information' became a popular term as the development of new technologies brought about the 'information revolution' and the alleged transformation of industrial societies into post-industrial societies.[56]

Whereas mainstream interpretations hailed this transformation for its potential to bring about democracy, peace and prosperity, more critical voices expressed scepticism. For Schiller, for example, new technologies served the 'new international *information* order' and 'the operation of the transnational corporate system … to serve the world business system'[57] and, in particular, 'corporate America's quest for hegemony in a new international economic order'.[58] For Schiller, the key question was to understand that in the 'information revolution':

> [W]hat is at issue is not technical change or resource availabilities, though of course they are related matters. At issue is the structural character of the world community and the quality of life and social existence to *all* people.[59]

---

55 P. Bourdieu, 'The Essence of Neoliberalism', *Le Monde diplomatique*, December 1998, p. 2.

56 D. Bell, *The Coming of Postindustrial Society: A Venture in Social Forecasting*, Peregrine, Harmondsworth 1974.

57 H.I. Schiller, 'Whose New International Economic and Information Order?' in R. Mansell (ed.), *The Information Society. Critical Concepts in Sociology. Vol I, History and Perspectives*, Routledge, London 2009, p. 149, emphasis in original. Originally published in (1980) 5(4) *Communication* 299–311.

58 *Ibid.*, p. 151.

59 *Ibid.*, p. 153.

For Cees Hamenlink, 'what is termed "information revolution" could, in a more sober analysis, be seen as equally non-revolutionary as its predecessor, the industrial revolution',[60] in relation to economy, politics and culture:

> *Economy*. The information techniques deployed in today's societies (and their planned innovations) are the perfect instruments to perpetuate the capitalist mode of production ... *Politics*. The development of information technology makes centralized control over decentralized activities simpler than ever before, thus allowing more latitude for deviant political behaviour. Moreover, the link between information technology and democratization is guided by unwarranted expectations about what machines per se can do ... *Culture*. Technical innovations in information tend to support a global process of cultural synchronization rather than autonomous diversity ... All this suggests that the myth of the information society ... does not hold promises for those who in today's society are the losers. In the information society they will simply be computer-controlled losers.[61]

Thus, between the opposite affordances of oppression and emancipation, the appropriation of the information revolution and its myth by capitalism paved the way for the increase in inequalities at both the national and international levels, a condition in which:

> [T]hose who control wealth or political power will have access to increasing volumes of information, which they can manipulate for their own ends at the expense of the majority of underprivileged people who will have very little information.[62]

For David Lyon, there were at least two reasons why 'it is hard to justify the claim that the "information society" takes us beyond industrial capitalism':

> On the one hand, information is being treated as though it were a commodity, to be priced within the marketplace. Vast transnational corporations such as IBM are involved in the commercial exploitation of information-related hardware, software, and services. On the other hand, the kinds of issues which have absorbed social analysts of industrial capitalism are reappearing in the information-intensive context – alienation and exploitation of [the] labor force, management and state monitoring and surveillance, and ethnic and class cleavages.[63]

---

60 C.J. Hamenlink, 'Is There Life after the Information Revolution?' in M. Traber (ed.), *The Myth of the Information Revolution*, SAGE, London 1986, pp. 7–20, at p. 8.

61 *Ibid.*, pp. 12–13.

62 P.A.V. Ansah, 'The Struggle for Rights and Values in Communication' in Traber (ed.), *supra* note 60, pp. 64–83, at p. 69.

63 D. Lyon, 'From "Post-industrialism" to "Information Society": A New Social Transformation?', in Mansell (ed.), *supra* note 57, p. 191. Originally published in (1986) 20(4) *Sociology* 577–88.

For Jennifer Daryl Slack and Fred Fejes, the information revolution not only favoured the most influential forces in society; the capitalist appropriation of technological development led to the emergence of an 'ideology of information', whose distinctive features reinforced the influence of capitalist ideology worldwide:

> [I]n particular, the equation of the development of information technologies with social progress; the quantification, commoditization, and privatization of information; the collapse of information, knowledge, and wisdom; the positioning of the information age as a whole new (and superior) way of life brought about by the new technologies; the positioning of the world as a market and as a source of labor and raw materials; an uncritical and overwhelming optimism/determinism about the future of political, economic, and social/cultural life and the role of information technologies in it; and the role of information and information technologies in the exercise of social power.[64]

Like myths, ideologies can also be seen as collective interpretative devices that, when applied to particular social phenomena, can reveal something important by obscuring something else. For Fredric Jameson, the fascination with the power of new technologies concealed the nature and the actual power of the forces that were their main beneficiaries:

> I want to suggest that our faulty representations of some immense communicational and computer network are themselves but a distorted figuration of something even deeper, namely, the whole world system of a present-day multinational capitalism. The technology of contemporary society is therefore mesmerizing and fascinating not so much in its own right but because it seems to offer some privileged representational shorthand for grasping a network of power and control even more difficult for our minds and imaginations to grasp: the whole new decentred global network of the third stage of capital itself.[65]

Ultimately, the capitalist appropriation of information technology transforms the ideological connotations of globalisation: from a cultural process of growing interdependence and secularisation into what Joseph Stiglitz described as:

> [A] system that might be called *global governance without global government*, one in which a few institutions – the World Bank, the IMF, the WTO – and few players – the finance, commerce, and trade ministries, closely linked to certain financial and commercial interests – dominate the scene, but in which many of those affected by their decisions are left almost voiceless.[66]

---

64 J.D. Slack and F. Fejes (eds.), *The Ideology of the Information Age*, Ablex, Norwood 1987, p. 11.

65 Jameson, *supra* note 22, pp. 37–38.

66 J. Stiglitz, *Globalization and its Discontents*, Penguin, London 2002, p. 22.

The Cold War promise of freedom and opulence in Western propaganda, based on the combination of capitalism and democracy, fell grossly short of the expectations it raised in the Second and Third Worlds. The 'winner' was not democracy but neoliberalism, and authoritarian regimes in China, Russia and elsewhere had no difficulties in adopting the latter to reject or even repress democratic 'springs' (remember the 1989 Tiananmen Square protests!). In these regimes, (dis)information is not construed as a pre-requisite for democracy, but as a fundamental resource to be used in the international competition and to shield their leaders and policies from public scrutiny.

As Polanyi predicted, the 'movement', or the expansion of information capitalism worldwide, was soon to be followed by a 'countermovement'.

4.3. THE CRISIS OF NEOLIBERAL DEMOCRACIES: COMMUNICATIVE FREEDOM AND SECURITISATION

To discuss (dis)information and democracy without problematising the crisis of neoliberal democracy is a simplification with profoundly misleading effects on the relevant debates and, ultimately, on the search for plausible solutions. What is missing is the role of capitalism and what, to quote Polanyi, can be described as a '(dis)information double movement'. The 'movement' is the digital expansion of neoliberal capitalism in the domestic and global communicative environments and the management of (dis)information as a valuable commodity and practice to enforce neoliberal 'strong discourse' and to destroy 'collectives'. The 'countermovement' is the opposition to this expansion, commodification and control which take the form of disruptive behaviours inside and outside the communicative sphere.

From this perspective, the crisis of neoliberal democracies is not brought about by a deliberate disinformation campaign waged by hostile foreign illiberal regimes or domestic political organisations. Neoliberal democracies are in crisis primarily because, in dealing with information as well as in other fields, neoliberalism undermines the credibility of democratic ideals and values.

Bennet and Livingston, for example, argue that the current 'disinformation order' is brought about by two main processes: first, the 'breakdown of trust in democratic institutions, a 'growing legitimacy crisis produced by the hollowing-out of centre parties as mechanisms for meaningful citizen engagement'; and, second, the 'growth of alternative information channels producing popular political mythologies, is mobilizing many citizens to join the upsurge in support for movements and parties outside the centre, particularly on the right'.[67]

---

[67] L.W. Bennett and S. Livingston, 'The Disinformation Order: Disruptive Communication and the Decline of Democratic Institutions' (2018) 33(2) *European Journal of Communication*, 122–139, at 127–128.

If the problem is to preserve and strengthen democracy, it is necessary to understand what the causes of this 'breakdown of trust' are and what can be done about them. As these authors acknowledge, referencing the work of Bartels and Crouch, and Della Porta, democratic institutions effectively represent only the interests of the 'upper economic demographics', 'the rising power of business elites and the reliance on market solutions to social problems as prescribed by neoliberal policy regimes', while 'corruption has contributed to the crisis of the democratic process and institutions'.[68]

However, in their argument, Bennet and Livingston choose to put these problems aside and, following Fred Zakaria, focus instead on the 'growth of alternative information channels' in order 'to understand the rise of undemocratic or "illiberal" politics preying on the weakness of core institutions'.[69] To neglect the causes of this weakness and to focus instead on the 'growth of alternative information channels' is a peculiar choice if our concern is to strengthen democracy rather than the control on information.

Yet, even within the more limited focus on alternative channels, this analysis is problematic for at least two reasons: first, because it confuses the problem of understanding the effects associated with the multiplication of channels with the problem of distinguishing between legitimate and illegitimate expressions of dissent; and, second, because it construes the expressions of dissent against 'moderate' and 'centre parties' as attacks on democracy and its institutions.

Most importantly, however, neglecting to look into the causes of the alleged weakness of democracy and democratic institutions contributes to hiding the effects of neoliberalism on the bond between the individual and society that is crucial for the credibility and effectiveness of democratic regimes and in particular:

- The growth of inequalities and poverty,[70] even among developed 'capitalist democracy[71] and in the EU.[72]
- The concentration of media and digital infrastructure in the hands of corporations.[73]

---

68 *Ibid.*, p. 127.

69 *Ibid.*, p. 129.

70 R. Duttagupta et al., 'Growth That Reaches Everyone: Facts, Factors, Tools', *IMF Blog*, 20 September 2017, https://blogs.imf.org/2017/09/20/growth-that-reaches-everyone-facts-factors-tools/.

71 IMF, 'Fiscal Monitor: Tackling Inequality', October 2017, https://www.imf.org/en/Publications/FM/Issues/2017/10/05/fiscal-monitor-october-2017; L.M. Bartels, 'Political Inequality in Affluent Democracies' (2017) *Social Science Research Council (Democracy Papers)*.

72 T. Chen et al., 'Inequality and Poverty across Generations in the European Union' *Staff Discussion Notes (SDNs), International Monetary Fund*, 24 January 2018.

73 B.H. Bagdikian, *The New Media Monopoly*, Beacon Press, Boston 2004.

- The ideological bias of institutional media when dealing with the causes of poverty, violence and oppression in developing countries.[74]
- The combination of state and corporate interests in the usage of digital technology for the illegitimate and illegal surveillance of innocent citizens.[75]
- The capitalist appropriation of the democratic affordances of the Internet and digital technologies more broadly, which saturates the social sphere with the 'interpellation' of people as 'consumers' rather than citizens.[76]

Constructing the crisis of neoliberal democracy as the crisis of democratic ideals and the growth of an alternative channel of expression as a threat to vulnerable democratic institutions creates distortions that damage democracy, protect neoliberalism and its effects from criticism, and ultimately strengthen the influence of radical dissent among people by simply alienating them from the institutions that should represent them.

A more radical 'working hypothesis' is that democracy is not in crisis because it is challenged by anti-democratic movements, but because its ideals have been drained of social and political significance by the effects of neoliberalism and the powers that support its epistemic and political programme. In the background of the digital age, this crisis generates exclusionary and disruptive tendencies that reinforce each other and that can be described in terms of 'securitisation' and 'communicative freedom'.

'Securitisation' is a concept originally coined by Ole Wæver[77] to describe a form of speech act with exclusionary and centralising effects on the political process. Applied to our discussion, the securitisation of information can be conceived as a discursive move with at least three implications. First, information is construed as the conduit of truth: not an element that has to be interpreted in the construction of truth, but the 'container' of truth itself. Second, once the relationship between truth and information is reduced to the

---

74 J. Lugo-Ocando, *Blaming the Victim: How Global Journalism Fails Those in Poverty*, Pluto Press, London 2015.

75 T. Allmer, *Critical Theory and Social Media: Between Emancipation and Commodification*. Routledge, Abingdon 2015; C. Fuchs, *Social Media: A Critical Introduction*, SAGE, London 2014; T. Allmer, 'Critical Surveillance Studies in the Information Society' (2011) 9(2) *tripleC* 566–592.

76 A. Feenberg, 'Subversive Rationalization: Technology, Power and Democracy' (1992) 35(3–4) *Inquiry* 301–322; A. Feenberg, *Transforming Technology: A Critical Theory Revisited*, Oxford University Press, Oxford 2002; J. Curran, N. Fenton and D. Freedman, *Misunderstanding the Internet*, Routledge, New York 2012; R.W. McChesney, *Digital Disconnect: How Capitalism is Turning Internet against Democracy*. New Press, New York 2013; L. Dahlberg and E. Siapera (eds.), 'Introduction: Tracing Radical Democracy and the Internet' in L. Dahlberg and E. Siapera (eds.), *Radical Democracy and the Internet: Interrogating Theory and Practice*, Palgrave Macmillan, Basingstoke 2017, pp. 1–16.

77 O. Wæver, 'Securitization and Desecuritization' in R. Lipschutz (ed.), *On Security*, Columbia University Press, New York 1995, pp. 46–86.

mechanical association between ends and means, the social construction of truth assumes the connotation of an automated process – one in which there is no room for interpretation or competing opinions. Needless to say, this is precisely the condition that the leaders of totalitarian regimes dream of. Third, even in more democratic contexts, the securitisation of information rapidly establishes and legitimates structures of inequality in the access to information based on exclusion and secrecy, as well as the profiling and therefore the surveillance of individuals to decide who can know, or not know, what. Some of these mechanisms, like the Echelon surveillance network,[78] were put in place during the Cold War and were revitalised and enhanced in the 'War on Terror'. While commercial information and communication remain unaffected, the securitisation of politically relevant information establishes a radical distinction between first- and second-class citizens: between those who can and those who cannot participate in the relevant political debates.

Once new technologies open up new channels of communication, some of which elude the influence of neoliberalism and the control of its apparatus, the 'securitisation' of information is a move that legitimises efforts to regain control through exclusion and centralisation. In the context of the 'new information and economic world order', the campaign against disinformation through the securitisation of information is an effort to criminalise political dissent based on the implicit epistemic assumption that the system governing this 'order' can tolerate only the production, circulation and consumption of information that is compatible with its ideological grounds and functional needs. In this system, the relevance of democratic ideals is instrumental to the preservation of capitalist ideology and is increasingly reduced to a mere façade that ultimately justifies its rejection.

The securitisation of information and, even more radically, its discursive 'weaponisation' (the discursive construction of information as a weapon and disinformation as a weapon pointed at us) are measures that seek to counter the disruptive affordances of digital technology as these apply to what Hannah Arendt and Jürgen Habermas have discussed in terms of 'communicative power' and 'communicative freedom'.[79]

Simplified to the extreme, while communicative freedom is 'the ability of participants in a discourse to take yes or no positions on validity claims', communicative power 'is generated by the mutual recognition of a validity claim

---

78 European Parliament, Temporary Committee on the Echelon Interception System, *On the Existence of a Global System for the Interception of Private and Commercial Communications (ECHELON Interception System) (2001/2098(INI))*, Session Document, Brussels 2001; M. Ward, 'Q&A: What You Need to Know about Echelon', *BBC News*, 29 May 2001, http://news.bbc.co.uk/2/hi/science/nature/1357513.stm.

79 J. Flynn, 'Communicative Power in Habermas' Theory of Democracy' (2004) 3(4) *European Journal of Political Theory* 433–454.

by two communicatively oriented speakers exercising their communicative freedom'.[80] This kind of power and freedom are constitutive of, rather than undermining, the possibility of popular sovereignty and 'the potential of a *common will* formed in non-coercive communication'[81] – in practice, democracy.

As Flynn puts it, discussing Habermas' notion of communicative freedom:

> When communication is free and open and the political culture is egalitarian, the normative reasons that are generated in such processes should steer the political decision-making process ... The generation of communicative power is thereby linked with the communicative action of citizens in their use of their 'communicative freedom', which is essentially the ability of participants in discourse to take yes or no positions on validity claims. On the smallest scale then, communicative power is generated by the mutual recognition of a validity claim by two communicatively oriented speakers exercising their communicative freedom.[82]

However, in the conditions of capitalist democracy, communication is neither free nor open as 'systemic coordination by market mechanisms and state power ... encroaches on the domain of the lifeworld, eroding the solidarity that can only be achieved communicatively' and 'members of modern democracies tend to take up the *client* or *consumer* role more often than that of *citizen*'.[83]

The digital expansion of communicative freedom/power destabilises neoliberal discourse and undermines the project associated with it. From this perspective, 'disinformation' is the concept that construes 'difference' as a threat and the new 'information disorder' is the notion describing the rejection *en masse* of neoliberal discourse and its influence in the social construction of reality. However, from the perspective of the neoliberal project, this expansion and its effects are interpreted as an increase in complexity or dysfunctional information, feeding a new need for a 'reduction of complexity' and new efforts to 'securitise' (dis)information. Ultimately, this dynamic results in a degenerative 'information spiral' where securitisation triggers disruptive expressions of communicative freedom/power that in turn feed a greater need for securitisation as well as more disruptions, and so on. In the end, this 'spiral' is the 'evidence' in the arguments about the hypocritical nature of 'liberal democracy' that is the central tenet in the political propaganda of radical movements.

Yet, on epistemic grounds, one of the most important effects is the political fragmentation of the social construction of reality. To suggest that digital technology facilitates the expressions of dissent and resistance to the neoliberal project is, of course, a completely different matter than to claim that the

80 *Ibid.*, p. 445.

81 J. Habermas, *Between Facts and Norms: Contribution to a Discourse Theory of Law and Democracy*, MIT Press, Cambridge, MA 1996, p. 36.

82 Flynn, *supra* note 79, pp. 438–443.

83 *Ibid.*, pp. 439–443.

same technology and dissent will combine to create a global and democratic regime of communication. Efforts to address the failure of neoliberalism through the 'securitisation' of information generate a countermovement in which excluded dissent becomes reorganised into alternative 'collectives' and 'sub-publics' capable of restoring loyalties and feeling of belonging and ultimately reinstating the 'collectives' destroyed by neoliberalism through a virtual escape, e.g. through 'echo chambers'. The neoliberal appropriation of digitalisation has managed to preserve capitalism, but not to repress expressions of dissent that are too often far from democratic because, as Polanyi predicted, society reacts to the disruptions of capitalism and people are lured into the communitarian utopia associated with radical identities and ideologies. Today, as in the 19th century, the dysfunctions of capitalism nurture social responses that damage democratic ideals.

Rather than being considered attacks on democracy, (dis)information can be construed as a form of disruptive use of communicative freedom/power that expresses frustration with the effects of the neoliberal appropriation of democratic affordances of this technology. These effects involve enhanced corporate and state surveillance, growing socio-economic inequality and exclusion, the dissolution of the social bond and the reinterpretation of the relationship between the individual and society in terms of consumers and the market.

5. CONCLUSIONS: THE STRENGTH OF DEMOCRACY

My final point is about the strength of democracy: this strength primarily depends not on the quality of circulating information, but on *the quality of its citizens* or, more precisely, on the quality of their critical or hermeneutic competences and their resolve to use these competences to think and act on behalf of a shared notion of the public good. Without these competences and resolve, there is no imaginable quality of information that can do the trick in their absence.

As Lincoln Dahlberg and Eugenia Siapera have noticed: '"Democracy" has become a universal signifier of political legitimacy.'[84] However, in the practices of neoliberal democracies, the effects of neoliberalism and the aim of effacing 'collectivities' erode the epistemic and political strength of democratic ideals, producing the 'breakdown of trust', the 'crisis of legitimacy' the hollowing-out of representative institutions and ultimately the growing popularity of anti-democratic ideologies and movements described by, *inter alia*, Bennett and Livingston. Compared to the 'strong discourse' of neoliberalism, the essence of democratic discourse is the identification of the citizen with the public as

[84] Dahlberg and Siapera, 'Introduction', *supra* note 76, p. 1.

both 'object', or 'the people organised as a discursive and decision-making public',[85] and 'subject', or what is commonly designed as the 'public good' or the 'res publica'.

While freedom of speech is commonly mentioned as a fundamental freedom of democratic societies, here I would like to focus on other conditions that, if forgotten, may seriously erode the strength of democratic ideals and regimes.

In our global and digital age, perhaps even more than in the past, for example, we should pay careful attention to the importance of equality and trust for democratic identification. Apart from the centuries-old debate about the specific connotations of these notions, what is important for the purposes of our discussion is their inter-connectedness: the ways in which each support the other in dealing with the effects of (dis)information. While basic equality is necessary to avoid the erosion of trust, a certain measure of trust is necessary to deal with inequalities that are part of human conditions and, to an extent, unavoidable.

While equality and trust are necessary for democratic identification, in a viable democratic regime they are also the grounds for the widespread participation of citizens in the political process. From the point of view of (dis)information, this means that the communicative expertise in the production and interpretation of relevant texts concerning the common good is a key and widespread competence of citizenship rather than a strategic asset of 'experts'.

And quite obviously, key to equality, trust and participation is the role of formal education. The digitalisation of education has not merely introduced digital technology in education; rather, as, for example, Karen Ferneding has observed, in education it has enforced the neoliberal appropriation of technology discourse.[86] In neoliberal discourse, education is a process in which individuals are trained to acquire the fundamental competencies and skills necessary for the functioning and reproduction of the socio-economic order as this is inspired by the free market utopia, but are given neither the competencies nor the inclinations to conceive of alternative futures or to participate in their making. In education, the strength of democracy depends largely on the possibility of transforming individuals into citizens willing and able to participate in the constitution of the public good as repositories of political sovereignty and therefore as responsible participants in the social construction of the future. In order to address the challenges of (dis)information in the digital age, democratic education relies on critical media literacy and on critical pedagogy. Essentially, the former is what gives citizens the capacity to use the media rather than be used by them, and includes distinct competencies such as the ability to identify and assess

85 C. Calhoun, *Critical Social Theory: Culture, History and the Challenge of Difference*, Blackwell, Oxford 1995, p. 241.

86 K.A. Ferneding, *Questioning Technology: Electronic Technologies and Educational Reform*, Peter Lang, New York 2003.

the legitimacy of relations of meaning and relations of power as these combine in a media text. In practice, critical media literacy gives the competencies to perform the kind of radical criticism of the meanings and powers involved in the social construction of reality that are also at the core of postmodernism. Critical pedagogy, if one follows Paulo Freire, Henry Giroux and others, is the educational practice that gives citizens not only the skills but also the inclinations or personality traits ('critical consciousness', 'integration', 'critical transitivity', etc.) that are required by citizens in their struggle to establish and preserve democratic ideals and regimes against their enemies. In other words, this approach prepares people with the dispositions to perform engaged and radical criticism that constitute the epistemic strength of democratic regimes and that Foucault attributed to the persona of the parrhesiastes.[87]

In the 'struggle' to protect democracy from its enemies, (dis)information is not a 'threat' in either the 'involuntary' or 'deliberate' connotation of this notion. As involuntary inaccuracy, disinformation is virtually unavoidable in human communication, but its detrimental effects in democratic societies are contained by pluralism and trust. First, freedom of communication and access to a plurality of sources facilitate the control of the accuracy of available information. Second, when individuals experience involuntary disinformation, identification with the 'public', participation in relations of trust and democratic education dissipate suspicions concerning the nature or intentions of inaccuracies. On the other hand, when dealing with deliberate disinformation or propaganda, the members of democratic societies are what Raymond A. Bauer called 'obstinate audiences'[88] or, in practice, selective recipients of information. One reason that is especially relevant in democratic regimes is that citizens are individuals whose relationship with other individuals and the abstraction we refer as to as the public involves rational and emotional aspects. Put simply, most citizens are attached to their democracy and its institutions, even when these are not working as well as they could and especially when the need for improvement become clear. In this way, deliberate disinformation or propaganda, especially if it originates in a foreign society, is not only inoffensive but may even produce the opposite effect of increasing rather than decreasing the cohesion of the democratic society. In summary, as long as trust, equality, participation and proper education are in place, democracies are very, very difficult to destabilise through disinformation.

Conversely, the example of a functioning democracy can be destabilising for non-democratic regimes. In international politics, the strength of democracy consists of its appeal for people living in regimes based on exclusion and oppression. Democracy is an appealing ideal because it addresses the problem

---

87 M. Stocchetti, 'Re-making the Truth in the Digital Age: Parrhesia and Human Interest' (2017) 3 *Comunicazioni sociali* 405–414.

88 R.A. Bauer, 'The Obstinate Audience: The Influence Process from the Point of View of Social Communication' (1964) 19(5) *American Psychologist* 319–328.

of power, or performativity, in combination with the problem of justice, or legitimisation. It does so by positing the 'citizen' and the 'public' as the fundamental relationship at the roots of both. The communicative environment of the digital age supports rather than weakens the strength of this appeal, and democratic regimes can perhaps subvert non-democratic ones by mere example.

My working hypothesis in this discussion is that while the rise of undemocratic movements does present democracies with important challenges, (dis)information *per se* is not a problem if the social construction of reality and the legitimisation of relations of power are based on democratic ideals rather than neoliberal ideology. Conversely, the greater the influence of neoliberalism, the greater and more divisive the effects of (dis)information. As a corollary, I would like also to suggest that, according to this perspective, the (dis)information of the digital age is not a threat, but rather a crucial test for political regimes as it strengthens democratic ones and weakens undemocratic ones.

In conclusion, if these are the strengths of democracy, how do we address the challenges of (dis)information in the digital age?

The efforts to 'save' democracy by controlling or securitising information should be engaged with suspicion, if not outright opposition. History over the past half-century shows that corporate and bureaucratic elites do not hesitate to sacrifice democracy to preserve their influence through exclusion, surveillance and repression. The efforts to save democracy by controlling and restricting information have the potential to strengthen disruptive uses of available information channels and ultimately support the spread of non-democratic ideologies in national and international communicative environments.

The reason why I think we need to oppose these efforts is that they will further undermine the relationship between the individual and the public. The idea that people should not be exposed to disinformation implies not only a lack of confidence in people's capacity to resist manipulation, but also the more dangerous suggestion that some people can decide for others what qualifies as information or disinformation. In other words, the efforts to control (dis)information has a detrimental impact on equality and trust.

If the goal is to strengthen democracy against the challenges of undemocratic ideologies and movements, the first and most obvious step in this direction is to give people serious reasons to appreciate the value and credibility of democratic ideals. This can be done by reducing inequalities and increasing participation, starting, for example, by identifying and addressing the roots of the discontent that feeds the radicalisation of a growing part of the population in democratic countries, instead of merely silencing, denying or rejecting the manifestations of discontent.

In democratic discourse, people are interpellated as members of a community in a relationship that bonds the citizen and the public to mutual rights and duties: the rights and the obligations associated with citizenship. The *raison d'être* of this relationship is the exercise of political power or, in constructionist terms, the social construction of the future. Thus, a second and related step is to reject the influence of neoliberal 'strong discourse' in public and private communication, and especially in education: the interpellation of individuals as consumers rather than citizens and the interpretation of the social world and its phenomena (health and illness, climate change, immigration, unemployment, etc.) in relation to their significance to the 'market'.

An alternative step to exclusion or repression would be to restore the credibility of institutional media by reducing their dependence on corporate control and increasing their openness to dissidence and criticism. Equally important would be to strengthen the credibility of democratic journalism by stopping the tendency towards precarity in the profession and supporting its professional requalification instead.

Democratic regimes are not, in principle, undermined by disinformation because the capacity to connect truth and power is a core competence of democratic citizenship. Disinformation becomes a problem when inequalities increase, social justice declines and political elites seek legitimation through exclusion rather than participation.

If the problem is to defend democracy rather than to control information, the fundamental challenge in the digital age is not one of (dis)information, but of neoliberal discourse and its effects on society. In this 'struggle', the epistemic grounds of social constructionism and the postmodern 'radical' critique, as I have argued earlier, are more part of the solution than the problem.

5. DEMOCRACY AND THE PRE-CONDITIONS OF COMMUNICATION

Sid Lukkassen*

1. INTRODUCTION

The growing concern over fake news or *disinformation* incites the European political community. For example, the EU has established an expert group to study this issue.[1] A recently adopted German media law called NetzDG is another response to this phenomenon. Many fear that disinformation and even the digital media as such could pose a challenge for democracy, the rule of law and even fundamental rights. In an attempt to delve into this growing fear, this chapter analyses the various aspects of fake news on the basis of the following theme:

The influence of social media and the digital revolution on the political foundations of society.

The underlying idea is that the core values on which representative democracy leans – as they were understood after the emergence of liberal democracy in 1848 (taking the Netherlands as a point of departure, because of the comparatively early liberal-democratic Constitution) – originate from a time when communication between politicians, compared to the present time, was a slow process.[2] The classic liberal example of a good politician was that of an 'enlightened statesman' – someone with the ability to distance him- or herself from the voter and the delusions of the day, in order to make space for a more thoughtful reflection. Nevertheless, is that idealistic image still viable in this (post)modern era? Nowadays, politicians have different means to express their reflections and respond directly to their voters, colleagues and fellow citizens through social media platforms. Experts have referred to this situation as the

* Dr. Sid Consultancy, the Netherlands. Email: sgmlukkassen@gmail.com.

1 EU Publications, *A Multi-dimensional Approach to Disinformation*. Press Office of the European Union, Luxembourg 2018, p. 42.

2 Also referred to as 'republic of letters' or 'Gutenberg Galaxis'. N. Bolz, *Am Ende der Gutenberg-Galaxis*, Munich 1995.

'digital economy' and, as such, we will have to shed light on the shifting economic reality of news production.[3]

2. THE DIGITAL EVOLUTION IN REPRESENTATIVE DEMOCRACY

In this chapter, I argue that a system of representative democracy as a type of regime is upheld by presuppositions on communicative proceedings and that a 'fatigue' or 'discomfort' about representative democracy stems from changes in these core suppositions. Therefore, here I will answer the question what the digital revolution means for both practical political expertise and the ideological foundations on which political decisions are made, as well as what kind of arguments are put forward in debates. When I describe a changing role for ideological foundations, I mean that intellectual labour used to be the basis of the process of convincing citizens politically, and that more 'flashy' forms of communication have supplanted that basis.

Media – and in particular the mainstream media (MSM) – have more influence than ever before when it comes to framing public discussions and political or social agenda formation. However, at the same time, these information currents are more fragmented than ever, due to emerging online media platforms. We live in the postmodern information age (also described as 'Informationskapitalismus'),[4] where the classic social pillars have become fragmented and each individual gathers news to his or her own liking: the consumer is 'both sender and receiver – every person is a broadcasting outlet'.[5]

These considerations comprise the following question:

Is a fair and sincere representative democracy still possible when it is based on the pre-condition of communicating with the electorate via modern media?

Central to any answer to this question is the understanding of 'Öffentlichkeit', which is understood as a public sphere and a communicative space not of the bourgeoisie but belonging to the citizens, together comprising the realm where citizenship is exercised.[6] We can safely assess that the character of this public sphere is increasingly digital: the rise of the blogosphere and phenomena such as

---

3 T. Mesenbourg, *Measuring the Digital Economy*, US Census Bureau, Suitland, MD 2001.

4 F. Shirrmacher, *Ego, das Spiel des Lebens*, Munich 2013, p. 13.

5 Lecture by M. Josten, http://human.nl/ep-44969-medialogica

6 J. Habermas, *Strukturwandel der Öffentlichkeit, Untersuchungen zu einer Kategorie der bürgerlichen Gesellschaft*, Taschenbuch 1962. The concept of *Öffentlichkeit* refers to the notion that in the 18th century, the striving for a democracy with space for active citizenship arose from literary philosophical milieus.

WikiLeaks have affected the news monopoly of traditional broadcasting systems. At first sight, this seems to strengthen the *Öffentlichkeit* – the model defended by Jürgen Habermas, advocating an objective political discussion without coercion. However, it remains unclear whether cyberspace stimulates users to remember the facts they read and encourages them to put those facts into perspective or context, in order to create a well-considered political discourse.

The polis culture,[7] with its physical collection of political actors, has emancipated itself through the French and Industrial Revolutions into the information economy. 'The nation-state was only a barrel of the dromocratic revolution', says French cultural theorist Paul Virilio: 'The dromocratic revolution will follow the democratic revolution in innovating an accelerated time in which energy technologies will gradually eliminate the myth of the territorial roots of the state.'[8] Virilio's 'dromocratic revolution' means that the content of the message no longer counts, but the speed with by it is delivered: 'The only thing that changes is the price of time.'[9]

The phenomenon described by Virilio becomes readily visible at the stock exchanges, where traders and states make their moves. The Polish/British sociologist Zygmunt Bauman noticed that when German Chancellor Angela Merkel and former French President Nicolas Sarkozy met for a discussion of Eurozone-related problems, the markets had already anticipated this – the mere rumour of their encounter caused rates to strongly fluctuate.[10] By their nature, nation-states are geopolitical entities that are geographically limited in terms of space and population. Yet global markets know no boundaries and their operational speed constantly increases.[11] This is known as the 'death of distance'.

As a general consensus, the essence of a representative democracy is reflected in the politicians' accountability to their national citizenry. Yet the question remains as to what extent this principle is valid in the era of the information economy. As Bauman demonstrates, politicians cannot plan ahead without having to anticipate answers from other global actors who appear to operate outside their sphere of influence.

Bauman's observations enable us to examine how the public domain is under siege and to understand why the legitimacy of a representative democracy is in doubt. The Italian-British sociologist Colin Crouch emphasised that 'a retreating government' encourages a call for more overt citizen participation in public services; however, it remains unclear how such encouragement might counter a 'democratic fatigue' without investigating its causes.[12] It brings us

7 In ancient Greece, a polis culture meant a body of citizens. It can also refer to the ancient Greek city-states.
8 P. Virilio, *Negative Horizon*, Cornwall 2008, p. 168.
9 *Ibid.*, p. 153.
10 Z. Bauman, *44 Letters from the Liquid Modern World*, Cambridge 2010.
11 N. Negoponte, *Being Digital*, New York 2003.
12 C. Crouch, *Post-democracy*, Cambridge 2012, p. 112.

back to the question of whether the ground rules of a representative democracy, as Virilio implies, are *incompatible* with the pre-conditions of a worldwide information society.

For that reason, we will focus on three areas to investigate the legitimacy of a representative democracy in its relationship with the sphere of communications throughout the digital revolution. The analysis will focus on the Dutch political system as a classic example of a representative democracy, but allows for counter-factual comparisons with foreign developments as an analytical tool. As my chosen method to obtain a conclusion, I will systematically cover the following three aspects of communication in the light of relevant literature – this methodology provides the structure for the rest of the text.

1. Media of communications
2. Velocity of communications
3. Space of communications

2.1. MEDIA OF COMMUNICATIONS

Since the 17th century, opponents of absolute monarchs have fought for freedom of speech and freedom of the press. In their perception, a free and independent press would enhance knowledge and diminish irrationality and ignorance. The French philosopher Alexis de Tocqueville stated that the media behaved like a searchlight, allowing people with unpopular opinions to find one another.[13] Individuals in a way get lost, but the media serve as beacons where they can find others. Thus, the free media are an important pre-condition for the formation of a civil society: a constellation of typical characteristics such as self-determination, meaning forms of sovereign and autonomous self-rule, and a separation of powers that does not want to be subject to an absolute monarch.[14]

De Tocqueville concludes that in a democracy, it will be hard for individuals to stick to their opinions once a majority of others no longer shares those beliefs. The media are therefore important to keep people informed of diverging existing opinions. Taking all this into account, we may conclude that the genesis of democracies correlates with the presence of a culture of public debate.

According to this understanding, the media served as an important safeguard against a tyranny of the majority. The digital revolution inverted this fear. By censoring a truth, a government implicitly admits its relevance. Today censorship may be redundant because for each truth, convenient or not, there

13 A. de Tocqueville, *Democracy in America* II, 1840 New York 1969, pp. 517–518.

14 M. Karskens, 'What is "Civil Society"?', in *Burgers en hun bindingen*, Damon 2000, pp. 11–31, at p. 17.

is the looming risk of drowning that truth in a vortex of one-liners, commercial slogans, loose facts and personal status updates. As observed by Sarah Palin's advisors in the documentary *Game Change*: 'Do not worry – in 48 hours all of this will have blown over.'[15] This is about weighing up the benefit of increasing transparency against the drawback of losing lasting significance: 'The consumer has triumphed over the citizen – the headline fathered the soundbite.'[16]

When an incident gathers the interest and attention of media, moral indignation frequently follows. In the Netherlands, Ernst Hirsch Ballin, former Minister of Justice, opted for new legislation because the TV news programme *Zembla* had stated that murderers were punished with community services. Although this turned out to be untrue, Hirsch Ballin stated that he nonetheless 'had to do something' – after so much publicity, one could not maintain that nothing had happened.[17] Here, we see the emergence of a new kind of media logic: new legislation sees the light as a result of a reality instigated by media.

To summarise, we may say that, in the footsteps of Tocqueville's findings, media play an important role in synchronising readers and voters into an informational ecosystem belonging to a politically engaged citizenry. A pre-condition is that the messaging stems from a certain journalistic independence and concurrent ethics that command the press to present reality in a rational way.

2.2. VELOCITY OF COMMUNICATIONS

The velocity of communications has meanwhile greatly increased in comparison to the past. Traditionally, the main aim of journalism was finding out the truth through investigation. The benchmark was quite high, set against a background of journalistic ethics. With and because of contemporary media, we see a demand for fast news and flexible coverage: in order to realise this, qualities of journalism such as objectivity, integrity and independence may be in jeopardy. Traditional media such as quality newspapers and public broadcasting have joined this tendency so as not to lag behind the higher velocity of other new media. In the past, the rule of thumb was to check multiple sources, compare and then evaluate them. Should this practice be abandoned, we can safely assume that faster and more sensational news can consequently be created, scoring more clicks and views.

15 J. Roach, *Game Change*, HBO 2012.
16 Crouch, *supra* note 12, pp. 47, 49.
17 E. Wit, 'Medialogica, afkicken van onze nieuwsverslaving', *Humus*, nr. 4, 2012, p. 15.

The increase in the velocity of communications also affects political parties. New political parties spring up like mushrooms in the Western world. Crouch sees a reverting pattern: new parties are often focused upon a clear brand with a strong leader, and a pragmatic, hardly coherent ideology that may appeal to many voters. In some cases these parties maintain strong ties to the corporate sphere. Often these young political entities are very 'media-savvy'. As a result, they may operate faster and in a more flexible way, allowing them to make their traditional opponents look hopelessly 'old-fashioned'.

2.3. SPACE OF COMMUNICATIONS

The University of Amsterdam created a research project in 2011 that showed that some 15,000 journalists are operating in the Netherlands, as opposed to 157,000 communication managers and PR experts who may be described as 'truth-creators'.[18] During the recent economic crisis, the number of journalists decreased, whereas the number of 'truth-creators' did not.

This finding aligns with Crouch's criticism of liberalism: in his view, 'liberal democracy' is often – erroneously – identified with representative democracy. Liberal democracy would supposedly grant a more significant role for corporate lobbyists, who have more power than the average citizen to influence legislation.[19] Whoever runs a big corporation has the money to hire truth-creators. He or she who pays is also the one who decides and, in the case of providing news, this also includes a worldview. Crouch notes that: 'To view the ills of democracy as just the fault of the mass media and the rise of spindoctors is to miss some far more profound processes that are currently at work.'[20]

The *homo economicus* cannot be identified with the *citoyen*, meaning the citizen in a politically engaged capacity. The calculative rationalism of modern times generates an information market where decisions may be mathematically gauged: authors argue that this forces decisions into a mathematical format.[21] The quick rise and fall of groups such as the Occupy movement demonstrates a discomfort and fatigue of the representative democracy as a whole. Representative democracy finds itself embedded in the info-economy rather than at the wheel. Can political decisions still qualify as *decisions* in the full

---

18 Josten, *supra* note 5.

19 Crouch, *supra* note 12, p. 3.

20 *Ibid.*, p. 6.

21 'All these numbers are nothing more than interpretations, whether a society, a state, the Eurozone will survive or not. It is virtually impossible to establish any connection between these numbers and their own identity as citizens.' F. Shirrmacher, *Ego, das Spiel des Lebens*, Munich 2013, p. 55.

sense of the word? Developments such as Brexit may suggest that citizens feel they have lost control.

According to the German journalist Frank Schirrmacher, the modern 'Beherrschungsdrang' found its apex in machines that now have the power to set standards for human society, with user-friendly functionality as the decisive impulse. Humans came to understand themselves in analogy to computers – now computers have learned to operate mankind. Schirrmacher argues that human communication has evolved into a worldwide, overarching algorithmic nervous system, both immaterial as well as autonomous and dominated by independent dynamics.

Crouch and Schirrmacher concur on the point that whoever pays increasingly becomes 'the one who decides', not because politicians would – without exception – be corrupt, but because those with the biggest budget for spin-doctors, press informers and data analysts are simply a step ahead. Therefore, a war erupts between 'truth-creators' who intend to influence the public debate and frame it according to their views. The 'truth-seekers' are left behind, confusedly asking themselves whether an objective truth still exists at all. Meanwhile the influence of lobbyists who happily engage in this battle from the background, should not be overlooked.

Through the rise of 'big data', humans are increasingly viewed as predictable, measurable and malleable. Computers can create highly accurate profiles by analysing human behaviour, to which companies and politicians may respond. This accumulation of data is often beyond the reach of national governments: big, international, global networks rise above the sovereignty of national democracies. Globalisation brought about an entanglement of channels of communication that cross national borders and extend into cyberspace.

3. POLITICAL MODELLING

What has been made clear so far is that the way in which society and its administration interact – let us call this the 'democratic feedback loop' – is itself supported by communicative assumptions. The underlying idea is that an elected government and parliament make policy: citizens develop opinions about this policy – under the influence of action groups, opinion makers and the like – and by means of elections, they then correct the composition of its representative bodies. This 'feedback' goes through communicative channels: the channels of political opinion and will-formation (*Willensbildung*). As a result, a change in the political constellation can also be explained by a change in communicative conditions.

This democratic feedback loop, the relationship between representation and conditions of communication, is explained in the following diagram.

Figure 1. Public opinion 'feedback' on policy through democratic processes, and vice versa

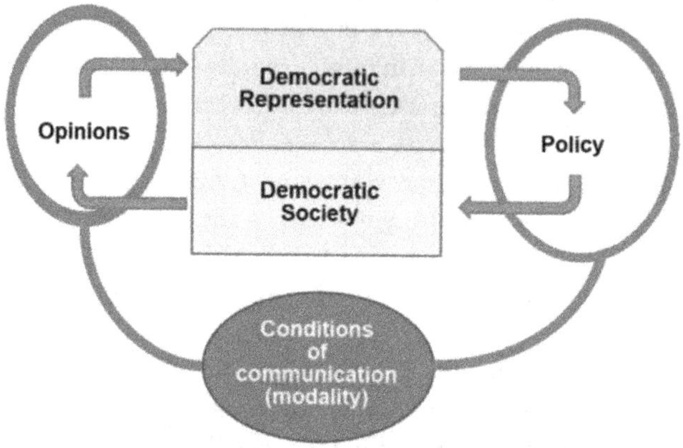

Source: Produced by the author, Christina Economides and Ton Nijhof.

Whenever communicative conditions of media, velocity and space are subject to substantive change, the feedback loop also changes. History has proved this through the transition of clan gatherings to the 'polis' and later to the town-hall meeting – the printing press, mass media and the digital revolution ensure that the level of organisation scales up and that the nation-state will be tied into a global communications network.

We find a striking example of this in the plenary debate in the Dutch Parliament on 2 October 2018, when the Minister of Foreign Affairs had to justify supporting Syrian rebels.

In this case the media and velocity of communication were determined by the government through a direct broadcast of this debate via the Internet (livestream), as well as traditional TV (NPO politics – *Nederlands Publiek Omroepbestel*). The political branch itself determined both. There is no doubt that representatives are aware of this live broadcast and shape their performance accordingly in view of later electoral interests. With the latter, the representatives shape public opinion in the expanding space of communications, occupied by reporters, editorial press channels, social media, etc.

What also determined the 'velocity of communications' in this instance was that the Minister was assisted in this debate by a large number of civil servants, who are carefully excluded from the picture. The room behind the ministers contains a workspace that can accommodate around 40 civil servants who advise the Minister 'live' when answering questions from the Parliament. The Minister can use a tablet or telephone (WhatsApp) for this purpose and sometimes the clerks hand the documents to him or her. It is not surprising that politicians are eager to use modern media of communication in debates. Likewise, during debates we see many Members of Parliament communicating via their tablet or telephone, to obtain additional information or to consult with executives of their political group or otherwise.

This situation means that the relationship between political representation and executive sovereignty is problematic. With whom has the controlling Parliament been in discussion? With the Minister, or perhaps with his officials?

Both the Minister and his officials are part of the 'executive power' that must, in principle, be controlled by the 'legislative power'. We can legitimately ask whether the power of public officials at that moment does not outstrip the course of events in Parliament.[22] After all, the speed of communication makes it possible for a Minister to be overthrown from the civil servants' room while broadcasting 'live' by providing the Minister with information *or by withholding it*. Because of the high communicative velocity, the Minister lacks the opportunity to have an in-depth discussion with his officials and to make political corrections to their suggestions.

In this scenario too, we see that communicative media, communicative velocity and communication space each exert a dynamic influence over the political process. This is done in a way that is incompatible with the spirit of Johan-Rudolph Thorbecke (1798–1872), the founder of the current parliamentary system in the Netherlands.

4. THE MEDIATIVE INFLUENCE UPON POLITICS AND VICE VERSA

'Media' is the plural of the concept of 'medium' and denotes the ways in which information can be disseminated. Some examples of these information carriers are newspapers, radio and TV. The Internet has been a rapidly emerging nexus of information in recent decades and become increasingly popular with the public, surpassing the mentioned traditional information carriers. It serves as an information carrier for, among other things, news websites of newspapers, but also hosts forums where visitors can converse on various topics.

The legislature and the executive power both make frequent use of various media. The members of the executive often have their own media, such as the 'Staatscourant', the Dutch governmental paper that publishes binding rules and laws. But TV channels and radio stations are also, for a considerable part, the domain of executive power.

This situation raises the question to what extent democracies depend on (I) communication media, (II) communication speed and (III) communication

22 Binnenlands Bestuur, 'Macht ambtenaren te groot voor Kamer', 25 May 2010, https://www.binnenlandsbestuur.nl/bestuur-en-organisatie/nieuws/macht-ambtenaren-te-groot-voor-kamer.167980.lynkx.

space for their functioning. Here, the phenomenon of the floating voter must be explained by the detaching society, which denotes a trend to delink, atomise and compartmentalise the social relations that connect citizens into a civil society and allow for a coherent life, as well as the role of the political party within this state of fragmentation. In democracies, political parties with different ideas attract people through an association with specific facets or the entirety of their ideology. These parties play the 'political game' by dividing tasks internally, which creates a top management that monitors party ideology.

This is exactly what brings us to the new media technology, because technological developments often precede economic developments, which in turn precede political developments. New circumstances require new answers, but the top executives of political parties owe their positions to older ideas. A new sound will therefore not be picked up quickly – those who knock on a political party's door, usually have to spend a few years sharing flyers and sticking up election posters in order to be able to gradually rise within the hierarchy.

Figure 2. Political participation in the 20th century illustrated by concentric circles

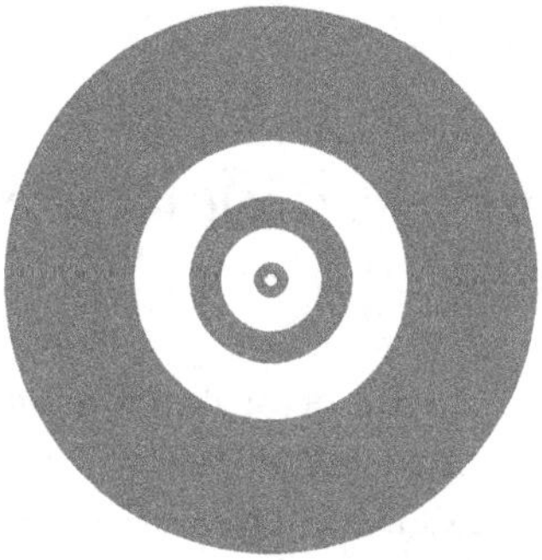

Source: Produced by the author, Christina Economides and Ton Nijhof.

The internal party structures that do not always fit in with a changing media world affect the relationship between a political democracy and its electorate. Political participation in the 20th century can be described as a model with concentric circles.[23] The middle circle, which is also the smallest, contains the party elite and their advisors, followed by the parliamentary representatives. Then come the active members: people who devote a lot of time and work to the party. These are political group staff and local council members. Next come the regular members, who do not dedicate much of their time to the party, but who do have an emotional bond with it. They are followed by the regular voters for

23 Crouch, *supra* note 12, p. 70.

the party, and then finally the largest circle: the general electorate, to which the party reaches out to win votes.

Typical of the phenomenon of 'post-democracy' is that pure professionals do most of the intellectual work for the party. Top management hires them even though they may not experience an emotional bond with the party or its political goals. The party does not win votes by having its members campaigning in the streets, but by profiling themselves in the media with powerful statements. The concentric circles that formed the intermediate links between party leadership and electorate in the 20th century are eliminated.[24] 'Global developments are characterized by an absence of democratic institutions and the growing dominance of global economic conglomerates: this is accompanied by the emergence of a global elite.'[25]

An economic concept from the private sector is transplanted to the public sector: the business strategist replaces the civil servant and the nation-state becomes the corporate state. News media become the echo chamber of specific elites, which reduces the role of political members in public debate and makes the concentric 'middle circles' of (traditional) political engagement superfluous: 'Democracy has not kept pace with the development of capitalism into truly global relations.'[26] A compensatory power is lacking for the right balance – energetic, bustling business executives face down against weary, pallid politicians.

This brings us back to the problem of democratic fatigue: the dilution of binding traditions, the relativism of values as well as norms and the deflation of civil society. The global firm becomes the key institution of the post-industrial world.[27] The 'Multioptionsgesellschaft' threatens to culminate into the fragmentation of the individual – both his inner life and identity.

This builds up to a development that the former advocates of press freedom already feared: the personality of the politician displaces the political programme as a distinguishing characteristic of a political party. 'Only through mass media is it possible to "sell" personalities. In this way the structural dependence of political parties on mass media grows considerably.'[28] This suggests that if the exposure of a personality in the mass media becomes the most important political criterion, political participation loses relevance and will have less impact.

The searchlight function of media was briefly mentioned. With this comparison, de Tocqueville argued that media are important to unite people and make joint action possible, now that citizens drift apart from each other by increased individualism. In addition, freedom of the press is a condition for

---

24 *Ibid.*, p. 72.

25 R. in 't Veld, *Kennisdemocratie opkomend stormtij*, The Hague 2010, §4.6.

26 *Ibid.*

27 *Ibid.*

28 *Ibid.*

maintaining freedom in general.[29] As a figure of speech, individuals are lost in the crowd, but the media show them the light they need to find their – political – way and guide them to reach one another.

So far, we still end up with the individual voter, who can dedicate as much time to inform him or herself politically as desired, but who ultimately will consider that their individual vote has an extremely limited influence. 'Whatever one does, it is impossible to raise the standard of enlightenment in a nation above a certain level', states de Tocqueville: 'Whatever facilities are made available for acquiring information and whatever improvements in teaching technique make knowledge available cheaply, men will never educate and develop their intelligence without devoting time to the matter.'[30] The disadvantage of lost time is set against the benefit of having a minimal impact upon an election – for many, it is just not worth it.

This means that more sources of information and a broader media landscape do not automatically produce a voter who is more aware of matters of state. A sparkling public debate is necessary to keep a lasting interest in public concerns alive in society.

We can safely state at this point that modern media are a major influence on the content of the political agenda and on the operations of the political industry. The reverse is also true: political parties chiefly put forth one clever and witty speaker, who preferably has a smooth and attractive appearance.

All these characteristics have priority over the ideology underlying their political actions. The reason is simple: such personal characteristics are crucial to generate sufficient attention in one of the many short media moments and to attract the electorate. The messenger is more decisive than the actual message. This means that the relatively few and scarce media moments are not emphatically filled only with political standpoints, but with appearances that *suggest* the underlying ideology. For instance, for some members of the Islam-inspired political party DENK in the Netherlands, the beard is probably more important as a signal to find their supporters; the humbly folded hands of the party leader of the SGP (Christian-reformed) is another possible example. The frame transcends the message and the picture outlines the political charge.

The consequence of this must be that political policy is being derived less from (ideological) basic principles and must respond directly to what is being addressed by the media. Images and framing have become more dominant within representative democracy. In the long term, this can undermine the consistency of policy-making. What is clear is that communicative media, velocity and space each have their own dynamics that influence political and social discussions, apart from the theoretical content. However, we observed that there were also

29 de Tocqueville, *supra* note 13, p. 181.
30 *Ibid.*, p. 197.

thinkers who made critical observations about the increasing dominance of media and technology.

5. VELOCITY OF COMMUNICATIONS AND POLITICS: FRAMING AND PRIMING

In 2012, during the directors' meeting of the Dutch liberals (VVD), the largest and currently governing party in the Netherlands, 'chief whip' Stef Blok addressed the audience in Utrecht. His main advice was to: 'Never step into the frame of another debater.' The advice roughly means that once one submits to going along with one's opponent in a discussion about their party's main theme, one will lose one's grip on the debate and be unable to change its direction. 'Framing is determining the definition of the main problem in order to "prime" it (to become owner of a theme).'[31]

This is related to the acceleration of communicative velocity – a larger information flow leads to greater pressure on the processing capacity, but also triggers a greater temptation to 'zap away'. Where attention spans are getting shorter, a politician must bring the conversation back to the main theme of his party almost immediately. Other important themes will remain unattended, showing only a selected part of the work of politicians and their parties.

An objection to this advice surfaced abruptly. Blok was asked: 'In these days when confidence in the government is declining, do people not want to see that politicians are able to exchange substantive and thorough ideas with each other in order to come up with new solutions? Do they only want to see politicians who stick to using the same old tricks and familiar hobby horses to please their supporters?' With such advice, the Spanish-American sociologist Manuel Castells might well be right in his conclusion: 'Political representation is obsolete now.'[32]

Blok answered with the following – for this investigation very significant – explanation: 'Most people watch TV, not to see me speak as a party leader, but more likely to see a singer or a dancer. And if, in the brief moment where I'm on i.e. the news, as long as I don't say anything irrelevant or strange, I have a slight chance that they will *not* move to another channel.' He also said that journalists repeatedly asked him the same question every day and that he always tried to give the same answer consistently. 'For if I elaborate on a question, and say something unusual, the political message disappears entirely from the news and only the unusual fragment will be broadcast.' We find support for this explanation

31 Medialogica, *RMO advies 26*, The Hague 2003, p. 37.
32 in't Veld, *supra* note 25, §4.6.

in scientific literature: 'In an entertainer society, politics have become a form of entertainment, and must compete with other forms of entertainment.'[33]

For example, teachers and textbooks compete with TV and chat applications for the students' attention. Let us explore this analogy of the position of the media within democracy, where – since de Tocqueville published on it – we agree that media have a responsible duty to inform the public and to prepare them for political citizenship. Let us suppose that parents found out that education, made up of 'eye-catching' and easily digestible, exciting bits of information, did not lead anywhere and did not adequately prepare pupils for their future. If that happened, the information market would adjust itself: poor education would perish, while good education would flourish.

In the case of mass media, however, such a self-correcting mechanism is absent. Parents will find out that their children perform badly on the jobs market. When will citizens discover that their media do not prepare them adequately for an effective existence as a *citoyen*? Moral outrage, a scandal, conflicts and personal intrigues give colour to news articles and thus increase their commercial value. A report of the undisputable facts will be edited into a spectacular plot like a 'race to power'.[34]

The question whether the velocity of the media influences the content of the news and the nature of the political debate, can be answered with a resounding 'yes'. The fast continuity of information suggests that the recipient has become accustomed to this situation. His or her ability to concentrate is adjusted to the showers of impulses, which usually results in a person being focused for approximately 30 seconds after something has caught his attention.[35] The political position should be stated within those 30 seconds – and thus only a few typical items will be discussed: the aforementioned political 'hobby horses'.

If in the past an incident occurred, political parties would usually announce a press conference later that week. Nowadays – thanks to platforms such as Twitter – they can respond immediately. This possibility creates the *expectation* of a reaction, which may implicate those who do not respond quickly and may seem to be involved in the scandal themselves (or suggest an internal conflict). The ability to respond immediately makes postponing a response suspicious. Thus, the *possibility* eventually turns into a *demand* to respond instantly. This demand, however, collides with daily activities and direct social interaction, such as the requirements of family life.

When we say 'democracy', we usually imply 'liberal democracy' – (Western) democracy, like liberalism, is based on the optimistic side of humanity and the Enlightenment. An assumption behind every democracy is that the electorate

---

33 Medialogica, *supra* note 31, p. 31.

34 Wit, *supra* note 17, p. 15, See also: Josten, *supra* note 5.

35 N. Carr, *De bibliotheek zonder boeken: Hoe verandert internet je manier van denken?*, Amsterdam 2011, p. 24.

makes a well-informed, rational consideration of which politician has the best abilities to represent them. But over time, it becomes more difficult for the voter to keep up with all the programs to inform him, and even when the voter is well-informed when he casts the vote – his influence will still be minimal.

The liberal philosopher John Stuart Mill pointed out that one should have some historical, cultural and social knowledge to be able to cast a vote in a well-founded way.[36] In other words, deciding on one's vote is not simply expressing one's own identity and sympathy: political judgement is a skill that must be cultivated carefully. It is questionable whether the acceleration of the supply of information – and with it the agitation, fragmentation and short-term orientation that this entails – is not disastrous for acquiring such knowledge and skill. After all, it is not reality or the development of our insights that is decisive for news velocity, but rather the media's longing for exciting articles as they compete over audiences and their limited attention spans.

6. COMMUNICATIVE SPACE AND POLITICS

Debates between John Rawls and Jürgen Habermas at the end of the 20th century demonstrated that democracy only works within a pluralistic society if there is a certain *Öffentlichkeit* – also known as the public sphere. The Canadian philosopher Charles Taylor describes this public sphere as 'a common space' in which members of a society meet to discuss matters of general interest. This is done 'face to face and by means of printed and electronic media'.[37] By *Öffentlichkeit*, we mean such a communicative space – a space where everyone is allowed to speak, provided that the speaker claims to speak truth, which means not fooling or tricking others, or bluffing with the use of rhetoric.[38] This is not a space of the bourgeois, but of the *citoyen* – not for the civilian but the citizen.

With this in mind, we must think for instance of the discursive culture that originated in the Dutch Republic in the 17th century, where citizens went to public places to talk about the ins and outs regarding the public interests. This *Öffentlichkeit* is closely related to a *democratisation of knowledge* that Rawls described: 'There are no experts: a philosopher has no authority over other citizens. Those who study political philosophy may know more about some things, but so may anyone else. Everyone appeals equally to the authority of human reason present in society.'[39]

---

36 J.S. Mill, 'Representative Government' in J. Gray (ed.), *On Liberty and Other Essays*, Oxford 1991, pp. 330–331.

37 Quoted in T. de Wit, *Leren wegkijken van je geloof*, Budel 2015.

38 Think here of the *Veil of Ignorance* reference.

39 J. Rawls, 'Reply to Habermas', lecture IX, 1995, p. 383, https://www.jstor.org/stable/2940843?seq=1.

However, is there really such an open public communicative space where one thinks and speaks about public interests? Are we not all attached to certain filters in our perception and attention span? Mattias Bjärnemalm, who at the time worked in the European Parliament for the Swedish Pirate Party, explained this in a personal interview. The Pirate Party originally assumed that the blogosphere (and thus the supply of information in cyberspace) would replace the traditional media.

Nonetheless, a complete transition to digital news remained out of the question, but the misrepresentation of news by the traditional media is covered in the blogosphere. Reporting as such, Bjärnemalm remarked, then becomes news itself. The *Öffentlichkeit* has therefore not been transferred to cyberspace, but has become fragmented into different channels. The 'filters' play a role here. Bjärnemalm showed that his phone gets dozens of notifications of new articles, blogs and status updates every minute. So naturally, his attention will likely go to what the people he deems important read and to articles that are repeatedly referred to.

On the subject of these filters, Google chairman Eric Schmidt stated: 'It is our responsibility to de-escalate tension on social media.'[40] Could this mean that critical contributions to somewhat controversial issues could become more difficult to find? In any case, it will become more important for political parties to map out filters. Bjärnemalm speculated that, for example, pirates and humanists would have overlapping areas of interest because they often filter news through the lens of rationality.

It is also interesting for parties to manipulate filters. For example, Google was paid to put the webpage for D66 (the Dutch 'left-liberal' party) in the top results for the query 'GroenLinks' (a political 'green' left-wing party in the Netherlands).[41] Google search algorithms can manipulate the preferences of floating voters by up to 20 per cent or more and in some demographic groups up to 80 per cent, with hardly any possibility to research the underlying algorithms and balance the search results fairly.[42]

Google admits it adjusts its algorithm 600 times per year, but the process is secret – a running candidate cannot see how he or she is affected. 'Search Engine Manipulation Effect (SEME) is a serious threat to a democratic government' said researchers Robert Epstein and Ronald Robertson, mainly because small

---

40 E. Schmidt, 'Eric Schmidt on How to Build a Better Web', 7 December 2015, http://www.nytimes.com/2015/12/07/opinion/eric-schmidt-on-how-to-build-a-better-web.html?_r=1.

41 J. Bertrams, 'Politieke partijen adverteren vooral op cpc basis', 2 March 2010, http://bertrams.net/2010/03/politieke-partijen-adverteren-vooral-op-cpc-basis.

42 R. Epstein and R. Robertson, 'The Search Engine Manipulation Effect (SEME) and its Possible Impact on the Outcomes of Elections', *PNAS*, 2015, https://www.pnas.org/content/112/33/E4512.

differences are often the decisive factor.[43] An effect of smartphones and search engines is that people become conditioned to look up information rather than to memorise, which means that the companies that shape our digital environment indirectly gain *psycho-power*: they shape the space where we shape our minds.

In India, the elected winner Narendra Modi did 25 per cent better in terms of search activity for 61 consecutive days prior to the election. 'In the United States we were able to boost the proportion of people who would like to have a candidate in between 37 and 63 per cent after just one search session … On all measures, it shifted to the direction of the candidate who was favoured in the rankings. Trust, liking and voting preferences all shifted predictably.'[44] The researchers argue that the US has a precedent in President Rutherford B. Hayes, who was supported by Western Union, which owned almost all electrical communication around 1876. Hayes won the election.

The controversy surrounding Cambridge Analytica, where the Facebook data of users was utilised for political campaigns without their explicit consent, marks the rise of *computational politics*.[45] This practice relies upon big data and powerful analytic software in order to exploit *information asymmetry*: the controllers of the data have large amounts of information on individuals, whereas the individuals are unaware of what the data hoarders and analysts know about them.

This means that discussions about 'net neutrality' and the power of search engines will become much more important: digital media are an increasingly important part of the political space where political opinions are developed and formed. What if political parties or their sponsors offer money to Internet providers to stop offering access to opinion pieces and websites of rival politicians? Or influence social media services to make such pieces less prominent in the feeds of users? This would affect the openness of that space and its fair and honest character (or at least appearance).

7. RESTRICTING CONVERSATION

In the past, salons and other social environments were the true embodiment of the *Öffentlichkeit* – the public space in which conversation about society and politics was conducted. Today, however, such societies have almost disappeared;

43 R. Epstein, 'How Google Could Rig the 2016 Election', 19 August 2015, https://www.politico.com/magazine/story/2015/08/how-google-could-rig-the-2016-election-121548.

44 *Ibid.*

45 R. Mercer, 'The Big Data Millionaire Waging War on the Mainstream Media', 26 February 2018, https://www.theguardian.com/politics/2017/feb/26/robert-mercer-breitbart-war-on-media-steve-bannon-donald-trump-nigel-farage.

in addition, the interest as well as the funding for regional newspapers is decreasing. This creates a political gap, as it raises the question how people will stay informed about regional policies. The American historian Christopher Lasch provided the following analysis:

> Before the rise of modern journalism, taverns and coffeehouses (often located on turnpikes or major crossroads) also served as media in their own right, places where news was gathered and circulated … As neighbourhood hangouts give way to suburban shopping malls – or, on the other hand, to private cocktail parties – the essentially political art of conversation is replaced by shoptalk or personal gossip. Increasingly, conversation literally has no place.[46]

Lasch wrote this when he examined the decline of democracy, which he understood as the impoverishment of public debate. In *The Revolt of the Elites and the Betrayal of Democracy* (1996), he identified three main causes:

- Firstly, *the emergence of a new cosmopolitan superclass*, operating globally and disconnected from the community, culture and locality.
- Secondly, widespread *political correctness*, meaning that curricula are increasingly focused on the wishes of minorities, while the traditions that bind us are being damaged and destroyed. Given the sensitivity of such curricula, words suddenly have different meanings, which results in the disappearance of a 'volonté générale': people simply do not understand each other anymore. Political correctness thus accelerates the breaking up of the public discourse into smaller subcultures, with incompatible identitarian narratives.
- Thirdly, *the decline of the communicative space*. The places where people traditionally gathered to exchange ideas were converted into fast food chains that are all about rapid turnover.[47]

Lasch argues that the American Dream initially included the existence of an intellectual or artistic culture in which everyone could participate and be equals – equality in the sense of mutual respect between those who actively participated in the community. However, because of the three factors mentioned above, this dream has derailed and given way to a consumer-based concept of democratic liberty.

---

46 C. Lasch, *The Revolt of the Elites*, New York 1995, pp. 122–123.

47 'Malls are populated by transients and serve corporations, not the community … Bars and restaurants are designed for high volume and rapid turnover. A paucity of benches discourages loitering. Background music takes the place of conversation.' *Ibid.*, p. 124.

8. THE RISE OF SYMBOL ANALYSTS

According to Lasch, the elite in the US hardly feel responsible for the state of affairs in the country. In the era of globalising data networks, they no longer involve themselves with the less fortunate fellow citizens in their own country: their loyalties are international. The elites literally do not know their place anymore: one day they are in Copenhagen, the next in Tokyo. Lasch describes them as symbol analysts who essentially hold a tourist view of the world. According to him, this does not encourage a perspective of heartening devotion to democracy: 'They live in a world of abstract concepts and symbols, ranging from quotations from the stock market to the visual representations produced by Hollywood and Madison Avenue. They specialize in interpreting and using symbolic information.'[48]

Lasch is not the only one who targets the superclass of symbol analysts; according to Crouch, they are also adept at 'using advertising and marketing techniques to acquire temporary images, which can be replaced and re-engineered after a relatively short period. Customers have difficulty in establishing [a firm's] track record. Invisibility becomes a weapon.'[49] Top management moves ever more easily between companies, while the behaviour of large capital is increasingly transient. How much influence do local democratic parties have here?

With his critique on the rise of symbol analysts, Lasch attacked modern journalism, but as a symptom of the information age as a whole. Information, although usually seen as a condition for debate, could be better understood as a by-product. Those who end up in a discussion that absorbs their full attention automatically search for relevant information. After all, we do not know what information we need until we ask the right questions.[50] In this concluding section, we now examine how looking up information has come to define the core of the journalistic profession:

> The core work of a correspondent isn't difficult. The editorial staff in the Netherlands called up and said something happened. They faxed or emailed the messages, and I explained those on the radio in my own words, and out of that I made an article for the newspaper. That is why my editors thought it was more important I was on the spot than that I knew what was going on.[51]

This quotation from the journalist Joris Luyendijk gives rise to serious concerns. Is the reporter of the future just a search engine user? Someone who skims blogs

[48] *Ibid.*, p. 35.
[49] Crouch, *supra* note 12, p. 38.
[50] Lasch, *supra* note 46, p. 161.
[51] J. Luyendijk, *Het zijn net mensen*, Amsterdam 2012, p. 25.

on the Internet, summarises them and forwards these to a local correspondent, who then reads it from a teleprompter? Initially, Luyendijk imagined a correspondent as a sort of historian on the spot: someone who hurdled to wherever something important happened, figuring out how it all happened and reporting on that.

'But I couldn't be bothered to exactly determine the situation', he writes. 'That was done ages ago. I went out as a presenter on location to share the news.'[52] On the news, you may see the Al-Aqsa Mosque or the skyscrapers of New York, but that is for the background – to complete the picture. The actual collection of the news has been done elsewhere.

Democracy presupposes a public debate, and a public debate assumes news based on facts. But even the reporting has been separated from the domain it actually covers; it dissolves into cyberspace. According to Luyendijk, editors in the middle of this web of news constantly examine the news of competitors and ask themselves: 'Do we already have this?' All these editorials gather their videos and information from the same sources.[53] When a contemporary journalist receives specific assignments, he first searches for articles on the Internet. From this, he filters the most relevant facts, numbers and statistics, and builds his own article around that. This is how reporting becomes 'Google journalism'.

We can say about the communicative domain that this domain is becoming less physical and more digital. Although the user has access to events around the world via the new media, it does not necessarily mean that his understanding of the world is better informed or more coherent, because the wide range of subjects can wipe out attention. By choosing one's own filters, there is also the risk that one can lock oneself into a select number of likes, of which one gets a number of updates by default until one is satisfied with the amount of information acquired. The wide range of coverage can undermine coherence, whereas the presence of 'filters' can prevent a broader awareness.

The emergence of the blogosphere and phenomena equivalent to WikiLeaks, have eroded the information monopoly of traditional media.[54] It is nevertheless questionable to what extent users can position the uncovered facts within a broader context and forge a coherent, politically valid argument. Forced by the changes in communication (media, velocity and space), the substantive professionalism of journalists also changes. Finally, these phenomena also influence the attention and the adaptation preferences of the public, who make up the electorate.

---

52 *Ibid.*

53 *Ibid.*, p. 26.

54 P. Pierik and G. Aalders, *Wikileaks, tussen cyberoorlog en informatierevolutie*, Soesterberg 2011.

9. CONCLUSION

After an in-depth analysis of the three core themes comprising the main question identified at the beginning, we can conclude on the following question:

Is it possible to have an honest and sincere representative democracy based on the pre-condition of communicating with the electorate using modern media?

Resulting from the previously mentioned developments regarding communicative media, velocity and space, we have to answer this question *negatively*. The supposedly enlightened statecraft as a guideline for political proceedings in the emergence of democracy as we know it would be shattered almost instantly in current times. Thorbecke, as an enlightened and distinguished statesman, could never have won the voter-conscious fights in a live debate on TV (or Twitter live reports).

Thorbecke, who laid the foundations of the Dutch Constitution and designed the institutions of the corresponding representative democracy, could not foresee that the party system would become an explicit part of the political area of influence. The designers of democracy never envisioned the collusion of political interests in that form. It is true that political collusions occurred within the representative bodies of the Netherlands in the 19th century, but most of the time only *after* candidates took office. These semi-formal collusions thus formed *during* the political process, whereas today the influence of party politics is always present and also ties in affiliated media.

Now I do take account of the possibility that some of these problematic effects upon civil society were already latently present in the rise of the mass media and that this adds some nuance to my overall morose analysis of the present situation. However, the digital economy has exacerbated many shortcomings: quantitative models and structures encompass and encroach upon quality-driven models. This is because the hunt for clicks, likes, shares and views makes hype-driven sensationalism into a viable business model.

Others may argue that the new social media facilitate grassroots movement such as the Arab Spring, the Occupy movement, women's marches and #MeToo, and make it easier to hold politicians to account. But I contend that the fragmentation of public discourse and the accelerated communicative pace offset these new gained advantages, making it even easier for the entrenched power structures to deflect attention, circumvent criticism and escape democratic accountability. In the Netherlands, we observed this clearly in 2018, when Parliament scrapped the possibility of citizens initiating a corrective referendum and the mainstream media simply changed the talking points, effectively dissolving the emancipatory hope for a participative democracy.

None of this means that democracy has no chance to survive at all under the pre-condition of communicating with the electorate via modern media. The verdict is that a sincere representative democracy is impossible. As has been shown, political and ideological sincerity is no longer indisputable, since for his or her success, the politician depends mainly on his or her appearance, the speed or the accent with which he or she speaks, the power of 'catchy' one-liners, the quality of his or her spin-doctors and political analysts – all factors which push a people's representative into the format of a 'savvy' media personality.

We have established that the nature of the medium can influence a discussion or even change its content. We have demonstrated how that happens with various political examples – this process emerges from the dynamics between the media, velocity and space of communication.

The examples given here have demonstrated that politicians who are hopefully sincere and representative can easily be outclassed by fast-paced mediagenic actors, and that the assumed objective press is mainly focused on profitable stories. Hopefully, the examples have also suggested that sincere representative politicians *can* adjust to the fast media-oriented players – yet the change in pre-conditions of communication makes politics far less sincere and representative than was assumed in the design of the original model. Nor is the press, the mass media, representative of the 'searchlight function', as de Tocqueville described it. This is how the influence of democracies shifts to (global) internet companies, which become bulwarks of economic, political and legal power.

The democracy of the 19th century is urgently in need of an overhaul, in order to be sincere and representative in the 21st century.

6. POST-TRUTH DISCOURSES AND THEIR LIMITS

A Democratic Crisis?

Johan Farkas and Jannick Schou*

1. INTRODUCTION

Western democracies are currently said to be under siege. 'Fake news' is flooding social media, 'alternative facts' are circulated by political elites and 'post-truth' sentiments roam throughout society. What was once deemed the normative foundations of democracy and freedom, namely reason and truth, have supposedly been shattered, leaving societies in a perpetual state of crisis. The French President Emmanuel Macron captured this dystopian *zeitgeist* in the spring of 2018 when he appeared before the joint houses of the US Congress: 'Without reason, without truth, there is no real democracy because democracy is about true choices and rational decisions. The corruption of information is an attempt to corrode the very spirit of our democracies.'[1]

Macron has not been alone in lamenting the contemporary devaluation of truth in Western liberal democracies. In recent years, a seemingly endless line of commentators from the academic, political, journalistic and commercial realms have argued that fake news and the post-truth era threaten democratic societies in substantive ways. Indeed, news outlets have overflowed with articles and op-eds dedicated to the post-truth condition, while a steady flow of books have sought to pinpoint its origins and potential resolution.[2] This range of post-truth voices has not emerged as a homogeneous or singular movement, agreeing on how and why democracy has ended up in its current predicament. Different fields and perspectives have blamed different factors for causing the crisis: from technology and media over politicians and institutions to the democratic masses

* Johan Farkas: School of Arts and Communication, Malmö University, Sweden. Email: johan.farkas@mau.se; Jannick Schou: Independent researcher, Denmark. Email: jannickschou@gmail.com.

1 E. Macron, 'Address to the US Congress', *CNN*, 25 April 2018, http://transcripts.cnn.com/TRANSCRIPTS/1804/25/ctw.01.html.

2 S. Fuller, *Post-truth: Knowledge as a Power Game*, Anthem Press, London 2018; B. McNair, *Fake News: Falsehood, Fabrication and Fantasy in Journalism*, Routledge, London 2017.

themselves. Still, across these post-truth discourses, we find a series of more or less unifying traits. For one thing, there is widespread agreement that we are facing grave societal dangers. The pillars of liberal democracies are supposedly crumbling and its structures are buckling under pressure. The rational spirit of democracy is said to be under attack or even dying. Post-truth discourses indeed seem to share a set of underlying normative premises about what democracy is and ought to be – namely a political system bound up with truth, reason and rationality. From this perspective, a decline of truth is necessarily equal to a decline of democracy itself.

This chapter presents the findings of a comprehensive investigation of contemporary post-truth discourses and their democratic underpinnings.[3] Instead of asking whether democracy really *is* suffering from a post-truth crisis, we examine the increasingly ubiquitous discourses presenting this claim. How and in what ways are Western democracies articulated as being in a state of crisis? What normative ideas are contained in such discourses? And what kind of democratic imaginaries do they produce? By investigating these developing political narratives and ideas – what we have elsewhere labelled as a new *politics of falsehood*[4] – it becomes possible to interrogate the very real democratic struggles they contain and foreclose. Based on the analysis presented in this chapter, we will suggest that a very particular idea about democracy has started to become hegemonic. As hinted at above, this is one premised on democracy being a truth-telling and rational project concerned with using facts as the foundation for consensus-based political decision-making. This kind of discourse is not neutral or innocent, but reproduces and enhances already existing political developments taking place in the last 30 years. Most notably, contemporary post-truth discourses rely on ideas connected to what critical scholars, such as Chantal Mouffe, have labelled as *post-politics* – that is, a mode of politics that values individual rights, consensus and technocratic forms of governance over equality, participation and the rule of and by the people.[5]

The chapter is a critical response to what we perceive to be two major problems facing contemporary debates on the proclaimed post-truth condition of democracy, both in scholarly and public discussions. First, there is a strong tendency to reify the basic political concepts used in the debate, taking for granted the meaning of concepts such as 'democracy', 'truth'

---

3 For a longer exposition of this research project and its core arguments, see J. Farkas and J. Schou, *Post-truth, Fake News and Democracy: Mapping the Politics of Falsehood*, Routledge, New York 2019.

4 J. Farkas and J. Schou, 'Fake News as a Floating Signifier: Hegemony, Antagonism and the Politics of Falsehood' (2018) 25(3) *Javnost – The Public* 298, https://doi.org/10.1080/13183222.2018.1463047.

5 C. Mouffe, *Agonistics: Thinking the World Politically*, Verso, London 2013; C. Mouffe, *On the Political*, Routledge, London 2005.

and 'rationality'. This is an infeasible premise – both conceptually and historically – as the development of these terms tell a very different and contested story. Second, there has so far been an absence of critical perspectives and historical contextualisation of present-day developments in advanced capitalist states. Critical voices have largely been missing from the debates on fake news and post-truth, while those who *have* engaged in debates have tended to overtake dominant narratives claiming that democracy is indeed experiencing a rapid 'truth crisis', which must be solved by restoring rationality and consensus. This chapter hopes to outline a fundamentally different take on these discussions on fake news, post-truth and democracy. Drawing on concepts from post-Marxist discourse theory, particularly as it has been developed by Ernesto Laclau and Chantal Mouffe,[6] we want to suggest that attention is needed to the ways in which different discourses hegemonise contemporary debates. We cannot take any shared meaning of key political terms for granted. Instead of seeking to find supposedly 'real' or 'neutral' definitions of fake news and post-truth, we need to investigate how they are mobilised as part of political conflicts. If there are any overarching commonalities in terms of how concepts such as democracy are mobilised – that is, common ideas about what democracy is and ought to be – then this is the outcome of political struggles for hegemony rather than a neutral starting point. Only through such a perspective can we begin to connect our contemporary democratic moment to wider historical developments taking place within advanced capitalist states.

2. APPROACH AND METHOD

This chapter presents a political analysis of contemporary post-truth discourses. It does so by building on what is known as discourse theory or the *Essex School of Discourse Analysis*.[7] The founding principle of this school, developed in an ongoing dialogue with Marxist, feminist and post-structuralist political philosophy since the 1980s, has been to reject essentialism and reified concepts like 'Society', 'Economy' and 'Democracy'. Society does not develop or exist as a closed totality with its own internal logics. Instead, the meaning of *all* political concepts is based on their relation to other signifiers (*moments*) within

6 E. Laclau and C. Mouffe, *Hegemony and Socialist Strategy: Towards a Radical Democratic Politics*, Verso, London 2014; E. Laclau, *New Reflections on the Revolution of Our Time*. Verso, London 1990.

7 E. Laclau, *On Populist Reason*, Verso, London 2005; D. Howarth, *Discourse*, Open University Press, Buckingham 2000; D. Howarth, *Poststructuralism and after: Structure, Subjectivity and Power*, Palgrave Macmillan, Basingstoke 2013; D. Howarth, A.J. Norval and Y. Stavrakakis, *Discourse Theory and Political Analysis: Identities, Hegemonies and Social Change*, Manchester Univerity Press, Manchester 2000; J. Torfing, *New Theories of Discourse: Laclau, Mouffe and Zizek*, Blackwell, Oxford 1999.

more or less coherent systems of meaning (*discourses*). All such discourses are necessarily contingent insofar as their existence cannot be attributed to any innate development or unfolding of history. At the same time, social reality cannot simply be changed through sheer imagination. Indeed, we are always already placed within circumstances not of our own making. As Marx remarked in *The Eighteenth Brumaire of Louis Bonaparte*: 'Men make their own history, but they do not make it as they please; they do not make it under self-selected circumstances, but under circumstances existing already, given and transmitted from the past.'[8] Discourse theorists account for this relation between change and stability – what they label as *political decisions* and *sedimentation* – by suggesting that social reality is always criss-crossed with antagonism and hegemonic struggles. Different groups are competing to impose particular understandings of reality onto others in order to establish moral, intellectual and popular domination, consent and control. Social reality is open in principle (*contingency*), yet closed in practice (*hegemony*).[9] The point of adopting a discourse-theoretical approach is to account for this closing of the social by deconstructing and systematically engaging with the formation of hegemonic discourse.[10]

If we accept these basic ideas, then certain arguments follow that directly impact our present investigation of post-truth discourses. It first of all becomes difficult to neatly separate the factual from the normative, as what is counted as factual is always embedded in particular historical circumstances and truth regimes.[11] All meaning is, at its core, the result of political decisions seeking to choose between competing alternatives. As Laclau suggests: 'There are no facts without signification, and there is no signification without practical engagements that require norms governing our behaviour. So there are not two orders – the normative and the descriptive – but normative/descriptive complexes in which facts and values interpenetrate each other in an inextricable way.'[12]

Acknowledging the intimate relation between the factual and the normative means recognising that what is counted as true and truthful is in itself a deeply political activity, no matter whether this takes place in the domain of science, politics or anywhere else for that matter. Establishing a specific truth as dominant in the world relies on political struggles as well as the rejection of other potential truths. Building on these premises, this chapter unpacks how contemporary

---

8 K. Marx, 'The Eighteenth Brumaire of Louis Bonaparte (in German)' (1952) 8 *MEW* 115.

9 O. Marchart, *Post-foundational Political Thought: Political Difference in Nancy, Lefort, Badiou and Laclau*, Edinburgh University Press, Edinburgh 2007.

10 Laclau, *supra* note 6.

11 J. Schou, 'Ernesto Laclau and Critical Media Studies: Marxism, Capitalism, and Critique' (2016) 14(1) *TripleC: Communication, Capitalism & Critique* 292, https://doi.org/10.31269/triplec.v14i1.740.

12 E. Laclau, *The Rhetorical Foundations of Society*, Verso, London 2014, p. 128.

political debates articulate and construct the relation between truth, democracy and falsehood. How is the so-called post-truth crisis constructed by public voices at the current conjuncture? How is democracy envisioned to function as a political system? And what kind of remedies are offered to solve the ongoing attack on Western democracies? Rather than seeking to deem whether democracy is *actually* facing a 'truth crisis', we are interested in interpreting and understanding how the *idea* of such a crisis is being constructed and what kind of performative impact it has. We are in this sense not interested in how new forms of false information circulate in society, something we have explored in previous works.[13] Rather, we seek to showcase how the notion of post-truth plays into already existing visions for democracy.

Methodologically, the chapter builds on a comprehensive empirical mapping of contemporary discourses in and around questions of fake news and the post-truth era. We rely on a broad set of empirical materials, including scholarly texts, journalistic articles, books and commentaries from public intellectuals, speeches from political figures as well as documents from different governmental branches published between 2015 and 2018 in the Western, English-speaking world. In line with discourse theory's rejection of universal methods, we have opted for an exploratory mode of analysis suitable for tracing a continuously evolving political field.[14] Since 2015, we have collected an archive of both academic and non-academic work. To systematise our data collection, we queried Google Scholar (the scholarly search engine) in August and September 2018 using the terms 'fake news', 'post-truth', 'post-factual' and 'post-factuality'. A similar technique was employed in the context of non-academic sources, which are central to the argument developed in this chapter, combining ongoing collection with subsequent focused searches on the websites of ten major news outlets. In total, we established an archive of over 125 academic publications, primarily from international scholarly journals, and 350 non-academic pieces, linked primarily to the *New York Times*, *The Guardian*, the BBC, CNN, Fox News, the *Washington Post*, Reuters, Buzzfeed and *Time Magazine*. We have analysed this substantive corpus of data through an explorative, qualitative approach using discourse theory as a guiding framework. This analysis involved a three-step process, including: (1) close textual readings of the included material and production of inductive notes;

13 J. Farkas, J. Schou and C. Neumayer, 'Platformed Antagonism: Racist Discourses on Fake Muslim Facebook Pages' (2018a) 15(5) *Critical Discourse Studies* 463, https://doi.org/10.1080/17405904.2018.1450276; J. Farkas, J. Schou and C. Neumayer, 'Cloaked Facebook Pages: Exploring Fake Islamist Propaganda in Social Media' (2018b) 20(5) *New Media & Society* 1850, https://doi.org/10.1177/1461444817707759; J. Farkas and M. Bastos, 'IRA Propaganda on Twitter: Stoking Antagonism and Tweeting Local News' (2018) *Proceedings of the 9th Annual International Conference on Social Media and Society*, https://doi.org/10.1145/3217804.3217929.

14 Torfing, *supra* note 7.

(2) construction of codes capturing themes, explanations and proposed solutions as found in the empirical material; and (3) grouping of codes into larger topics and categories. Based on this approach, our focus has been to establish key threads across the studied material, mapping underlying premises that structure the semantic space at our current societal conjuncture. As this discursive space is continuously developing, the analysis presented should not be seen as exhaustive or final.[15]

3. MAPPING POST-TRUTH DISCOURSES

Having now presented the theoretical and methodological backdrop to this chapter, we turn to our analysis. This is structured in three main sections: first, we examine how democracy is articulated as being in a state of crisis within contemporary post-truth discourses; second, we look into what actors and institutions are said to have caused this crisis, including justifications for why they are to blame; and, third, we focus on the different solutions proposed to solve the post-truth crisis. Following our analysis, we discuss the implications of these increasingly hegemonic discourses. We do so by linking them to contemporary critical analyses of the historical development of liberal democracy in advanced capitalist states, particularly as proposed by the discourse theorist Chantal Mouffe.

3.1. WHAT IS WRONG?

The idea that Western liberal democracies have entered a so-called post-truth era has become increasingly widespread and dominant. In this emergent political landscape – labelled as a 'post-fact, post-truth, we've-had-enough-of-experts era'[16] – the very foundations of truthfulness, facts and evidence have been put into question. Lies are said to be abundant and truth has become 'whatever public opinion is persuaded by'.[17] Across the political landscape, it is claimed, 'emotional response prevails over factual evidence',[18] making truth 'of secondary importance'.[19] In this line of reasoning, citizens have become 'passive consumers

15 For an elaboration of the analytical approach of this research project, see J. Farkas and J. Schou, *supra* note 4,

16 M. McCartney, 'Evidence in a Post-truth World' (2016) 355 *British Medical Journal* 1, https://doi.org/10.1136/bmj.i6363.

17 B. Jameson, 'God, Post-truth' (2018) 121(3) *Theology* 186, https://doi.org/10.1177/0040571X17749145.

18 P. Dahlgren, 'Media, Knowledge and Trust: The Deepening Epistemic Crisis of Democracy' (2018) 25(1–2) *Javnost – The Public* 25, https://doi.org/10.1080/13183222.2018.1418819.

19 'Post-truth Politics: Art of the Lie', *The Economist*, 10 September 2016, https://www.economist.com/news/leaders/21706525-politicians-have-always-lied-does-it-matter-if-they-leave-truth-behind-entirely-art?fsrc=scn/tw/te/pe/ed/artofthelie.

of bullshit'[20] who engage in and are victims of 'wilful ignorance and distortions of reality'.[21] Citizens are even said to be losing the basic ability to distinguish between true and false, causing a 'political subordination of reality',[22] or even a 'vanishing of reality'[23] with the potential of 'bringing down democracy'.[24]

Questions of democracy and participation are central to contemporary post-truth discourses. Often, it is presupposed that liberal democracy fundamentally revolves around truthfulness and reason: 'Facts hold a sacred place in Western liberal democracies. Whenever democracy seems to be going awry, when voters are manipulated or politicians are ducking questions, we turn to facts for salvation. But they seem to be losing their ability to support consensus.'[25] The notion that lies are flourishing, truth is destabilised and Western democracies are threatened has become seemingly ubiquitous: 'Facts and reliable information are essential for the functioning of democracy.'[26] Indeed, as summarised by Lance Bennett and Steven Livingston, the spread of lies and fake news undermines core democratic values: 'Given the daunting mix of institutional decline, public sphere disruptions, and the growing attacks on journalism and enlightenment values, it may be that we have entered a "post-truth" order ... If so, democracies based on norms of debate, deliberation, compromise and reason will not fare well.'[27] The idea that what is under siege are the 'enlightenment values' that underlie liberal democracies is also widespread; indeed, it has served as a substantial part of the discursive landscape. What we are witnessing, it is claimed, is the rapid collapse of the fundamental ideals that underpin democracy: 'This is not a battle between liberals and conservatives. It is a battle between two ways of perceiving the world, two fundamentally different approaches to reality: and as between those two, you *do* have to choose.

20 J. Stuart, '"Bullshit is a Greater Enemy than Lies": Lessons from Three New Books on the Post-truth Era', *The Guardian*, 22 May 2017, https://www.theguardian.com/us-news/2017/may/22/post-truth-era-trump-brexit-lies-books.

21 The Learning Network, 'On "The Age of Post-truth Politics"', *New York Times*, 6 September 2018, https://learning.blogs.nytimes.com/2016/09/06/summer-reading-contest-winner-week-10-on-the-age-of-post-truth-politics.

22 L. McIntyre, *Post-truth*, MIT Press, Cambridge, MA 2018.

23 M. Kakutani, *The Death of Truth: Notes on Falsehood in the Age of Trump*, Tim Duggans Books, New York 2018, p. 77.

24 M. Kakutani, 'The Death of Truth: How We Gave up on Facts and Ended up with Trump', *The Guardian*, 14 July 2018, https://www.theguardian.com/books/2018/jul/14/the-death-of-truth-how-we-gave-up-on-facts-and-ended-up-with-trump.

25 W. Davies, 'The Age of Post-truth Politics', *New York Times*, 24 August 2016, https://www.nytimes.com/2016/08/24/opinion/campaign-stops/the-age-of-post-truth-politics.html.

26 K. Viner, 'How Technology Disrupted the Truth', *The Guardian*, 12 July 2016, https://www.theguardian.com/media/2016/jul/12/how-technology-disrupted-the-truth?CMP=soc_568.

27 W.L. Bennett and S. Livingston, 'The Disinformation Order: Disruptive Communication and the Decline of Democratic Institutions' (2018) 33(2) *European Journal of Communication* 122, https://doi.org/10.1177/0267323118760317.

Are you content for the central value of the Enlightenment, of free societies and of democratic discourse, to be trashed by charlatans – or not? … The truth is out there, if only we demand it.'[28]

Portraying truth as something that is 'out there' – beyond dispute – runs throughout post-truth discourses. As stated by *The Economist*: 'Helped by new technology, a deluge of facts and a public much less given to trust than once it was, some politicians are getting away with a new depth and pervasiveness of falsehood. If this continues, the power of truth as a tool for solving society's problems could be lastingly reduced.'[29] Writing for *The Guardian*, Hadley Freeman similarly argues: 'We live in a blog culture where it's pitched as a triumph of democracy that everyone can claim authority, which means anyone who says that, actually, there is an objective truth is condemned. Feelings rather than facts are what matter, these purveyors of bullshit claim.'[30]

These discourses, arguing that democracy's capacity to function is mainly dependent on reason and consensus, often articulate the decline of truth as having an almost larger-than-life agency of its own. This manifests itself through a highly naturalised or medicalised vocabulary. Thus, numerous voices have argued that fake news is 'spreading and replicating like a virus',[31] behaving like a 'wildfire on social media'[32] or 'killing people's minds', as stated by Apple CEO Tim Cook.[33] It has a viral nature, representing nothing less than a new form of 'epidemic'[34] or 'epidemics'.[35] In this narrative, fake news has become 'a plague on the Web',[36] posing 'a serious security threat to our societies', as argued

[28] M. d'Ancona, *Post-truth: The New War on Truth and How to Fight Back*, Ebury Press, London 2017, pp. 5–6, emphasis in original.

[29] 'The Post-truth World: Yes, I'd Lie to You Dishonesty', *The Economist*, 10 September 2016, https://www.economist.com/briefing/2016/09/10/yes-id-lie-to-you.

[30] H. Freeman, 'From Deliciously Ella to Donald Trump', *The Guardian*, 14 January 2018, https://www.theguardian.com/us-news/2017/jan/14/difference-bullshitting-lying-donald-trump.

[31] J. Parsons, 'How to Stop "Fake News": Psychologists Believe We Can Be "Inoculated" against Misinformation', *Daily Mirror*, 23 January 2017, https://www.mirror.co.uk/science/how-stop-fake-news-psychologists-9675939.

[32] M. Fox, 'Fake News: Lies Spread Faster on Social Media Than Truth Does', *NBC News*, 8 March 2018, https://www.nbcnews.com/health/health-news/fake-news-lies-spread-faster-social-media-truth-does-n854896.

[33] A. Heath, 'Fake News is Killing People's Minds, Says Apple Boss Tim Cook', *The Telegraph*, 10 February 2017, https://www.telegraph.co.uk/technology/2017/02/10/fake-news-killing-peoples-minds-says-apple-boss-tim-cook.

[34] M. Amrita, 'Understanding the Plague of Fake News and How to Combat it', *Medium*, 12 December 2017, https://medium.com/melissa-persauds-portfolio/understanding-the-plague-of-fake-news-and-how-to-combat-it-862d4920e61b.

[35] C. Shao et al., 'The Spread of Fake News by Social Bots', *ArXiv*, 2017, https://arxiv.org/abs/1707.07592v2.

[36] B. Stelter, 'The Plague of Fake News is Getting Worse: Here's How to Protect Yourself', *CNN Media*, 1 November 2016, http://money.cnn.com/2016/10/30/media/facebook-fake-news-plague/index.html.

by Sir Julian King, Commissioner for the Security Union in the EU.[37] In taking on this viral nature, circulated through digital networks and technologies, fake news supposedly traverses borders and operates at all scales. The post-truth condition has become a 'global problem',[38] the 'equivalent of a public-health crisis'.[39] In this viral vocabulary, democracies are said to be in a state where 'a large share of the populace is living in an epistemic space that has abandoned conventional criteria of evidence'.[40] This 'fake news epidemic'[41] has proven 'alarmingly resistant to treatment. Indeed, the treatment has often strengthened the disease'.[42] Instead of stopping the plague and putting out the wildfires, societies amplify and worsen the critical post-truth condition: 'we've entered a post-truth world – there's no going back now'.[43] Unless radical measures are taken, 'this cannot end well'.[44] Indeed, according to some: 'It's no exaggeration to say that relying on emotions and personal opinions over facts will very likely destroy our political system.'[45]

3.2. WHO DID IT?

In post-truth discourses, a series of actors and developments are seen as primary causes of the sudden rupture in the rational fabric of democracy. In particular, we find that three actors are targeted as the main drivers of contemporary changes: social media, journalism and the democratic masses.

The first key signifier linked to the rise of the post-truth condition is *social media*, understood as a more or less homogeneous technological actor.

---

37 European Commission, 'Tackling Online Disinformation: Commission Proposes an EU-Wide Code of Practice', 2018, http://europa.eu/rapid/press-release_IP-18-3370_en.htm.

38 K. Connolly et al., 'Fake news: An Insidious Trend That's Fast Becoming a Global Problem', *The Guardian*, 2 December 2016, https://www.theguardian.com/media/2016/dec/02/fake-news-facebook-us-election-around-the-world.

39 K. Steinmetz, 'How Your Brain Tricks You into Believing Fake News', *Time Magazine*, 9 August 2018, http://time.com/5362183/the-real-fake-news-crisis.

40 S. Lewandowsky, U.K.H. Ecker and J. Cook, 'Beyond Misinformation: Understanding and Coping with the "Post-truth" Era' (2017) 6(4) *Journal of Applied Research in Memory and Cognition* 360, https://doi.org/10.1016/j.jarmac.2017.07.008.

41 J. Horowitz, 'For Pope Francis, Fake News Goes Back to the Garden of Eden', *New York Times*, 24 January 2018, https://www.nytimes.com/2018/01/24/us/politics/pope-francis-fake-news.html.

42 d'Ancona, *supra* note 28.

43 M. Norman, 'Whoever Wins the US Presidential Election, We've Entered a Post-truth World – There's No Going Back Now', *The Independent*, 8 November 2016, http://www.independent.co.uk/voices/us-election-2016-donald-trump-hillary-clinton-who-wins-post-truth-world-no-going-back-a7404826.html.

44 N. Enfield, 'We're in a Post-truth World with Eroding Trust and Accountability. It Can't End Well', *The Guardian*, 16 November 2017, https://www.theguardian.com/commentisfree/2017/nov/17/were-in-a-post-truth-world-with-eroding-trust-and-accountability-it-cant-end-well.

45 G. Tsipursky, 'Towards a Post-lies Future: Fighting "Alternative Facts" and "Post-truth" Politics' (2017) *The Humanist* 13.

Once hailed as an empowering democratic force, uniting the world through global connectedness and engagement, social media has increasingly been recast as a destabilising entity: 'one might say that if the internet ushered in a more diverse and decentralised public sphere of global reach and accessibility, it has also created the pathways down which fake news and other malicious forms of content can spread'.[46] The transformation from technological hero to villain has been rapid. Less than a decade ago, social media platforms were said to give 'genuine cause for hope' by enabling 'dissent from official government and/or corporate-interest propaganda'.[47] Scholars and journalists highlighted decentralised protest movements such as Occupy Wall Street and the so-called Iranian 'Twitter revolution'[48] as examples of how and why social media could empower individuals and collectives to circumvent elite interests and change society for the better through bottom-up initiatives.

In contrast to these optimistic accounts, social media is now increasingly (re)cast as a corrosive force that 'effectively sways voters, suppresses rivals, sows confusion, defames opposition, and spreads fake news'.[49] Instead of supporting democracy, it now represents one of its greatest threats: 'popular platforms such as Twitter and Facebook are powerhouses that enable misinformation to spread on a massive scale'.[50] Across post-truth discourses, social media are thus said to have 'disrupted the truth',[51] giving rise to a dangerous 'political culture of distrust that undermines shared assumptions about social reality'.[52] The epicentres of the negative turn in public discourse came in the wake of the 2016 US presidential elections when it was revealed that a data analytics firm, Cambridge Analytica, used social media data on millions of Americans to target them with political ads. Additionally, it became clear that a Russian firm, the Internet Research Agency, had used thousands of fake social media accounts to infiltrate US debates. Negative sentiment towards social media quickly extended far beyond

---

46 McNair, *supra* note 2, p. 59.

47 M. Boler and S. Nemorin, 'Dissent, Truthiness, and Skepticism in the Global Media Landscape: Twenty-First Century Propaganda in Times of War' in J. Auerbach and R. Castronovo (eds.), *The Oxford Handbook of Propaganda Studies*, Oxford University Press, Oxford 2013, p. 411.

48 'Editorial: Iran's Twitter revolution', *Washington Times*, 16 June 2009, https://www.washingtontimes.com/news/2009/jun/16/irans-twitter-revolution; M. Castells, *Networks of Outrage and Hope: Social Movements in the Internet Age*, Polity Press, Cambridge 2012.

49 M. Boler and E. Davis, 'The Affective Politics of the "Post-truth" Era: Feeling Rules and Networked Subjects' (2018) 27 *Emotion, Space and Society* 75, https://doi.org/10.1016/j.emospa.2018.03.002.

50 H. Webb and M. Jirotka, 'Nuance, Societal Dynamics, and Responsibility in Addressing Misinformation in the Post-truth Era: Commentary on Lewandowsky, Ecker, and Cook' (2017) 6(4) *Journal of Applied Research in Memory and Cognition* 414, https://doi.org/10.1016/j.jarmac.2017.10.001.

51 Viner, *supra* note 26.

52 Dahlgren, *supra* note 18, p. 26.

these specific cases and into the realm of politics in general, establishing a direct link between the rise of social media and the post-truth era.

Whereas previous forms of mass communication, curated by journalists or other gatekeepers, ensured an informed public sphere, social media give users the 'impetus to participate digitally, through user-generated content, liking, and sharing' with little to no emphasis on factuality.[53] This leads, according to post-truth discourses, to a threatening situation in which users increasingly engage in debates 'without even thinking twice, let alone checking to determine if it is true'.[54] As a result, we have entered a post-truth era in which 'fear, rumour and gossip can spread alarmingly fast with feelings and emotions often carrying more weight than facts and evidence'.[55]

Notions of 'echo chambers' and 'filter bubbles' are central to this discursive link between social media and post-truth.[56] These terms capture ways in which 'people gather with like-minded and thereby collectively screen out information and views that do not sit well with the group consensus'.[57] On social media, algorithmic selection of content is said to entrench political polarisation and create 'positive feedback loops' that 'fuels the spread of fake news'.[58] Increasingly, we are witnessing the 'replacement of verification with social media algorithms that tell us what we want to hear'.[59] Each user has become 'trapped in a filter bubble' that forms 'large-scale alternative realities'.[60] Within these realities, citizens are only presented with information they agree with. 'We', in other words, 'become so secure in our bubbles that we start accepting only information, whether it's true or not, that fits our opinions', as formulated by US President Barack Obama in his farewell address.[61] This is said to pose a fundamental threat to democracy

53 J. Harsin, 'Regimes of Posttruth, Postpolitics, and Attention Economies' (2015) 8(2) *Communication, Culture and Critique* 330, https://doi.org/10.1111/cccr.12097.

54 'The Post-truth World', *supra* note 29.

55 E. Speed and R. Mannion, 'The Rise of Post-truth Populism in Pluralist Liberal Democracies: Challenges for Health Policy' (2017) 6(5) *Kerman University of Medical Sciences* 249, https://doi.org/10.15171/ijhpm.2017.19.

56 J. Ball, 'How Can We Fight back against Fake News and Post-truth Politics?', *New Statesman*, 16 May 2017; S. Lewandowsky, J. Cook and U.K.H. Ecker, 'Letting the Gorilla Emerge from the Mist: Getting Past Post-truth' (2017) 6(4) *Journal of Applied Research in Memory and Cognition* 418, https://doi.org/10.1016/j.jarmac.2017.11.002; C. Laybats and L Tredinnick, 'Post-truth, Information, and Emotion' (2016) 33(4) *Business Information Review* 204, https://doi.org/10.1177/0266382116680741.

57 Dahlgren, *supra* note 18, p. 25.

58 P.R. Berthon and L.F. Pitt, 'Brands, Truthiness and Post-fact: Managing Brands in a Post-rational World' (2018) 38(2) *Journal of Macromarketing* 218, https://doi.org/10.1177/0276146718755869.

59 d'Ancona, *supra* note 28.

60 I. Kalpokas, 'On Guilt and Post-truth Escapism' (2018) 13 *Philosophy & Social Criticism*, https://doi.org/10.1177/0191453718794752.

61 B. Obama, 'President Obama Farewell Address: Full Text', *CNN Politics*, 11 January 2018, https://edition.cnn.com/2017/01/10/politics/president-obama-farewell-speech/index.html.

not only because such bubbles drive political polarisation, but also because they make citizens vulnerable 'to lines of deliberate attack from those trying to deceive or discourage us: we believe we're in groups of like-minded people, and this leaves us open to be exploited by malicious actors'.[62] In this regard, it should be noted that empirical scholarship increasingly challenges this notion of 'filter bubbles', despite its centrality in post-truth narratives.[63]

The notion of 'malicious actors' is also central to post-truth discourses. These are often linked to concepts such as '(social) bots' and 'trolls', referring respectively to software-driven social media accounts and deceptive online behaviour thriving on ambivalence and antagonism.[64] These create a digital landscape in which '[o]rdinary people experience ... propaganda posts as something shared by their own trusted friends, perhaps with comments or angry reactions, shaping their own opinions and assumptions'.[65] Once part of the 'dark corners of the Internet', social media has increasingly become 'so poisoned by incivility that trolling can rightly be said to be the new normal'.[66] Combined with bots that increase 'the circulation of false information as they automatically retweet posts without verifying the facts', trolling has effectively made social media vehicles of post-truth.[67] Citizens are said to be flooded with 'fake sites, bots, trolls – things that regenerate themselves, reinforcing opinions with certain algorithms', as said by the German Chancellor Angela Merkel.[68] In other words, according to post-truth discourses, the rise of post-truth is fuelled by social media that have become 'tools of very ugly kinds of politics'.[69]

The second set of actors intimately connected to the post-truth era in contemporary discourses is the field of journalism and more specifically its role as an autonomous practice, professional institution and societal gatekeeper of knowledge: 'The fragmentation of news sources has created an atomised world in which lies, rumour and gossip spread with alarming speed.'[70] While a strong

---

62 J. Ball, *Post-truth: How Bullshit Conquered the World*, Biteback Publishing, London 2017.

63 A. Bruns, *Are Filter Bubbles Real?*, Polity Press, Cambridge 2019.

64 Webb and Jirotka, *supra* note 50; N. Vasu, B. Ang and S. Jayakumar, 'Fake News: National Security in the Post-truth Era' (2018) *Nanyang Technological University*; J. Hannan, 'Trolling Ourselves to Death? Social Media and Post-truth Politics' (2018) 33(2) *European Journal of Communication* 214, https://doi.org/10.1177/0267323118760323; Kakutani, *supra* note 23.

65 M. Haigh, T. Haigh and N.I. Kozak, 'Stopping Fake News: The Work Practices of Peer-to-Peer Counter Propaganda' (2018) 19(4) *Journalism Studies* 2062, https://doi.org/10.1080/1461670X.2017.1316681.

66 Hannan, *supra* note 64.

67 K. Shu et al., 'Fake News Detection on Social Media: A Data Mining Perspective' (2017) 19(1) *ACM SIGKDD Explorations Newsletter* 31, https://doi.org/https://doi.org/10.1145/3137597.3137600.

68 Connolly et al, *supra* note 38.

69 S. Sismondo, 'Post-truth?' (2017) 47(1) *Social Studies of Science* 4, https://doi.org/10.1177/0306312717692076.

70 'Post-truth Politics', *supra* note 19.

connection between journalism and post-truth is found across contemporary discourses, specific details and explanations often diverge considerably. On the one hand, a number of voices emphasise that post-truth represents the *result* of declining societal trust in journalism. On the other hand, some argue that post-truth is instead what *creates* journalism's decline. From the first perspective, the catalyst of post-truth is said to be declining trust in journalism since the late 20th century. According to this understanding, post-truth politics is largely sparked by an 'increasingly privatised and fragmented public news that began with the "sound bite" and "photo opportunity" to bypass public discussion in the regime of the 24-h[our] news cycle'.[71] Thus, the rise of post-truth designates not only an increase in fake news and lies online, but, more substantially, a decline of quality and integrity within the journalistic field: 'We have a bad news problem, not a fake news problem', as formulated by the founder of the fact-checking website Snopes.[72] News organisations have increasingly engaged in 'horse-race election coverage, the daily twists of the stock market – and not enough deal consistently and seriously with issues that affect people's lives'.[73] Slowly, but steadily, journalism's pursuit of 'truth and justice' has been replaced by a 'carnival of gossip and spectacle'.[74] Accordingly, this line of reasoning suggests, the spread of false information online can be 'traced to growing legitimacy problems in many democracies'.[75] Citizens no longer trust journalistic sources and seek out alternative (fake) ones. Some authors do, however, also emphasise that the 'plague of fake news' amplifies existing 'threats to the integrity of journalism'.[76] For example, social media is said to contribute negatively by enabling 'fake election news to outperform real news',[77] causing financial distress to news organisations, while supporting malicious actors. Accordingly, 'the fake news

---

71 M. Peters, 'Post-truth and Fake News: Responses to the Editorial "Education in a Post-truth World"' (2017) 49(6) *Educational Philosophy and Theory* 564, http://dx.doi.org/10.1080/00131857.2017.1288782.

72 D. Mikkelsen, 'We Have a Bad News Problem, Not a Fake News Problem', *Snopes*, 17 November 2016, https://www.snopes.com/news/2016/11/17/we-have-a-bad-news-problem-not-a-fake-news-problem.

73 M. Zimdars, 'My "Fake News List" Went Viral. But Made-up Stories are Only Part of the Problem', *Washington Post*, 18 November 2016, https://www.washingtonpost.com/posteverything/wp/2016/11/18/my-fake-news-list-went-viral-but-made-up-stories-are-only-part-of-the-problem/?utm_term=.b037b313a4fb.

74 N. Fenton and D. Freedman, 'Fake Democracy, Bad News' (2018) 54 *Socialist Register* 1, http://research.gold.ac.uk/22330/1/Fenton-Fake_democracy.pdf.

75 Bennett and Livingston, *supra* note 27.

76 W.Y. Wang, '"Liar, Liar Pants on Fire": A New Benchmark Dataset for Fake News Detection' (2017) 1 *Proceedings of the 55th Annual Meeting of the Association for Computational Linguistics*, https://doi.org/10.18653/v1/P17-2067.

77 S. Levin, 'Facebook Promised to Tackle Fake News. But the Evidence Shows it's Not Working', *The Guardian*, 16 May 2017, https://www.theguardian.com/technology/2017/may/16/facebook-fake-news-tools-not-working.

phenomenon both embodies and intensifies' the crisis of journalism and post-truth conditions.[78]

The third prominent cause of the post-truth conditions found in contemporary discourses hones in on the democratic people or masses. Writing for the *Huffington Post*, Masur captures this position in arguing that: 'The most important thing in a functional society is a well-informed public. What we have now is not only uninformed but misinformed masses. That's something that should scare us all.'[79] Whereas citizens were once able to stay informed about public affairs, they now get overwhelmed by the massive 'barrage of misinformation that comes our way these days'.[80] This links directly to the role of social media and journalism, as the public now only hears 'what it wants to hear, because many people get their news exclusively from sources whose bias they agree with'.[81] Some argue that younger citizens are especially to blame, as the 'social media generation may not be equipped – or sufficiently interested – to actually understand what news is, and how it differs from other kinds of information'.[82] Others point to the exact opposite conclusion, arguing that so-called millennials 'know more than anybody that context is key, and the same story told from different perspectives can hold many different meanings … By understanding communication as something individualized, they can process information efficiently and improve its accuracy'.[83] Yet others point to 'rightwing social network users' as being primary consumers and disseminators of '[l]ow-quality, extremist, sensationalist and conspiratorial news'.[84] At the moment, then, there are a number of both different and connected ideas about the relationship between citizens and the post-truth era. Some argue that the problem for citizens is not necessarily a biased selection of sources or abandonment of truth-telling, but instead the amount of sources available that causes a crisis: 'citizens are encircled by millions of channels, newspapers, websites, blogs and

78 McNair, *supra* note 2.

79 M. Masur, 'Bernie Sanders Could Replace President Trump with Little-Known Loophole', *Huffington Post*, 14 November 2016, https://www.huffingtonpost.com/entry/bernie-sanders-could-replace-president-trump-with-little_us_5829f25fe4b02b1f5257a6b7.

80 H. Berghel, 'Alt-News and Post-truths in the "Fake News" Era' (2017) 50(4) *Computer* 114, https://doi.org/10.1109/MC.2017.104.

81 K. Higgins, 'Post-truth: A Guide for the Perplexed' (2016) 540(7631) *Nature* 6, https://doi.org/10.1038/540009a.

82 N. Richardson, 'Fake News and Journalism Education' (2017) 27(1) *Asia Pacific Media Educator* 5, https://doi.org/10.1177/1326365X17702268.

83 K. Moore, 'How Do We Navigate a "Post-truth" World? Follow The Millennials', *Forbes*, 7 September 2017, https://www.forbes.com/sites/karlmoore/2017/09/07/how-do-we-navigate-a-post-truth-world-follow-the-millennials/#1622be0b7072.

84 A. Hern, 'Fake News Sharing in US is a Rightwing Thing, Says Study', *The Guardian*, 6 February 2018, https://www.theguardian.com/technology/2018/feb/06/sharing-fake-news-us-rightwing-study-trump-university-of-oxford.

social media feeds creating an information – or misinformation – overload'.[85] Mobilising the concept of *infoglut*, Dahlgren similarly argues that 'challenges of acquiring knowledge in a media environment … ushers in an uncertain epistemic future' for democracy.[86] Meanwhile, others argue that the answer lies in our brains, which 'Tricks You Into Believing Fake News'.[87] Playing off the charges against social media and journalism, the problem with citizens remains that they are either too easy to deceive, live in their own secluded realities or simply no longer care about the truth.

3.3. WHAT IS TO BE DONE?

A large part of contemporary discourses on post-truth and democracy has not just been about diagnosing what is wrong with the state of democracy; it has also been concerned with prescribing solutions and remedies. In this regard, a large set of different policy initiatives, both implemented and proposed, can be highlighted. In France, new legal means are put in place to combat the spread of fake news.[88] In Germany, a controversial law came into effect on 1 January 2018, known as the Network Enforcement Act (NetzDG), requiring online platforms to remove hate speech within 24 hours.[89] Both laws attracted criticism from multiple sides, including human rights groups arguing that they risk violating freedom of speech.[90] They have also been criticised for contributing to a rise in censorship laws against 'fake news' worldwide.[91] In addition to legislation, specialized units and task forces have been launched, including the EU's EastStratcom Task Force, serving to 'address and respond to disinformation

---

85 H. Taş, 'The 15 July Abortive Coup and Post-truth Politics in Turkey' (2018) 18(1) *Journal of Southeast European and Black Sea* 3, https://doi.org/10.1080/14683857.2018.1452374.

86 Dahlgren, *supra* note 18; M. Andrejevic, *Infoglut: How Too Much Information is Changing the Way We Think and Know*, Routledge, New York 2013.

87 Steinmetz, *supra* note 39.

88 J. McAuley, 'France Weighs a Law to Rein in "Fake News", Raising Fears for Freedom of Speech', *Washington Post*, 10 January 2018, https://www.washingtonpost.com/world/europe/france-weighs-a-law-to-rein-in-fake-news-raising-fears-for-freedom-of-speech/2018/01/10/78256962-f558-11e7-9af7-a50bc3300042_story.html.

89 P. Olterman, 'Tough New German Law Puts Tech Firms and Free Speech in Spotlight', *The Guardian*, 5 January 2018, https://www.theguardian.com/world/2018/jan/05/tough-new-german-law-puts-tech-firms-and-free-speech-in-spotlight.

90 Humans Rights Watch, 'Germany: Flawed Social Media Law', 14 February 2018, https://www.hrw.org/news/2018/02/14/germany-flawed-social-media-law; McAuley, *supra* note 88.

91 J. Mchangama and J. Fiss, 'The Digital Berlin Wall: How Germany (Accidentally) Created a Prototype for Global Online Censorship', *Justitia*, November 2019, http://justitia-int.org/wp-content/uploads/2019/11/Analyse_The-Digital-Berlin-Wall-How-Germany-Accidentally-Created-a-Prototype-for-Global-Online-Censorship.pdf.

activities by external actors', particularly from Russia.[92] In the Czech Republic, the government created a similar unit, dubbed as a 'fake news police', also with the purpose of countering disinformation.[93] The same applies to the UK, where a security unit was established to contest and actively intervene in cases of fake news.[94] Finally, European research-based initiatives have also been launched, such as the Social Observatory for Disinformation and Social Media Analysis, funded by the EU to 'support to a European community that will jointly fight disinformation!'[95] While these geopolitical interventions deserve detailed analyses in their own right, the following section seeks to outline wider discursively constructed visions for solving the post-truth condition rather than specific interventions.

Somewhat unsurprisingly, one of the general themes emerging throughout contemporary discourses is that the institutions that once safeguarded and produced truth, reason and rationality should be re-established. This goes particularly for the fields of politics, science and journalism. Writing for the European Council on Foreign Relations, Sebastian Dullien and Jeremy Shapiro thus argue: 'It is time to recognize that the integrity of information about current events and persons of public interest is part of the critical infrastructure of liberal democracy. If that infrastructure is compromised, the stability of the political system (and of liberal democracy itself) is threatened. Attacks on information integrity are therefore national security problems. And national security problems require a distinct response from domestic issues.'[96]

Similar sentiments have been attached to science, as numerous voices have argued for the need to reclaim the truth-telling capacity of this field by ensuring 'that researchers and technologists have a seat at the table when important decisions are made'.[97] This has also made scholars call for the development of new

---

92 East Stracom, 'Questions and Answers about the East StratCom Task Force', 5 December 2018, https://eeas.europa.eu/regions/eastern-europe/2116/questions-and-answers-about-east-stratcom-task-force_en.

93 A. Faiola, 'As Cold War Turns to Information War, a New Fake News Police Combats Disinformation', *Washington Post*, 18 January 2017, https://www.washingtonpost.com/world/europe/as-cold-war-turns-to-information-war-a-new-fake-news-police/2017/01/18/9bf49ff6-d80e-11e6-a0e6-d502d6751bc8_story.html.

94 P. Walker, 'New National Security Unit Set up to Tackle Fake News in UK', *The Guardian*, 23 January 2018, https://www.theguardian.com/politics/2018/jan/23/new-national-security-unit-will-tackle-spread-of-fake-news-in-uk.

95 Soma Observatory, 'Who Leads this Effort?', http://www.disinfobservatory.org/#somaproject.

96 S. Dullien and J. Shapiro, 'How to Avoid a Post-truth World', *European Council of Foreign Relations*, 16 January 2017, https://www.ecfr.eu/article/commentary_how_to_avoid_a_post_truth_world.

97 J.L. Vernon, 'Science in the Post-truth Era' (2017) 105(1) *American Scientist* 2, https://www.americanscientist.org/article/science-in-the-post-truth-era.

'strategies to counter a current flood of deception and misinformation'.[98] Indeed, for some, '[a]n understanding of the nature of science is absolutely fundamental to combat post-truth, which is the antithesis of science'.[99] Finally, journalism has also been called upon, as the proclaimed saviour and watchdog of democracy, truth and critical thinking. As McNair puts it, the declining truth-telling capacity of the journalistic field is (seemingly) equal to the breakdown of liberal democracy:

> If the crisis of trust in journalistic elites and the loss of authority of elites in other spheres such as politics and academia are not addressed in the coming years, it is quite possible that the entire structure of liberal democracy which has driven global evolution forward since 1945 will collapse in the face of rising authoritarianism and 'post-truth' cultural movements such as that embodied by the alt-right in the United States or in Putin's Kremlin, or will be eroded to the point where it is unrecognizable as the generally progressive, if messy and imperfect polity we see (still).[100]

Rather than simply arguing for the re-establishment of the authority of politics, science and journalism, others have also proposed more tangible ideas as to how truth should be reclaimed. Amongst these is a very strong notion that technology can provide the solution to the existing problems. Indeed, 'technological solutionism'[101] is in many ways deeply ingrained in post-truth discourses. In this narrative, technology is portrayed in a double fashion as both a poison and a cure: 'Technology helped fake news. Now technology needs to stop it.'[102] While the post-truth era was in large part caused by the rise of new technologies, the solution might still be more technology. Artificial intelligence, machine learning, natural-language processing and similar developing tools could, some suggest, be a way of mitigating the onslaught of fake news and misinformation.[103] Although new technologies certainly have

---

98 R. Struminger, J. Winking and A. Ross, 'How Will Science Survive in the Age of Alternative Facts?', *Huffington Post*, 20 July 2017, https://www.huffingtonpost.com/entry/how-will-science-survive-in-the-age-of-alt-facts_us_596fa33be4b0110cb3cb427f.

99 L. Ackland, 'Post-truth and the Rejection of Science', *Australasian Science*, August 2017, http://www.australasianscience.com.au/article/issue-mayjune-2017/post-truth-and-rejection-science.html.

100 McNair, *supra* note 2.

101 E. Morozov, *To Save Everything, Click Here: Technology, Solutionism, and the Urge to Fix Problems That Don't Exist*, Penguin, London 2013.

102 J. Cook, 'Technology Helped Fake News. Now Technology Needs to Stop it', *Bulletin of the Atomic Scientists*, 17 November 2017, https://thebulletin.org/2017/11/technology-helped-fake-news-now-technology-needs-to-stop-it.

103 E. Gent, 'Sock Puppet Accounts Unmasked by the Way They Write and Post', *New Scientist*, 6 April 2017, https://www.newscientist.com/article/2127107-sock-puppet-accounts-unmasked-by-the-way-they-write-and-post.

flaws, 'computers may be the only things capable of keeping up with the sheer volume'.[104] From a policy perspective, the European Commission has similarly argued for technological measures in order to make 'detection and analysis of online disinformation more accurate and timely'.[105] This includes the use of 'artificial intelligence … for verifying, identifying and tagging disinformation', '[c]ognitive algorithms that handle contextually-relevant information' and '[i]nnovative technologies, such as blockchain', which can 'enable transparency and traceability, and promote trust in news displayed on the Internet'.[106] Social media companies have largely co-opted this rhetoric, presenting themselves as leading actors in the fight against fake news through 'improvements in machine learning and artificial intelligence, which can proactively identify suspicious behavior at a scale that was not possible before'.[107]

Going one step further than simply arguing for technological fact-checking, Lewandowsky and colleagues propose what they label as 'technocognition'. This encompasses 'an inter-disciplinary approach to the design of information architectures that incorporates principles borrowed from behavioral economics to "nudge" … against the spread of misinformation' with the purpose of building 'bridges between the socially-defined epistemic islands that define the post-truth era'.[108] From this perspective, it is not only false information itself that needs to be corrected but also the citizens currently living in alternative epistemic bubbles or realities. As citizens have moved beyond the realm of facts, they need to be pushed back into society. This requires technological solutions that can get them 'nudged out of their filter bubbles',[109] altering their 'minds by making them more responsive to genuine evidence'.[110]

4. DISCUSSION: THE DANGERS OF POST-TRUTH DISCOURSES

Based on the analysis presented above, we can begin to see how a certain set of ideas have become increasingly hegemonic in contemporary debates on truth,

---

104 E. Gent, 'Post-truth: Technology is a Big Part of the Problem, But it's Also a Solution', *Singularity Hub*, 27 December 2017, https://singularityhub.com/2016/12/27/post-truth-technology-is-a-big-part-of-the-problem-but-its-also-a-solution.

105 European Commission, *Tackling Online Disinformation: A European Approach*, Brussels 2018, p. 15, https://ec.europa.eu/digital-single-market/en/news/communication-tackling-online-disinformation-european-approach.

106 *Ibid.*, p. 11.

107 Facebook, 'Russian Ads Released by Congress', 19 May 2018, https://newsroom.fb.com/news/2018/05/russian-ads-released-by-congress.

108 Lewandowsky, Ecker and Cook, *supra* note 40, p. 362.

109 *Ibid.*, p. 364.

110 N. Levy, 'Nudges in a Post-truth World' (2017) *Journal of Medical Ethics* 498, https://doi.org/10.1136/medethics-2017-104153.

democracy and politics. Centred on notions of fake news and post-truth, voices from across institutional fields have in large part come to promote an overarching ideal of democracy that places truth, reason and rationality at its core. It is these elements that are under attack, it is claimed, and it is consequently these elements that should be protected. In this section, we want to critically reflect on how and in what ways this democratic imaginary, currently underpinning post-truth discourses, relates to wider changes in Western democracies. In doing so, we want to shift gears slightly, moving from an analysis of contemporary discourses to a discussion of their potential implications and shortcomings.

Since the early 1990s, a number of critical political philosophers and sociologists have started to question the development of Western (liberal) democracies. Under labels such as 'post-politics' and 'post-democracy', diverse scholars such as Chantal Mouffe,[111] Jacques Rancière,[112] Colin Crouch[113] and Wolfgang Streeck[114] have pointed out how fundamental transformations have taken place to liberal democracy since the 1970s and 1980s. In conjunction with wider developments in the political economy of advanced capitalist states, largely sparked by the economic crisis of the 1970s and the failures of Keynesianism, Western democracies have increasingly been hollowed-out. More concretely, public deliberation, democratic inclusion and participation have been replaced by technocratic solutions, individual obligations and market-based modes of governance. This neoliberal offensive, which has taken place since the 1980s, has had serious repercussions for democracy.[115] Indeed, Ian Bruff names this as the rise of *authoritarian neoliberalism* – that is, a mode of politics that no longer relies on democratic compromise and popular sovereignty, but increasingly works through coercion, non-democratic legal mechanisms and (if necessary) outright violence.[116] There are many ways of understanding and unpacking these developments. For our present purposes, we want particularly to focus on this *de-democraticisation* of democracy as it has been analysed by Mouffe. Her starting point is to place contemporary liberal democracies within their wider political history. She does so by suggesting that liberal democracy has to be understood as a contingent compromise between two seemingly opposite political philosophical traditions. She names this *the democratic paradox*: 'liberal

111 C. Mouffe, *For a Left Populism*, Verso, London 2018; C. Mouffe, *The Return of the Political*, Verso, London 1993.

112 J. Ranciere, *Disagreement: Politics and Philosophy*, University of Minnesota Press, Minneapolis 1999.

113 C. Crouch, *Post-democracy*, Polity Press, Cambridge 2004.

114 W. Streeck, *How Will Capitalism End? Essays on a Failing System*, Verso, London 2016.

115 N. Olsen, *The Sovereign Consumer: A New Intellectual History of Neoliberalism*, Palgrave Macmillan, Cham 2018; T. Biebricher, 'Neoliberalism and Democracy' (2015) 22(2) *Constellations* 255.

116 I. Bruff, 'The Rise of Authoritarian Neoliberalism' (2014) 26(1) *Rethinking Marxism* 113, https://doi.org/10.1080/08935696.2013.843250.

democracy is an articulation that combines two different traditions: liberalism, with its emphasis on individual liberty and universal rights; and democracy, which privileges the idea of equality and "rule by the people", i.e. popular sovereignty'.[117]

According to Mouffe, the political development that has taken place in the last 30 years has forcefully tipped the balance between the poles of this compromise, so that the liberal component has started to overtake the democratic. Indeed, as part of the increasingly widespread adoption of neoliberal policies, the liberal part of liberal democracy has come to dominate or even cancel out its democratic counterpart. This means, Mouffe argues, that many of the political achievements linked to the democratic tradition have been rolled back. Ideas that were formerly seen as integral to the political order have been 'dismissed as "archaic"'.[118] This has, on the one hand, meant that the contemporary liberal hegemony has been progressively more neutralised and sedimented, appearing as the *only* possible way of organising democracy.[119] On the other hand, this neutralisation serves to consolidate a 'post-political trend … [that] deprives democratic citizens of an agonistic debate where they can make their voices heard and choose between real alternatives'.[120] This post-political *zeitgeist* is, according to Mouffe, based on two fundamental assumptions, namely a *rationalist* and an *individualist* understanding of democracy and politics. Post-politics tends, first of all, to reduce democracy and political participation to the individual. In taking the individual as its starting point, collective identities and political projects are either reduced to 'aggregated' collectives (made up of supposedly rational beings) *or* simply seen as the starting point for 'deliberative' modes of communication. Secondly, individualism is coupled with 'the rationalist belief in the availability of a universal consensus based on reason'.[121] For Mouffe, it is precisely this combination of individualism and reason, alongside institutional and economic changes, that constitutes the backbone for a post-political climate in which conflicting voices of the democratic people have been systematically dismantled.

To our mind, Mouffe's discussion of post-politics – and the wider field of literature this connects to – is important for our present analysis of post-truth discourses. This is so in two main regards. Firstly, it gives us significant clues as to the underlying *causes* of contemporary discourses. Indeed, one of the points that Mouffe has made time and again is precisely that the rise of populism and right-wing demagogues represents a *response* to the increasingly post-political

117 Mouffe, 2013, *supra* note 5, p. 29.
118 *Ibid.*, p. 124.
119 C. Mouffe, *The Democratic Paradox*. Verso, London 2000, p. 5.
120 Mouffe, 2013, *supra* note 5, p. 119.
121 *Ibid.*, p. 11.

condition of democracy. These kinds of political groupings often represent – or claim to represent – genuine alternatives to the established order, as well as the reclaiming of popular sovereignty (the people). In a similar sense, it seems legitimate to speculate whether current political conflicts over truth and democracy represent a similar trajectory: could it not be that the (supposed) denial of truth and authority comes from a desire to move *beyond* a post-political condition? Those who are blamed for spreading post-truth sentiments often represent otherwise denied and silenced voices (however problematic these might be). Secondly, and more substantially, Mouffe's discussion is helpful because it helps pinpoint the underlying ideals that have driven, and continue to drive, contemporary processes of de-democratisation. It seems that it is in many ways precisely these ideas that are currently being mobilised in contemporary post-truth discourses. Indeed, these hegemonic discourses often presuppose the notion that democracy more or less exclusively needs to be grounded in reason, rationality and consensus. Moreover, they presuppose that these concepts are stable and that, given the right conditions, it is possible to establish a rational and 'objectively truthful' mode of governance. Yet, along with Mouffe, we want to insist these ideas are far from neutral; they represent only one part of the political history of liberal democracy.

In this sense, it seems to us that current discussions on the post-truth era of democracy have in many ways internalised the post-political language of individualism, rationalism and consensus that has flourished since the 1980s. What needs to established, according to these, are not spaces for popular sovereignty and political participation, but instead more rigid forms of truth-based governance and technocratic policing. Consequently, the plea for regrounding democracy in truth seems to be a plea for further entrenching post-political sentiments. All too often, protecting democracy has come to mean safeguarding and expanding its liberal underpinnings, neglecting or even suppressing the democratic tradition. Contemporary discourses thus end up reproducing the very set of problems that might have caused a crisis of democracy in the first place; as a supposed remedy for the post-political condition, more post-politics is ordained.

5. CONCLUSION

This chapter has engaged with contemporary political discourses on post-truth and democracy currently dominating Western democracies. Through an analysis of both academic and non-academic sources – ranging from media commentaries, research articles, books and governmental policies – we have sought to showcase how a new hegemonic discourse is currently being formed. This discourse is, we argue, both contentious and consensual. It is, on the one hand, made up of conflicting ideas about the current state of democracy, while nonetheless, on the other hand, being underpinned by a series of homogeneous ideological premises. To put it in very condensed terms, these premises present democracy as bound up with truth, rational decision-making and consensus. As a consequence, post-truth discourses portray the rise of so-called fake news and alternative facts as a direct threat to the very core of liberal democracy. However, as we have argued in the discussion, these increasingly hegemonic discourses reproduce and repurpose a post-political vocabulary mobilised by political elites since the 1970s and 1980s. In so doing, these discourses tend to smuggle in an implicit model of democracy that emphasises rationalism, reason and truth, while neglecting or even suppressing popular sovereignty, difference and equality.

By pointing to the articulation of this new hegemonic discourse, this chapter contributes to our understanding of the present political climate and conjecture of democracy. It adds to the few accounts provided so far by critical scholars concerning democracy and the post-truth era.[122] It does so, not least, by highlighting how a contemporary *politics of falsehood* is becoming increasingly dominant, depending on a specific, and often limited, normative ideal of democratic participation.[123] Furthermore, the chapter critically problematises the all too widespread tendency to take notions like truth, democracy and fake news for granted. It documents how these terms are deeply politically charged and constructed. They are not merely descriptions of the world, but discursive weapons used to intervene and shape social reality. This also means that future research would do well to take the constructed and contested nature of such labels into account. Doing so does not mean denying the very real problems posed by disinformation, propaganda and online politics;[124] it means taking seriously the foundational role of discourses in understanding and shaping politics.

From the arguments presented in this chapter, no easy solutions can or should be deduced. The history of democracy is not driven by any necessary movement towards more egalitarian or inclusive societies. Instead, democracy remains a frail and in many ways contradictory compromise that must be continuously deepened and defended. One way of deepening democracy might be to start reclaiming the democratic tradition by insisting on the need

---

122 Fenton and Freedman, *supra* note 74; N. Fenton, 'Fake Democracy: The Limits of Public Sphere Theory' (2018) 25(1–2) *Javnost – The Public* 28, https://doi.org/10.1080/13183222.2018.1418821; R. Mejia, K. Beckermann and C. Sullivan, 'White Lies: A Racial History of the (Post)Truth' (2018) 15(2) *Communication and Critical/Cultural Studies* 109, http://doi.org/10.1080/14791420.2018.1456668.

123 Farkas and Schou, *supra* note 4.

124 Farkas, Schou and Neumayer, *supra* note 13; J. Farkas and C. Neumayer, 'Disguised Propaganda from Digital to Social Media', in J. Hunsinger, L. Klastrup and M.M. Allen (eds.), *The International Handbook of Internet Research*, 2nd ed., Springer, New York 2018, http://doi.org/10.1007/978-94-024-1202-4_33-1.

to establish inclusive and participatory spaces of politics over technocratic and technological solutions. Rather than rallying behind calls for reason and consensus, it is high time to realise that democracy is *not* just (and never has been) about truth alone. More substantially, it is about the *voice of the people* and what they, collectively, deem appropriate. As a consequence, there might be value in pursuing the building of, what Mouffe defines as, new left populist movements concerned with bringing back political contestation, affect and the voice of the *demos.*[125] While critiques of Mouffe have rightly highlighted that any such attempt to repoliticise democracy should carefully avoid falling into the trap of 'fetishising the moment of the political',[126] valuing autonomy and conflict above and beyond the wellbeing of people,[127] it seems increasingly clear that the *status quo* no longer holds. Thus, while Mouffe's ideas cannot be seen as a clear-cut plan of how to move forward,[128] they still provide a productive starting point for critically thinking through our present historical moment and develop genuine democratic alternatives. Contemporary democracy might very well be facing a deep-seated crisis. However, whether truth-based post-politics represents a viable option is much more dubious. What needs to take place to address current democratic deficits is not the cancellation or shutting down of political conflict, either by policing what is deemed as false or algorithmically sorting the voices who have access to the public sphere; instead, we need genuine political alternatives and open discussions. Only then might we become capable of reinvigorating liberal democracies and deal with the entrenched political issues that continue to haunt our present age.

---

125 Mouffe, *supra* note 119.

126 Y. Stavrakakis, 'Challenges of Re-politicisation: Mouffe's Agonism and Artistic Practices' (2012) 26(5) *Third Text* 551, https://doi.org/10.1080/08935696.2013.843250.

127 S. White, 'Response to Chantal Mouffe', in W. Williams (ed.), *Religion and Rights: The Oxford Amnesty Lectures*, Manchester University Press, Manchester 2011.

128 J. Schou, 'Hvordan skabes et alternativ? Om det radikale demokratis mulighedsbetingelser' (2017) 3(20) *Politik* 138, https://doi.org/10.7146/politik.v20i3.97158.

7. ELITE THEORY, MEDIA REGULATION AND 'FAKE NEWS'

Daniel Barnhizer and Adam Candeub*

1. INTRODUCTION

Democratic institutions rely upon the rule of law, and the rule of law depends upon rational analysis of public matters. 'Fake news' undermines the rule of law as it derives its strength from appetitive and emotional responses in a manner that threatens both the rule of law and a political culture's willingness to trust in democratic institutions. Even worse, however, the phenomenon of 'fake news' creates an atmosphere in which political, media, and cultural elites can exploit fear *about* fake news in order to forward their own agenda and undermine democratic institutions in favour of political control by a dominant oligarchic elite. In this chapter, we place the 'fake news' concern in the context of media regulation in the US. Looking to so-called elite theory, we examine media ownership, reviewing the empirical research showing the elite nature of media ownership and control. We examine how the Internet disrupted this elite, creating 'elite churn' in the form of a new media oligarchy. We suggest that the 'fake news' phenomenon may simply be a justification for a power grab by this new Internet elite, which can leverage gaps in US media regulation. As such, calls to limit and regulate civic discourse to counter fake news on the Internet may be misplaced and may result in limiting free speech. Rather, the cure for fake news, which has always existed, is not to further empower this new elite. Instead, it is to promote consumer-oriented freedom on the Internet – perhaps combined with stronger antitrust enforcement – to allow a bottom-up corrective pressure.

2. DEFINING 'FAKE NEWS'

The term 'fake news' exploded into the public consciousness, at least in the US, during the presidential election of 2016 and its aftermath, and in the UK

* Daniel Barnhizer: College of Law, Michigan State University, US. Email: barnhize@law.msu.edu; Adam Candeub: College of Law, Michigan State University, US. Email: Candeub@law.msu.edu.

during the run-up to the 2016 referendum on EU membership.[1] Despite the pervasiveness of the term, like many political and social concepts, the meaning of the term 'fake news' eludes consensus (as many supposedly meaningful terms in politics often do). In October 2018, for instance, the UK government banned the use of the term in strategy and policy documents, requiring instead that official statements use allegedly more precise terms 'misinformation' and 'disinformation' to refer to phenomena otherwise collected within the fake news umbrella.[2]

But fake news encompasses more than mere disinformation or misinformation. In one sense, the term refers to Internet-based entities that craft false stories specifically for the purpose of causing gullible readers to visit a particular website and generate ad revenue for the writer.[3] Following the 2016 US presidential election, President Donald Trump used social media extensively to characterise traditional media outlets such as CNN as fake news organisations to draw attention to media hostility to his presidency and administration.[4] In yet another sense, Professors Hunt Allcott and Matthew Gentzkow, in a detailed study about the extent to which readers recall fake news articles, define fake news to be:

> News articles that are intentionally and verifiably false, and could mislead readers … Our definition includes intentionally fabricated news articles, such as a widely shared article from the now-defunct website denverguardian.com with the headline, 'FBI agent suspected in Hillary email leaks found dead in apparent murder suicide'. It also includes many articles that originate on satirical websites but could be misunderstood as factual, especially when viewed in isolation on Twitter or Facebook feeds.[5]

We define fake news more broadly. At its heart, fake news covers misinformation, disinformation and non-information. Specifically, it involves information disseminated to a large audience in such a way that it either: (a) presents false information as if it were true (misinformation if unintentional, disinformation if intentional); (b) presents true information in a manner that exaggerates

---

1 P. Mihailidis and S. Viotty (2017). Spreadable Spectacle in Digital Culture: Civic Expression, Fake News, and the Role of Media Literacies in 'Post-Fact' Society. *American Behavioral Scientist*, 61(4), 441–454. doi: 10.1177/0002764217701217, p. 442; S. Jukes (2018). Back to the Future. *Journalism Practice*, 12(8), 1029–1038. doi: 10.1080/17512786.2018.1494512, p. 1035; H. Allcott and M. Gentzkow (2017). Social Media and Fake News in the 2016 Election. *Journal of Economic Perspectives*, 211–236. doi: 10.3386/w23089, p. 212.

2 M. Murphy (2018). Government Bans Phrase 'Fake News', 23 October. Retrieved from https://www.telegraph.co.uk/technology/2018/10/22/government-bans-phrase-fake-news.

3 Allcott and Gentzkow, *supra* note 1, pp. 213–214.

4 H. Britzky (2017). Everything Trump has called 'FAKE NEWS', 9 July. Retrieved from https://www.axios.com/everything-trump-has-called-fake-news-1513303959-6603329e-46b5-44ea-b6be-70d0b3bdb0ca.html.

5 Allcott and Gentzkow, *supra* note 1, pp. 213–214.

non-relevant facts to suggest a false inference from those facts (disinformation); (c) selectively presents true facts while deliberately hiding other true facts to create a false narrative; or (d) hides true facts in a manner that suggests these did not occur (non-information). Fake news in the form of misinformation and disinformation also has an emotional and anti-intellectual component. Whether done for profit or political advantage, fake news seeks to convince recipients by appealing to emotional priors and bypassing critical faculties that might cause the recipient to question the veracity of the report. While much of the modern fake news phenomenon is sensationalist 'clickbait' created by companies to drive viewers to their ad revenue-generating websites,[6] fake news is presented for the purpose of instigating an emotional response that drives news consumers to sympathise or identify with a particular political party or cultural group without regard to concepts of shared community or greater public good.

Although the term 'fake news' was not popularised until 2016, the phenomenon has likely existed for as long as the concept of 'news' itself.[7] And fake news has a long history in the US. A historically egregious example of fake news lies in the work of Walter Duranty, Moscow correspondent for the *New York Times* in the 1930s. Duranty vociferously denied the existence of the Stalin-engineered famine in Ukraine, claiming people were 'hungry but not starving' and 'there is no famine or actual starvation'.[8] This suppression of news regarding the Ukranian genocide being committed by the Stalin regime was neither negligence nor ignorance by Duranty. As his biographer Sally J. Taylor documents,[9] Duranty admitted he knew about the famine when he visited the British Embassy in Moscow in June 1932. An official dispatch to the British Foreign Office in London preserves his interview, proving Duranty's complicity. The American publishing elites awarded Duranty in 1931 a Pulitzer Prize for his reporting on the Ukraine. In our typology of fake news, Duranty was deliberately hiding true facts – the existence of the Ukranian famine – in a manner intended to suggest that the famine was not occurring. Moreover, he disseminated this fake news for the purpose of driving news consumers to sympathise with and appreciate the Soviets, and to distrust leaks of the real story of the human tragedy in Ukraine.

---

6 Z. Tufekci (2018). It's the (Democracy-Poisoning) Golden Age of Free Speech, 15 February. Retrieved from https://www.wired.com/story/free-speech-issue-tech-turmoil-new-censorship; see also A. Guess, B. Nyhan and J. Reifler (2018). Selective Exposure to Misinformation: Evidence from the Consumption of Fake News during the 2016 U.S. Presidential Campaign. Unpublished manuscript, Dartmouth College. Retrieved from https://www.dartmouth.edu/~nyhan/fake-news-2016.pdf, pp. S5–S7.

7 Chrisbolman (2018). The Real History of Fake News, 2 February. Retrieved from https://chrisbolman.com/fake-news-history; J. Soll (2016). The Long and Brutal History of Fake News, 18 December. Retrieved from https://www.politico.com/magazine/story/2016/12/fake-news-history-long-violent-214535.

8 W. Duranty (1933). Russians Hungry, But Not Starving. *New York Times*, 31 March, p. A13.

9 S.J. Taylor (1990). *Stalin's Apologist: Walter Duranty, the New York Times Man in Moscow*. New York: Oxford University Press.

But in comparison to Duranty's genocide cover-up, the actual proven cases of 'fake news' in the 2016 US presidential election seem small beer. Stories about John Podesta, adviser to presidential candidate Hillary Clinton, running a child prostitution ring out of a Washington DC pizzeria reached around half a million Internet viewers.[10] Likewise, it now appears that a relatively small number of Russian operatives or sympathisers were deliberately spreading fake news regarding a number of political candidates on social media sites such as Facebook and Twitter.[11]

Despite the attention given to the fake news phenomenon, it is actually difficult to locate a 'big lie' *believed and acted upon by* the American people during the 2016 elections. Indeed, even those who view fake news as a serious threat recognise there is little information about the extent and impact of fake news. As noted by Lazer: 'How common is fake news, and what is its impact on individuals? There are surprisingly few scientific answers to these basic questions.'[12] And as reported by Guess, Nagler and Tucker: 'It is important to be clear about how rare this behaviour [sharing of fake news articles] is on social platforms: The vast majority of Facebook users in our data did not share any articles from fake news domains in 2016 at all.'[13] As suggested by Allcott and Gentzkow:

> How much [fake news] affected the [2016] election results depends on the effectiveness of fake news exposure in changing the way people vote. As one benchmark, Spenkuch and Toniatti … show that exposing voters to one additional television campaign ad changes vote shares by approximately 0.02 percentage points. This suggests that if one fake news article were about as persuasive as one TV campaign ad, the fake news in our database would have changed vote shares by an amount on the order of hundredths of a percentage point.[14]

---

10 P. Mihailidis and S. Viotty (2017). Spreadable Spectacle in Digital Culture: Civic Expression, Fake News, and the Role of Media Literacies in 'Post-Fact' Society. *American Behavioral Scientist*, 61(4), 441–454. doi: 10.1177/0002764217701217, pp. 443–45.

11 A. Prokop (2019). All of Robert Mueller's Indictments and Plea Deals in the Russia Investigation, 22 March. Retrieved from https://www.vox.com/policy-and-politics/2018/2/20/17031772/mueller-indictments-grand-jury; D. Barrett, S. Horwitz and R.S. Helderman (2018). Russian Troll Farm, 13 Suspects Indicted in 2016 Election Interference. *Washington Post*, 16 February. Retrieved from https://www.washingtonpost.com/world/national-security/russian-troll-farm-13-suspects-indicted-for-interference-in-us-election/2018/02/16/2504de5e-1342-11e8-9570-29c9830535e5_story.html.

12 D.M.J. Lazer et al. (2018). The Science of Fake News: Addressing Fake News Requires a Multidisciplinary Effort. *Science Advances*, 359(6380), 1094–1096. doi: 10.1126/science.aao2998, p. 1095.

13 A. Guess, J. Nagler and J. Tucker (2019). Less Than You Think: Prevalence and Predictors of Fake News Dissemination on Facebook. *Science Advances*, 5(1), 1–8. doi: 10.1126/sciadv.aau4586, p. 1.

14 Allcott and Gentzkow, *supra* note 1.

In an interview with National Public Radio regarding the Allcott and Gentzkow[15] study, Matthew Gentzkow further summarised the study's conclusions:

> And if you just sort of, you know, read the news online or watch cable TV, you get the impression that we were inundated by a flood of fake news. And, you know, the fact that the average voter saw one of these kind of crazy made up stories during the election is still pretty striking, but it's way short of. A world where this was a wave that crashed over everybody in advance of the election and [*sic*] we were all seeing dozens of these stories every day.[16]

Other studies regarding reactions of consumers of false information such as propaganda suggest that even if consumers are exposed to fake news, the impact may not be significant. Notably, it is important to recognise at the outset that study design may have a significant effect on the perceived willingness of individuals to claim belief in false information that relates to their partisan preferences. Bullock, Gerber, Hill and Huber report that survey-based studies of individuals' belief in the accuracy of news stories may suffer from a 'cheerleading bias' that leads individuals to claim belief in false claims that favour their partisan preferences, and that this effect is diminished when partisans are offered a small financial reward ($0.17 per question in this study) for identifying correct information.[17] It is unclear how much the cheerleading bias affects actual voting behaviour, but it is important to recognise that sharing of and surveyed belief in fake news may reflect a bias that is not replicated in the voting booth or in actual (as opposed to merely stated) preferences.

Some uses of false information may also cause individuals to discredit the false information. As Marquez notes, 'survey evidence [in China] suggests that the more exposure to the most obvious forms of indoctrination, such as political education classes or newspapers like the *People's Daily*, is actually associated with more *negative* attitudes towards the government among university students and other groups'.[18] While fake news in the US only occasionally involves actual government propaganda, the over-the-top nature of claims made in fake news stories by private parties or political aspirants is analogous. Similarly suggesting that repeated exposure to false information is analogous to fake news, Wessel,

15 *Ibid.*

16 R. Siegel (interviewer) and M. Gentzkow (interviewee) (2017). Economist Calculates Impact of Fake News on Trump's election, 23 January. Retrieved from https://www.npr.org/2017/01/23/511267145/economist-calculates-impact-of-fake-news-on-trumps-election.

17 J. Bullock, A. Gerber, S. Hill and G. Huber (2015). Partisan Bias in Factual Beliefs about Politics. *Quarterly Journal of Political Science* 10(4) 519–578. doi: http://dx.doi.org/10.1561/100.00014074, pp. 539, 560.

18 X. Márquez (2017). *Non-democratic Politics: Authoritarianism, Dictatorship, and Democratization*. London: Palgrave Macmillan, p. 137.

Thies and Benlian[19] found that there is some evidence that fake news in the form of false quantitative information such as artificially inflated Facebook Likes in the context of private crowdfunding campaigns actually has a negative effect on the success of such campaigns. Although Facebook Likes are not technically fake news in the sense of news articles, this conclusion may suggest that fake quantitative information may cause consumers of that information to distrust and discount the value of that information in making decisions as to whether to rely on that information. But as discussed below, Pennycook, Cannon and Rand[20] observe that repetitive observations of fake news articles may increase perceived accuracy, rendering this analogy uncertain.

Other research presents mixed or moderately negative effects relating to the dissemination and consumption of fake news. In one study, Gunther, Beck and Nisbet[21] suggest that belief in fake news stories 'is very strongly linked to defection from the Democratic ticket by 2012 Obama voters'. While this study acknowledges that its data cannot prove a causal link between the defections and fake news, it also illustrates one of the more general problems in such research. The study is based upon only three 'fake news' items, two anti-Clinton and one pro-Trump: (1) 'Hillary Clinton is in very poor health due to a serious illness'; (2) 'Pope Francis endorsed Donald Trump for president prior to the election'; and (3) 'During her time as U.S. Secretary of State, Hillary Clinton approved weapons sales to Islamic jihadists, including ISIS'.[22]

Beyond the concentration of fake news consumption among the most highly conservative (and therefore unlikely to change their votes) voters,[23] the choices of which 'fake news' stories to study are problematic. While the Pope's endorsement story is obviously false and objectively determinable, the two anti-Clinton fake news stories are matters of interpretation. With respect to Clinton's health, it is undisputed that Clinton has suffered from multiple blood clots (including one in her brain), that she fainted in 2012 and suffered a concussion from the resulting fall, suffered from pneumonia during the 2016 campaign and nearly collapsed at a 2016 memorial service for the victims of the 9/11 attacks.[24] Reasonable minds

---

19 M. Wessel, F. Thies and A. Benlian (2016). The Emergence and Effects of Fake Social Information: Evidence from Crowdfunding. *Decision Support Systems*, 90, 75–85. doi: 10.1016/j.dss.2016.06.021, pp. 83–84.

20 G. Pennycook, T.D. Cannon and D.G. Rand (2018). Prior Exposure Increases Perceived Accuracy of Fake News. *Journal of Experimental Psychology: General*, 147. doi: 10.1037/xge0000465.

21 R. Gunther, P.A. Beck and E.C. Nisbet (2019). 'Fake News' and the Defection of 2012 Obama Voters in the 2016 Presidential Election. *Electoral Studies*. doi: 10.1016/j.electstud.2019.03.006, p. 2.

22 *Ibid.*

23 Guess, Nyhan and Reifler, *supra* note 6, pp. 6–7.

24 T.C. Frankel (2016). Hillary Clinton Has Not Been Quick to Share Health Information. *Washington Post*, 12 September.

could differ on the seriousness of these health issues and characterising them as 'fake news' is difficult in light of the lack of objective falsifiability. Gunther, Beck and Nisbet appear to rely upon a Snopes.com fact-check of a different claim – that Clinton suffers from Parkinson's disease – to characterise this statement as fake news.[25] Likewise, the claim about approval of weapons sales 'to jihadists, including ISIS' is mixed. The fact-checking website Snopes.com recasts this claim as 'Wikileaks e-mails confirm that Hillary Clinton *directly and knowingly* sold weapons to ISIS'.[26] While there is no evidence that Clinton approved weapons sales to ISIS, the Snopes.com fact-check concludes that: 'One could certainly make the case (from material published by WikiLeaks and elsewhere) that during Hillary Clinton's tenure as Secretary of State, the US provided weapons (either directly or indirectly) to various factions in Libya and Syria, that some of those weapons might have ended up in the hands of groups such as the Muslim Brotherhood, al-Qaeda, and ISIS, and that the latter was a foreseeable outcome of the former.'[27] While the initial claim studied by Gunther, Beck and Nisbet might qualify as fake news, it is only as an exaggeration. What remains unclear even after their study is whether reasonable minds could conclude that Clinton was a flawed candidate based on the summary claim that she 'approved weapons sales to jihadists, including ISIS,' but not based upon the arguably true claim that Clinton either negligently or recklessly approving weapons sales that would foreseeably flow to jihadists (including ISIS). In both of the anti-Clinton stories, survey respondents could reasonably have believed a valid interpretation of the claim without being the victims of 'fake news'.

Other studies examine the *reach* of fake news, as opposed to its *impact*. In a 2018 article, for example, Guess, Nyhan and Reifler report that in the 2016 US election, more than a quarter of the US voting age population visited a pro-Trump or pro-Clinton fake news website.[28] Consumption of fake news was also heavily skewed towards pro-Trump voters.[29] However, at the same time, the authors report that almost 60 per cent 'of all visits to fake news websites came from the

25 While Gunther, Beck and Nisbet (*supra* note 21) do not detail how they determined that particular stories qualified as 'fake news', an earlier report on their research attaches a hyperlink to this claim that directs to Snopes.com. See R. Gunther, E.C. Nisbet and P. Beck (2018). Trump May Owe His 2016 Victory to 'Fake News', New Study Suggests, 18 February. Retrieved from http://theconversation.com/trump-may-owe-his-2016-victory-to-fake-news-new-study-suggests-91538. This hyperlink refers to a page titled 'Did a Physician Confirm Hillary Clinton Has Parkinson's Disease?': D. Emery (2016). Did a Physician Confirm Hillary Clinton Has Parkinson's Disease?, 9 September. Retrieved from https://www.snopes.com/fact-check/hillary-clinton-has-parkinsons-disease.

26 K. Lacapria (2016). WikiLeaks Confirms Hillary Clinton Sold Weapons to ISIS?, 13 October. Retrieved from https://www.snopes.com/fact-check/wikileaks-cofirms-hillary-clinton-sold-weapons-to-isis/.

27 *Ibid.*

28 Guess, Nagler and Tucker, *supra* note 13, p. 4.

29 Guess, Nyhan and Reifler, *supra* note 6, pp. 4–5.

decile of news consumers with the most conservative information diets'.[30] This disproportionate concentration of consumption among the group of consumers least likely to change their voting patterns does not provide significant support for the proposition that fake news had a meaningful impact on the outcome of the election. In suggesting future research projects, the authors conclude that: 'While fake news is unlikely to have changed the outcome of the 2016 election,[31] exposure to it or similarly dubious and inflammatory content can still undermine the quality of public debate, promote misperceptions, foster greater hostility toward political opponents and corrode trust in government and journalism.'[32] Similarly, other studies report that fake news disseminates through social media faster and to a greater extent than true information.[33] Pennycook, Cannon and Rand observe that repeated exposures to fake news stories increase the likelihood that readers will believe subsequent exposures to the same or similar stories. But 'this effect was relatively small'[34] and this study did not analyse the extent to which fake news actually influenced voter behaviour in the 2016 US election: 'Although it is unclear to what extent fake news influenced the outcome of the Presidential Election, there is no question that many people were deceived by entirely fabricated (and often quite fanciful) fake news stories.'[35]

While it is tempting to ascribe political losses, perceived losses in the quality of public debate, hostility towards political opponents and loss of trust in government and journalism to the fake news phenomenon, these effects are hypothetical. It is beyond the scope of this chapter to survey the entire literature on fake news, but the impact of the phenomenon is at best uncertain and may in fact be quite minimal.

3. ELITE THEORY AND THE FAKE NEWS PHENOMENON

Elite theory is a school of political thought that developed in the early 20th century, primarily through the writings of Italian sociologists and political scientists Vilfredo Pareto, Gaetano Mosca and Robert Michels.[36] The elite theory school approached the question of political organisation from an arguably cynical and

---

30 *Ibid.*, pp. 6–7.
31 Allcott and Gentzkow, *supra* note 1.
32 Guess, Nyhan and Reifler, *supra* note 6, p. 12.
33 S. Vosoughi, D. Roy and S. Aral (2018). The spread of true and false news online. *Science* 359(6380), 1146–1151, doi: 10.1126/science.aap9559.
34 Pennycook, Cannon and Rand, *supra* note 20, pp. 10–11.
35 Allcott and Gentzkow, *supra* note 1, p. 2.
36 R.A. Nye (1977). *The Anti-democratic Sources of Elite Theory: Pareto, Mosca, Michels.* London: SAGE, pp. 7–8.

disillusioned intuition that control of any political entity rested in the hands of an elite group or even an oligarchy of elites that coordinated and guided the desires of the masses to maintain their elite position in the governing hierarchy. Thus, elite theory is an approach to political theory that claims that politics is best understood through the generalisation that nearly all political power is held by a relatively small and wealthy group of people sharing similar values and interests, and mostly coming from relatively similar privileged backgrounds. For Pareto, Mosca and Michels, the elites could be distinguished from the masses by some criterion of excellence. Notably, however, the nature of that superior character could vary widely – parties could enter the elite class as a result of superior intellect, morality, wealth, military or charismatic qualities.

This sentiment is descriptive, predictive and normative – for the elite theory school of thought, oligarchic control of any organisation (including democratic states) is necessary, desirable (in at least some senses and for some purposes) and inevitable.[37] The movement towards elites is simply a result of human nature in an organisational structure. Thus, Michels, in his so-called iron law of oligarchy, states: 'It is organisation which gives birth to the dominion of the elected over the electors, of the mandatories over the mandators, of the delegates over the delegators. Who says organization, says oligarchy.'[38] Importantly, and often missed, is the possibility that Michels was speaking of the tendency of organisations towards oligarchy – as Hamilton notes: 'That translation … is not accurate. The original reads "*sagt Tendenz zur Oligarchie*" – says tendency to oligarchy.'[39] Thus, while democratic institutions bear the seeds of oligarchy, as discussed below, the tendency towards oligarchy may be harnessed by democratic tendencies to facilitate circulation of elite viewpoints at the top of power hierarchies.

Pareto, like Michels, sees the domination of elites as a natural state. But for Pareto, the 'elite' is not a stable group. Summarising his view of the 'circulation of elites,' he states that: 'Except during short intervals of time, people are always governed by an elite. I use the word elite in its etymological sense, meaning the strongest, the most energetic, and the most capable. … Hence, the history of man is the history of the continuous replacement of certain elites: as one ascends, the other declines. Such is the real phenomenon, though to us it may often appear under another form.'[40]

---

37 R.L. Michels (1915). *Political Parties: A Sociological Study of the Oligarchical Tendencies of Modern Democracy*. (E. Paul and C. Paul, Trans.). New York: Hearst's International Library Co. (original work published 1911).

38 *Ibid.*, p. 401.

39 R.F. Hamilton (2001). *Mass Society, Pluralism, and Bureaucracy: Explication, Assessment, and Commentary*. Westport, CT: Praeger, p. 92.

40 V. Pareto (1979). *Rise and the Fall of the Elites* (H.L. Zetterberg, Trans.). New York: Arno (original work published 1901), p. 436.

In a normative sense, elite theory is a critique of both the democracy of the masses and of collectivist political systems:

> [A]s political participation is made more universal, political leaders must adapt their ideas to 'a fairly low moral level' to 'play upon all the sensitive springs of conduct … [and] take advantage of their weaknesses ….' In this infernal dialectic the least scrupulous, those who lie most persuasively, dissemble most effectively and pitch their appeals to the lowest passions will gain ascendency. The only foreseeable result of this process, says Mosca, is the utter triumph of Rousseau's most vulgar ideology: 'Collectivism and communism, like all doctrines that are based on the passions and the blind faith of the masses, tend to destroy multiplicity of political forces.' Thus, for Mosca, as for Pareto, it is democracy which leads inevitably to socialism and threatens the roots of modern civilization.[41]

Three recurring themes in elite theory are particularly relevant to the fake news phenomenon. First, 'the elite' need not be a single homogeneous group of actors, such as in pure non-democratic strongman regimes. Rather, in most situations, the elite in a given organisation comprises multiple groups of actors situated at key points of political, social, economic, religious and military power. Second, the elite circulate dynamically, sometimes slower and sometimes faster, through positions in the power hierarchy, and in some cases new entrants to the elite classes may emerge from the masses. Third, building on Pareto's conception of the circulation of elites, Mosca[42] posited two tendencies of political organisations that either facilitate relatively smooth transitions of power between elite groups (the democratic tendency) or that resist change in order to maintain one body of elite in power (the aristocratic tendency). While neither tendency is ever absolute in any given political system, the aristocratic temptation for any elite group to attempt to 'rig the system' to deny other elite powers access to the elite hierarchy is strong. Nonetheless:

> It is rather difficult if not impossible to nullify completely either one of these two tendencies. The absolute predominance of the aristocratic tendency would presuppose that the ideas and conditions of human association never change; experience shows the absurdity of that assumption. On the other hand, the democratic tendency could absolutely triumph only on condition that the sons would not inherit the means, contacts, and advantages in training which enabled their progenitors to capture all the choice positions.[43]

---

41 Nye, *supra* note 36, p. 19; G. Mosca (1939). *The Ruling Class* (H.D. Kahn, Trans., A. Livingston, Ed.). New York: McGraw-Hill, pp. 155–156, 190–193, 307.

42 G. Mosca (1962). The Final Version of the Theory of the Ruling Class (J.H. Meisel, Trans.). In J.H. Meisel *The Myth of the Ruling Class: Gaetano Mosca and the 'Elite'*. Michigan: University of Michigan Press (original work published 1933), pp. 388–389.

43 *Ibid.*, p. 389.

Elite theory presents a useful lens for analysing the fake news phenomenon in the context of democratic institutions. Fake news may be fairly characterised as an appeal to the base desires, fears, jealousies and other irrationalities of the masses. Claims in the US that close associates of Hillary Clinton were running a child prostitution service through a Washington DC pizzeria[44] or that Donald Trump stated that Neo-Nazis were 'very fine people'[45] are absurd and have been debunked. But true believers on both sides of the American political aisle cling to these beliefs with a deeply emotional fervour. At the same time, however, as discussed above, the actual impact of fake news articles is uncertain at best and may in fact be *de minimis*.

Into this emotionally charged political arena, the elites can inject themselves, promising to provide order and clarity for a clouded public discourse. As empirical evidence has shown, US newspaper and media companies tend to be privately owned, as opposed to public corporations.[46] And we see this pattern again with the large social media firms. For example, Twitter is privately owned and Facebook, while a publicly traded corporation owned by disaggregated shareholders, has a system of stock classes that vests control with creator and co-founder Mark Zuckerberg. These privately-owned news media organisations are both closely associated with the American left political elite[47] and possess the ability to control through algorithmic weighting the information and news stories that users see and that will be suppressed. As part of a new information elite that has successfully entered the market for news that was previously bottlenecked by a few traditional publishing and broadcasting news agencies, the new social media interests have strong incentives to both maintain their new

44 P. Mihailidis and S. Viotty (2017). Spreadable Spectacle in Digital Culture: Civic Expression, Fake News, and the Role of Media Literacies in 'Post-fact' Society. *American Behavioral Scientist*, 61(4), 441–454. doi: 10.1177/0002764217701217, p. 443–445; A.D. Holan (2016). PolitiFact's 2016 Lie of the Year: Fake News, 13 December. Retrieved from https://www.politifact.com/truth-o-meter/article/2016/dec/13/2016-lie-year-fake-news.

45 S. Moran (2019). CNN Contributor Benched for Fighting Charlottesville Hoax Meets Trump, 31 August. Retrieved from https://www. breitbart.com/politics/2019/08/30/steve-cortes-cnn-contributor-benched-for-fighting-charlottesville-hoax-met-with-trump.

46 S. Djankov, C. McLiesh, T. Nenova and A. Shleifer (2003). Who Owns the Media? *Journal of Law and Economics*, 46, 341–381. doi: 10.1086/377116 C. Hanretty (2014). Media Outlets and Their Moguls: Why Concentrated Individual or Family Ownership is Bad for Editorial Independence. *European Journal of Communication*, 29(3), 335–350. doi: 10.1177/0267323114523150; G. Mastrini and M. Becerraz (2008). The International Encyclopedia of Communication. In *The International Encyclopedia of Communication*. Hoboken: John Wiley & Sons, Ltd. Retrieved from https://onlinelibrary.wiley.com/doi/book/10.1002/9781405186407.

47 J. Bowden (2018). Twitter CEO Jack Dorsey: I 'Fully Admit' Our Bias is 'More Left-Leaning', 19 August. Retrieved from https://thehill.com/policy/technology/402495-twitter-ceo-jack-dorsey-i-fully-admit-our-bias-is-more-left-leaning; D. Boylan (2018). Silicon Valley an 'Extremely Left-Leaning Place', admits Zuckerberg, 10 April. Retrieved from https://www.washingtontimes.com/news/2018/apr/10/zuckerberg-admits-silicon-valley-extremely-left-le.

aristocratic positions of elite power in the news (and advertising) media, but also an apparent aristocratic desire to prevent the masses of media consumers from challenging that position of elite authority. Consequently, elite theory potentially provides a rich framework for understanding American media, particularly its current phase characterised by the dominance of oligarchic control of search engines (Google), news curation (Facebook), and social discourse and interaction (Twitter, Instagram/Facebook and Snapchat).

4. MEDIA REGULATION AND MEDIA ELITES

Media regulation in the US largely represents a compromise between government and an elite in the form of media owners.[48] The US, without an official government-owned news service, has allowed media concentration, but has limited it to some degree with ownership regulations. From its beginnings in 1934, the Federal Communication Commission (FCC) has placed significant ownership restrictions on broadcast radio, television and cable companies, exercising a type of soft control. And at least to some degree (and as discussed below), American news coverage responded to these financial and political influences.

Media regulation as a response to elites incorporating Mosca's democratic tendencies in the circulation of elites can be seen in the inception of the FCC. President Franklin D. Roosevelt felt that, as a group, newspaper editors were ideologically hostile to his New Deal. He therefore used the FCC's power over granting radio licences to prohibit newspapers from expanding their news organisations into broadcasting.[49] Following this overtly politicised beginning, the relationship between American elite media ownership and both legislators in the US Congress and regulators in the FCC stabilised and remained so for many decades as complex systems of regulation were created. For instance, in 1941, the FCC promulgated the first national ownership limits, the Chain Broadcasting

---

48 R. Akhavan-Majid and G. Wolf (1991). American Mass Media and the Myth of Libertarianism: Toward an 'Elite Power Group' Theory. *Critical Studies in Mass Communication*, 8(2), 139–151. doi: 10.1080/15295039109366787, p. 139; G. Cowan and D. Westphal (2010). *Public Policy and Funding the News. Public Policy and Funding the News.* USC Annenberg School for Communication & Journalism, Center on Communication Leadership & Policy. Retrieved from https://fundingthenews.usc.edu/files/2015/07/Funding-the-News_report-optimized.pdf, pp. 7–14.

49 J. Dunaway (2008). Markets, Ownership, and the Quality of Campaign News Coverage. *Journal of Politics*, 70(4), 1193–1202. doi: 10.1017/s0022381608081140; B.H. Sparrow (1999). *Uncertain Guardians: The News Media as a Political Institution*. Baltimore: Johns Hopkins University Press.

Rule, which were upheld in a landmark case, *National Broadcasting Co. v. United States*.[50] These rules limited the national broadcasting networks' control of individual broadcasters' decisions. These regulations also included a structural ownership rule limiting a radio network from owning more than one broadcast station within a market area. These limitations reflected the FCC's earlier presumption that a single entity holding more than one broadcast licence in the same community contravened the public interest. These rules also incidentally placed ownership limits on the incipient television networks.

On the heels of the US Supreme Court's decision in *National Broadcasting Co.*, the FCC promulgated further structural regulations limiting national ownership of radio. The FCC prohibited FM radio station owners from owning more than six stations nationally in order to 'obviate possible monopoly and encourage local initiative'.[51] The FCC also limited broadcast ownership locally. In the 1950s, the FCC, building on this informal practice and expanding it to the new technology of television, adopted what became known as the 'Rule of Seven', which limited common ownership to seven FM-band stations, seven AM-band stations and seven television stations nationally (up to five of which could be VHF-band stations).[52] The Rule of Seven remained in place for roughly 30 years until the FCC increased the limit to 12 in the 1980s.[53]

In the face of increasing competition from expanded cable networks and the Internet, the FCC essentially gave up on broadcast regulation in the 1990s and early 2000s. In 2018, it scrapped its cross-ownership rules that prohibited newspapers and broadcast stations from having joint ownership. Under FCC Chairman Ajit Pai, further elimination of rules were indicated.

However, in the early 2000s, social media burst onto the scene in a manner that radically changed the mechanisms by which most Americans consumed news and that democratised the dissemination of news. Before the Internet and social media, high barriers to entry restricted news dissemination to just a handful of sources. After the advent of the Internet and social media, Americans began consuming news from an ever-growing number of online producers

---

50 *Broadcasting Co. v. United States*, 319 U.S. 190, 206–208, 224–227 (1943).

51 See In re Amendment of Section 73.3555 (formerly Sections 73.35, 73.240 and 73.636) of the Commission's Rules Relating to Multiple Ownership of AM, FM and Television Broadcast Stations, 100 F.C.C. 17, 21 (1984) (quoting Federal Communications Commission, Sixth Annual Report 68 (1940)).

52 A. Candeub (2008). Media Ownership Regulation, the First Amendment, and Democracy's Future. *UC Davis Law Review*, 41, 1547–1611; In re Amendment of Sections 3.35, 3.240 and 3.636 of the Rules and Regulations Relating to Multiple Ownership of AM, FM & Television Broadcase Stations, 18 F.C.C. 288, 294, 297 (1953); In re Amendment of Section 3.636 of the Commission's Rules and Regulations Relating to Multiple Ownership of Television Broadcast Stations, 43 F.C.C. 2797, 2798, 2800–2801 (1954).

53 Candeub, *supra* note 52.

of news content. Moreover, of this new class of news producers, many came from outside the long-established media ownership circles. This is particularly relevant, given the decline of print media such as newspapers, which appear to be fading from the US media marketplace.[54]

At the same time, the FCC has refrained for the most part from regulating the Internet. With the blessing of the Supreme Court in *National Cable & Telecommunications Association v. Brand X Internet Services*,[55] the FCC ruled that it could choose to classify the Internet in a way that mandates the most minimal level of regulation. While the FCC under President Obama's Chair switched course towards a more regulatory approach, the FCC returned to its deregulatory position under Chairman Pai, who was appointed by President Trump.

Ironically, the FCC justified much of the deregulation of media ownership restrictions and other regulation of 'incumbent' media on the grounds that competition from the Internet obviated the economic justifications for these restrictions. They existed (or so the story went) because of the potential abuse of broadcasters' dominant market position. With a competitive Internet to check a less competitive broadcast industry, the need for regulation to check either diminished.

But elite theory suggests a different justification of media regulation. It was not economic, but political – a truth that President Roosevelt certainly understood. By decentralising ownership, at least to some extent, democratically elected politicians undermined elite media power. The regulations served as a check on a hijacking of democracy for personal purposes by a small number of people.

5. ELITE CIRCULATING: FROM TELEVISION AND RADIO NETWORKS TO SILICON VALLEY

The democratisation of news production occurred because nearly everyone has access to a smartphone and video camera. Production of 'news', whether it is a video of a political speech, a violent political rally or videos of one's cat looking cute, has become phenomenally inexpensive. But the other factor driving the democratisation of news production is social media. Social media, which is the

---

[54] D. Cho, M.D. Smith and A. Zentner (2016). Internet Adoption and the Survival of Print Newspapers: A Country-Level Examination. *Information Economics and Policy*, 37, 13–19. doi: 10.1016/j.infoecopol.2016.10.001; H.I. Chyi and O. Tenenboim (2016). Reality Check. *Journalism Practice*, 11(7), 798–819. doi: 10.1080/17512786.2016.1208056.

[55] *National Cable & Telecommunications Association v. Brand X Internet Services*, 545 U.S. 967 (2005).

dominant way people receive news today,[56] provide distribution platforms for individuals or groups to get their news and viewpoints out to a wide audience for nominal cost. YouTube, Facebook, Twitter, Instagram, Snapchat and many more platforms have emerged as both platforms for news dissemination that allow virtually anyone to become a citizen journalist at minimal expense.

With this democratisation of news production and dissemination, the traditional landscape of heavily curated news distribution by elite media ownership interests quickly broke down. When news cycles were dominated by a few media companies, those companies selected the news to distribute and determined the issues that would be highlighted in their broadcasts and print pages. But with democratisation, populist voices suddenly generated a significantly greater diversity of news stories and viewpoints that were not well represented under the previous system. With more stories, voices and viewpoints from which to choose, many news consumers began rejecting standard accounts of global events fed by traditional American media producers. While there may be other social factors driving the growing distrust of traditional media (and perhaps even social and political institutions generally),[57] the new online media at the very least facilitated that growing distrust by both increasing available content and viewpoints and by providing an outlet for those acting on that distrust.

At the same time, this democratisation empowered a new set of elites – the Silicon satrapies of Facebook, Twitter and Google. They have the power to edit, shadow ban,[58] de-platform[59] and, indeed, control the flow of all of

---

56 Pew Research Center (E. Shearer and J. Gottfried) (September 2017). News Use across Social Media Platforms 2017. Retrieved from https://www.journalism.org/2017/09/07/news-use-across-social-media-platforms-2017; Pew Research Center (E. Shearer and K. Matsa) (September 2018), News Use across Social Media Platforms 2018. Retrieved from https://www.journalism.org/2018/09/10/ news-use-across-social-media-platforms-2018.

57 A.J. Moore (2017). *Critical Elitism: Deliberation, Democracy and the Problem of Expertise*. Cambridge: Cambridge University Press, pp. 1–15.

58 'Shadow banning' is the practice by social media platforms of deliberately adjusting algorithms that control how often a particular user's posts appear to other users on the platform. The user is able to access the platform normally, but will be unaware that followers and other users will not see the shadow banned user's posts. B. Molina (2018). Shadow Banning: What is it, and Why is Trump Talking about in on Twitter, 27 July. Retrieved from https://www.usatoday.com/story/tech/nation-now/2018/07/26/shadow-banning-what-and-why-trump-talking-twitter/842368002.

59 'Deplatforming,' according to Wikipedia (https://en.wikipedia.org/wiki/Deplatforming), 'is a form of political activism or prior restraint by an individual, group, or organization with the goal of shutting down controversial speakers or speech, or denying them access to a venue in which to express their opinion. Tactics used to achieve this goal among community groups include direct action, [*sic*] and Internet activism. It is also a method used by social media and other technology companies to selectively suspend, ban, or otherwise restrict access to their platform by users who have allegedly violated the platform's terms of service, particularly terms regarding hate speech. … The term *deplatforming* also refers generally to tactics, often

this decentralised content production. And, indeed, they have the incentive to do so. Their economic purpose is to keep eyes on their screens to watch their advertisers. Therefore, their interest is not necessarily consistent with their users. Through the lens of elite theory, we argue that the 'fake news' brouhaha can be seen as an effort of the new Silicon Valley elites to exert aristocratic control in order to cement their new elite status in the vacuum created by the decline of the incumbent media.

6. RESPONDING TO FAKE NEWS

To the extent that the 'fake news' phenomenon exists, it threatens the rule of law and democratic institutions on two levels. The first threat arises from the ability of fake news to 'short circuit' rational or semi-rational interactions by news consumers in political discourse. Given that democratic institutions require participants to rationally promote self-interested political positions, fake news undermines that goal. The first threat is *de minimis* – fake news has existed in every political system and there are few indications that news consumers are significantly more susceptible to fake news even in the light of improved distribution mechanisms.

In contrast, the second threat is very real. It arises from the reaction by traditional and social media news producers, as well as legislators and regulators, who have responded to the perceived increase in fake news with proposals for restricting speech by policing viewpoints and speakers. While some may argue that traditional and social media organisations do not wish to restrict speech, it is in fact happening on multiple levels. On the private side of the equation, social media and many traditional media firms have responded to the perceived fake news phenomenon by adjusting (based on third-party fact-checkers or internal policy) the algorithms that control whether particular posts appear on news feeds, whether material is flagged as fake news or whether particular users are permitted to post at all. Such actions clearly restrict speech and consolidate power to limit the spread of information and discussion from outsider groups. Beyond algorithmic control, Facebook founder Mark Zuckerberg has advocated for the creation of a purportedly independent 'supreme court' that would censor content appearing on social media websites:

> But over the long term, what I'd really like to get to is an independent appeal. So maybe folks at Facebook make the first decision based on the community standards

organized using social media, for preventing controversial speakers or speech from being heard. Deplatforming tactics have included disruption of speeches, attempts to have speakers disinvited to a venue or event, and various forms of personal harassment including efforts to have an individual fired or blacklisted.'

> that are outlined, and then people can get a second opinion. You can imagine some sort of structure, almost like a Supreme Court, that is made up of independent folks who don't work for Facebook, who ultimately make the final judgment call on what should be acceptable speech in a community that reflects the social norms and values of people all around the world.[60]

While framed in idealistic terms, the pernicious side of such an institution would be to act as the arbiter of truth and ultimately prevent any dissemination of speech on the major social media outlets that fails to conform with a politicised definition of 'truth'. Non-mainstream voices will be the most at risk of being marginalised in such a context.

Elite theory principles suggest that traditional news producers and established social media owners are self-interested and are not altruistic. Consequently, even if such interests do possess nominally altruistic motives in desiring to control the curation and distribution of news products, these motives will express themselves in restrictions on the ability of outsiders to enter the market and produce diverse news. Empirical evidence shows that newspapers and media outlets pursue readers, viewers and profits – at the same time often reflecting the private, personal views of their owners and managers: 'The organizational structure of editorial boards and newspaper personnel policies ... play a considerable role in determining editorial viewpoints.'[61] Similarly, dominant Internet platforms can seek viewers' attention, while at the same time promoting their own personal or corporate editorial viewpoints.

The incentive to label insurgent outsider intervention in the news production and dissemination markets as 'fake news' is strong. By labelling news articles generated by those outside the elite as 'fake news', entrenched elite in social media can erect barriers to entry in the form of denied access to the distribution networks that most Americans use to consume news. Similarly, social media sites restrict speech by de-platforming or shadow banning users and alternative platforms. While some of the speech restricted by such actions may be actual fake news, no algorithmic regulation of platform content can fully discriminate between real and fake news, particularly if fake news judgements are made on the basis of interpretation rather than objectively determinable fact. Thus, for example, the social media platform Twitter appeared to engage in a form of shadow banning aimed at prominent conservative-leaning US Republicans,

---

60 E. Klein (2018). Mark Zuckerberg on Facebook's Hardest Year, and What Comes Next, 2 April. Retrieved from https://www.vox.com/2018/4/2/17185052/mark-zuckerberg-facebook-interview-fake-news-bots-cambridge; see also S.O. Bloomberg (2019). Zuckerberg's Facebook 'Supreme Court' Can't Handle All the Disputes, 25 June. Retrieved from https://www.washingtonpost.com/business/zuckerbergs-facebook-supreme-court-cant-handle-all-the-disputes/2019/06/24/02e7ffd4-96a1-11e9-9a16-dc551ea5a43b_story.html.

61 D.E. Ho and K.M. Quinn (2009). Viewpoint Diversity and Media Consolidation: An Empirical Study. *Stanford Law Review*, 61, 781–868, p. 787.

including the chair of the Republican National Committee, by making it more difficult for users to search for those accounts.[62] Though Twitter claimed that this effect was accidental, the fact remains that it affected only conservative posters and did not affect their leftist political counterparts.[63] Similarly, a Project Veritas investigative project released videos of Twitter employees confirming the practice of shadow banning, Twitter's bias against conservative views and that 'conservative and pro-Trump content was subject to far harsher scrutiny than liberal posts.'[64] Algorithmic or deliberate human judgements can easily be abused in order to favour some viewpoints or identities over others.

The threat of entrenchment and restriction of entry by high-value alternative news products into the market outweighs the relatively trivial threat that news consumers will be taken in by actual fake news. As Mosca[65] states, political structures, such as the separation of powers, that prevent any one group from gaining a monopoly on political power and that facilitate the circulation of elites produce the most lasting regimes able to avoid 'violent convulsions'. Yet political structures are not enough:

> But more is needed: a great deal of education, which is always a slow process, and long experience in devising the most practical means of domesticating the base instincts which so often are joint to the will to power – instincts which again and again reasserted themselves after a protracted period of political and social peace, just when they seemed to be extinct forever.[66]

If this is correct, the proper response that preserves the rule of law and related democratic institutions requires resisting calls by entrenched interests for greater restrictions and regulation of news production and dissemination by users. Rather, consumer education and awareness regarding the evaluation of news products as 'real' or 'fake' provides a potential for real benefits in terms of devaluing fake news and promoting the dissemination of multiple news products and viewpoints. While warnings that content may be (or is) fake news are subject to the abuses discussed above, such warnings do show some effect

---

62 A. Thompson (2018). Twitter Appears to Have Fixed 'Shadow Ban' of Prominent Republicans Like the RNC Chair and Trump Jr.'s Spokesman, 25 July. Retrieved from https://www.vice.com/en_us/article/43paqq/twitter-is-shadow-banning-prominent-republicans-like-the-rnc-chair-and-trump-jrs-spokesman.

63 *Ibid.*

64 H. Parry (2018). Project Veritas Films Twitter Staff Undercover, 11 January. Retrieved from https://www.dailymail.co.uk/news/article-5260111/Undercover-video-Twitter-staff-talking-censorship.html; Project Veritas. (n.d.). American Pravda: Twitter. Retrieved from https://www.projectveritas. com/twitter.

65 Mosca, *supra* note 42, p. 390.

66 *Ibid.*, p. 391.

in ameliorating the belief in fake news.[67] However, other innovative approaches to news consumer education do show promise. In one study, for example, news consumers were 'inoculated' against fake news through participation in a game in which they were trained to emulate a fake news producer and to use common techniques for creating fake news with the goal of attracting as many followers as possible while maintaining credibility.[68] This training trained participants 'to be more attuned to specific deception strategies'[69] rather than merely warning them that particular news stories are, in the opinion of other parties, fake news. If this effect holds, then education may be an effective prophylactic against the proliferation of and belief in fake news.

Beyond education, renewed and reinvigorated antitrust enforcement against the dominant platforms such as Google, Facebook and Twitter is warranted. Their power and ability to impose preferences regardless of the market impact stems in large part from the market power they enjoy. Zuckerberg, Dorsey and other Internet moguls tolerate ideological slant in their firms because they do not fear competitors – with differing views or otherwise. They are, to use the language of market power, the price givers. If that price includes an ideological slant, consumer cannot go elsewhere.

Although they appear to be picking up, US antitrust efforts have been half-hearted. To its credit, the EU courts and the EU Commission have been more energetic,[70] but have yet to require major structural changes. Elite theory would argue that technology and Internet firms might need significant 'elite churn' of the sort that prolonged market power impedes and that antitrust enforcement may facilitate. To the degree that regulation is necessary, it should limit the power of dominant social media firms and search engines to edit and discriminate against users.

In the end, however, there is no silver bullet, no panacea for the dissemination and belief of false information spread by others for personal or partisan gain. A fundamental proposition of elite theory is that organisations tend towards

---

67 B. Nyhan, E. Porter, J. Reifler and T. Wood (2019). Taking Fact-Checks Literally But Not Seriously? The Effects of Journalistic Fact-Checking on Factual Beliefs and Candidate Favorability. *Political Behavior*. doi: 10.1007/s11109-019-09528-x; Pennycook, Cannon and Rand, *supra* note 20, p. 12.

68 J. Roozenbeek and S.V.D. Linden (2019). Fake News Game Confers Psychological Resistance against Online Misinformation. *Palgrave Communications*, 5(1). doi: 10.1057/s41599-019-0279-9, p. 3.

69 *Ibid.*, p. 7.

70 E. Schulze (2019). If You Want to Know What a US Tech Crackdown May Look Like, Check out What Europe Did, 7 June. Retrieved from https://www.cnbc.com/2019/06/07/how-google-facebook-amazon-and-apple-faced-eu-tech-antitrust-rules.html. S. Cao (2018). Why Tech's 'Big 4' All Faced Antitrust Probes in Europe, But Not in the US, 15 February. Retrieved from https://observer.com/2018/02/eu-antitrust-probe-apple-amazon-facebook-google.

oligarchic control by elite groups. If we accept that the new media elite control large swaths of the social media landscape and the ability to restrict insurgent voices from disseminating dissident voices, then it follows that the elite has incentives to restrict dissident voices and sources of news that could compete and displace the elite from power. To the extent that the promotion of dissident voices and sources of news comprises both real and fake news, then some degree of fake news will always be present, regardless of the viewpoint advocated by that fake news. Our choices then range between trusting the state to control dissemination of news media, trusting entrenched interests to police themselves, trusting individuals to discriminate between real and fake news or some combination thereof. We suggest that the best response is dynamically prophylactic – the response to fake news requires active training of individuals to recognise fake news, state-based structural responses that do not favour entrenchment of current media elites, and self-regulation of elite media interests competing on the basis of reliability and truth. This combination cannot prevent the dissemination of fake news or the entrenchment of elite media interests altogether, but it may preserve the democratic tendencies of smooth circulation of elites as new viewpoints gain support of the masses and rise to displace previous elites who no longer effectively represent those interests.

7. CONCLUSION

Fake news is not a new phenomenon – it is a necessary consequence of any system of information gathering and dissemination. But the political turmoil of 2016 brought fake news to the public's attention and, in turn, generated public support for regulatory mechanisms to reduce the impact of fake news on the information used by voters and decision makers. In the abstract, such an impulse to increase the reliability of information systems, particularly in democratic institutions, is well-founded. Absent reliable information, or in the presence of false information that in many cases is crafted to generate emotional responses toward opposing viewpoints, parties, proposals, or persons, democratic institutions become driven less by reason and the rule of law and more by base impulses.

In reality, however, actualisation of that abstract goal of eliminating fake news may be more problematic than accepting fake news as merely an unavoidable consequence of the messy world of human communications. In the first instance, it is difficult to define exactly what is and what is not 'fake news'. Second, it is unclear whether fake news actually impacts voter and decision-maker behaviour in meaningful ways. And third, the ever present question of *quis custodiet ipsos custodes?* (who guards the guards?) raises problems of lack of transparency and transference of extraordinary hidden political, social and economic power to any authority given the power to decide what is real and what is fake.

This last problem implicates the elite theory conception of the circulation of elites. Modern Internet social media platforms are quickly becoming dominant players in the market for news, but are also the primary mechanisms by which alleged fake news articles disseminate quickly and broadly to the news-consuming public. As this new Internet elite gradually displaces traditional news media, calls for increased regulation of fake news may simply serve to cement this new elite in power and may serve to limit civic discourse as owners of such platforms gain powers to use their ability to supress dissenting information and views. We believe such direct regulation of fake news is a dead end that will artificially limit the ability of new voices to communicate their messages to the public. Instead, the best response to fake news requires improving user education and encouraging greater freedom of expression, as well as carefully examining the new Internet elite's market power concentration.

PART II

EXPERIENCE OF DEALING WITH DISINFORMATION

8. TRUE STORY! CHALLENGES TO DEMOCRACY NOT COVERED BY THE MEDIA

Lessons from the (Non-)Coverage of the Greek Financial Crisis

Georgios TERZIS*

1. INTRODUCTION

It is almost a truism to state that what is not there is sometimes more important than what it is. Before the 2008 financial crisis, between 2002 and July 2007, approximately 300 stories with a 'banking crisis' tag were written in the UK. Most were found in the back of newspapers and were discussing the Japanese economy. Once the story of the financial crisis first broke in the US, over 3,000 stories with the same tag could be found – this time on the front pages as major stories – between August 2007 and mid-2009.[1] The numbers alone explain that few people were aware of the financial crisis 'truth' that hit them before it was a hot news issue.[2]

Once the media coverage started, three stages of narratives emerged: initial surprise at the situation; a blame game between countries, banks, politicians and individuals; and dramatic headlines depicting the demise (or, on occasion, the strengthening) of the eurozone. These stages produced two different types of media coverage – one from the 'high-end quality' journalism with reports that included some serious analysis and an attempt to create a consistent picture

* Brussels School of Governance (BSG) (an alliance between the Institute for European Studies and Vesalius College), Vrije Universiteit Brussel, Belgium. Email: georgios.terzis@vub.be. An earlier version of this chapter was published in S. MERTENS, (ed.), *Perspectieven op Internationale Journalistiek (Perspectives on International Journalism)*, Brussels: Academia Press, 2013.

1 'Aditya Chakrabortty on media reporting of the financial crisis', YouTube (around 7:00–9:30), 4 August 2011, http://www.youtube.com/watch?v=zAXEdoJTrBE.

2 J. SCHENKER, 'The story not reported' *Covering the Crisis: the role of media in the financial crisis*, 2010, p. 109 and S. SCHIFFERES, 'Aftershock: how the BBC called the crisis', *Covering the Crisis: the role of media in the financial crisis*. Maastricht: EJC Publications, 2010, p. 117.

and the other the tabloid-style journalism in which the focus was on 'scumbag millionaires' and 'fat cats working at the banks',[3] and discussions concerning which countries were to blame for financial failings (Greece, Italy, Portugal, Spain and Ireland) and which were to blame during the efforts of creating reform (for the most part, Germany).

Those failings of the press to act as an *early warning system*[4] and subsequently to cover some of the fundamental truths behind the crisis were mainly attributed to the fact that most reporters around the world were not sufficiently trained to report a story of this magnitude, including financial reporters who are experienced on reporting companies and microeconomics instead of macroeconomics and international debt cases.

This effect is even more apparent with international finance news, which is more technical in nature and thus requires a certain degree of background knowledge in order to be able to dive into the data. And it is for these reasons that a certain elite media (the *Financial Times* and *The Economist*) and some international news agencies (*Reuters* and *Bloomberg*) have enjoyed immense power over the framing of the issue of the Greek financial crisis.

As a result, an inter-media agenda-setting phenomenon occurred whereby the above media set the tone and framework, and thus their particular truth on it, for most of the media coverage around the world. We have seen, for example, more than enough times American, African and Asian foreign correspondents, with a minimal level of knowledge of economics and/or Greek and Eurozone policies, 'copying and pasting' the *Financial Times*' or *The Economist*'s main arguments in their reporting on the Greek financial crisis. The world's media indeed followed the *Financial Times*/*The Economist* framework day in and day out, both qualitatively (the same type of arguments and biases) and quantitatively (daily coverage and then a halt when the *Financial Times* and *The Economist* stopped reporting the issue). The rest was filled with different ethnic stereotypes that ranged from the slightly biased selection of data to the overt fabrication or alteration of them in order to fit the stereotype and describe the story with maximum compression and effect.

In all of this, some of the most important true stories have again failed to rise from the constraints of today's media and journalism straitjackets and be covered substantially and consistently in order to make a difference. On the contrary, they can be used as case studies of media failures to expose the fundamental processes that are at work in our current media and political systems that allow only certain types of truths to emerge while suppressing others and failing to address our current challenges to democracy. The non-coverage of these truths

[3] E. Engelen, 'Financial crisis and storytelling by distributive coalition', *Covering the Crisis: the role of media in the financial crisis*, Maastricht: EJC Publications, 2010, p. 41.

[4] B. McNair, *An Introduction to Political Communication*. London: Routledge, 2003.

in Greece is our case study in this chapter, which indeed argues that what is not there is sometimes more important than what it is.

2. NEWS SELECTION AND THE NON-COVERED 'TRUTHS' OF THE GREEK FINANCIAL CRISIS

The Greek financial crisis became one of the biggest stories ever to be covered by the global media, with more front-page articles than the collapse of Lehman Brothers. This is quite a considerable level of media attention for a country of 11 million people that accounts for only 2.5 per cent of the eurozone economy. The reason for this publicity according to the reports in the international press, is that 'the story' holds valuable lessons for the world's policy-makers as well as average citizens who see how their taxes and pensions could be affected by things happening outside their country.[5]

Yet, despite this coverage, there are some fundamental truths that are consistently overlooked or are simply implied 'between the lines' mainly because they are long-term processes rather than events that are highly valued by journalists and editors using their standard criteria in the selection of stories. The vast majority of the coverage focused on easy generalisations and dangerous selective nationalistic stereotyping, such as a photo of only five men dressed in Nazi uniforms in a demonstration of thousands of people during the visit of the German Chancellor Angela Merkel to Athens.[6]

2.1. TRUE STORY 1: THE NON-MERITOCRACY CATCH-22 OF GREEK POLITICAL PARTIES

Since its creation, modern Greece has suffered from clientelistic relationships in its political and economic life. These relationships and their monetary (bribing) or non-monetary (exchange of favours) aspects have defined the maintenance of people's social mobility, wealth and eventually status for the last two centuries.[7]

The modern cradles of these relationships are the political parties that govern Greece, which are undemocratically run on clientelistic or family-based networks and are thus non-meritocratic institutions. It is hardly a coincidence that both the

---

5 R. Picard, *The Euro Crisis in the Media*. London: I.B. Tauris, 2015.

6 Associated Press Reporter, 'Naked fury: Nude demonstrator is one of 50,000 protesters in Athens as Angela Merkel is met with burning swastikas and Greek riot police battle crowds with teargas', *Daily Mail*, 10 October 2012, https://www.dailymail.co.uk/news/article-2214972/Angela-Merkel-Athens-Protestors-dress-Nazis-burn-swastikas-throw-rocks-police.html.

7 K. Featherstone, 'The challenge of liberalization: parties and the state in Greece after the 1993 elections' (1994) 1(2) *Democratization Journal* 280.

father and grandfather of a former Prime Minister George Papandreou also held the same position, while the earlier Prime Minister Konstantinos Karamanlis was the nephew of an earlier prime minister, and the current Prime Minister Kyriakos Mitsotakis is also the grandson of a former prime minister.

These institutions promote, for reasons other than merit, a majority of mediocre incompetent politicians in their ranks. They, in turn, create an incompetent non-meritocratic bureaucracy, which promotes their cronies and castrates the majority of those who were hired by a previous government despite the level of their competence.[8]

This incompetent bureaucracy fails first to sufficiently defend the national interests of the country in international fora like the EU and lets down its own society internally by failing to create institutions of 'fair play' among its citizens. The result is a non-meritocratic society based on unfair competition due to different levels of access to state resources (civil servant positions, tenders, procurements, etc.). Finally, it is this non-meritocratic society that reproduces/votes the non-meritocratic incompetent parties back into power based on its self-interests.

As we have seen in the case of Greece, as in many other democracies, the internal workings of political parties are considered almost sacred or simply too boring and are not sufficiently and systematically covered by the mainstream media. And that is the first lesson of the non-covered 'truth' of the 'corruption' of political parties in liberal democratic systems: the non-meritocracy's Catch-22, the undemocratic and non-meritocratic political parties that govern a country give birth to and protect a vicious circle of incompetence that challenges democratic systems and, if not contained, eventually suffocates them.

2.2. TRUE STORY 2: 'CORRUPTION COMPETITION': THE EPIDEMIC THAT INFESTS EVERYTHING AND ERODES BASIC TRUST

As we know from current social research, the value of the wealth of individuals is only relative to the wealth of other individuals around them. This perception is particularly acute in *nouveau riche* societies such as Greece and is one of the main reasons behind the 'corruption competition' among the Greek elites that was sometimes driven to extremes normally reserved for Russian oligarchs, African dictators or Middle East princesses. It manifested itself as conspicuous consumption by the upper and upper-middle classes of the country that control the private sector (and the black economy). Just before the crisis, it led to real

---

8 C. Lyrintzis, 'Greek politics in the era of economic crisis', LSE Research, 2011, http://eprints.lse.ac.uk/33826/1/GreeSE_No45.pdf.

estate prices in areas around Athens higher than those in Lake Geneva and some luxury brand shops in Athens making more money than in Paris.[9]

In this game, instead of controlling and punishing whenever necessary, the Greek political elites (and subsequently the high echelons of the public sector) joined in, and bribes to public officials and tax evasion of millions of euros were considered almost negligible, since the benchmark has been set at hundreds of millions.

The failure of consecutive Greek governments to address the endemic and spiralling problem of corruption as a challenge to democratic values and the failure of the Greek press to cover it provides us with our second lesson. Unfortunately, for countries that enter this process, the end of this corruption competition is the abyss of a negative spiral of corruption and a rotten environment in which everything is infested and no one is beyond suspicion or indeed innocent of willingly or unwillingly participating in the corruption chorus. Such a situation erodes trust in democracy even further.

2.3. TRUE STORY 3: THERE ARE NO 'SHIELDS' TO PROTECT FROM THE GLOBALISATION 'BARBARIANS'

As explained above, the inefficient cronyistic political and economic systems led to an economy in Greece featuring the accumulation of local wealth by mainly uncompetitive companies, which were created and survived due to favouritism, like in many other places around the world where similar conditions exist, but the significant new factor in this widespread business corruption was that it was within the eurozone. Today the vast majority of these Greek companies are 'lost' in a globalised and euro-denominated economy that cannot offer the protection of favouring local firms for state contracts or of currency devaluations and import tariffs.

A side-effect of the diminishing private sector competitive power has been more people being 'forced' due to a lack of choice to work in the public sector on salaries close to the poverty line, creating the façade of reduced unemployment, while at the same time widening the inequality gap among its citizens and accumulating more public debt. This in turn also impeded the competitiveness of the country, since it needed to raise more taxes both from individuals and companies to service this debt.

And this is the third 'truth' from the Greek financial crisis that most of the media failed to address for many years: in today's globalised financial world, a fully integrated economy such as the Greek one unfortunately cannot offer

9 T. Pappas, 'The causes of the Greek crisis are in Greek politics', 2010, https://www.opendemocracy.net/en/openeconomy/causes-of-greek-crisis-are-in-greek-politics.

many protectionist 'shields' for its uncompetitive private sector or even for its public sector. In the long run, either competition will catch up with them and/or the country will financially bleed to death, not only because of the direct and indirect subsidies of the uncompetitive sectors but also because of the massive opportunity costs involved and the lost generations of talented citizens who never realised their potential, widening inequalities and economic migration. This non-reported 'truth' poses an unbearable financial but also ideological challenge to our democratic systems.

3. LESSONS LEARNT: MEDIA WATCHDOGS, MEDIA LAPDOGS, GREEK DONKEYS AND THE 'BIG FAT GREEK FUNERAL' MEDIA FESTIVAL

The failures of the above-mentioned non-coverage are of course a reflection of the failure of the Greek media and the national media governance system. It is indicative that the magnitude of the corruption when it finally received (only due to international pressure) the appropriate level of coverage by the Greek national media (which have been subservient to the national elites and until then had exposed corruption selectively only to reflect the competition among these corrupt elites) has confirmed the feeling of the average citizen that the Greek media are not watchdogs but lapdogs of the establishment.

Servile donkeys might be a more accurate description, since certain ex-ministers admitted that some Greek journalists were even on the government's secret payroll. A number of journalists not only turned a blind eye to the above 'inconvenient truths', but like Greek donkeys were actually assisting and sometimes doing the work (on behalf) of the Greek governments. It is indicative again that although many Greek journalists were aware that the government has been 'cooking the books' in order to enter the eurozone, their national pride and the IOUs to the government prevailed over their professional identity and ethics, and all kept their mouths shut and pens down on the issue; instead, most of them enthusiastically and actively promoted the entry of Greece to the eurozone.

As a result, when the crisis actually hit, the communication system of the Greek government was totally unprepared for this scale of crisis communication. Having been used to the Greek donkeys that turned to lapdogs in the worst-case scenario, it was not prepared at all for the scrutiny led by the pitbulls of the international press when these arrived in Athens.

All political public relations attempts failed miserably, while internal political communication was in a state of shambles. Different ministries were delivering different messages on the same day, while even the office of the Prime Minister seemed to have a different opinion every other day. The 'inexperienced' Greek government could not be proactive as it should in response to this type of crisis (especially when it came to financial markets that depend on perceptions as much as reality on the ground) and instead was reactive until the very last moment. On the few occasions that it tried to be proactive, its inexperience led it to believe that a 'total transparency' Scandinavian-style of the country's finances was the appropriate remedy for years of misinformation and disinformation of the Greek citizens and the international community. This 'dose' of transparency instead turned out to be a poison rather than medicine.

The 'Big Fat Greek Funeral' was at full speed around the world. The international media and their foreign correspondents framed the crisis in terms of four stereotypes or 'truths': lazy employees, a big public service sector, lack of taxation and a closed economy/professions. All these of course are stereotypes and none stands up to strict quantitative scrutiny when one compares Greece with other countries that did not suffer the same level of financial crisis despite 'scoring worse' in some or all of the above. But the 'Big Fat Greek Funeral' festival of stereotypes had started in the international media circus in Athens and if the Greek government could not stop it, nothing could.[10]

The majority of the Greek press was indeed a press that did not represent the fourth power in a system of checks and balances of a liberal democracy, but more closely resembled a communist media governance system of good news serving the goals of the government. As a result, the lesson from the lack of coverage of the Greek financial crisis is that in today's globalised economy and political world, liberal democracies cannot afford not to have an independent press that looks into possible abuses by governments and businesses. The early warning system that this provides will generally act to safeguard democratic development.

4. EPILOGUE

All the above lead to a perilous road for any democracy. After the financial crisis, public cynicism in Greece (but also around the world), not only towards individual politicians but also towards the political system of democracy itself, has reached levels that are having a tremendous impact and are putting in doubt three out of the four basic premises of liberal democracy, namely the (a) rational, (b) choice, (c) of the majority, (d) in a constitutional framework.[11]

There is no reason to panic about the threat to the fourth premise above, at this moment at least. Constitutionality is guaranteed by several national and international institutions. Greece is not going to have another dictatorship, since

10 See the report by the World Economic Forum regarding the number of working hours per country (https://www.weforum.org/agenda/2018/02/greeks-work-longest-hours-in-europe) and government debt (https://www.weforum.org/agenda/2019/05/european-countries-with-most-government-debt-chart).

11 McNair, *supra* note 4, pp. 16–17.

it is still part of the EU, while the possibility of the return of the ex-king is quite small, despite his expensive public relations campaign in Greece and abroad for several years.[12]

However, despite the fact that elections maintain their constitutionality in Greece, the *rational* choice of the majority has reached dangerously low levels. This is first because both the election campaigns are conducted and the votes of most citizens are cast in emotional rather than rational terms. And of course, outside of the election campaigns, the average citizen today receives disproportionate amounts of 'fake', one-sided or non-news that masquerades as news, while really impactful news is not reported, as we have seen above.

Second, there is no 'real' *choice*, since in a growing number of liberal democracies (especially those with majoritarian or strong presidential systems), citizens are asked to choose 'the least worst' among the two or three non-meritocratically promoted candidates, as was demonstrated above. This is not just one of the roots of Greece's current problems, but is also the Achilles' heel of a number of liberal democracies today. These political parties produce the 'illusion of choice' among undemocratically elected by their parties and thus most of the time, if not always, mediocre and incompetent candidates.

This is a situation that more and more citizens have noticed and thus stay home during election days rather than vote. Third, then, a growing number of citizens do not vote or vote with a blank vote. Sooner or later the *majority* will not actively participate in the election of its 'democratically' elected leaders.

This disillusionment with three of the four basic premises of liberal democracies is putting a huge strain on the fourth, its constitutional framework, and this is best reflected in the rise of populism, social unrest and demonstrations targeting the very institutions of democracy and its leaders, and their slogan outside the Greek Parliament: 'To be burned, to be burned, the brothel parliament' ('Na kaei, Na Kaei, To Mpourdelo h Vouli!' or «να καεί, να καεί το μπουρδέλο η Βουλή»). This slogan was not just the cry of some dissident isolate anarchists, but was heard from angry middle-class citizens and partly reflects the feelings of a big part of the Greek population that is now asking for a 'firm hand' and a 'strong leader', and is gazing with some admiration towards Turkey's Recep Tayyip Erdogan and even further to Russia's Vladimir Putin, while there is talk about the 'success' of the Beijing model. And this is one of the ultimate current challenges. Due to the disillusionment with the current state of democracy as well as capitalism, the supporters of Plato's approach that a technocratic intellectually efficient class of 'rulers' should possess absolute control of political power in Greece and elsewhere might soon outnumber those of Aristotle's democratic 'polity'. This is the ultimate challenge because as we know from Paracelsus, the *dose is the poison*. Small and even increasing doses of crises could make a nation

[12] See, for example, https://www.hellomagazine.com/tags/greek-royals.

and its institutions stronger if they manage to overcome them, but when the dose is very high and sudden, it could be catastrophic or even fatal.

5. THE ROAD AHEAD AND THE ROLE OF THE 'TRUE' NEWS STORIES

Greece will never emerge from the current crisis unless it opens up the closed shop profession of the Greek politicians to real competition, stops the clientelistic business environment and supports an independent media system and critical press to monitor and report abuses of these processes.

Democratising the political parties and making them more meritocratic is a *sine qua non* for societies like Greece that need to cut their connection with their cronyistic traditions and modernise in order to be able to compete in today's globalised world. This is actually the first prescription that the International Monetary Fund (IMF) should give to this and any other country that it tries to assist, since it is the root cause of most of the financial problems that it is called to assist with.

Unfortunately for Greek politicians, the instructions to open the 'closed shop' of their profession to fair competition cannot come from the European troika as they did with other professions. Instead, they have to take the political risk and consequently the potential cost to themselves. Because indeed, Greece has not received so much global attention since the times of Alexander the Great, and indeed, its discredited economy and democracy would be restored only if the Greek politicians like Alexander the Great finally decide to cut the Gordian Knot of the Greek non-meritocratic political parties. In order for this to materialise, an independent and critical press needs to be allowed to flourish and to report the 'true stories' that matter, raising these issues high in its agenda and thus the public agenda, and forcing politicians to act upon these issues, and by doing so safeguarding our democratic systems.

9. THE SCOURGE OF FAKE NEWS IN GREECE

Thanos SITISTAS*

1. INTRODUCTION

'Avrianismos' is a term that comes from one of Greece's most popular newspapers of the 1980s and 1990s. The *Avriani* newspaper was often accused of wrongfully targeting politicians and other public figures, and doing so in an opportunistic way, meaning that it would support a political party according to its current interests. Nowadays, the definition of 'Avrianismos' could simply be put as 'journalistic populism'. And where there is populism, fake news – especially that which is based on common misconceptions and prejudice – tends to thrive. In the age of information overload, the problem has exacerbated:

> In the late 1980s, the first private television stations were established in Greece allowing people to express their opinions, which would not be expressed otherwise that freely. However, this situation also allowed people with extreme or absurd opinions to express themselves. In this framework, some fans of conservatism in Greece, who identified with the right-wing, extreme-right, even centre-right political parties in Greece, took advantage of the concept of Greek civilization superiority. They have been appearing in private television aiming at justifying that position, by stressing the risk of the Greek civilization being threatened by many enemies, each for their own reasons.[1]
>
> Since the beginning of the financial slump in Greece press freedom has worsened. A previously rather unknown but long history of state intervention in the media, censorship, and interplay between major media magnates and government officials has become apparent.[2]

---

* Senior Editor at ellinikahoaxes.gr, Greece. Email: info@ellinikahoaxes.gr/sitistas@ellinikahoaxes.gr.

1 E. KOURDIS, 'The Velopoulos-Liakopoulos phenomenon. A semiotic view of the explosion of Greek conspiracy theories and urban Legends in the economic crisis', Aristotle University of Thessaloniki, January 2016, https://ikee.lib.auth.gr/record/286515/files/TheVelopoulos%20Liakopoulos%20 Phenomenon.pdf.

2 T. VAN DER HEIJDEN, 'Media landscape in Greece must reform quickly', *Euroscope*, 28 November 2014, https://bit.ly/39Eneno.

The quality and influence of mainstream media has deteriorated, especially since 2010 and the beginning of the economic crisis in Greece. Many printed media and some TV stations went bankrupt, while others (including digital media) had to adapt to the new economic conditions by laying off experienced journalists and hiring inexperienced ones in their place, who were tasked to 'produce' as many articles as possible, either by translating foreign tabloids or by copying content from others. This left no room for fact-checking and, as a result, even mainstream media reproduce fake stories from abroad. However, some benefited from this change, especially those that offered populist and unprofessional content, by becoming Greece's equivalent of British tabloids such as *The Sun* and the *Daily Mail*.

Another point that needs to be taken into account is the fact that website advertising income sharply declined during the years of economic crisis, which resulted in fewer journalists being hired and who were forced to produce more articles and perform many roles at the same time, in some of which they had no relevant expertise. Although Greeks seem to acknowledge that the quality of online news is rather poor, they rank first among Europeans in trusting the Internet (websites, social media, etc.) to act as a reliable source of news.[3]

2. WHAT DO GREEKS READ ON THE INTERNET?

Out of Greece's 50 most popular websites (according to data from Alexa, February 2019), only 17 can be considered as news portals, although at least five of them should be considered tabloids. Out of these, only seven produce strictly original content (for the most part), eight partially produce original content, with at least three of them reproducing content from other sources most of the time and two websites containing no original content. At least three websites often present far-right content, conspiracy theories, pro-Russian content and disinformation. These websites receive heavy traffic, with millions of clicks and hundreds of thousands of unique users every month.

To be more specific, if we take a closer look at Greece's 50 most popular websites, we find:

1. At number 13 in Alexa's list, makeleio.gr, which is a highly controversial, far-right, conspiracy theory-peddling website.
2. At number 21 in Alexa's list, pentapostagma.gr, which also promotes disinformation and occasionally far-right content, and often presents pro-Russian context.

---

3 T. Sitistas, 'Eurobarometer: where do Greeks choose to stay informed?', *Ellinika Hoaxes*, 11 June 2017, https://www.ellinikahoaxes.gr/2017/06/11/trust-gap-between-traditional-and-new-media-europe/.

3. At number 45 in Alexa's list, pronews.gr, which is also a frequent disinformer and promoter of occasional far-right and pro-Russian content.

The above three often post clickbait, homophobic, anti-immigrant, and anti-NATO/EU content.

Today we know that the manipulation of facts, fake news, information warfare and information overload pose a direct threat to the democratic values of modern societies and Greeks seem to acknowledge that.

New means of conveying information much faster than before, like social media and the Internet as a whole, have made the proliferation of fake news much easier than ever before and Greeks rank first in the EU in terms of accessing news from the Internet.

A 2017 study by the European Broadcasting Union (EBU), based on the data published in the 86th Eurobarometer survey, gave an idea of European citizens' perception of the trustworthiness of several types of media, and included EU Member States as well as acceding and candidate countries, showed that Greeks ranked first among all Europeans.

On the other hand, only 36 per cent of EU citizens tend to trust the Internet and a mere 21 per cent of EU citizens say they trust social networks.[4] A 2018 study of Eurobarometer showed that only four per cent of Greeks fully trust news they read in news outlets (online newspapers and news magazines) and only three per cent fully trust news they read on online social networks and messaging apps. A total of 55 per cent of Greeks also stated that every day (or almost every day), they come across news or information that misrepresents reality or is even false. Only 12 per cent of Greeks are absolutely confident that they are able to identify fake news. In addition, almost 90 per cent of Greeks are confident or somewhat confident that fake news poses a direct threat to democracy.[5]

This means that Greece is in a tough spot. Although Greeks seem to be aware of possible manipulation of facts through online platforms (social media, news outlets, etc.), they still prefer to receive news from these sources.

3. COMMON MISCONCEPTIONS

Surprisingly, Greeks seem to support authoritarian leaders and states. Although there is no official data, our experience in Ellinika Hoaxes show that leaders like

4 EBU, 'Trust Gap between Traditional and New Media Widening Across Europe', 23 May 2017, https://www.ebu.ch/news/2017/05/trust-gap-between-traditional-and-new-media-widening-across-europe.

5 EU Directorate-General for Communication, 'Flash Eurobarometer 464: Fake News and Disinformation Online', 2018, http://data.europa.eu/euodp/en/data/dataset/S2183_464_ENG.

Bashar al Assad and Muammar Gaddafi enjoy a significant degree of popularity. Any negative mention of these people usually causes a response (seen in the comments) by many who strongly believe that they are (or were) victims of things like the 'New World Order' because they stood up for their people. Those who oppose such regimes, like the White Helmets in Syria, are automatically branded as 'jihadists' or 'Western agents'. It is worth noting regarding the latter that a systematic and prolonged misinformation campaign originating from the Kremlin has convinced many people (and not only in Greece) that the White Helmets are evil. These misconceptions are systematically shared via social media and always lack verification.[6]

The latest controversy comes from government officials who adopted a rhetoric friendly to Nicolas Maduro's regime in Venezuela, although it is known that nearly 90 per cent of Venezuelans now live in poverty and inflation is projected to hit 10 million per cent next year according to the International Monetary Fund. Citizens have trouble purchasing staples like bread and milk, and despite the fact that most Western countries recognised Juan Guaido as legal or interim President and called for elections, including the US, Canada, the UK, France, Germany and all of the country's Latin American neighbours except Mexico,[7] Greek government officials, and a significant part of the public, expressed warm feelings for Maduro's regime. In line with the Greek government and the public was the pro-government media as well, adopting a positive point of view for Nicolas Maduro, which more or less coincides with Russia's opinion on the legitimacy of Maduro's regime.

However, it is well known that the electoral authorities banned the largest opposition political parties from taking part in the May 2018 elections and key politicians were barred from running, while the three opposition candidates who faced Maduro joined the elections at the last minute to 'legitimise' the electoral process. The EU had already warned Maduro since February 2018 that it would not recognise the election result. Following 10 January 2019, when Maduro's new mandate began, most of the international community – including the vast majority of the major European nations – did not recognise him as a legitimate president.[8]

6 O. Solon, 'How Syria's White Helmets became victims of an online propaganda machine', *The Guardian*, 18 December 2017, https://www.theguardian.com/world/2017/dec/18/syria-white-helmets-conspiracy-theories.

7 I. Bremmer, 'Foreign powers align against Venezuela's Nicolas Maduro', *Kathimerini*, 10 February 2019, http://www.ekathimerini.com/237517/article/ekathimerini/comment/foreign-powers-align-against-venezuelas-nicolas-maduro.

8 C. Abellan Matamoros, 'Venezuela: European countries send Maduro major ultimatum', *euronews*, 27 January 2019, https://www.euronews.com/2019/01/26/venezuelan-president-maduro-accuses-washington-of-coup-attempt.

4. THE RUSSIAN PARADOX

However, the most striking example is that of the popularity of Russia in Greece. Russian President Vladimir Putin is regarded as the great leader-protector of Orthodox Christianity, the man that upholds the moral values that the West has supposedly lost, and as someone who will eventually help Greece to overcome the influence of EU and the US, which for many is the reason (among others) why Greece entered an economic crisis in 2009 and eventually defaulted on its debts. Far-right and less frequently far-left figures consider Putin an ally in the resistance against the West, notably the US and Germany. Putin is the most popular politician in Greece, with 30 per cent of Greeks considering him to be the ideal leader. On the other hand, only 0.8 per cent consider Alexis Tsipras, the then Prime Minister, as the best possible choice to lead Greece.[9]

Greece's lasting economic crisis brought forward the idea that Russia could help overcome it. Rumours that circulated in 2011 and 2015 called for Moscow to provide Greece with a loan up to $10 billion in order to escape the grip of Greece's Western creditors. In 2015, the Greek government allegedly asked for, or was offered, an emergency loan from Russia, although this was never given. Most of these rumours were never confirmed (although some were even peddled by officials belonging to the pro-Grexit/pro-Russian faction, which was later removed from the government), but Russia's image in Greece was elevated.

Russia's influence in Greece goes far beyond the deployment of 'fake news', as the Atlantic Council, a think tank in Washington, DC, observed back in November 2017:

> Russian oligarchs with close ties to the Kremlin have bought stakes in Greek media. Russia's state-owned gas giant, Gazprom, purchased large stakes in Greek energy firms. And most notably, Putin has maintained a close relationship with the Greek leadership. Whereas Russia sees an ally in the left-wing government [this has changed – see below], it also supports a party on the opposite side of the political spectrum: the far right and ultra nationalist Golden Dawn party.[10]

European Values, a non-governmental organisation (NGO) based in the Czech Republic, claimed in May 2018 that Greece and Cyprus are the least effective among the EU countries when it comes to combating Russian-spread fake news. The NGO accused Greece that it not only avoided making efforts to curtail the influence of Russia in Greece, but that it collaborated in order to spread 'fake news' showing Russia in a favourable light.

---

9 DiaNEOsis, 'What Greeks Believe', March 2018, https://www.dianeosis.org/wp-content/uploads/2018/06/Ti_Pistevoun_Oi_Ellines_2018_Upd_%20040618.pdf.

10 Atlantic Council, 'The Kremlin's Trojan Horses 2', November 2017, https://www.atlanticcouncil.org/publications/reports/the-kremlin-s-trojan-horses-2-0.

Although the findings of European Values might be slightly exaggerated, some facts need to be taken into account when we look at the influence of Russian fake news in Greece. As already mentioned, Russian leader Vladimir Putin enjoys great popularity in Greece. Russia is seen by many as a 'homogeneous' nation, with a common religious background, goals and enemies. However, this misconception is misleading, because Russia's foreign policy is always dictated by its own interests, which at the moment *does not* coincide with those of Greece (for example, see below on the EastMed pipeline).

However, this fails to discourage a large portion of the electronic media from promoting ideas of a Greek-Russian approach on issues ranging from economic to armament collaborations. It is worth noting that these media very often reproduce fake news and propaganda touted by Kremlin-controlled media, such as Sputnik, RT and TASS. Greece lacks a protection mechanism to stop the dissemination of Russian fake news because, unlike other European countries that have taken active measures to 'shield' themselves against this, Greece does not have anything like that, except for a few private initiatives which are few and far between.[11]

Although Russia's 'soft power' has not changed when it comes to the Greek media, the Greek government came very close to severing diplomatic ties with Russia in August 2018 when two diplomats were expelled for trying to influence Greek officials and public opinion on the Prespa agreement. This agreement was reached on 12 June 2018 between Greece and North Macedonia under the United Nations' auspices, resolving a long-standing dispute over the latter's name. Russia responded with tit-for-tat measures, and although both sides later claimed that all issues were resolved, the Greek–American rapprochement on diplomatic and military level practically meant that the Greek government would no longer allow Russian interference.[12]

However, Russian 'soft power' in Greece is projected to last for many decades by those who rely upon ambiguous prophecies and a common religious background. This should not be expected to change anytime soon.

---

11 T. Sitistas, 'Greece and Cyprus "Kremlin partners" on fake news according to European think tank', *Ellinika Hoaxes*, 17 May 2018, https://www.ellinikahoaxes.gr/2018/05/17/greece-and-cyprus-kremlin-collaborators; Atlantic Council, *supra* note 10; D. Alandete, 'Which European democracies are best combating Russian disinformation?', *El Pais*, 13 May 2018, https://elpais.com/elpais/2018/05/11/inenglish/1526039604_758778.html.

12 A. Osborn, 'Russia expels Greek diplomats in retaliatory move', *Reuters*, 6 August 2018, https://www.reuters.com/article/us-greece-russia-envoy/russia-expels-greek-diplomats-in-retaliatory-move-idUSKBN1KR1L2; A. Koutantou and M. Kambas, 'Greece, Russia to expel diplomats in Macedonia tussle ahead of NATO summit', *Reuters*, 11 July 2018, https://www.reuters.com/article/us-greece-russia-diplomats/greece-russia-to-expel-diplomats-in-macedonia-tussle-ahead-of-nato-summit-idUSKBN1K10PU.

5. *TO KSANTHO GENOS*: THE BLOND RACE

For many years, even before the Greek Revolution of 1821, a myth has been cultivated in Greece that Russia, the 'blond race' (meaning the fair coloured hair of the Russian people), is a close ally of Greece that is always standing beside it. Despite the fact that there is no historical evidence to substantiate this view (in fact, Russian foreign policy has often been against Greece), this perception is common even to this day.

In circa 1751, Greek cleric and scholar Theoklitos Polyeides published *The Vision of Agathangelos*, which refers to a priest-monk by the name of Ieronymos Agathangelos who supposedly experienced a prophetic vision while he was in Messina in Italy in 1279 in which several prophecies were foretold to him. It is well known that the 'prophecies' were a forgery and were conceived and written by Polyeides and they are obscure, ambiguous and vague so that they can be interpreted in many ways. According to the 'prophecies', Greece would become the world's leading country through Orthodox Christianity, following the creation of a new Byzantine Empire by 1840, with the help of the 'blond race', which Agathangelos foresaw coming from Russia. Later additions amplified the 'blond race' notion in the prophetic myth, and while by the mid-18th century the Ottoman Empire was in decay, the notion is still well entertained by Greek nationalist circles. Specifically, the 'blond race' story was linked even more with *The Vision of Agathangelos*, after the Russo-Turkish wars of 1768–1774 and 1787–1792, both resulting in Russian victories.[13] These events increased the belief in Russia's role as the savior-protector of Greece, despite the fact that the 1770 Orlov revolt in Greece, instigated by Russia to distract Ottoman forces from their engagement in the Russo-Turkish wars of 1768–1774, ended in complete failure and led to massacres amongst the Greek population.[14] According to professor of history Lucien J. Frary, a rebellion in Acarnania against the (appointed by the Great Powers) Bavarian Regency's ecclesiastical reforms in 1836 was inspired by the Agathangelos stories. The first three published editions would appear between 1837 and 1838 (until then, the 'prophecies' circulated in pamphlets), when Russophiles were gaining more influence in the government and the Holy Synod.[15]

---

13 P. Mitev, I. Parvev, M. Baramova and V. Racheva (eds.), *Empires and Peninsulas: Southeastern Europe between Karlowitz and the Peace of Adrianople, 1699–1829*, LIT Verlag, Münster 2010, p. 268.

14 G.F. Nafziger and M.W. Walton, *Islam at War: A History*, Praeger Publishers, Westport CT 2003, p. 76.

15 L.J. Frary, *Russia and the Making of Modern Greek Identity, 1821–1844*, Oxford University Press, Oxford 2015.

A large number of 'prophecies' by Greek saints and monks, which for the most part have an irredentist character and claim that Istanbul (Constantinople in Greek) will once again come under Greek control, either by divine intervention or assistance from the Russians (or both), are widespread in many electronic publications. The most famous 'prophecies' come from a (now sanctified by the Greek Church) monk by the name 'Elder Paisios', who supposedly, among others, prophesied about the 'blond race' and their role in helping Greece restore its so-called Byzantine glory.

His most famous prophecies – some totally fictitious, the rest usually exaggerated or misrepresented by the Greek media – include the following:

- Hexamilia [Six miles – referring to the six nautical miles of Greek territorial waters] 'When the Turkish fleet starts [its attack] against Greece and reaches six miles, it will actually be destroyed. They have the koliva (memorial wheat) in their belts', meaning that their death will be imminent.
- 'Turks may harm a couple of [Greek] islands. They will be hungry in Greece, which will last for several months.'
- 'Then the Russian will intervene [in favour of Greece] and it will be as the Saint Kosmas prophecy says.'
- 'Turkey will be dissolved by its own allies. Their nation will be wiped out, and all of Turkey will turn into a desolate desert. One will have to walk for seven hours before coming across another person!'
- 'Turkey will be partitioned into 3–4 pieces. The countdown has already begun. We [the Greeks] will get our share, the Armenians and the Kurds will get theirs. The Kurdish "issue" has already been arranged to be resolved.'
- 'I remembered then that St. Methodius of Patara said in his prophecy "... and the Russians will keep Eptalofon [Seven Hills, associated with Constantinople], and the blond race will plant cabbage". Those are the Russians who will keep the city as long as the cabbages last [i.e. 5–6 months] [and they will pass it on to the Greeks].'

Although these 'prophecies' often contradict each other, they are widely popular in Greece. As mentioned above, any article (mostly on online media) referring to prophecies by saints, monks and elders is shared hundreds if not thousands of times via social media.

Thus, it is quite common that Greeks view Putin, Russian weapons technology and generally Russian superiority as if they are better than those of the EU/NATO/US. These myths have been systematically cultivated over the years, and fake news has played its part in enhancing these misconceptions. Russia, which over the last few decades has overcome the shock of the collapse of the Soviet Union, has gradually become a capitalist superpower, leading its admirers in Greece to expect that Russia will come to its rescue if need be.

However, pro-Russian news and several popular websites do not mention that at present, Greece's interests are on a collision course with those of Russia. For instance, reports about EastMed, a Greek-Cypriot-Israeli pipeline that will bring East Mediterranean gas to Europe and will help diversify its natural gas imports (most of the EU's natural gas comes from Russia), usually remain obscure, are never mentioned or are mentioned in a demeaning or disapproving manner.

Another issue that has troubled Greek–Russian relations recently is the North Macedonia name issue. In July 2018, Greece decided to expel two Russian diplomats, suspected of meddling in the politically sensitive issue of 'Macedonia'. They were accused of attempting to influence rally organisers, who protested against the Prespa agreement. There were also reports that the same individuals attempted to bribe Greek officials. The root cause behind Russia's attempt to undermine the Prespa agreement is that it would lift Greece's standing veto and would allow North Macedonia to join NATO, thus depriving Russia of a significant foothold in the Balkans.

In the days leading up to the signature of the Prespa agreement, there was a spike in fake news, ranging from the true content of the agreement to what was really going on in the demonstrations involving those protesting against the agreement.

There were two stories that gained great traction, especially through social media. Popular news outlets published a picture of a woman allegedly killed by the Greek riot police. The story went on to become viral via social media, although it was debunked in just a few hours by Ellinika Hoaxes.

The second fake news story that went viral claimed that NATO military riot police from the South-Eastern Europe Brigade (SEEBRIG), which resides in Tyrnavos, was used to crash the protests. Facebook posts and articles in various blogs and websites published a picture of a Greek police officer, claiming that he was the Romanian Commander of SEEBRIG and was the one who was coordinating his forces against the Greek demonstrators. Thousands of readers and social media users fell for this story and called for his immediate assassination by any means possible. This claim was also debunked by Ellinika Hoaxes.

The Greek legal system provides criminal penalties for defamation; however, in most prosecuted cases, defendants are acquitted or simply forced to pay a symbolic fee. Defamation articles, usually based on fake news, are seldom prosecuted and are almost never punished. In fact, the first ever conviction of a website owner for spreading fake news about vaccines took place in 2016 and was largely based on a fact-check published by Ellinika Hoaxes in 2014.

6. ECONOMIC CRISES AND FAKE NEWS IN GREECE

Each new major crisis, whether economic or otherwise, causes an outbreak in fake news and conspiracy theories. Greeks have the long-standing notion that all their hardships come, for the most part, from Western governments, individuals and institutions. For instance, Germany, the US, George Soros, various NGOs, etc., are targeted even by the mainstream media. Especially in Greece, the financial crisis had an impact on the quality of journalistic work and the freedom of the press has diminished significantly, while at the same time has multiplied and exacerbated beliefs in conspiracy theories. One characteristic example was the alleged collaboration of SYRIZA's controversial Minister of Finance, Yanis Varoufakis, with George Soros, a conspiracy theory peddled even by popular right- and left-wing political figures, as well as the mainstream media.

Press freedom sharply eroded in Greece during the economic and financial crisis of 2010–2015, with the country falling from 35th place in 2009 in the Reporters Without Borders Press Freedom Index to 99th place in 2014, well below all Western Balkans countries as well as states with repressive media policies such as Gabon, Kuwait and Liberia. Although there seemed to be an improvement in the following years (Greece's was ranked 91st in 2015, 89th in 2016, 88th in 2017 and 71st in 2018), local media are considered far from independent, because the country's widespread patronage system has negatively impacted the press and has silenced the voices of independent and investigative journalists, especially after the establishment of the private TV channels and radio stations.[16]

As Open Democracy has stated:

> The market is controlled by a few powerful interests who dominate the national discussion through their newspapers, television stations, and online outlets, stifling the influence of voices and narratives outside the establishment and exerting strict control over independent journalists.

In this context, shutting down Greece's public broadcaster Hellenic Broadcasting Corporation (ERT) in 2013 by the then Conservative-Socialist coalition government further damaged pluralism in the domestic media landscape.

The economic crisis revealed the unsustainability of Greek media and their dependence on state advertisement and tax breaks, which in turn forced these media to publish stories favourable to the government. Things would become even worse when public funds dried up, leading to many media bankruptcies, while the government resorted to more aggressive tactics like coercion, censorship and shutdowns. Journalists themselves would resort to self-censorship and the printing of 'acceptable' stories in order to keep their jobs.[17] In this volatile environment, the tough solutions about Europe's economic crisis came with a political cost. Between 2013 and 2015, voters throughout the EU vented their

16 P. Iosifidis, 'Greek media and independent journalism under austerity', *Open Democracy*, 25 May 2016, https://www.opendemocracy.net/en/opendemocracyuk/greek-media-and-independent-journalism-under-austerity/.

17 Van Der Heijden, *supra* note 2.

fury against the austerity measures decided in Brussels and implemented by their governments. Most blamed the 'dictatorial' way in which the EU had dealt with the crisis. In the European elections of 2014, populist movements on the right and the left of the political spectrum made spectacular gains. This was already more obvious in Greece by 2012, when the Neo-Nazi, ultra-nationalist party Golden Dawn received seven per cent of the total votes, and elected MPs for the first time in the Greek Parliament. The same party won three seats in the European Parliament in 2014. In 2015 in Greece, five years after the beginning of the economic crisis, the radical left-wing SYRIZA (Coalition of Radical Left) party won the national elections, promising to scrap austerity by repealing all unpopular economic measures taken by previous governments. SYRIZA collaborated with ANEL (Independent Greeks) a national-conservative, populist party to form a government. It is worth noting that every single Greek government since the beginning of the economic crisis in 2009, adopted populist rhetoric, promising to prevent or scrap austerity. George Papandreou, the leader and later Prime Minister (2009–11) of the centre-left PASOK party, was quoted in 2009 as saying 'Money exists'. Prior to the 2014 elections, Antonis Samaras, elected Prime Minister in 2012 on an anti-austerity rhetoric, and leader of centre-right Nea Dimokratia party, proclaimed 'For the past two years, I'm ripping up Memorandums'. However, every single government was forced to sign or support three bailout plans (2010, 2012 and 2015) with harsh economic measures, in order to avoid the defaulting of the Greek economy.[18] Alexis Tsipras would become Prime Minister (2015–19) of the EU's first populist government. SYRIZA, however, relied on a strategy of transformation – from radical left to social democrat – to ensure its longer-term political survival. 'Greece was the first country that experienced the peak of populism. And then it was deflated', according to George Pagoulatos, Professor at the Athens University of Economics and Business.[19]

Populism and fake or 'acceptable' and 'favourable' news usually go hand in hand, and the same is true of the radical politicians who gained popularity in Greece. The 2015 SYRIZA–ANEL government (ANEL is a conservative right-wing populist party that collaborated with SYRIZA to form a government) was elected by promising to scrap austerity and fight back against the EU establishment that 'tramples upon the weak countries'. In this context, the use of populist rhetoric against the EU and especially Germany was not uncommon. Prime Minister Tsipras was quoted as saying 'Go back Madame Merkel',

---

18 V. Samara, 'The eight years that shook society and the political scene, *news 24 7*, 20 August 2018, https://www.news247.gr/politiki/ta-okto-chronia-poy-sygklonisan-tin-koinonia-kai-to politiko-skiniko.6641393.html.

19 M. Birnbaum, 'Greek elections are expected to bring a populist experiment to an end, *The Washington Post*, 5 July 2019, https://www.washingtonpost.com/world/euroe/greece-experimented-with-leftist-populism-now-its-going-back-to-the-status-quo/2019/07/04/c0dd41ce-99b8-11e9-9a16-dc551ea5a43b_story.html.

referring to the perceived notion that the German Chancellor, Angela Merkel, was responsible for Greece's economic hardships.

The Greek government eventually complied with EU mandates and continued austerity, despite the fact that a referendum (which was supported by SYRIZA–ANEL) rejected by a majority of over 61 per cent the European Commission, the International Monetary Fund and the European Central Bank bailout plan. Despite the result of the referendum, on 13 July 2015 the government of Tsipras reached an agreement with the European authorities for a three-year bailout with even harsher austerity conditions than those rejected by the voters. This represented a 'drastic turnaround' for Prime Minister Tsipras' position, as he had been elected on an anti-austerity platform.[20]

It is worth noting that right up to the point of the referendum, pro-SYRIZA and even the centre-left media promised that the government would scrap austerity. For instance, on its front page, the *Avgi* newspaper wrote on 26 June 2015 'Memorandum, forget it' ('Memorandum' refers to the Economic Adjustment Programme for Greece, better known as the bailout programme). The following day, the same newspaper would write 'NO to blackmails and ultimatums, social bankruptcy, memorandums and austerity'. After the bailout programme was signed, and even harsher austerity was imposed, the newspaper claimed that the new bailout was much more preferable than the ones imposed by the previous governments. Such populist and often fake stories reflect the impact that these forms of media had on Greek voters.

7. THE ECONOMIC CRISIS AND CONSPIRACY THEORIES

The 2009 economic crisis that still troubles Greece gave birth to new conspiracy theories, while amplifying pre-existing ones. These conspiracy theories are all too often intertwined with fake news, and pre-existing misconceptions, to enhance their traction on public opinion and gain more popularity.

A survey conducted in June 2014 by the University of Macedonia, the International Hellenic University and the University of Oxford was presented at a conference on anti-semitism in Berlin. The survey found that urban legends and conspiracy theories have increased in the previous few years. According to the data, 75.25 per cent of the people who participated in the survey believed that the Greek economic crisis was planned by various non-institutional organisations, 68.66 per cent supported the theory that a drug to cure cancer has been found

20 G. Steinhauser and T. Fairless, 'Greece Requests Three-Year Bailout in First Step Toward Meeting Creditors' Demand', *The Wall Street Journal*, 8 July 2015, https://www.wsj.com/articles/greek-prime-minister-pledges-concrete-proposals-to-bridge-creditor-impasse-1436348229.

but has not been made available to the public yet, and 58.74 per cent claimed that the attack on the Twin Towers was the result of a well-organised plan of the US to impose its foreign policy. A total of 27 per cent of survey participants also believed that Neil Armstrong's moon landing in 1969 was staged in a remote location and 60.86 per cent believed that former Greek Prime Minister Costas Simitis has Jewish origins. 'This kind of suspicion is linked with two major findings: the low social trust of Greeks and a lack of education', said Dr Elias Dinas of the University of Oxford.[21]

8. THE GREEK PROBLEM OF MEDIA LITERACY AND FREEDOM OF THE PRESS

According to the 2018 Media Literacy Index:

> The countries worst equipped to resist the post-truth, fake news and their ramifications are the countries in Southeast Europe – all the way from Croatia to Turkey – as well as their close neighbours Hungary and Cyprus. As a rule, the reasons for the low results are poor or mediocre education performance and controlled media. Such countries are the most likely to be vulnerable to fake news and ensuing negative effects.[22]

Greece scored 39 out of 100 in media literacy and 32 out of 100 in media freedom. More specifically, on the Freedom of the Press (Freedom House) Index, on a scale of 0 to 100, Greece scored 44. On the Press Freedom Index (Reporters Without Borders), on a scale of 0 to 100, Greece scored 30.89. On the PISA score in reading literacy (OECD), Greece scored 467 (the higher the score, the better; 500 is very good and below 300 is a very poor result), on the PISA score in scientific literacy (OECD), it scored 455 and on the PISA score in mathematical literacy (OECD), it scored 454. On the share of population with a university degree (Eurostat), it scored 26.4 per cent. On trust in others (Eurostat, European Quality of Life Survey), it scored 5.3 out of 10. On the E-participation Index (UN), it scored 0.610 out of 1. Combining all of the above factors, Greece ranked 27th out of 35 European countries in the 2018 Media Literacy Index.

It is worth noting that although the privately-owned TV stations spread various conspiracy theories in the Greek public, these theories did not become the subject of broad scientific research in Greece, perhaps because of their exaggeration or even because of the metaphysical element involved in their dissemination.

---

21 G. Antoniou, E. Dinas, S. Kosmidis and L. Saltiel, 'Antisemitism in Greece: Evidence from a Representative Survey', August 2014, https://www.osservatorioantisemitismo.it/wp-content/uploads/2014/09/Antisemitism_in_Greece_survey.pdf.

22 The 2018 Media Literacy Index, http://osi.bg/downloads/File/2018/MediaLiteracyIndex2018_publish ENG.pdf.

However, this does not mean that such conspiracy theories do not enjoy popularity among the Greeks, especially those referring to the so-called 'Greek superiority' and the uniqueness of the Greek element (Hellenocentrism), and the dozens of stories about how Greece is in the crosshairs of imaginary enemies, including Zionism, the US, Germany and the EU, which are viewed as being responsible for, among other things, orchestrating the Greek economic crisis. Zizakou mentions that Greek conspiracy theories and urban legends tend to place lies and distortions behind a lot of significant personalities and stories.[23] Antoniou et al. found in their survey that urban legends and conspiracy theories have increased in the last few years and are attributed to the low level of social trust shown by Greeks and their lack of education.[24]

9. GREECE AND POPULISM: A RECENT EXAMPLE

Greeks have always been very susceptible to populist politicians. Perhaps the most recent and characteristic example is that of Kyriakos Velopoulos, President of the 'Elliniki Lysi' (Greek Solution) party, which was established in 2016. Even though this party is relatively new, according to the polls, soon it will be able to pick up seats by itself.[25]

As mentioned above, a significant percentage of Greeks believe in the supremacy of the Greek element, and usually because of that, Greece is placed in a position where it has to fend off powerful enemies by itself. According to the Pew Research Center:

> The most chauvinistic attitudes towards culture were recorded across Eastern Europe with Romania (66 percent), Bulgaria (69 percent) and Russia (also 69 percent) on top. The highest score of any country across Europe was actually recorded in Greece where 89 percent of people agreed with the statement 'our people are not perfect but our culture is superior to others'.[26]

If we add the common belief that Putin's Russia is the only 'reasonable ally' against Greece's enemies, we have an explosive mixture of conspiracy theories

---

23 See *supra* note 18.

24 G. Antoniou, E. Dinas, S. Kosmidis and L. Saltiel, 'Antisemitism in Greece: Evidence from a Representative Survey', 2014, https://osservatorioantisemi-c02.kxcdn.com/wp-content/uploads/2014/09/Antisemitism_in_Greece_survey.pdf; Kourdis, *supra* note 1.

25 Open Society Foundations, 'North Macedonia: What's Next?', January 2019, https://www.opensocietyfoundations.org/publications/north-macedonia-what-s-next.

26 Pew Research Center, 'Eastern and Western Europeans Differ on Importance of Religion, Views of Minorities, and Key Social Issues', 29 October 2018, https://www.pewforum.org/2018/10/29/eastern-and-western-europeans-differ-on-importance-of-religion-views-of-minorities-and-key-social-issues/.

and fake news that can be bent by someone (in our case Kyriakos Velopoulos) to create a populist movement, with significant support from Greek voters.

Velopoulos became known as a book salesman through TV shows. As a journalist, he worked in a number of radio and television stations, such as TV Thessaloniki, *ΕΡΜΗΣ* (HERMES), BEST, TOP, ORION and TeleAsty, where he presented his two major shows, *Η ΒΟΥΛΗ* (VOULI) and *ΕΛΛΗΝΟΡΑΜΑ* (ELLINORAMA), on which he promoted his books. Today, he appears on Kontra Channel, Extra Channel and Alert TV, where he presents his shows that include book and food supplement sales, and political and geopolitical analysis of current affairs in Greece, the Eastern Mediterranean, the Balkans and the Middle East. His shows are rebroadcasted by a number of other regional channels, giving him access to a national audience. He also controls the voicenews.gr website, which is dedicated mostly in promoting his agenda. He was a member of the Popular Orthodox Rally, the right nationalist populist party of Georgios Karatzaferis, for which he was a candidate in the 2004 Greek parliamentary elections. In the parliamentary elections of 2007 and 2009, he was elected in the B prefecture of Thessaloniki. Since 2016, he has been President of the Greek Solution political party (Ελληνική Λύση).

The problem with Mr Velopoulos is that his 'fierce' analyses in current affairs (including immigration, the so-called death of core Western values, etc.) are packed with fake news and conspiracy theories. For instance, he has claimed that Archbishop Christodoulos – a very popular religious figure in Greece – who died of cancer in 2008, was assassinated by foreign powers that were afraid of his popularity among the Greeks (a widely held conspiracy theory that has been debunked).[27] He has also claimed that wildfires that often devastate forests in Greece are the result of arson by those that wish to build wind turbines in their place, despite the fact that Greek law forbids any economic use of burned land.[28]

Last but not least, Velopoulos has claimed that toothpastes contain fluoride, which, according to him, is a by-product of nuclear waste, while at the same time promoted his own herb-based toothpastes, which are fluoride-free.[29] He also often makes bold claims about the superiority of Russian-made weapons systems, which (if bought) could make Greece a regional superpower. His most profound lie was when he claimed to possess and put up for sale letters that were

27 T. Sitistas, 'Christodoulou's death and conspiracy theories', *Ellinika Hoaxes*, 21 September 2018, https://www.ellinikahoaxes.gr/2018/09/21/christodoulos-death-rumors-and-facts.

28 T. Sitistas, 'No wind turbines were built after fires in Evia on August 1, 2016', *Ellinika Hoaxes*, 6 August 2018, https://www.ellinikahoaxes.gr/2018/08/06/euboea-wildfires-wind-turbines-hoax/.

29 T. Sitistas, 'Velopoulos claims that fluoride toothpaste is a derivative of nuclear waste', *Ellinika Hoaxes*, 26 September 2017, https://www.ellinikahoaxes.gr/2017/09/26/velopoulos-hoax/.

handwritten by Jesus himself.[30] All of these stories were debunked by Ellinika Hoaxes.

Velopoulos is an adamant supporter of a Greek–Russian alliance and a fierce opponent critic of EU and US policies. He presents himself and his party as the only ones that fight against evil (a term that is often not defined) foreign powers, institutions and individuals that seek to 'dismember' Greece. Those 'enemies' include the US, the EU, Germany, Angela Merkel, the Open Society Foundation, George Soros, the mainstream media, immigrants and refugees. Velopoulos' populistic rhetoric matches that of the Kremlin and other EU right-wing populist leaders and officials, like Hungary's Viktor Orban, Italy's Matteo Salvini and France's Marie Le Pen, all of whom either promote Eurosceptic views or are in open conflict with Brussels.

It should therefore come as no surprise, that anti-EU parties were on course 'to win one-third of seats in the European Parliament election in May 2019, which could "undermine and cause irreparable damage" in areas such as trade, security and defence', according to a recently published study by the European Council of Foreign Relations (ECFR), a Berlin-based think tank.[31]

As Politico points out:

> Currently around 23 percent of MEPs belong to anti-EU parties ranging from the far left to the far right, but this number could jump to at least 33 percent, according to the report. Despite deep divisions across the anti-European movement, the report said legislators are likely to form alliances to inhibit Europe's ability to work on 'foreign policy, Eurozone reform, and freedom of movement'. In addition, these alliances could 'limit the EU's capacity to preserve European values relating to liberty of expression, the rule of law, and civil rights'.[32]

Euroscepticism, often based on fake news, opportunism, propaganda and conspiracy theories, has undoubtedly driven a wedge between EU Member States, causes hostility towards the EU and enhances (sometimes pre-existing) divisions across Europe about the basic nature, purpose and architecture of the EU. Although the problems presented in relation to EU cohesion by these populist parties like Five Stars in Italy and Rassemblement National in France have been thoroughly discussed, the same is not true of Greece's populist fervour.

---

30 T. Sitistas, 'Velopoulos claims that Jesus's hand written letters are genuine', *Ellinika Hoaxes*, 11 November 2018, https://www.ellinikahoaxes.gr/2018/11/11/velopoulos-jesus-letters/.

31 S. Dennison and P. Zerka, 'The 2019 European Election: How Anti-Europeans Plan to Wreck Europe and What can be Done to Stop it', *European Council on Foreign Relations*, February 2019, https://www.ecfr.eu/specials/scorecard/the_2019_European_election.

32 E. Schaart, 'Study: Anti-EU parties set to win third of seats in May election', *politico.eu*, 2 November 2019, https://web.archive.org/web/20190211174656/https:/www.politico.eu/article/study-anti-eu-parties-set-to-win-third-of-seats-in-may-election/.

Euroscepticism is on the rise in Greece and no one can predict its future repercussions. What we can say for sure is that as long as nothing is done to address the issue, Greece could witness far-right populist parties participating in governments by cooperating with more or less mainstream parties (like ANEL joining SYRIZA to form a government in 2015).

10. CONCLUSION

Greece was already poorly equipped to battle fake news even before 2009. The economic crisis that started ten years ago managed to make things even worse. Greeks already had a poor understanding of what caused the country's economic downfall and they would rather attribute it to 'foreign powers', both existing (e.g. Germany) and imaginary (e.g. Zionism), than accepting even the slightest responsibility. From that point on, it was relatively easy for fake news and conspiracy theories to thrive. The same is true of populist politicians, who took advantage of Greek's lack of media literacy to promote promises that were simply too good to be true. As Greece emerges from ten years of harsh austerity, the challenges remain the same. Athens still has a long way to go before it becomes economically independent, and populist politicians taking advantage of the continuing hardships still manage to gain lots of traction among voters.

10. DIGITAL DISINFORMATION IN A DEEPLY DIVIDED SOCIETY

Reflections from Northern Ireland

Paul REILLY*

1. INTRODUCTION

Despite its supposed central role in electoral 'shocks' such as Donald Trump's election as US President in November 2016, 'fake news' remains one of the most popular misnomers of the 21st century. Members of the public broadly agree that it refers to 'news articles that are intentionally and verifiably false'.[1] Yet, it is also a pejorative term used by politicians to discredit media outlets that are critical of their conduct in office. By way of response, scholars characterise the current 'post-truth' era as a crisis born of the entire information ecosystem, not just the mainstream media. They argue that information disorders, such as the intentional sharing of false information to cause harm to others (disinformation) and the inadvertent sharing of such information (misinformation), are more appropriate conceptual frameworks for analysing the threat of information pollution to liberal democracies.[2] Nevertheless, much of the empirical research in this field has concentrated on the supposed effects of digital disinformation, manufactured in 'fake news factories' for the financial gain of their 'workers' and amplified on social media by bots, on voting behaviour during national elections and referenda between 2015 and 2017.[3] This is despite the fact that these 'pure' forms of 'fake news' have been virtually non-existent in most countries during this period.[4]

---

* Information School, University of Sheffield, UK. Email: p.j.reilly@sheffield.ac.uk.

1 H. ALLCOTT and M. GENTZKOW, 'Social media and fake news in the 2016 election' (2017) 31(2) *Journal of Economic Perspectives* 211, p. 213.

2 C. WARDLE 'Fake news. It's complicated', *First Draft News*, 2017, available at: https://firstdraftnews.com:443/fake-news-complicated.

3 D. GHOSH and B. SCOTT, '#Digitaldeceit: the technologies behind the precision propaganda on the Internet', New America, Public Interest Technology and Shorenstein Center, 2018.

4 A. CHADWICK, C. VACCARI and B. O'LOUGHLIN, 'Do tabloids poison the well of social media? Explaining democratically dysfunctional news sharing' (2018) *New Media & Society*, 1, 4.

There have been few studies exploring the impact of digital disinformation within deeply divided societies. Anti-Muslim riots in Myanmar in July 2014 were blamed on an unsubstantiated rumour spread on Facebook claiming that the proprietor of a Muslim tea shop had raped a Buddhist employee.[5] The circulation of false stories on the same platform suggesting that Muslims were planning to violently overthrow the Buddhist majority were linked to sectarian violence in Sri Lanka in March 2018.[6] Although there have been no such incidents in Northern Ireland to date, the limited empirical data available thus far suggests that false or fabricated content about contentious parades and related protests have a very short lifespan on social media and thus have limited influence on 'real-world' events.[7] This chapter builds on this work by presenting the first in-depth study of digital disinformation in 'post-conflict' Northern Ireland. It does so by providing an overview of the emergent literature on information disorders, as well as efforts to mitigate their impact on democratic processes such as elections and referenda. It then moves on to explore how propaganda was deployed by state and non-state actors during the 30-year conflict known colloquially as 'the Troubles'. Recent empirical research on the role of Facebook and Twitter in spreading disinformation during contentious parades and related protests will be elaborated upon in order to explore how Northern Irish citizens have responded to deliberately false content shared via social media. Public opinion data from organisations such as Ofcom will also be analysed in order to explore the apparent decline in public trust in both professional news media and political institutions in the divided society, which are key characteristics of the information crisis facing contemporary democracies.[8]

2. THE CHALLENGE OF 'FAKE NEWS' TO MEDIA AND POLITICS

2.1. FAKE NEWS AND TRUST IN MAINSTREAM MEDIA

Over the past 18 months, the term 'fake news' has become synonymous with US President Donald Trump's efforts to cast doubt upon the credibility of the mainstream media, presumably in response to their unfavourable coverage of him in the run-up to the 2016 US presidential election. Subsequent research showed that there were in fact nearly three times as many fake news items

---

5 S. Stanley, 'Misinformation and hate speech in Myanmar', 16 May 2017, available at: https://firstdraftnews.org/misinformation-myanmar.

6 A. Taub and M. Fisher, 'Where countries are tinderboxes and Facebook is a match', *New York Times*, 22 April 2018.

7 P.J. Reilly, 'Rumours, mis- and disinformation in divided societies: Twitter and the Ardoyne parade dispute', *New Social Media, New Social Science?*, 12 April 2018.

8 LSE Commission on Truth, Trust and Technology, *Tackling the Information Crisis: A Policy Framework for Media System Resilience*. London: LSE Press, 2018.

that were supportive of Trump compared to his Democratic opponent Hillary Clinton; these were said to have had a modest but significant impact on the voting decisions of those who had previously voted for Barack Obama in 2012, resulting in Trump victories in key swing states including Pennsylvania and Wisconsin.[9] Far-right groups were said to have wielded undue influence on the news agenda in the run-up to the election through their strategic use of disinformation, memes and social bots to share content with partisan news outlets and mainstream media.[10] Trump may have been the most well-known, but he was not the only politician during this period to accuse professional journalists of peddling 'fake news'. Pertinent to this chapter, Democratic Unionist Party (DUP) Member of the Legislative Assembly (MLA) Jeffrey Donaldson dismissed the 'fake' media reports in October 2017, which suggested that £1 billion funding resulting from the party's confidence and supply deal with the minority Conservative government was under threat.[11]

Whether similar efforts to de-legitimise mainstream media are successful or not remains to be seen. Certainly, perceptions of media bias and sensationalism have been linked to a decline in public trust in news media organisations in countries such as Germany, Spain and the UK in recent years.[12] However, a public consultation into disinformation across EU Member States found that traditional newspapers were still the most trusted information source, with social media being the least trustworthy.[13] An audience-based study conducted across nine EU countries also found that more participants agreed (40 per cent) that the news media did a good job in helping separate fact from fiction than disagreed (25 per cent).[14] The UK 2018 Edelman Trust Barometer pointed to a significant increase in public trust in traditional media (from 48 per cent in 2017 to 61 per cent in 2018); in contrast, social media was only trusted by 24 per cent of respondents, with many calling for greater government regulation of these companies.[15] One interpretation of these findings is that this 'renewal' in public

---

9 H. Allcott and M. Gentzkow, *supra* note 1; R. Gunther, P.A. Beck and E.C. Nisbet, 'Fake news may have contributed to Trump's 2016 victory', 8 March 2018, available at: https://assets.documentcloud.org/documents/4429952/Fake-News-May-Have-Contributed-to-Trump-s-2016.pdf.

10 A. Marwick and R. Lewis, *Media Manipulation and Disinformation Online*. New York: Data & Society Research Institute, 2017.

11 A. McGonagle, 'Jeffrey Donaldson brands claims that DUP's £1bn from Tories under threat as "fake news"', *The Irish News*, 31 October 2017.

12 N. Newman and R. Fletcher, *Bias, Bullshit and Lies: Audience Perspectives on Low Trust in the Media*. Oxford: Reuters Institute for the Study of Journalism, 2017.

13 European Commission, 'Summary report of the public consultation on fake news and online disinformation', 2018, p. 2, available at: https://ec.europa.eu/digital-single-market/en/news/summary-report-public-consultation-fake-news-and-online-disinformation.

14 N. Newman and R. Fletcher, *supra* note 12, p. 6.

15 A total of 70 per cent of respondents felt social media companies did not do enough to prevent 'illegal and unethical' behaviours on their platforms. For more, see: https://www.edelman.co.uk/magazine/posts/edelman-trust-barometer-2018.

trust in traditional media correlates with an increasing cynicism about social media companies' commitment to eliminate 'anti-social' behaviour from their respective platforms.

2.2. INFORMATION DISORDERS

'Fake news' fails to encapsulate the complexities of how false information is created and shared on social media in order to sow confusion and disunity in democracies. It has been characterised as a 'floating signifier' deployed by politicians to project an image of how they think society should be structured.[16] The term was specifically criticised for being a form of propaganda on behalf of populist, reactionary ideologies such as those espoused by Trump.[17] Much of the empirical work in this area has characterised it as a problem co-constructed by a small but vocal minority of professional journalists and politicians and distributed via social media platforms.[18] A more nuanced framework for understanding this 'information crisis' was provided by researcher Claire Wardle, who asserted that these are problems relating to the pollution of information ecosystems, rather than being confined to professional news media. She identified three different types of 'information disorder' affecting democratic states:

1. misinformation: sharing false information without harmful intent;
2. disinformation: intentionally sharing false information to cause harm to others; and
3. malinformation: sharing accurate information with the purpose of causing harm to others.

This chapter focuses primarily on the second of these, namely the use of social media to disseminate false information with the intention of causing harm to others. It builds on a long history of scholarship addressing the use of propaganda, which can be defined as the purposeful manipulation of representations (including images, texts and videos) with the 'intention of producing any effect in the audience (e.g. action or inaction; reinforcement or transformation of feelings, ideas, attitudes or behaviours) that is desired by the propagandist'.[19] As far back as the late 1980s, it was argued that corporate

---

16 J. Farkas and J. Schou, 'Fake news as a floating signifier: hegemony, antagonism and the politics of falsehood' (2018) 25(3) *Javnost – The Public, Journal of the European Institute for Communication and Culture* 298.

17 J. Harcood-Coote, 'Stop talking about fake news!' (2019) 62(9) *Inquiry* 10.

18 R.K. Nielsen and L. Graves, '"News you don't believe": audience perspectives on fake news', Oxford: Reuters Institute for the Study of Journalism, 2017, p. 1.

19 E.L. Briant, *Propaganda and Counter-terrorism: Strategies for Global Change*. Manchester: Manchester University Press, 2015, p. 9.

media were ideological institutions that employed distorting filters in order to manipulate populations and 'manufacture consent' for elite hegemony.[20] Indeed, contemporary definitions of disinformation are congruent with the black and grey propaganda identified in this work; the former refers to covert campaigns that use falsehoods to generate behavioural change within a target audience, while the latter is characterised by uncertainty about the accuracy of the information as well as the validity of the source.[21] While acknowledging that these are not digitally oriented practices, it is undeniable that they can be 'turbocharged' by social media, which host public expression and organise access to it via mobile devices.[22] Yochai Benkler and colleagues defined this as a form of 'network propaganda' insofar as the 'architecture of a media ecosystem makes it more or less susceptible to disseminating these kinds of manipulations and lies'.[23] Much of the disinformation about Clinton and Trump during the 2016 US presidential election emanated from an insular right-wing media ecosystem, in which conspiracy theories and 'fake news' created by far-right groups online were amplified by partisan news outlets such as Breitbart and Fox News.[24] Repetition, a key component of such disinformation campaigns, was facilitated by online platforms that encouraged users to click, like and share content.[25] Its 'virality' was said to be considerably higher if it had a powerful narrative, a visual component, provoked high-arousal emotions and originated from sources that were trusted by digital citizens.[26] There has also been some research indicating that a new generation of tech-savvy journalists consider tweets to be as 'newsworthy' as headlines from more established sources, which may increase the risk that they will inadvertently focus attention on disinformation being shared online.[27] This suggests that, for the foreseeable future, social media will remain a fertile terrain for those who attempt to sow disunity through the sharing of disinformation online, especially when it is amplified by the news media.

While network propaganda may have shaped some voting decisions during the US presidential election and UK EU referendum in 2016, its agenda-setting

---

20 E.S. Herman and N. Chomsky, *Manufacturing Consent: The Political Economy of the Mass Media*. New York: Pantheon Books, 1988.

21 E.L. Briant, *supra* note 19, p. 9.

22 T. Gillespie, 'Governance of and by platforms' in J. Burgess, T. Poell and A. Marwick (eds.), *SAGE Handbook of Social Media*. London: SAGE, 2017, p. 1.

23 Y. Benkler, R.M. Faris and H. Roberts, *Network Propaganda: Manipulation, Disinformation and Radicalization in American Politics*. Oxford: Oxford University Press, 2018, p. 24.

24 *Ibid.*, p. 220.

25 C. Wardle, *supra* note 2.

26 L. Shifman, *Memes in Digital Culture*. Cambridge, MA: MIT Press, 2015; C. Wardle, *supra* note 2.

27 S.C. McGregor and L. Molyneux, 'Twitter's influence on news judgement: an experiment among journalists' (2018) *Journalism* 1.

power should not be overstated.[28] False information shared on social media with the intention of polarising opinion does not necessarily have uniform effects on audiences. Citizens use heuristics to evaluate the credibility of political information encountered online.[29] Like journalists, they invariably check the source and content of the message before deciding whether it is authentic.[30] External sources, such as pre-existing social networks, are consulted in cases where it is difficult to determine the veracity of this content. This feeds into the ongoing debate over whether social media platforms create 'filter bubbles' and 'echo chambers' in which the algorithmic curation of newsfeeds, as well as the tendency of people to only engage in online groups populated by like-minded individuals, limits exposure to opposing views and reinforces pre-existing opinions. The empirical investigation of these claims has been a primary focus of Internet studies for the past decade. For example, one study found that people are exposed to ideologically diverse opinion courtesy of the sharing of content produced by traditional media on Facebook, albeit that they are still most likely to click on those stories that are congruent with their opinions.[31] This appears to corroborate the characterisation of news consumption as a ritual that *confirms* rather than *challenges* worldviews.[32] Recent research by Dubois and Blank has argued that much of the evidence for the echo chamber thesis is based on studies of news consumption practices on Twitter.[33] They argue that political information seeking and news consumption practices are invariably conducted across multiple platforms; those with diverse media diets and an interest in politics are less likely to find themselves in 'echo chambers' due to their constant exposure to alternative viewpoints. Yet, one should be cautious about ascribing rationality to the information behaviours practised by social media users. There is already some evidence that 'civic-minded' citizens share tabloid news via their social media accounts, irrespective of its accuracy, in order to spark debate with others. While the intentional sharing of fabricated news may be subject to the correction of other social media users, many 'democratically dysfunctional news sharing behaviours' on these platforms remain unchallenged.[34]

---

28 C.J. Vargo, L. Guo and M.A. Amazeen, 'The agenda-setting power of fake news: A big data analysis of the online media landscape from 2014 to 2016' (2018) 20(5) *New Media & Society* 2049.

29 E. Thorson, Belief echoes: the persistent effects of corrected misinformation' (2016) 33(3) *Political Communication* 460, p. 475.

30 E.C. Tandoc, Z.W. Lim and R. Ling, 'Defining "fake news": a typology of scholarly definitions' (2018) 6(2) *Digital Journalism* 137.

31 E. Bakshy, S. Messing and L.A. Adamic, 'Exposure to ideologically diverse news and opinion on Facebook' (2015) 348(6239) *Science* 1130.

32 J. Carey *A Cultural Approach to Communication from Communication as Culture.* New York: Routledge, 1992.

33 E. Dubois and G. Blank, "The echo chamber is overstated: the moderating effect of political interest and diverse media' (2018) 21(5) *Information, Communication & Society* 729. doi: 10.1080/1369118X.2018.1428656.

34 A. Chadwick et al., *supra* note 4.

3. THE PROPAGANDA OF WAR AND PEACE IN NORTHERN IRELAND

In order to contextualise this study of digital disinformation in 'post-conflict' Northern Ireland, it is necessary to first develop a historical understanding of the role of propaganda in the deeply divided society. Disinformation has frequently been deployed by both elites and non-elites in support of the two main competing narratives on the constitutional status of the contested entity. For the sake of brevity, their complexities cannot be fully elaborated here, but the conflict (known colloquially as 'the Troubles') was invariably framed as the clash of two distinct strands of ethnic nationalism.[35] Catholics, nationalists and republicans tended to oppose partition and support reunification with the rest of Ireland, whereas Protestants, unionists and loyalists supported the maintenance of the union with Great Britain.[36] Prior to the conflict, news media were complicit in efforts by both the UK and the regional Stormont government to portray a 'society without division', going so far as not to mention the word 'partition' in their coverage.[37] They were subject to even more restrictions in their reporting of the 30-year conflict (1968–1998). The Troubles were frequently characterised as a 'propaganda war supported by a shooting war'.[38] The news media were effectively banned from interviewing or transmitting footage of republicans and had to rely instead on 'official' sources such as the Northern Ireland Office (NIO) and the British Army in their coverage of terrorist atrocities. In this way, the UK government actively promoted the notion that journalistic norms of 'impartiality' should be abandoned in favour of coverage that designated these groups as 'the enemy' of the state.[39]

The republican movement established newspapers such as *An Phoblacht* to counter media coverage that framed them as 'terrorists' who were unrepresentative of the nationalist community.[40] Publications such as *The Loyalist* were launched to provide a similar narrative stream for loyalist terrorist groups, such as the Ulster Volunteer Force (UVF). However, both loyalists and republican paramilitaries were unable to match the 'psyops' of the British Army in the early 1970s, the term used to describe the use of propaganda to 'influence the

35 K. O'Sullivan-See, *First World Nationalisms: Class and Ethnic Politics in Northern Ireland and Quebec*. Chicago: University of Chicago Press, 1986, p. 148.

36 A. Edwards and C. McGrattan, *The Northern Ireland Conflict (Beginners Guide)*. London: Oneworld, 2010.

37 D. Miller, *Don't Mention the War: Northern Ireland, Propaganda and the Media*. London: Pluto Press, 1994, p. 28.

38 R. Clutterbuck, *The Media and Political Violence*. London: Macmillan, 1983, p. 87.

39 P. Schlesinger, and P. Elliott, *Televising Terrorism: Political Violence in Popular Culture*. London: Comedia, 1983, p. 121.

40 L. Curtis, 'Reporting republican violence' in B. Rolston and D. Miller (eds.), *War and Words: The Northern Ireland Media Reader*. Belfast: Beyond the Pale Publications, 1996, p. 324.

opinions, emotion, attitudes and behaviour of enemy, neutral and friendly groups during a military action'.[41] The Information Policy Unit in Northern Ireland, created by the British Army in 1971, was charged with discouraging publicity for violence perpetrated by loyalist paramilitaries and the security forces while simultaneously discrediting the Provisional Irish Republican Army (PIRA) and the republican movement. Early successes included the British media blaming PIRA for the McGurk's Bar atrocity in December 1971, with one journalist reproducing the army's version of events 'word for word'.[42] In reality, a group identifying themselves as the 'Empire Loyalists' (later identified as the UVF) had claimed responsibility for the attack on the North Belfast bar. Although these operations ceased a few years later, both direct and indirect pressure continued to be placed upon broadcasters to reproduce the British narrative on the conflict and portray republican terrorists as 'criminals'. There was also evidence that official sources were 'placing' stories with unsuspecting media organisations and were working with academics and journalists in order to promote 'good news stories' showing the British Army helping local communities.[43]

Despite Sinn Féin's burgeoning electoral success, the UK government continued to attempt to limit media coverage devoted to the political wing of the PIRA. Most notably, the 1988 UK Broadcasting Ban made it illegal for Sinn Féin members to make statements on television.[44] Propaganda was also deployed by the NIO and the UK government in order to protect security forces personnel from prosecution for their role in 'extra-judicial executions'. For instance, unidentified 'official sources' were responsible for the false story circulated in the British media in March 1988 stating that three PIRA members shot dead by the Special Air Service (SAS) in Gibraltar were armed and had planted a car bomb.[45] Despite some evidence of a 'belief echo' amongst British audiences when evidence first began to emerge casting doubt on these claims, this incident demonstrated the limits of the UK government's information management policy in shaping media coverage of the conflict. *Death on the Rock*, a Thames Television documentary that aired in April 1988, provided evidence that the three PIRA members had been unarmed and shot dead by the SAS team without warning. UK Foreign Secretary Sir Geoffrey Howe failed in two attempts to ban the programme from being aired.[46] This illustrated the tension between the public service remit of UK broadcasters and the efforts by the British state to use

---

41 L. Curtis, *Ireland, the Propaganda War: The Media and the 'battle for Hearts and Minds.* Belfast: Sásta, 1988, p. 229.

42 *Ibid.*, p. 91.

43 D. Miller, *supra* note 37, p. 124.

44 E. Moloney, 'Closing down the airwaves: the story of the broadcasting ban' in B. Rolston (ed.), *The Media and Northern Ireland.* London: Palgrave, 1991, p. 46.

45 D. Miller, *supra* note 37, p. 212.

46 R. Bolton, 'Death on the Rock' in B. Rolston and D. Miller (eds.), *War and Words: The Northern Ireland Media Reader.* Belfast: Beyond the Pale Publications, 1996, pp. 118–141.

these organisations for disinformation campaigns about their 'war on terrorism'. While there may have been severe restrictions placed on news media, it would be misleading to characterise professional journalists and media organisations as a 'subordinate apparatus of the state' during the conflict.[47] Indeed, *Death on the Rock* illustrated how some journalists actively pushed back on state propaganda designed to justify the unlawful use of force against PIRA.

The late 1980s saw the NIO and UK government propaganda shift from portraying terrorists as 'criminals' to 'victims of circumstances'.[48] A series of television commercials were commissioned for the 'Confidential Telephone Number', a service designed to gather intelligence about the activities of loyalist and republican paramilitaries. Probably the most well-known of these was 'I Wanna Be Like You Dad', which depicted the son of a paramilitary prisoner getting involved in terrorist activity and ended with the father standing at the graveside of his son, killed due to his involvement in terrorism.[49] This was followed by a series of adverts after the 1994 paramilitary ceasefires which 'sold' the benefits of peace to citizens in the deeply divided society. The news media were not immune to these efforts to bolster support for the fledgling peace process. Op-eds and editorials in newspapers such as the *Belfast Telegraph* and *Irish News* were overwhelmingly supportive of the Good Friday (or Belfast) Agreement, and their coverage purposefully differentiated political fronts such as Sinn Féin from the violence of their respective terrorist organisations.[50] At the same time, the republican party developed a sophisticated public relations capacity that enabled it to consolidate internal support for the peace process while expanding its electoral base.[51]

Dissidents have had little opportunity to articulate their opposition to the peace process in the news media over the past two decades. McLaughlin and Baker argued that this was indicative of the pervasiveness of the 'propaganda of peace', which mobilised citizens in support of a neoliberal agenda that conflated economic prosperity with peace and treated the Agreement as a 'self-evident good' beyond critique.[52] This has resulted in loyalist and republican dissidents being branded as 'dangerous and transgressive threats to the peace

---

47 P. Schlesinger and P. Elliott *Televising Terrorism: Political Violence in Popular Culture*. London: Comedia, 1983, p. 110.

48 A. Finlayson and E. Hughes, 'Advertising for peace: the state and political advertising in Northern Ireland 1988–1998' (2000) 20(3) *Historical Journal of Film, Radio and Television*, 397, p. 397.

49 *Ibid.*, p. 404.

50 G. Wolfsfeld, *The News Media and Peace Processes: The Middle East and Northern Ireland*. Washington DC: United States Institute of Peace, 2001, p. 36.

51 I. Somerville and A. Purcell, 'A history of republican public relations in Northern Ireland from "Bloody Sunday" to the "Good Friday Agreement"' (2011) 5(3) *Journal of Communication Management* 192, p. 208.

52 G. McLaughlin and S. Baker, *The Propaganda of Peace: The Role of the Media and Culture in the Northern Ireland Peace Process*. Bristol: Intellect, 2010.

process', irrespective of whether they were engaged in 'spoiler' political violence campaigns.[53] While it appeared relatively benign in comparison to the disinformation campaigns of the Troubles, this helped elites manufacture consent for a consociationalist peace settlement that entrenched divisions between the two ethno-sectarian blocs and did little to address conflict-legacy issues experienced by both communities. In this context, dissidents resorted to using digital media to articulate their opposition to the peace process. A study of websites maintained by political actors and residents' groups in the mid-2000s suggested that the Internet had limited value as a propaganda tool for these actors.[54] Political parties used their websites to position themselves as either critics or supporters of the Good Friday Agreement. For example, there were few references to PIRA in the history section of the Sinn Féin website, which asserted its democratic credentials and used rhetorical appeals similar to those of the Socialist Democratic and Labour Party (SDLP).[55] Yet, there was little evidence to suggest that this online propaganda had a significant impact upon the political attitudes and behaviour of citizens. These websites appeared to function as 'islands of political communication' that were unlikely to provide a high degree of visibility for groups who received very little coverage in the mainstream media. Indeed, their relative obscurity arguably made them ideal platforms for the sharing of internal propaganda with like-minded individuals, rather than fomenting disunity amongst the general population.[56]

4. SOCIAL MEDIA, DISINFORMATION AND HYBRID MEDIA EVENTS IN NORTHERN IRELAND

The early signs were that Web 2.0, the section of the Web revolving around user-generated content, would make it easier for dissidents to disseminate black and grey propaganda designed to undermine public confidence in the Agreement. In contrast to the limited interactivity afforded by their websites a decade earlier, they could use these platforms to share disinformation with target audiences such as professional journalists, who were increasingly likely to source stories on social media.[57] This was potentially very significant for those groups who were marginalised due to their perceived threat to the peace process and

53 P. Hoey, *Shinners, Dissos and Dissenters: Irish Republican Media Activism since the Good Friday Agreement*. Manchester: Manchester University Press, 2018, p. 8.

54 P.J. Reilly, *Framing the Troubles Online: Northern Irish Political Groups and Website Strategy*. Manchester: Manchester University Press, 2011.

55 *Ibid.*

56 P. Hoey, *supra* note 53, p. 55.

57 A. Chadwick, *The Hybrid Media System: Politics and Power*. Oxford: Oxford Studies and Digital Politics, 2013.

wished to counter mainstream media narratives that presented the Agreement as sacrosanct. The evidence to date suggests that social media have ushered in a new era of political partisanship amongst a small but vocal minority of citizens who use these sites to find and share political information. In the case of Sinn Féin, the party with the most sophisticated online communication strategy, its social media profiles were frequently flooded with sectarian comments made by anonymous loyalists and unionists in the late noughties.[58] Since 2014, the republican party itself has been linked to orchestrated social media campaigns by so-called 'Shinnerbots' that seek to attack and silence its critics. For example, these anonymous Sinn Féin supporters were responsible for the online bullying and harassment of Maíria Cahill in October 2014, in the wake of her allegations that senior PIRA figures had attempted to cover up her sexual assault by a senior republican.[59] Researchers such as Hoey argued that they have effectively 'drowned out' other voices during partisan political debates online.[60] Yet, with the exception of the aforementioned UK EU referendum in 2016, there has been little evidence to date suggesting that digital disinformation has influenced the voting decisions of citizens in Northern Ireland. The region's only fact-checking organisation conducted 49 fact-checks between April 2016 and September 2018, none of which referred to disinformation shared via social media.[61]

4.1. THE 2012 UNION FLAG PROTESTS

In contrast to elections, there has been mounting evidence that disinformation is being shared online during hybrid media events, those 'media events whose significance for media professionals, politicians, and non-elites is being reconfigured by the growth of social media'.[62] Loyalist and republican dissidents have invariably been responsible for the sharing of false or misleading information on social media, designed to inflame sectarian tensions surrounding contentious parades and protests. Fears amongst community workers and other key stakeholders that the spread of false information online

---

58 P.J. Reilly, 'Ourselves alone (but making connections): the social media strategies of Sinn Féin' in P. Nixon, R. Rawal and D. Mercea (eds.), *Chasing the Promise of Internet Politics*. London: Routledge, 2013, p. 168.

59 N. Emerson, 'Just whose side are the Shinnerbots on?', *Irish News*, 30 October 2014.

60 Hoey argues that this is illustrative of Sinn Féin's command of social media and has an antecedent in their strategies to circumvent British censorship during the conflict. For more on this, see: https://www.thetimes.co.uk/edition/ireland/shinnerbots-drown-out-unionists-on-social-media-xsv02q9q8.

61 For more on this and the other fact-checks, see: https://factcheckni.org/category/facts.

62 C. Vaccari, A. Chadwick and B. O'Loughlin, 'Dual screening the political: media events, social media, and citizen engagement' (2015) 65 *Journal of Communication* 1041, 1044.

might spark intercommunal violence (see Reilly,[63] for instance) appeared to be realised during the union flag protests in December 2012. Loyalists took to the streets to demonstrate their anger at the decision of Belfast City Council to alter its protocol on the flying of the union flag over City Hall, reversing its previous policy of flying the flag all year round in favour of only doing so on 18 designated days. The Alliance Party bore the brunt of loyalist anger as this was its amendment to an original proposal by Sinn Féin seeking its permanent removal. Several of its constituency offices were picketed on a daily basis in the weeks following the vote, with a death threat made against its East Belfast MP Naomi Long and a petrol bomb attack on a police vehicle outside her constituency office in December 2012.[64] The DUP and the Ulster Unionist Party (UUP) were widely criticised for distributing 40,000 'anti-Alliance' leaflets to households across Belfast in the run-up to the vote, which presented the party as a threat to unionist and loyalist identity.[65] Yet, irrespective of the link between the leaflet and this campaign of intimidation, none of the parties could have anticipated the scale of the protests, with approximately 10,000 people recorded as being involved in protest-related incidents in the week before Christmas.[66]

While much of the media coverage focused on the role of public Facebook pages in the coordination and organisation of the flag protests, they would also provide a platform for those who wished to post sectarian comments about the 'other' community and 'troll' public figures, including the spokespersons for the flag protest movement.[67] Facebook and Twitter were frequently characterised as a 'sectarian battleground' due to the noticeable increase in anti-Catholic and anti-Protestant sentiments on these platforms during this period.[68] There was also a noticeable increase in rumours and misinformation rather than disinformation on social media during the flag protests. Public Facebook pages such as Loyalist Peaceful Protest Updater (LPPU) were used to share misinformation, such as claims that An Garda Siochána had been involved in the policing of the flag protests and that security staff from a Belfast office building had been approached by the Police Service of Northern Ireland (PSNI)

---

63 P.J. Reilly, 'Community worker perspectives on the use of new media to promote conflict transformation in Belfast' (2012) 49(15) *Urban Studies* 3385.

64 P. Nolan, D. Bryan, C. Dwyer, K. Hayward, K. Radford and P. Shirlow, 'The Flag Dispute: Anatomy of a Protest', Supported by the Community Relations Council & the Department of Foreign Affairs and Trade, Ireland, 2014.

65 A. Kane, 'Confidence requites more than a flag', *Eamonn Mallie*, 14 December 2012, http://eamonnmallie.com/2012/12/confidence-requires-more-than-a-flag.

66 P. Nolan et al., *supra* note 64, p. 4.

67 O. Young, 'New media and young people in interface areas of Belfast' (2014) 14 *Shared Space*.

68 P. Nolan et al., *supra* note 64, p. 70.

for CCTV footage of the flag protesters.[69] In terms of the former, it should be noted that commentators in the same thread asked for corroborative evidence and several categorically refuted this claim. It was also one of the few rumours spread on social media that surfaced in media coverage of the protests, with Justice Minister David Ford and a PSNI spokesperson denying the claim in a newspaper article published on 8 January 2013.[70] Twitter was also used by citizens to share claims about alleged police brutality and threatening behaviour and physical assaults inflicted on members of the public by flag protesters. The responses to these claims, which were rarely corroborated by visual evidence, were unsurprisingly polarised. Critics of the protesters were quick to condemn any wrongdoing on their part, whereas claims of PSNI brutality were held up as further evidence of its complicity in Sinn Féin's war against unionist and loyalist culture. In sum, citizens' acceptance of rumour and misinformation shared on social media at the height of the flag protests depended upon whether it was congruent with their view on the loyalist culture war narrative.

4.2. THE 2014 AND 2015 ARDOYNE PARADE DISPUTES

In contrast to the flag protests, there was more disinformation than misinformation during the Ardoyne parade disputes. The Ardoyne parade dispute provided further evidence of how social media were being used to promulgate disinformation during hybrid media events in Northern Ireland. The Parade Commission decision to reroute the annual Twelfth of July parade away from the nationalist Ardoyne district of North Belfast in July 2013 led to several nights of violence between loyalist protesters and the PSNI. The parade passed off without incident in July 2014, despite the efforts of several disinformation propagators on Twitter to inflame sectarian tensions surrounding the parade. A study of 1,842 #Ardoyne tweets posted between 11 and 14 July 2014 revealed that rumours and disinformation about the contentious parade had a very short lifespan and typically went unreported by the news media.[71] Most notably, there were two Photoshopped images shared on the microblogging platform presumably with the intention of generating further hostility between the nationalist residents and loyalist protesters. The first appeared to show a picture of Oscar Knox, a five-year-old who had died from a rare form of cancer, on

69 P.J. Reilly and F. Trevisan, 'Researching protest on Facebook: developing an ethical stance for the study of Northern Irish flag protest pages' (2015) 19(3) *Information Communication and Society* 419.

70 A. McKernon, 'Flags crisis – "no substance" to claims about drafting Gardai', *Irish News*, 8 January 2013, p. 5.

71 P.J. Reilly, 'Tweeting for peace? Twitter and the Ardoyne parade dispute July 2014' (2016) 21(11) *First Monday*.

an 'Eleventh Night' bonfire near Randalstown. This provoked outrage amongst many tweeters, but was quickly refuted by the Randalstown Sons of Ulster Flute band, who posted a picture of their Eleventh night bonfire to show that the image had been digitally altered.[72] By way of response, loyalists also distributed disinformation on social media depicting the nationalist Ardoyne residents as intolerant towards their culture. At 7.30 pm on 12 July, a picture was shared on Twitter showing one of the nationalist protesters holding aloft a placard with a mock road sign declaring that the Orange Order were not welcome in the area. The crude Photoshopping of the placard led to much scepticism amongst tweeters about its authenticity. Like the Knox case, it took only a few minutes before visual proof that the photograph had been manipulated was shared on Twitter. A picture uploaded by BBC Northern Ireland journalist Kevin Sharkey revealed that the slogan had in fact read 'Love Thy Neighbour' rather than expressing local opposition to the contentious parade.[73] In both cases, it was notable that the number of retweets of these digitally manipulated images declined sharply after corrections were shared. Tweeters also directly challenged the disinformation propagator responsible for manipulating the image of the protester with the placard.[74]

The 2015 parade was marred by loyalist rioting after protesters faced off against PSNI officers enforcing the Commission ruling prohibiting the march from returning home via its traditional route. A total of 24 police officers were hurt after loyalists began to throw missiles at their lines, with erroneous rumours circulating online that PSNI Chief Constable George Hamilton was amongst those injured. A study of 5,546 tweets posted between 12 and 15 July 2015 provided further evidence of how Twitter was used by citizens to share and debunk misinformation.[75] Claims and counter-claims were made about the incident in which John Aughey, a member of the Orange Order, drove his car into a crowd of nationalist residents in North Belfast, critically injuring a 16-year-old girl. The West Belfast Ulster Political Research Group shared reports that his car had been attacked by republicans, making no reference to Aughey's attempted murder of the teenager.[76] Loyalists speculated whether the victim had been trapped under the vehicle as had been claimed by other tweeters. Within a few minutes, journalists confirmed that the girl had been seriously injured and that Aughey had been arrested at the scene.[77] There were few tweets alleging that the

72 'If everyone could retweet this and confirm! There was no Oscar Knox memorabilia/flags or objects on Randalstown bonfire. Oscar was a hero!' @RandalstownSOU, Twitter, 12 July 2014, 12.30 am.

73 P.J. Reilly, *supra* note 7.

74 P.J. Reilly, *supra* note 71.

75 P.J. Reilly, *supra* note 7.

76 P.J. Reilly, 'Local journalists have key role to play in combating "fake news" in Northern Ireland', *Democratic Audit UK*, 10 September 2018.

77 P.J. Reilly, *supra* note 7.

car had been attacked by republicans after these media reports began to circulate on social media. Further corrective information about the status of the victim was provided a few hours later, when local MLAs including Sinn Féin's Gerry Kelly confirmed that her injuries were not life-threatening.

The Chief Constable himself was the subject of misinformation later that evening. A viewer of Russia Today's livestream showing the standoff tweeted that a senior police officer closely resembling Hamilton had been injured by an object thrown by one of the rioters. This misinformation flow was corrected within a few hours by local journalist Rodney Edwards, who confirmed that the Chief Constable had not been present at the scene during the riot.[78] Further corroborative evidence of this 'debunk', a 'corrective message that establishes that the prior message was misinformation',[79] was provided by the Chief Constable later that evening; Hamilton tweeted that he had not been injured and thanked members of the public for their concern. Elsewhere, tweeters worked to prevent the spread of rumours and misinformation that might incite violence in North Belfast. One tweeter apologised for one of their own tweets, posted a few days prior to the Twelfth and retweeted three times, disclosing a rumour they had heard about a deal being struck to allow the return leg of the parade to proceed past the Ardoyne shops.[80] This correction showed how some citizens were aware that such misinformation might have a negative impact on community relations in the contested interface area.

These were crudely Photoshopped images and unsubstantiated claims rather than the sophisticated disinformation campaigns seen during elections and referenda in 2016. While it was highly unlikely that these 'agents' were motivated by financial gain like those 'workers' in 'fake news factories', it was more plausible that they were seeking to inflame sectarian tensions surrounding these events. North Belfast remains a highly segregated area where the logic of inter-community separation embedded during the conflict has remained largely intact.[81] Rival interface communities remain engaged in a form of ethnic poker, whereby both retain zero-sum perceptions of space and politics.[82] In these circumstances, it might be argued that disinformation spread on social media was likely to reinforce existing (negative) attitudes towards 'out-groups'. However, the potential impact of such activity on events on the ground should

78 *Ibid.*

79 M.S. Chan, C.R. Jones, K.M. Jamieson and D. Albarracin, 'Debunking: a meta-analysis of the psychological efficacy of messages countering misinformation' (2017) 28(11) *Psychological Science* 1537.

80 P.J. Reilly, *supra* note 7.

81 P. Shirlow and B. Murtagh, *Belfast: Segregation, Violence and the City*. London: Pluto Press, 2006.

82 W.J.V. Neill, *Urban Planning and Cultural Identity*. London: Routledge, 2004, p. 205.

not be overstated. Professional journalists played an active role in fact-checking unsubstantiated claims and refrained from amplifying disinformation in their coverage. There was also no clear evidence to suggest that false information circulated on social media contributed to the violent clashes between loyalists and the PSNI during the 2015 Ardoyne impasse, nor any similar incident of civil unrest.

4.3. EFFECTS OF DIGITAL DISINFORMATION MAY BE DIFFICULT TO DETECT

There are two caveats that should be acknowledged when analysing the circulation of disinformation on Twitter during these contentious parades and protests. First, it is difficult to make too many inferences about the attitudes of those who viewed this content but did not comment on it. Indeed, many of these 'watchers' may have continued to believe such false information, even after it had been debunked. The empirical evidence to date suggests that 'debunks' may unintentionally provide a degree of legitimacy to the original claim and deliver the publicity sought by those agents responsible for its creation and dissemination.[83] Thorson asserts that even in those cases where misinformation is debunked, there will still be some people who will refuse to believe the correction.[84] These 'belief echoes' are caused by the affective 'pull' of the original piece of misinformation being much stronger than the correction, as well as the extent to which the false information appears to corroborate pre-existing political views and prejudices.[85] There has also been evidence of 'partisan selective sharing', when citizens only share fact-checking messages that are congruent with their political ideologies and ignore those that appear to support the views of their political opponents.[86] The failure of elected representatives to resolve the Ardoyne parade dispute meant that loyalists and nationalist residents were perhaps more likely to believe misinformation and disinformation that correlated with their respective views of each other. In this context, it is conceivable that loyalists would believe that nationalist protesters carried anti-Orange Order placards, even after the evidence for such a claim had been debunked.

---

83 C. Shao, G.L. Ciampaglia, O. Varol, A. Flammini and F. Menczer, 'The spread of low-credibility content by social bots' (2018) 9 *Nature Communications* 4787; C. Wardle, *supra* note 2.

84 E. Thorson, *supra* note 29.

85 D.J. Flynn, B. Nyhan and J. Reifler, 'The nature and origins of misperceptions: understanding false and unsupported beliefs about politics' (2016) 38(1) *Political Psychology* 127.

86 J. Shin and K. Thorson, 'Partisan selective sharing: the biased diffusion of fact-checking messages on social media' (2017) 67(2) *Journal of Communication* 233.

Second, this chapter has drawn on easily obtained data from Twitter rather than 'hard' data that are out of reach of the researcher.[87] Only an estimated 18 per cent of Northern Irish adults were said to be using Twitter during this period.[88] It is inconceivable that disinformation about the flag protests and the Ardoyne dispute was not being shared on private Facebook pages, encrypted messaging apps such as WhatsApp or indeed via face-to-face conversations. In contrast to the aforementioned propaganda campaigns of the British state and paramilitaries during the Troubles, which were extensively documented, much of this content is ephemeral and therefore inaccessible to researchers. Therefore, it may not be possible to fully assess the current scale of digital disinformation in the deeply divided society due to the many channels through which it originates and circulates.

5. BUILDING SOCIETAL RESILIENCE AGAINST DIGITAL DISINFORMATION

Perhaps the most pertinent issue is how Northern Irish citizens respond to political disinformation shared on social media. As discussed earlier, public perceptions of the Troubles were heavily influenced by a combination of the psyops of the British Army and the news media's reliance on 'official sources'. In these circumstances, citizens might be understandably wary of the veracity of information they encounter on platforms such as Facebook and Twitter. Certainly, there has been some evidence to suggest that the online news consumption practices may inadvertently increase their exposure to digital disinformation. One recent survey found that only 59 per cent of Northern Irish Internet users checked the accuracy of factual information found online, compared to 67 per cent of users across the UK.[89] This was congruent with a 2016 study that found that only 55 per cent of Internet users understood that the accuracy of the information generated in search engine results was variable, below the UK average of 62 per cent.[90] Yet, paradoxically, there are also some signs that Northern Irish citizens are increasingly sceptical of all information they encounter online. For example, one survey found that only half of participants (50.2 per cent) trusted content posted on websites of news

87 J. Burgess and A. Bruns, 'Easy data, hard data: the politics and pragmatics of Twitter research after the computational turn' in G. Langlois, J. Redden and G. Elmer (eds.), *Compromised Data: From Social Media to Big Data*. London: Bloomsbury Publishing, 2015, pp. 93–111.

88 Ofcom, 'Internet use and attitudes: 2017 Metrics Bulletin', 3 August 2017, p. 10.

89 *Ibid.*, p. 12.

90 Ofcom, 'Internet use and attitudes: 2016 Metrics Bulletin', 4 August 2016, p. 15.

media organisations. Northern Irish social media users were rated as slightly more trustworthy than either professional journalists or elected representatives at Stormont, albeit that all three groups were ranked amongst the least-trusted groups. Reasons why participants did not trust the news media included their 'dumbing' down of the news, the tendency to exaggerate the differences between the main political parties, and the failure to promote healthy debates on key political issues.[91]

The media diets of Northern Irish citizens may, at the very least, ensure that they are only likely to be inadvertently exposed to the information pollution spread by disinformation propagators on social media. Recent research suggests that, despite the perceived low level of public trust in journalists, television remains the main source of news for 72 per cent of adults aged over 16 in Northern Ireland.[92] UTV Live, independent broadcaster UTV's flagship early-evening news programme, regularly achieves 47.2 per cent audience share in its 6 pm timeslot, making it one of the most-watched regional news bulletins in the UK.[93] In contrast, just seven per cent of respondents said that they used a website or app as their primary source of news.[94] Furthermore, another study found that only 21.2 per cent of citizens said they trusted social media as a source of information.[95]

These news consumption practices have a number of implications for the 'resilience' of Northern Irish citizens towards online misinformation and disinformation. On the one hand, the widespread scepticism about information posted online appears to be a positive development. The dominant position occupied by television news in the regional information ecosystem would also appear to assuage fears that they were getting their news from unverified sources. While acknowledging that media consumption is a ritual that typically reinforces worldviews, the diversification of media diets could potentially help address the mutual suspicion that surrounds contentious parades such as Ardoyne, which provides a fertile terrain for digital disinformation during the annual Twelfth demonstrations. If the predominantly unionist readership of the *News Letter* read the *Irish News*, the largest nationalist paper in the region, and *vice versa*, it would at the very least provide more communicative spaces in which both sides could discuss these contentious issues. Yet, declining trust in professional journalists is arguably a more pressing problem and is particularly problematic in a society emerging from a 'propaganda war'. If these trends continue, then they might threaten the long-term survival of an independent and free news media

91 S. McGookin, 'Lucidtalk poll: local media – old and new – face issues of trust and performance', *Northern Slant*, 12 March 2018.
92 Ofcom, 'Communications Market Report: Northern Ireland', 3 August 2017, p. 28.
93 *Ibid.*, p. 27.
94 *Ibid.*, p. 28.
95 S. McGookin, *supra* note 91.

within Northern Ireland, which is a pre-requisite for reducing the pollution of the information ecosystem.

The fact-checking and professional norms of mainstream media are not in and of themselves a solution to the so-called 'fake news' problem in this deeply divided society. The tendency of professional journalists to source stories online increases the possibility that they themselves will inadvertently contribute to these flows on social media, especially given their role as key influencers on platforms such as Twitter. Belief echoes and partisan selective sharing also militate against the simplistic notion that debunks issued via mainstream media will automatically nullify disinformation shared on social media. The central role of tabloid media in democratic dysfunctional news-sharing practices suggests that some forms of journalism may be directly and indirectly contributing to the polarised political debates seen on these platforms. Similarly, calls for mass digital literacy initiatives to tackle digital disinformation fail to acknowledge the impracticalities of training millions of people on how to distinguish 'good' from 'bad' content;[96] they also perpetuate the false premise that a digitally literate population will not be vulnerable to these information disorders. Even if a consensus could be reached on how to define digital literacy, it would seem unrealistic that the entire media ecosystem could be transformed in such a way as to fully eradicate the sources of disinformation. After all, the evidence from the 2016 US presidential election was that disinformation emanated from a small right-wing media ecosystem that accounted for no more than 30 per cent of the population.[97] Rather, politicians, journalists and community representatives in Northern Ireland should work together to develop collective narratives on contentious issues that resonate with members of both main communities, thus making it much harder for disinformation propagators to share false information that inflames sectarian tensions around these issues. Future research should explore how such collective narratives on contentious issues can be constructed in a 'post-conflict' society that remains deeply divided along sectarian lines.

6. CONCLUSION

Propaganda has frequently been deployed by both elite and non-elite actors in support of the two main competing narratives surrounding the constitutional status of Northern Ireland. While the British state used psyops and information management to frame the PIRA as 'criminals' and protect security forces' personnel from prosecution, loyalist and republican paramilitaries developed

---

96 S. Vaidhyanathan, *Antisocial Media: How Facebook Disconnects Us and Undermines Democracy*. Oxford: Oxford University Press, 2018.

97 Y. Benkler, R.M. Faris and H. Roberts, *supra* note 23, p. 189.

their own media to counter negative media representations and articulate their respective ideologies. Information disorder in the 'post-conflict' society shares many of the same traits as this 'propaganda war'. Although there has been no evidence to date showing that it has influenced the voting decisions of citizens, loyalist and republicans have spread disinformation on social media with the intention of inflaming sectarian tensions and reinforcing negative stereotypes of outgroups during contentious parades and protests. Thus far, its effects appear to have been stymied by the corrections issued by citizens and professional journalists on platforms such as Twitter. Citizens directly challenged those responsible for sharing disinformation during the Ardoyne parade dispute, while news media organisations fact-checked unsubstantiated claims and refrained from amplifying misinformation in their coverage of both of these hybrid media events. The absence of a coordinated approach also appeared to contribute to the relatively short lifespan of these misinformation and disinformation flows. These were crude Photoshopped images created by seemingly unaffiliated tweeters, not the sophisticated disinformation campaigns of the 2016 US presidential election and UK EU referendum. Clearly this may have raised suspicions amongst some tweeters about the authenticity and veracity of the information provided by these disinformation propagators. However, the potential impact of social media upon 'real-world' events in Northern Ireland should not be overstated. Previous research has suggested that platforms such as Facebook and Twitter are more likely to host antagonistic debates about contentious political issues, as opposed to directly influence events on the ground. There have also been no incidents of sectarian violence thus far that have been attributed to false information shared online. Nevertheless, it is reasonable to presume that disinformation on social media has the potential to cause harm to citizens in deeply divided societies, especially in contested interface areas such as North Belfast, who continue to be affected by sporadic low-level intercommunal violence. Future research should focus on how such information circulates on encrypted messaging apps and private social media profiles during contentious parades and related protests. A particular focus should be the interplay between intentionally and verifiably false information and civil disturbances that occurs during contentious episodes.

Despite a recent decline in public trust in professional journalism in Northern Ireland, television news remains the main source of news for most adults, with social media being the least trusted. However, the growth in democratically dysfunctional sharing of tabloid news on social media suggests that accidental exposure to false and misleading information remains a strong possibility, as does professional journalists' increasing reliance on social media to source stories. Moreover, evidence from the 2016 US presidential election suggests that disinformation can emanate from a small part of the media ecosystem. This raises questions as to the feasibility of 'cleansing' the Northern Irish information ecosystem, or any other for that matter, of all forms of misinformation and disinformation. News consumption is after all a ritual designed to confirm worldviews; those who believe loyalists or nationalist residents are sectarian are more likely to believe Photoshopped images confirming these prejudices are authentic, even when faced with evidence to the contrary. In the absence of a political consensus on how to address complex conflict-legacy issues, digital disinformation looks likely to persist and possibly thrive in the deeply divided society. In this regard, the current genre of information disorders may have much more in common with the 'propaganda war' than previously thought.

11. DISINFORMATION AND FEAR PROPAGANDA AS JUSTIFICATION FOR THE WAR ON TERROR DURING GEORGE W. BUSH'S PRESIDENCY

Ewelina Waśko-Owsiejczuk*

1. INTRODUCTION

After the terrorist attacks of 11 September 2001,[1] there was a peculiar atmosphere of fear, compassion and solidarity with the US, which was meticulously used by the George W. Bush administration to introduce significant changes in US security policy. The US President's administration effectively used traditional media alongside the White House website to disinform and spread propaganda and fear. By using disinformation and fear propaganda in the War on Terror, the Bush administration intended to convince public opinion that all detained and tortured prisoners were dangerous terrorists. Propaganda of intimidation by the White House aimed to divert attention from violations of basic human rights guaranteed by the international community. This chapter will analyse the era of George W. Bush's government, during which the presidential administration used disinformation to try to convince the public that the regime of Saddam Hussein had weapons of mass destruction to justify the start of the American war in Iraq in March 2003, which had no legitimacy in international law. As it turned out, the Bush administration presented false

* Department of History and International Relations, University of Bialystok, Poland. Email: wasko-owsiejczuk@uwb.edu.pl.

1 A group of 19 terrorists belonging to the al-Qaeda organisation hijacked four passenger planes, two of which hit the skyscrapers of the World Trade Center in New York. The third plane was directed at the Pentagon, while the fourth crashed in a field in southern Pennsylvania. The alleged target of the last of the hijacked planes was the White House or the Capitol. As a result of the attacks, nearly 3,000 people were killed. See E. Waśko-Owsiejczuk, *Polityka bezpieczeństwa narodowego Stanów Zjednoczonych Ameryki w latach 2001–2009*, Avalon, Kraków 2014, pp. 144–145.

information, disinforming the public. The second tool employed by the Bush administration was the appeal to fear, the purpose of which was to convince the public of a constant threat from terrorists. Through the use of this tool, the Bush administration could introduce new (controversial) regulations – e.g. the Patriot Act, the creation of secret CIA prisons around the world, and the utilisation of enhanced interrogation techniques. Appeal to fear also had a huge impact on the results of the US presidential election in 2004, when George W. Bush ran for re-election and won, despite the fact that public opinion was very divided at the time. The results of the polls showed that more than half of Americans did not trust Bush, yet at the same time, the same percentage of the population expressed acceptance for his presidency. In this chapter, I will try to answer the following research questions: how did the Bush administration use disinformation and fear propaganda? What impact did these tools have on public opinion and the result of the 2004 presidential election and US policy? Analysis of the above issues is intended to show how disinformation and propaganda are also common in democratic societies and not only in authoritarian regimes.

2. DISINFORMATION AND PROPAGANDA: THEORETICAL ASPECTS

Discussion of the issues found in this article should be preceded with a presentation of key definitions for analysis. What is disinformation and propaganda? At the outset, it is worth emphasising that neither disinformation nor propaganda is a new phenomenon; both have been used since antiquity. However, as was rightly pointed out by Natalie Nougayrède, 'never before has there been the technology to so effectively disseminate it'.[2] Generally understood, disinformation refers to the method of transmitting information (true or false) in such a way as to make the recipient (e.g. the opponent or competitor) believe in a falsehood in order to encourage specific behaviour that is favourable and in line with the expectations of the presenter. It is worth emphasising that disinformation is not simply lying, that is, passing on false information; it should be considered in terms of deception. Thus, disinformation usually means the transmission of a number of different pieces of information, most of which are true, and only one (crucial for triggering the intended effect) piece of information that is false. Sometimes disinformation is used to

2 More on the subject of the use of disinformation and propaganda in particular historical periods, See J. Posetti and A. Matthews, 'A short guide to the history of "fake news" and disinformation', www.icfj.org/sites/default/files/2018-07/A%20Short%20Guide%20to%20History%20of%20Fake%20News%20and%20Disinformation_ICFJ%20Final.pdf.

provide true information in a way that makes it seem false.[3] Disinformation is characterised by systematic activities, professional preparation and organisation, as well as the consistent use of mass media. It presupposes the implementation of a specific programme with the aim of changing the views identified in the consciousness, and even the subconscious, of a mass audience. The key is appropriately selecting the narrative, previously prepared by the disinforming entity. Disinformation methods include, among other things, negation of facts, reversing the facts, placing bits of truth in lies, modification of the motif and circumstances, and camouflage.[4] Alexander Lanoszka explains that 'a disinformation campaign is a systematic government effort aimed at using disinformation to mislead a particular audience – whether a government or key members of society – in order to influence the policy process'.[5] In the literature, we can find a definition of strategic disinformation as the systematic dissemination of false political information and fabrication of the message in order to provide a false picture of the situation, resulting in its erroneous assessment.[6]

Although the definition of disinformation overlaps to a certain extent with propaganda, there are subtle differences between the two. As some researchers have pointed out, propaganda is 'consciously designed to serve the interests, either directly or indirectly, of the propagandists and their political masters. The aim of propaganda is to persuade its subject that there is only one valid point of view and to eliminate all other options'.[7] Propaganda is defined as a mechanism to convey specific beliefs or doctrine: 'Clever use of images, slogans and symbols, referring to our prejudices and emotions; it is a communication of a certain point of view, aimed at inducing the recipient to voluntarily accept this point of view as his own.'[8] It is the same organised effort (e.g. by state authorities) to spread certain ideas in order to shape the position and obtain the expected reaction from a given social group (a potential opponent, the international

3 'Słownik podstawowych pojęć związanych z komunikacją społeczną', http://www.prbezkomentarza.pl/wp-content/uploads/2018/05/Słownik-pojęć-PR.pdf, p. 3; D. Fallis, 'What is disinformation?' (2016) 63(3) *Library Trends* 422; compare with: L. Bennett and S. Livingston, 'The disinformation order: disruptive communication and the decline of democratic institutions' (2018) 3(2) *European Journal of Communication* 124.

4 A. Januszko-Szakiel, 'Dezinformacja jako narzędzie medialnej manipulacji świadomością' in J. Aksman (ed.), *Manipulacja: pedagogiczno-społeczne aspekty. Cz. 1, Interdyscyplinarne aspekty manipulacji*, Oficyna Wydawnicza AFM, Kraków 2010, pp. 212–213.

5 A. Lanoszka, 'Disinformation in international politics' (2019) 4(2) *European Journal of International Security* 3.

6 T. Kacała, 'Dezinformacja i propaganda w kontekście zagrożeń dla bezpieczeństwa państwa' (2015) 24(2) *Przegląd Prawa Konstytucyjnego* 52. For more on the impact of disinformation on politics, see A. Lanoszka, *supra* note 5, 1.

7 Lanoszka, *supra* note 5, pp. 3–4.

8 Kacała, *supra* note 6, p. 53.

community or one's own society). The aim of propaganda is to change attitudes and influence public opinion. It works by creating a collective force on a large scale and its claims have no real basis. The mission is to create a movement whose leader remains unnamed. It is worth emphasising that propaganda operates in the imperative mode and is one-sided. Negative propaganda is often referred to as 'black PR' and consists of writing offensive, engaging content or ridiculing serious discussions. These are deliberate, harmful actions towards another entity.[9] Historical examples of the effective use of propaganda, especially within the same society, are fascist Italy, Nazi Germany and the Soviet Union. Since public media is usually used to spread propaganda, this gave rise to a widespread belief that this sort of media disseminates lies through its messages. One example may be propaganda of the American government during the Vietnam War called the 'Optimism Campaign'.[10] Propaganda and disinformation are not only used by undemocratic regimes; according to Chomsky, 'propaganda is to democracy what the bludgeon is to a totalitarian state'.[11] Moreover, Chomsky claims that in democracies, the media have been used many times as a propaganda tool to provide public support for going to war,[12] which will be analysed later on in this chapter. As has been rightly pointed out by some researchers, both disinformation and propaganda have a huge impact on shaping the national security environment by building the way in which citizens perceive social reality.[13]

3. FEAR PROPAGANDA AFTER 9/11

The scale and form of terrorist attacks carried out in the US on 11 September 2001 surprised and scared not only Americans themselves, but also the international community.[14] The use of passenger planes as a tool for attacking symbols of the superpower and the deaths of nearly 3,000 people shocked the whole world[15] and caused panic in various US cities. Live TV broadcasts showed

---

9 'Słownik podstawowych pojęć związanych z komunikacją społeczną', *supra* note 3.

10 E.E. Moïse, 'Lyndon Johnson's war propaganda', *New York Times*, 20 November 2017, https://www.nytimes.com/2017/11/20/opinion/johnson-propaganda-vietnam-westmoreland.html.

11 'Noam Chomsky interviewed by unidentified interviewer', 1992, https://chomsky.info/199201__.

12 N. Chomsky, *Media Control: The Spectacular Achievements of Propaganda*, Seven Stories Press, New York 1991.

13 Kacala, *supra* note 6, p. 51

14 The 9/11 attacks, which were seen as an attack on the entire civilised world, caused a huge wave of compassion and solidarity with America around the world.

15 E. Waśko-Owsiejczuk, 'Wydarzenia 11 września 2001 r. w świetle prasy polskiej' (2009) VII *Białostockie Teki Historyczne* 139.

the drama of the events – the initially repetitive image of aircrafts flying into the World Trade Center towers, then the burning buildings, people jumping out from the windows of the skyscrapers in desperation, the collapsing of the buildings and the extracting of survivors from the rubble. The dramaturgy of events was even bigger given the fact that the terrorist attacks occurred on the same day, separated only by short intervals. A third plane hit the Pentagon, destroying part of the building, and the fourth hijacked plane crashed in the fields of Pennsylvania, as a result of the heroic deeds of the passengers. Paralysis in communication and the ubiquitous presence of the security services, fire brigades, medical services, police and military increased the sense of fear among Americans, which was additionally fuelled by the administration of President George W. Bush. Fear propaganda was used with the aim of facilitating the introduction of changes in security policy, especially legal provisions that would otherwise be considered unacceptable to Americans, as these provisions significantly limited the rights and civil liberties of citizens. The atmosphere of danger was constantly being fuelled, with the threat of subsequent attacks on the US being stressed as something very real. It was therefore necessary to introduce greater domestic security, tighten regulations and broaden the scope of the President's powers and the competences of special services and the police. Faced with an uneasy dilemma – freedom or security – the American public trusted President Bush, who in a message to the nation assured them that he would find and punish the perpetrators of the attacks.[16] Announcing the War on Terror, he appealed to other nations at the same time: 'Every nation, in every region, now has a decision to make. Either you are with us, or you are with the terrorists. From this day forward, any nation that continues to harbor or support terrorism will be regarded by the United States as a hostile regime.'[17] Traditional media made it significantly easier for the Bush administration to convince the public for the need to retaliate; moreover, as Douglas Kellner stresses, the media spectacle sparked war hysteria and promoted military solutions to the problem of global terrorism.[18] It is worth adding that in the pre-war period in Iraq, a series of articles containing disinformation about the possession of weapons of mass destruction by the Hussein regime were published in the *New York Times*, presenting the story as fact rather than just a possibility.[19] As some researchers

16 'Statement by the President in his Address to the Nation', White House, 11 September 2001, https://georgewbush-whitehouse.archives.gov/news/releases/2001/09/20010911-16.html.

17 'Address to a Joint Session of Congress and the American People', United States Capitol, Washington DC, 20 September 2001, https://georgewbush-whitehouse.archives.gov/news/releases/2001/09/20010920-8.html.

18 D. Kellner, '9/11, spectacles of terror, and media manipulation: a critique of Jihadist and Bush media politics' (2004) 1(1) *Critical Discourse Studies* 41.

19 Posetti and Matthews, *supra* note 2.

pointed out, many American networks had 'wrapped themselves in the American flag and swapped impartiality for patriotism'.[20]

President Bush could count on the support of both the international community and US citizens in retaliating against terrorists. The results of a survey conducted by the Gallup Institute before the attacks (7–10 September 2001) indicated that he was popular among 51 per cent of the respondents. Another poll carried out after the attacks on the World Trade Center and the Pentagon on 14–15 September indicated an increase in support for the President by 35 per cent. At the end of September 2001, Bush enjoyed the trust of nearly 90 per cent of Americans.[21] His decision to carry out a military operation in Afghanistan[22] in October 2001, where Osama bin Laden, the leader of terrorist organisation al-Qaeda, was allegedly hiding, was met with the approval of 90 per cent of Americans surveyed. The rhetoric used by the Bush administration was quite significant here, which not only supported fighting terrorists in Afghanistan, but also the liberation of civilians from the brutal Taliban regime.[23] Over 90 per cent of respondents accepted the actions of the President in his declaration of the War on Terror. As much as 78 per cent of the population were in favour of carrying out military actions against other states that cooperated and supported terrorists.[24] With such strong support from both Americans and the international community, the administration of President Bush was able to implement their planned activities without major obstacles. Considering the fact that more than half of Americans surveyed were afraid of further terrorist attacks on the US,[25] the President could resort to various tools, change the law, expand his own powers, and even limit civil liberties and rights. A sense of security was more important than the freedom and liberty of Americans. The impulsiveness and unpredictability on the part of the terrorists caused great anxiety and fear in American society, who expected the President to act decisively.[26]

The use of fear propaganda by the Bush administration was noted and criticised by many politicians and researchers. Stephen Tanner wrote that the

---

20 O. Boyd-Barrett, 'Judith Miller, the *New York Times*, and the propaganda model' (2004) 5(4) *Journalism Studies* 438.

21 '2001 Poll Trend, Presidential Ratings – Job Approval', Gallup, www.gallup.com/poll/116500/presidential-approval-ratings-george-bush.aspx.

22 The purpose of the military intervention in Afghanistan was to capture America's greatest enemy, Osama bin Laden, as well as other al-Qaeda members, to liquidate terrorist training camps and to overthrow the Taliban regime. See E. Waśko-Owsiejczuk, 'Europe's position in US security policy at the beginning of the 21st century' (2017) 1 *International and Security Studies* 177.

23 'Presidential Address to the Nation', White House, 7 October 2001, https://georgewbush-whitehouse.archives.gov/news/releases/2001/10/20011007-8.html.

24 'Public overwhelmingly backs bush in attacks on Afghanistan', Gallup, www.gallup.com/poll/4966/Public-Overwhelmingly-Backs-Bush-Attacks- -Afghanistan.aspx.

25 'Terrorism', Gallup, https://news.gallup.com/poll/4909/terrorism-united-states.aspx.

26 Waśko-Owsiejczuk, *supra* note 1, p. 149.

use of messages relaying information that Iraq would be able to prepare an attack in 45 minutes using weapons of mass destruction must have caused fear and paralysis in society: 'Bush used fear, driving paranoia among US residents.'[27] Zbigniew Brzezinski presented a similar position criticising Bush's attitude and policy, and accused Bush of referring to American patriotism, while at the same time spreading fear, to pursue 'arrogant policy'. The purposeful procedure was to use phrases such as 'Let's take them out' or 'Axis of Evil'[28] during presidential speeches. Al Gore, in his book *The Assault on Reason*, described the role of fear, which in his opinion was meticulously used by the Bush administration to create political circumstances for attacking Iraq: 'When the president of the United States stood before the nation and made citizens imagine a terrorist attack using nuclear weapons, he was really talking about terrorists who were not related to Iraq. Our nation survived the horror of September 11, 2001, so when the president said: imagine this fear – it was quite easy to skip the reasoning process, which in other circumstances would lead to the question: wait a minute, Mr. President, and where is the evidence?'[29] According to him: 'Terrorism consists of fueling fear for political purposes. A particular goal of such action is to distort the political reality of the nation by raising fear in the whole society; fear that is disproportionate to the real danger posed by terrorism.'[30]

4. THE WAR ON TERROR: DESPERATE TIMES CALL FOR DESPERATE MEASURES …

The reaction of the White House to the attacks was fast and unwavering. On 14 September 2001, the US President announced a state of emergency, while strengthening the social conviction that at any moment another terrorist attack could occur. In his statements, Bush often emphasised that the new threat required new tools to combat it. The introduction of the state of emergency widened the scope of executive power, while laying the foundations for the War on Terror, which Bush did during an emotional speech before Congress on 20 September, where he claimed: 'Our war on terror begins with al Qaeda, but it does not end there. It will not end until every terrorist group of global reach has been found, stopped and defeated'.[31] The War on Terror declared by

27 S. Tanner, *Wojny Bushów, ojciec i syn jako zwierzchnicy sił zbrojnych*, Wydawnictwo Dolnośląskie, Wrocław 2007, p. 210.

28 Z. Brzeziński, *Druga szansa*, Świat Książki, Warsaw 2008, p. 120.

29 A. Gore, *Zamach na rozum*, Sonia Draga, Katowice 2008, p. 43.

30 *Ibid.*, p. 43.

31 'Address to a Joint Session of Congress and the American People', *supra* note 17.

Bush required changes to American laws. The most controversial of these were as follows:

- The Memorandum of Notification of 17 September 2001 – a programme of secret prisons was launched, which involved detaining suspected terrorists without time limits in various places in the world. New CIA privileges were granted, e.g. ability to transfer prisoners outside the legal and lawful procedures abroad, where they were interrogated and subjected to torture.[32]
- The Patriot Act of 21 October 2001 – this allowed special services to collect metadata from telecommunications companies, to conduct property searches without prior notice to the owner and to have access to documentation relating to telephone bills, online accounts and online activities.[33]
- The military order of the President of 13 November 2001 on the detention, treatment and trial of foreigners in the War on Terror – this enabled the special services to arrest and indefinitely detain people suspected of terrorism without being charged. It deprived detainees of the right to trial in an independent court. Defendants were subject to the jurisdiction of military tribunals that ruled on guilt and punishment, including, for example, the death penalty, and at the hearing, confessions obtained through torture were allowed.[34]
- The President's memorandum of 7 February 2002 – this excluded people suspected of terrorism, who were given the status of 'illegal enemy combatants', from protection under the Third Geneva Convention on the Treatment of Prisoners of War, which forbids mutilation, torture, humiliation and execution without a court verdict.[35]

---

32 See E. Waśko-Owsiejczuk, 'Zwalczanie terroryzmu po 9/11 – nowe procedury, uprawnienia i narzędzia amerykańskich służb specjalnych' in Z. Siemiątkowski and A. Zięba (eds.), *Służby Specjalne we współczesnym państwie*, Dom Wydawniczy Elipsa, Warsaw 2016, pp. 247–259; E. Waśko-Owsiejczuk, 'Globalizacja tortur – o programie tajnych więzień CIA na świecie' (2016) 45 *Politeja. Pismo Wydziału Studiów Międzynarodowych i Politycznych Uniwersytetu Jagiellońskiego* 207.

33 See Waśko-Owsiejczuk, 'Zwalczanie terroryzmu po 9/11', *supra* note 32; Waśko-Owsiejczuk, 'Globalizacja tortur', *supra* note 32.

34 The order violated the fundamental rights to a fair trial: lack of specific charges (suspicion was sufficient), right to testify or appeal. Human rights were infringed upon and violated by the use of arbitrary detention, kidnapping and forced transfers of detainees, and the use of reinforced interrogation techniques, which are considered torture under international law. The accused were also deprived of the opportunity to contact a lawyer and family. See Waśko-Owsiejczuk, 'Globalizacja tortur', *supra* note 32.

35 This was not a new date because, according to international law and martial law, persons recognised as 'hostile fighters' may be detained for the duration of the armed conflict. However, a significant distinction was made between legal and illegal fighters. The difference between them is that the former was entitled to the status of prisoners of war and protection under the Third Geneva Convention. President Bush recognised that people suspected of carrying

- The Department of Defense Memorandum of 2 December 2002 – this approved resistance-breaking techniques used during the interrogation of suspected terrorists, which placed prisoners in stressful positions, subjecting them to high or low temperatures, isolation, forced nudity, attacks by dogs and beatings.[36]

The scale of the abuse of power by the authorities and the special services was evident in various published reports (governmental, congressional and non-governmental reports, as well as reports by organisations supporting human rights protection) and showed the errors and manipulation of government agencies empowered to investigate innocent people.[37] As a result of the Snowden affair,[38] the international community could see just how far the US special services had gone in terms of their surveillance policy.[39] After the 9/11 attacks, President Bush saw his power significantly expand. He was the one to decide which suspects to investigate and detain; this was no longer the role of US judicial authorities. Judgment was issued by a military tribunal, the trials of the defendants were often secret, and the evidentiary proceedings took place without the possibility to respond to the accusations against the allegations and evidence submitted.[40] The publication of evidence of US torture of detainees subjected to, *inter alia*, waterboarding, low or very high temperatures, sleep deprivation,

out terrorist activities should be included in the group of 'illegal enemy fighters' because they were members of non-state groups – terrorist organisations that are not protected by the Third Geneva Convention. Depriving them of their right to contact with family and a lawyer, according to the Bush administration, had the goal of preventing concealed messages from America's enemies to get out and collecting information to prevent further attacks in the US. See Waśko-Owsiejczuk, 'Globalizacja tortur', *supra* note 32.

36 See Waśko-Owsiejczuk, 'Zwalczanie terroryzmu po 9/11', *supra* note 32; Waśko-Owsiejczuk, 'Globalizacja tortur', *supra* note 32.

37 See E. Waśko-Owsiejczuk, 'National security letters: a controversial FBI tool to fight terrorism' (2015) 7(2) *Internal Security* 71.

38 Edward Snowden worked at the NSA and was responsible for the Internet security system, thanks to which he had access to secret documentation, which he copied and made available to the media in 2013. For more on the scandal, see 'National Security Archive Electronic Briefing Book No. 436', The Snowden Affair Web Resource Documents the Latest Firestorm over the National Security Agency, https://nsarchive2.gwu.edu/NSAEBB/NSAEBB436.

39 In June 2013, the *Washington Post* and *The Guardian* revealed the details of the government eavesdropping program (PRISM), launched in 2007, which enabled the NSA to access the content of emails, private messages on social networks, conversations carried out via Skype voice messengers, saved data, file transfers and information about Internet activity. The information published in the following months, which pointed to the surveillance of not only citizens of other countries but also of world leaders, such as the German Chancellor Angela Merkel or the UN officials, were particularly harmful for the image and credibility of the secret services. See G. Greenwald and E. MacAskill, 'NSA Prism program taps in to user data of Apple, Google and others', *The Guardian*, 6 June 2013, http://www.theguardian.com/world/2013/jun/06/us-tech-giants-nsa-data.

40 Waśko-Owsiejczuk, 'Globalizacja tortur', *supra* note 32.

isolation for a period of multiple weeks,[41] surprised the Bush administration. The above practices were scrupulously concealed by US government. President Bush himself repeatedly stressed in the media that Americans did not break the law and did not torture detainees.[42] However, a report of the Senate Intelligence Commission published in December 2014 showed that information provided to the public by US government agencies was not always true. An example of this was one of the agency's greatest successes – locating Osama Bin Laden's hiding place, which was allegedly revealed through testimonies obtained during the torture of detained al-Qaeda members. The report not only undermined the accuracy of information previously presented by the CIA, but also showed the ineffectiveness of the programmes launched after the 9/11 attacks. According to the document, the al-Qaeda leader's hideout was found through traditional methods in the form of electronic intelligence rather than through the testimonies of tortured persons. Moreover, the document states that the methods used during the interrogations were much more brutal and the conditions in which prisoners were detained were much worse than what was previously reported by the agency to both decision-makers and the public.[43]

Using fear propaganda, threatening with further attacks, the President's collaborators assured the American people that they were keeping dangerous terrorists away from the US. The Bush administration wanted to convince the public that all those detained and tortured were dangerous terrorists. Propaganda based on intimidation had the aim of diverting attention away from violations of basic rights guaranteed by the international community. These tactics proved effective. Fear of terrorists was so strong that even a dozen or so years after the attacks on the US, most Americans opposed closing the Guantanamo Bay base and transporting prisoners to prisons in the US, and supported methods of interrogation using torture.[44] This may testify to the effectiveness of the US government's propaganda of fear, whose presence could still be observed even after the change of power in the White House.

5. THE WAR IN IRAQ: IN SEARCH OF AN EXCUSE

When planning the military operation in Iraq, the US government was aware that it required not only a specific reason but also a legal basis to enter another

41 People suspected of terrorism were detained in CIA 'secret prisons' located in various places around the world. See Waśko-Owsiejczuk, 'Globalizacja tortur', *supra* note 32.

42 'Bush: "we don't torture"', https://www.cbsnews.com/news/bush-we-dont-torture.

43 'Committee Study of the Central Intelligence Agency's Detention and Interrogation Program', Senate Select Committee on Intelligence, https://www.intelligence.senate.gov/study2014/minority-views.pdf.

44 'Americans continue to oppose closing Guantanamo Bay', Gallup, www.gallup.com/poll/171653/americans-continue-oppose-closing-guantanamo-bay.aspx.

sovereign state. Initially, the actions of the Bush administration focused on an attempt to manipulate the provisions contained in the United Nations (UN) Security Council Resolution of 2002, pointing to serious consequences for Iraq, which would occur if the organisation's guidelines were not observed by the Hussein regime. Although there is no mention of military intervention in the document, the Bush administration, in its own interpretation, recognised this provision in the resolution as a legal gateway for military action.[45] Fear propaganda was constantly used at this time. In almost every public statement, President Bush emphasised that the US was at war and that the enemy of America was unpredictable and could attack again at any moment. Using fear propaganda, he warned:

> Saddam Hussein is a threat to peace ... Iraq's weapons of mass destruction are controlled by a murderous tyrant who has already used chemical weapons to kill thousands of people. This same tyrant ... holds an unrelenting hostility toward the United States ... The danger is already significant, and it only grows worse with time ... We know that Iraq and the al Qaeda terrorist network share a common enemy – the United States of America ... We've learned that Iraq has trained al Qaeda members in bomb-making and poisons and deadly gases. And we know that after September the 11th, Saddam Hussein's regime gleefully celebrated the terrorist attacks on America ... Understanding the threats of our time, knowing the designs and deceptions of the Iraqi regime, we have every reason to assume the worst, and we have an urgent duty to prevent the worst from occurring ... As Americans, we want peace. But there can be no peace if our security depends on the will and whims of a ruthless and aggressive dictator. I'm not willing to stake one American life on trusting Saddam Hussein ... We refuse to live in fear.[46]

The tactics of the Bush administration were based on the presentation of a planned war with the Hussein regime as a fight between good and evil, where the US as a superpower would lead the mission for the freedom, peace and security of the whole world. The main argument of the Bush administration, aside from combating terrorism – Hussein's cooperation with al-Qaeda and the liberation of civilians from the tyrant's power – was based on the assumption

---

45 UN Security Council Resolution 1441 of 2002 set a deadline of 30 days for the Iraqi authorities to comply with earlier UN guidelines, such as the presentation of evidence of disarmament and destruction of weapons of mass destruction and ballistic missile programmes greater than 150 km. In addition, the Iraqi authorities were to provide unrestricted access by UN inspectors to all facilities, including underground buildings, equipment, devices and documentation, as well as officials and other persons who had to be heard without the involvement of Iraqi authorities and services. Paragraph 13 of Resolution 1441 speaks of serious consequences for Iraq, which would occur if UN resolutions were not respected. See Waśko-Owsiejczuk, *supra* note 1, pp. 207–208.

46 'President Bush outlines Iraqi threat', 7 October 2002, https://georgewbush-whitehouse.archives.gov/news/releases/2002/10/20021007-8.html, p. 1.

that the Hussein regime had weapons of mass destruction. Trying to influence public opinion, Bush warned that: 'Year after year, Saddam Hussein has gone to elaborate lengths, spent enormous sums, taken great risks to build and keep weapons of mass destruction … Some have said we must not act until the threat is imminent. Since when have terrorists and tyrants announced their intentions, politely putting us on notice before they strike?'[47] Hussein's connection to terrorism was made by stressing that al-Qaeda members responsible for the terrorist attacks on the US were in Iraq and were supported by the Saddam regime, and such statements were made in order to maintain the atmosphere of fear that had proved to be a useful tool in policy implementation.

In addition to using fear propaganda, the Bush administration used disinformation. The speech of Colin Powell, Secretary of State, on 5 February 2003, during the UN Security Council meeting, in which he presented evidence to convince the public that Saddam Hussein was in possession of weapons of mass destruction at that time, could serve as an example of this. Powell showed satellite images, claiming that the forbidden weapons were taken to other locations before the inspections by the UN and that the inspectors were shown empty warehouses.[48] The reasons for commencing the Iraq war turned out to be false and the evidence presented also turned out to be falsified. Americans failed to find weapons of mass destruction and failed to prove a connection between Hussein and Al-Qaeda. President Bush met with tremendous criticism, being accused of using 'social anxiety against terrorism to create political circumstances to attack Iraq'.[49]

Disinformation was used not only at the stage of seeking a pretext to organise a war in Iraq, but also after its launch, giving the public a distorted, often idealised picture of the situation in Iraq. Rather than the optimistic picture painted by the Bush administration, which claimed that US soldiers received a positive reception from civilians in Iraq, researchers assert that 'it turned out quickly that, contrary to American proclamation, no one greeted hostile troops with flowers, and Iraqis fought as much as they could'.[50] The White House used propaganda of success, manipulating the message sent out by the mainstream media. An example of this was the famous TV coverage of coalition forces entering Baghdad on 9 April 2003, heralding the overthrow of Hussein's regime. Media around the world showed images of liberated Iraqis trying to bring down Saddam Hussein's monument. Researchers have analysed other sources of information concerning this event and have found that the message presented

47 'President delivers "State of the Union"', White House, 28 January 2003, http://georgewbush-whitehouse.archives.gov/news/releases/2003/01/20030128-19.html.
48 See Waśko-Owsiejczuk, *supra* note 1, pp. 209–210.
49 A. Gore, *Zamach na rozum*, Wydawnictwo Sonia Draga, Katowice 2008, p. 43.
50 M. Dziekan, *Historia Iraku*, Wydawnictwo Akademickie Dialog, Warsaw 2007, p. 198.

by the mainstream media was not in fact accurate. While the mainstream media tried to give the impression that a crowd of many thousands had gathered at the square, the reality was that there were only about 150 people present at the time of filming.[51] In spite of the increasingly frequent media reports about the chaos that was overtaking liberated Iraq,[52] President Bush continued to claim that the internal situation of the country was improving: 'We have made good progress. Iraq is more secure. The economy of Iraq is beginning to improve.'[53]

6. THE PRESIDENTIAL ELECTION IN 2004 IN THE SHADOW OF THE WAR ON TERROR

The shock caused by the 9/11 attacks revived Americans' expectations of the presidential candidate in the 2004 campaign. Economic policy, which is usually at the centre of the election campaign, was relegated to second place, as the priority became ensuring security and preventing any repeat of a terrorist attack. Knowing the expectations of his citizens, George W. Bush used the American public's mood in his electoral strategy during his re-election campaign. The aim was to emphasise his merits in combating terrorism and to show that Americans were still in danger and that only he could protect them from further attacks. Summing up the three years of the fight against terrorism, on 2 August 2004, Bush said: 'In the three years since our country was attacked, we've taken steps to overcome new threats. We will continue to do everything in our power to defeat the terrorist enemy and to protect the American people … we're still not safe … We are a nation in danger.'[54]

Taking into account the emotions accompanying the 9/11 attacks, statements by President Bush regarding the threat that still existed had a considerable impact on the electorate's decisions. Bush assured Americans that the state under his rule was growing in strength and that winning the fight against terrorism was only a matter of time. Interestingly, after the start of the war in Iraq, neither weapons of mass destruction nor evidence of links between Hussein and al-Qaeda were found. Results of public research indicated that over 54 per cent of Americans

---

51 S. Tanner, *Wojny Bushów, ojciec i syn jako zwierzchnicy sił zbrojnych*, Wydawnictwo Dolnośląskie, Wrocław 2007, p. 248.

52 P. Foster, 'America's rebuilding of Iraq is in chaos, say British', *The Telegraph*, 17 June 2003, www.telegraph.co.uk/news/worldnews/middleeast/iraq/1433251/Americas-rebuilding-of-Iraq-is-in-chaos-say-British.html.

53 'President Bush, Secretary Rumsfeld discuss progress in Iraq', White House, 8 August 2003, https://georgewbush-whitehouse.archives.gov/news/releases/2003/08/20030808-1.html.

54 'Three years of progress in the War on Terror', White House, 11 September 2004, https://georgewbush-whitehouse.archives.gov/news/releases/2004/09/20040911.html.

considered the sending of troops to Iraq to be an error and 55 per cent did not believe that the war in the Persian Gulf had increased the security of the US against terrorists.[55] Yet Bush continued to stand by his actions as though they had been justified: 'In Iraq, we saw a threat and we realized that after September the 11th, we must take threats seriously before they fully materialize. Saddam Hussein now sits in a prison cell; America and the world are safer for it.'[56]

It is worth noting that the US presidential election campaign in 2004 was of a competitive nature not so much in terms of the programmes proposed as for the character traits of the candidates running for the office of president. It was therefore an image campaign, during which Bush assured voters: 'American people know I know how to lead. ... I made some tough decisions. But people know where I stand. This nation of ours has got a solemn duty to defeat this ideology of hate, and that's what they are ... if we remain strong and resolute, we will defeat this enemy.'[57] The outcome of the election showed the extent to which the public was convinced that Bush's War on Terror was warranted and, more importantly, that he had chosen the right way to combat the global threat. Opinion polls conducted at that time suggest that public opinion was divided: 44 per cent of Americans surveyed described Bush as 'a trustworthy leader', while 55 per cent expressed some doubts in this matter. At the same time, 54 per cent of respondents expressed their approval for Bush's presidency. The assessment of key issues in Bush's policy was as follows: policy towards Iraq – 52 per cent of Americans rated the policy positively and 44 per cent negatively; Bush's foreign policy – 50 per cent rated positively and 43 per cent negatively.[58] The results of the survey showed that on the one hand, more than half of Americans did not trust Bush and, at the same time, the same percentage of society expressed acceptance for his presidency. In spite of these doubts, Bush's appeal to the nation to allow him to continue the War on Terror he began was heard. The Americans did not want to change the president during the war. After the 9/11 attacks, Bush became a national hero who in an era of tragedy was able to unite the whole nation and restore lost faith in the strength and power of the country. Bush won the election despite the growing number of fallen American soldiers in Iraq and despite growing evidence that American soldiers were using torture on suspected terrorists. The US presidential campaign in 2004 was dominated by rhetoric based on fear. During almost every appearance in the media, at press conferences, in meetings with residents

55 'Poll: sending troops to Iraq a mistake', 25 June 2004, http://edition.cnn.com/2004/ALLPOLITICS/06/24/poll.iraq.

56 'Transcript of debate between Bush and Kerry', http://news.bbc.co.uk/nol/shared/bsp/hi/pdfs/01_10_04_debate1.pdf.

57 *Ibid.*

58 See L. Pastusiak, *George W. Bush. Jaki człowiek taki prezydent?*, Wydawnictwo Adam Marszałek, Toruń 2004, pp. 302–303.

of individual states, the President emphasised the nature of the threat, fuelling fear and arousing emotions. He knew just how strongly Americans would react to memories of the attacks on the World Trade Center and the Pentagon. The tactics of the campaign proved to be effective and he won the presidential election in 2004.

7. CONCLUSIONS

The terrorist attacks carried out on 11 September 2001 in the US created a convenient situation for the introduction of controversial policy pursued by the White House in the months following the attacks, which in other circumstances would not gain acceptance from either American society or the wider international community. The administration of President George W. Bush used effective tools in the form of disinformation and propaganda of fear, exerting influence on the mindset of society. Traditional media, which picked up the belligerent rhetoric of the White House, proved extremely useful in the dissemination of the propaganda of fear. The Bush administration managed to convince the public about the continuing threat of terrorism and the need to introduce new tools, procedures and powers for special services, whose main task was to prevent another attack on the US. The fear of terrorism was so huge that Americans accepted the new laws restricting their freedom and civil rights, as well as agreeing to the use of torture against people suspected of terrorism. Security became a priority at the price of freedom and values on which the foundations of American democracy were based. And although the unlawful war in Iraq did not meet with such limitless acceptance in public opinion as President Bush had expected, the evident use of disinformation and the disclosure of false reasons for war did not prevent him from being re-elected. Conducted in the shadows of the War on Terror, the presidential election in 2004 showed just how strongly the Bush administration succeeded in rooting fear of terrorism in the American people.

12. PERFORMANCE ANALYSIS OF FACT-CHECKING ORGANISATIONS AND INITIATIVES IN EUROPE

A Critical Overview of Online Platforms Fighting Fake News

Tanja PAVLESKA, Andrej ŠKOLKAY, Bissera ZANKOVA, Nelson RIBEIRO and Anja BECHMANN*

1. INTRODUCTION

The advent of information and communication technologies opened up a myriad of opportunities for people to create and disseminate content through multiple services and platforms. However, not always and not all of the actors take advantage of this bright side of the Internet. Very often (purposefully or not), content of dubious veracity or unverified origin is also created and spread. This type of content is what has popularly become classified as 'information pollution', for which fake news is the most common expression and is often interchangeably used for any type of information pollution.

Fake news is often simply defined as *spreading false content for political purposes*. However, from a broader perspective, fake news may refer to rumours,

* Tanja Pavleska: Department of Open Computer Systems and Networks, Jozef Stefan Institute (JSI), Slovenia. Email: atanja@e5.ijs.si; Andrej Školkay: School of Communication and Media (SCM), Slovakia. Email: askolkay@hotmail.com; Bissera Zankova: Media 21 Foundation, Bulgaria. Email: bzankova@gmail.com; Nelson Ribeiro: School of Human Sciences, Universidade Católica Portuguesa (UCP), Portugal. Email: nelson.ribeiro@fch.lisboa.ucp.pt; Anja Bechmann: School of Communication and Culture – Media Studies, Aarhus University, Denmark. Email: anjabechmann@aias.au.dk. This research has been supported by the CSA H2020 COMPACT Project, 'Compact: From research to policy through raising awareness of the state of the art on social media and convergence', Grant Agreement 762128, 2017–2020.

gossip or generally information that is not checked, is not objective and, in the worst-case scenario, is completely misleading. The most controversial property of fake news is their potential to influence how society as a whole or groups within society behave and perceive reality. This not only impacts the quality of contents on the Web, but also undermines the trust of the users in the platforms, in the online applications and in the other users creating and sharing content. As reported in the Reuters Institute Digital News Report,[1] only a quarter (24 per cent) of the respondents think that 'social media do a good job in separating facts from fiction, compared to 40% for the news media'. The data cited points out that 'users feel the combination of a lack of rules and viral algorithms are encouraging low quality and allowing fake news to spread quickly'. In that regard, Vertesi[2] also calls for the need to pay more attention to the topic of digital information technology in daily life and in knowledge work within science and technology studies.

However, these developments in the online world do not imply that traditional media are immune to fake news reporting.[3] The media presentation of reality and the quality of journalistic work have in particular been largely questioned because distrust in the media is on the rise. Thus, it comes as little surprise that we have witnessed the emergence of dozens of fact-checking and debunking organisations in Europe over the last few years.[4]

Although many journalistic articles and academic studies report on some aspects of these activities, tools, organisations and their work,[5] there is no study, let alone a holistic one, that either determines factors for measuring performance or inspects the influence of those factors on any aspect of the performance of fact-checking efforts. Yet, this particular issue seems to be approached by a multitude of disciplines:

- Economically, we can speak about the efficacy of the efforts, their social impact, return on investment, value for money, effect on consumer behaviour

---

1 N. Newman, R. Fletcher, A. Kalogeropoulos, A. David, L. Levy and R.K. Nielsen. 2017. 'Reuters Institute Digital News Report 2017'. Oxford: Reuters Institute for the Study of Journalism.

2 J. Vertesi, 2016. 'Seizing the digital'. *Engaging Science, Technology, and Society* 2, pp. 180–192, doi:10.17351/ests2016.75.

3 The 2018 Edelman Trust Barometer, https://www.edelman.com/trust-barometer.

4 M. Stencel, 2017. 'A big year for fact-checking, but not for new U.S. fact-checkers'. *Reporterslab*, 13 December, https://reporterslab.org/big-year-fact-checking-not-new-u-s-fact-checkers; P. Bae Brandtzaeg and A. Følstad. 2017. 'Trust and distrust in online fact-checking services'. *Communications of the ACM* 60(9): pp. 65–71; L. Graves and F. Cherubini. 2016. *The Rise of Fact-Checking Sites in Europe*. Oxford: Reuters Institute for the Study of Journalism.

5 See: https://journalistsresource.org/studies/society/internet/fake-news-conspiracy-theories-journalism-research/; and https://journalistsresource.org/tip-sheets/reporting/tools-verify-assess-validity-social-media-user-generated-content/.

and risk assessments of potential failures, or their contribution to the media development in general.

- Politically, we may concentrate on investigating either general questions like 'which entities deserve public/civil support and how is this provided in the most transparent and sustainable way?' and 'what are the practical implications of their functioning?' or some more specific questions, such as 'what is the correlation between information disorder and the political developments in a country?', 'how can regulation impact and be impacted by these efforts?' and 'how are fundamental rights affected by the success or failure of these initiatives?'.
- Psychologically and from a socio-economic aspect, investigating these issues may provide deeper and novel insights into the human bias phenomenon, the role of social behaviour and groupthink (echo chambers), and the formation of social networks in the proliferation of a certain piece of information, the urge to lower the human cognitive dissonances as a factor in the formation of information disorder, etc.

Nevertheless, research has provided arguments for negative perceptions on the general usefulness and trustworthiness of these organisations by social media users.[6] Economic theory suggests that any organisation pursuing special goals must apply a measurement of performance to follow its progress towards the achievement of these goals.[7] As Caruntu and Caruntu[8] point out, the measurement of economic and financial performance has started to gain even greater importance than before. It is therefore recommended that companies, organisations and any goal-oriented project should use a combination of financial, economic and non-financial indicators to measure their performance.

This chapter aims at developing a methodology for performance analysis of fact-checking and debunking organisations.[9] Europe as a case study was chosen to provide a counterweight to the US-dominated discussion on fake news, but also as a market with historically strong regulatory approaches to information infrastructure (e.g. privacy regulation). However, the same approach is applicable to a non-European context as well.

The methodology presented in this study comprises the development of a scheme of performance indicators and the design of a taxonomy of

6 Bae Brandtzaeg and Følstad, *supra* note 4.

7 M.J. Epstein, J.F. Manzoni and A. Davila (eds.). 2010. *Performance Measurement and Management Control: Innovative Concepts and Practices*. Bingley: Emerald Group Publishing.

8 A.L. Caruntu and R.C. Caruntu. 2012. 'Theoretical approaches regarding the economic and financial performance measurement'. *Annals of the 'Constantin Brâncuşi' University of Târgu Jiu, Economy Series*, Issue 4/2012.

9 From this point on, by 'fact-checking', we imply 'fact-checking and debunking'. For the sake of brevity, only 'fact-checking' will be used.

fact-checking systems as an upgrade of an existing conceptual framework. To provide a proof of concept of the practical value and implementation of the methodology, an empirical study is carried out and the methodology is piloted into a set of implemented and working online platforms. This enables the extraction of a set of recommendations for the performance evaluation and improvement of fact-checking processes and organisations.

Based on the outcome from this research, the findings and the results are analysed and structured into a proposal for a general research and assessment framework of the performance of fact-checking organisations. As such, it is the first implementable methodology-oriented framework empirically employed in the context of combating information disorder.

To develop the topics presented above, the next section introduces the basic concepts and definitions employed throughout the work in this study. Related work and state of the art are also included in this section. The basic features of fact-checking organisations are elaborated upon in Section 3. Section 4 proceeds with the methodology of the work, introducing the guiding principles for designing and carrying out the theoretical and the empirical parts of the study. An empirical study is then built and its piloting in 50 EU fact-checking organisations is discussed, before the discussion moves on from the description of the field work through the presentation and the analysis of the results to the final recommendations and conclusions. The chapter concludes with pointers to future directions on the work on developing trustworthy information infrastructure, of which fact-checking organisations are becoming an integral part.

2. BACKGROUND CONCEPTS AND RELATED WORK

The discussion over cases concerned with fake news,[10] hoaxes, fact-checking and clickbait (monetisation and traffic attraction) is often impeded by the absence of a theoretical framework on underlying this research area. Some suggest novel terms for this research field, such as *attention hacking.*[11] Others introduce additional terms to come to a consensus on the definition of fake news, such as *information disorder*, *information pollution* and *disinformation campaigns.*[12] Yet others prefer more general terms, such as *distribution of harms*, as coined by

10 V.L. Rubin, Y. Chen and N.J. Conroy. 2015. 'Deception detection for news: three types of fakes'. *Proc. Assoc. Info. Sci. Tech.* 52: pp. 1–4. doi:10.1002/pra2.2015.145052010083.

11 A. Marwick and R. Lewis. 2017. *Media Manipulation and Disinformation Online.* New York: Data & Society Research Institute.

12 C. Wardle and H. Derakhshan. 2017. *Information Disorder: Toward an Interdisciplinary Framework for Research and Policymaking.* Strasbourg: Council of Europe, p. 5.

Rubin et al.[13] Bounegru et al.[14] argue that 'fake news is not just another type of content that circulates online, but that it is precisely the character of this online circulation and reception that makes something into fake news'. According to Marwick and Lewis,[15] it 'generally refers to a wide range of disinformation and misinformation circulating online and in the media'. In media market theories, fake news is defined as 'distorted signals uncorrelated with the truth' that emerge in the market because it is 'cheaper to provide than precise signals'.[16] From a political economy perspective, fake news has a long history that is linked to the commodification of journalism in a market economy.[17]

However, there seems to be a consensus that the current communication environment within and between many countries worldwide is much more politically and socially challenged than in the past periods of grey[18] and black[19] propaganda, conspiracy theories and fabricated content.[20] Although Collins Dictionary has included 'fake news' on the 2017 Word of the Year shortlist, some researchers like Wardle and Derakhshan[21] oppose the use of the term. In their view, it is a conceptually inadequate and politically abused term. In the same vein, Marwick et al.[22] call for a greater focus on *attention* and *frame hacking*, providing a perspective that is more oriented towards data infrastructure manipulation sensitivity rather than vague discussions on veracity, truth and objectivity. Therefore, Wardle and Derakhshan introduce a new conceptual framework, defining what they prefer to call *the key terminology of information disorder* – misinformation, disinformation and malinformation – and distinguishing between information that is false and information that is designed to harm. In this chapter, we follow Wardle and Derakhshan's conceptual framework for information disorder and adopt the following working definitions:

- *Definition 1*: misinformation is when false information is shared, but no harm is meant.

---

13 Rubin, Chen and Conroy, *supra* note 10, pp. 1–4.

14 L. Bounegru, J. Gray, T. Venturini and M. Mauri (eds.). 2017. 'A Field Guide to Fake News: A Collection of Recipes for Those Who Love to Cook with Digital Methods' (Chapters 1–3) Public Data Lab, Research Report, p. 5.

15 Marwick and Lewis, *supra* note 11.

16 H. Allcott and M. Gentzkow. 2017. 'Social media and fake news in the 2016 election'. *Journal of Economic Perspectives* 31(2): pp. 211–236.

17 M. Hirst. 2017. 'Towards a political economy of fake news'. *Political Economy of Communication* 5(2): pp. 82–94.

18 Information of questionable origin that is never sourced and whose accuracy is doubtful.

19 False information and material that purports to be from a source on one side of a conflict, but is actually from the opposing side. It is typically used to vilify, embarrass or misrepresent the enemy.

20 Invented or produced some false messages in order to deceive someone.

21 Wardle and Derakhshan, *supra* note 12, p. 6.

22 Marwick and Lewis, *supra* note 11.

- *Definition 2*: disinformation is when false information is knowingly shared to cause harm.
- *Definition 3*: malinformation is when genuine information is shared to cause harm, often by moving information designed to stay private into the public sphere.

Clearly, information disorder can have a detrimental effect on the 'social transformation' facilitated by the Internet. Moreover, it can also bring harm to the public like any other type of harmful content. Recognising this, a political intervention was undertaken by the EU in this regard: the European External Action Service East Stratcom Task Force that ran the 'EU vs Disinformation' campaign.[23] The Task Force was established after the EU heads of state and government stressed 'the need to challenge Russia's ongoing disinformation campaigns in March 2015'. Between September 2015 and November 2017, the Task Force and its partners have identified and debunked over 3,500 disinformation cases. Despite these concrete efforts, research on whether fact-checking is effective at correcting false beliefs (and under what conditions) has been contradictory at times.[24] Nyhan and Reifler[25] argue that misinformation can be very difficult to correct and may have lasting effects even after it is discredited. Therefore, simply debunking it is not sufficient; it must be replaced by an alternative causal explanation.[26]

Some scholars implicitly or explicitly point to the contextual and cultural dimensions of spreading hoaxes and fake news.[27] Different interests are involved in the process, and the public expression of opinions often results in considerable ambiguity. In order to properly understand the digital discourse, it may be necessary to identify and elucidate the practices of communication from historical, cultural, and other aspects, which would require exhaustive comparative analysis.[28] This is in part a global issue that requires a global approach. Therefore, several global tools have been developed by IT companies to verify and re-establish trusted sources of online information, such as Google fact-checking and Facebook repost-verification. Rather than establishing the veracity of a certain piece of information, these tools only offer news and

23 See https://euvsdisinfo.eu/about.

24 M.P.S. Chan, C.R. Jones, K.H. Hall Jamieson and D. Albarracín. 2017. 'Debunking: a meta-analysis of the psychological efficacy of messages countering misinformation'. *Psychological Science* 28(11): pp. 1531–1546.

25 D. Nyhan and J. Reifler. 2015. 'Displacing misinformation about events: an experimental test of causal corrections'. *Journal of Experimental Political Science* 2(1): pp. 81–93.

26 *Ibid.*

27 See http://www.worldvaluessurvey.org/WVSContents.jsp?CMSID=Findings.

28 S.E. Bird. 2003. *The Audience in Everyday Life: Living in a Media World*. New York: Routledge.

facts on more aspects of the piece of information, allowing users themselves to decide on 'what would be their own truth'. Furthermore, tech-industry players may not have their interests tuned into laying out a critical approach to the use and manipulation of data infrastructures, or to ensuring the transparency of such use. As a result, very often they may even defeat the purpose of fact-checking simply by their nature of operation. For instance, in late 2017, fake news stories were accidentally promoted with prominent ads promoted by Google on websites like PolitiFact and Snopes, which are fact-checking sites created precisely to dispel such falsehoods.[29] Hence, it is not surprising that the public in many countries is also worried about the proliferation of fake news across the different media and the rise of distrust in the news in general.[30]

Considering the variety of stakeholders concerned by the problem, several initiatives and organisations have also been established with the common objective of raising awareness and addressing challenges related to trust and truth in the digital age: the non-governmental organisation (NGO) *First Draft*[31] (in 2016), the global *Partner Network* of journalism (e.g. BBC, Reuters), human rights (e.g. Amnesty International) and technology (e.g. YouTube) organisations, to name but a few. To join these efforts at a European level, in November 2017 the European Commission announced its next step in the fight against fake news: setting up a High-Level Expert Group and launching a public consultation.[32] Interestingly, the actions of the Commission also include 'assessment of measures already taken by platforms, news media companies and civil society organisations to counter the spread of fake news online, as well as positions on the roles and responsibilities of the relevant stakeholders'.[33] However, no details have been disclosed about the methodological framework to be applied and whether effectiveness and efficiency of fact-checking initiatives will fall within the scope of the evaluation.

Some EU Member States had already taken measures to combat information disorder. For example, the Czech Republic set up a specialist 'anti-fake news' police unit called the Centre against Terrorism and Hybrid Threats, which has been operating since 2017. Both the Italian and the Slovak police announced a fight against fake news in January 2018. Simultaneously, Sweden engaged in

---

29 D. Wakabayashi and L. Qiu. 2017. 'Google serves fake news ads in an unlikely place: fact-checking sites'. *New York Times*, 17 October, p.17.

30 R. Cellan-Jones. 2017. 'Fake news worries "are growing" suggests BBC poll'. *BBC News*, 22 September. http://www.bbc.com/news/technology-41319683; J. Rankin. 2017. 'EU anti-propaganda unit gets €1m a year to counter Russian fake news'. *The Guardian*, 25 November. https://www.theguardian.com/world/2017/nov/25/eu-anti-propaganda-unit-gets-1m-a-year-to-counter-russian-fake-news.

31 See https://firstdraftnews.com/about/#network.

32 See http://europa.eu/rapid/press-release_IP-17-4481_en.htm.

33 *Ibid.*

plans to create a new public authority tasked with countering disinformation and boosting the population's resilience in the face of possible influence operations, called 'psychological defence' (*psykologiskt försvar*) authority. Similarly, in January 2018, the UK revealed plans to establish a new 'national security communications unit' to curb the presence of hoax news stories online and stop social media campaigns carried out by foreign adversaries. Many of these initiatives have no professional or permanent institutional background. A debate could be raised here on whether any effort to make them institutional would result in their approval by the public and what repercussions this would have on human rights, national security and public safety.

3. PROPERTIES OF FACT-CHECKING ORGANISATIONS

There is no single definition of fact-checking organisations summarising their basic features. A variety of approaches among scientists exist to determine and describe these organisations. By and large, scientists take into account the different traits and features to devise their models of fact-checking organisations. Thus, a recent study by Brandtzaeg and Føolstad[34] divides fact-checking services into three general categories based on their areas of concern: (1) political and public statements in general; (2) online rumours and hoaxes; and (3) specific topics, controversies and particular conflicts or narrowly scoped issues and events. At the time of writing, we counted 137 active fact-checking projects around the world, up from 114 in early 2017. A third of these are located in the US.[35] In Europe alone, 34 permanent political fact-checking sources have been identified as active in 20 different European countries, from Ireland to Turkey.[36] These organisations are categorised in terms of their mission and methods. Based on this categorisation, Graves and Cherubini found that fact-checking outlets occupy a spectrum between *reporters*, *reformers* and a third, overlapping category including organisations which have cultivated a role as independent *experts*.

Fact-checkers around the globe have also formed an entire professional network. The International Fact-Checking Network (IFCN) is a unit of the Poynter Institute dedicated to bringing fact-checkers together worldwide. The IFCN was launched in September 2015 to support fact-checking initiatives by promoting best practices and exchanges among organisations in this field.

---

34 Bae Brandtzaeg and Følstad, *supra* note 4.
35 Stencel, *supra* note 4.
36 Graves and Cherubini, *supra* note 4.

The association also adopted a code of principles in 2016.[37] It addresses 'organizations that regularly publish nonpartisan reports on the accuracy of statements by public figures, major institutions, and other widely circulated claims of interest to society'. The principles represent professional commitments to non-partisanship and fairness, transparency of sources, transparency of methodology and open and honest corrections. These comprise the principles and values on which the activities of fact-checking organisations are premised; notwithstanding the fact that these organisations are similar to journalistic and other associations (like NGOs), they have not adopted criteria for the self-assessment of their performance. Moreover, only some of the European fact-checkers joined this global network.

Analysing more in depth these organisations, some scholars explore the methodology they use. Rubin et al.[38] provide a map of the current landscape of veracity (or deception) assessment methods, their major classes and goals. Two major categories of methods exist: (1) *linguistic approaches*, in which the content of deceptive messages is extracted and analysed to associate language patterns with deception; and (2) *network approaches*, in which network information, such as message metadata and structured knowledge network queries, can be harnessed to provide aggregate deception measures. Interestingly, most of the insights on deception research originate from disciplines without automation or deception detection in mind.

Despite their diversity, the functional characteristics of fact-checking organisations are denoted by their names. Experts have (rightly) observed that while the spreading of misinformation/disinformation/malinformation is mainly dominated by very active users, fact-checking is still more of a grassroots activity.[39] Furthermore, as Rubin and Conroy[40] and Wineburg et al.[41] demonstrate, one serious drawback of fact-checking and debunking activities relates to the fact that human observers perform poorly in the detection of fake news and machines even slightly outperform humans on certain tasks. The mathematical modelling of information diffusion processes showed that there is a threshold value for the fact-checking probability that guarantees the

37 See https://www.poynter.org/international-fact-checking-network-fact-checkers-code-principles.

38 Rubin, Chen and Conroy, *supra* note 10, pp. 1–4.

39 C. Shao, G. Luca Ciampaglia, A. Flammini and F. Menczer. 2016. 'Hoaxy: a platform for tracking online misinformation'. In *Proceedings of the 25th International Conference Companion on World Wide Web (WWW '16 Companion)*. Switzerland: Republic and Canton of Geneva.

40 V.L. Rubin and N. Conroy. 2012. 'Discerning truth from deception: human judgments & automation efforts'. *First Monday* 17: pp. 3–5.

41 S. Wineburg, S. McGrew, J. Breakstone and T. Ortega. 2016. *Evaluating Information: The Cornerstone of Civic Online Reasoning*. Stanford Digital Repository. http://purl.stanford.edu/fv751yt5934.

complete removal of the hoax from the network, which does not depend on the spreading rate, but only on the gullibility and forgetting probability.[42] This also raises a series of fundamental issues: how efficient are the tools and platforms aimed at combating information disorder? Which factors affect their performance? And how should this be evaluated in the first place?

In the following section, we move on to defining the methodology of work that will help us pursue the goal of answering the above questions.

4. METHODOLOGY OF WORK

Pertinent to the definition of a proper set of performance indicators is the analysis of the contextual traits of the systems/organisations where the evaluation is to be performed. Unlike most of the approaches that pre-define the performance indicators based on the needs of their research objectives, we extract the baseline of the methodology from the existing frameworks and reports on the performance issues of two sectors: the governmental and non-governmental sectors. Combining the insights of the analysis of these two sectors not only enables us to extract a general set of indicators that highlights the advantages of both sectors, but also allows these efforts to complement each other in a way that can improve both the evaluation and the performance of the organisations.

As most of the fact-checking organisations are in essence non-governmental, we first analyse and extract the relevant performance indicators for the non-governmental sector, and then complement it with the insights from other contexts.

In addition to defining performance indicators, an initial survey was also designed containing a basic set of questions addressing the identified indicators. This survey was piloted in several fact-checking organisations. In parallel, unstructured interviews were carried out with experts who are directly involved in the implementation of the fact-checking methodology of these organisations. Both types of feedback (from the survey and from the interviews) enabled us to perform a second iteration of improvements of our methodology and progress towards defining a more relevant and granular set of indicator-related questions for the empirical study provided in Section 5. A conceptual framework was adopted to guide the structure of the elaborated issues and was adjusted to the context of fact-checking in order to ensure the greatest relevance of this work

42 M. Tambuscio, G. Ruffo, A. Flammini and F. Menczer. 2015. 'Fact-checking effect on viral hoaxes: a model of misinformation spread in social networks'. In *Proceedings of the 24th International Conference on World Wide Web (WWW '15 Companion)*. New York: ACM, pp. 977–982.

among the efforts for combating information disorder. In order to verify the relevance, a basic taxonomy of fact-checking systems was also developed as part of the methodology.

4.1. DEVELOPING PERFORMANCE INDICATORS

It has become clear by now that the introduction of performance indicators and metrics allows an organisation to build a holistic quality management system. Although measuring performance may come once policies, procedures and feedback mechanisms are adopted and clarified, performance indicators can also be introduced incrementally, depending on the strategic goal and the foreseen outcomes. This is also the logic behind the development of indicators followed in this work.

4.1.1. Performance Indicators Relevant for Non-Governmental Organisations

Scriven[43] was among the first researchers who discerned the bifurcated role of evaluation: its formative and summative nature. The formative evaluation pursues the provision of useful information to the team, with team improvement as the ultimate goal. Chianca[44] also calls this type of evaluation *process evaluation*. For the purposes of this chapter, the process is represented by the *internal coordination* indicator.

Summative evaluation, on the other hand, is performed to provide information to the decision-makers who run the team, as well as to potential users who judge the value or merit of the programme in relation to important criteria. Scriven[45] finds that the two types of evaluation are interwoven, above all on a practical scale. When it comes to NGOs, fact-checking organisations notwithstanding, their goal of *pursuing social change* makes them predominantly function as natural open systems, where performance is highly dependent on and sensitive to instability and rapid change in the external environment.[46] We recognise this crucial interaction between the outside environment and

---

43 M. Scriven. 1967. 'The methodology of Evaluation'. In: R. Tyler, R. Gagne and M. Scriven (eds.) *Perspectives of curriculum evaluation*. AERA Monograph Series on Curriculum Evaluation. Chicago: Rand McNally, pp. 36–83.

44 T.K. Chianca and J.S. Risley. 2005. 'Applying the success case method as part of the institutional evaluation of a nonprofit organization'. Paper presented at the Meeting of the American Evaluation Association/Canadian Evaluation Society, Toronto, Canada.

45 M. Scriven. 1991. *Evaluation Thesaurus* (4th ed.). London: SAGE.

46 W.R. Scott. 1987. *Organizations: Rational, Natural, and Open Systems* (2nd ed.). Hemel Hempstead: Prentice Hall; A. Fowler et al. 1992. 'Distant obligations: speculations on NGO funding and the global market'. In: *Review of African Political Economy*, No. 55, Sheffield, November, pp. 9–29.

the internal organisation setting, and enlist *external coordination* as another indicator that is relevant for the evaluation of performance.

Clearly, the performance of NGOs can be evaluated with respect to, on the one hand, the accomplishment of the project goals and, on the other hand, their overall societal impact. However, as many researchers have noted, there is a pervasive problem in that the monitoring and evaluation of organisations is mainly concentrated on expenditure, activities and outputs, but not on the effects and impacts of the work carried out by the organisations, e.g. on humans, society and the environment.[47] In the most comprehensive overview of NGO impact and impact evaluation methods to date, Riddell et al.[48] looked at evidence from 60 separate reports of 240 projects undertaken in 26 developing countries. They reported that 'in spite of growing interest in evaluation, there is a lack of reliable evidence on the impact of NGO development projects and programs'. Thus, *tracking impact* is an important indicator to address in the process of performance evaluation.

Despite the aim of tracking their impact, Fowler has argued that the 'limitations of the instruments that NGOs use to monitor, evaluate and review' are one reason why NGOs have not been able to substantiate their achievements.[49] There has been considerable debate over the value of logical frameworks as planning and monitoring tools.[50] Logical frameworks have been useful in encouraging the identification of indicators at the planning stage, but much less so in ensuring their actual use during project monitoring or evaluation.[51] In practice, the widespread focus on the *identification* of indicators reflects a bias towards planning rather than monitoring and evaluation that is built into most NGOs, and other agencies. *Tracking progress* is thus an important part of continuous performance awareness.

Very often, NGOs set the scene for anticipating exceedingly high expectations of what can be achieved.[52] It is widely recognised that the achievements of many objectives, such as empowerment, institutional strengthening and

---

47 A. Fowler (ed.). 1997. *Striking a Balance: A Guide to Enhancing the Effectiveness of Non-governmental Organizations in International Development.* London: Earthscan; R. Riddell et al. 1997. *Searching for Impact and Methods: NGO Evaluation Synthesis Study.* Available at http://pdf.usaid.gov/pdf_docs/PNACD416.pdf; C. Roche. 1999. 'Impact assessment and advocacy'. In: *Impact Assessment for Development Agencies: Learning to Value Change.* Oxford: Oxfam, pp. 192–234.

48 Riddell et al., *supra* note 47.

49 Fowler, *supra* note 47, p. 160.

50 T. Wallace et al. 1997. *Standardising Development: Influences on UK NGOs' Policies and Procedures.* Oxford: Worldview.

51 R. Davies. 1997. 'Moving from logical to network frameworks: a modular matrix approach to representing and evaluating complex programs' A Briefing Note prepared for the ODI Workshop 'Indicators of Poverty: Operational Significance', London, 8 October (unpublished).

52 R. Davis. 2001. 'Monitoring and evaluating NGO achievements'. Available at http://www.cepa.lk/content_images/publications/documents/491-S-OI_%20Rick%20Davis-%20Monitoring%20and%20Evaluating%20NGO%20Achievemen.pdf.

the development of civil society, are difficult to define in advance. Hence, *clarity of objectives* is another relevant indicator for the performance evaluation of fact-checking organisations.

All of the aspects discussed above require the involvement of stakeholders in the elaboration of evaluation criteria, which should be an ongoing process. Such a method also presupposes a high degree of transparency of the organisation's activities. This is especially relevant for fact-checking organisations, where absence of transparency has been detected as a major issue that affects stakeholders' perceptions of the trustworthiness of an organisation.[53] Therefore, *accounting for transparency* (of the methodology used, funding sources, etc.) is a factor we employ in the set of performance indicators.

Addressing the identified set of indicators in the appropriate manner allows for a feedback loop to be established between the inputs and outputs of the quality management system of an organisation, enabling the introduction of necessary measures into the operations and functions of the organisation, and the achievement of desirable goals. Nevertheless, NGOs exist in an environment that exhibits contextual traits which are not inherently present within the structure and management of NGOs, but are interlocked in the communication pathways with these external systems. This is the case, for example, for government-related systems, whose presence raises additional issues, but also facilitates the coping with some inherently non-governmental issues. The next section introduces such indicators that emerge from the interactions between these two sectors.

4.1.2. *Performance Indicators from Governmental Contexts*

The choice of objectives in a system/organisation is also deemed to be critical for the governmental sector. In the context of governmental performance, indicators' systems provide a systematic collection of information to measure and monitor particular activities.[54] They can serve a variety of specific objectives, such as allocation and control of resources, quality evaluation, cost, coverage, transparency and communication with citizen stakeholders, and efficiency evaluation. As revealed by the OECD 'regular collection, use, and/or dissemination of information help to distinguish between ad hoc use of indicators and indicator systems'.[55] An essential characteristic of indicators is that they are not static and should be viewed as evolving in a dynamic and collaborative

---

53 Bae Brandtzaeg and Følstad, *supra* note 4.

54 OECD. 2008. 'Promoting performance using indicators to enhance the effectiveness of subcentral spending'. Working Papers on Fiscal Federalism N5. Available at https://www.oecd-ilibrary.org/docserver/5k97b11g190r-en.pdf?expires=1581756313&id=id&accname=guest&checksum=B6392BC458A3DFCA5099FCC830DDFB2B.

55 *Ibid.*

context.[56] Certainly, this stands not only for NGO-relevant indicators, but also for any organisation residing in a human-centric environment. In a governmental context, performance indicators can be used to establish the current organisation's performance, measure improvement over time, set targets to motivate continuous improvement and as part of a self-assessment which could be included in third-party verification.

In addition to external evaluation, self-assessment is a very important part of the continuous performance evaluation on both a short-term and on a long-term basis. The self-assessment criteria can be adopted by the organisation as a result of an internal discussion with the staff and/or an external discussion with stakeholders. Furthermore, *self-assessment* is an important part of tracking the progress of the performance. It encourages the team's involvement and responsibility and enables it to reflect on the role and contribution of any of the group to the process. Thus, self-assessment ties most of the other performance indicators together. In our empirical study, we also pay special attention to self-assessment.

When we speak of the governmental sector, it is inevitable that we will touch upon regulatory frameworks and policies. In the context of performance evaluation, the OECD Framework for Regulatory Policy Evaluation was devised to assist countries in evaluating the process of their regulatory policy.[57] In addition, it recommends an overarching method of evaluating performance based on data and information on the design, implementation and results. Thus, it becomes important to assess the *alignment between the regulatory policies* by determining where the state-responsibility meets the NGOs' objectives.

Some obstacles to the proper application of this approach within NGOs can be the identification of the relevant outcomes, which, as stated before, can be vague or too ambitious. However, establishing the connection among the sequence of inputs, activities, outputs and outcomes is only a logical way to assess any organisational performance. In that sense, the choice of proper indicators contributes to enhancing the efficiency and effectiveness of an objective by reducing information asymmetries which exist among the various management levels and encouraging performance improvements by altering the incentives for carrying out the necessary work to achieve the planned goals. Thus, *incorporating incentives* into the design of an indicator scheme is not even optional; incentives are inevitable, regardless of whether their implementation is implicit or explicit in terms of achieving the objectives. Therefore, an incentive policy in an organisation's work is the final performance indicator we enlist in the indicators scheme.

56 OECD, *supra* note 54.

57 OECD. 2014. 'Framework for regulatory policy evaluation'. Available at: https://read.oecd-ilibrary.org/governance/oecd-framework-for-regulatory-policy-evaluation_9789264214453-en#page19.

Among the well-established performance indicators, *effectiveness* and *efficiency* are two broad categories used to evaluate the genuine advancement of the work of organisations. While effectiveness indicators measure how many targets are reached and relate actual to expected values, efficiency indicators measure how 'well' resources (like people, machines and money) are deployed to produce a given output (like products, services and profit). As is the case for NGOs, the accomplishment of outcomes is naturally considered the most relevant indicator for measuring effectiveness in this context as well.

These two broad categories of indicators are also adopted in our approach and are embedded into the empirical study. Moreover, they integrate (either implicitly or explicitly) all of the indicators identified in this section and unify them under the common term *performance indicators*. For instance, the presence of incentives is relevant for both efficient operation and effective outcomes. The same is true for most other performance indicators.

In summary, in addition to *internal coordination*, *external coordination*, *tracking impact*, *tracking progress*, *clarity of objectives* and *accounting for transparency*, the complementary analysis of the governmental sector allows for the identification of *self-assessment procedures* and *incentives policy* as additional indicators. The analysis of all of the identified indicators is either implicitly or explicitly embedded into the analysis of the *effectiveness* and *efficiency* indicators whose maximisation is the most desirable performance aspect.

4.2. THE WDF CONCEPTUAL FRAMEWORK

In order to establish a common ground with the approaches taken or yet to be taken in the field, but also to ensure a level of conceptual rigour, our work follows a well-defined conceptual framework. As underlying premises for studying the combating of information disorder by the fact-checking organisations surveyed in this study, we have adopted the conceptual framework for information disorder of Wardle and Derakhshan.[58] This framework (hereinafter referred to as the WDF) represents a qualitative sublimation of the types, phases and elements of information disorder (as shown in Figure 1).

The three types of information disorder have already been defined and explained earlier. The phases essentially follow the logical lifecycle of information: *creation* refers to the steps taken towards 'creating the message'; *production* encompasses the transformation of the message into a media product, denoting its initial presence in the media; and *distribution* refers to the spreading of the message across various media and its proliferation to the public. The elements

[58] Wardle and Derakhshan, *supra* note 12.

of information disorder are divided into: *messages* – the information of interest, e.g. the (potentially) fake news; *agents* – the controllers of the messages; and *interpreters* – the 'audience' or 'consumers' of the messages. Certainly, their roles and functions are further divided and analysed into subprocesses.

Figure 1. The WDF conceptual framework for information disorder

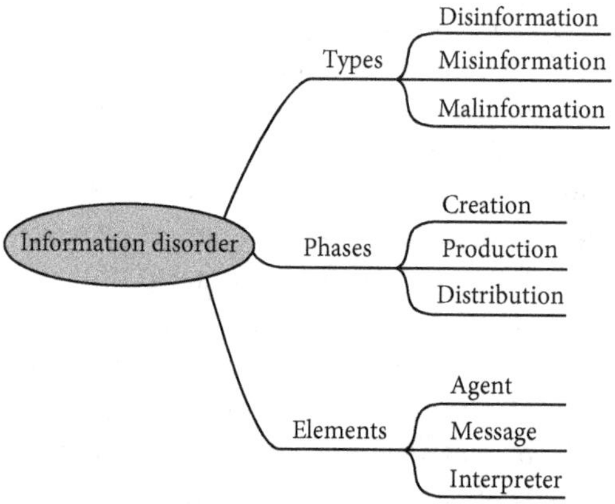

Source: Produced by the authors.

All of the above concepts provide the guidelines for developing further our methodology, from designing the survey, through structuring and elaboration on the scheme of performance indicators, to the necessary adjustment to the narrower context addressed by this study: fact-checking. This 'narrower context', for example, implies that while the WDF requires addressing the 'creation' phase of a message, the fact-checking process is clearly not tackling this issue and this phase would thus be irrelevant for our analysis. Therefore, a relevant mapping between the context of fact-checking organisations and the WDF needs to be performed. This is demonstrated in the following Section.

4.3. MAPPING THE WDF TO THE CONTEXT OF FACT-CHECKING

In order to be able to perform the required mapping, it is first necessary to establish the link between the conceptual framework and the structural organisation of the components of a fact-checking system. However, there is no known taxonomy of fact-checking systems that defines such components. Moreover, there is even not an approach that establishes the process of fact-checking as one that could be functionally organised into a systematic operational unit. This is probably due to the fact that the fact-checking process is mainly seen as a human-effort expertise, which makes it difficult to unify the operations across organisations. However, relying solely on human effort is increasingly becoming an unrealistic assumption, and the latest developments in the field call for the need to establish a common taxonomy of fact-checking systems.

In this section, we will only provide the basis for defining such a taxonomy. The further development of this taxonomy is beyond the scope of this chapter and will be subject to our future work.

The first step towards the definition of a fact-checker's taxonomy is the identification of existing systems that bear a resemblance in their objectives to the process of fact-checking and debunking. An example would be computational trust systems, which are already highly automated and supported by a well-defined taxonomy.[59]

Based on the known approaches that try to systematise the fact-checking processes,[60] and complemented by the taxonomy of trust systems, we are able to determine the following three main components that a fact-checking system would integrate: *information gathering*, *decision-making* and *response*. These can further be divided into subsystems that can again be equipped with both human and computational mechanisms, as shown in Table 1.

Table 1. **Basic taxonomy of fact-checking systems**

	Fact-checking system	
Information-gathering	**Decision-making**	**Response**
Information sources	Good vs. bad messages	Targets choice
Information classification	Good vs. bad agents	Incentives
Information aggregation	Level of successful vs. unsuccessful interpreters	Punishments
Newcomer policy		

Source: Compiled by the authors.

For the purposes of our mapping, it is sufficient to consider only the three major parts of the fact-checking system. With such a defined taxonomy, we are able to perform the mapping of the WDF in a fact-checking context. This is shown in Table 2. By merging these two approaches, not only will our analysis benefit from having a conceptual grounding, but the WDF can also be revised through the lens of more practical approaches. For instance, if we provide a feedback

59 S. Marti and H. Garciamolina. 2006. 'Taxonomy of trust: categorizing P2P reputation systems'. *Computer Networks* 50(4): pp. 472–484.

60 N.J. Conroy, V.L. Rubin and Y. Chen. 2015. 'Automatic deception detection: methods for finding fake news'. *Proc. Assoc. Info. Sci. Tech.* 52: pp. 1–4; S. Guha. 2017. 'Related fact checks: a tool for combating fake news'. *arXiv:1711.00715 [Cs]*. Available at http://arxiv.org/abs/1711.00715; N. Hassan et al. 2017. 'ClaimBuster: the first-ever end-to-end fact-checking system'. *Proceedings of the VLDB Endowment* 10(12): pp. 1945–1948.

loop from the taxonomy to the phases of information disorder, it can be noted that the framework does not account for the full lifecycle of information: storage and destruction are missing in this regard to ensure that the complete set of the fact-checking activities that could be related to the elements of information disorder has been taken into account.

Table 2. Mapping WDF relevance to fact-checking

			Fact-checking system		
			Information-gathering	**Decision-making**	**Response**
WDF	Information disorder type	Disinformation	•	•	•
		Misinformation	•	•	•
		Malinformation	•	•	•
	Information disorder phase	Creation			
		Production	•		
		Distribution	•	•	•
	Information disorder element	Agents	•	•	•
		Messages	•	•	•
		Interpreters	•	•	•

Source: Compiled by the authors.

This, on the one hand, could mean that the WDF only accounted for the possibility of relying on human effort in the fact-checking process; on the other hand, it does reveal an important space for improvement. Additional improvements can also be made at the lower organisational level of the framework. This will be addressed in our future work.

The convenience of WDF lies primarily in the fact that it joins together the general issues of several different contexts to construct common guidelines and recommendations for a variety of stakeholders. Moreover, putting this framework into practice enables us to design a constructive feedback loop from practice to theory and to show how the two can benefit from each other. This kind of approach pushes the whole field on from having only a conceptual framework and a step closer to designing a common reference model for information disorder.

5. EMPIRICAL STUDY

Clearly, the scientific validity of many of the above-described methods and approaches depends on the cooperation of the target organisations (and the maturity of their projects). As a primary database of fact-checking organisations combating information disorder we used the list compiled by Graves and Cherubini.[61] This list, however, turned to be incomplete (for example, it listed only one fact-checking organisation for the Czech Republic, whereas we were able to identify three more – manipulatori.cz, hoax.cz and evropskehodnoty.cz – and one international project run in cooperation with the Czech Centre for Investigative Journalism).[62] Based on our extended search, 50 European organisations located in 27 countries were approached. The majority of these were contacted through their official website or through their publicly available email address. In 12 cases, however, an online form was the only available form of communication. In addition, Facebook was used to establish contact with seven of them, as this appeared to be the only possible way. The period in which all of the organisations were contacted was in December 2017 and January 2018. Despite the online communication, we also asked local contacts for help in several cases, such as in Finland, Italy, Latvia, Norway, Poland and the UK. The feedback rate (number of feedbacks vs. the overall number of surveys distributed), although relatively low, allowed us to carry out highly relevant and statistically meaningful analysis. The processed results and the analysis are given below.

5.1. RESULTS AND ANALYSIS

The results, although derived from a modest statistical set, provide important insights. Few of them were expected, but most of them can certainly be claimed novel. We have collected data from 15 countries, 11 of which were obtained through the online survey and four through the offline survey (30 per cent feedback rate). Other fact-checking organisations promised to provide their feedback as well. In addition to the surveys, four semi-structured interviews were also carried out. These helped us iterate through and refine the initial set of questions into a final coherent survey.[63]

The overall content of the survey was divided into three sections: two major sections corresponding to the two major sets of indicators (efficiency and effectiveness), and one additional section to help us capture some more subtle contextual traits and interpret more adequately the responses provided in the first two sections.

---

61 Graves and Cherubini, *supra* note 4.

62 P. Holcová, S. Černá, E. Żemła, J. Goda and A. Kőműves. 2017. 'Propaganda targets Czechs, Slovaks and Hungarians differently'. *The Spectator*, 27 November.

63 See https://goo.gl/forms/XV1DDjudPGZIFYLv2.

5.1.1. *Efficiency of Fact-Checking Organisations*

In order to investigate the efficiency of fact-checking organisations, we questioned various aspects of performance-related issues. In that regard, we inspected the volume and fluctuation of the organisations' staff, metrics related to the number of detected hoaxes/debunked fake news stories, user reach, type of content analysed and tools employed for the analysis.

The number of people engaged in the fact-checking process varies greatly among organisations (from 3 to 30). However, there is no staff reduction noted over the years and most (~64 per cent) of the organisations have increased the number of employees. This speaks of the realisation of the problem and their efforts to keep track of the arising issues. If we consider the distribution of users reached over the duration of a given project, it can be seen that most of the projects have a similar rate of expansion of their user base, with the oldest projects having a significantly larger audience. This, on the one hand, dictates the requirement of having proper dissemination practices adjusted to the type of user base, but, on the other hand, reveals an opportunity to exploit the user feedback in order to quickly detect, repair and improve a large number of performance issues. However, both of these appear to be exploited to an insufficient extent.

The number of debunked news stories/hoaxes (taken as the average number of news stories for the past three-months) varies considerably across countries and is very much context-dependent. However, for this information, it was necessary to see if it could reveal some context-related peculiarities, such as huge variations in the number of hoaxes between regions. It turns out (see below) that the number of detected fake news and hoaxes is very much dependent on the political situation and specific political events in a given country (elections, campaigns, etc.). Clearly, this number also depends on the type of content analysed by the fact-checking organisation and the share of such content among the information sources. In that context, Figure 2 shows a relatively satisfactory distribution of the type of content analysed by the fact-checkers. However, it is important to note that there is still a significant division between the organisations with respect to textual and audiovisual content; in other words, most of them are 'specialised' in one type of content only. Visual content, although known to have a far greater impact on the proliferation of fake news than text,[64] is given the least attention. Hence, increasing and adjusting efforts in this regard may result in a significant improvement in the rate of detecting fake news and thus of the effectiveness of fact-checking organisations.

---

[64] Wardle and Derakhshan, *supra* note 12.

All of the metrics discussed so far can directly be related to the methodology employed by the organisations in performing their work, such as the share between the potential automated services/tools employed for combating fake news and the human effort invested in the process.

Figure 2. The type of content analysed by the fact-checking organisations

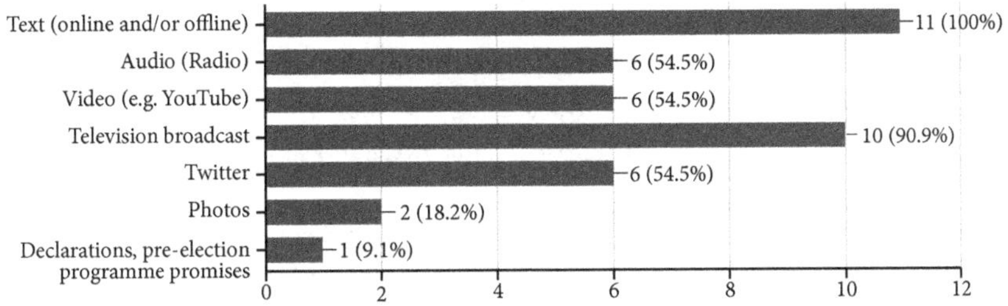

Source: Produced by the authors.

In this regard, only three organisations reported the use of both human effort and computational tools. However, it is not clear which aspect of the fact-checking process human experts cover and which is reserved for the computational techniques. Nevertheless, it is clear that the extent to which automated services are employed in these projects is very low. On the one hand, this prevents the organisations from exploiting the full range of fact-checking possibilities in a more efficient manner, and on the other hand blocks the potential contribution to the development of news technical means for combating fake news that could emerge from the processing of large text documents through crowdsourced users' interactions. Hence, there is considerable space for improvements and introducing innovations in this context. Similar suggestions have only recently been put forward.[65] There is a proposal for a complete (end-to-end) technical fact-checking solution based on machine learning and natural language processing named ClaimBuster,[66] components of which have already been implemented in real-world technical systems. Thus, it is clear that certain improvements are starting to be developed in the field of computational facilitation of fact-checking. However, it is important to note that these are all operational measures, as is the fact-checking itself. Proactive steps need to be taken as the best measure against information disorder. This is also revealed through the results of the survey in the final section, where the fact-checking organisations themselves

---

65 G.L. Ciampaglia. 2018. 'Fighting fake news: a role for computational social science in the fight against digital misinformation'. *Journal of Computational Social Science* 1(1): pp. 147–153.

66 Hassan et al., *supra* note 60. See also: https://www.rand.org/research/projects/truth-decay/fighting-disinformation/search.html.

call for greater awareness and proper resource allocation in the fight against information disorder.

5.1.2. *Effectiveness of Fact-Checking Organisations*

While efficiency can help analyse the functionality and operation of the employed means for fact-checking, it is less of an indication in reference to the overall impact of the project. In order to inspect impact-related issues, additional analysis is required that relates to the effectiveness of the fact-checking efforts. In that context, we analysed the long-term strategy of the organisations (represented by their objectives for internal and external impacts) and the mechanisms for evaluation of their impact.

As part of the long-term strategy, we asked for a concrete business and/or sustainability plan. Few such strategies were reported with only two organisations having a concrete business model, and three having developed a concrete sustainability plan. Mapping this information onto the planned longevity of each of the projects, it is to some extent understandable why the 'newcomers' have not had such operational considerations. However, most of the organisations/projects have been running long enough to have such plans already elaborated in their sustainability portfolio. This would also imply that mechanisms for transparency and accountability should be in place, which are directly related to increasing the credibility and trustworthiness of organisations. Properly accounting for these inter-dependent factors for sustainable operation will help fact-checking organisations to build a strategy which provides a more effective outcome of their work and a realistic set of operational objectives.

Related to the issue of sustainability is the type of impact envisaged by the objectives of the projects. Figure 3 demonstrates that almost all of the projects envisage political and human impact, and most of them are aware of the societal impact the work may have in general.

Figure 3. Envisaged impacts of the project

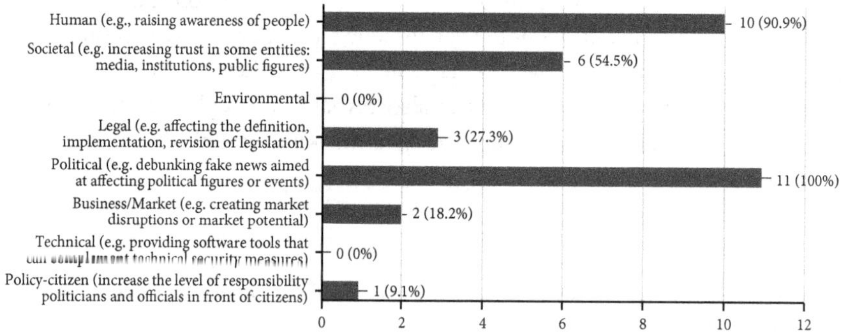

Source: Produced by the authors.

Despite the potential of the projects to have an even wider and greater impact, none of them considers environmental and technical impacts in their objectives, and only a few actually assess these impacts in some way. Most of the organisations did not assess any impact, regardless of envisaging it as part of their objectives. Only one reported concrete measures taken in this respect: 'Prepared a video instruction how to use the site search tool; Monthly trainings that help increase citizen awareness.'[67] Clearly, monitoring and evaluation of impact as part of the tracking of the organisations' progress and impact is a measure of paramount importance to be taken into account for increasing the effectiveness and efficiency of fact-checking projects. Much has been done in this regard in the field of public health and health-related projects; for example, the Payback model[68] is the most well-known and is used for project impact evaluation in disciplines other than health. It may be worth exploring this possibility in the context of fact-checking projects as well.

Figure 4. Frequency of revision of the employed tools

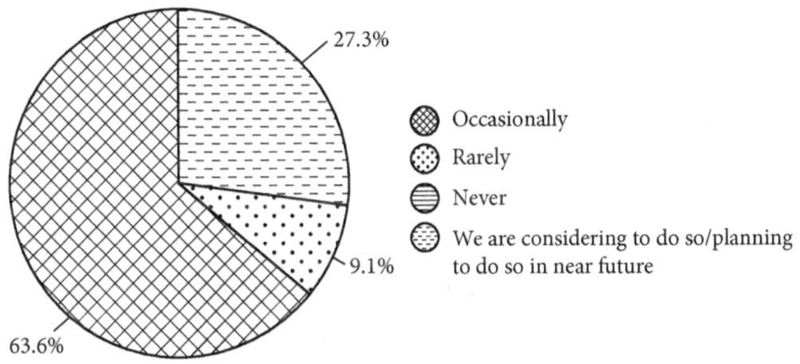

Source: Produced by the authors.

As part of the internal considerations, it is important not only to have the proper tools in place, but also to revise them and allow them to evolve together with the changing environment. In that sense, frequency of revision of the employed tools was explored, and the results are shown in Figure 4. Most organisations do pay attention to the revision of tools, a significant number of them still have not yet considered this. Taking into account that this is a crucial requirement for effective fact-checking, raising awareness of these performance-related issues appears to be a necessity at the European level.

The majority of organisations select their target sources and media by some predefined criteria, the most common of which is 'public interest about the

---

67 See https://www.facebook.com/slovoidilo.ua/videos/1604236676294784.

68 M. Buxton and S. Hanney. 1996. 'How can payback from health services research be assessed?' *Journal of Health Services Research & Policy* 11: pp. 35–43.

information'. Furthermore, they employ some mechanisms for information source evaluation (credibility, independence, trustworthiness, etc.), mainly in order to evaluate the independence of their information sources (news articles, politicians' speeches, tweets, etc.), although a few still do not perform such checks. However, even those that do pay attention to the independence of sources only rely on human expertise and subjective evaluations. This is another area in which technology can provide great support and can play a crucial role in improving the effectiveness and efficiency of fact-checkers. More importantly, such an approach would increase both the transparency and accountability of organisations and, ultimately, their perceived trustworthiness. For instance, one formal apparatus that offers the possibility to assess source dependence and to reason with subjective beliefs at the same time can be found in subjective logic.[69]

Many of the organisations also provided evidence of an agenda-setting impact (e.g. legacy media referencing the results of their work) as part of their effectiveness assessment. This mere fact highlights the importance of fact-checking efforts that complement the current strategies for addressing information disorder. Almost all of the organisations reported that they have noted a high dependency between the number of fake news stories and specific public events (elections, campaigns, etc.), which makes them direct testifiers of the interplay between the offline and the online world in a particular information context. Considering the above, together with the scale and speed at which fake news issues arise, a case can be made that efficient and effective efforts for combating information disorder could soon become part of some general set of cybersecurity measures. This adds even higher weight and value to the work (both theoretical and practical) carried out in this study.

As part of the external considerations, we explored the interaction of fact-checking organisations with stakeholders. This includes the nature of interactions, the means of dissemination of the work and results, and the direct collaboration with stakeholders. Interestingly, social media platforms are exploited very little as a means to interact with the stakeholders. Only one of the organisations reported using social media for this purpose (see Figure 5). Although social platforms are used to promote and disseminate the work of fact-checking organisations, an interactive mode of promotion could be an obvious point where improvements could be sought and achieved.

69 A. Jøsang. 2016. *Subjective Logic: A Formalism for Reasoning under Uncertainty.* Geneva: Springer International Publishing.

Figure 5. Nature of interaction with stakeholders

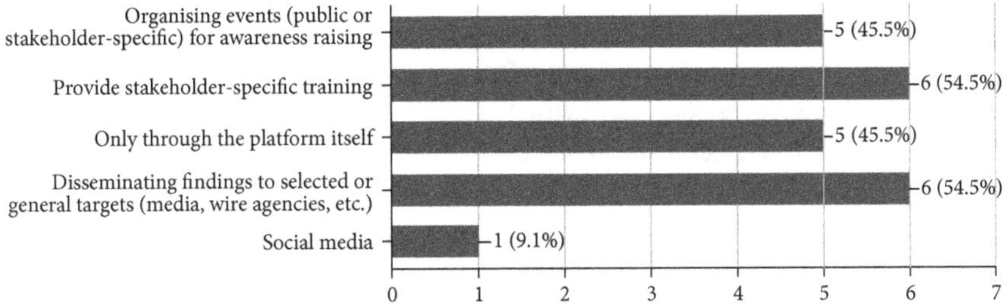

Source: Produced by the authors.

This is especially the case considering that almost all organisations reported on employed efforts to gather user feedback about one or more aspects of their work. Despite their seemingly identical work, there are organisational and operational traits that may differ among these fact-checking organisations. For instance, some of them only deal with debunking political statements, others only check the veracity of tweets, and some only deal with visual content. Nevertheless, there is a strong collaboration among most of the European fact-checking organisations reported by the respondents of the survey (see Figure 6).

Moreover, the results show that there is a deep involvement in the regulatory issues related to the combating of information disorder online at both a national level and a European level. Most of the organisations (~55 per cent) reported that they 'do not find the requirements for quality of online content aligned with the national/regional media policies (e.g. code of ethics of journalism)'.

Figure 6. Collaboration with other similar (regional, EU, and wider) initiatives

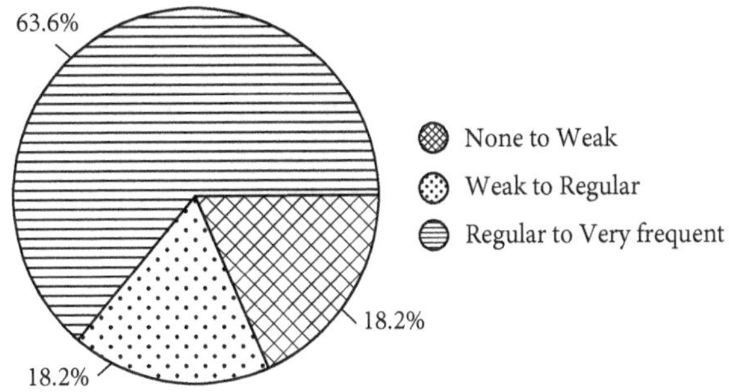

Source: Produced by the authors.

Although no experience with case law was noted (in the sense that none of the organisations have been called to court on some fake news-related issues), two organisations reported direct involvement in the removal of harmful content by IT companies or media outlets. Moreover, three organisations responded that they had at some point employed 'strategic silence' (i.e. deliberately not publicly revealing a debunked fake news article) in order to prevent the further proliferation of fake news. This, in and of itself, is a strong argument for considering the possibility of a self- or co-regulatory effort that can be made by these organisations to even further increase their cooperation and societal role and, ultimately, to contribute for more effective and efficient regulation and Internet governance *per se*.

Finally, in order to gain an insight into the difficulties faced by organisations in realising their performance objectives, we asked them what the biggest challenges and issues encumbering the pursuit of their goals were. In that regard, lack of resources and insufficient stakeholder awareness on the issues relating to information disorder were reported as the major problems affecting the workflow of fact-checkers (see Figure 7).

Figure 7. The most challenging issues involved in combating hoaxes and fake news

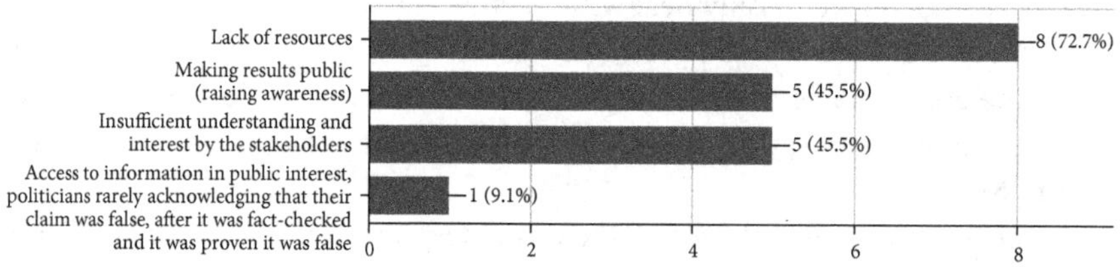

Source: Produced by the authors.

This points to the necessity of bridging the gap between an organisation's objectives and the public understanding of its own role in the fulfilment of those objectives. In order to achieve this, it may be necessary to also engage external efforts in this process of raising awareness so as to give more credibility to the fact-checking movement and increase the publicity of the issues related to it. In this regard, it is important to note that in at least 11 EU Member States (which were also part in our sample), there is more than one fact-checking organisation, and in six of them, there are more than two such organisations. In order to cope with the drawback of insufficient awareness and understanding of the issues related to fact-checking, some of the organisations run their websites in multiple languages (e.g. stopfake.org integrates its contents in 12 languages, and EUversusDisinfo in three languages).

5.2. DISCUSSION

In this section, we summarise the key findings and distil the main recommendations that result from this study. These are divided into parts following the same logical flow according to which they were previously introduced.

5.2.1. *Key Findings*

Efficiency: the number of people (the staff) varies across organisations, but is either constant or increasing. This speaks of the ability of fact-checking organisations to act as stand-alone companies capable of preserving their human capital. However, only two organisations have a business and long-term sustainability plan in place.

There is an obvious lack of multi-stakeholder cooperation, especially such that involves experts with different backgrounds and expertise, such as the social scientists, lawyers, politicians, mathematicians, IT specialists, electrical engineers and civil activists, to name but a few. That being said, it can be discerned that although a clear general goal is set for all of the fact-checking organisations, there is a lack of clarity in the sub-goals and objectives that concern the internal processes in the organisations' operation.

In that sense, there is a lack of automated means that can be employed in the process of fact-checking, but also a lack of information about the advances in a number of scientific areas, which causes activists to apply rather traditional, less functional and/or too costly methods in order to combat information disorder issues in their activities. The vast majority of the organisations rely solely on human expertise to perform all tasks related to fact-checking. This relates not only to the efficiency of performing the tasks, but also to the effectiveness of the entire effort.

Related to this issue is that of specialisation in the analysed content: although various types of content are addressed by the fact-checking organisations, each organisation specialises in a concrete type (mainly text), overlooking potentially significant and impactful information.

Effectiveness: the obvious absence of long-term sustainability plans also concerns the effectiveness of the fact-checking organisations. Thus, it comes as no surprise that most of the organisations do not have means for tracking the organisations' progress in relation to the pursued goals. Moreover, no means for tracking and evaluating any impact are in place and the self-assessment procedures are largely missing.

The dissemination practices employed by most of the fact-checkers are non-interactive and one-sided, and therefore lack the mechanisms that would ensure the effective fulfilment of their goals.

There is also a lack of mechanisms for information source evaluation (credibility, independence, trustworthiness, etc.) and a heavy reliance on human expertise. Not only is there an absence of automated means for the facilitation of the fact-checking processes, but the tools that are employed in some aspects of the work are only occasionally revised.

Lack of resources and insufficient stakeholder awareness of the issues relating to information disorder are the major problems affecting the workflows of fact-checkers. This points to the need to bridge the gap between an organisation's objectives and the public understanding of its own role in the fulfilment of those objectives.

Methodological remarks: we initially faced the fundamental problem of unwillingness to cooperate and to provide the requested data. In a way, this also motivated us to evolve our methodology and search for more efficient and effective means of getting the desired feedback, following a similar set of recommendations as those that came out of our work. Some of the organisations were also contacted multiple times, including through their national contacts. A common argument provided by some privately funded organisations was that their private funding meant they were not open to external assessment. Others expressed worries about 'commercial secrecy' or sources of funding (*vis-à-vis* their competitors in the field). Very often the unwillingness to cooperate was due to the high level of interest among researchers and journalists in the activities of fact-checkers, resulting in a flood of questionnaires, emails and calls. Although some information is freely and publicly available on the websites of the fact-checking organisations, this information is in most cases identical for all of the organisations.

One (relative) drawback of the methodology employed in this work is the one that usually comes with a survey of this kind: the data obtained and the responses are largely based on self-assessment by the respondents. However, in our survey, we were aiming for as much comparable feedback as possible in order to lessen the drawback raised by self-assessment. Questions that were of a more descriptive nature were posed with the aim of gaining deeper contextual insights about the organisations.

5.2.2. *Recommendations*

Efficiency: having proper sustainability and business plans in place, fact-checking organisations can act as stand-alone companies that account for their own human capital. Through firm establishment within the network of related initiatives, they may even become part of a well-defined self/co-regulatory effort capable of directly affecting the regulatory landscape, the shaping of national policies and the implementation of national security strategies. However, this can only be achieved by bringing together stakeholders from a diverse set of backgrounds and with various forms of expertise in a transparent and eloquent manner. This will also reduce the gap between the fact-checkers' objectives and the public understanding of those objectives, alleviating one of the major problems these organisations are currently facing.

The successful 'marriage' between technology and human efforts must be considered by organisations and adjusted to their context of operation within the particular environment. Although regular use of software-based fact-checking practices may not work properly in some specific linguistic contexts, implemented and employed properly, such methods would dramatically increase the fact-checking capacity and the possible impacts of this in many respects (e.g. allowing for real-time detection and warning impact, addressing various types of content, choosing relevant information sources, and engaging wider audiences and as a result increasing awareness among stakeholders). The presence of such solutions is also an incentive for public involvement in and of itself, positively affecting the effectiveness of the overall fact-checking process.

Effectiveness: in addition to considering the employment of automated tools and services as part of the fact-checking process, revision of the employed tools at all levels is a crucial requirement for effective fact-checking. Raising awareness of these performance-related issues appears as a necessity on a European level. Such requirements should also become part of the internal self-assessment procedures of organisations.

In order to address the lack of self-assessment procedures, among which tracking impact and tracking progress are the major ones, implementing systems for monitoring and evaluation of impact are of paramount importance in terms of increasing both the effectiveness and efficiency of fact-checkers.

While it is clear that the trustworthiness of fact-checkers is critical and that fact-checking organisations must strive for transparency in their working process, foundations, internal organisation and funding sources, it may be less obvious that this issue is closely linked to the issue of guarantees needed to prevent fact-checking organisations from behaving like online censors. Thus, there is a need for stronger and independent civil society control and of broader stakeholder involvement.

Once established as credible bodies within the regulatory network of actors, mechanisms for the accountability of fact-checkers should be put in place and their effectiveness must be ensured. This will also make it possible to appropriately deal with the issue of lack of trustworthiness.

Methodological improvements: the next logical step of this methodology would be a formalisation effort that could lead to the quantification of results and a concrete assessment of the efficiency and effectiveness of fact-checking organisations. The nature of the addressed issues is suitable for such an approach and promises valuable insights if this is further pursued.

We firmly believe that the comparative analysis presented here is not only meaningful in a statistical sense, but also extremely useful for providing the guiding insights into a topic that is relatively new and highly relevant in many respects (political, economic, technological, scientific, and societal). This is an important point, given that there is no similar research data available, let alone empirical studies performed of this kind.

6. CONCLUSION AND FUTURE WORK

The research presented in this chapter is a contribution both to the development of fact-checking systems and the fight against information disorder in general. It not only concerns itself with the functionality and the performance of the system as a whole, but it also engages in understanding how the components of the fact-checking system interact with and depend on each other. Through the development of the relevant indicators for performance evaluation of fact-checking organisations and the definition of a taxonomy for fact-checking systems, we both invest our efforts in the functional improvement of the fact-checking process and nurture the higher goal of improving democratic structures and the European governance processes *per se*. On a practical level, the working principles developed and followed here also contribute to the general practices of NGO performance evaluation. We believe that this research can form the basis for defining a generic methodology for performance evaluation of fact-checking and debunking organisations.

In addition to obtaining theoretical insights into the workings of fact-checking organisations, here we have presented the first empirical research of practically implemented (mainly human-based) fact-checking systems, supporting the recommendations for performance improvements with arguments coming directly from the 'battlefield'. Based on the main findings from this fast-track research, an important set of policy recommendations and proposals can further be developed. The ones of the highest priority should refer to: the need for interdisciplinarity in the approaches and multistakeholderism in the solutions; the need for sustainability plans (coordinated efforts through common networks would support sustainability to a great extent); employing technology both as a methodological support and as a means for self-evaluation; and more interactive ways of raising awareness about information disorder of the general public and the stakeholder community.

It is important to note that the current research is only the starting point on a novel research journey relating to topics that are very current and also very dynamic. Additional and continuous research is required to establish a sound basis for adopting this methodology and enabling it to capture the emergent properties of the societal model of information creation and spreading.

As a next step, it would undoubtedly be interesting and useful to gain insights from a larger sample of organisations whose number is on the rise. Fact-checking initiatives from non-European countries will also be included to allow for additional comparative analysis. Moreover, quantitative analysis needs to be developed that encompasses more precise criteria and indicators (especially relating to the assessment of the methodologies used), as well as a more granularly defined taxonomy. This will also allow for the methodology to be formalised and integrated into a software solution that will serve the same purpose for a broader stakeholder community.

PART III

SOLUTIONS TO DEAL WITH DISINFORMATION AND THEIR CRITIQUE

13. DISINFORMATION AND FAKE NEWS IN CURRENT JURISPRUDENCE OF THE STRASBOURG COURT

An Unsolved Problem

Monika Hanych and Marek Pivoda*

1. INTRODUCTION

Numerous claims of fear or apprehensions have been expressed about the threats posed by the proliferation of disinformation and fake news within the current democratic society.[1] Even though dissemination of misleading, untruthful or false stories has been recognised as an effective means to achieve various personal, political or other goals long before its online boom, it has to a great extent been the remarkable expansion of new technologies which brought to light a clear pressing social need to find more efficient tools to counter such practices.[2] As a rich debate about appropriate ways of tackling the phenomenon of fake news takes place among scholars, within national governments and international organisations, our chapter aims to contribute to

* Monika Hanych, Faculty of Law, Masaryk University, Czech Republic. Email: monika.hanych@gmail.com; Marek Pivoda, Faculty of Law, Masaryk University, Czech Republic. Email: marek.pivoda@mail.muni.cz.

1 See e.g. S. Morgan, 'Fake News, Disinformation, Manipulation and Online Tactics to Undermine Democracy' (2018) 3 *Journal of Cyber Policy* 39; J.A. Kuypers, *The 2016 American Presidential Campaign and the News: Implications for American Democracy and the Republic*, Lexington Books, Lanham 2018. See also the Directorate-General for Communication: 'More than eight in ten respondents (85%) think that the existence of fake news is a problem in their country (within EU), at least to some extent. A similar proportion (83%) say that it is a problem for democracy in general'. European Commission, Directorate-General for Communication, *Fake News and Disinformation Online*, Flash Eurobarometer 464, 2018, p. 51.

2 S. Burshtein, 'The True Story on Fake News' (2017) 29(3) *Intellectual Property Journal* 397, pp. 407–411; A. Alemanno, 'How to Counter Fake News? A Taxonomy of Anti-fake News Approaches' (2018) 9(1) *European Journal of Risk Regulation* 1.

the debate by mapping the current approach of the European Court of Human Rights (hereinafter 'ECtHR' or 'the Court'), a leading institution in forming current European human rights system by its substantive case law and legal interpretations.

Fighting false information through the court system represents only one of the multiple approaches to combating the dissemination of false information. Nevertheless, seeking protection through the courts remains one of the core mechanisms within the legal framework upon which the democratic society is built.[3] Therefore, we believe that it is of great importance to address the topic from the perspective of judicial approach. It is only by means of detailed analysis of the existing case law that we are able to assess the effectiveness of judicial protection against false stories.

This chapter proceeds as follows. First, it briefly introduces the concept and definition of fake news as a starting point for the purpose of case law analysis (Section 2). Then it demonstrates the Court's approach towards the issue of disinformation through the inductive analysis of its existing case law (Section 3). Subsequently, it identifies key actors relevant to judicial proceedings and their roles within the process (Section 4). Finally, it assesses the overall effectivity of judicial means of tackling the proliferation of false information and suggests possible solutions (Section 5).

2. CONCEPT AND DEFINITION OF FAKE NEWS/ DISINFORMATION

Prior to proceeding to the analysis of the role of the judiciary in combating fake news, we have to clarify the scope of the subject matter of our interest. Since much has been said regarding the definition of fake news,[4] we certainly do not aim to provide the readers with a lengthy definition of such term. However, our focus is on scrutinising the subject matter from the perspective of the ECtHR and so we simply accept one of the existing and generally accepted definitions and categories as a starting point in order to be able to identify the relevant decisions of the Court.

Generally, the term 'fake news' refers to false or misleading stories that appear to be news, spread on the Internet or using other media, usually created to influence political, social or cultural views or as a joke.[5] An examination

---

3 Regarding the ECtHR's role as an actor in the field of new technologies and human rights in general, see T. Murphy and G.Ó Cuinn, 'Works in Progress: New Technologies and the European Court of Human Rights' (2010) 10(4) *Human Rights Law Review* 601.

4 See the discussion on the issue of definition of 'fake news' in other chapters in this volume.

5 Definition of 'misinformation' available at: https://dictionary.cambridge.org/dictionary/english/fake-news.

of 34 academic articles that used the term 'fake news' between 2003 and 2017 resulted in a typology of the following kinds of fake news: *news satire*, *news parody*, *fabrication*, *manipulation*, *advertising* and *propaganda*.[6] Similar categories were also identified by the Stanford Practicum Research Team on Fake News and Misinformation: (1) *Bogus Click-Bait*, i.e. entirely fabricated stories designed to gain ad revenue by tricking social media users into viewing and sharing them; (2) *Conspiracy Theories*, i.e. baseless and usually outlandish claims, typically asserting some nefarious secret plot – unlike intentionally false stories, the promoters of conspiracy theories often believe their own claims; (3) *Reckless Reporting*, i.e. false stories or unsubstantiated rumours that are reported without regard for the truth; (4) *Political Propaganda*, i.e. false stories designed to achieve a particular political outcome; (5) *Hoaxes*, i.e. fake stories that are typically created as a joke or to make people look foolish for believing them; and finally (6) *Misleading News*, i.e. all news content that is sensational, biased, slanted, unfair or that otherwise leaves the reader with an inaccurate impression.[7]

As can be seen, the definitions of fake news, disinformation, misinformation or misleading, untruthful or false stories vary, as there has been no clear consensus among scholars or within society in general.[8] Therefore, in this chapter, we generally use these terms interchangeably and only where relevant or appropriate, the certain term within specific context (and explanation) is used. As we have at least narrowed our focus and established our starting point, we can proceed further to the actual analysis of the approach of the ECtHR. The next section aims to provide a first glance at the existing case law of the leading international human rights institution. Through an inductive analysis of the case law of the Court and the European Commission of Human Rights, we seek to map the development of the use of the notion of 'fake news' in human rights adjudication over time as well as to identify the potential means to tackle dissemination of misleading information through the Court nowadays.

---

6 C. Tandoc Jr., Z.W. Lim and R. Ling, 'Defining "Fake News": A Typology of Scholarly Definitions' (2018) 6(2) *Digital Journalism* 137.

7 Stanford Law School Fake News and Misinformation Policy Lab Practicum, *Fake News and Misinformation: The Roles of the Nation's Digital Newsstands, Facebook, Google, Twitter and Reddit*, Stanford Law School, 2017, p. 10, https://law.stanford.edu/wp-content/uploads/2017/10/Fake-News-Misinformation-FINAL-PDF.pdf.

8 For instance, Carol A. Watson claims that 'fake news is not produced by traditional or established media sources that adhere to journalistic standards and ethics'. See C.A. Watson, 'Information Literacy in a Fake/False News World: An Overview of the Characteristics of Fake News and its Historical Development' (2018) 46(2) *International Journal of Legal Information* 93, p. 93.

3. THE DEVELOPMENT OF THE COURT'S APPROACH TO THE ISSUE OF DISINFORMATION/FAKE NEWS

Firstly, it should be noted that the European Convention on Human Rights (hereinafter 'the Convention') contains no explicit provision concerning the question of fake news.[9] According to our analysis, the ECtHR has not yet acquired an opportunity to directly comment on the topic of dissemination of false news in digital platforms. However, there is a pending case *Dareskizb Ltd v. Armenia*[10] dealing with the question of whether national legal provisions strictly prohibiting the dissemination of false news are compatible with freedom of expression.[11]

When closely examining the existing case law, we may discover that the Court has already discussed several crucial aspects of the proliferation of misleading information. The issue of fake news is mainly connected with two rights established by the Convention: freedom of expression guaranteed by Article 10 of the Convention (see Section 3.1) and the right to respect for private and family life stipulated in Article 8 of the Convention (see Section 3.2), sometimes also connected to prohibition of discrimination in Article 14. In the following subsections, we analyse the existing case law of the Court in relation to Articles 8 and 10 in order to obtain general insights on how the Court might approach the issue of fake news when asked to do so.

It should be noted that in such cases, where the application was brought by the person who was the subject of the false statement (under Article 8) or by the person who has produced certain information (Article 10), the protection should not vary as the rights under these articles deserve equal respect.[12] Moreover, various factors rather than only one taken in isolation determine the outcome of the case. Therefore, the Court's approach to these types of cases can thus be described as highly context-specific.[13] As there are different ways of ensuring respect for private life, there is also a wide margin of appreciation for contracting states to apply, regardless of whether the obligations on it are

9 European Convention for the Protection of Human Rights and Fundamental Freedoms, available at: https://www.echr.coe.int/Documents/Convention_ENG.pdf.

10 *Dareskizb Ltd v. Armenia* App no 61737/08 (ECtHR, 16 December 2008).

11 However, the case might not be an accurate representative example, as the legal provisions in question include the requirement of prior verification by the state authorities before publication. See *Dareskizb Ltd v. Armenia – Statement of Facts and Questions*, available at: http://hudoc.echr.coe.int/eng?i=001-171218.

12 *Perinçek v. Switzerland* App no 27510/08 (ECtHR, 15 October 2015) para. 198.

13 *Ibid.*, para. 208.

positive or negative.[14] The role of the Court is then to review, in the light of the case as a whole, the compatibility of the steps taken at the national level with the provisions of the Convention that are being relied upon.[15] In other words, the Court's main role is to assess whether the reasons given by the national authorities to justify the actual measures of interference are relevant and sufficient.[16]

3.1. FAKE NEWS AND DISINFORMATION WITHIN THE SCOPE OF FREEDOM OF EXPRESSION

3.1.1. *Preliminary Observations*

A close connection between freedom of expression and democratic society has always been essential. Free speech represents one of the basic conditions for the progress of democratic society as well as for each individual's fulfilment and development.[17] Should we aim to study the relationship between dissemination of false stories and free speech properly, we have to first mention the main theoretical arguments for the functions of freedom of speech in modern society: (1) the argument concerned with the importance of discovering truth; (2) free speech as an aspect of self-fulfilment; (3) the argument deriving from citizen participation in a democracy; and (4) free speech as a means of critique of government.[18] These theoretical concepts are foundations of the right to freedom of expression as guaranteed by the Convention and thus should be kept in mind when analysing particular rationales behind the Court's decisions.

Article 10 of the Convention guarantees 'freedom to hold opinions and to receive and impart information and ideas without interference by

14 The Court has reiterated that although the essential object of many provisions of the Convention is to protect the individual against arbitrary interference by public authorities, there may in addition be positive obligations inherent in an effect respect of the rights concerned. See the Research Report, 'Positive Obligations on Member States under Article 10 to Protect Journalists and Prevent Impunity', available at: https://www.echr.coe.int/Documents/Research_report_article_10_ENG.pdf. The Court also held in *Dink v. Turkey* that 'States are required to create a favourable environment for participation in public debate by all the persons concerned, enabling them to express their opinions and ideas without fear'. See *Dink v. Turkey* App nos 2668/07, 6102/08, 30079/08, 7072/09 and 7124/09 (ECtHR, 14 September 2010) para. 137.

15 *Ibid.*, para. 198.

16 *Handyside v. United Kingdom* App no 5493/72 (ECtHR, 7 December 1976) para. 50.

17 *Rekvényi v. Hungary* App no 25390/94 (ECtHR, 20 May 1999) para. 42.

18 E.M. Barendt, *Freedom of Speech*, 2nd ed., Oxford University Press, Oxford 2016, pp. 7–23.

public authority and regardless of frontiers'.[19] Freedom of speech affords the 'opportunity to take part in the public exchange of cultural, political and social information and ideas of all kinds'.[20] According to the ECtHR, freedom of speech covers not only freedom to receive and impart information or ideas that are favourable or regarded as inoffensive or as a matter of indifference, but also those that offend, shock or disturb.[21] On the other hand, in relation to the content, the Court noted that particular classes of speech, such as lewd and obscene speech, have no essential role in the expression of ideas if their main purpose is to insult.[22] Furthermore, it has been stated that Article 10 protects not only the substance of the ideas and information expressed but also the form in which they are conveyed.[23] The Court's interpretation of 'information and ideas' concerns the broad scope of formats and kinds of speech, including not only texts but also pictures,[24] historical truth,[25] information covered by medical confidentiality[26] and others.

But what about the truthful nature of such ideas? The Court has reiterated that 'the public has a right to receive information as a corollary of the specific function of journalists, which is to impart information and ideas on matters of public interest'.[27] In principle, journalists and the media ought to impart the information in good faith in order to provide the public with reliable information. However, this does not necessarily mean that they are obliged to tell the truth. The primary task of a journalist is to seek out 'the best

---

19 Article 10 of the Convention reads:

1. Everyone has the right to freedom of expression. This right shall include freedom to hold opinions and to receive and impart information and ideas without interference by public authority and regardless of frontiers. This Article shall not prevent States from requiring the licensing of broadcasting, television or cinema enterprises.
2. The exercise of these freedoms, since it carries with it duties and responsibilities, may be subject to such formalities, conditions, restrictions or penalties as are prescribed by law and are necessary in a democratic society, in the interests of national security, territorial integrity or public safety, for the prevention of disorder or crime, for the protection of health or morals, for the protection of the reputation or rights of others, for preventing the disclosure of information received in confidence, or for maintaining the authority and impartiality of the judiciary.

20 *Müller and Others v. Switzerland* App no 10737/84 (ECtHR, 24 May 1988) para. 27.

21 See *Palomo Sánchez and Others v. Spain* App nos 28955/06, 28957/06, 28959/06 and 28964/06 (ECtHR, 12 September 2011) para. 53; *Morice v. France* App no 29369/10 (ECtHR, 23 April 2015) para. 124.

22 *Rujak v. Croatia* App no 57942/10 (ECtHR, 2 October 2012) para. 29.

23 See *Karataş v. Turkey* App no 23168/94 (ECtHR, 8 July 1999).

24 *Von Hannover v. Germany (No. 2)* App no 40660/08 (ECtHR, 7 February 2012) para. 103.

25 *Chauvy and Others v. France* App no 64915/01 (ECtHR, 29 June 2004).

26 *Editions Plon v. France* App No 58148/00 (ECtHR, 18 May 2004).

27 *Observer and Guardian v. United Kingdom* App no 13585/88 (ECtHR, 26 November 1991) para. 59.

obtainable truth'.[28] Supposedly, a certain degree of public interest should be preserved when assessing the scope of the right to freedom of expression in connection with the spread of disinformation.

In this regard, it is important to distinguish between statements of facts and value judgements. As the Court stated, 'while the existence of facts can be demonstrated, the truth of value judgments is not susceptible of proof. The requirement to prove the truth of a value judgment is impossible to fulfil and infringes freedom of opinion itself, which is a fundamental part of the right secured by Article 10'.[29] Yet, in *Jerusalem v. Austria*, the Court has also stipulated the particular requirement of 'sufficient factual basis' even for statements amounting to value judgements, as failing this test could result in the value judgement being excessive.[30] This approach could be useful when dealing with the question of fake news. Comparably, fake news sometimes aims to proliferate mixed statements of facts and mere speculations or other value judgements (*vis-à-vis* the above-mentioned categories of *Conspiracy Theories*, *Reckless Reporting* and *Misleading News*). When fiction is presented, there can obviously be no requirement that the statements be 'true'. However, sometimes 'fiction' introduces real characters or facts, as may be seen in the practice of dissemination of fake news. In addition, if those statements become more than mere value judgements, the requirement of a sufficient factual basis might be justified.[31]

Nevertheless, Article 10 of the Convention cannot be read in isolation: regarding the topic of creation and/or dissemination of false information, there are at least two more articles to be followed in conjunction with Article 10 of the Convention. So far, at least in relation to certain types of hate speech (and there is a possibility of applying the argumentation similarly to several kinds of fake news as well), the Court has developed a tradition of applying Article 17 of the Convention with its so-called abuse clause.[32] Such an

28 See T. McGonagle, '"Fake News": False Fears or Real Concerns?' (2017) 35(4) *Netherlands Quarterly of Human Rights* 203, p. 208, citing C. Bernstein, 'The Idiot Culture: Reflections of Post-Watergate Journalism' (1992) *The New Republic* 22, p. 24.

29 *Pedersen and Baadsgaard v. Denmark* App no 49017/99 (ECtHR, 17 December 2004) para. 76; *Lingens v. Austria* App no 9815/82 (ECtHR, 8 July 1986) para. 46.

30 See *Jerusalem v. Austria* App no 26958/95 (ECtHR, 27 February 2001); see also *Lindon, Otchakovsky-Laurens and July v. France* App nos 21279/02 and 36448/02 (ECtHR, 22 October 2007) para. 55. However, it is necessary to add that this case concerned extracts from a novel consisting of mixed facts and fiction, so the passages were not merely value judgements but were also allegations of fact.

31 See W. Schabas, *The European Convention on Human Rights: A Commentary*, Oxford University Press, Oxford 2016, p. 477.

32 Article 17 of the Convention reads: 'Nothing in this Convention may be interpreted as implying for any State, group or person any right to engage in any activity or perform any act aimed at the destruction of any of the rights and freedoms set forth herein or at their limitation to a greater extent than is provided for in the Convention.'

application leads to a categorical exclusion from the protection of the right to freedom of expression under Article 10 for some expressions. These are neither considered through the Court's general test of interference with the freedom of expression nor its factual or legal elements.[33] To fall within the ambit of Article 17 instead of Article 10 nevertheless requires a very strong imperative to be breached: such statements need to amount to any activity infringing the essence of the values underlying the Convention and calculated to destroy or restrict the rights and freedoms guaranteed by it.[34]

In a similar way, some restrictions might be imposed on freedom of expression in connection to the basis of Article 16 of the Convention, which restricts the political activities of aliens.[35]

3.1.2. Legitimate Aim and Striking the Balance

As can be seen from our preliminary remarks, the question whether the prohibition of dissemination of fake news might be compatible with Article 10 of the Convention is relevant and the Court has already addressed some aspects relating to this issue. As described above, the scope of freedom of expression is quite broad. Fake news (especially *Hoaxes*, *Bogus Click-Bait* and *Conspiracy Theories*) might under certain circumstances be regarded as a form of expression in line with the requirement of pluralism and broadmindedness. Nevertheless, Article 10(2) of the Convention allows for certain limitations of the right to free expression and thus fake news might as well be subject to those limitations.

The exercise of freedom of expression may be subject to certain formalities, conditions, restrictions and penalties, since it explicitly carries, unlike the similarly formulated Articles 8, 9 and 11 of the Convention, particular duties and responsibilities.[36] Such limitations must be prescribed by law, follow a legitimate aim and be necessary in a democratic society.[37] The Court has often addressed the requirement of duties and responsibilities in cases concerning the press. In *Fressoz and Roire*, it expressly identified that 'the right of journalists to impart information on issues of general interest requires that they should act in good faith and on an accurate factual basis and provide "reliable and precise" information in accordance with the ethics of journalism'.[38] It might

33 H. Cannie and D. Voorhoof, 'The Abuse Clause and Freedom of Expression in the European Human Rights Convention: An Added Value for Democracy and Human Rights Protection?' (2011) 29(1) *Netherlands Quarterly of Human Rights* 54.

34 *Fatullayev v. Azerbaijan* App no 40984/07 (ECtHR, 22 April 2010) para. 81.

35 Article 16 reads: 'Nothing in Articles 10, 11 and 14 shall be regarded as preventing the High Contracting Parties from imposing restrictions on the political activity of aliens.'

36 Article 10(2) of the European Convention for the Protection of Human Rights and Fundamental Freedoms.

37 *Ibid.*

38 *Fressoz and Roire v. France* App no 29183/95 (ECtHR, 21 January 1999) para. 54.

be argued that similar obligations should apply in cases where 'ordinary' or semi-professional individuals create and disseminate content that presents itself as valid news.

When assessing the compliance of provisions prohibiting the spread of fake news with the Convention, the Court has to examine whether the law is accessible, foreseeable and sufficiently precise in its formulation to enable an individual to regulate his or her conduct.[39] In this regard, the lacking, vague or too broad definition of fake news might be problematic. Furthermore, the potential wide discretion of specific authorities empowered to decide on the nature of the news spread might also seem problematic in terms of the demands of the Convention, especially when no criteria for the assessment are prescribed by law. Moreover, the legal system must afford a measure of legal protection against arbitrary interferences by public authorities with the rights safeguarded by the Convention.[40] On the other hand, the Court emphasised many times that it has always understood the term 'law' in its 'substantive' sense and not its 'formal' sense, which means it has included both written and unwritten law. 'Law' therefore must be understood to include both statutory law and judge-made 'law'.[41] In other words, possibly for most of the countries under the Convention, the solid judicial interpretation of broad terms such as false information, fake news or online expressions would be an adequate response to the Court's call for fulfilling the condition 'prescribed by law'.

As far as the legitimate aim is concerned, there are several justifications for the limitation of free expression. The Convention recognises the following ones: national security, territorial integrity or public safety, prevention of disorder or crime, protection of health or morals, protection of the reputation or rights of others, prevention of the disclosure of information received in confidence, or maintenance of the authority and impartiality of the judiciary. Such justifications are quite broad and a lot of them might cover the purpose of actions combating the dissemination of false information. For example, fake news including defamation and hate speech might be tackled on the basis of protection of the reputation and rights of others.[42] Similarly, fake news disseminated in order to undermine the election process by a foreign power might be prohibited under

---

39 *Sanoma Uitgevers B.V. v. The Netherlands* App no 38224/03 (ECtHR, 14 September 2010) para. 81–82.

40 *Ibid.*

41 *Sanoma Uitgevers B.V. v. The Netherlands* App no 38224/03 (ECtHR, 19 September 2010) para. 83.

42 See e.g. *Balsytė-Lideikienė v. Lithuania* App no 72596/01 (ECtHR, 4 November 2011), a case concerning the publication of calendars describing various historical dates in an offensive and xenophobic way. See C. Francis, 'Trial or Truth: Law and Fake News' (2018) 3 *Edinburgh Student Law Revue* 100, p. 106.

special circumstances in order to protect national security or public order.[43] Nevertheless, it should be noted that the evaluation of a legitimate aim pursued always depends on the specific circumstances of each individual case and any restriction should be interpreted narrowly.

Finally, when assessing the necessity of the taken action, the Court has to consider whether the state authorities have struck a fair balance between the competing interests of an individual and of the society as a whole.[44] The interference must correspond to a 'pressing social need' and, in particular, must remain proportionate to the legitimate aim pursued.[45]

In *Medžlis Islamske Zajednice Brčko and Others v. Bosnia and Herzegovina*, the Court dealt with the application of a religious community of Muslims and three non-governmental organisations (NGOs) of ethnic Bosnians in the Brčko District. By the decisions of the domestic courts, the applicants were held liable for defamation of an editor who had been proposed for the position of director of the multi-ethnic public radio station. Since they sent a letter to the highest district authorities in which they accused the editor of being disrespectful in regard to another ethnicity and religion, they interfered with her rights under Article 8 of the Convention.[46] This case is important regarding the issue of fake news since the Court explicitly stated that when the applicants (the NGOs) drew attention to matters of public interest, they were exercising a public watchdog role of similar importance to that of the press. As they could be characterised as a social watchdog, they were also required to act in good faith in order to provide accurate and reliable information. Moreover, they were bound to do so by the requirement to verify the veracity of the allegations submitted.[47]

In *Solov v. Ukraine*, the Court managed to comment on the issue of dissemination of false information directly. The applicant allegedly distributed a number of copies of a forged special edition of the parliamentary newspaper, which included a statement attributed to the Speaker of the Parliament, claiming that presidential candidate and incumbent at the time President Leonid Kuchma had died.[48] The Court found the conviction of the applicant too severe and not necessary in a democratic society. In assessing relevant circumstances, it stated that the fact that the applicant had not intentionally produced or published false information himself and had referred to it in conversations with others

---

43 *Ibid.*

44 See also C. Grabenwarter, *European Convention on Human Rights: Commentary*, C.H. Beck, Verlag 2014, Commentary to Art. 10.

45 *Aquilina and Others v. Malta* App no 28040/08 (ECtHR, 14 September 2011) para. 40.

46 *Medžlis Islamske Zajednice Brčko and Others v. Bosnia and Herzegovina* App no 17224/11 (ECtHR, 27 June 2017).

47 *Ibid.*, para. 85.

48 *Solov v. Ukraine* App no 65518/01 (ECtHR, 6 September 2005).

as a personalised assessment of factual information as a crucial criterion.[49] Furthermore, it stated that:

> Article 10 of the Convention as such does not prohibit discussion or dissemination of *information received* even if it is strongly suspected that this information might not be truthful. To suggest otherwise would deprive persons of the right to express their views and opinions about statements made in the mass media and would thus place an unreasonable restriction on the freedom of expression.[50]

In this regard, it is particularly important to emphasise the fact that in this case, the Court dealt with the false information received from a third party. Therefore, in our opinion, it should not be suggested that the Court openly approved that the dissemination of false statements (fake news) is not subject to restrictions under Article 10(2).

On a similar note, the ECtHR commented on the issue of the breaching of the right to freedom of expression in the context of an electoral campaign in *Brzeziński v. Poland*. During a political campaign for municipal elections, the applicant, who was standing for the post of municipal councillor, issued a brochure with his colleague, in which they criticised members of the outgoing local government. The targeted local politicians brought an action against the applicant under the Local Elections Act which allows political candidates to apply for an injunction to prevent dissemination of campaign material or statements containing false or misleading information, requiring the respective court to examine the application within 24 hours. As a result, the national courts ordered the applicant to cease distributing his brochure, to apologise and correct the misleading information contained therein; he was also ordered to pay a certain sum of money to charity and to pay the legal costs. Consequently, the Court proclaimed that the decisions of the national courts had interfered with the applicant's freedom of expression. Although the Court emphasised the importance of the fight against the dissemination of false information during the prelection period, it nevertheless reiterated the importance of free circulation of information. According to the Court, the contested statements had been made in the context of a debate on public issues which were important for the local community and the language used in the brochure had remained within the limits of admissible exaggeration or provocation, having regard to the ordinary tone of the political debate at local level.[51]

Another integral part of the freedom of expression is to seek historical truth which might be often a base for a deep societal schism or long-standing conflict,

---

49 *Ibid.*, para. 113.

50 *Ibid.*

51 *Brzeziński v. Poland* App no 47542/07 (ECtHR, 25 July 2019).

as it can be difficult to come to a consensus on the truth or the interpretation of historical events in society. The Court noted that it is not its role 'to arbitrate the underlying historical issues which are part of a continuing debate between historians that shapes opinion as to the events which took place and their interpretation'[52] and that it is also not its role to arbitrate in such debates.[53] On the other hand, although jurisprudence in the area of freedom of expression is particularly liberal, the Court has not forgotten to use the abuse clause in its case law in relation to expressions which should be completely excluded from the scope of the Convention. These were the cases of the expressions purporting to justify Nazism,[54] revisionism of well-established historical truths such as the Holocaust[55] or anti-Semitism[56] for violating the values of the Convention and incurring a form of abuse of the law outlawed by Article 17.

Therefore, when assessing a certain expression, the Court first decides upon whether the particular expression falls within the ambit of protection of the Convention (under Article 10) or not (under Article 17), and only once the result of the evaluation is positive will the Court review whether the interferences with the exercise of the right to freedom of expression posed by the national authorities are necessary in a democratic society. During such a process, the Court has to weigh up several factors, especially the following: the manner in which the impugned statements were phrased and the way in which they could be construed, the specific interest or right affected by the statements, the impact of the statements and the lapse of time since the events to which the statements related.[57] Similarly to the position in relation to 'hate speech', the Court's assessment of the necessity of interferences with statements relating to historical events (which can often include false or misleading information and are thus of interest here) has also been 'quite case-specific' and 'has depended on the interplay between the nature and potential effects of such statements and the context in which they were made'.[58] Nevertheless, not to be forgotten, one general principle to be extracted from above-mentioned information is that under the Court's case law, the expression on matters of public interest is generally entitled to strong protection, whereas expression that promotes or justifies violence, hatred, xenophobia or another form of intolerance cannot normally claim protection.[59]

As can be seen from the presented case law, the Court has already dealt with many aspects concerning the proliferation of fake news regarding freedom of

52 *Fatullayev v. Azerbaijan* App no 40984/07 (ECtHR, 22 April 2010) para. 87.

53 *Perinçek v. Switzerland*, *supra* note 12, para. 214; *Chauvy and Others*, *supra* note 25, para. 69.

54 *Lehideux and Isorni v. France* App no 24662/94 (ECtHR, 23 September 1998).

55 *Garaudy v. France* App no 65831/01 (ECtHR, 24 June 2003).

56 *M'Bala M'Bala v. France* App no 25239/13 (ECtHR, 20 October 2015).

57 *Perinçek v. Switzerland*, *supra* note 12, paras 216–219.

58 *Ibid.*, para. 220.

59 *Ibid.*, para. 230.

expression guaranteed by the Convention. Even though it has not yet had the chance to adjudicate on the core of the issue itself, we might argue that there are certainly a number of arguments which could support the combat against fake news through the ECtHR: first, the Court takes into consideration the truthful nature of the statements expressed; second, it recognises certain duties and responsibilities of the speakers when assessing their conduct; third, it carefully examines the pressing social need and proportionality of the restrictions, taking into account a number of aspects, such as the severity of the limitation, the intention of the speakers, the impact of the statements and the nature of the false information. Despite all of these, the Court's contribution to the fake news debate remains highly casuistic and case-specific. Therefore, it remains impossible to create a definitive list of both general and specific rules to be followed in order to avoid the collision of the freedom of expression with the other rights protected by the Convention.

3.2. FAKE NEWS AND DISINFORMATION WITHIN THE SCOPE OF THE RIGHT TO RESPECT FOR PRIVATE AND FAMILY LIFE

3.2.1. *Preliminary Observations*

Where the false claims touch upon what may be subsumed under the heading of one's private life, a remedy may be pursued in a claim according to Article 8 of the Convention for misuse of private information, irrespective of whether it is defamatory according to Article 10 or not. This is quite a radical development within the jurisprudence of the ECtHR over the last decade.[60]

Article 8 of the Convention guarantees protection of the right to a private life, the right to family life, the right to residence and the right to correspondence, and is thus a crucial starting point for the protection of individual privacy.[61] Nevertheless, at present, there is no single generally accepted definition of what this article covers.[62] This leads to a necessity to follow the Court's interpretation

60 J. Hartshorne, 'An Appropriate Remedy for the Publication of False Private Information' (2012) 4(1) *Journal of Media Law* 93.

61 It should be noted that the creators of the Convention intentionally used the term 'private life' instead of 'privacy' to create a broader scope for interpretation. See J. Kmec, D. Kosař, J. Kratochvíl and M. Bobek, *Evropská úmluva o lidských právech. Komentář (European Convention on Human Rights. Commentary)*, C.H. Beck, Prague 2012.

62 According the Court, the concept of 'private life' is a broad term that is not susceptible to an exhaustive definition which can embrace multiple aspects of the person's physical and social identity. See *S. and Marper v. United Kingdom* App nos 30562/04 and 30566/04 (ECtHR, 4 December 2008) para. 66.

of the scope of the article in each individual case. The key purpose of Article 8 is to protect against arbitrary interferences in private and family life, home and correspondence. This obligation is primarily of the negative kind; nevertheless, states also have positive obligations to ensure that Article 8 rights are respected even between private parties.[63]

Article 8 belongs among the relative rights of the Convention, as does Article 10; therefore, the collision of two of these rights does not necessarily always lead to the same result. On the contrary, in each case the Court must weigh up the conflicting interests of the individual circumstances. Moreover, the concrete interpretation of rights stems from the evolving nature of the interpretation of the Convention, known as 'a living instrument' anchored to the reality of the Member States. This means that the Court reflects the present-day conditions, developing standards and social changes.[64] These must be common or shared amongst the contracting states.[65]

Despite securing general protection of everyone's right to respect four key aspects of privacy (i.e. private and family life, home and correspondence), Article 8 also contains several limitations. Its exercise may be restricted if the interests of national security, public safety or the economic wellbeing of the country, the prevention of disorder or crime, the protection of health or morals, or the protection of the rights and freedoms of others prevail over the private life of a particular subject. Similarly to Article 10, the limitations must be prescribed by law, follow a legitimate aim and be necessary in a democratic society.[66]

Furthermore, the Court does not always necessarily need to flag which of the four aspects of Article 8 is violated; the interests protected by the article are so closely interconnected that the interference can subsume more than one aspect.[67] Therefore, it should be noted that a missing or incomplete identification of the aspect violated under Article 8 does not prevent the Court from carrying out the decision-making analysis.

3.2.2. Legitimate Aim and Striking the Balance

In relation to fake news or false information within the scope of Article 8 of the Convention, there are two possible collisions: (1) the protection of reputation

---

63 *Evans v. United Kingdom* App no 6339/05 (ECtHR, 10 April 2007) para. 75.

64 *Tyrer v. United Kingdom* App no 5856/72 (ECtHR, 25 April 1987) para. 31; *Glor v. Switzerland* App no 3444/04 (ECtHR, 30 April 2009) para. 75.

65 G. Letsas, 'The ECtHR as a Living Instrument: Its Meaning and its Legitimacy', 14 March 2012, available at: http://dx.doi.org/10.2139/ssrn.2021836, p. 24.

66 See e.g. Grabenwarter, *supra* note 44, p. 207; *Dubská and Krejzová v. Czech Republic* App nos 28859/11 and 28473/12 (ECtHR, 15 November 2016) para. 176.

67 *Klass and Others v. Germany* App no 5029/71 (ECtHR, 6 September 1978) para. 41.

(defamation); and (2) the protection of one's image and photographs. These cases will usually fall under the fake news categories of *Bogus Click-Bait, Reckless Reporting, Political Propaganda* or *Misleading News*. However, this distinction is far from exhaustive, as the categories can overlap or be transformed into a mixed or evolved type of false news or disinformation.

Regarding decision-making in the event of a possible violation of one's private or family life, the Court usually considers a number of elements relevant to an individual case: 'Since there are occasions when people knowingly or intentionally involve themselves in activities which are or may be recorded or reported in a public manner, a person's reasonable expectations as to privacy may be a significant, although not necessarily conclusive, factor.'[68] Thus, one of the key relevant factors would typically be whether a person could reasonably expect to be publicly visible. Nevertheless, when gathering the information by technological means (e.g. a systematic or permanent record), the Court evaluates each case on its individual basis, even where the information has not been gathered by any intrusive or covert method.[69]

When examining the necessity of an interference in a democratic society in the interests of the 'protection of the reputation or rights of others', the Court may be required to verify whether the domestic authorities struck a fair balance when protecting two values guaranteed by the Convention which may come into conflict with each other in certain cases. Typically, on the one hand, there would be freedom of expression protected by Article 10 and, on the other, the right to respect for private life enshrined in Article 8.[70]

The right to protection of one's reputation is a right which is protected by Article 8 as part of the right to respect for private life. Nevertheless, in order for this article to come into play, an attack on a person's reputation must attain a certain level of seriousness and in a manner causing prejudice to the personal enjoyment of the right to respect for private life.[71] Moreover, the complaint of a loss of reputation which is the foreseeable consequence of one's own actions is not regarded as a breach of Article 8 by the Court.[72] For example, when a criminal offence is committed, typically the information regarding the judicial trial, background information about the crime or the characteristics of the perpetrator are seen by the Court as not undermining the purpose of Article 8, especially if such information is of a kind which is typically taken into account by a judge during his or her decision-making process. The possible collision would

68 *P.G. and J.H. v. United Kingdom* App no 44787/98 (ECtHR, 25 September 2001) para. 57.
69 *Rotaru v. Romania* App no 28341/95 (ECtHR, 4 May 2000) paras 43–44.
70 *Axel Springer AG v. Germany* App no. 39954/08 (ECtHR, 7 February 2012) paras 83–84.
71 *Ibid.*
72 *Axel Springer AG v. Germany*, *supra* note 70, paras 83–84.

turn up once the purpose of (media) informing would be to show the person before, during or after a trial in a deprecatory, misleading or false manner.[73] We can therefore assume that in future judicial cases concerning false information, the Court would regard this aspect as one of the keystones in its proportionality puzzle.

The information spread about an individual should also respect his or her right to establish and develop relationships with other human beings. This includes not only personal relationships but also those connected to activities of a professional or business nature, since for the majority of people, they are a significant, if not the greatest, opportunity for developing relationships with the outside world. Moreover, it is not always possible to distinguish clearly which of an individual's activities form part of his or her professional or business life and which do not.[74] Therefore, the misleading or false information about one's privacy, personal, professional or business activities should most of the time be excluded from protection under Article 8. However, the falsity itself does not always necessarily need to be the crucial aspect for the judicial decision-making process regarding fake news. Once the privacy of a person is breached in a serious manner, it may make no difference whether the information turned out to be true or not.[75] On the other hand, in some cases, even misleading, manipulative or wrong information can be of a legitimate aim, e.g. publishing. These will be valid especially in cases which are of such a nature that the public interest prevails over one's privacy, e.g. because it helps to open up a crucial public debate on a topic of great public importance.[76]

As to the concrete criteria regarding the balancing test, when assessing the proportionality of interference within Article 8 (in the cases of both the

---

73 *M.L. and W.W. v. Germany* App nos 60798/10 and 65599/10 (ECtHR, 28 June 2018) para. 111; *Lillo-Stenberg and Sæther v. Norway* App no 13258/09 (ECtHR, 16 January 2014) para. 41.

74 *Niemietz v. Germany* App no 13710/88 (ECtHR, 16 December 1992) para. 29.

75 Hartshorne, *supra* note 60.

76 *Von Hannover v. Germany (No. 2), supra* note 24, paras 102 and 109. A case concerning the situation described above occurred in November 2018 in the Czech Republic: while the Czech Prime Minister was facing allegations that he had defrauded the EU of funds and his son was supposed to be a key witness to a case, his son was found by two Czech journalists hiding in Switzerland, having previously been kidnapped and held in Crimea in order to prevent from testifying in the case. The original media report was flagged by some as problematic and even misleading or manipulative: the Prime Minister's (possibly mentally ill or at least very frightened) son did not know he had been recorded by a hidden camera and did not give consent to publish the improvised interview which the journalists undertook with him at his flat. On the other hand, the story subsequently opened up a new wave of investigations about the Prime Minister's possible fraud and even about his behaviour towards his family and lying to the public. Such reasons would most probably be seen by the Court as being of the utmost public interest and thus as being worthy of coverage even by problematic means or methods that were intrusive into the right of the Prime Minister's son to a private and family life.

protection of reputation and the protection of one's image or photographs), the Court provides six common criteria to be taken into account in its assessment: (1) its contribution to a debate of general interest; (2) how well known the person concerned is; (3) what the subject of the report is; (4) the prior conduct of the person concerned; (5) the content, form and consequences of the publication; and (6) the circumstances in which the photos were taken.[77]

Regarding the sensitive photographs, the most exposed criteria the decision-making analysis takes into account are especially whether the taking of the photographs amounted to an intrusion into the individual's privacy, whether the photographs related to private matters or public incidents and whether the material obtained was envisaged as being for a limited use or was likely to be made available to the general public.[78]

Therefore, although there has been almost no case law from the Court regarding fake news under the right to respect private and family life, in a number of cases the important aspects related to false or misleading information have been addressed by the Court. However, as the Court's approach remains highly casuistic and case-specific, it is necessary to wait for the Court's future evaluation in cases concerning false information in a more specific or explicit way.

4. IDENTIFYING KEY ACTORS IN JUDICIAL PROCEEDINGS: WHY DOES IT MATTER?

The previous sections of this chapter mainly focused on the substantive part of the issue, i.e. the extent to which fake news might be fought before the ECtHR. Nevertheless, the procedural 'side of the coin' should not be forgotten. In reviewing the efficiency of judicial proceedings in the fight against fake news, it is crucial to ask the following questions: (1) who is supposed to bring legal action against the dissemination of false information?; and (2) who is liable for the dissemination of fake news?

As we can see from our case analysis, the claim is usually brought before the ECtHR either by those whose right to a private and personal life has been infringed or by those who were somehow limited in their ability to spread the information freely. It is due to a specific nature of the proceedings before the ECtHR that the application is always lodged against a particular state.[79] However, before the case gets to Strasbourg, parties are obliged to exhaust all

77 *Von Hannover v. Germany (No. 2)*, *supra* note 24, paras 108–113.
78 *P.G. and J.H. v. United Kingdom* App no 44787/98 (ECtHR, 25 September 2001) para. 58.
79 See Article 34 of the Convention.

the available effective domestic remedies.[80] This signifies the importance of focusing on the original parties of the dispute.

Regarding the question of an active legitimisation (i.e. who is entitled to bring a lawsuit against fake news), it should be noted that the number and type of potential claimants will always depend on the relevant legislation and a particular category of fake news. First and foremost, people directly affected by false information can be entitled to seek protection from national courts either under private law actions (privacy actions, defamation actions, etc.),[81] administrative law (offence laws) or *ultima ratio* criminal law (when included in penal codes). Nevertheless, when authorised by legislation, national states themselves might be the ones responsible for seeking an action. This might prove effective, especially in categories of fake news such as *Political Propaganda*, *Bogus Click-Bait* and *Hoaxes* in which no particular person may be directly affected.[82] However, regarding the states themselves, it would be naïve to expect them to adopt a proactive approach, especially if no one is directly affected. This is mainly due to (in many cases) the lack of national experts, means or time.[83] That is why it is more probable that states would mostly deal only with individual cases based on criminal charges. Nevertheless, civil society in the form of various NGOs could represent a potentially influential player in that regard.[84]

As to the second question, it might be argued that one should bring legal action against the particular person infringing one's rights. This is certainly possible in some cases, as we can see above. However, it is important to emphasise that one of the most troubling aspects of fake news is the common difficulty of tracking down its original source.[85] Indeed, fake news is often

---

80 *Ibid.*, Article 45.

81 See e.g. Stanford Law School Fake News and Misinformation Policy Lab Practicum, *supra* note 7, pp. 16–31.

82 See e.g. *Aksu v. Turkey* App nos 4149/04 and 41029/04 (ECtHR, 15 March 2012), which concerned a whole ethnic group (the Roma). The Court *inter alia* held that the negative stereotyping of an ethnic group was capable, if it reached a certain level, of having an impact on the group's sense of identity and on its members' feelings of self-worth and self-confidence. It could thus affect their 'private life' within the meaning of Article 8(1) of the Convention. On this basis, any person of Roma origin who had felt offended by passages in a book and dictionary entries about the Roma in Turkey could seek redress by engaging this article.

83 Let alone the administrations which try to use fake news as a means of political propaganda themselves.

84 For instance, the Court stated in *Steel and Morris v. United Kingdom* (App no 68416/01 (ECtHR, 15 May 2005) para. 89) that: 'In a democratic society even small and informal groups … should be able to carry out their activities effectively and there is a strong public interest in allowing these groups and individuals out of the mainstream to contribute to the public debate by disseminating information and ideas on matters of public interest such as health or the environment.'

85 B. Vojak, 'Fake News: The Commoditization of Internet Speech' (2017) 48 *California Western International Law Journal* 123, pp. 131–132.

spread anonymously and therefore it is difficult to even consider the person responsible.[86] Consequently, it is sometimes argued that platforms providing the opportunities for the spread of fake news should be held responsible for such illegal content.[87] The ECtHR itself addressed such a possibility in *Delfi v. Estonia*[88] and *MTE v. Hungary*,[89] which concerned the question of intermediary liability. Such an intermediary can be held liable in certain circumstances; however, a fuller discussion of this issue is beyond the scope of this chapter.[90]

To summarise this section, it is crucial to consider several procedural issues when assessing the effectiveness of judicial means with regard to fake news. Firstly, in order to be able to effectively lead a legal action, it is necessary to identify a probable perpetrator, which in the cases of creating or spreading false information online can be per se impossible. Secondly, even if identified, the state has to have the effective legal remedies and legal framework under which the harm from false information falls. Moreover, such a legislature must attain a certain level of quality in order to be applicable in accordance with the Court's case law. Therefore, taking legal action against a perpetrator of misinformation can amount to financially and time-consuming activity with no clear result or prospect of success in such an uncertain environment and circumstances.

5. CONCLUSION

In this chapter, we have focused on the possibility of using judicial means as an avenue to combat the spread of disinformation. Primarily, we aimed to examine whether the jurisprudence of a leading European human rights court (the ECtHR) can provide us with certain guidance regarding the treatment of fake news in judicial proceedings.

Even though the ECtHR has not yet had the chance to decide on a case directly concerning the issue of the proliferation of fake news on social media

---

86 See E. Savino, 'Fake News: No One is Liable, and That is a Problem' (2017) 65 *Buffalo Law Review* 1101.

87 L.K. Royster, 'Fake News: Political Solutions to the Online Epidemic' (2017) 96 *North Carolina Law Review* 270, pp. 286–294.

88 *Delfi AS v. Estonia* App no 64569/09 (ECtHR, 16 June 2015).

89 *Magyar Tartalomszolgáltatók Egyesülete and Index.hu Zrt. v. Hungary* App no 22947/13 (ECtHR, 2 February 2016).

90 For the wider context, see G.F. Frosio. 'Reforming Intermediary Liability in the Platform Economy: A European Digital Single Market Strategy' (2017) 112(19) *Northwestern University Law Review*; G.F. Frosio, 'From Horizontal to Vertical: An Intermediary Liability Earthquake in Europe' (2017) 12(7) *Journal of Intellectual Property Law & Practice* 565; C. Angelopoulos and S. Smet, 'Notice-and-Fair-Balance: How to Reach a Compromise between Fundamental Rights in European Intermediary Liability' (2016) 8(2) *Journal of Media Law* 266; M. Husovec, *Injunctions against Intermediaries in the European Union: Accountable But Not Liable?*, Cambridge University Press, Cambridge 2017.

platforms, the principles valid for assessing the issue remain in its core the same as in other freedom of expression cases. Firstly, the Court's task is not to take the place of domestic courts, as they are better placed to interpret local facts and laws, but to review the domestic decisions that they made under Article 10 in the light of the case as a whole and determine the proportionality of the outcome. This includes balancing different aspects such as the truthful nature of the statements expressed, duties and responsibilities of the speakers, the severity of the limitation on the freedom of expression, the intention of the speakers, the impact of the statements and the nature of the false information.

Similarly, with regard to the right to private and family life under Article 8, the Court takes into account several factors, such as the reasonable expectations of individuals and the level of seriousness of the infringement of one's personal reputation. Only once the Court considers all the relevant criteria, can it conclude whether the reasons put forward by the state were relevant and sufficient, and reflected an acceptable assessment of the relevant facts.

Above that, in both cases under Article 8 or 10, where a political debate, politician or a similar public figure is concerned, the Court is especially cautious about speech restrictions (e.g. as in *Brzeziński v. Poland* mentioned above). While politicians need to show more tolerance towards criticism, there is also a lower margin of appreciation for the national authorities when it comes to expressions made by political opposition or critics of state power. And whilst states are therefore allowed to take steps against spreading false information in a political debate (especially during an election), the flow of information is also crucial. States are thus in an unenviable situation of balancing very important interests (and positive obligations) on all sides.

Although the analysis of the Court's case law concerning substantive aspects of the spread of fake news provides a certain form of guidance, the examination of a procedural side of judicial protection indicates some potential drawbacks. Firstly, due to the largely anonymous origins of online false information, it may be difficult to identify a probable perpetrator, i.e. a person to be held legally liable. Certain forms of online platforms' responsibility may represent one of the potential means. Furthermore, even if national legal systems provided for certain kind of remedies that would be appropriate in the case of false information dissemination, taking legal action might still be an unpredictable and rather financially and time-consuming means.

14. FAKE NEWS AND FREEDOM OF EXPRESSION AND INFORMATION

The Legal Framework and Policy Actions at the EU Level to Address Online Disinformation

Cristina PAUNER CHULVI*

1. INTRODUCTION

Recent events have sparked a heated debate about the influence of fake news. Some suggest that fake news led to a spate of surprise election results, including the rejection of the Colombian peace agreement by referendum, the Leave campaign's victory in the Brexit referendum and, very significantly, Donald Trump's win in the US presidential elections.

Fake news, of course, is not a new phenomenon. Publishing unverified stories – in lay terms, bad journalism – is the equivalent of what was always referred to as propaganda or yellow journalism. With the explosion of information and communication technologies, however, fake news has taken on a new dimension. While online media, such as blogs, social networks and websites, are excellent at helping people to communicate and provide access to huge amounts of information, they also allow fake news to reach anyone. This situation has changed the functional nature of the right to information, which was always tied directly to the right to freedom of opinion.[1] The key difference,

* University Jaume I – Castellon, Spain. Email: pauner@uji.es. This work is part of the research projects on the implementation of the General Data Protection Regulation in Spain funded by Spain's Ministry of Science, Innovation and Universities (RTI2018-095367-B-I00) and the Valencian Government (AICO/2019/205). The work was carried out during a research fellowship at the Centre for Commercial Law Studies at Queen Mary University of London.

1 Spain's constitutional jurisprudence and European jurisprudence make it clear that freedom of expression and freedom of information are central to a functional democracy. Without these two freedoms, democracy cannot be protected. Freedom of expression is one of the pillars of a free and democratic society, since it ensures that public opinion can be formed freely, which is essential for the exercise of other fundamental rights. Examples include Spanish Constitutional Court Judgment 6/1981 of 16 March 1981; and judgment of the European Court of Human Rights of 24 May 1988, *Müller and Others v. Switzerland.*

therefore, between fake news published in traditional media and fake news published online is that the latter have a greater impact and go viral because they are shared around the world on social media.

Fake news might seem like a new phenomenon, but the only thing that is new is the platforms used to share it – the sites on which all the stories are fabricated. The sites are designed to look reliable and use sensationalist titles to attract readers. The controversies that these malicious news stories create are mainly the fault of the authors and sites that create them, but the social media platforms that help them go viral and the advertising platforms that fund them are also to blame.

Traditional media have also been guilty of disseminating false or unverified news, albeit far less often. When traditional media publish fake news, it is usually connected to the current structural crisis of journalism as a sustainable model. Over the last decade or so, there has been a seismic shift in the business model of the press, which has been unable to generate a profit through its traditional advertising model. Furthermore, the press faces new demands from its readers and new challenges in terms of distribution and sales channels. The big media companies are responding to the overall decline in the number of advertisers and subscribers by cutting jobs or restructuring their payrolls, sometimes in drastic fashion.

The transformation has also included new methods to churn out stories quickly, sometimes almost instantaneously. In today's digital age, in which news must be constantly up to date, journalists do not have enough time to verify that their stories are accurate, even though accuracy is one of the basic requirements of good-quality, error-free news. Newspapers work against the clock to make sure they are the first to report on an event. They send out news alerts right away to generate more traffic, even though they still need to write the actual story. Even the story itself 'is no longer a finished product written by an independent professional, but is a constantly evolving, open process involving many different non-professional voices and distributed through a range of channels and platforms'.[2]

The danger of fake news is that it creates a society unable to agree on basic facts, making it impossible to build a functional democracy. Disinformation strikes the very foundations of democratic societies, which are built on the assumption that citizens make informed decisions when they go to the polls. The information that citizens receive about public affairs, about the work of

2 J.C. Suárez Villegas and J. Cruz Álvarez, 'Problemas éticos de la instantaneidad informativa en el entorno digital', in B. Lloves and F. Segado (eds.), *I Congreso Internacional de Comunicación y Sociedad Digital*, UNIR, Logroño 2013, p. 11. Regarding the change in the story-writing process, see G. Brock, *Out of Print: Newspapers, Journalism and the Business of News in the Digital Age*, Kogan Page, London 2013.

our representatives and public institutions, lets us form an opinion about them so we can oversee how they are run. But we can no longer form a fair opinion if the information we receive is false and misleading or, in a word, untrue. Legal protections can therefore be afforded only to real news about issues and people connected to matters of general interest, which is essential for democratic scrutiny and is the only thing that legitimately shapes public opinion.

In his book *A Preface to Democratic Theory*, Robert Dahl lists eight requirements to create a decisive majority. The first four requirements define the form of suffrage. The fifth requires that 'all individuals possess identical information about the alternatives'.[3] Uncontrolled news flows online are therefore a good development, given how much power the traditional press used to have in setting the political agenda. Access to new channels that foster progress has made the world far more democratic. There is, however, also a downside to uncontrolled news flows: consensus requires certain shared foundations, but the spread of disinformation sometimes makes it impossible for such foundations to exist. If certain groups create their own reality, reaching agreements will be impossible.

The threat is so serious and fake news stories are so widespread that the media and public authorities are on high alert. Around the world, there is great concern about the problem of fake news. In Europe, some governments have introduced a series of measures to counter the threat. Germany, Italy and France launched several safeguards against the massive spread of fake news stories, as explained later in this chapter. But they are well aware that, in today's globalised world, national measures to combat fake news will have little impact or success, so action is now being taken at the EU level. EU institutions have asked large tech firms to help them stem the flood of fraudulent information on the Internet, calling for the same kind of commitment already made to fighting hate speech in social media.[4] In the international arena, the UN expressed its concern about the issue in its recent document 'Fake News, Disinformation and Propaganda'.[5] In the declaration, the UN said that disinformation and propaganda are

3 R. Dahl, *A Preface to Democratic Theory*, University of Chicago Press, Chicago 1956, p. 71.

4 The 'Code of conduct on countering illegal hate speech online', approved on 31 May 2016, is one of the initiatives that was developed as part of the European Commission's Digital Single Market Strategy. See http://ec.europa.eu/justice/fundamental-rights/files/hate_speech_code_of_conduct_en.pdf, footnote no. 20.

5 'Joint Declaration on Freedom of Expression and "Fake News", Disinformation and Propaganda', of 3 March 2017, adopted by the special rapporteurs on freedom of expression and opinion of the United Nations, the Organization of American States, the Organization for Security and Co-operation in Europe and the African Commission on Human and Peoples' Rights, available at: http://www.ohchr.org/EN/NewsEvents/Pages/DisplayNews.aspx?NewsID=21287.

implemented to mislead the population and interfere with the public's right to receive a variety of information and to form their own opinion.

Attempts to stamp out fake news and calls for stricter regulation of online content to prevent fake news from being read raise many questions regarding what the democratic response to disinformation should be. What constitutes fake news? When biased but legitimate information becomes propaganda and a lie, is it fake news? Who will monitor the content circulating on social media? To what extent are search engines and social media responsible? Is it feasible to create an algorithm that will stamp out fake news without blocking any real news? What criteria would be used to distinguish between fake news and real news? Is 'truth' the right criterion? How should governments respond to this phenomenon? Might it be preferable, in terms of democracy, to let people judge news stories for themselves and decide which ones they want to receive, without any third-party involvement?

On the face of it, it seems dangerous to make online service providers, such as social media platforms, partly responsible for filtering news stories, because doing so would make access to online content subject to business interests. Similarly, if this role were in the hands of government, it could be deemed a form of censorship and could lead to something akin to a Ministry of Truth.

2. NEWS FLOWS IN TODAY'S WORLD: DIGITAL PLATFORMS AND THEIR ROLE IN DISSEMINATING NEWS AND INFORMATION

To analyse how fake news spreads, we must first identify the two parties involved in the process: the platforms and websites that create fake news, and the social media that help them go viral.

Many of the fake news stories on websites were originally fabricated by spammers, who try to lure in Internet users so that they can earn pay-per-click advertising revenue. These fake newspapers and websites deliberately imitate real news websites, but publish hoaxes and propaganda that look like real news stories. Initially, the main motive of fake new sites was to manipulate facts, but that became a secondary motive once it became clear that fake news was a very lucrative business, generating huge sums of money in advertising revenue thanks to the sheer number of hits they attract.

Later, fake news stories began to go viral through social media platforms like Facebook and Twitter through a process that has been dubbed an 'information cascade'. Fake news sites try to attract attention on social media to divert Internet traffic towards them. By doing so, they multiply the impact of the stories while generating vast sums of money through social media advertising services. The news industry has therefore become more consumer-focused, and a media service's value now depends more on how viral its stories are than on how true or well written they are. Today, what matters is not whether a news story is true, but whether people are posting about it. The way news stories spread therefore depends on social media rather than traditional media, because it is the social media platforms that select and filter information using their complex, opaque, unpredictable algorithms and platforms.[6]

In the information society, a large proportion of the population obtain their news in their feed on Facebook, Google and other social media, rather than searching for it in several different traditional media. The social media platforms use secret algorithms to customise the stories they show each user based on the data they have about that user, and basically they show a stream of information selected by the person's friends, family and contacts. These algorithms therefore 'control' which news stories social media users see. Strictly speaking, social media platforms do not decide what each person reads and which news stories get published in the media, but when a platform becomes the dominant source of access to information, as has occurred with Facebook (dubbed the newspaper of the 21st century), traditional media adapt to social media guidelines and prepare their stories based on how social media operate.[7] Such is the scale of Facebook's influence on the press that there is a huge commotion whenever any changes are made to the algorithm used to select news stories, since the changes can reduce the number of views a story gets. This is contrary to the initial idea of an open, diverse, decentralised World Wide Web, which is being replaced by platforms that centralise information, sometimes even prohibiting external links.

Because news stories are filtered to match our personal interests, the version of the world presented to us every day serves only to confirm and reaffirm our pre-existing beliefs. The invisible tailored filtering in the background sanitises the news stories we read before they reach us. In 2011, Eli Pariser coined the term 'filter bubble'[8] to describe this situation. He showed how Google's customised search settings prevent two people from ever finding the same information, even if they use exactly the same search terms. The algorithms determine what we do and do not see, limiting our knowledge of a broader range of ideas and reliable information, and we are less likely to stumble upon other sources of knowledge.

---

6 There have been numerous studies on algorithms and their influence on the news sector in different parts of the world, especially in the UK and the US. Notable recent studies include E.A. Kirley, 'The robot as cub reporter: law's emerging role in cognitive journalism' (2016) 7(3) *European Journal of Law and Technology* 1 and B. Wagner, 'Algorithmic regulation and the global default: shifting norms in Internet technology' (2016) 1 *Etikk i praksis. Nord J Appl Ethics* 5.

7 K. Viner, 'How technology disrupted the truth', *The Guardian*, 17 July 2016.

8 The seminal work on this topic is E. Pariser, *The Filter Bubble: What the Internet is Hiding from You*, Penguin, New York 2011.

If the algorithm hides diverse news sources and even removes contradictory sources (i.e. those that challenge our personal beliefs), the diverse range of viewpoints in society are likely to be pulled as far apart as possible, creating truly divergent social groups.

There are two reasons why news stories that are doing the rounds in social media are accepted and deemed trustworthy. First, users are more inclined to believe a story if it comes from an acquaintance. They see the traditional media as inherently biased, but their response to their contacts is built on trust. Second, people find it harder to detect bias in stories selected by social media algorithms than when the editorial choices are made by traditional media. Because traditional media have existed for so long, society has developed ways to spot the ideological assumptions they make and can see when information is real, when it is false and when it uses caricature, irony or humour. The news selection methods of social media, on the other hand, are not well known. The lack of transparency about their algorithms makes it hard for the public to spot ideological bias from the people who work for those companies. Moreover, users do not have suitable indications they can use to check whether a story is true or not.

The filtering algorithms have already proved unable to assess the quality and reliability of news stories, as exemplified by Facebook's failed experiment when its editorial team was accused of bias. In its quest for neutrality, Facebook sacked 18 editors responsible for classifying news stories and replaced them with algorithms, only to discover, just a few days later, that the algorithms could not distinguish between real and fake news.[9]

Social media's algorithms therefore fail to cleanse the communication sector of lies. Not only that, but the platforms actually help dangerous content to spread and at the same time they narrow people's vision of the world they live in. This has been described as 'the social power of algorithms'.[10] Social networks are hugely powerful because they control 'who publishes what to whom, and how that publication is monetized'.[11] All the social media companies have platforms that allow the traditional media to publish exclusive content directly through their social media service, which can then be shared by their users.[12] We know

---

9 'Facebook despide al equipo que filtraba sus noticias … y el algoritmo se vuelven loco', *El Confidencial*, 31 August 2016; and 'Facebook has repeatedly trended fake news since firing its human editors', *Washington Post*, 16 October 2016.

10 L. Rainie and J. Anderson, 'Code-dependent: pros and cons of the algorithm age', *Pew Research Center*, February 2017, p. 25; and D. Beer, 'The social power of algorithms' (2017) 20(1) *Information, Communication & Society* 1.

11 E. Bell, 'Facebook is eating the world' (2016) *Columbia Journalism Review*, https://www.cjr.org/analysis/facebook_and_media.php.

12 The Discover App by Snapchat, Instant Articles by Facebook, Apple News by Apple, Accelerated Mobile Pages by Google, and Moments by Twitter.

little to nothing, however, about how these services select news stories, as the inner workings of their systems are not transparent, and are not subject to any form of external regulation.

Therefore, although these companies were not founded with the intention of taking on responsibilities in the area of freedom of the press, they are becoming ever more relevant in the area of social information. Furthermore, as explained below, the solutions being put forward by the EU to combat fake news emphasise that these companies must be active partners.

3. HOW THE EU AND ITS MEMBER STATES REACT TO THE SPREAD OF FAKE NEWS

The search for answers to the dangers that fake news poses to democracy is taking place on many fronts. A fact-checking frenzy broke out in the American media during the US presidential election campaign, but the protection afforded to freedom of speech in the First Amendment of the Constitution makes the battle against fake news particularly difficult in the US.[13]

In the EU, all governments fear that made-up stories which look like real news might shape the course of political events, especially in the run-up to elections. National and European public bodies and authorities have therefore joined the battle against lies by supporting a model that not only regulates news but also involves the industries concerned, which are being asked to develop filtering systems and make users take responsibility for making critical decisions about the content they consume.[14]

Germany is one of the countries that has gone down the regulatory route. In March 2017, the Federal Government introduced a bill with fines of up to €50 million for social media platforms that fail to remove defamation, hate speech and fake news.

The French parliament has passed two laws that allow electoral candidates to request a court order preventing the publication of 'false information' in the three months prior to a national election.[15] It also authorises the regulatory body for the audiovisual media (the Conseil Supérieur de l'Audiovisuel)

---

13 See J. Rosen, 'The delete squad: Google, Twitter, Facebook and the global battle over the future of free speech', *New Republic*, 29 April 2013.

14 See Teruel Lozano's excellent paper on the shift towards regulated online content: G.M. Teruel Lozano, 'Libertad de expresión en Internet, control de contenidos de las páginas web y sus garantías constitucionales' (2011) 25 *Revista Aranzadi de Derecho y Nuevas Tecnologías* 81.

15 Law n° 2018-1202 and Organic Law n° 2018-1201 on the battle against manipulation of information (JORF n. 0297 of 23 December 2018).

to suspend the licences of television and radio stations that are considered to be controlled by a foreign state or under the influence of that state, and it forces platforms like Facebook and Twitter to reveal the source of funding of sponsored content.

Italy was also considering a bill to prevent manipulated online news in order to ensure online transparency and to encourage media literacy. The proposal, which is currently on hold, would allow civil and criminal procedures to be brought against anyone who published exaggerated or biased news stories containing data or information that is blatantly unfounded or false.

In Spain, the government's National Security Strategy in 2017 identified fake news as a threat. Furthermore, the digital newspaper *El Confidencial* and the television station *La Sexta* introduced fact-checking segments, combining the journalistic corroboration process with video footage.[16]

The EU has put forward its own reforms to combat disinformation, with four main lines of action. First, the proposals would strengthen the East Stratcom initiative launched by the European Council in March 2015 to counter the Russian disinformation campaign. A team of 400 volunteers would publish two weekly bulletins exposing the lies that the Kremlin is trying to pass as truth in Europe. In addition, the EU has called for the battle against fake news to be included in its security policy agenda. Second, it will publicly challenge those who spread disinformation and it has called on its member states to support independent fact-checkers. Third, the EU would use real information to combat propaganda and disinformation. This is not a new tactic, as it has already been employed by traditional media and by digital tools similar to websites like FactCheck, PolitiFact and Snopes. More recently, some projects focused on journalism are fighting false news by warning users or by providing experts with technological instruments, namely NewsGuard or SOMA projects.[17] Fourth, and most importantly, it has called for similar action to what has already been done to tackle hate speech in social media. The idea is to pass EU measures similar to the Code of Conduct that the European Commission drafted to counter online

[16] La Sexta introduced Spain's TV viewers to this new focus on public fact-checking in 2013, with the programme *El Objetivo*. The show's 'Verification Tests' segment regularly fact-checks the most widely quoted claims made by public figures. See N. Hernández, 'Estos son los datos, suyas las conclusiones' (2017) 33 *Cuadernos de Periodistas* 9; and B. Echevarría, 'Más "fact-checking" contra la posverdad' (2017) 33 *Cuadernos de Periodistas* 17.

[17] NewsGuard has trained analysts who research online news brands to review and rate news and information online. They provide online users with reliability indicators – green, yellow or red – and 'nutrition label' write ups (NewsGuard, https://www.newsguardtech.com). The Social Observatory for Disinformation and Social Media Analysis (SOMA) offers support to experts in their work against disinformation, providing them with technological infrastructure based on the collaborative verification platform Truly Media (SOMA, http://www.disinfobservatory.org).

hate speech, racism and xenophobia,[18] which was signed by Facebook, Twitter, YouTube and Microsoft at the end of May 2016.

All these measures have been accompanied by a powerful regulatory initiative launched by the European Commission. First, the Commission set up a High Level Expert Group on fake news and online disinformation[19] in late 2017. Second, the Commission also launched a broad public consultation process[20] with more than 26,000 interviewees and conducted a Eurobarometer opinion poll covering all 28 member states. Third and finally, on 26 April 2018, the European Commission adopted a Communication on 'Tackling online disinformation: a European approach',[21] which highlights the challenges associated with online disinformation and proposes a set of potential measures to tackle online disinformation. The measures include an EU-wide Code of Practice on Disinformation, support for an independent network of fact-checkers, and a series of actions to stimulate quality journalism and promote media literacy. The Code of Practice on Disinformation was presented on 26 September 2018 and it includes measures in relation to five complementary lines of action: disrupting the advertising revenues of certain social media accounts and websites that spread disinformation; making political advertising and issue-based advertising more transparent; addressing the issue of fake accounts and online bots; empowering consumers to report disinformation and access different news sources, while improving the visibility and findability of authoritative content; and empowering the research community to monitor online disinformation by providing them with privacy-compliant access to the platforms' data.

The actions envisaged in the Communication, including the Code of Practice, will contribute to protecting free and fair election processes. In this respect, the EU plan to combat fake news before elections to the European Parliament were held in May 2019, included an 'election package' adopted by the Commission on 12 September 2018 to protect the democratic process from foreign interference and illegal manipulation.

---

18 European Commission, 'Code of conduct on countering illegal hate speech online', Technical Report, 2016. The results of the Code of Conduct's application were analysed in October and November 2016 and were subsequently published. The Commission concluded that the results were disappointing. The report is available at: http://www.politico.eu/wp-content/uploads/2016/12/factsheet-code-conduct.pdf.

19 High Level Group, *A Multi-dimensional Approach to Disinformation, Report of the Independent High Level Group on Fake News and Online Disinformation*, March 2018.

20 European Commission, *Report on Fake News and Disinformation Online*, Flash Eurobarometer 494, February 2018 (published in April 2018).

21 Communication from the Commission to the European Parliament, the Council, the European Economic and Social Committee and the Committee of the Regions, 'Tackling online disinformation: a European approach', Brussels, 26 April 2018, COM(2018) 236 final.

The set of measures presented by the European Commission consists of a Communication[22] and a Recommendation[23] on election cooperation networks. These documents encourage member states to set up national election cooperation networks and take part in a European cooperation network to alert citizens about threats, to exchange on best practices, to discuss common solutions and to encourage common projects.

4. SOCIAL MEDIA'S RESPONSE TO FAKE NEWS: SOLUTIONS OFFERED

As part of this collective strategy to combat fake news in Europe, the authorities called on technology companies to get involved. Initially, they refused to play an active role. In fact, until recently, tech firms refused to be considered media, including Facebook, the most powerful of them all and a primary source of access to news. Tech firms were reluctant to accept responsibility for controlling the stories they publish, preferring to present themselves as neutral intermediaries whose role was to offer 'the best possible experience' to their 'community'. At the same time, however, because Facebook is a platform used to share news, it has had to deal with issues related to truthfulness, privacy, publication and content-sharing. In other words, issues related to freedom of speech, freedom of information and online sharing.

Since the Internet giants are providers of news services, they do have certain duties because of how powerful they are as news providers. They cannot be considered totally neutral technology companies. When a search term produces different results depending on the user's search history, choice of browser or ideology and interests, a decision-making process is taking place in the background. The platform is actively 'serving' news in a certain way, which amounts to making editorial decisions. That is why, slowly but surely since late 2016, Facebook has begun accepting a new type of responsibility, creating a space for people to receive news in a *safe* and *certified* way. This intermediate position acknowledges that a social media platform cannot become an arbiter of truth, but can be an essential partner in the fight against blatant hoaxes.

Accepting responsibility does not turn the social media platforms into editors as, strictly speaking, these companies do not publish anything. But Facebook, Twitter and Google are part of what has been dubbed the 'freedom of

---

22 Communication from the Commission to the European Parliament, the European Council and the Council, 'A Europe that delivers: institutional options for making the European Union's work more efficient', 13 February 2018, COM(2018) 095 final.

23 Commission Recommendation (EU) 2018/234 of 14 February 2018 on Enhancing the European nature and efficient conduct of the 2019 elections to the European Parliament.

speech infrastructure',[24] and as such they have civic and democratic responsibilities. They have a duty to cooperate in preventing the spread of fake news using transparent methods, explaining how their algorithms work and how they select which news stories to show.

As a first step, online service providers have begun to combat fake news by rolling out certain mechanisms that filter and block content. These filtering systems have been considered the best way to achieve a balance between protecting freedom of speech and protecting users from harmful online content. Very often, filtering is done in accordance with the conditions that users must accept when they contract or use a service. The 'community standards' that social media impose as a matter of corporate policy, for instance, stipulate that the platforms can remove content that is illegal or that they deem inappropriate or that might harm the company's image. In addition to this private-sector initiative, governments are forcing service providers to use filters to control and identify certain content, block it and, if appropriate, remove it. This approach is somewhat controversial. On the one hand, fake news twists public opinion and can threaten the very system of democracy, but on the other hand, the solutions put forward could be considered to generate biased information (a private company's political stance or ideological bias could be incorporated into an algorithm) or even constitute censorship. Both bias and censorship can ruin democracy, which relies on freedom of expression and freedom of information.

Social media now tend to combat fake news using one of three methods, or a combination of the three: recruiting human revisers and editors, normally from traditional media; cooperating with other platforms; and applying algorithmic technology solutions.

Human-led solutions involve bringing in independent experts with fact-checking skills to help select and verify news stories before they appear in social media news feeds. Systematic data-checking and fact-checking in the public sphere is considered a basic component of good journalism and has been an essential part of the work carried out by the editorial offices of the traditional press. These procedures have spread from the traditional press to other media (television and online), and are now commonplace around the world.

Those who believe that social media should use the same procedures argue that human judgement is more reliable than technology and algorithms, which struggle to detect trolling (provocative, irrelevant or off-topic messages) on online platforms and subtle shades of meaning by people exercising their freedom of expression. Cost is the main drawback of this proposal, because social media form such a huge ecosystem and hiring enough staff to act swiftly

24 This expression is used in J.M. Balkin, 'The future of free expression in a digital age' (2008) 36 *Pepperdine Law Review* 106, available at: https://ssrn.com/abstract=1335055.

and effectively would cost a fortune. Also, evaluators would not be impartial and would have to make subjective decisions, and social media platforms would need to specify how they determine whether a news story is fake or real.

Crowdsourcing solutions open the assessment process up so that users of social networks can evaluate news stories and classify them as they see fit. Once a news story has been tagged, users are free to decide whether they think it is credible or not. In the crowdsourcing model, volunteers produce news stories collectively, in a similar manner to how the Wikipedia is produced. Thanks to this system, crowdsourced news stories are less likely to be accused of bias or censorship since, theoretically, anyone can take part. There is still the potential, however, for manipulation by the very groups who spread fake and biased stories.

New algorithmic solutions take it as read that many fake news producers tag their stories with metadata meant to appeal to the algorithms that select and prioritise which stories appear first when users visit a social media platform. The algorithms for selecting news stories are therefore being refined so that they prioritise pages considered more reliable and make less credible stories less prominent.

Although tech companies claim that the algorithms have no ideological bias, clearly they are not necessarily balanced, since those who create the algorithms determine how they operate and what results they produce. This system has the advantage that it is cheap and easy to implement.

In addition to this offensive waged against fake news by the large tech firms, programmatic advertising firms also use filters based on whitelists of sites with reliable news and blacklists of sites with questionable content.[25] They do so to ensure that advertisers do not spend money on media that spread fake news.

5. FILTERING SYSTEMS AND CONSTITUTIONAL GUARANTEES OF FREEDOM OF EXPRESSION AND INFORMATION

Controlling the news stories that circulate online is a controversial topic, since it forces us to define how far freedom of expression and freedom of information should go in the digital environment. In theory, publishing and posting news

25 Programmatic advertising uses automated systems to publish online advertisements and generate brand awareness. Thanks to this system, advertising spaces can be auctioned in real time based on users' activity, clicks and searches. If the result matches the brand's target market, the advertisement appears, irrespective of the context. AppNexus and RocketFuel are two of the advertising firms that have developed blacklists of websites they believe include incitement to hate and sites they believe publish fake news, and they do not offer such sites to their brands. Similarly, there are whitelists of media approved for advertisers.

and opinions online is considered a form of freedom of expression and freedom of information. Websites that publish online news are protected by these freedoms, within the same limits as the traditional media. It is therefore important to distinguish between illegal content and harmful content.[26] Since illegal content is a criminal offence, it is prohibited and is forced to be taken down by legally established procedures; harmful content, on the other hand, might go against certain values or principles, so the publication of harmful material can be subject to proportionate limitations or restrictions. Fake news falls into the second category. It poses a threat to plural news coverage and robs the general public of their right to access real news. I therefore believe that certain restrictions on those who publish fake news are perfectly legitimate.

It is also necessary to determine how much social media platforms should do to combat fake news and to what extent they should be held accountable. There needs to be careful consideration about what these private companies should do, how much power they should have and how suitable the tools are that they use to evaluate and select news stories. Do attempts to counter fake news by applying filters and removing content constitute a form of censorship, driven by the desire to spread the 'truth' by establishing an official story, thereby restricting freedom of expression? This is a predicament for online service providers, which, as private companies, 'are not in a position to properly weigh up legal rights and legal assets, because they are governed by market rules'.[27]

5.1. THE LEGAL DISTINCTION BETWEEN VALUE JUDGEMENTS AND FALSE INFORMATION

Invoking truth as the absolute yardstick might be contrary to the principle of freedom of expression and information, since truth is not a concept that exists from a legal perspective. This freedom, enshrined in international texts such as Article 10 of the European Convention on Human Rights (ECHR), includes the freedom to hold opinions and the freedom to receive and impart information. Nevertheless, these two freedoms are not on a level footing. Facts are susceptible of proof, so those who make statements of fact can be expected to demonstrate them; value judgements, on the other hand, cannot be verified and therefore cannot be required to be true.[28] 'However,

26 See M.L. Fernández Esteban, 'Internet y los derechos fundamentales' (2000–2001) 6–7 *Anuario Jurídico de La Rioja* 321, pp. 334–335; and 'Illegal and harmful content on the internet. Communication from the Commission to the Council, the European Parliament, the Economic and Social Committee and the Committee of the Regions', 16 October 1996, COM(96) 487 final.

27 J. de Miguel Bárcena, 'Las transformaciones del derecho de la información en el contexto del ciberperiodismo' (2016) 173 *Revista de Estudios Políticos* 141, p. 159.

28 ECtHR judgment of 15 March 2011, *Otegi Mondragon v. Spain*, para. 53.

even when freedom of speech is being exercised, opinions must be founded, or at least sincere. Furthermore, "even where a statement amounts to a value judgement… [there needs to be] sufficient factual basis [i.e. an external reference] for the impugned statement, since even a value judgement without any factual basis to support it may be excessive" (ECtHR judgment of 27 February 2001, *Jerusalem v. Austria*, para. 43).'[29]

These same criteria for the protection of freedom of expression and the right to information adopted by the ECtHR are shared by the Court of Justice of the European Union (CJEU) and the Spanish Constitutional Court.[30] The CJEU has set out its position on freedom of expression and freedom of the press within the boundaries marked out by Article 51 of the Charter of Fundamental Rights of the European Union (CFREU), whose interpretation is limited to cases in which EU powers are being exercised or EU law is applicable.[31] The CJEU applies the same interpretation as the ECtHR in terms of the freedoms established in Article 11 of the CFREU.

Freedom of expression was formally incorporated into EU law by Article 11 of the CFREU. This freedom is a fundamental right which is contained in all member states' constitutions[32] as well as through Article 10 of the ECHR. The jurisprudence of the CJEU has analysed the scope of freedom of expression in connection with regulations on intellectual property rights,[33] electronic commerce,[34] data protection[35] and audiovisual communications.[36]

---

[29] I. Serrano Maillo, 'El derecho a la libertad de expresión en la jurisprudencia del Tribunal Europeo de Derechos Humanos: dos casos españoles' (2011) 28 *Teoría y Realidad Constitucional* 579, p. 582; square brackets indicate additions by Serrano not found in the original ECtHR judgment being cited.

[30] See the judgments of the CJEU: Case C-368/95, *Familiapress v. Austria*, 26 June 1997, para. 18; and Case C-112/00, *Schimdberger v. Austria*, 11 July 2002, para. 101. See also the judgments of the Spanish Constitutional Court: Cases 127/2018 of 26 November 2018; 79/2014 of 28 May 2014; and 77/2009 of 23 March 2009, among others.

[31] E. Linde Paniagua, 'El ámbito de aplicación: el talón de Aquiles de la Carta de Derechos Fundamentales de la Unión Europea' (2008) 15 *Revista de Derecho de la Unión Europea* 27, p. 39.

[32] In the UK, which has no written constitution, the right to freedom of expression under Article 10 of the ECHR is enshrined in constitutional law through the Human Rights Act of 1998.

[33] For example, Case C-145/10, *Eva-Maria Painer v. Standard VerlagsGmbH and Others*, 1 December 2011.

[34] Case C-71/02, *Herbert Karner Industrie-Auktionen GmbH v. Troostwijk GmbH*, 25 March 2004; or Case C-245/01, *RTL Television GmbH v. Niedersächsische Landesmedienanstalt für privaten Rundfunk*, 23 October 2003.

[35] Case C-131/12, *Google Spain SL v. AEPD & Mario Costeja González*, 13 May 2014.

[36] CJEU judgments: Case C-250/06, *United Pan-Europe Communications Belgium SA v. Bélgica*, 13 December 2007, Rec. 2007; and Case C-336/07, *Kabel Deutschland Vertrieb und Service GmbH & Co. KG v. Niedersächsische Landesmedienanstalt für privaten Rundfunk*, 22 December 2008.

The restrictions on freedom of expression are subject to tests to determine whether they are necessary and proportional.[37]

The same focus is found in the recognition of freedom of expression and freedom of information in Article 20 of the Spanish Constitution and in its interpretation by the Constitutional Court. The Court has taken a similar approach since its very first rulings. Most notably, regarding 'real news', it has stated that 'real' does not mean 'true'. Instead, the Court ruled that 'Article 20.1 d) covers news that is compiled and distributed honestly, even if its total accuracy is controversial'.[38] Rather than taking an objectivist stance to news, allowing only uncontested versions of facts, the Constitutional Court ruled that 'incorrect assertions are inevitable in a free debate, so if truth were imposed as a condition for this right to be recognised, the only way of ensuring one's legal security would be to remain silent'.[39] In a separate ruling, the Constitutional Court explained why incorrect assertions are lawful, quoting a judgment by the ECtHR:

> Freedom of expression constitutes one of the essential foundations of such a society, one of the basic conditions for its progress and for the development of every man. Subject to paragraph 2 of Article 10 (art. 10-2), it is applicable not only to 'information' or 'ideas' that are favourably received or regarded as inoffensive or as a matter of indifference, but also to those that offend, shock or disturb the State or any sector of the population. Such are the demands of that pluralism, tolerance and broadmindedness without which there is no 'democratic society' (ECtHR judgment of 7 December 1976, Handyside case, par. 65), since subjective divergences of opinion is part of the very structure of the institutional nature of the right to information.[40]

But neither can it be concluded that information is entirely subjective based merely on the reporter's subjective belief that whatever he or she is saying is true. A story that goes against the public interest or does not serve to inform in any way – such as rumours, malice, insults and contempt – is not news or information.[41] Even when a story does serve to inform, constitutional protection

37 For recent cases in which the EU judge has moved away from the classic tests derived from Article 10 of the Convention, see M. Rodríguez-Izquierdo Serrano, 'La libertad de expresión y la jurisprudencia del Tribunal de Justicia de la Unión Europea' (2014) 2 *Estudios de Deusto* 93.

38 Constitutional Court ruling 121/2002 of 20 May 2002, Conclusion of Law no. 5.

39 Constitutional Court ruling 6/1988 of 21 January 1988, Conclusion of Law no. 5.

40 Spanish Constitutional Court ruling 171/1990 of 12 November 1990, Conclusion of Law no. 9. Although the Constitutional Court cites paragraph 65 of the *Handyside* case judgment by the ECtHR, this is a mistake, since the quoted excerpt is from paragraph 49.

41 Constitutional Court ruling 214/1991 of 11 November 1991, Conclusion of Law no. 6.

is not afforded to '*false or biased stories*, slanderous stories, stories that invade people's privacy, and stories that breach legal principles and values such as good faith, national security and the proper functioning of public institutions'.[42]

This legal framework clearly sets out the scope of what should be considered fake news and what distinguishes fake news from other concepts. So, although some opinions will be correct and some incorrect, they are never false (or 'fake'), because the truthfulness of value judgements and assessments is not a black-and-white matter, even if someone fervently disagrees with them. Similarly, although partisan news stories that interpret facts according to a certain party-political line are examples of journalistic malpractice, they are not illegal exercises of freedom of expression. Also, although parodies, jokes and satire may include wrong or incorrect statements, making them technically 'false', because such statements appear in the context of irony or humour, they cannot be classified as news.

Fake news refers only to when people spread fictitious or fraudulent information knowing full well that it is inaccurate. Defining fake news in this way incorporates the idea of 'dishonesty', which is a helpful way of distinguishing fake, unacceptable news from the types of news that – as discussed earlier – enjoy constitutional protection despite containing errors. The aim, then, is to assess the quality of sites and ensure that those set up solely to publish made-up stories, unverified news, rumours and pure fabrications for financial gain can be identified, tagged and in some cases removed altogether, and to keep them from gaining viral momentum.

Identifying fake news obviously cannot be automated, not least because, given the term's ambiguity, it is difficult to create a regulatory framework at the EU level (and more so at the global level) that defines what a fake news story is in all member states, especially given how different countries define the content and scope of freedom of expression so differently, often based on deep-rooted cultural differences. For instance, the governments of countries like Poland and Hungary, which are becoming increasingly authoritarian, will see the boundaries between fake news and freedom of expression very differently from, say, France or Germany.

And given the sea of news stories inundating the Internet, it is also debatable whether algorithms can effectively distinguish fake news from the types of information protected by freedom of expression, such as opinions and satire, without increasing the threat of online censorship.

---

42 Constitutional Court ruling 51/1985 of 10 April 1985; A. Azurmendi Adarraga, 'De la verdad informativa a la "información veraz" de la Constitución Española de 1978: una reflexión sobre la verdad exigible desde el derecho de la información' (2005) 18(2) *Comunicación y Sociedad* 9, p. 20.

5.2. SOCIAL MEDIA'S ACCOUNTABILITY IN THE SPREAD OF FAKE NEWS

Classifying and tagging the information that users read is the responsibility of social media companies, since they are the ones who design the algorithm-based filters and content-blocking systems. Although users know that the first principle in Facebook's community standards is that 'people should have the freedom to share whatever information they want', everyone also knows that the platform's algorithm applies filters to huge quantities of data – such as user comments – to check and determine whether content is appropriate. The algorithm can be programmed to discard texts containing insults, for instance, or to remove comments from a certain part of the world that repeatedly request a bank account number. However, these standards embedded in the company's technology are not transparent to most of the population, and they are frequently updated and modified, which fuels the fear that a private company will introduce a form of censorship without the support of the user base. The Spanish Constitution deals with prior restraint in Article 20.2, but in principle it does not take into account the filtering, and subsequent blocking or removal, of online content, since these take place when the content has already been published and is not performed by government bodies. Nevertheless, as the legal scholars have established, blocking and removing content does harm the public's right to access online information[43] and could have a chilling effect.[44]

Indeed, the CJEU has refused to allow generic filtering systems, stating that they are contrary to freedom of expression. Certain decisions by the CJEU have suggested that the filtering system is not very effective at distinguishing between legitimate content and content that breaches copyright law, which means that freedom of information is not protected. Specifically, in the series of *SABAM* judgments, the CJEU stated that a filtering system introduced by court order in Belgium to protect intellectual property rights breached Article 11.1 of the CFREU.[45] It has stressed the need for countries to harmonise the various

---

43 G.M. Teruel Lozano, 'La libertad de expresión y censura en Internet' (2014) 62(2) *Estudios de Deusto* 41, p. 63.

44 That is why Josu de Miguel has called for Article 20.2 of the Constitution to change its definition of prior restraint to take into account the new risks posed by technological advances: J. de Miguel Bárcena, 'Las transformaciones del derecho de la información en el contexto del ciberperiodismo' (2016) 173 *Revista de Estudios Políticos* 141, p. 160.

45 These cases are linked to the question of fake news because the contested filtering system may infringe the right to protection of personal data of the ISP's customers 'as it would involve a systematic analysis of all content and the collection and identification of the users' IP address from which unlawful content on the network is sent' (CJEU judgments Case C-70/10, *Scarlet v. SABAM*, 24 November 2011, paras 50–51; and Case C-360/10, *Netlog v. SABAM*, 16 February 2012, para. 33).

fundamental rights covered by the Charter, referring to the 'proportionality' required by Article 52 of the Charter, which means that blocking is permitted, as long as the blocks do not deprive Internet users of their right to access lawful information.[46]

This position is not a total prohibition on filtering systems, but it does mean that only very specific content can be blocked, and clear, pre-determined, objectively justifiable criteria are required for the use of any measures that go above and beyond the legal requirements in terms of how they restrict third-party content.[47] This brings us to the key requirement: the need for transparent processes for evaluating and selecting the stories that are shared. Intermediaries must provide information on how their algorithms work, because those algorithms ultimately affect people's right to access information, and people need to have the option to contest that power.

Because more and more decisions are being made by algorithms, Europe's new General Data Protection Regulation restricts automated individual decisions, including profiling, that significantly affect the user (in Article 22) and creates a right to an explanation, allowing users to demand an explanation about any automated decision affecting them.

This need to know how the algorithm works can also be applied to the field of communication, because transparency is essential if news stories and journalists are to be trusted and it is the most important element for developing objective verification criteria.[48]

As discussed earlier, it is important to understand that an algorithm, by definition, will never be able to distinguish between true and false stories. It is impossible to create a 'truth algorithm'. Nevertheless, algorithms can be useful if, for instance, they help users to evaluate the quality of websites that produced a story by analysing the accuracy of the data on those sites. The algorithms can highlight the information that users should double-check in a story before they form an opinion about it or they can identify fake news stories and provide context for them.

This form of mediation through artificial intelligence, however, is not enough on its own. Algorithms should always, at the very least, also have a human fact-checking team. Automatic and automated fact-checking are no substitute for humans, since humans are better than computers at analysing the context of messages and the judgements and vague statements that they contain. One advantage a machine does have, however, is that it can scan the Web for simple,

---

46 CJEU judgment Case C-70/10, *Scarlet Extended*, 24 November 2011, para. 31.

47 See paragraph 4.a) of the Joint Declaration on Freedom of Expression and 'Fake News', Disinformation and Propaganda.

48 B. Kovach and T. Rosenstiel (eds.), *The Elements of Journalism*, 3rd ed., Three River Press, New York, 2014.

black-and-white statements and leave humans to deal with the many shades of grey. I therefore believe that an ideal way to screen fake news stories is to combine algorithms with human fact-checking teams.

The latest fact-checking techniques being implemented in traditional and social media must at least be consistent with the international standards set out in the International Fact-Checking Network's code of principles,[49] which stresses that transparency is vital. Signatories to the code of principles must abide by a series of commitments: (i) *non-partisanship and fairness* – signatories must use the same standard for all fact-checking and must not concentrate on one side of the facts; (ii) *transparency of sources* – sources are provided so that readers can check results for themselves; (iii) *transparency of funding and organisation* – signatories must say what financial support they received to write their articles and detail the professional background of the key people in the organisation's fact-checking team; (iv) *transparency of methodology* – signatories must clearly explain how they selected, researched, wrote, edited, published and corrected their news stories; and (v) *an open and honest corrections policy* – signatories must do everything possible to ensure readers can see corrected versions.

Fact-checking should not result in the removal of content. Instead, it would be better for external fact-checkers or automated fact-checking systems to tag stories that have factual issues. Users would then see a logo with a link to the fact-checkers' report and it would be up to them to form their own opinion about the story. For this solution to work, the public will need to become media literate so they can critically analyse digital information or have access to new tools to analyse the sources and the accuracy of the news stories they consume online. This could be achieved, for example, by ensuring that news stories are traceable or by creating fact-checking manuals to help people detect fake news.[50]

6. CONCLUSIONS

In the last two years, there has been growing concern that the general public are becoming increasingly suspicious of traditional sources of news and information – newspapers, radio stations and television channels. Instead, they are turning to the Internet, reading social media posts, even though the sources

49 http://www.poynter.org/fact-checkers-code-of-principles.

50 Such as the fact-checking manual produced by expert journalists from the BBC, Storyful, ABC and Digital First Media, as well as by other fact-checking specialists. The manual has versions adapted to different news contexts. The various manuals are available at: http://verificationhandbook.com.

of the stories are unclear and it is not easy to find out whether the information is true and has been corroborated.

Fears that the general public would consume the propaganda and fake news reached their height following the announcement of the US presidential election results in 2016, with many suggesting that fake news in the months preceding the election swayed the result. The rise of fake news is becoming a threat to democracy. It constitutes an assault on the right to information, pluralism and the right of citizens to freely form an opinion. It even leads to mistrust of the media in general.

Fake news – meaning deliberately erroneous or false information – is nothing new. Bad journalism and manipulation have always existed. What is new is that once these fake news stories have been created by malicious sources, they now go viral on social media. Users consume them, believing they are reliable, even though they have not been subject to any quality control whatsoever. They have simply been shared by the user's inner circle of acquaintances. Content-sharing platforms have therefore been asked to help fight against this problem. Just as these companies have already accepted their social responsibility in the fight against online piracy and the spread of illegal content, they are considered vital partners in fighting back against the spread of fake news on social media. In fact, large tech firms have started rolling out systems to filter the content they carry so that they can be fact-checked.

However, the use of such methods by private companies to control content poses serious questions to democracy. First, it is difficult to come up with a general definition for 'fake news' that distinguishes it from legitimate forms of freedom of expression, such as jokes and partisan opinions. Second, there is the danger of a private organisation being given wide-ranging, decisive powers to restrict the right to freedom of information and freedom of expression. Finally, there is a lack of transparency in the algorithms used by social media to select news stories and, if controls are used, to block them.

The challenge posed by fake news requires a paradigm shift in terms of the tools used to combat it and the entities involved in the battle.

Fact-checking needs to be the main tool used. In free democratic societies, the free flow of information must be guaranteed and restrictions must be kept to a minimum, so the Internet should not be over-regulated and, most importantly, criminal prosecution should not be a tool used to combat fake news. Fact-checking has always been the cornerstone of journalistic practice and can be used to select information that is trustworthy, as long as the criteria used are transparent and end users have the final choice about which content they want to consume. In the search for true news and information, the forms of cooperation from tech firms that are currently on the table (technological designs, human fact-checking and user collaboration) can have a positive impact. They must, however, be governed by the principle of transparency so that the public understand the formulas and criteria used to control what they can access and what is given priority on their social media news feeds. Furthermore, content controls should result in a tag that warns the user that the content is largely or totally inaccurate so that he or she can decide whether to consume it.

In terms of which parties should be involved in combating fake news, calls have been made for the state, the media, tech firms and civil society to participate, and rightly so. In Spain, the Pro-Freedom of Information Platform (Plataforma en Defensa de la Libertad de Información) has put forward a set of ten proposals[51] to serve as the basis for discussions to create joint strategies to fight the spread of fake news and its effects on journalism and society. The proposals call on all parties at all stages of the news supply chain to combat, and not to encourage, the spread of fake news, which requires parties to agree upon a definition of what is and is not a hoax or a fake news story. As part of this collective commitment, the media have a duty to state the source of the stories that they write or report on and to ensure that the information and content they deliver is traceable, except if the sources were confidential. The public authorities, meanwhile, must support media and digital literacy drives that help the public to spot fake news, and they must provide people with tools to help them check whether news stories, headlines and websites are reliable. Finally, content-distribution platforms should be considered news companies, given that news represents such a significant portion of the activity on their platforms, so they too should develop mechanisms that penalise hoaxes, including tools that can filter them out from shared content feeds.

51 Plataforma en Defensa de la Libertad de Información, 'Contra la posverdad: 10 fórmulas para hacer frente a las noticias falsas', 21 February 2017, http://libertadinformacion.cc/contra-la-posverdad-10-formulas-para-hacer-frente-a-las-noticias-falsas.

15. FIGHTING ONLINE DISINFORMATION

Did the EU Code of Practice Forget about Freedom of Expression?

Aleksandra KUCZERAWY*

1. INTRODUCTION

The problem of disinformation online is a source of growing concern for EU policy-makers. During the political events of 2016, it became clear that the spreading of so-called 'fake news' can create risks to democratic political processes, including the integrity of elections.[1] With EU elections on the way, policy-makers attempted to mitigate these risks as quickly as possible.[2] In early 2018, the EU Commission set up a new High-Level Expert Group (HLEG) on Fake News and Online Disinformation to advise the Commission on the phenomenon of disinformation, defining the roles and responsibilities of stakeholders, and formulating recommendations.[3] The HLEG released its final Report in March 2018.[4] Next, in May 2018, the Commission released

* Centre for IT and IP Law (CiTiP), KU Leuven, Belgium. Email: aleksandra.kuczerawy@kuleuven.be.

1 See J. WINSTON, 'How the Trump campaign built an identity database and used Facebook ads to win the election', *Medium*, 18 November 2016, https://medium.com/startup-grind/how-the-trump-campaign-built-an-identity-database-and-used-facebook-ads-to-win-the-election-4ff7d24269ac; C. CADWALLADR, 'British courts may unlock secrets of how Trump campaign profiled US voters', *The Guardian*, 1 October 2017, https://www.theguardian.com/technology/2017/oct/01/cambridge-analytica-big-data-facebook-trump-voters; 'Vote Leave's targeted Brexit ads released by Facebook', *BBC News*, 26 July 2018, https://www.bbc.com/news/uk-politics-44966969.

2 See EUROPEAN COMMISSION, 'Tackling online disinformation, providing an overview of EU joint and coordinated action against disinformation', https://ec.europa.eu/digital-single-market/en/tackling-online-disinformation.

3 EUROPEAN COMMISSION, 'Experts appointed to the High-Level Group on Fake News and online disinformation', 12 January 2018, https://ec.europa.eu/digital-single-market/en/news/experts-appointed-high-level-group-fake-news-and-online-disinformation.

4 EUROPEAN COMMISSION, 'Final report of the High-Level Expert Group on Fake News and Online Disinformation: a multi-dimensional approach to disinformation', March 2018, https://ec.europa.eu/digital-single-market/en/news/final-report-high-level-expert-group-fake-news-and-online-disinformation.

a Communication 'Tackling online disinformation: a European approach'.[5] Both documents set a number of goals ranging from enhanced transparency in political advertising to the closure of fake accounts, the demonetisation of purveyors of disinformation and the promotion of media literacy.[6] Moreover, the HLEG invited the European Commission to promote a general, Europe-wide Code of Practice as a multi-stakeholder approach.[7] In September 2018, the European Commission published the Code of Practice on Disinformation (hereinafter 'the Code').[8]

The Code is described as a voluntary, self-regulatory mechanism agreed on by representatives of online platforms, leading social networks, advertisers and advertising industry. The Code observes that the dissemination of disinformation is facilitated by and impacts a broad segment of actors in the ecosystem. For this reason, all stakeholders have roles to play in countering the spread of disinformation.[9]

The purpose of the Code is to identify actions that the signatories could put in place in order to address the challenges posed by disinformation online. The EU policy-makers define 'disinformation' as 'verifiably false or misleading information' which is both 'created, presented and disseminated for economic gain or to intentionally deceive the public' and may cause public harm, intended as 'threats to democratic political and policymaking processes as well as public goods such as the protection of EU citizens' health, the environment or security'.[10] The term does not cover misleading advertising, reporting errors, satire and parody, or clearly identified partisan news and commentary.[11] Moreover, the term does not apply to issues arising from the creation and dissemination of illegal content online (notably defamation, hate speech and incitement to violence).[12] Nevertheless, disinformation is considered harmful to the democratic state and the society and therefore requires steps to be taken to minimise its impact.

---

5 European Commission, Communication from the Commission to the European Parliament, the Council, the European Economic and Social Committee and the Committee of Regions, 'Tackling online disinformation: a European approach', 26 April 2018, COM(2018) 236 final, https://eur-lex.europa.eu/legal-content/EN/TXT/HTML/?uri=CELEX:52018DC0236&from=EN.

6 See European Commission, 'Communication – tackling online disinformation: a European approach', 26 April 2018, https://ec.europa.eu/digital-single-market/en/news/communication-tackling-online-disinformation-european-approach.

7 European Commission, *supra* note 4, p. 31.

8 European Commission, Code of Practice on Disinformation, 26 September 2018, https://ec.europa.eu/digital-single-market/en/news/code-practice-disinformation.

9 *Ibid.*, p. 1.

10 *Ibid.*

11 *Ibid.*

12 European Commission, *supra* note 4, p. 10.

This chapter does not dispute the position that disinformation may have a negative impact on democracy or that the problem needs to be addressed. However, enlisting private platforms to suppress the dissemination of online content that is not illegal may have unintended consequences. The chapter also does not discuss the problem of misuse of personal data for political micro-targeting, which is another element of the disinformation conundrum, as evidenced by the case of Cambridge Analytica. The aim of this chapter is to look at the Code of Practice on Disinformation from the perspective of the right to freedom of expression. In particular, it focuses on two questions: (1) what are the policy implications of co-opting private entities to regulate speech?; and (2) what safeguards could be introduced into the Code to help mitigate the risks to freedom of expression?

2. WHAT IS IN THE CODE?

The HLEG report observed that 'disinformation is a multifaceted problem, which cannot be addressed by a single measure' and that 'an overarching, multi-dimensional approach' is needed.[13] The Code proposes actions and describes commitments in five areas: (1) scrutiny of ad placements; (2) political advertising and issue-based advertising; (3) integrity of services; (4) empowering consumers; and (5) empowering the research community. The Code also contains a plan for monitoring its effectiveness and implementation.

2.1. SCRUTINY OF AD PLACEMENTS

The Code considers that advertising and monetisation incentives lead to behaviour such as misrepresentations about oneself or the purpose of one's properties.[14] As a response, the signatories of the Code commit to deploy policies and processes to disrupt such incentives. The signatories acknowledge, in particular, that there is a need to 'significantly improve the scrutiny of advertisement placements'.[15] As explained in the Code, all parties involved in the online advertising (and advertising-related) market need to work together to improve transparency across the ecosystem. This means, according to the Code, that they should effectively scrutinise, control and limit the placement of advertising on accounts and websites belonging to purveyors of disinformation.[16]

---

13 *Ibid.*, p. 12.

14 European Commission, *supra* note 8, p. 5.

15 *Ibid.*, p. 4.

16 *Ibid.*

Moreover, the signatories should make commercially reasonable efforts to ensure they do not accept remuneration from or promote accounts and websites which consistently misrepresent information about themselves.[17] The signatories should also 'avoid' misplacing ads on disinformation sites through, for example, the use of brand safety tools. To acquire information about purveyors of disinformation, the Code suggests implementing indicators of trustworthiness and cooperation with fact-checking organisations or the independent network of fact-checkers.[18]

2.2. POLITICAL ADVERTISING AND ISSUE-BASED ADVERTISING

The Code acknowledges the need to ensure transparency in the area of political and issue-based advertising. In particular, such transparency means that users should be able to understand why they have been targeted by a given advertisement.[19] Therefore, the signatories commit to comply with the requirement that all advertisements should be clearly distinguishable from editorial content.[20] Moreover, the relevant signatories commit to enable public disclosure of political advertising, which could include the identity of the actual sponsor and the amounts spent.[21] The signatories also commit to put reasonable efforts to publicly disclose 'issue-based advertising' in a way that would not limit reporting on political discussion and the publishing of political opinion.[22] The Code encourages signatories to engage with expert stakeholders that could help to develop methods that both achieve transparency and also uphold fundamental rights, given the implications relating to freedom of expression.[23]

2.3. INTEGRITY OF SERVICES

Maintaining integrity of services requires certain efforts on the side of the signatories. The Code refers to the findings of the EC Communication, which highlighted the importance of efforts to close fake accounts, as well as the importance of establishing 'clear marking systems and rules for bots to ensure

17 *Ibid.*
18 *Ibid.*, p. 7.
19 *Ibid.*, p. 5.
20 *Ibid.*
21 *Ibid.*
22 *Ibid.*
23 *Ibid.*, p. 6.

their activities cannot be confused with human interactions'.[24] Moreover, the signatories recognise the importance of ensuring that online services include and promote safeguards against disinformation and against misrepresentations.[25] The signatories therefore commit to put in place clear policies regarding identity and the misuse of automated bots on their services and to enforce these policies within the EU.[26] The signatories also commit to put in place policies on what constitutes impermissible use of automated systems and to make this policy publicly available on the platform and accessible to EU users.[27] However, these measures should not prevent anonymous or pseudonymous use of accounts and services, in accordance with Article 8 of the European Convention on Human Rights.[28]

2.4. EMPOWERING CONSUMERS

The Code gives a lot of attention to the empowerment of consumers. Consumer empowerment could be achieved through tools allowing for a customised and interactive online experience to facilitate content discovery and access to varied sources with alternative viewpoints.[29] For this reason, the signatories commit to invest in features and tools that make it easier for people to find diverse perspectives about topics of public interest.[30] Empowerment also means that users should be able to report disinformation through easily accessible tools.[31] Moreover, the Code highlights the importance of diluting the visibility of disinformation and improving the findability of trustworthy content.[32] The signatories should invest in technological means to prioritise relevant, authentic and authoritative information in search, feeds or other automatically ranked distribution channels.[33] Consumer empowerment can also be strengthened by enabling users to understand why they have been targeted by a given political or issue-based advertisement. And, finally, the Code links the empowerment of users with digital media literacy. The signatories commit to partner with civil society, governments, educational institutions and other stakeholders to support efforts aimed at improving critical thinking and digital media literacy.[34]

---

24 *Ibid.*, p. 3.
25 *Ibid.*, p. 6.
26 *Ibid.*
27 *Ibid.*
28 *Ibid.*
29 *Ibid.*, p. 7.
30 *Ibid.*
31 *Ibid.*
32 *Ibid.*
33 *Ibid.*
34 *Ibid.*

2.5. EMPOWERING THE RESEARCH COMMUNITY

The Code also aims to empower the research community. Following the HLEG report and the Communication, the Code recognises the importance of enabling privacy-compliant access to data for fact-checking and research activities, as well as providing data on the functioning of the services.[35] Such access should include data for independent investigation by academic researchers and general information on algorithms.[36] The signatories therefore commit not to prohibit or discourage good faith research into disinformation and political advertising, but rather to encourage research into these topics. The signatories also commit to support good-faith independent efforts to track disinformation and understand its impact, including the independent network of fact-checkers facilitated by the European Commission.[37] Doing so may involve sharing of privacy-protected datasets, undertaking joint research or otherwise partnering with academics and civil society organisations. The signatories also commit to convene an annual event to foster discussions with academia, the fact-checking community and members of the value chain.[38]

2.6. MONITORING EFFECTIVENESS

Finally, the Code foresees periodic monitoring of its effectiveness. The signatories commit to write an annual account of their work to counter disinformation in the form of publicly available self-assessment reports.[39] The reports may include details of any measures taken and the progress made to improve transparency regarding disinformation. The reports should be reviewable by third parties, which are selected by the signatories themselves.[40] The role of the third party is to review and evaluate the level of progress made by the signatories against the commitments of the Code in an objective manner. The signatories should also work with the European Commission and other key stakeholders to develop the most effective approaches to publicly disclose 'issue-based advertising'.[41]

Moreover, the signatories of the Code commit to assess its effectiveness after 12 months. During the first assessment period, the signatories will meet regularly to analyse its progress, implementation and functioning, and discuss possible

35 *Ibid.*, p. 4.
36 *Ibid.*, p. 8.
37 *Ibid.*
38 *Ibid.*
39 *Ibid.*
40 *Ibid.*, pp. 8–9.
41 *Ibid.*, p. 9.

follow-up actions. In addition, the signatories are called upon to cooperate with the European Commission in assessing the reporting on the functioning of the Code.[42]

3. FREEDOM OF EXPRESSION CONCERNS

The Code of Conduct on Disinformation commences with a declaration that it is 'mindful of the fundamental right to freedom of expression and to an open Internet, and the delicate balance which any efforts to limit the spread and impact of otherwise lawful content must strike'.[43] Moreover, the Code is not meant to replace or interpret the existing legal framework, in particular the EU Charter of Fundamental Rights and the European Convention on Human Rights.[44] Yet, one cannot deny that the Code will have an impact on the exercise of the right to freedom of expression and access to information online. The EU Charter of Fundamental Rights and the European Convention on Human Rights belong to different legal regimes.[45] However, both instruments have a common approach to the protection of the right to freedom of expression.

3.1. PRINCIPLES OF THE RIGHT TO FREEDOM OF EXPRESSION IN EUROPE

The right to freedom of expression in Europe has a broad scope of application. It applies to the rights of everyone, which means it is not limited to citizens or natural persons only.[46] The right protects any expression regardless of its content, its form (any word, picture, image or action to express an idea, etc.),[47]

42 *Ibid.*, p. 10.

43 *Ibid.*, p. 1.

44 *Ibid.*, p. 2.

45 The Charter of Fundamental Rights is an instrument of the EU and the European Convention on Human Rights is an instrument of the Council of Europe. In theory, the legal orders of the two international organisations are distinct from one another. However, all EU Member States are also signatories to the European Convention. In order to be eligible for membership of the EU, candidates must be members of the Council of Europe and must ratify the Convention. This means that all EU Member States are bound by the Convention. Moreover, as clarified by Article 52.3 of the Charter, the meaning and scope of the right to freedom of expression is the same as those guaranteed by the Convention. This means that the Charter should be interpreted in accordance with the Convention and the jurisprudence of the European Court of Human Rights (ECtHR).

46 See, for example, ECtHR, *Autronic AG v. Switzerland*, 22 May 1990; L. Woods, 'Freedom of expression in the European Union', *European Public Law*, Vol. 12, No. 3, 2006, p. 378.

47 M. Macovei, 'Freedom of expression – A guide to the implementation of Article 10 of the European Convention of Human Rights', *Human rights handbooks*, No. 2, 2004, p. 15.

its speaker or the type of medium used.[48] The Internet plays a fundamental role in providing access to diverse and pluralistic information.[49] It acts as a tool for citizens to actively participate in building and strengthening democratic societies.[50] As pointed out by the European Court of Human Rights (ECtHR) in *Yildrim*: '[The] Internet has now become one of the principal means by which individuals exercise their right to freedom of expression and information, providing as it does essential tools for participation in activities and discussions concerning political issues and issues of general interest.'[51]

Information of a commercial nature is protected, although in this case states have a wider margin of appreciation to restrict freedom of expression. Interestingly in relation to the topic of disinformation, in the case of political speech the margin of appreciation is more narrow and there is little scope for restrictions.[52] It is crucial to remember that the right to freedom of expression protects not only information and ideas that are favourably received or deemed inoffensive, but also those that offend, shock or disturb the state or any sector of the population.[53] Such broad protection is demanded in a democratic society where pluralism, tolerance and broadmindedness have to be preserved.[54]

The right to freedom of expression is not absolute. In the EU, restrictions can take the form of 'formalities, conditions, restrictions or penalties' and are permissible under three conditions. In particular, the restriction must be (1) prescribed by law, (2) introduced for the protection of a legitimate aim (e.g. protection of the rights of others)[55] and (3) necessary in a democratic society (proportionate). The rules defining the conditions for lawful interference with expression are addressed to the states and not to private entities. In principle, therefore, the potential to curb interference by private entities, such

48 *Ibid.*, p. 7.

49 See, for example, Council of Europe, Recommendation CM/Rec(2016)1 of the Committee of Ministers to Member States on protecting and promoting the right to freedom of expression and the right to private life with regard to network neutrality, 13 January 2016.

50 Council of Europe, Recommendation CM/Rec(2014)6 of the Committee of Ministers to Member States on a Guide to human rights for Internet users, 16 April 2014.

51 ECtHR, *Ahmet Yıldırım v. Turkey*, 18 March 2013, para. 54.

52 See ECtHR, *Wingrove v. United Kingdom*, 25 November 1996, para. 58; ECtHR, *Ceylan v. Turkey* [GC], 8 July 1999, para. 34. See also D. Voorhoof, 'Freedom of expression under the European human rights system. From Sunday Times (n° 1) v. U.K. (1979) to Hachette Filipacchi Associés ("Ici Paris") v. France (2009)', *Inter-American and European Human Rights Journal*, Vol. 2 Nos 1–2, 2010, pp. 3–49, p. 23.

53 ECtHR, *Handyside v. United Kingdom*, 7 December 1976, para. 49; see also ECtHR, *Perna v. Italy*, *o.c.*, para. 39.

54 See, *Handyside v. United Kingdom*, *supra* note 53, para. 49

55 Article 10(2) ECHR – including national security, territorial integrity or public safety, for the prevention of disorder or crime, for the protection of health or morals, for the protection of the reputation or the rights of others, for preventing the disclosure of information received in confidence, or maintaining the authority and impartiality of the judiciary.

as the signatories of the Code, is more limited. The Code, after all, has been characterised as a self-regulatory instrument. However, considering the role of the European Commission, there is reason to question this characterisation. The development of the Code was initiated by the European Commission, which also participated in the development process, approved its shape and defined its objectives. Such a level of involvement can hardly qualify an instrument as self-regulatory. The recent study on disinformation and propaganda uses a term 'induced self-regulation',[56] but it might be appropriate to think of the Code as a co-regulatory scheme. While the full analysis of the self- or co-regulatory nature of the Code is beyond the scope of this chapter, it is worth pointing out the conundrum.[57] While the Code is certainly not a binding legal act, it should, as a co-created (or at least supported) instrument, respect the European rules on the right to freedom of expression.

3.2. RESTRICTIONS ON LAWFUL SPEECH

The Code displays a certain awareness of the risks it creates for the right to freedom of expression and access to information. For example, it clarifies that the signatories should not be compelled by governments to delete or prevent access to otherwise lawful content or messages solely on the basis that they are thought to be 'false'.[58] Nor should they adopt voluntary policies to this effect. The awareness does not prevent the Code from introducing measures that seek to limit the dissemination and impact of otherwise lawful content (even if it is 'disinformation'). This feature of the Code is perhaps the most remarkable one. The content targeted by the Code does not actually amount to illegal content. It may be intentionally deceitful or may cause public harm, but this does not equate to illegality. The Code therefore allows for (and incentivises) restrictions on speech that as such is lawful.

Strictly speaking, the Code does not advocate directly for censorship measures such as removal of content; rather, it encourages the signatories to invest in technological means to prioritise relevant, authentic, accurate and

[56] See J. Bayer et al., 'Disinformation and propaganda – impact on the functioning of the rule of law in the EU and its Member States', study commissioned by the European Parliament's Policy Department for Citizens' Rights and Constitutional Affairs and requested by the European Parliament's Committee on Civil Liberties, Justice and Home Affairs, February 2019, p. 105.

[57] See a similar discussion on the Code of Conduct on Hate speech in A. Kuczerawy, 'The Code of Conduct on Online Hate Speech: an example of state interference by proxy?', 20 July 2016, https://www.law.kuleuven.be/citip/blog/the-code-of-conduct-on-online-hate-speech-an-example-of-state-interference-by-proxy.

[58] European Commission, *supra* note 8, p. 3.

authoritative information.[59] The positive phrasing used by the Code does not diminish its potential negative effect on the right to freedom of expression. Not removing content, but merely downgrading it or otherwise decreasing its visibility does not change the goal of the proposed measures, which is to limit access to and the spread of the targeted content, and therefore interfere with its dissemination. Any restriction imposed on the means of information dissemination inevitably interferes with the right to receive and impart information.[60] After all, users devote only a certain amount of time and attention to search for information. If information is buried at the bottom of search results or on an undiscovered profile that never surfaces, the chances of reaching any audience are rather low.

Apart from the fact that the targeted content is legal, there is another worrying aspect of the Code. The Code encourages prioritising content that is relevant, authentic, accurate and authoritative; however, it does not clarify who classifies the content. There is no indication how to determine if content actually fulfils the requirements of relevance, authenticity, accuracy or authoritativeness. Assessing the legality of content is not a trivial task, but assessing its accuracy or relevance may be even more complicated. Moreover, the assessment risks becoming arbitrary in the absence of specific criteria. Mistakes in the assessment of content may and do happen constantly. Nevertheless, the Code does not provide any information about a possibility of appealing a decision that incorrectly labelled content as disinformation. Are all these decisions left entirely to the signatories? The Code mentions the involvement of fact-checking organisations and the new independent network of fact-checkers facilitated by the European Commission upon its establishment. These organisations could provide indicators of trustworthiness and information on purveyors of disinformation and could potentially partner with the signatories to achieve some of the goals of the Code.[61] However, their role is not clearly specified in the Code.[62]

3.3. DELEGATED PRIVATE ENFORCEMENT

The Code is by no means the first EU initiative that enlists online service providers to regulate speech of their users. A similar approach can be found in recent initiatives such as the Code of Conduct on Hate Speech or the

59 *Ibid.*, p. 7.

60 See the case law of the European Court of Human Rights: ECtHR, *Autronic AG v. Switzerland*, 22 May 1990, para. 47; ECtHR, *Murphy v. Ireland*, 10 July 2003, para. 61.

61 European Commission, *supra* note 8, p. 4.

62 More information on fact-checking organisations in general can be found in the HLEG report (European Commission, *supra* note 4, e.g. pp. 15, 16 and 24), but their role in the Code is not described in a detailed manner.

proposed Regulation on preventing dissemination of terrorist content online.[63] While discussions continue about the precise scope of application and definitions used in each of these initiatives, their general goal is to target content broadly understood as illegal.[64] In particular, they target hate speech, incitement to violence and terrorist content, which should (at least in theory) be easier to recognise than disinformation.

The Code on disinformation, as explained above, does not require the removal of content, but merely its demotion. However, in a similar fashion to the initiatives on hate speech and terrorist content, the Code enlists private companies to enforce public policy objectives. In this particular case, the objective is to fight with disinformation. Effectively, the instrument co-opts private companies to regulate online speech. The Code creates a situation that encourages private entities to interfere with the freedom of expression of Internet users. Co-opting private entities to regulate speech of their users allows states to achieve regulatory objectives in a discreet manner. Any possible interference, strictly speaking, is not by the state; after all, the Code is a soft law instrument, there is no penalty foreseen and the introduced measures are voluntarily administered by companies that choose to subscribe.

Delegated private enforcement is less visible and less obvious than classic state intervention.[65] It makes it possible to conveniently sidestep certain safeguards otherwise applicable to direct state interference.[66] As a result, speech could be suppressed without the protections that the legal system normally grants when the limitation originates from the state.[67] This is because the protections provided in the human rights instruments do not formally apply to private companies. The introduced measures may, as a result, enforce rules in a way that interferes with the fundamental rights of users.[68]

---

63 The Code of Conduct on Countering Illegal Hate Speech Online, http://ec.europa.eu/justice/fundamental-rights/files/hate_speech_code_of_conduct_en.pdf; EUROPEAN COMMISSION, 'Proposal for a Regulation of the European Parliament and of the Council on preventing the dissemination of terrorist content online', 12 September 2018, COM(2018) 640 final, https://ec.europa.eu/commission/sites/beta-political/files/soteu2018-preventing-terrorist-content-online-regulation-640_en.pdf.

64 See, for example, A. KUCZERAWY, 'The proposed Regulation on Preventing the Dissemination of Terrorist Content Online: safeguards and risks for freedom of expression', research paper for CDT, 6 December 2018, https://cdt.org/files/2018/12/Regulation-on-preventing-the-dissemination-of-terrorist-content-online-v3.pdf.

65 See D.E. BAMBAUER, 'Orwell's Armchair', *University of Chicago Law Review*, Vol. 79, 2012, p. 863. See also S.F. KREIMER, 'Censorship by proxy: the First Amendment, Internet intermediaries, and the problem of the weakest link', U. *Pa. L. Rev.*, Vol. 155, No. 11, 2006, p. 28.

66 See C. ANGELOPOULOS ET AL., 'Study of fundamental rights limitations for online enforcement through self-regulation', Institute for Information Law (IViR), 2016, p. 61.

67 D. TAMBINI, D. LEONARDI and C. MARSDEN, 'The privatisation of censorship: self-regulation and freedom of expression', in D. TAMBINI, D. LEONARDI, and C. MARSDEN (eds.), *Codifying Cyberspace: Communications Self-Regulation in the Age of Internet Convergence*, Routledge/UCL Press, Abingdon 2008, p. 411.

68 See ANGELOPOULOS ET AL., *supra* note 66.

Enlisting private entities to make decisions impacting fundamental human rights, such as freedom of expression, may be necessary in certain situations in order to provide a quick and effective solution. However, in order to ensure proportionality and the effective protection of fundamental rights, states should clearly delineate the limits of the delegated decision-making power. Indeed, states cannot absolve themselves from responsibility by delegating their obligations to private bodies.[69] As already observed by Frydman and Rorive in 2002, 'it is not enough to get the ISPs to do the job of the police, it is also necessary to give them guidelines defining the limits of the right to free speech and offering procedural guarantees against censorship'.[70]

The states' duty to provide for safeguards can be derived from the doctrine of positive obligations.[71] According to the doctrine, states must not only refrain from unnecessary interference with fundamental rights, but must also actively protect individuals from excessive interference by others. Under the European Convention on Human Rights, states clearly have a positive obligation to ensure effective enjoyment of the right to freedom of expression.[72] Under the Charter of Fundamental Rights, the doctrine is less developed. However, there exists an obligation to ensure effective protection of the Charter rights.[73] In my opinion, the theories of positive obligations and effective protection require states to take measures to protect the right to freedom of expression from interference by other private parties, in particular in situations where the state itself directly encourages the interference.[74] The requirement to ensure effective protection could be satisfied by implementing procedural safeguards into instruments that co-opt private entities to regulate (or, to put it more bluntly, to censor) speech online. At the moment, the Code on disinformation lacks safeguards to ensure respect for fundamental human rights and prevent over-compliance.[75]

69 See ECtHR, *Costello-Roberts v. United Kingdom*, 25 March 1993, Series A no. 247-C, para. 27.

70 B. Frydman and I. Rorive, 'Regulating Internet content through intermediaries in Europe and the USA', *Zeitschrift für Rechtssoziologie*, Vol. 23, No. 1, 2002, pp. 41–59, at p. 59.

71 For more on the positive obligation to protect the right to freedom of expression in content regulation, see A. Kuczerawy, 'The power of positive thinking: intermediary liability and the effective enjoyment of the right to freedom of expression', *JIPITEC* Vol. 8, 2017.

72 See ECtHR, *Özgür Gündem v. Turkey*, 16 March 2000, para. 43; ECtHR, *Verein gegen Tierfabriken Schweiz (VgT) v. Switzerland*, 28 June 2001, para. 38; ECtHR, *Appleby and Others v. United Kingdom*, 6 May 2003, para. 47; ECtHR, *Dink v. Turkey*, 14 September 2010, para. 137.

73 See, for example, CJEU, *Coty Germany GmbH v Stadtsparkasse Magdeburg*, Case C-580/13, 16 July 2015, para. 29; CJEU, *Digital Rights Ireland Ltd and Seitlinger and Others*, Joined Cases C-293/12 and C-594/12, 8 April 2014, para. 66; and CJEU, *Maximillian Schrems v. Data Protection Commissioner*, Case C-362/14, 6 October 2015, para. 91.

74 See more in A. Kuczerawy, *Intermediary Liability and Freedom of Expression in the EU: From Concepts to Safeguards*, Intersentia, Cambridge 2018.

75 See Bayer et al., *supra* note 56, p. 106.

4. POSSIBLE SAFEGUARDS

Safeguarding the right to freedom of expression requires introduction of procedural measures that would improve fairness and proportionality and install elements of due process in the Code. This chapter proposes a handful of measures that might be considered, namely: (1) introducing notifications to the content provider; (2) counter-notification; (3) appeal mechanisms; and (4) improved monitoring of the functioning of the Code. More safeguards could be developed over time, on the basis of the results contained in the monitoring reports.

4.1. NOTIFICATION TO THE CONTENT PROVIDER

As a matter of principle, content providers should be informed of any decisions to interfere with the dissemination of their content.[76] The notification should inform the content provider that a complaint has been filed against his or her content and about the nature of the complaint. Such notifications would help to ensure transparency, which is a necessary first step for any further actions against incorrect assessment of content. Ideally, notification should be sent before any decision about the content is taken, although exceptions could be foreseen for particularly time-sensitive cases. The notification should state the reason for the selected action and provide an explanation of the rights of the content provider as well as any possibility to reply and to appeal the decision. However, the notifications should take into account applicable data protection requirements. Intermediaries that receive the complaint should not be compelled to disclose personal data about a user without an order by a judicial authority. Hampering criminal investigation should not be a concern, since the targeted content is not illegal. It could be debated whether such a notification would alarm the purveyor of disinformation and allow them to re-upload the content on the same or different platform. Yet, a more efficient elimination process should not be the sole reason to give up on procedural fairness and the rights of content providers.

4.2. COUNTER-NOTIFICATION

The ability to file a counter-notification would allow content providers to file an objection to the complaints made against their content, and therefore,

[76] See, for example, European Commission, 'Recommendation on measures to effectively tackle illegal content online', Brussels, 1 March 2018, COM(2018) 1177 final, pp. 5 and 11.

operationalise the rights to a fair hearing, adversarial proceedings and equality of arms. Moreover, it would provide an opportunity to clarify in case of misqualification (or mislabelling) of content. Only when the content provider is given an opportunity to express their views and to present their defence can the decision-making process be considered fair. Taking decisions that have an impact on the dissemination of content without hearing from the content provider, and possibly also without their knowledge, should only be done in exceptional circumstances. However, these exceptions must be crafted carefully and defined explicitly in the Code. Ideally, a possibility to file a counter-notification should be available before any potential actions against the content are decided. Only then can the information in the counter-notifications be taken into account in the decision-making process prior to interference and only then can the safeguard actually become a meaningful manifestation of due process, procedural justice and the presumption of innocence.

4.3. APPEAL MECHANISM

The procedure that enlists platforms to make decisions about content should include a step allowing for the correction of any initial decision. It is clear that decisions that involve balancing between the right to the freedom of expression and other fundamental rights (e.g. the right to privacy) may be difficult. Mistakes resulting from inaccurate assessments may happen, but in such cases, a path for a relief should be available. Therefore, users should be equipped with the right to appeal decisions that lead to the demotion of their content. It is of course necessary to remember that there is no 'must-carry' obligation of content for private platforms. Platforms in principle cannot be forced to reinstate content they do not wish to carry, although recently attempts to reinstate content through court orders are gaining popularity.[77] Generally, however, content is put back not as a result of a court order, but following a public outcry and negative media attention.[78] Despite this fact, appeal mechanism should be available to users, especially in schemes developed in cooperation with legislature.

---

77 See more in J. Schmid and S. Bouderbala, 'Facebook denies "censoring" 19th-century vagina painting', *Phys.org*, 1 February 2018, https://phys.org/news/2018-02-facebook-denies-censoring-19th-century-vagina.html. D. Meyer, 'Court tells Facebook: stop deleting "offensive" comment', *ZDNet*, 13 April 2018, https://www.zdnet.com/article/court-tells-facebook-stop-deleting-offensive-comment.

78 For example, this happened in the case of the removal of the iconic 'Vietnam napalm girl' picture or the prehistoric 'Venus of Willendorf' figurine. See more in S. Levin, J.C. Wong and L. Harding, 'Facebook backs down from "napalm girl" censorship and reinstates photo', *The Guardian*, 9 September 2016, https://www.theguardian.com/technology/2016/sep/09/facebook-reinstates-napalm-girl-photo; and 'Facebook apologises for censoring prehistoric Venus statue', *Phys.org*, 1 March 2018, https://phys.org/news/2018-03-facebook-apologises-censoring-prehistoric-venus.html.

4.4. TRANSPARENCY AND MONITORING

How the Code functions in practice should be closely monitored by the gathering of evidence on its implementation and application. Only through a collection of certain practical information is it possible to monitor whether the Code is fulfilling its objectives and whether any corrective measures are necessary. Accordingly, the Code describes how the signatories should monitor and report its effectiveness. Mainly, the signatories commit to provide regular accounts of their work to counter disinformation in the form of a publicly available self-assessment reports that are reviewable by self-selected third parties. The reports submitted so far suggest that compliance with the Code's commitments is not going as smoothly as expected. In January 2019, the European Commission observed that there had been some progress, notably in removing fake accounts and limiting the visibility of sites that promote disinformation. However, it urged the signatories to intensify their efforts, in particular in monitoring and reporting, and to increase their cooperation with fact-checkers and the research community.[79] For the next reports, the Commission advised the signatories to develop a 'more systematic approach to enable a proper and regular monitoring and assessment, on the basis of appropriate performance data'.[80] In February 2019, with less than three months to go before the European elections, the Commission signalled that it was 'deeply concerned by the platform's failure to provide specific benchmarks to measure progress, by the lack of detail on the actual results of the measures already taken and lack of detail showing that new policies and tools are deployed timely and with sufficient resources across all EU Member States'.[81] In May 2019 the Commission highlighted that 'the data provided still lacks the level of detail necessary to allow for an independent and accurate assessment of how the platforms' policies have actually contributed to reducing the spread of disinformation in the EU'.[82] The first monthly reports on the functioning of the Code clearly showed that the measures taken so far by the signatories of the Code are not entirely satisfactory. The self-assessment nature

[79] See European Commission, 'Code of Practice against disinformation: Commission calls on signatories to intensify their efforts', press release, 29 January 2019, http://europa.eu/rapid/press-release_IP-19-746_en.htm. See also 'First results of the EU Code of Practice against disinformation', 29 January 2019, https://ec.europa.eu/digital-single-market/en/news/first-results-eu-code-practice-against-disinformation.

[80] European Commission, Code of Practice against disinformation, 29 January 2019, https://ec.europa.eu/commission/news/code-practice-against-disinformation-2019-jan-29_en.

[81] European Commission, 'First monthly intermediate results of the EU Code of Practice against disinformation', 28 February 2019, https://ec.europa.eu/digital-single-market/en/news/first-monthly-intermediate-results-eu-code-practice-against-disinformation.

[82] European Commission, 'Code of Practice against disinformation: Commission recognises platforms' efforts ahead of the European elections', 17 May 2019, http://europa.eu/rapid/press-release_STATEMENT-19-2570_en.htm.

of the reports allows the signatories to choose what they report or do not report. Platforms use different metrics to describe their activities, for example, the number of accounts classified and added to a certain list or a number of accounts or pages removed.[83] Apart from following the progress made by the signatories, the reports make it difficult to draw any meaningful conclusions about the impact of the Code on the right to freedom of expression. It would be beneficial to establish certain standards in terms of what information must be contained in the reports.[84] Contrary to what the European Commission expressed, such standards or specific benchmarks should be provided by the state and not the signatories themselves. Moreover, it would be useful to agree what information could reflect the impact on the right to freedom of expression. Possibly, more detailed information could be included on the number of removals (due to its classification as disinformation). Even if the Code does not directly advocate for removals, analysis of the reports shows that such removals actually do take place on the platforms' own initiative.

5. CONCLUSION

The Code of Practice on disinformation was introduced as an element of a broader campaign against disinformation that could potentially influence the elections for the European Parliament. A few months into its existence, the reception of the Code has been somewhat lukewarm. From gentle nudges by the European Commission to straightforward criticism, the Code seems to have only partially achieved its goals.[85] A Report on the implementation of the Action Plan against Disinformation issued in June 2019 summarises some of the achievements of the Code, but highlights that more needs to be done by the platforms to effectively tackle disinformation.[86] Moreover, the Report suggests

---

83 For a comparison, see the specific company reports: European Commission, 'First monthly intermediate results of the EU Code of Practice against disinformation', 28 February 2019, https://ec.europa.eu/digital-single-market/en/news/first-monthly-intermediate-results-eu-code-practice-against-disinformation.

84 See also 'Informing the "disinformation" debate', joint report by Access Now, Civil Liberties Union for Europe, European Digital Rights, 18 October 2018, p. 8.

85 *Ibid.* See also Sounding Board of the Multistakeholder Forum on Disinformation Online, 'The Sounding Board's unanimous final opinion on the so-called Code of Practice', 24 September 2018, https://www.beuc.eu/documents/files/3OpinionoftheSoundingboard.pdf. See also N. Schmidt and D. Dupont-Nivet, 'Facebook and Google pressured EU experts to soften fake news regulations, say insiders', 21 May 2019, https://www.opendemocracy.net/en/facebook-and-google-pressured-eu-experts-soften-fake-news-regulations-say-insiders.

86 European Commission, Joint Communication to the European Parliament, the European Council, the Council, the European Economic and Social Committee and the Committee of Regions, 'Report on the implementation of the Action Plan against Disinformation', Brussels, 14 June 2019, JOIN(2019) 12 final, https://eeas.europa.eu/sites/eeas/files/joint_report_on_disinformation.pdf, p. 5.

that not all signatories performed equally well. It points out the lack of engagement from the advertising industry, which has limited progress in increasing the transparency of websites hosting ads.[87] Nevertheless, it maintains that the coordinated EU approach 'contributed to expose disinformation attempts and to preserve the integrity of the elections, while protecting freedom of expression'.[88]

Given the information provided by the signatories, it is difficult to factually assess the impact of the Code on the exercise of the right to freedom of expression. Nevertheless, the possibility of interference with lawful speech remains troublesome. This is especially the case since the interference by private companies, which are not bound by fundamental rights instruments, is incentivised by an EU institution. Moreover, the interference with freedom of expression is state-sanctioned, yet without any meaningful safeguards that provide at least minimal balance, proportionality and oversight in the scheme. Enlisting private companies to regulate speech of their users may seem to be a practical and efficient approach, as it places the burden directly on the platforms that offer technical means to address the problem. However, it could also be seen as the passing of a hot potato instead of approaching the problem responsibly in accordance with the rule of law. Involving private platforms in addressing the problem of online disinformation may be inevitable. As pointed out by Thompson, involving intermediaries in making autonomous decisions about content 'is, in fact, something that cannot practicably be forestalled, on pain of completely undermining the way the Internet operates'.[89] However, if this is the way to go, it should be accompanied by safeguards that could introduce balance and elements of due process. The safeguards proposed in this chapter are not particularly sophisticated. For this reason, they are a relatively low hanging fruit that should not be difficult to implement. In practical terms, an addition of a notification, counter-notification or an appeal mechanism may slow down the process of handling disinformation. However, a striving for efficiency should not trump respect for human rights. Moreover, the proposed safeguards may raise the costs of the implementation of the Code and as a result may discourage other platforms from signing up. Realistically speaking, any meaningful solution will constitute inconvenience for platforms and require the investment of additional resources. Signatories of the Code must realise this, unless their involvement is merely a PR move that is not really intended to achieve any of the Code's

---

87 *Ibid.*

88 *Ibid.*, p. 9. See also footnote 26 of the Report on the implementation of the Action Plan against Disinformation pointing to research indicating that there was less disinformation than expected in the run-up to the European elections. See N. Marchal et al., 'Junk news during the EU parliamentary elections: lessons from a seven-language study of Twitter and Facebook', Oxford Internet Institute, DataMemo 2019.3, https://comprop.oii.ox.ac.uk/wp-content/uploads/sites/93/2019/05/EU-Data-Memo.pdf.

89 M. Thompson, 'Beyond gatekeeping: the normative responsibility of Internet intermediaries', *Vanderbilt Journal of Entertainment & Technology Law*, Vol. 18, No. 4, 2016, p. 793.

commitments. According to the recent Report on the implementation of the Action Plan against Disinformation, the European Commission was planning to assess the effectiveness of the Code by the end of 2019. If not satisfied with the results, the European Commission may propose further initiatives, including those of a regulatory nature.[90] The experience of the past year has yielded additional insights on the problem of disinformation. The insights obtained will hopefully be utilised by policy-makers as disinformation is clearly a highly complex problem that requires proportionate and evidence-based response. Imprudent solutions that do not sufficiently safeguard fundamental rights may lead to unintended consequences in terms of legitimate public debate and democracy.

90 European Commission, *supra* note 86, p. 5. It remains to be seen if the European Commission is willing to strengthen its initiatives to combat disinformation by addressing the issues that stem from the monetisation of commercialisation of personal for advertising purposes. As indicated earlier, discussion of this topic is beyond the scope of this chapter. For more on this, see Y. Blaschke, 'Digital rights as a security objective: fighting disinformation', *EDRi*, 5 December 2018, https://edri.org/digital-rights-as-a-security-objective-fighting-disinformation. See also Schmidt and Dupont-Nivet, *supra* note 85.

16. REGULATING INTERNET CONTENT WITH TECHNOLOGY

Analysis of Policy Initiatives Relevant to Illegal Content and Disinformation Online in the European Union

Trisha MEYER, Christopher T. MARSDEN and Ian BROWN*

1. INTRODUCTION

Within the European Union (EU), online disinformation has been addressed from a variety of regulatory angles. Legislation and policy initiatives against defamation, incitement to hatred and violence,[1] or banning certain misleading advertising techniques[2] all seek to limit the spread of disinformation. Moreover, within the context of electoral campaigns, the problem can be tackled by regulating the spending and transparency of political campaigns, enforcing data protection rules and bolstering against cyberattacks.[3] More broadly,

* Trisha Meyer: Brussels School of Governance (BSG) (an alliance between the Institute for European Studies and Vesalius College), Vrije Universiteit Brussel (VUB), Belgium. Email: trisha.meyer@vub.be; Christopher T. Marsden: @SussCIGR Centre for Information Governance and Research, University of Sussex, UK. Email: c.marsden@sussex.ac.uk; Ian Brown: Research ICT Africa, South Africa. Email: ibrown@researchictafrica.net. This chapter is based on their expert report: C. MARSDEN and T. MEYER, 'Regulating Disinformation with Artificial Intelligence. The Effects of Disinformation Initiatives on Freedom of Expression and Media Pluralism', European Parliament, doi: 10.2861/003689.

1 As found, for instance, in Articles 19 and 20 of the UN International Covenant on Civil and Political Rights (1966); the EU Multistakeholder Code of Conduct on Countering Illegal Hate Speech Online (May 2016); and the proposed EU Regulation on Prevention of Dissemination of Terrorist Content Online (COM(2018) 640 final – 2018/0331 (COD)).

2 Such as Directive 2006/114/EC concerning Misleading and Comparative Advertising; Directive 2010/13/EU on Audiovisual Media Services (the Coordination of Certain Provisions Laid Down by Law, Regulation or Administrative Action in Member States concerning the Provision of Audiovisual Media Services).

3 As recently addressed, for instance, in the European Commission Elections Package, which contains (amongst others) a proposed EU Revised Regulation on the Statute and Funding of European Political Parties and European Political Foundations (COM(2017) 0481

institutional support is also provided to safeguard media pluralism,[4] encourage fact-checking[5] and enhance media literacy.[6]

It is clear that disinformation has taken on new proportions in this age of social media. Within the EU, 2018 triggered a flurry of additional reflections and actions on online disinformation. Table 1 provides a timeline of disinformation policy-related initiatives at a European level from 2015 to the present day, ranging from cybersecurity and strategic communications to tackling illegal content and disinformation online. Social media platforms in particular have been in the spotlight in relation to curbing the spread of disinformation on their networks.

---

final – 2017/0219 (COD)); European Commission Guidance on the Application of Union Data Protection Law in the Electoral Context (COM(2018) 638 final); and European Commission Recommendation on Election Cooperation Networks, Online Transparency, Protection against Cybersecurity Incidents and Fighting Disinformation Campaigns in the Context of Elections to the European Parliament (C(2018) 5949 final).

4 The EU's most impactful tools are its competition rules on abuse of a dominant position, state aid and merger control (Articles 101 and 102 of the Treaty on the Functioning of the European Union (TFEU)). It also takes a monitoring and capacity-building approach, as illustrated amongst other things through its support of the Media Pluralism Monitor and capacity building and training of journalists. See, for instance, European Commission, Media Pluralism Monitor, 2020, https://ec.europa.eu/digital-single-market/en/media-pluralism-monitor-mpm; and European Commission, 'Media Freedom and Investigative Journalism – Call for Proposals', 2019, https://ec.europa.eu/digital-single-market/en/news/media-freedom-and-investigative-journalism-call-proposals.

5 The EEAS East StratCom Task Force is the EU's most ambitious internal debunking effort. It was set up after the European Council mandated the High Representative and the Member States to develop an action plan on strategic communications in its March 2015 Conclusions. The Task Force's mandate pertains to addressing Russia's ongoing disinformation campaigns through strategic communications and research. This can consist, among other things, of better explaining EU policies and strengthening the media in the Eastern Partnership region, and explaining, correcting and raising awareness of disinformation narratives through amongst others the Disinformation Review (http://www.EUvsDisinfo.eu, @EUvsDisinfo) and analysing and reporting on disinformation trends. See EEAS, 'Questions and Answers about the East StratCom Task Force', 2017, https://eeas.europa.eu/headquarters/headquarters-homepage/2116/-questions-and-answers-about-the-east-stratcom-task-force_en.

6 The European Commission plays a supporting role in digital and media literacy through programmes, prizes, coordination and sharing of best practices among Member States. For instance, one of the actions has been to develop a Digital Competence Framework for Citizens. The European Commission has also supported worldwide safer Internet efforts for over 20 years through the Safer Internet Action Plan and its successor programmes. For instance, in 2018 it launched a series of #SaferInternet4EU initiatives in coordination with safer Internet centres across Europe. See European Commission, 'Launch of the #SaferInternet4EU Initiatives on Safer Internet Day', press release, 6 February 2018, https://ec.europa.eu/digital-single-market/en/news/launch-saferinternet4eu-initiatives-safer-internet-day.

Table 1. EU disinformation-related policy initiatives (2015–2020)

Year	Initiatives
2015	• European Council Conclusions Calling for Strategic Communications Action Plan (March 2015) • EEAS East StratCom Task Force (March 2015) • European Commission Communication on European Agenda on Security (April 2015) • Europol Internet Referral Unit (July 2015) • EU Internet Forum on Terrorist Content Online (December 2015)
2016	• EU Multistakeholder Code of Conduct on Countering Illegal Hate Speech Online (May 2016) • European Parliament Resolution on EU Strategic Communication to Counteract Propaganda (November 2016)
2017	• EU Directive on Combatting Terrorism (Article 21, March 2017) • European Council Conclusions on Internal Security and the Fight against Terrorism (June 2017) • European Commission Communication on Tackling Illegal Content Online (September 2017) • EU Proposed Revised Regulation on the Statute and Funding of European Political Parties and European Political Foundations (September 2017)
2018	• European Commission Recommendation on Measures to Effectively Tackle Illegal Content Online (March 2018) • European Commission High-Level Expert Group Report on Fake News and Online Disinformation (March 2018) • EDPS Opinion on Online Manipulation and Personal Data (March 2018) • European Commission Communication on a European Approach to Tackling Online Disinformation (April 2018) • European Commission and HR Joint Communication on Increasing Resilience and Bolstering Capabilities to Address Hybrid Threats (June 2018) • European Council Conclusions calling for Disinformation Action Plan (June 2018) • Proposal for EU Regulation on Prevention of Dissemination of Terrorist Content Online (September 2018) • European Commission Recommendation on Election Cooperation Networks, Online Transparency, Protection against Cybersecurity Incidents and Fighting Disinformation Campaigns in the Context of Elections to the European Parliament (September 2018) • European Commission Guidance on the Application of Union Data Protection Law in the Electoral Context (September 2018) • Proposal for EU Regulation establishing the European Cybersecurity Industrial, Technology and Research Competence Centre and the Network of National Coordination Centres (September 2018) • EU Multistakeholder Code of Practice on Disinformation (September 2018) • Online platforms/advertising industry roadmaps for implementation of the Code of Practice on Disinformation (October 2018) • European Commission and EEAS Joint Action Plan against Disinformation (December 2018) • European Commission Report on Implementation of the April Communication on a European Approach to Tackling Online Disinformation (December 2018)

(continued)

Table 1 *continued*

Year	Initiatives
2019	• Online platforms/advertising industry baseline reports on implementation of the Code of Practice on Disinformation (January 2019) • Facebook, Google and Twitter monthly reports on implementation of the Code of Practice (commitment up to European Parliament elections, February–May 2019) • Set up of EU Rapid Alert System on Disinformation (March 2019) • European Commission and EEAS Joint Report on implementation of the Action Plan against Disinformation (June 2019) • Online platforms/advertising industry self-assessment reports on implementation of the Code of Practice on Disinformation (October 2019)
2020	• External assessment of effectiveness of the Code of Practice on Disinformation (expected Spring 2020) • Consultation on Proposal for Digital Services Act (expected Spring 2020) • Proposal for Digital Services Act (expected 2020–2021)

Source: Compiled by the authors.

Use of technology has often been heralded as the silver bullet to deal with social problems online. Over time, technological solutions to detect and remove illegal/undesirable content have become more effective, but they also raise questions about who is the 'judge' in determining what is legal/illegal and desirable/undesirable in society. Underlying this use is a difficult choice between different elements of law and technology, public and private solutions, with trade-offs between judicial decision-making, scalability and the impact on users' freedom of expression.

Importantly, EU initiatives beyond disinformation also call for proactive measures by online intermediaries to aid the removal of illegal content. The proposed EU Regulation on the Prevention of Dissemination of Terrorist Content Online targets rapid removal of terrorist content by online intermediaries.[7] Article 17 of the 2019 Copyright in the Digital Single Market Directive obliges intermediaries to conclude license agreements with rightsholders, or in absence thereof, holds them liable for the availability of unauthorised copyrighted content. Without sufficient user safeguards, this will likely lead to broad filtering and over-blocking of content.[8] These policy

[7] Most remarkable/controversial is the proposed one-hour rule to take terrorist content offline 'following a removal order from national competent authorities'. See the proposed EU Regulation on Prevention of Dissemination of Terrorist Content Online (COM(2018) 640 final – 2018/0331 (COD)).

[8] EU Directive 2019/790 on Copyright in the Digital Single Market, https://eur-lex.europa.eu/eli/dir/2019/790/oj. For critical commentary, see for instance European Academics, 'Safeguarding User Freedoms in Implementing Article 17 of the Copyright in the Digital Single Market Directive: Recommendations from European Academics', 2019, https://www.ivir.nl/recommendationsarticle17/.

developments fit into a context where social media platforms and search engines are increasingly scrutinised on competition grounds and are called upon to take more responsibility in the online ecosystem.

There has sometimes been an almost instinctive eagerness on the part of policy-makers to believe that technology can solve the 'new' problem of disinformation, while the reality is that its roots lie much deeper. Evidence of disingenuous news is as old as the cuneiform tablets of Hammurabi.[9] Telling falsities serves powerful interests and citizens are at times unwilling or unable to discount proven untruths, due to confirmation bias, peer pressure and other media literacy factors.[10]

In this chapter we review a sample of policy initiatives dealing with illegal content and disinformation online. We focus in particular on initiatives that address the use of technology in moderating the availability of content online. Sections 2 and 3 focus on what and how they recommend to curb certain types of content online, while Section 4 reviews the commitments and recommendations made towards transparency in interventions aimed at decreasing the prevalence of disinformation. We also conducted semi-structured interviews with a range of European and international experts on disinformation, governance of online platforms and freedom of expression. In the conclusions, Section 5, we argue for more independent, transparent and effective appeal and oversight mechanisms to minimise the impact of inaccuracies when regulating illegal content and disinformation through technology.

2. ILLEGAL CONTENT ONLINE

Of crucial importance when studying technology-based solutions to illegal content and disinformation online, Articles 12–15 of the E-Commerce Directive[11] set out the limits of liability of Internet intermediary service providers for illegal activity and content on their networks. 'Information Society Service Providers' (ISSPs or intermediaries) are not subject to liability for their customers' content so long as they have no actual or constructive knowledge of that content – if they 'hear no evil, see no evil and speak no evil'.

---

9 Discussed in L. Enriques, 'Financial Supervisors and RegTech: Four Roles and Four Challenges', *Oxford University, Business Law Blog*, 9 October 2017, http://disq.us/t/2ucbsud.

10 R. Fletcher and R.K. Nielsen, 'Are People Incidentally Exposed to News on Social Media? A Comparative Analysis', (2018) 20(7) *New Media & Society* 2450–2468, https://doi.org/10.1177/1461444817724170.

11 EU Directive 2000/31/EC on Certain Legal Aspects of Information Society Services, in particular Electronic Commerce, https://eur-lex.europa.eu/legal-content/EN/ALL/?uri=CELEX%3A32000L0031.

Article 12 protects the ISSP where it provides a 'mere conduit' with no knowledge of, or editorial control over, content or receiver ('does not initiate the transmission, select the receiver of the transmission, and select or modify the information contained in the transmission'). However, as Articles 13 and 14 stipulate, liability increases as the intermediary's editorial control increases. Where intermediaries provide hosting services (Article 14), they are protected from liability, subject to two tests:

- 'the provider does not have actual knowledge of illegal activity or information and, as regards claims for damages, is not aware of facts or circumstances from which the illegal activity or information is apparent'; or
- 'the provider, upon obtaining such knowledge or awareness, acts expeditiously to remove or to disable access to the information'.[12]

As mere ciphers for content, ISSPs have a safe harbour from liability; should they engage in any filtering of content, they become potentially liable. They have to take action when they are notified of illegal activity or content on their networks.

Intermediaries have been acting as the fabled 'three wise monkeys' in relation to Internet content liability since the dawn of the commercial Internet, as is reflected in the pioneering case law.[13] Thus, 'masterly inactivity', except when prompted by law enforcement, is economically the most advantageous policy open to them. Articles 12–15 of the E-Commerce Directive have not been amended since being implemented in national law in 2002, but have been subject to extensive judicial interpretation across Europe.[14] There is widespread use of notice and action processes, especially blocking injunctions, to reduce the availability of illegal content online. Intermediaries also take voluntary action, often based on their terms of service. Commission President Ursula von der Leyen announced in her political guidelines that '[a] new Digital Services Act

12 *Ibid.*, Articles 12–14.

13 C. Marsden, 'Internet Co-regulation and Constitutionalism: Towards European Judicial Review' (2012) 26(2–3) *International Review of Law, Computers & Technology* 215–216. For UK law, see *Shetland Times Ltd v. Jonathan Wills and Another*, 1997 FSR (Ct Sess. OH), 24 October 1996; *Godfrey v. Demon Internet Service* [2001] QB 201. For US law, see *Cubby v. CompuServe* (1991) 766 F. Supp. 135; *Playboy Enterprises, Inc. v. Frena*, 839 F. Supp. 1552 (M.D. Fla. 1993); *Stratton Oakmont Inc. v. Prodigy* 1995 NY Misc. 23 Media L. Rep. 1794; *American Civil Liberties Union v. Reno* (1997) 21 US 844 of 27 June No 96–511; and Digital Millennium Copyright Act 1998, s 512(k)(1)(A–B).

14 For comprehensive academic commentary, see, for instance, M. Husovec, *Injunctions against Intermediaries in the European Union. Accountable But Not Liable?* Cambridge: Cambridge University Press, 2017; E. Rosati, *Copyright and the Court of Justice of the European Union.* Oxford: Oxford University Press, 2019; G. Sartor, *Providers Liability: From the eCommerce Directive to the Future*, In-depth Analysis for EP IMCO Committee, IP/A/IMCO/2017-07, Brussels: European Parliament, 2017.

will upgrade our liability and safety rules for digital platforms, services and products',[15] hereby indicating that the E-Commerce Directive is now up for review. Stakeholder consultations on the Digital Services Act are scheduled to start in 2020.

The dangers of a regime that incentivises companies to take down content on notice, but not proactively search for illegal and otherwise harmful content, has been recognised officially. In 2014 the European Council declared that it would '[r]aise awareness among judges, law enforcement officials, staff of human rights commissions and policymakers around the world of the need to promote international standards, including standards protecting intermediaries from the obligation of blocking Internet content without prior due process'.[16]

However, as we will illustrate in the following paragraphs, it is clear that change is coming, especially for online platforms. The European Commission's Digital Single Market strategy, consultation and communication on online platforms and its assessment of the formally self-regulatory Code of Conduct on Countering Illegal Hate Speech Online all employ the 'bully pulpit' to argue for greater responsibility by online platforms.[17] Moreover, in response to pressure from those affected negatively by the legal 'masterly inactivity' approach of intermediaries,[18] the European Commission explained in its September 2017 Communication on Tackling Illegal Content Online what further action online platforms should be required to consider, which is summarised in the table below.[19]

---

15 U. von der Leyen, 'A Union that Strives for More. My Agenda for Europe', 2019, https://ec.europa.eu/commission/sites/beta-political/files/political-guidelines-next-commission_en.pdf.

16 EU Human Rights Guidelines on Freedom of Expression Online and Offline, 2014, https://www.consilium.europa.eu/uedocs/cms_data/docs/pressdata/EN/foraff/142549.pdf, para. 34.

17 European Commission Communication on a Digital Single Market Strategy for Europe (COM(2015) 192 final), para. 3.3; European Commission, 'Public Consultation on the Regulatory Environment for Platforms, Online Intermediaries, Data and Cloud Computing and the Collaborative Economy', 2015, https://ec.europa.eu/digital-single-market/news/public-consultation-regulatory-environment-platforms-online-intermediaries-data-and-cloud; European Commission Communication on Online Platforms and the Digital Single Market: Opportunities and Challenges for Europe (COM(2016) 288), p. 9; European Commission, 'Fighting Illegal Online Hate Speech: First Assessment of the New Code of Conduct', press release, 6 December 2016, http://ec.europa.eu/newsroom/just/item-detail.cfm?item_id=50840.

18 M. Lemley, 'Terms of Use' (2006) 91(2) *Minnesota Law Review* 459–483. On intermediary and access provider liability, see generally C. Marsden, 'Regulating Intermediary Liability and Network Neutrality', in I. Walden (ed.), *Telecommunications Law and Regulation*, 5th ed. Oxford: Oxford University Press, 2018, pp. 733–788. On intermediary liability in copyright, see specifically T. Meyer, *The Politics of Online Copyright Enforcement in the EU. Access and Control*. Cham: Palgrave Macmillan, 2017.

19 European Commission Communication on Tackling Illegal Content Online: Towards an Enhanced Responsibility of Online Platforms (COM(2017) 555 final), https://ec.europa.eu/digital-single-market/en/news/communication-tackling-illegal-content-online-towards-enhanced-responsibility-online-platforms.

Table 2. Summary of online platform action called for in the European Commission Communication on Tackling Illegal Content Online (2017)

Section	Online platform action
3. *Detecting and notifying illegal content*	
3.1. Courts and competent authorities	'Online platforms should be able to take swift decisions as regards possible action' on illegal content 'without a court order or administrative decision, especially where a law enforcement authority identifies and informs' (p.7) 'Online platforms should systematically enhance cooperation with competent authorities' (p.8)
3.2. Notices	'Online platforms are encouraged to make use of existing networks of trusted flaggers' (p. 8) In a limited number of cases, 'platforms may remove content upon notification of trusted flaggers without further verifying the legality of the content themselves' (p. 9) 'Online platforms should establish an easily accessible and user-friendly mechanism that allows their users to notify content considered illegal' (p. 9) 'Online platforms should put in place effective mechanisms to facilitate the submission of notices that are sufficiently precise and adequately substantiated' (p. 9)
3.3. Proactive measures by online platforms	Platforms should not limit themselves to reacting to notices, but 'should adopt effective proactive measures to detect and remove illegal content' (p. 10)
4. *Removing illegal content*	
4.1. Ensuring expeditious removal and reporting crime to law enforcement authorities	'Online platforms should prioritise removal in response to notices received from law enforcement bodies and trusted flaggers' (p. 14) Fully automated removal should be applied 'where the circumstances leave little doubt about the illegality of the material' (such as where removal is notified by law enforcement authorities, p. 14) 'Online platforms should report to law enforcement authorities whenever they are made aware of or encounter evidence of criminal or other offences' (p. 15)
4.2. Ensuring transparency	'Online platforms should provide a clear, easily understandable and sufficiently detailed explanation of their content policy in their terms of service' (p. 16) 'Online platforms should publish transparency reports' (p. 16)
4.3. Safeguards against over-removal and abuse of the system	'Online platforms should offer simple online counter-notice procedures' (p. 17) while also discouraging bad-faith notices and counter-notices

(*continued*)

Table 2 *continued*

Section	Online platform action
5. *Preventing the re-appearance of illegal content*	
5.1. Measures against repeat infringers	'Online platforms should take measures' (such as account suspension or termination) 'which dissuade users from repeatedly uploading illegal content of the same nature' (p. 18)
5.2. Automatic re-upload filters	Platforms are strongly encouraged 'to fingerprint and filter out (take down and stay down) content which has already been identified and assessed as illegal' (p. 19)

Source: European Commission Communication on Tackling Illegal Content Online: Towards an Enhanced Responsibility of Online Platforms (COM (2017) 555 final), https://ec.europa.eu/digital-single-market/en/news/communication-tackling-illegal-content-online-towards-enhanced-responsibility-online-platforms.

As a follow-up to the Communication, the European Commission issued a Recommendation on Measures to Effectively Tackle Illegal Online Content[20] in March 2018. The Recommendation provides guidance and considerations, again primarily for hosting providers. In a similar fashion to the September 2017 Communication,[21] it calls for proactive measures, but also states that human verification should be included where possible. A distinction is made between 'all types of illegal content' and 'terrorist content', where the Commission specifically calls for the use of automated means to remove, block or prevent the re-uploading of terrorist content. Importantly, due process safeguards are recommended, as informing the user whose content has been blocked or removed and providing the option of a counter-notice are emphasised (with the exception of manifestly illegal content that relates to criminal offences involving a threat to the life or safety of persons). The Commission also encourages transparency through clear explanations and regular reports on content moderation policies, and cooperation with Member States, trusted flaggers and among hosting providers is recommended.

In sum, the EU has a well-established tradition on liability protections for digital intermediaries through the E-Commerce Directive and the relevant case law. At the same time, momentum has built within the EU to request online platforms to take proactive measures in tackling illegal content. This shift in European Commission thinking became particularly noticeable in the proposed Prevention of the Terrorist Content Dissemination Online Regulation[22]

20 European Commission Recommendation on Measures to Effectively Tackle Illegal Online Content (COM(2018) 1177 final), https://ec.europa.eu/digital-single-market/en/news/commission-recommendation-measures-effectively-tackle-illegal-content-online.

21 European Commission Communication on Tackling Illegal Content Online, *supra* note 19.

22 Proposed EU Regulation on Prevention of Dissemination of Terrorist Content Online (COM(2018) 640 final – 2018/0331 (COD)).

and the adopted Copyright in the Digital Single Market Directive.[23] The Communication[24] and the Recommendation[25] on tackling illegal content online confirm that the European Commission deems more stringent requirements for online platforms desirable beyond these policy areas of anti-terrorism and copyright. Interview respondent Chris Sherwood[26] described the current trend on intermediary liability as '[t]he E-Commerce Directive slowly dying a death by a thousand cuts. It is being undermined by topical legislation, all "without prejudice to" the E-Commerce Directive'.

3. DISINFORMATION ONLINE

We use disinformation to refer to intentional faking of news.[27] Evidence of large-scale harm is still inconclusive, though abuses resulting from the 2016 US presidential election and the UK referendum on leaving the EU ('Brexit') have been uncovered. The problem of large-scale state-sponsored social media inaccuracy was first identified in Ukraine in 2011, when the Russian government was accused of deliberately faking news of political corruption.[28] Disinformation can also be economically profitable to economic actors who employ 'clickbait' tactics to lure users into reading/viewing false articles and advertisements.[29]

In the European context, the High-Level Expert Group (HLEG) report on Fake News and Online Disinformation kickstarted policy discussions in

---

23 EU Directive 2019/790 on Copyright in the Digital Single Market, *supra* note 8.

24 European Commission Communication on Tackling Illegal Content Online, *supra* note 19.

25 European Commission Recommendation on Measures to Effectively Tackle Illegal Online Content, *supra* note 20.

26 Expert interview with Chris Sherwood (Head of Policy at OLX Group, 19 April 2019).

27 This is in line with the European institutions, the HLEG on Fake News and Online Disinformation, and the regional and global United Nations rapporteurs on freedom of information's use of the term: N. Bentzen, 'Understanding Propaganda and Disinformation', European Parliament Research Service, 2015, http://www.europarl.europa.eu/RegData/etudes/ATAG/2015/571332/EPRS_ATA(2015)571332_EN.pdf; HLEG on Fake News and Online Disinformation, 'A Multi-dimensional Approach to Disinformation: Report of the Independent High Level Group on Fake News and Online Disinformation', 2018, https://ec.europa.eu/digital-single-market/en/news/final-report-high-level-expert-group-fake-news-and-online-disinformation, p. 10; UN Special Rapporteur on Freedom of Opinion and Expression et al., 'Joint Declaration on Freedom of Expression and "Fake News" Disinformation and Propaganda', UN Doc. FOM.GAL/3/17, 3 March 2017, https://www.osce.org/fom/302796?download=true.

28 See S. Sanovich, 'Computational Propaganda in Russia: The Origins of Digital Misinformation', *Oxford Computational Propaganda Research Project, Working Paper No. 2017(3)*, 2017, http://comprop.oii.ox.ac.uk/wp-content/uploads/sites/89/2017/06/Comprop-Russia.pdf.

29 K. Lamb, 'I Felt Disgusted: Inside Indonesia's Fake Twitter Account Factories', *The Guardian*, 23 July 2018, https://www.theguardian.com/world/2018/jul/23/indonesias-fake-twitter-account-factories-jakarta-politic.

March 2018.[30] The HLEG report reviewed current practices on disinformation and recommended a multi-dimensional approach, focusing on transparency and accountability-enhancing practices, media and information literacy, empowerment of users and journalists, diversity and sustainability of the media ecosystem, and research on the impact of and responses to disinformation.[31]

It is important to note that in recommending responses and actions, the HLEG focused primarily on 'improv[ing] the findability of, and access to, trustworthy content', as it states that 'filtering out disinformation is difficult to achieve without hitting legitimate content, and is therefore problematic from a freedom of expression perspective'.[32]

In April 2018, the European Commission responded to the HLEG report and published a Communication on a European Approach to Tackling Online Disinformation.[33] The Commission highlighted five priority areas for action. Like the HLEG, media literacy and pluralism are mentioned, but (more) attention is also paid to elections, strategic communication and the role of online platforms.[34]

The Commission then convened a Multistakeholder Forum whose produced an EU Code of Practice on Disinformation, published in September 2018. The emphasis here lies heavily on commitments from online intermediaries, such as social media platforms, search engines and advertisers.[35] The Multistakeholder Forum was composed of a Working Group and a Sounding Board. The Code of Practice includes the following commitments as shown in Table 3.

Table 3. Summary of online platform and advertiser commitments in the EU Code of Practice on Disinformation (2018)

Section	Commitments
1. *Scrutiny of ad placements, political and 'issue-based' advertising*	'Disrupt advertising and monetisation incentives for relevant behaviours' (p. 5)
	Ensure that advertisements are 'clearly distinguishable from editorial content' (p. 5)
	'Enable public disclosure of political advertising' (p. 5)
	'Use reasonable efforts towards devising approaches to publicly disclose "issue-based advertising"' (p. 5)

(*continued*)

30 HLEG on Fake News and Online Disinformation, *supra* note 27.
31 *Ibid.*, pp. 22–30.
32 *Ibid.*, p. 31.
33 European Commission, Communication on Tackling Online Disinformation: a European Approach (COM(2018) 236 final), https://eur-lex.europa.eu/legal-content/EN/TXT/?uri=CELEX:52018DC0236.
34 *Ibid.*, pp. 6–16.
35 EU Code of Practice on Disinformation (2018), https://ec.europa.eu/digital-single-market/en/news/code practice-disinformation.
We conducted expert interviews with the directors of two organisations on the Sounding Board: Monique Goyens (Director-General of the European Consumer Organisation – BEUC, 31 August 2018) and Renate Schroeder (Director of the European Federation of Journalists – EFJ, 7 September 2018).

Table 3 *continued*

Section	Commitments
2. *Integrity of services*	'Put in place clear policies regarding identity and the misuse of automated bot' (p. 6)
	'Put in place policies on what constitutes impermissible use of automated systems and to make this policy publicly available on the platform and accessible to EU users' (p. 6)
3. *Empowering users*	'Help people make informed decisions when they encounter online news that may be false, including by supporting efforts to develop and implement effective indicators of trustworthiness in collaboration with the news ecosystem' (p. 7)
	'Invest in technological means to prioritise relevant, authentic and authoritative information' (p. 7)
	'Invest in features and tools to make it easier to find diverse perspective' (p. 7)
	'Support efforts aimed at improving critical thinking and digital media literacy' (p. 7)
	'Encourage market uptake of tools that help consumers understand why they are seeing particular advertisements' (p. 7)
4. *Empowering the research community*	'Support good faith independent efforts to track and research disinformation and political advertising, including the independent network of fact-checkers facilitated by the European Commission' (p. 8)
	'Convene an annual event to foster discussions within academia, the fact-checking community and members of the value chain' (p. 8)[36]

Source: Compiled by the authors.

The Sounding Board, composed of representatives of the media, civil society, fact-checkers and academia, was scathing in its opinion on the self-regulatory approach:

> [T]he 'Code of practice' as presented by the working group contains no common approach, no clear and meaningful commitments, no measurable objectives or KPIs, hence no possibility to monitor process, and no compliance or enforcement tool: it is by no means self-regulation, and therefore the Platforms, despite their efforts, have not delivered a Code of Practice.[37]

In sum, the recommendations in the HLEG report[38] focus primarily on the role that social media platforms can play in supporting the media ecosystem,

36 *Ibid.*, pp. 4–8.

37 *Ibid.*

38 HLEG on Fake News and Online Disinformation, *supra* note 27.

fact-checking and literacy efforts. The European Commission Communication[39] includes recommendations on media literacy and pluralism as well, although in a significantly reduced form. It adds reflections on election processes and strategic communication, which were given further attention during previous Commission President Jean-Claude Juncker's State of the Union address in September 2018.[40] Importantly, the Communication picked up on the HLEG's reflections on a transparent digital ecosystem and set up the EU Multistakeholder Forum.

The resulting EU Code of Practice[41] focuses on (electoral) ads, includes a short section on automated bots and addresses the platforms' role in supporting/enabling literacy, fact-checking and research. It mainly recaps existing measures and does not aim to provide industry standards. It should be noted that media trust (source transparency) indicators are mentioned in each of these proposals. Discussions on increasing media trust are ongoing at several levels, including in the Multistakeholder Forum.[42]

4. TRANSPARENCY IN TECHNICAL INTERVENTIONS

The previous sections make it clear that the multi-faceted nature of disinformation calls for varied action. The HLEG stressed that 'the best responses to disinformation are multi-dimensional, with stakeholders collaborating in a manner that protects and promotes freedom of expression, media freedom, and media pluralism'.[43] At the same time, there is an emphasis, especially in the European Commission reports on illegal content online, on solutions that encourage online intermediaries to take (proactive) action to clean up their platforms. In this section, we analyse four areas where technical intervention has often been requested: (political) advertising; fact-checking/trustworthiness; automated processes; and content/account moderation. We focus in particular on how transparency has been integrated into the requests.

39 European Commission Communication on Tackling Online Disinformation, *supra* note 33.

40 European Commission President Juncker announced an Elections Package during his 2018 State of the Union address. See European Commission, 'State of the Union 2018: European Commission Proposes Measures for Securing Free and Fair European Elections', press release, 2018 (IP/18/5681), http://europa.eu/rapid/press-release_IP-18-5681_en.htm.

41 EU Code of Practice on Disinformation, *supra* note 35.

42 See e.g. Reporters Without Borders, 'RSF and its Partners Unveil the Journalism Trust Initiative to Combat Disinformation', 3 April 2018, https://rsf.org/en/news/rsf-and-its-partners-unveil-journalism-trust-initiative-combat-disinformation; Santa Clara University Markkula Center for Applied Ethics, 'The Trust Project', 2017, https://thetrustproject.org. Media trust indicators were also discussed during an expert interview with Renate Schroeder (Director of the EFJ, 7 September 2018).

43 HLEG on Fake News and Online Disinformation, *supra* note 27, p. 3.

Why transparency? Transparency allows for better understanding of the effects of technological responses. Explanation, reporting, review and appeal are all components of transparency and are crucial to any technology-based approach that seeks to minimise harm to the freedom of expression. Table 4 maps the requested technical interventions as found in the key policy initiatives discussed above.

Table 4. Requested technical interventions in EU policy initiatives relevant to illegal content and disinformation online

Technological concern per policy initiative	European Commission Communication on Tackling Illegal Content Online (September 2017)	European Commission Recommendation Measures to Effectively Tackle Illegal Content Online (March 2018)	EU HLEG Report on Fake News and Online Disinformation (March 2018)	European Commission Communication on Tackling Online Disinformation (April 2018)	EU Code of Practice on Disinformation (September 2018)
(Political) advertising			X	X	X
Source transparency and fact-checking			X	X	X
Automated processes (automated filtering, automated ranking, etc.)	X	X	X	X	X
Content/ account moderation	X	X			

Source: Compiled by the authors based on analysis of policy initiatives.

Recommendations on *(political) advertising* are only included in more recent proposals dealing specifically with disinformation. This draws attention to the use of advertising for the purposes of disinformation, even though existing legislation[44] already provides protection and remedies for consumers. The proposals call for transparency on the source and placement of ads, as well as informing users why they are seeing certain ads. The European Commission Communication on Tackling Online Disinformation takes this approach one step further and recommends restricting targeting options for political advertising.[45] The HLEG report also highlights the 'follow-the-money'

[44] For instance, EU Directive 2006/114/EC concerning Misleading and Comparative Advertising.

[45] European Commission Communication on Tackling Online Disinformation, *supra* note 33, p. 7.

approach, which aims at restricting advertising and thus revenues of promoters of disinformation.[46]

Similarly, *source transparency and fact-checking* are only discussed in disinformation initiatives. Linking to the previous paragraph on advertising practices, the broader question at hand when reflecting on economic drivers underlying disinformation is clickbait practices, which the policy initiatives additionally recommend tackling through trustworthiness or source transparency indicators and the prioritisation of 'relevant, authentic and authoritative'[47] and alternative content.

Further, all policy initiatives included in this chapter deem *automated processes* appropriate, with an important qualification that the references to automation differ significantly between the proposals on illegal content online and disinformation online. While the early proposals discuss automated filtering and removal of content and accounts, the later proposals restrict themselves to providing transparency in the use of automated ranking and automated bots. Indeed, the Communication on Tackling Illegal Content Online considers that 'fully automated deletion or suspension of content is acceptable when its illegality has already been established'.[48] In the same vein, the Recommendation on Effective Measures to Tackle Illegal Content Online calls for automated prevention (filtering) of re-uploading of terrorist content, although there is acknowledgement in the proposals that human oversight is necessary 'where detailed assessment of the relevant context is required'.[49] The more recent policy proposals, specific to disinformation, propose a lighter touch to automation.

Finally, it is striking that the recent proposals specific to disinformation do *not* address *content/account moderation*. This is probably because invasive technical interventions of this nature are deemed less appropriate and important than ensuring a rich media system. Nonetheless, interventions on the (de)prioritisation, blocking and removal of content and accounts are part and parcel of the online intermediaries' actions and policies. The silence of the disinformation initiatives on content/account moderation is thus unfortunate, as they could have provided guidance on transparency, appeal and review in the removal of disinformation. Recommendations on content/account moderation can instead be found in the European Commission's Recommendation and Communication on Tackling Illegal Content Online.[50] The European

---

46 HLEG on Fake News and Online Disinformation, *supra* note 27, p. 32.

47 EU Code of Practice on Disinformation, *supra* note 35, commitment 8.

48 European Commission Communication on Tackling Illegal Content Online, *supra* note 19, p. 14.

49 European Commission Recommendation on Measures to Effectively Tackle Illegal Online Content, *supra* note 20, para. 20.

50 European Commission Communication on Tackling Illegal Content Online, *supra* note 19.

Commission makes an exception where notification and appeal of removal is not deemed appropriate for criminal offences.[51]

5. CONCLUSIONS

Neither law nor technology is neutral: both embody the values and priorities of those who have designed them. But while recent EU policy initiatives on disinformation have prioritised the use of technology to deprioritise and remove misleading content and accounts, concomitant assessments of the impact of such technology-based solutions on human rights in general, and freedom of expression and media pluralism in particular, have been limited.[52]

We warn against technocentric optimism as a solution to disinformation online, which proposes the use of automated detection, (de)prioritisation, blocking and removal by online intermediaries *without human intervention*. International law has long required that restrictions on freedom of expression must be provided by law, be legitimate, be proven necessary and be the least restrictive means to pursue the aim. As Milton Mueller, one of our interview respondents, stated:

> Disinformation is a very long-term historical problem with human society. The fact that we can automate it and scale it up the way we can with social media is interesting, but I don't think it is qualitatively different from what we have seen. With the exception that it is more globalised, so foreign governments or foreign actors can partake and have access in ways that are both good and bad.[53]

Automated technologies are limited in their accuracy, especially for expression where cultural or contextual cues are necessary. Legislators should not push

---

51 European Commission Recommendation on Measures to Effectively Tackle Illegal Online Content, *supra* note 20, para. 10; European Commission Communication on Tackling Illegal Content Online, *supra* note 19, p. 17.

52 UN Special Rapporteur on the Promotion and Protection of the Right to Freedom of Opinion and Expression, 'Report to the United Nations Human Rights Council on A Human Rights Approach to Platform Content Regulation', A/HRC/38/35, 2018, https://freedex.org/wp-content/blogs.dir/2015/files/2018/05/G1809672.pdf.
See also UN Special Rapporteur on Freedom of Opinion and Expression et al., *supra* note 27; Access Now, Civil Liberties Union for Europe, and European Digital Rights (EDRi), 'Informing the "Disinformation" Debate', 2018, https://edri.org/files/online_disinformation.pdf. We discussed the implications of technology-driven solutions for freedom of expression in expert interviews with David Kaye (UN Special Rapporteur on Freedom of Opinion and Expression, 3 July 2018) and Joe McNamee (former Executive Director at EDRi, 6 September 2018).

53 Expert interview with Milton Mueller (Professor at Georgia Institute of Technology School of Public Policy; Director Internet Governance Project, 6 August 2018).

this difficult judgement exercise in disinformation on to online intermediaries. When automated technologies are used, we argue that far more independent, transparent and effective appeal and oversight mechanisms are necessary in order to minimise the impact of inevitable inaccuracies.

To protect freedom of expression, disinformation is best tackled through *media pluralism and literacy* initiatives. *Source transparency indicators* are preferable over (de)prioritisation of disinformation, as these allow for diversity of expression and choice. Users also need to be given the opportunity to understand how their search results or social media feeds are built and make changes where desirable.

We advise against regulatory action that would encourage increased use of automated technologies for content moderation purposes, without *strong human review and appeal processes*. When technical intermediaries need to moderate content and accounts, detailed and transparent policies, notice and appeal procedures, and regular reports are crucial. We believe this is valid for automated removals as well.

There is scope for standardising (the basics of) notice and appeal procedures and reporting, and creating a *self- or co-regulatory multistakeholder body*, such as the UN Special Rapporteur's suggested 'social media council'.[54] The Special Rapporteur recommends that this multistakeholder body could, on the one hand, have the competence to deal with industry-wide appeals and, on the other hand, could work towards a better understanding and minimisation of the effects of technological interventions on freedom of expression and media pluralism.

Lack of independent evidence or *detailed research* in this policy area means that the risk of harm remains far too high for any degree of policy or regulatory certainty. *Greater transparency* is needed in the variety and effect of disinformation reduction techniques used by online platforms and content providers in order to enable societies to move towards more effective mechanisms to reduce the harms of disinformation, while protecting freedom of expression and other human rights.

---

54 UN Special Rapporteur on the Promotion and Protection of the Right to Freedom of Opinion and Expression, *supra* note 52.

17. THE WAR AGAINST FAKE NEWS IN THE DIGITAL AGE AND THE WEAPONS IN OUR INTELLECTUAL ARSENAL

Stamos ARCHONTIS*

1. INTRODUCTION

If we want to properly discuss the topic of fake news, we first need to understand the difference between printed and digital media. In the era before the Internet, in order to launch and, most importantly, maintain a sustainable and profitable news organisation, substantial financial and social capital was required. As a result, the number of news outlets (and thus the sources of information) was limited. There were of course small, local newspapers and television stations, but these attracted only a tiny portion of the total audience.

The development and widespread availability of the Internet in the past two decades spearheaded a new era of information, bringing about a fundamental change in the way we consume news – unparalleled access to a variety of opinions and perspectives, as well as an unprecedented ability for every citizen to become both a consumer and a distributor of information. This meant that a variety of independent news outlets began to pop up in the form of amateur blogs and later as social media pages.[1]

The problem quickly became apparent. On the one hand, this new, faster and unrestrained access to information was a powerful and extremely useful tool that had the potential to improve people's everyday life as well as improve the speed of information exchange in the field of scientific research. However, on the other hand, this access also gave everyone the ability to write and share anything they wanted through social media without even a moderate form of content review.

* Researcher at ellinikahoaxes.gr, Greece. Email: stamosarchontis@ellinikahoaxes.gr.

1 L. RAINIE, 'Internet, Broadband, and Cell Phone Statistics', Pew Research Center: Internet, Science & Tech, 31 December 2019, https://www.pewresearch.org/internet/2010/01/05/internet-broadband-and-cell-phone-statistics.

There is a clear distinction between news and opinion, and this line is set by journalists' commitment to facts and impartial analysis of any given claim. Without this mindset, journalism is nothing short of gossiping. Yet, the average citizen is not a trained journalist; therefore, they have probably not invested time and energy into learning how to assess the validity of any given news article. This leaves us with millions of people who have appointed themselves as journalists, constantly sharing and, more often than not, writing news articles of questionable accuracy. This situation has, in part, given rise to the problem of fake news in the form we see today. This phrase is not just a catchy slogan; it describes a whole political and cultural landscape where facts are viewed as an *à la carte* system in which we pick and choose what reality fits our *a priori* beliefs and sensibilities.

This is not to say that major newspapers and news stations are without fault; quite the opposite in fact, since we have seen major fake or misleading news stories appear in well-established media outlets over the years. A notable example is a series of fabricated articles published by the well-known German magazine *Der Spiegel*. These articles were scathing criticisms of US politics and were written by one reporter, who, as it turned out, fabricated the vast majority of them. While the reporter was fired, the problem remains. A professional news organisation published stories that were apparently not checked thoroughly for authenticity, resulting in an international scandal and a letter of condemnation from the US ambassador to Germany.[2]

And of course, this is just a modern example. Fake news pre-dates the Internet and there are a plethora of examples regarding hoaxes propagated by popular publications. The most notable example would be the story about the 'Central Park Zoo escape' of 1870, when the *New York Herald* published a 10,000-word article detailing how the animals at the Central Park Zoo in New York had escaped, causing mayhem on the streets, killing innocent civilians and injuring policemen. The article caused widespread panic even though at the end of the article there was a small note explaining that the whole story was fake. Of course, most readers did not read the article all the way through and the fact that the newspaper had not published a similar story in the past made the readers believe that it was a legitimate news article. This in turn led a number of civilians to try and escape the area near Central Park, a state of panic that could have potentially caused harm.[3]

---

2 K. Connolly and J. Le Blond, 'Der Spiegel Takes the Blame for Scandal of Reporter Who Faked Stories', *The Guardian*, 23 December 2018, https://www.theguardian.com/world/2018/dec/23/anti-america-bias-der-spiegel-scandal-relotius.

3 Museum of Hoaxes, 'The Central Park Zoo Escape', http://hoaxes.org/archive/permalink/the_central_park_zoo_escape/.

Regardless of such examples, an established news organisation has a reputation to uphold. Thus, it has an incentive to be as thorough as it can in terms of fact-checking the content it publishes. This vested interest in accurate reporting does not diminish the instances of inaccurate articles, but it certainly has kept that trend in check in the past. Fast-forward a few years and what we see is a surge of misleading or outright false news articles, blog posts and social media posts being spread both by actual news organisations as well as self-proclaimed journalists.

The aforementioned access to information facilitated by social media and related sites may seem like a net-positive development, but it has some serious drawbacks, the most notable of which is the lack of oversight regarding the accuracy of the published content; anyone can post virtually anything they want in any social media site using just a smartphone. Moreover, each individual social media platform can, realistically, only test for profanity in material such as photos rather than testing the accuracy of the published content. We are talking about millions, if not hundreds of millions of posts every day, making the task of manually reviewing this vast amount of content rather challenging. However, in the past few years we have seen that the practice of hiring accredited fact-checkers in order to handle this task has been adopted by social media platforms, like the third-party fact-checking program initiated by Facebook.[4]

The second issue is the potential reach of every citizen. The fact that every citizen now has a platform to freely voice their concerns and opinions is, without a doubt, a positive development for any modern democracy. However, the problem arises when these opinions are branded or advertised as facts and are in fact used as sources in actual news articles. The only thing you need is a smartphone and Internet access, and you can potentially reach millions of people regardless of who you are. Some of the most influential social media accounts are run by ordinary citizens who managed to amass large followings over the years.

Although most of these lifestyle and educational pages are very useful and interesting, amongst them we also find a few worrying examples such as conspiracy theory sites. The vast majority of these news outlets peddle unsubstantiated information, often promoting potentially dangerous nationalistic agendas. Sites like these have fuelled the far-right agenda in Europe over the past decade, leading to the rise of extremist groups like the AfD in Germany and the Neo-Nazi 'Golden Dawn' party in Greece. And these changes unfortunately

---

4 C. Silverman, 'Facebook Is Turning To Fact-Checkers To Fight Fake News' *BuzzFeed News*, 15 December 2016, https://www.buzzfeednews.com/article/craigsilverman/facebook-and-fact-checkers-fight-fake-news.

permeate through the walls of parliaments; they affect the lives of everyday people, natives and immigrants alike, leading to acts of violence against the latter, in virtually every country which has accepted refugees in recent years.[5]

Furthermore, inaccurate information has led to the establishment and propagation of groups like the anti-vaccination movement, a wave of people who actively promote pseudoscientific misinformation which has resulted in the re-emergence of diseases such as measles in several European countries and the US. We are now at a point where measles outbreaks with dead children as a result has become a new reality, and health professionals have actually named the wave of anti-vaccination activism as one of the main causes.[6]

Yet, vaccines are only one of the examples we can cite regarding potentially dangerous medical fake news. Alternative cancer cures is another area where misleading online news sites can have a serious impact on people's lives. There is ample example of charlatans peddling pseudoscientific 'alternative medicine' cures for serious medical conditions like various forms of cancer. These sites sell herbal or religious treatments to desperate cancer patients, often with fatal results. In Greece this phenomenon is unfortunately quite common and while legal action has been taken against several of these individuals, their cases are still undergoing review by the courts.

Misinformation is by definition detrimental to public discourse, but in the modern era it is more than just a nuisance; it can potentially endanger

---

5 A. Gmurczyk, 'A New Europe, *National Rebirth Of Poland*, 18 October 2016, https://en.nop.org.pl/2016/10/18/adam-gmurczyk-a-new-europe/; N.G. Michaloliakos, 'They are rejoicing in vain … Golden Dawn is not over!', *Golden Dawn*, 21 June 2019, http://xrisiavgi.com/en/view/golden-dawn-and-thepatriots-who-partner-with-the-bolshevists-article-of-n.g.; Deutsche Welle, 'AfD: What You Need to Know about Germany's Far-Right Party', *dw.com*, 28 October 2019, https://www.dw.com/en/afd-what-you-need-to-know-about-germanys-far-right-party/a-37208199; S. Tipaldou and K. Uba, 'Golden Dawn: How the Greek Far Right Wrote the Playbook Others Now Use to Go Mainstream', *The Conversation*, 17 August 2018, http://theconversation.com/golden-dawn-how-the-greek-far-right-wrote-the-playbook-others-now-use-to-go-mainstream-100987; A. Carassava, 'Attacks on Migrants "Planned by Far-Right Party" Golden Dawn in Greece' *The Times*, 20 June 2017, https://www.thetimes.co.uk/article/attacks-on-migrants-planned-by-far-right-party-in-greece-90jd7nssb.

6 S. Boseley, 'Measles Cases at Highest for 20 Years in Europe, as Anti-Vaccine Movement Grows', *The Guardian*, 21 December 2018, https://www.theguardian.com/world/2018/dec/21/measles-cases-at-highest-for-20-years-in-europe-as-anti-vaccine-movement-grows; Clark County Washington, 'Clark County Measles Case Count up to 36 Confirmed, 12 Suspect', 29 January 2019; World Health Organization, 'WHO EpiData, January–December 2017', 19 February 2018, http://www.euro.who.int/en/health-topics/disease-prevention/vaccines-and-immunization/publications/surveillance-and-data/who-epidata/2018/who-epidata,-no.-12018; World Health Organization, 'WHO EpiData, No. 1/2019, January 2018– December 2018', 11 June 2019, http://www.euro.who.int/en/health-topics/disease-prevention/vaccines-and-immunization/publications/surveillance-and-data/who-epidata/2019/who-epidata-no-12019; S. Mundasad, 'Measles Resurgence "Due to Vaccine Hesitancy", WHO Warns', *BBC News*, 29 November 2018, https://www.bbc.com/news/health-46387167.

people's lives. This reality makes proper analysis and refutation of inaccurate information a top priority. Unfortunately, the legal system has yet to catch up with the potential risks associated with online journalism, specifically with topics that revolve around medical information and pseudoscientific claims.[7]

This brings us to the role of fact-checkers. As previously mentioned, news organisations, whether traditional or 'new media', have, through their actions, proven that they need proper monitoring from independent institutions in order to ensure the accuracy of the information they publish. This role has been 'unofficially' assumed by a new kind of journalism model called 'fact-checking'. It may be argued that the role of a journalist necessarily includes a thorough investigation and double-checking of facts before publication, but the way in which the news reporting landscape has been shaped in recent years makes that reasonable request obsolete. News organisations try to publish new articles every minute in order to keep up with competition and this reality has accorded accuracy and quality a lower priority status.[8] Consequently, mistakes, whether intentional or deliberate, have become a common occurrence, resulting in a steady decrease of the public's confidence in mainstream media. This in turn pushes more people to embrace 'new media' as their primary news sources. And while there are now many quality online news outlets, there are even more inaccurate and potentially dangerous sources.

Sites such as Snopes are amongst the most famous fact-checking groups worldwide. They were started by volunteers, who took it upon themselves to help the public learn which claims were not factual, as well as teaching people how to spot shady claims in the process. However, the most incredible fact is that this initiative was not an outlier. There were dozens, if not hundreds, of similar efforts across the globe from people who tried to make the Internet haystack a bit more navigable. In Greece the first site which tried and succeeded in doing so is Ellinika Hoaxes.

By trial and error, as well as comparing notes with other fact-checkers worldwide, Ellinika Hoaxes have developed a set of tools which enable their team to assess the validity of claims they encounter online from most sources. In this chapter we will attempt to walk the reader through the most notable

---

7 T. Sitistas, 'Oncologists Recommend Medical Treatments with the Use of Precious Stones', *Ellinika Hoaxes*, 1 July 2019, https://www.ellinikahoaxes.gr/2019/07/01/kriara-crystalotherapy-pseudoscience/; T. Sitistas, '"Dr. Mouroutis", a "Doctor" with Fake Credentials', *Ellinika Hoaxes*, 10 August 2019, https://www.ellinikahoaxes.gr/2017/04/27/mouroutis-fake-credentials/; T. Sitistas, 'Academic and Scholar with Just a Primary School Degree', *Ellinika Hoaxes*, 10 August 10 2019, https://www.ellinikahoaxes.gr/2017/06/07/paschalidis-tri-antropo-model-debunked/.

8 R. Saisho, 'Speed vs Accuracy in Times of Crisis', *Reuters Institute, University of Oxford*, 2015, https://reutersinstitute.politics.ox.ac.uk/sites/default/files/research/files/Speed%20vs%20Accuracy%20in%20Times%20of%20Crisis.pdf.

examples of those tools and provide real-life examples of how they helped us as a fact-checking group in our battle against misinformation.

However, before we start with our analysis, it would be prudent to dismiss the notion that in order to work successfully as a professional (or even part-time) fact-checker, you need to be a professional journalist. It does require a great deal of experience, but it is a skill which anyone can master, given enough time, patience and dedication.

The Internet provides us with all the tools we need to do this job, and the only challenge is to learn how to use them. It is also a good idea to keep in mind that fact-checking is a serious responsibility, not only because you assume the role of the individual that will put a stamp of accuracy on a given news article, but because a mistake on your part can have implication on a journalist's career. Claiming that a professional journalist has misrepresented the facts on a given story is a serious accusation which can impact their professional development, and it should be treated as such. We need to be as certain as possible before publishing our analysis and should not jump to conclusions before we have all of the available facts. The methods and tools we will discuss in the following sections are meant to act as a starting point which will help you build and develop your skills and experience.

2. THE PROBLEMS OF EXAGGERATED TITLES AND CLICKBAITING

Considering the various aspects which comprise a news article, one quickly realises that the first and perhaps most telling indicator of potential problems with its content can be found in the title. A trend which every social media user has probably observed is that a lot of the titles we come across do not accurately reflect the content of the article we read. This tactic is called 'clickbait', denoting a title which is designed to make the article appealing to the reader even though it may not be entirely accurate.

Every news organisation wants to persuade people to click on their articles and generate traffic on their site, so their promotional strategy is built around that requirement. While this is not necessarily a problematic tactic, we do need to be more careful about an article with a title which seems exaggerated. It may seem like a trivial concern, but actually the majority of social media users share articles without ever reading them, relying solely on whether or not they agree with the title, and this behaviour in turn incentivises various media to keep sensationalising the titles of their articles.

Two very interesting research papers regarding this topic explain in part why clickbait titles prompt more reposts or retweets from readers. According to a 2018 study in the *Journal of Computer-Mediated Communication*, the majority of social media users access these sites with a smartphone or a tablet. Reading the news through those devices causes their attention span to be limited. As a result, they read only the title and, depending on whether or not they agree with it, they press the like button and/or share the article. Furthermore, a study on the behaviour patterns of Reddit accounts showed that almost 73 per cent of users upvoted an article without first viewing the content.[9]

This pattern outlines a problematic user behaviour, which explains in part why we have so many reposts of inaccurate new stories every day. At the same time, this gives us a very easy way to detect a potentially problematic article for review. There are several universal indicators for a clickbait title, like the use of capital letters, exclamation points, phrases like 'you won't believe what we found' and so on. Each country and culture has its own versions of this tactic. Therefore, reading as many of these articles as you can will help you become familiar with those patterns and learn to recognise them quickly.

Regardless of the aforementioned facts, it should be stressed that a suspicious title does not necessarily mean that the content is problematic; it means that, based on the evidence thus far, articles with sensationalist titles are statistically more likely to misrepresent the contents of the news piece in question. It is really important to avoid black-and-white thinking when analysing articles we come into contact with.

3. ASSESSING THE ACCURACY OF PHOTOS

While the examination of a title can be very useful, it is by far the easiest indicator when we are analysing a news article. However, the content itself can be much more challenging. Luckily, over the years, a number of tools have been developed which can help us tackle every issue we might face. In Greece we come into regular contact with memes or simply photos in articles which are used to make specific claims. For example, a photo of soldiers marching through a plain field might be used in an article which claims that Turkey has sent troops to the northern Greek border; therefore, being able to find out whether or not the photo is genuine, and trace its origin, is really important. There are a couple of tools we can use in instances like this. Due to the fact that most of the time an article of this sort uses stock photos, it is quite easy to trace the origin using Google Images. The process is relatively simple, as we only need to download the

---

[9] J. Dunaway, K. Searles, M. Sui and P. Newly, 'News Attention in a Mobile Era' (2018) 23(2) *Journal of Computer-Mediated Communication* 107–124, doi: 10.1093/jcmc/zmy004; M. Glenski, C. Pennycuff and T. Weninger, 'Consumers and Curators: Browsing and Voting Patterns on Reddit' (2017) 4(4) *IEEE Transactions on Computational Social Systems* 196–206, doi: 10.1109/tcss.2017.2742242.

photo from the article in question, then open a Google search engine for photos and upload it there. This will generate all public articles or social media posts which include the photo in question.

Google is the easiest way to check a photo for authenticity in terms of context. If, on the other hand, we want to examine whether or not a photo is genuine or the product of editing, we need another tool. For this purpose, we can use a site like FotoForensics, which is free to use and was developed by professional programmers. On this site we can upload the photo we want to examine and check for colour changes, pixel inconsistencies and quality, and even the photo's metadata, which can often reveal the date the file was created and modified, so that we can draw conclusions about possible tampering.

If the story you are working on is about a historical event, there is a slight chance you will not be able to find the photos you need online. In this instance, you might need to contact or even visit relevant museums which feature collections regarding the topic at hand. It is a rare occurrence, as nowadays most of these collections have been digitised, but keep in mind that, in a situation like this, you might need to engage in old-fashioned investigative journalism.

On rare occasions, the photo you are looking for might not appear anywhere, leading you to the conclusion that it might be genuine. However, in some cases, the photo in question might be fake, but we are not able to find its source because it has not yet been posted online. Whether or not a photo is genuine does not always mean that the context in which it is presented is accurate. Photos are a convenient way to spot weak points in an article, but in the end they are only one aspect of our analysis. Even if the photo is fake, we should not rely solely on that issue with the article in question. Our analysis needs to include every single problem we find with the article, including but not limited to the photos it uses.

4. INVESTIGATING SOURCES

While the aforementioned sites are very helpful to a fact-checker, it is essential to keep in mind that we should not focus our attention on any single tool, but should use all of them in concert in order to efficiently organise our analysis. An interesting, albeit not always appreciated, aspect of an article is whether or not it includes sources. This is particularly important when the article covers a scientific topic, although it is of course not limited to this field. A new discovery or a new drug that is being developed always has an accompanying research paper or at the very least an official listing in a governmental agency which tracks clinical trials if the discovery concerns the testing of a medication. When we read an article regarding a scientific topic without a direct link to such material or at the very least a reference to the name of title of the research paper or the researcher in charge, then it is very likely that the content of the article is not accurate. In most cases with missing references, the journalist either blindly copied information from a social media post or another article without themselves fact-checking the accuracy of the source they used.

In articles where the author is making conspiracy claims or unsubstantiated, anti-science assertions, it is essential that we find out the source of this claim in order to fact-check it and refute it in case it is not accurate. In order to find the source when the article does not give any information whatsoever, you need to investigate blindly and this means taking all the information the article provides and using it as search parameters. For example, let us imagine that we have an article regarding a new research paper which claims that a specific vaccine causes cancer. The article does not mention a title or a name, which leaves us only with the details of the article. Most of the time, these articles contain abstract descriptions of the study findings or, in some cases, numbers from that study. For instance, the article might mention that the study used data from 2,000 participants with an age range of 10 to 15, and this will be our search parameter. We use the keywords 'study', 'vaccines', '2,000 participants' and 'age 10 to 15' in a search engine like Google and start a thorough examination of the results. Ideally we would only look in research paper databases like 'Scopus', 'ScienceDirect' or 'PubMed', but it is a common occurrence for these articles to reference a 'study' posted on a blog and not one published in an established, peer-reviewed scientific journal; this in turn means that we need to cast a wider net in order to find our source.

Assuming we are able to locate the source of the claim, we need to examine it thoroughly in order to assert whether or not the claim made by the article is accurate. If we are dealing with a 'blog study', it is quite simple to explain that this material has no legitimacy as a source of scientific information and thus the article spreads unscientific assertions. We should still read the material in question in order to explain the content, but there is no point in fact-checking that source itself. If, on the other hand, the source is an actual research paper, our job becomes a bit more difficult as we need to read the paper carefully and see if the article has reported the findings accurately.

Research papers may appear intimidating at first glance, but there is a way even for someone without an academic background to read them and get a rough estimation of their findings. Most research papers have a section called 'Discussion' and another section called 'Conclusions'. These two are often the only parts of the paper which do not include technical terminology and describe the process followed by the researchers, as well as the findings, using simple language. Thus, lay readers are provided with a solid understanding of what the researchers did and what they found. It is still possible that the picture may change when you read the technical aspects of the paper, and for that reason it is always a good idea to have at least one scientist in your fact-checking team – and more than one if possible.

You are also encouraged to use secondary sources such as official websites of scientific bodies like the American Cancer Institute, the World Health Organization (WHO) and the Center for Disease Control and Prevention (CDC), as all of them publish articles regarding specific studies from time to time, especially if the study in question has been profusely publicised by the mainstream media. Most of the time when news sites use the findings of a new study, they exaggerate the results, forcing scientific bodies such as the aforementioned to step in and explain the results in a more comprehensive manner. Therefore, you can use these articles as a guide to write your analysis, and also as a source, given the fact that they usually contain all the necessary primary sources you might need.

The same principle applies to every topic in politics or economics. Parsing a given article and using its components in order to fact-check it is the best tactic a fact-checker can employ. More often than not, you may confront an article that covers a topic regarding international news; in this case, the sources available to you might be in a different language. In cases like this, you have many options. The best is to cultivate a relationship with a trustworthy fact-checking group which operates in the country in question so that you can request their assistance. There are lists of such groups that have been vetted by independent organisations and that might be of use to you. Another option is to hire someone who can translate the news article from a local news site or to try and translate it yourself, although this option should be the last resort, as the available translation tools often tend to misrepresent the context of the translated text in certain languages.

5. TECHNICAL ASPECTS OF AUTHENTICITY

A problematic aspect of journalism today is that a specific story can be modified or even completely distorted as it passes from one news site to the next. The author of each individual article may add or remove information, making the original news piece unrecognisable. In addition, individual social media posts may complicate the story further, as it is not uncommon for single tweets from civilians, containing unsubstantiated claims, to become international news because a politician used them without fact-checking them first. A notable example is a retweet made by the US President Donald Trump of a fake statistic regarding crime rates in the US. The original tweet was from a Neo-Nazi account, which the president was not aware of, and yet he distributed this information without fact-checking it, resulting in the spreading of serious and potentially dangerous misinformation on millions of people.[10]

[10] M. Pearce, 'Once again, Trump tweets a meme linked to a brazen racist', *Los Angeles Times*, 3 July 2017, https://www.latimes.com/nation/la-na-trump-reddit-20170703-story.html.

Also, when the story you are working on includes social media posts from politicians or any other public figure, you need to make sure that you are dealing with the official account of that individual and not a parody account. There are many instances of established news organisations publishing an array of articles based on social media post by fake accounts. The most amusing of these instances is the creation of 'Tiger Beat' by the satirical page *The Onion*. The site created a mock cover of the teen magazine *Tiger Beat* featuring former US President Barack Obama alongside the boyband Jonas Brothers with the title 'I sing in the shower'. And while many people understood the joke, especially given the fact that *The Onion* is a well-known satirical site, the *New York Times* thought the cover was genuine and reported on an article profiling 'Tiger Beat', explaining how the cover helped Obama's popularity with young Americans. The newspaper eventually realised its mistake and issued a correction, but the main point in this story is that even a large news organisation, which supposedly has many layers of scrutiny to avoid mistakes, can actually fall victim to online pranks such as this.[11]

Based on the aforementioned examples, apart from being familiar with the way in which news sites operate, you need to have a solid grasp of the way in which a website functions in general. First of all, you need to make sure that the article you read is not from a satirical website like *The Onion*. The aforementioned example of the *New York Times* mistake is not an outlier; these types of mistakes are actually quite common. In addition, you cannot trust a picture of a tweet, not even a live broadcast of someone's computer showing the tweet. Anyone can alter the space where the content of a tweet or a Facebook post is displayed by simply using the 'inspect element' tool in their browser, such as in Firefox. Using this option, it is possible to rewrite the content of that space and make it appear to be a totally different message. In order to verify that a tweet or a post is genuine, we need to have a link to an archived webpage containing the original tweet.

Any changes an individual makes through 'inspect element' only affects their browser, so if they present an archived page containing the tweet, we can be sure that the content of that tweet is genuine; otherwise, we cannot be sure of the authenticity. This tactic is not limited to social media posts. Any article you wish to fact-check should be archived before you proceed with analysis.

More often than not, the website which posted the article will make subsequent changes in order to cover inaccuracies or mistakes, possibly denying

---

11 J. Caramanica, 'Tiger Beat: Still Squeaky Clean After All These Years', *The New York Times*, 16 April 2011, https://www.nytimes.com/2011/04/17/weekinreview/17tigerbeat.html; Huffington Post, 'New York Times Fooled By The Onion Obama Magazine Cover', 6 December 2017, https://www.huffpost.com/entry/new-york-times-fooled-onion_n_853151?guce_referrer_us=aHR0cHM6Ly+9ndWNlLm9hdGguY29tLw&guce_referrer_cs=GzhCVBdEd9Mn_e7nN8olHw&_guc_consent_skip=1581700748.

having made the mistake in the first place. This means that you need to have a verifiably genuine copy of the original article. The most convenient option is Wayback Machine, a site which asks you for the link of the original article and saves the whole page as it appeared on the day you saw it. You can then copy the link that Wayback Machine generates and have access to that edition of the article regardless of the subsequent changes the news site might make.

Although some might view it as overkill, it is good practice to use Wayback Machine for every single source you provide in your article. Some webpages might shut down over the years, some might be restructured, losing previous content in the process, and thus the links you provide in your article might become useless. If you have everything archived, you can be sure that, no matter what happens, every source you have provided will be available.

Keep in mind that your work is only as good as the level of proof you attach to it. A serious dedication to rigorous examination of the facts is a prerequisite for any person wishing to work as a fact-checker, and thus the aforementioned steps should be considered as a necessary toolkit in your work process.

6. CLOSING REMARKS

The purpose of this chapter is not to provide a full documentation of the tools used by every fact-checker, but to help the reader fully grasp the extent of the problem we face regarding fake news. The methods and tools described here serve as a starting point which can help every aspiring fact-checker in developing their own tools and improving their experience through practice. While writing an original news story may be a laborious task, fact-checking a published article may sometimes be more demanding.

Keep in mind that this job does not have a strict set of instructions or a guidebook. The process you will follow for analysing news will, in large part, be a custom formula of your own making, which will of course be based on experiences and tools developed by more experienced fact-checkers. There are ample examples of successful fact-checking groups, such as Snopes, which can help you in your first steps. Analysing the process followed by these groups in every article they examine can help you develop your own style.

Finally, we need to mention an aspect of fact-checking which often goes unmentioned. You are going to make mistakes. Even though this whole process is about checking for mistakes, it is entirely possible to misread or misunderstand a given article. You may falsely conclude that a news story is inaccurate and publish that conclusion. Our job is to make sure that the public is accurately informed. We do not claim that we are infallible and this needs to be communicated to our readership. One of the roadblocks in the pursuit of fair and impartial public discourse is appeal to authority. So, the last thing a fact checking group needs to cultivate is the perception that they themselves are a form of authority which their audience need to blindly trust. Given enough time, it is inevitable to amass an audience which will trust your opinion, especially if you produce quality work consistently, but you need to remind them constantly that they should critically question everything they read, including you, and demand evidence for every claim they encounter.

Healthy scepticism, critical thinking and the right to question the information we are presented with constitute the bedrock of every civilised society and modern democracy. The tools we use to distribute information might change, but the goal of keeping the public accurately informed should remain the same. In this respect, both traditional journalism and fact-checking as a separate form of reporting have a major role to play in the coming years.

18. IN THE NAME OF SCIENTIFIC ADVANCEMENT

How to Assess What Constitutes 'Scientific Research' in the GDPR to Protect Data Subjects and Democracy

Heidi Beate BENTZEN*

One of the biggest failures of Facebook is to excessively legalize its terms and conditions and forget something so important as the reasonable expectation of the user.[1]

– Christopher Wylie, Cambridge Analytica whistleblower

1. INTRODUCTION

The Cambridge Analytica scandal was not the first scandal involving research on Facebook data and is likely not to be the last. An academic researcher obtained data from 87 million Facebook users under the pretence of scientific research and sold it on to the commercial company Cambridge Analytica,

---

* Centre for Medical Ethics, Faculty of Medicine, University of Oslo and Norwegian Research Center for Computers and Law, Faculty of Law, University of Oslo, Norway. Affiliated researcher at HeLEX Centre for Health, Law and Emerging Technologies, University of Oxford, UK. Email: h.b.bentzen@medisin.uio.no. The author wishes to thank Professors Lee Andrew Bygrave and Dag Wiese Schartum for their valuable discussions and document review. This chapter reports research conducted as part of the 'Governance of Health Data in Cyberspace' project. The project is a joint undertaking between the University of Oxford, the University of Iceland, Uppsala University and the University of Oslo. In addition to the named author and individuals, the following individuals have contributed to the chapter through group discussion, peer support and/or document review: Sarah Coy, Eik Haraldsdóttir, Jennifer Viberg Johansson, Guðbjörg Andrea Jónsdóttir, Jane Kaye, Deborah Mascalzoni, Salvör Nordal, Nisha Shah and Jorien Veldwijk. This work was supported by NordForsk grant number 81105 and the Economic and Social Research Council (part of UK Research and Innovation), and by the Research Council of Norway grant number 238999.

1 P. GUIMÓN, 'Brexit wouldn't have happened without Cambridge Analytica', *El País*, 27 March 2018. Available at: https://elpais.com/elpais/2018/03/27/inenglish/1522142310_757589.html.

which subsequently used the data with the aim of influencing democratic elections.[2] A few years earlier, Facebook conducted a psychological experiment designed to determine whether it could alter emotional states on nearly 700,000 of its users without their knowledge, consent or ethical review.[3] Facebook admitted to having been unprepared for the negative reactions that followed, conceding that the research should have been conducted differently.[4] The editor-in-chief of the *Proceedings of the National Academy of Sciences of the USA* (*PNAS*), which published the research, expressed concern that Facebook's data collection 'may have involved practices that were not fully consistent with the principles of obtaining informed consent and allowing participants to opt out'.[5] Nevertheless, the research project appears to have been legal, but not necessarily ethical or well conducted.[6]

In acknowledgement of the importance of scientific research, the EU General Data Protection Regulation 2016/679 (GDPR) offers it a number of concessions. However, the GDPR does not provide a definition of 'scientific research', making it unclear which practices are afforded this privileged position. As the examples above illustrate and as elaborated below, use of research data for other purposes – including those that may pose a threat to democracy – is a well-recognised and frequent problem. Unethically and/or poorly conducted research is similarly a known problem, which may also pose a challenge to democracy.

Sometimes, personal data is seemingly not collected for scientific research purposes, although that may be the primary purpose. Some businesses are, for instance, built for the purpose of obtaining and reselling sensitive data for research, although the business model can be hidden from plain sight. 23andMe, a direct-to-consumer genetic testing company with over five million customers worldwide, is a prime example. By offering genetic testing kits to the public, including the European public, and simultaneously asking them to

---

2 Facebook was fined £500,000 by the Information Commissioner's Office (ICO) in the UK for the serious breaches of data protection law, the maximum fine possible prior to the GDPR. See Information Commissioner's Office, 'Data Protection Act 1998. Supervisory powers of the Information Commissioner. Monetary Penalty Notice', 24 October 2018. Available at: https://ico.org.uk/media/action-weve-taken/mpns/2260051/r-facebook-mpn-20181024.pdf.

3 A. D. Kramer, J. E. Guillory and J. T. Hancock, 'Experimental evidence of massive-scale emotional contagion through social networks' (2014) 111 *PNAS* 8788–8790.

4 M. Schroepfer, 'Research at Facebook', 2 October 2014. Available at: https://newsroom.fb.com/news/2014/10/research-at-facebook.

5 I. M. Verma, 'Editorial expression of concern: experimental evidence of massive-scale emotional contagion through social networks' (2014) 111 *PNAS* 10779

6 Facebook, due to being a private company, was not bound to the US rules on consent in the Common Rule, and the research fell outside the scope of ethical review by Cornell University's Institutional Review Board because Facebook conducted the research for internal purposes. For details, *Ibid*.

consent to research, the company has not only been able to build one of the world's largest biobanks, it has also been able to get the people who provide the biological samples to foot the bill for the sample collection. 23andMe has entered into a number of large business deals with the pharmaceutical industry to give them access to data, for instance a US$60 million deal with biotechnology company Genentech, a subsidiary of the pharmaceutical company Roche, and a US$300 million equity investment from GlaxoSmithKline (GSK) along with a collaboration allowing GSK to mine 23andMe's customer data.[7] 23andMe also partners with Pfizer, Lundbeck, Janssen, Biogen and Alynlam Pharmaceuticals.[8] Anne Wojcicki, CEO and co-founder of 23andMe. is quoted as saying that 'I think that this illustrated how pharma companies are interested in the fact that we have a massive amount of information'.[9] Obviously, she is right – research data is big business.

Not all research is good research. In fact, much research is not very good at all in the sense that it is often conducted in a manner that is not sufficiently methodologically rigorous.[10] *The Lancet* published a paper claiming that most research is 'avoidable waste'.[11] In addition, it is more likely for a research finding to be false than true, as shown in the most-cited paper of *PLoS Medicine* ever.[12] The paper demonstrates that most research findings are false for most research designs and for most fields, and that many claimed research findings are nothing more than accurate measures of the prevailing bias.[13]

Clearly, there is also excellent research being conducted, but it increasingly suffers as a result of bureaucratic demands incompatible with the rigour true scientific advancements require.[14] Obviously, this is the type of obstacles the

---

7 M. Herper, 'Surprise! With $60 million Genentech deal, 23andMe has a business plan', *Forbes*, 6 January 2015. Available at: https://www.forbes.com/sites/matthewherper/2015/01/06/surprise-with-60-million-genentech-deal-23andme-has-a-business-plan/#702680222be9. 'GSK and 23andMe sign agreement to leverage genetic insights for the development of novel medicines', *23andMe*, 25 July 2018. Available at: https://mediacenter.23andme.com/press-releases/gsk-and-23andme-sign-agreement-to-leverage-genetic-insights-for-the-development-of-novel-medicines.

8 M. Molteni, '23andMe's pharma deals have been the plan all along', *Wired*, 3 August 2018. Available at: https://www.wired.com/story/23andme-glaxosmithkline-pharma-deal.

9 *Ibid.*

10 D. G. Altman, 'The scandal of poor medical research' (1994) 308 *BMJ* 283–284. R. Smith, 'Medical research – still a scandal', *BMJ Opinion*, 31 January 2014. Available at: https://blogs.bmj.com/bmj/2014/01/31/richard-smith-medical-research-still-a-scandal.

11 I. Chalmers and P. Glasziou, 'Avoidable waste in the production and reporting of research evidence' (2009) 374 *The Lancet* 86–89.

12 J. P. Ioannidis, 'Why most published research findings are false' (2005) 2 *PLoS Med* e124. See also R. Smith 'Time for science to be about truth rather than careers', *BMJ Opinion*, 9 September 2013. Available at: https://blogs.bmj.com/bmj/2013/09/09/richard-smith-time-for-science-to-be-about-truth-rather-than-careers.

13 Ioannidis, *supra* note 12, 699–700.

14 S. Kleinert and R. Horton, 'How should medical science change?' (2014) 383 *The Lancet* 197–198.

GDPR aims to avoid so that brilliant research will not be impeded. However, by not defining 'scientific research', the GDPR may extend the privilege it affords such research to an unintentionally broad range of actors and activities. This may in its utmost consequence endanger the research participants' legitimate expectations, trust and fundamental rights, and – as illustrated by the Cambridge Analytica case – may even endanger democracy as such.

Thus, I aim to identify the criteria for assessing what constitutes 'scientific research' in the GDPR. Health research is used as an example throughout, as it often entails the processing of large amounts of sensitive data and provides a good illustration of unclear boundaries. Unless the 'scientific research' term is clarified, it cannot function as a safeguard against misuse. To answer the research question of what the definition of 'scientific research' in the GDPR is and ought to be, I conduct a legal dogmatic analysis. First, an introductory overview of the privileged position data processing for scientific research purposes enjoys in the GDPR is provided. Second, a thorough review of the Court of Justice of the European Union (CJEU) and the European Court of Human Rights (ECtHR) jurisprudence on the subject matter is conducted in an effort to distil potential assessment criteria for what constitutes scientific research. Third, these assessment criteria are subject to a concluding *de lege ferenda* analysis, against the background of, *inter alia*, Helen Nissenbaum's theory on contextual integrity.[15] A lack of definition can, as demonstrated by the examples in this chapter, constitute a threat to the rule of law. This analysis is intended as a necessary building block to aid in the protection of fundamental rights and democracy.

2. THE PRIVILEGED POSITION OF SCIENTIFIC RESEARCH IN THE GDPR

Labouring under the assumption that all scientific research is beneficial, several special rules and derogations have been added to the GDPR to advance research. Recital 157 GDPR is particularly complimentary towards the potential of registry-based research. It states that '[b]y coupling information from registries, researchers can obtain new knowledge of great value with regard to widespread medical conditions' and '[r]esearch results obtained through registries provide solid, high-quality knowledge which can provide the basis for the formulation and implementation of knowledge-based policy, improve the quality of life for a number of people and improve the efficiency of social services'.[16]

[15] H. F. Nissenbaum, *Privacy in Context: Technology, Policy, and the Integrity of Social Life* (Stanford Law Books, 2010).

[16] Recital 157 GDPR.

2.1. LAWFUL BASIS FOR DATA PROCESSING

In order for the consent of a data subject to be valid, it must be 'freely given, specific, informed and unambiguous'.[17] However, for scientific research purposes, it is acknowledged that it can sometimes be impossible to fully identify the purpose at the time of data collection, rendering it equally impossible to obtain a specific consent. Hence, for these cases, an exception exists where data subjects are allowed to give their consent to certain areas of scientific research.[18] The controller must then seek other ways to ensure that the essence of the consent requirements is served and may apply further safeguards such as transparency.[19]

For medical research, consent is for ethical reasons usually required for the research participation as such.[20] When relying on other lawful bases than consent for the data processing, one separates the data processing even more clearly from that of the research participation, because scientific research can, but does not need to, depend on consent for the data processing.[21]

Other lawful bases for scientific research involving the processing of personal data include necessity for the performance of a task carried out in the public interest, necessity for the purposes of legitimate interests pursued by the

---

17 *Ibid.*, Article 4(11).

18 *Ibid.*, Recital 33.

19 Article 29 Data Protection Working Party (WP259 REV.01), *Guidelines on consent under Regulation 2016/679* (2018) 29. The European Data Protection Board has in Endorsement 1/2018 endorsed the guidelines.

20 Processing of personal data for scientific research purposes must also comply with other relevant legislation, such as that on clinical trials; cf. Recital 156 GDPR. Regulation 536/2014/EU applies for the purpose of consenting to the participation in scientific research activities in clinical trials; see Recital 161 GDPR.

21 Article 6(1)(a) GDPR. Note that not everyone agrees with this interpretation. In Sweden, consent is only deemed appropriate for private research. For public research, necessity must be the lawful basis for data processing. See Statens Offentliga Utredningar, 'Personuppgiftsbehandling för forskningsändamål' (2017) 50 *SOU* 163–167. The National Health Services Health Research Authority in the UK has published a GDPR operational guidance in which it states that 'the legal basis for processing data for health and social care research should NOT be consent. This means that requirements in the GDPR relating to consent do NOT apply to health and care research' (emphasis in original). This seems to go even further than the Swedish interpretation, in that it appears to relate to both public and private research. See NHS Health Research Authority, 'GDPR guidance for researchers and study coordinators. Consent in research', 19 April 2018, https://www.hra.nhs.uk/planning-and-improving-research/policies-standards-legislation/data-protection-and-information-governance/gdpr-guidance/what-law-says/consent-research. Furthermore, there is some disagreement, predominantly voiced in German scholarship, as to whether and how far public interest may apply to private bodies; see for instance P. Kramer, 'Art. 6 Rechtmäßigkeit der Verarbeitung' in H. Auernhammer, M. Eßner, P. Kramer and K. von Lewinski (eds.), *Heymanns Kommentare DSGVO BDSG* (5th ed., Carl Heymanns Verlag, 2017) 105.

controller or by a third party, and in some cases also necessity for compliance with a legal obligation to which the controller is subject.[22]

Processing of special categories of personal data such as health and genetic data is in general prohibited.[23] However, such data can be processed where this is necessary for scientific research purposes, provided that a legal basis exists in EU or Member State law and appropriate safeguards for the rights and freedoms of the data subject are in place.[24]

2.2. PURPOSE LIMITATION

The purpose limitation principle is one of the core principles of data protection law. It is defined as follows: 'Personal data shall be collected for specified, explicit and legitimate purposes and not further processed in a manner that is incompatible with those purposes.'[25] In order to ascertain compatibility, 'the context in which the personal data have been collected, in particular the reasonable expectations of data subjects based on their relationship with the controller as to their further use' should amongst other factors be taken into account.[26] A derogation is made from the compatibility dimension of the purpose limitation principle for scientific research purposes, for which further processing shall not be considered incompatible with the initial purposes.[27]

2.3. STORAGE LIMITATION

Another core principle is that of storage limitation.[28] When data is no longer necessary for the purposes for which it has been processed, it should be

---

22 Article 6(1)(e), (f) and (c) GDPR. The EDPS has stated that: 'Democratically-accountable parliaments … must always be able to control companies who, at the end of the day, are only accountable to their shareholders. That is why we must not be seduced by the Siren justifications of bad practices on grounds of "building community" or "connecting people" et cetera. That is why, under the GDPR, "public interest" is something to be defined by elected representatives in a law, not on the whim of a profit seeking company.' See EDPS, 'Speech to LIBE on the Facebook/Cambridge Analytica Case. Giovanni Buttarelli', 25 June 2018. Available at: https://edps.europa.eu/sites/edp/files/publication/25-06-18_speech_giovanni_hearing_libe_en.pdf, at 3. Some argue that universities are not 'public authorities' performing 'tasks'. See British Academy For The Humanities And Social Sciences and Economic & Social Research Council, *A British Academy and Economic & Social Research Council submission to the Department of Culture, Media and Sport (DCMS) call for views on the General Data Protection Regulation derogations* (2017) paragraph 16.

23 Article 9(1) GDPR.

24 Articles 9(2)(j) and 89(1) GDPR.

25 Article 5(1)(b) GDPR.

26 Recital 50 GDPR.

27 Article 5(1)(b) GDPR.

28 Article 5(1)(e) GDPR.

anonymised or erased. The right to erasure ('the right to be forgotten') does not apply if processing is necessary for scientific research purposes, subject to appropriate safeguards and that erasure 'is likely to render impossible or seriously impair the achievement of the objectives of that processing'.[29] Thus, further data retention can be lawful in the name of scientific research.

2.4. TRANSPARENCY

Personal data shall also be processed in a transparent manner.[30] At the time of data collection, the data subject should be informed according to the lists provided in Articles 13 and 14 GDPR to ensure fair and transparent data processing and enable the exercise of data subject rights.[31] However, if the personal data has not been obtained from the data subject and information provision is impossible or would involve a disproportionate effort, it is not necessary to impose the obligation to provide information. This is, again, subject to appropriate safeguards and the fact that erasure 'is likely to render impossible or seriously impair the achievement of the objectives of that processing'.[32] In conducting the assessment, the number of data subjects, the age of the data, and the adopted safeguards should be considered. Appropriate measures such as making the information publicly available should be taken.[33]

2.5. DATA SUBJECT RIGHTS

The data subject has a number of rights, some of which – subject to safeguards – can be derogated by EU or Member State law 'in so far as such rights are likely to render impossible or seriously impair the achievement of the specific purposes, and such derogations are necessary for the fulfilment of those purposes'.[34] Specifically, the rights the law may provide for derogations from are the right of access by the data subject, the right to rectification, the right to restriction of processing and the right to object to processing of personal data for scientific research purposes if the processing is 'necessary for the performance of a task carried out for reasons of public interest'.[35]

---

29 Articles 5(1)(e), 17(3)(d) and Recital 65 GDPR.
30 Article 5(1)(a) GDPR.
31 Articles 13 and 14 GDPR.
32 Article 14(5)(b) and Recital 62 GDPR.
33 Article 14(5)(b) GDPR.
34 Article 89(2) and Recital 156 GDPR.
35 Articles 15, 16, 18 and 21(6) GDPR.

2.6. THIRD-COUNTRY DATA TRANSFER

In residual cases, where no other grounds for transfer to third countries are applicable, transfer is still possible for the purposes of the compelling legitimate interests pursued by the controller following a thorough assessment of a number of factors, one of which is the consideration of 'the legitimate expectations of society for an increase of knowledge'.[36]

2.7. CODE OF CONDUCT

Even though Member States are allowed to maintain or introduce further conditions, including limitations, on the processing of health, genetic, and biometric data, these conditions cannot hamper the free flow of the data within the EU.[37] To contribute to the proper application of the GDPR and to specify its application, sector-specific codes of conduct can be drawn up.[38] For health research, a code of conduct is in the making, spearheaded by the European biobank network BBMRI-ERIC.[39] There is a strong push for an even more research-friendly interpretation of the GDPR, some of which is aimed at the drafting of the code of conduct.[40]

3. WHAT CONSTITUTES SCIENTIFIC RESEARCH?

3.1. THE TERM 'SCIENTIFIC RESEARCH' WITHIN THE CONTEXT OF THE GDPR

Despite not providing a definition for 'scientific research', Recital 159 GDPR offers some guidance on what the term is intended to include. It states that the term 'should be interpreted in a broad manner' and that it includes 'for example technological development and demonstration, fundamental research, applied research and privately funded research', as well as 'studies conducted in the public interest in the area of public health'.[41]

The formulations in Recital 159 GDPR seem not to have been reassuring to the Article 29 Data Protection Working Party. In guidelines endorsed by

---

36 Article 49(1) and Recital 113 GDPR.

37 Article 9(4) and Recital 53 GDPR.

38 Articles 40(1) and (2) GDPR.

39 Code of Conduct for Health Research. Available at: http://code-of-conduct-for-health-research.eu/faq. In addition, some Member States such as Italy and Belgium are drafting national codes of conduct.

40 B. Knoppers, 'Broaden human-rights focus for health data under GDPR' (2018) 558 *Nature* 189.

41 Recital 159 GDPR.

the European Data Protection Board (EDPB), the Working Party considered that the notion of scientific research 'may not be stretched beyond its common meaning and understands that "scientific research" in this context means a research project set up in accordance with relevant sector-related methodological and ethical standards, in conformity with good practice'.[42] Former European Data Protection Supervisor Giovanni Buttarelli likewise expressed that the biggest challenge for the freedom of scientific research lies in defining what genuine scientific research truly is. With reference to scientific research carried out by the private sector or by other privately funded research potentially also benefiting from the provisions relating to scientific research in the GDPR, he stated that we must be careful so that we do not stretch the definition of scientific research beyond its intended limits.[43] Recently, European Data Protection Supervisor Wojciech Wiewiorówski issued a preliminary opinion on data protection and scientific research in which the special data protection regime for scientific research is understood to apply where relevant sectoral standards of methodology and ethics apply, and the research is carried out with the aim of growing society's collective knowledge and wellbeing.[44]

Some Member States have in their national implementation of the GDPR defined sub-terms of scientific research. Ireland has, for instance, defined 'health research'.[45]

It is necessary to await clarification from the EU legislator or the CJEU before one with certainty can say how the term 'scientific research' is to be understood within the context of the GDPR. In the following sections, I conduct a legal and ethical analysis of the term that can hopefully serve to provide guidance and reflections in the meantime.

3.2. POTENTIAL ASSESSMENT CRITERIA

It could be argued that certain general terms, which may include 'scientific research', are to be interpreted in conformity with how they are interpreted in other EU legislation and in particular in the Treaties. Advocate General Tanchev describes a method for how this can be accomplished in his Opinion

---

42 WP259 REV.01 p. 28.

43 European Data Protection Supervisor, 'Fifth World Congress for Freedom of Scientific Research Speech by Giovanni Buttarelli', 12 April 2018, at 2. Available at: https://edps.europa.eu/sites/edp/files/publication/18-04-12_fifth_world_congress_freedom_scientific_research_en.pdf.

44 European Data Protection Supervisor, 'Preliminary Opinion on Data Protection and Scientific Research', 6 January 2020, at 12.

45 Data Protection Act 2018 (Section 36(2)) (Health Research) Regulations 2018 (S.I. No. 314/2018), provision 19.

in Case C-617/15 in relation to the term 'establishment': where no statutory definition has been included, and the court has not provided guidance, the term must be determined by recourse to sources beyond the legal instrument in question.[46]

There is a general void of data protection case law from the CJEU dealing with scientific research and, accordingly, as of March 2020, no clarification from the Court of what the term 'scientific research' encompasses in respect of the GDPR.

Article 13 of the Charter of Fundamental Rights of the European Union establishes freedom of the arts and sciences, specifying that the arts and scientific research shall be free of constraint. The Charter does not include a definition of scientific research.

As stated in the Treaty on the Functioning of the European Union (TFEU), the EU has an objective of 'strengthening its scientific and technological bases by achieving a European research area where researchers, scientific knowledge and technology circulate freely, and encouraging it to be more competitive, also in its industry'.[47] Legal obstacles to research cooperation shall be removed.[48] This shows the strong emphasis the EU places on scientific research and the link to industry; however, the TFEU does not include a statutory definition of scientific research.

Nevertheless, the CJEU has addressed scientific research in a number of cases in relation to other areas of EU law. A review of these cases – supplemented with a review of the cases from the ECtHR addressing scientific research – may indicate what the CJEU will consider 'scientific research' also within the context of the GDPR.

As none of the CJEU judgments mentioned below relate to the GDPR or the field of data protection, they are only legally binding for the interpretation of the GDPR if one assumes that the term 'scientific research' is autonomous. Furthermore, Advocate General Opinions and ECtHR judgments are included, which – even if they had dealt directly with the GDPR – would have carried substantial weight in the absence of other guidance, but would not have been legally binding for the interpretation. This review is a humble effort to deduce potential assessment criteria from real-life cases, some of which may be referred to if the question of the definition of 'scientific research' in the GDPR should ever come before the CJEU.

---

46 Case C-617/15 *Hummel Holding A/S v. Nike Inc. Nike Retail BV*, Opinion of Advocate General Tanchev, ECLI:EU:C:2017:13 (Court of Justice of the European Union) 24–50. Thank you to Luca Tosoni for making me aware of this Opinion.

47 Article 179(1) TFEU. See also H.B. Bentzen and N. Høstmælingen, 'Balancing protection and free movement of personal data: the new European Union General Data Protection Regulation' (2019) 170 *Annals of Internal Medicine* 335–337.

48 Article 179(2) TFEU.

The potential assessment criteria further elaborated upon below can be grouped into three main categories: (1) the role of the legal entity; (2) the role of those carrying out the activity; and (3) quality standards including scientific methodology.

3.2.1. The Role of the Legal Entity

The entity where the supposed scientific research activity takes place may be relevant. As pointed out by Advocate General Trstenjak in Case C-159/11 *Azienda Sanitaria Locale di Lecce* in reference to the Italian Università del Salento, 'the University's role, by law, consists in scientific research'.[49] This will frequently be the case for universities. However, universities are not the only institutions mentioned by the CJEU as entities where scientific research is carried out.

Research institutes may – as the name indicates – carry out scientific research. In the judgment in Case C-94/07 *Raccanelli*, the Max-Planck-Gesellschaft zur Förderung der Wissenschaften eV, which is established as an association operating in the public interest under German private law, is described as managing 'a number of scientific research institutes in Germany and other European States'.[50] However, names may be misleading, as shown in Case C-475/11 *Konstantinides*, in which a surgeon advertised himself on a website using terms to cover his professional activity such as 'German Institute' and 'European Institute', thus creating the impression that he provided services within a permanent institutional structure linked to scientific research, which prompted a complaint by the professional association.[51] Advocate General Cruz Villalón noted in his Opinion the importance attributed in Germany to the use of categories linked to the scientific research sector, and the important attraction this has from a commercial point of view.[52] The surgeon provided his services in a private clinic without any research activities.[53]

---

49 Case C-159/11 *Azienda Sanitaria Locale di Lecce v. Ordine degli Ingegneri della Provincia di Lecce, Consiglio Nazionale degli Ingegneri, Associazione delle Organizzazioni di Ingegneri, di Architettura e di Consultazione Tecnico-economica (OICE), Etacons srl, Ing. Vito Prato Engineering srl, Barletti – Del Grosso e Associati srl, Ordine degli Architetti della Provincia di Lecce, Consiglio Nazionale degli Architetti, Pianificatori, Paesaggisti e Conservatori*, Opinion of Advocate General Trstenjak, ECLI:EU:C:2012:303 (Court of Justice of the European Union) para. 77.

50 Case C-94/07 *Andrea Raccanelli v. Max-Planck-Gesellschaft zur Förderung der Wissenschaften eV. Reference for a Preliminary Ruling: Arbeitsgericht Bonn – Germany* ECLI:EU:C:2008:425 (Court of Justice of the European Union (Fifth Chamber)) para. 6.

51 Case C-475/11 *Kostas Konstantinides*, Opinion of Advocate General Cruz Villalón, ECLI:EU:C:2013:51 (Court of Justice of the European Union) paras. 9 and 53.

52 *Ibid.*, para. 34.

53 *Ibid.*, para. 67.

Committees and organisations may also conduct scientific research. In a case regarding food supplements, Case C-107/97 *Rombi and Arkopharma SA*, in the Opinion of Advocate General Fennelly, a European Commission-appointed committee of independent scientific experts is specifically referred to: 'cases show that, in exercising their discretion in relation to public health protection, the Member States must take into account the results of international scientific research and, in particular, the work of the Community's Scientific Committee for Food'.[54] France was criticised in the Opinion for having relied on two opinions by national authorities that could not be corroborated by international scientific research.[55] In a judgment regarding contamination of smoked salmon, Case C-121/00 *Hahn*, the same committee was mentioned as one to be taken account of. This time others were mentioned alongside it: 'the results of international scientific research, in particular the work of the Scientific Committee for Food and of the Codex Alimentarius Committee of the FAO (United Nations Food and Agriculture Organization) and the WHO (World Health Organization)'.[56] It goes on to mention the Community's scientific committees in general and the Scientific Committee on Veterinary Measures Relating to Public Health in particular.[57]

All these examples from the CJEU relate to public research entities. As is clear from Recital 159 GDPR, privately funded research is also covered by the term 'scientific research'. In the ECtHR case of *Elberte v. Latvia*, the State Centre for Forensic Medical Examination made an agreement with a pharmaceutical company to cooperate for the purposes of scientific research.[58] Pharmaceutical companies often have scientific research divisions conducting privately funded research, so their research is an example of what may be covered by the GDPR 'scientific research' term.

Not all those who conduct scientific research are affiliated with traditional research entities. An example can be seen in the ECtHR case of *Bubon v. Russia*, in which a lawyer also had contracts with well-known Russian publishing houses and legal magazines, for whom he wrote articles for law journals and online legal information databases and networks on topics of legal and

---

54 Case C-107/97 *Criminal Proceedings against Max Rombi and Arkopharma SA, the Party Liable at Civil Law, and Union fédérale des consommateurs 'Que Choisir?' and Organisation générale des consommateurs (Orgeco), Union départementale O6*, Opinion of Advocate General Fennelly, ECLI:EU:C:1998:500 (Court of Justice of the European Union) para. 40.

55 *Ibid.*, para. 43.

56 Case C-121/00 *Criminal Proceedings against Walter Hahn. Reference for a Preliminary Ruling: Bezirksgericht Innere Stadt Wien – Austria* ECLI:EU:C:2002:611 (Court of Justice of the European Union (Fifth Chamber)) para. 30. This was later repeated in Case C-95/01 *Ministère public v. John Greenham and Leonard Abel*, Opinion of Advocate General Mischo, ECLI:EU:C:2002:301 (Court of Justice of the European Union) paragraph 37.

57 *Hahn*, *supra* note 56, paras 40–41.

58 *Elberte v. Latvia* Application no. 61243/08 (European Court of Human Rights Fourth Section) 13 January 2015, para. 14.

social interest.[59] According to the applicant, this work usually required extensive scientific research.[60] However, this was merely stated as a fact of the case and the Court did not assess it. Another example can be the ECtHR case of *Hertel v. Switzerland*, in which a retired man with a degree in technical sciences conducted private research in his own laboratory.[61]

3.2.2. *The Role of those Carrying Out the Activity*

Frequently, the work being carried out at research entities is scientific research. A doctoral student with a grant contract with one of the Max Planck Institutes was in the *Raccanelli* judgment described as a researcher. Whether he could be considered a worker within the meaning of then-Article 39 EC depended on whether 'his activities are performed for a certain period of time under the direction of an institute forming part of that association [Max-Planck-Gesellschaft zur Förderung der Wissenschaften eV] and if, in return for those activities, he receives remuneration'.[62] In the ECtHR Grand Chamber case of *Gillberg v. Sweden*, a medical researcher at the University of Gothenburg refused on the basis of confidentiality to grant access to study data which included 'a very large amount of privacy-sensitive data about … children and their relatives'.[63] The ECtHR noted that 'the applicant was a public official researcher exercising public authority at a public institution, namely the University of Gothenburg. He was not the children's doctor or psychiatrist and he did not represent the children or the parents'.[64] The researcher was therefore not bound by professional secrecy to refuse disclosing the data to other researchers seeking access.[65]

However, not all work at universities and other entities where scientific research is typically carried out is scientific research. The judgment in Case C-40/14 *Utopia* shows where the border may be drawn. Utopia/Marshall Bioresources is a company importing live animals for laboratory research from the US to France.[66] There are rules providing for relief of import duties for animals specifically prepared for laboratory use intended for establishments

59 *Bubon v. Russia* Application no. 63898/09 (European Court of Human Rights Third Section) 7 February 2017, paras 6 and 7.

60 *Ibid.*, para. 7.

61 *Hertel v. Switzerland* 59/1997/843/1049 (European Court of Human Rights) 25 August 1998, para. 7.

62 *Raccanelli, supra* note 50, paras 37 and 53.

63 *Gillberg v. Sweden* Application no. 41723/06 (European Court of Human Rights Grand Chamber) 3 April 2012, para. 11.

64 *Ibid.*, para. 64.

65 *Ibid.*, paras 79–97.

66 Case C-40/14 *Direction générale des douanes et droits indirects, Chef de l'Agence de poursuites de la Direction nationale du renseignement et des enquêtes douanières, Direction régionale des douanes et droits indirects de Lyon v. Utopia SARL. Request for a Preliminary Ruling from the Cour de cassation (France)* ECLI:EU:C:2014:2389 (Court of Justice of the European Union (Eighth Chamber)) para. 14.

primarily engaged in scientific research. Also, the importer was found to be entitled to relief from import duties, although Utopia itself does not conduct scientific research: 'where animals specially prepared for laboratory use, which an importer brings into the European Union, are intended for a public establishment or an authorised private establishment which is principally engaged in education or scientific research, that importer, although it is not itself such an establishment, may be entitled to the relief from import duties provided for by that article for goods of this type'.[67] Ancillary activities closely related to scientific research may therefore possibly be included in the term.

Drawing the line between scientific research and other purposes can be challenging. One of the questions that was referred to the CJEU for a preliminary ruling in the judgment in Case C-34/10 *Brüstle* was whether the expression 'uses of human embryos for industrial or commercial purposes' in Directive 98/44/EC (relating to the patentability of biotechnological innovations), included commercial exploitation and especially use for the purpose of scientific research.[68] The Court answered this affirmatively, noting that: 'Although the aim of scientific research must be distinguished from industrial or commercial purposes, the use of human embryos for the purposes of research which constitutes the subject-matter of a patent application cannot be separated from the patent itself and the rights attaching to it.'[69] Patient treatment and scientific research can also at times be difficult to distinguish. In the ECtHR case of *Bataliny v. Russia*, a patient in a psychiatric hospital under forced treatment was subjected to scientific research by being treated with a new antipsychotic medication.[70] The Court found that this unconsented scientific research amounted to inhumane and degrading treatment within the meaning of Article 3 of the European Convention on Human Rights and hence a violation of this article.[71]

Once scientific data has been generally accepted, it may be applied in practice, and thus the purpose may change. For instance, in *Bataliny v. Russia*, once sufficient scientific data exists, the medications may be used routinely in clinical care. The administration of the medication will then no longer be perceived as scientific research, but as healthcare. Advocate General Mischo's Opinion in Case C-95/01 *Greenham and Abel* about whether there can be national legislation prohibiting the marketing of food supplements lawfully

---

67 *Ibid.*, para. 35.

68 C-34/10 *Oliver Brüstle v. Greenpeace e.V. Reference for a Preliminary Ruling: Bundesgerichtsh of – Germany* ECLI:EU:C:2011:669 (Court of Justice of the European Union (Grand Chamber)) para. 23. This judgment was later referred to in *Parrillo v. Italy* Application no. 46470/11 (European Court of Human Rights Grand Chamber) 27 August 2015, paras 59–61.

69 *Brüstle, supra* note 68, para. 43.

70 *Bataliny v. Russia* Application no. 10060/07 (European Court of Human Rights First Section) 23 July 2015, paras 13 and 38.

71 *Ibid.*, paras 90 and 91.

sold in other Member States refers to Article 1(3) of Directive 2001/15/EC, after which the use of nutritional substances in food shall result in safe products 'as established by generally accepted scientific data'.[72] In the Opinion of Advocate General Ruiz-Jarabo Colomer in Case C-157/99 *Smits and Peerbooms* regarding compulsory sickness insurance, it was explained that when assessing the national Dutch legislation, 'treatment is not recognised as normal where it is not provided or recommended because it has not been sufficiently endorsed by international or national scientific research. What matters is the extent to which a particular treatment is regarded as the appropriate professional procedure; if it has a valid scientific basis, it is recognised as a benefit within the meaning of the ZFW [Law on sickness funds]'.[73] However, research is not necessarily generally accepted. As explained in the Opinion of Advocate General Poiares Maduro in Case C-41/02 *Commission v. The Netherlands* regarding food additives, 'uncertainty might derive from conflicting scientific results. Secondly, in order to achieve scientific certainty it might be necessary to collect data which are not yet available, since the novelty of the product means, for example, that all its effects on health cannot be known. Lastly, the impossibility of achieving scientific certainty may only be a material one inasmuch as the costs involved in conducting scientific research or in adopting legislative measures act as a deterrent'.[74]

3.2.3. *Quality Standards Including Scientific Methodology and Scientific Publication*

The pursuit of scientific research as central to the EU is evident in Article 13 of the Charter of Fundamental Rights of the European Union, which provides that scientific research should be free of constraint and academic freedom must be respected. Hence, in the Opinion of Advocate General Mengozzi in Case C-219/11 *Brain Products GmbH*, the impact on the pursuit of scientific research was used as an argument not to ban the marketing of a product intended for cognitive science researchers.[75] The ECtHR Grand Chamber judgment

---

72 Case C-95/01, Opinion of Advocate General Mischo, *supra* note 56, paras 1 and 68.

73 Case C-157/99 *B.S.M. Geraets-Smits v. Stichting Ziekenfonds VGZ and H.T.M. Peerbooms v. Stichting CZ Groep Zorgverzekeringer*, Opinion of Advocate General Ruiz-Jarabo Colomer, ECLI:EU:C:2000:274 (Court of Justice of the European Union) para. 4. Similarly, see Case C-385/99 *V.G. Müller-Fauré v. Onderlinge Waarborgmaatschappij OZ Zorgverzekeringen UA and E.E.M. van Riet v. Onderlinge Waarborgmaatschappij ZAO Zorgverzekeringen*, Opinion of Advocate General Ruiz-Jarabo Colomer, ECLI:EU:C:2002:602 (Court of Justice of the European Union) para. 11 and footnote 38.

74 Case C-41/02 *Commission of the European Communities v. Kingdom of the Netherlands*, Opinion of Advocate General Poiares Maduro, ECLI:EU:C:2004:520 (Court of Justice of the European Union) para. 33.

75 Case C-219/11 *Brain Products GmbH v. BioSemi VOF and Others*, Opinion of Advocate General Mengozzi, ECLI:EU:C:2012:299 (Court of Justice of the European Union) paras 16 and 56.

in *Parrillo v. Italy* regarding an Italian ban on embryo donation for scientific purposes includes a dissenting opinion of Judge Sajó with a similar reasoning.[76] Judge Sajó recognised 'the strong social interest in the scientific research at stake'. He went on to state that a blanket ban on donation to medical research 'is not only overly restrictive of the individual's freedom of self-determination, it also disregards the constitutional values recognised in Article 33 of the Italian Constitution and the value system of the Convention, which recognises the Article 10 interest in scientific research'. He concluded that:

> Whether or not the Government's desire to protect the potential for life outweighs the applicant's interest in using her own genetic material to contribute to life-saving science is a question that cannot be dismissed out of hand. The judgment in this case lacks any sort of proportionality analysis; nor does it consider the important third-party interest in the health benefits arising from scientific discovery ... The law disregards the interest in preventing actual human suffering through scientific research in the name of the protection of a *potential* for life which, moreover, cannot ever materialise in the circumstances of the case.[77]

In the Opinion of Advocate General Mengozzi in Case C-15/13 *Technische Universität Hamburg-Harburg*, it was expressed that the autonomy of universities in relation to research is 'an expression of values of a constitutional nature common to the legal systems of the Member States and enshrined in the Charter'.[78]

The GDPR distinguishes between scientific research, historical research, statistical purposes and archiving purposes in the public interest. In the Joint Concurring Opinion of Judges Sajó, Vučinić and Kūris in the ECtHR case of *Mustafa Erdoğan and Others v. Turkey*, they state that:

> As a matter of principle, social and legal scientists' contributions to public discourse and other 'extramural' utterances that are based on their research, professional expertise and competence serve the public interest. It is for this reason that social and legal scientists' judgments, those of value no less than those of fact, where these academics freely express their views and opinions on matters belonging to the area of their research, professional expertise and competence, deserve the highest level of protection under Article 10.[79]

---

76 *Parrillo v. Italy, supra* note 68.

77 *Ibid.*, Dissenting Opinion of Judge Sajó, paras 13, 18 and 19, emphasis in original.

78 Case C-15/13 *Technische Universität Hamburg-Harburg, Hochschul-Informations-System GmbH v. Datenlotsen Informationssysteme GmbH*, Opinion of Advocate General Mengozzi, ECLI:EU:C:2014:23 (Court of Justice of the European Union) para. 73.

79 *Mustafa Erdoğan and Others v. Turkey* Application nos. 346/04 and 39779/04 (European Court of Human Rights Second Section) 27 May 2014, Joint Concurring Opinion of Judges Sajó, Vučinić and Kūris, para. 6.

There has been criticism that some of the research provisions are better tailored to that of biomedical research than social science research.[80] Statistics can be a part of scientific research, but can also be separate from it, by for instance being used for quality assurance purposes.

A reference to 'sound' scientific research is evident in the Opinion of Advocate General Trstenjak in Case C-319/05 *Commission v. Germany*, where it is stated that both the dangers and effect of medicinal products 'must be examined using information based on sound scientific research'.[81] This is repeated in his Opinion in Case C-140/07 *Hecht-Pharma GmbH*.[82] There are references to the 'results of international scientific research' in numerous judgments from the CJEU.[83] In the Opinion of Advocate General van Gerven in Case C-290/90 *Commission v. Germany* regarding whether a French firm's eye lotions are medicinal products, he noted that a Member State must plausibly demonstrate 'on the basis of the results of international scientific research and, in particular, the findings of specialized committees operating at Community level, that a given product is a medicinal product for the purposes of Directive 65/65. If the Commission wishes to contest the data furnished by the Member State, it must do so on the basis of equally reliable data'.[84] Advocate General Bobek clarified in his Opinion in Case C-672/15 *Noria Distribution SARL* about food supplements:

> [W]hat the case-law seems to me to be primarily concerned with is the *quality* of the data relied on (in terms of its credibility, accuracy, and relevance), not necessarily the

80 British Academy For The Humanities And Social Sciences and Economic & Social Research Council, *supra* note 22, para. 8.

81 Case C-319/05 *Commission of the European Communities v. Federal Republic of Germany*, Opinion of Advocate General Trstenjak, ECLI:EU:C:2007:364 (Court of Justice of the European Union) para. 44.

82 Case C-140/07 *Hecht-Pharma GmbH v. Staatliches Gewerbeaufsichtsamt Lüneburg*, Opinion of Advocate General Trstenjak, ECLI:EU:C:2008:352 (Court of Justice of the European Union) para. 63.

83 See for instance Case C-304/84 *Criminal Proceedings against Claude Muller and Others* ECLI:EU:C:1986:194 (Court of Justice of the European Union (Fifth Chamber)) para. 24; Case C-42/90 *Criminal Proceedings against Jean-Claude Bellon* ECR I-4863 (Court of Justice of the European Union (First Chamber)) para. 17; Case C-192/01 *Commission of the European Communities v. Kingdom of Denmark* ECLI:EU:C:2003:492 (Court of Justice of the European Union) para. 46; Case C-24/00 *Commission of the European Communities v. French Republic* ECLI:EU:C:2004:70 (Court of Justice of the European Union (Sixth Chamber)) para. 53; and Case C-446/08 *Solgar Vitamin's France, Valorimer SARL, Christian Fenioux, L'Arbre de Vie SARL, Source Claire, Nord Plantes EURL, RCS Distribution, Ponroy Santé, Syndicat de la Diététique et des Compléments Alimentaires v. Ministre de l'Économie, des Finances et de l'Emploi, Ministre de la Santé, de la Jeunesse et des Sports, Ministre de l'Agriculture et de la Pêche* ECLI:EU:C:2010:233 (Court of Justice of the European Union (Third Chamber)) para. 55.

84 Case C-290/90 *Commission of the European Communities v. Federal Republic of Germany*, Opinion of Advocate General van Gerven, ECLI:EU:C:1992:125 (Court of Justice of the European Union) point 5. A similar statement is made in Case C-319/05, Opinion of Advocate General Trstenjak, *supra* note 81, para. 47 in relation to Directive 2001/83.

> *origin* of the data (national or international). Whether or not full risk assessments in practice rely on sources from 1, 2 or 10 countries appears rather irrelevant in itself. What is relevant is whether the data relied on is convincing and not contradicted by other significant stream of research.[85]

Quality is alluded to in several judgments. In the Opinion of Advocate General Bobek in the *Noria Distribution SARL* case, it is stated that 'the risk assessment must be based on data of a certain quality. For example, Article 5 of the Directive refers to "generally accepted scientific data"'.[86] In the judgment in Case C-446/08 *Solgar Vitamin's France* about maximum amounts of vitamins and minerals in food supplements, the requirement of 'a risk assessment based on generally accepted scientific data' was stated.[87] The same requirement was highlighted in the *Noria Distribution SARL* judgment.[88]

In the same vein, in the *Noria Distribution SARL* judgment, 'a comprehensive scientific assessment of the risks for public health, based not on general or hypothetical considerations, but on relevant scientific data' is required.[89] Similarly, in the Opinion of Advocate General Léger in Case C-215/04 *Marius Pedersen AS* about waste shipment, it is stated that a risk assessment 'must be made on the basis of relevant scientific research and not on that of general considerations'.[90] In the judgment in Case C-17/93 *Van der Veldt* regarding salt content in bread, the Court specified that 'risk must be measured, not according to the yardstick of general conjecture, but on the basis of relevant scientific research'.[91] This statement was repeated in the Opinion of Advocate General Poiares Maduro in Case C-41/02 *Commission v. The Netherlands* about vitamin-fortified foods.[92] In the Opinion of Advocate General Bobek in Case C-528/16 *Confédération paysanne and Others* regarding mutagenesis, a different phrasing is used, denoting the same, that '"risk uncertainty" does not mean mere general doubts. Concrete risks for human health or the environment must be identified, supported by a minimum amount of serious and independent

85 Case C-672/15 *Procureur de la République v. Noria Distribution SARL*, Opinion of Advocate General Bobek, ECLI:EU:C:2016:961 (Court of Justice of the European Union) para. 89.

86 *Ibid.*, para. 77.

87 *Solgar Vitamin's France*, *supra* note 83, para. 32.

88 Case C-672/15 *Criminal Proceedings against Noria Distribution SARL* ECLI:EU:C:2017:310 (Court of Justice of the European Union (First Chamber)) para. 16.

89 *Ibid.*, para. 42.

90 Case C-215/04 *Opinion of Advocate General Léger. Marius Pedersen A/S v. Miljøstyrelsen* ECLI:EU:C:2005:178 (Court of Justice of the European Union) para. 37.

91 Case C-17/93 *Criminal Proceedings against J.J.J. Van der Veldt. Reference for a Preliminary Ruling: Rechtbank van eerste aanleg Gent – Belgium* ECLI:EU:C:1994:299 (Court of Justice of the European Union (Fifth Chamber)) para. 17.

92 Case C-41/02, Opinion of Advocate General Poiares Maduro, *supra* note 74, footnote 36.

scientific research. A fear of a risk, or risk of a risk, is not enough' and, further, 'protective measures "cannot validly be based on a purely hypothetical approach to the risk, founded on mere assumptions which have not yet been scientifically verified"'.[93]

Scientific research can be dynamic. This can be exemplified by the development in tobacco-related research. In the Opinion of Advocate General Kokott in Case C-477/14 *Pillbox 38* regarding the regulation of e-cigarettes and menthol cigarettes, 'the current state of scientific research' is referred to.[94] It is stated that 'conventional tobacco products are well known on the market and their health risks have been widely researched, whilst a feature of e-cigarettes, at least at present, is that they are novel and – in large parts of the population – still relatively unknown'.[95] Furthermore, Advocate General Kokott went on to state that 'Both sides rely on scientific studies in support of their respective arguments. However, both sides also recognise that further research into e-cigarettes is still required in order to establish a more reliable basis for evaluating this novel product and the risks to human health which it may cause'.[96] Rules made in the context of policy of protecting human or animal health must be reviewed if the basis for their adoption changes, such as 'further information becoming available through scientific research', as held by the CJEU in Case C-54/85 *Mirepoix* regarding national legislation prohibiting the use of a pesticide.[97] In general, the Court frequently holds in its judgments that risk assessments need to be based 'on the most reliable scientific data available and the most recent results of international research'.[98] This is also in line with Article 114(3) of

---

93 Case C-528/16 *Confédération paysanne, Réseau Semences Paysannes, Les Amis de la Terre France, Collectif vigilance OGM et Pesticides 16, Vigilance OG2M, CSFV 49, OGM dangers, Vigilance OGM 33, Fédération Nature & Progrès v. Premier ministre, Ministre de l'agriculture, de l'agroalimentaire et de la forêt*, Opinion of Advocate General Bobek, ECLI:EU:C:2018:20 (Court of Justice of the European Union) paras 49 and 148.

94 Case C-477/14 *Pillbox 38 (UK) Limited v. Secretary of State for Health*, Opinion of Advocate General Kokott, ECLI:EU:C:2015:854 (Court of Justice of the European Union) para. 64.

95 *Ibid.*, para. 49.

96 *Ibid.*, para. 63.

97 Case C-54/85 *Ministère public v. Xavier Mirepoix. Reference for a Preliminary Ruling: Tribunal de police de Dijon – France* ECLI:EU:C:1986:123 (Court of Justice of the European Union (Third Chamber)) point 16. Later and similarly, see Case C-333/14 *The Scotch Whisky Association and Others v. The Lord Advocate, The Advocate General for Scotland*, Opinion of Advocate General Bot, ECLI:EU:C:2015:527 (Court of Justice of the European Union) para. 103; and Joined Cases C-78/16 and C-79/16 *Giovanni Pesce and Others (C-78/16), Cesare Serinelli and Others (C-79/16) v. Presidenza del Consiglio dei Ministri (C-79/16), Presidenza del Consiglio dei Ministri – Dipartimento della Protezione Civile, Commissario Delegato per Fronteggiare il Rischio Fitosanitario connesso alla Diffusione della Xylella nel Territorio della Regione Puglia, Ministero delle Politiche Agricole Alimentari e Forestali, Regione Puglia*, Opinion of Advocate General Bot, ECLI:EU:C:2016:340 (Court of Justice of the European Union) para. 103.

98 Case C-41/02 *Commission of the European Communities v. Kingdom of the Netherlands* ECLI:EU:C:2004:762 (Court of Justice of the European Union (Third Chamber)) para. 53.

the Treaty on the Functioning of the European Union, after which 'any new development based on scientific facts' will be taken into account for a high level of protection concerning health, safety, environmental protection and consumer protection.

Adherence to scientific methodology can be of importance in the assessment of whether an activity is 'scientific research'. In the ECtHR Grand Chamber case of *Aksu v. Turkey*, three publications – one book and two dictionaries – that had received government funding were claimed to be insulting toward the Roma community in Turkey.[99] The Court noted that the book had been written by an academic and the method was scientific, referring to the fact that the academic 'had collected information from members of the Roma community, local authorities and the police. He also stated that he had lived with the Roma community to observe their lifestyle according to scientific observation principles'.[100] Similarly, in the ECtHR case of *Sapan v. Turkey*, importance was placed on the fact that the applicant was an academic adhering to scientific methodology: 'L'auteur de ce livre est une universitaire qui a analysé le phénomène de star et l'apparition de ce phénomène en Turquie avant d'étudier l'arrivée du chanteur sur la scène musicale et sa consécration comme star. L'ouvrage litigieux traite donc, à travers Tarkan et par le biais d'outils scientifiques, du phénomène de société que sont les stars.'[101] In other words, the author was an academic who with the use of scientific methodology analysed the star phenomenon and the appearance of this phenomenon in Turkey through the star singer Tarkan.

In the ECtHR case of *Brincat and Others v. Malta*, which concerned whether the Maltese government had failed to protect again asbestos, it was necessary to determine if the Maltese government knew or ought to have known in the early 1970s of the dangers associated with exposure to asbestos.[102] The Court

---

Similarly, see Case C-236/01 *Monsanto Agricoltura Italia SpA and Others v. Presidenza del Consiglio dei Ministri and Others* ECLI:EU:C:2003:431 (Court of Justice of the European Union) para. 113; *Commission v. Denmark*, *supra* note 83, para. 51; Case C-95/01 *Criminal Proceedings Pending before That Court against John Greenham and Léonard Abel* ECLI:EU:C:2004:71 (Court of Justice of the European Union (Sixth Chamber)) para. 47; Case C-333/08 *European Commission v. French Republic* ECLI:EU:C:2010:44 (Court of Justice of the European Union (Third Chamber)) para. 92; Case C-343/09 *Afton Chemical Limited v. Secretary of State for Transport* ECLI:EU:C:2010:419 (Court of Justice of the European Union (Fourth Chamber)) para. 60; Case C-282/15 *Queisser Pharma GmbH & Co. KG v. Bundesrepublik Deutschland* ECLI:EU:C:2017:26 (Court of Justice of the European Union (Fourth Chamber)) para. 56; *Noria Distribution SARL*, *supra* note 88, para. 49; Case C-528/16, Opinion of Advocate General Bobek, *supra* note 93, para. 49.

99 *Aksu v. Turkey* Application nos. 4149/04 and 41029/04 (European Court of Human Rights Grand Chamber) 15 March 2012, paras 3 and 69.

100 *Ibid.*, paras 71 and 72.

101 *Sapan v. Turkey* Application no. 44102/04 (European Court of Human Rights Second Section) 8 June 2010, para. 34. The official version is only available in French.

102 *Brincat and Others v. Malta* Application nos. 60908/11, 62110/11, 62129/11, 62312/11 and 62338/11 (European Court of Human Rights Fifth Section) 24 July 2014, para. 3.

stated that it had to rely on 'objective scientific research' to assess this and took account of a list submitted by the applicants 'which contains references to hundreds of articles or other publications concerning the subject at issue published from 1930 onwards – many of them taken from reputable British medical journals'.[103] Hence, publication in reputable scientific journals may be an assessment factor for whether the work is scientific research. A handbook written by an academic is distinguished from scientific publications by not containing original ideas, citations, sources, or a bibliography. This was stated by the parties to the ECtHR case of *Hasan Yazici v. Turkey* and in the Turkish court case referenced by the ECtHR.[104]

The cases seem to imply a certain quality standard of scientific research, describing it as sound, serious, independent and adhering to scientific methodology. The scientific research may be published in scientific journals. In fact, in the Opinion of Advocate General Poiares Maduro in *Commission v. The Netherlands*, there is a reference to 'the findings of a scientific study – the quality of which is subject to special scrutiny'.[105]

Some may operate under the guise of scientific research. The following quote from the ECtHR Grand Chamber case of *Perinçek v. Switzerland* can serve as an example of a disguised agenda: 'Holocaust denial, even if dressed up as impartial historical research, must invariably be seen as connoting an antidemocratic ideology and anti-Semitism.'[106]

3.2.4. Potential Assessment Criteria Based on Jurisprudence

There are three main potential assessment criteria to be derived from jurisprudence: the role of the legal entity; the role of the persons carrying out the activity; and quality standards including scientific methodology and scientific publication.

The legal entity where the supposed scientific research activity takes place may be relevant, bearing in mind that not all those who conduct scientific research are affiliated with traditional research entities. Research institutes may carry out scientific research, but the entity's name can be misleading. Furthermore, committees and organisations may also conduct scientific research. Both publicly and privately funded research is covered by the term.

---

[103] *Ibid.*, para. 106. Many Maltese medical graduates used to continue their studies in Britain, hence the specific reference to British medical journals.

[104] *Hasan Yazici v. Turkey* Application no. 40877/07 (European Court of Human Rights Second Section) 15 April 2014, paras 17, 35 and 44.

[105] Case C-41/02, Opinion of Advocate General Poiares Maduro, *supra* note 74, para. 34.

[106] *Perinçek v. Switzerland* Application no. 27510/08 (European Court of Human Rights Grand Chamber) 15 October 2015, para. 253.

The role of the person or persons carrying out the activity may be relevant. Frequently, the work being carried out at research entities is scientific research, but not all work at universities and other entities where scientific research is typically carried out is scientific research. However, ancillary activities closely related to scientific research may possibly be included in the term. Drawing the line between scientific research and other purposes can be challenging.

Quality standards including scientific methodology may be relevant. The courts typically refer to scientific research as being sound, serious, independent and adhering to scientific methodology. The work having been subject to the special scrutiny that scientific publication involves may also be a factor.

4. *DE LEGE FERENDA*

The assessment criteria that can be derived from jurisprudence may not provide sufficient safeguards. A recent research study may be illustrative. Stanford researchers used approximately 300,000 photographs from online dating sites – with ethical approval from Stanford University's IRB, but without the data subjects' knowledge or consent – to classify based on facial image who is heterosexual and who is gay. Half the images were from each group. The algorithm was very accurate, being able to correctly classify between 81 per cent and 91 per cent of the men and between 71 per cent and 83 per cent of the women according to sexual orientation, depending on the number of photographs available.[107] Tools such as these can be misused by countries where homosexuality is illegal, and it is difficult to see any need for such a tool apart from the researchers' warning and awareness-raising that those with bad intentions can do the same.[108] This poses a threat both to individuals' fundamental rights and to democracy. However, revisiting the potential assessment criteria for scientific research that could be deducted from the legal analysis, the Stanford study seems to fulfil all of them. It is only if one supplements those criteria with a respect for context and a requirement that the research needs to be ethical that fundamental rights and values are protected.

An editorial in the prestigious scientific journal *Nature* stated that a common theme in scientific research controversies such as the Stanford study and Cambridge Analytica is that '[d]ata were used in ways well beyond what users expected or intended. Bundled together and trawled by algorithms, innocuous data points can reveal information that users might reasonably

107 Y. Wang and M. Kosinski, 'Deep neural networks are more accurate than humans at detecting sexual orientation from facial images' (2018) 114 *J Pers Soc Psychol* 246–257, at 250.

108 *Ibid.*, 255.

expect to stay private and that might be used in ways they are not happy with.'[109] In other words, context and data subjects' legitimate expectations matter and must be respected.

When ascertaining the compatible use dimension of the purpose limitation principle, the GDPR Recital notes that 'the context in which the personal data have been collected, in particular the reasonable expectations of data subjects based on their relationship with the controller as to their further use' be taken into account.[110] Philosopher Helen Nissenbaum's theory on contextual integrity may offer elements that can be useful in defining the appropriate boundaries of scientific research that ought to enjoy the GDPR privileges.[111] The key concept revolves around a right to *appropriate* flow of personal data: Nissenbaum argues that within each individual context, there are informational norms that prescribe the types of information, the data subjects as well as those sending and receiving the data, and information transmission principles that apply.[112] When context-relative informational norms are contravened, we experience it as a privacy violation.[113]

The former European Data Protection Supervisor stated in a speech to the European Parliament Committee on Civil Liberties, Justice and Home Affairs that: 'Legitimate interest is appropriate where a company can assess that the risk to the individual is minimal. But for the most intimate sphere, our communications and behaviour when connected, we cannot now give any opportunity for loopholes. Consumers expect their data to be used within the context it was collected or by entities with which they have a relationship.'[114] This describes what Charles Ess denotes as a shift in data privacy from individual to relational conceptions of selfhood, a notion that aligns well with Nissenbaum's theory on contextual integrity and the gist of the purpose limitation principle's compatible use dimension.[115] By emphasising the intimate sphere and our communications and behaviour when connected, a sense of identity is described as interwoven with various relationships that define individuals as relational selves.[116]

---

109 'Cambridge Analytica controversy must spur researchers to update data ethics' (2018) 555 *Nature* 559–560. Another research study that can be mentioned alongside these is the Harvard 'Taste, ties, and time' study. See K. Lewis et al., 'Tastes, ties, and time: A new social network dataset using Facebook.com' (2008) 30 *Social Networks* 330–342. See criticism in for instance M. Zimmer, "But the data is already public': on the ethics of research in Facebook' (2010) 12 *Ethics and Information Technology* 313–325.

110 Recital 50 GDPR.

111 Nissenbaum, *supra* note 15.

112 *Ibid.*, 140–141.

113 *Ibid.*, 127.

114 EDPS, *supra* note 22, at 4.

115 C. Ess, 'New selves, new research ethics?' in H. Fossheim and H. Ingierd (eds.), *Internet research ethics* (Cappelen Damm, 2015) at 48–50.

116 *Ibid.*, 49.

There are research guidelines that respect contextual integrity and combine individual and relational conceptions of selfhood, such as the Norwegian internet research guidelines.[117] Four factors in the guidelines are deemed particularly relevant in the ethical assessment: the accessibility of the data in the public sphere; the sensitivity of the data; the vulnerability of the data subjects; and the interaction with the data subjects.[118] These guidelines successfully bridge the understanding of public and private life online by respecting the expectation of publicity and the context – for instance, social media or online dating – where the data is available.

Recital 33 GDPR, which allows for broad consent in certain circumstances, only applies when the scientific research complies with recognised ethical standards. It can also be argued that the principle of accountability similarly implies adherence not just to the letter of the law, but also to the spirit of it, which may encompass an ethical standard for scientific research that is undertaken in accordance with the GDPR.[119] The European Data Protection Supervisor has in fact signalled that genuine scientific research equals ethical scientific research and has indicated that the EDPB can play a decisive role going forward by delivering sound guidance complementing and reinforcing the GDPR on the matter.[120] Aligning with this interpretation of the GDPR accountability principle, the above-mentioned *Nature* editorial concluded that: 'All researchers have a duty to consider the ethics of their work beyond the strict limits of law or today's regulations. If they don't, they will face serious and continued loss of public trust.'[121]

Adding an additional criterion – an ethical assessment including respect for context – will make the definition of 'scientific research' more robust and safeguard against cases such as Cambridge Analytica and studies in the same vein as the Stanford study.

5. CONCLUDING REMARKS

'Scientific research' in the GDPR ought to be assessed according to four main criteria: (1) the role of the legal entity; (2) the role of the person(s) carrying out

117 NESH, 'The National Committee for Research Ethics in the Social Sciences and the Humanities, A Guide to Internet Research Ethics', 2nd ed., June 2019. Available at: https://www.etikkom.no/globalassets/documents/publikasjoner-som-pdf/forskningsetisk-veileder-for-internettforskning/a-guide-to-internet-research-ethics.pdf. Ess, *supra* note 115, 57–59.

118 NESH, *supra* note 117, at 5.

119 Article 5(2) GDPR.

120 European Data Protection Supervisor, *supra* note 43, 2–3.

121 'Cambridge Analytica controversy must spur researchers to update data ethics', *supra* note 109.

the activity; (3) quality standards, including scientific methodology and scientific publication; and (4) an ethical assessment, including respect for context. In combination, these four criteria provide robust safeguards, protecting both individuals and democracy.

The United Nations Special Rapporteur on the Right to Privacy, Joseph A. Cannataci, has in Article 3 of his *Recommendation on the Protection and Use of Health-Related Data* included these four criteria alongside the main criteria of the OECD's Frascati Manual in the definition of 'scientific research', which reads:[122]

> 'scientific research' means creative and systematic work undertaken in order to increase the stock of knowledge and/or to devise new application of available knowledge. The activity must be novel, creative, uncertain, systematic, and transferable and/or reproducible. Factors for determining whether an activity is scientific research include the role of the legal entity where the activity is carried out; the role of the natural person(s) carrying out the activity; quality standards including use of scientific methodology and scientific publication; and adherence to research ethical norms. Research within any discipline that may process health-related data, including medical and health sciences, natural sciences, engineering and technology, social sciences, humanities and fine arts, is scientific research. The scientific research may be basic research, applied research or experimental development, and policy analysis, health services and epidemiology are all examples of scientific research. Scientific research can be both publicly and privately funded and conducted, and may in some cases be conducted for profit.[123]

This definition provides a more sustainable protection of fundamental rights, and ought to serve as an inspiration for further definition efforts of the concept of 'scientific research'.

The introductory quote by Cambridge Analytica whistleblower Christopher Wylie seems fitting. Forgetting about the reasonable expectation of the user, which – as Nissenbaum explains – is tied to the context in which the data processing happens and the integrity of that context is a recipe for a loss of trustworthiness. The GDPR concessions for scientific research are an acknowledgement of its importance, so misuse of research data for other purposes and unethically and/or poorly conducted research represents

---

122 OECD, Frascati Manual 2015. Available at: http://www.oecd.org/sti/frascati-manual-2015-9789264239012-en.htm.

123 The United Nations Special Rapporteur On The Right To Privacy, 'Recommendation on the Protection and Use of Health-Related Data', 5 December 2019. Available at: https://www.ohchr.org/Documents/Issues/Privacy/SR_Privacy/UNSRPhealthrelated dataRecCLEAN.pdf. The author of this chapter is a member of the United Nations Special Rapporteur on the Right to Privacy's Task Force on Privacy and the Protection of Health-Related Data, and contributed to the drafting of the Recommendation.

a problem to the reputation of all research. Trustworthiness is typically seen as comprised of two main elements – transparency and accountability – both of which are key principles of the GDPR. Opaque data processing avoids democratic control and may endanger fundamental rights and freedoms, and even democracy itself. Hence, these principles must be the core focus for data processing for scientific research purposes going forward.

INVITED CONTRIBUTION

19. TACKLING MIS- AND DISINFORMATION IN THE CONTEXT OF SCIENTIFIC UNCERTAINTY

The Ongoing Case of the COVID-19 'Infodemic'

Mihalis KRITIKOS*

1. INTRODUCTION

Since the World Health Organization (WHO) declared the 2019–20 coronavirus (COVID-19) outbreak a Public Health Emergency of International Concern (PHEIC) on 30 January 2020,[1] and a pandemic on 11 March 2020,[2] several countries around the world have put in place measures to combat the health crisis. Such measures included travel bans,[3] restrictions on public movement and allowing trips only to buy food, medicines or other essential products.[4]

---

* Scientific Foresight Unit (STOA), European Parliament Research Service (EPRS), European Parliament. E-mail: mihalis.kritikos@europarl.europa.eu. The views represented in this contribution are solely of the author and do not necessarily represent the viewpoint on the European Parliament.

1 WHO, 'Statement on the second meeting of the International Health Regulations (2005) Emergency Committee regarding the outbreak of novel coronavirus (2019-nCoV)', 30 January 2020, https://www.who.int/news-room/detail/30-01-2020-statement-on-the-second-meeting-of-the-international-health-regulations-(2005)-emergency-committee-regarding-the-outbreak-of-novel-coronavirus-(2019-ncov).

2 WHO, 'WHO Director-General's opening remarks at the media briefing on COVID-19', Press release, 11 March 2020, https://www.who.int/dg/speeches/detail/who-director-general-s-opening-remarks-at-the-media-briefing-on-covid-19---11-march-2020.

3 P. CONNOR, 'More than nine-in-ten people worldwide live in countries with travel restrictions amid COVID-19', *Pew Research Center*, 1 April 2020, https://www.pewresearch.org/fact-tank/2020/04/01/more-than-nine-in-ten-people-worldwide-live-in-countries-with-travel-restrictions-amid-covid-19/.

4 WORLDAWARE, 'COVID-19 Alert: European Countries Continue Enforcing Movement & Business Restrictions', 8 April 2020, https://www.worldaware.com/covid-19-alert-european-countries-continue-enforcing-movement-business-restrictions-april-8.

In such imposed, limited circumstances, people have been increasingly resorting to the Internet to socialise and to find therein reliable information about all aspects related to the outbreak, containment and fighting of the disease, as well personal hygiene advice.[5] Social media platforms have long been an essential source for staying informed, but also for mis- and disinformation. The COVID-19 pandemic has only amplified this; it has been estimated that Internet traffic has increased by more than 70 per cent, which, at the same time, puts more pressure on the communications infrastructure around the world.[6] As people are encountering a large volume of coronavirus-related material on social media platforms, the virus has provided sufficient grounds for a tsunami of misinformation, disinformation and conspiracy theories, among others.[7]

In February 2020, Tedros Adhanom Ghebreyesus, WHO Director-General, referred to the combat against disinformation and related practices around COVID-19 and the pandemic as fighting an 'infodemic'. This phenomenon has been described as an overabundance of information, rendering it difficult to find trustworthy sources thereof and to differentiate from falsehood,[8] and to find reliable guidance. In other words, 'infodemic' is an uncontrolled propagation of highly socially dangerous information.[9] The 'infodemic' is a specific challenge given that 'fake news spreads faster and more easily than the virus, and it is just as dangerous.'[10] Cristina Tardáguila, Associate Director of the International Fact-Checking Network (IFCN), has called COVID-19

---

5 M. McKee, M.C.I. van Schalkwyk and D. Stuckler, 'The second information revolution: Digitalization brings opportunities and concerns for public health', (2019) 29 *European Journal of Environmental Public Health* 3–6.

6 C. Kang, D. Alba and A. Satariano, 'Surging Traffic Is Slowing Down Our Internet', *New York Times*, 26 March 2020, https://www.nytimes.com/2020/03/26/business/coronavirus-internet-traffic-speed.html.

7 D.M.J. Lazer, M.A. Baum, Y. Benkler, A.J. Berinsky; K.M. Greenhill, F. Menczer, M.J. Metzger, B. Nyhan, G. Pennycook, D. Rothschild, et al., 'The science of fake news' (2018) 359 *Science* 1094–1096.

8 S.H. Spencer, 'False Claims of Nationwide Lockdown for COVID19', *FactCheck.org*, 16 March 2020, https://www.factcheck.org/2020/03/false-claims-of-nationwide-lockdown-for-covid-19/.

9 W. Joe, 'Coronavirus: Indian man "died by suicide" after becoming convinced he was infected', *The Telegraph*, 12 February 2020, https://www.telegraph.co.uk/global-health/science-and-disease/coronavirus-indian-man-died-suicide-becoming-convinced-infected/; and S. Busari and B. Adebayo, 'Nigeria records chloroquine poisoning after Trump endorses it for coronavirus treatment', *CNN*, 23 March 2020, https://www.cnn.com/2020/03/23/africa/chloroquine-trump-nigeria-intl/index.html.

10 T.A. Ghebreyesus, 'Speech at the Munich Security Conference', 15 February 2020, https://www.who.int/dg/speeches/detail/munich-security-conference; N. Vigdor, 'Man Fatally Poisons Himself While Self-Medicating for Coronavirus, Doctor Says', *New York Times*, 24 March 2020, https://www.nytimes.com/2020/03/24/us/chloroquine-poisoning-coronavirus.html.

'the biggest challenge fact-checkers have ever faced'.[11] Other commentators have even argued that the pandemic has a far greater reach than the virus itself[12] or that it is shaping up to be a mis- and disinformation problem of greater proportion than even the meddling that marked the 2016 US presidential election and the Brexit referendum in the UK.[13]

The 'infodemic' hence deserves the attention of decision-makers, commentators, including academics, and the public at large. The aim of this chapter is to critically analyse, from the perspective of the functioning of a democracy, the early efforts to combat mis- and disinformation in the context of scientific uncertainty, focusing on the ongoing case of the COVID-19 'infodemic'. The chapter is largely based on the information from the media and public discourse. It first outlines the development of the problem, sketching its political, cybersecurity and (public) health dimensions, also outlining some of its consequences for democracy (Section 2). The chapter then provides an overview and evaluates the relevant initiatives assumed by the WHO, the main social media platforms and, eventually, the EU to tackle mis- and disinformation (Section 3). Next, the chapter examines some of the informational challenges associated with the spread of falsehood surrounding the pandemic, e.g. its novelty, and the scarcity and the (still) unverified nature of much of the information concerning COVID-19 (Section 4). Although at the time of writing (April 2020) the crisis is still ongoing, Section 5 takes stock of and offers a few preliminary suggestions as to how the 'infodemic' should be dealt with, while maintaining the democracy standards to which Europe has always adhered to. In particular, it is argued that, with regard to fact-checking, *inter alia*, striving for efficiency should not trump the respect for fundamental rights and freedoms, for scientific and ethical plurality. Thus, other tools may need to employed, in particular open-science and data-sharing initiatives.

2. OUTLINING THE PROBLEM

The COVID-19 'infodemic' has touched upon a wide array of topics, ranging from politics, cybersecurity to – perhaps most importantly – individual and public health.

11 E. Suárez, 'How fact-checkers are fighting coronavirus misinformation worldwide', *Reuters Institute*, 31 March 2020, https://reutersinstitute.politics.ox.ac.uk/risj-review/how-fact-checkers-are-fighting-coronavirus-misinformation-worldwide.

12 apolitical, 'Coronavirus: How governments can tackle the "infodemic"', 24 March 2020, https://apolitical.co/en/solution_article/coronavirus-how-governments-can-tackle-the-infodemic.

13 M. Vella, 'Big Tech has exactly one job to do in a pandemic', *Quartz,* 26 March 2020, https://qz.com/1825450/why-pandemic-misinformation-is-so-hard-to-for-big-tech-to-tackle/.

First and foremost, medical mis-, disinformation and related unverifiable content pertaining to the COVID-19 pandemic are being propagated at an alarming rate on social media platforms.[14] The pandemic is particularly vulnerable to media manipulation as scientists and decision-makers are operating in an unchartered territory in which uncertainty, confusion and political anxiety reign, and in which an array of misinformation, disinformation and flawed amateur analysis fills in the void.[15] To date, false or unverified claims about COVID-19 are proliferating on social media platforms, in the form of unsubstantiated information about the source and timeline of the virus, the symptoms and effects thereof, the situation in hospitals, testing practices, etc. There have also been multiple false claims about cures, treatments and prevention methods – e.g. colloidal silver, vitamins and essential oils or that drinking excessive amounts of water could ward off the disease;[16] there too have been unfounded posts warning about the use of anti-inflammatory drugs, overhyping the effectiveness of the treatment hydroxychloroquine.[17] Amongst these claims, mis- and disinformation regarding the launch and the effectiveness of a miraculous vaccine, the source of the fatal illness and who should wear protective masks have been the largest trends. In response, for example, BuzzFeed maintains a list of debunked coronavirus claims relating to its origin, potential treatments and faked government communications about it.[18] In recent research, it was reported that misleading or false claims about the actions or policies of public authorities, including governments and international bodies like the WHO, are in the single largest category of claims identified, appearing in 39 per cent of the relevant sample.[19]

Second, the 'infodemic' is a cybersecurity problem as it involves attacks on cognitive infrastructure, on people themselves, and on systems of information and beliefs.[20] Cyberattacks come in various forms, from disinformation

---

14 R. Kouzy, J. Abi Jaoude, A. Kraitem et al., 'Coronavirus Goes Viral: Quantifying the COVID-19 Misinformation Epidemic on Twitter', (2020) 12(3) *Cureus* e7255, doi:10.7759/cureus.7255.

15 C. Warzel, 'What We Pretend to Know About the Coronavirus Could Kill Us', *New York Times,* 3 April 2020, https://www.nytimes.com/2020/04/03/opinion/sunday/coronavirus-fake-news.html.

16 Vella, *supra* note 13.

17 E. Hannon, 'Twitter, Facebook Delete World Leaders' Misleading Coronavirus Posts. Could Trump Be Next?', *Slate,* 31 March 2020, https://slate.com/news-and-politics/2020/03/twitter-facebook-delete-brazil-bolsonaro-maduro-misleading-coronavirus-posts.html.

18 J. Lytvynenko, 'Here Are Some Of The Coronavirus Hoaxes That Spread In The First Few Weeks', *BuzzFeed,* 24 January 2020, https://www.buzzfeednews.com/article/janelytvynenko/coronavirus-disinformation-spread.

19 J.S. Brennen, F. Simon, P.N. Howard and R.K. Nielsen, 'Types, sources, and claims of COVID-19 misinformation', *Reuters Institute*, 7 April 2020, https://reutersinstitute.politics.ox.ac.uk/types-sources-and-claims-covid-19-misinformation.

20 J. Morgan and R. DiResta, 'Information Operations are a Cybersecurity Problem: Toward a New Strategic Paradigm to Combat Disinformation', *Just Security,* 10 July 2018,

campaigns to hostile operations on critical infrastructure. In the case of the 'infodemic', fake news has viralised fear and prompted confusion, which in effect have brought forward the vulnerabilities of a physically and communicatively connected world.[21] The world is currently experiencing the largest range of attacks which exploit a single theme for years, possibly ever.[22]

Third, the 'infodemic' is a highly political problem as mis- and disinformation have been increasingly designed to, both implicitly and explicitly, fuel divisions in European countries, whether this concerns identity, or societal or political rifts among EU Member States.[23] For example, China has become the leading country in pandemic disinformation in Europe[24] and Russian state media have allegedly engaged in disinformation campaigns. They have allegedly used malicious reporting in an attempt to create panic – e.g. by framing alternative narratives concerning the origin of the virus (e.g. that COVID-19 is a US biological weapon), the containment strategies and the efforts to treat – and to sow distrust amongst western nations and weaken trust in European health care systems[25] (e.g. that European democracies are not effective in combating the pandemic). More broadly, these campaigns seem to have been used in an attempt to undermine faith in the unity and effectiveness of the EU, while portraying Russia and China as the new 'saviours' of European nations,[26] further undermining the climate of debate and trust in critical health institutions.[27] Similar disinformation efforts are also allegedly

---

https://www.justsecurity.org/59152/information-operations-cybersecurity-problem-strategic-paradigm-combat-disinformation/.

21 C. Colomina, 'Coronavirus: Infodemics and disinformation', *Barcelona Centre for International Affairs,* March 2020, https://www.cidob.org/en/publications/publication_series/opinion/seguridad_y_politica_mundial/coronavirus_infodemics_and_disinformation.

22 A. Scroxton, 'Coronavirus now possibly largest-ever cyber security threat', *ComputerWeekly.com*, 18 March 2020, https://www.computerweekly.com/news/252480238/Coronavirus-now-possibly-largest-ever-cyber-security-threat.

23 EU Disinfo Lab, 'Covid-19 Disinformation: Narratives, Trends, and Strategies in Europe', 2 April 2020, https://www.disinfo.eu/publications/covid-19-disinformation-narratives-trends-and-strategies-in-europe.

24 J. Dempsey, 'Judy Asks: Is the Coronavirus Breeding Disinformation Across Europe?', *Carnegie Europe,* 9 April 2020, https://carnegieeurope.eu/strategiceurope/81508; J. Kao and M. Shuang, 'How China Built a Twitter Propaganda Machine Then Let It Loose on Coronavirus', *ProPublica,* 26 March 2020, https://www.propublica.org/article/how-china-built-a-twitter-propaganda-machine-then-let-it-loose-on-coronavirus.

25 EUvsDisinfo, 'EEAS Special Report: Disinformation on the Coronavirus – Short Assessment of the Information Environment', 19 March 2020, https://euvsdisinfo.eu/eeas-special-report-disinformation-on-the-coronavirus-short-assessment-of-the-information-environment/.

26 M.G. Sirotniková, 'Democracy Digest: Slovakia's Infections "Infodemic"', *Reporting Democracy,* 3 April 2020, https://balkaninsight.com/2020/04/03/democracy-digest-slovakias-infectious-infodemic/.

27 Dempsey, *supra* note 24.

coming out of Iran,[28] whereas in the US, a number of politicians – including the President – have cast doubt over established scientific consensus on vaccinations,[29] amplified health-related conspiracy theories and attempted to play down the severity of the pandemic.

At the same time, spreading misinformation about COVID-19 and the pandemic has become part of a polarised political narrative and of manipulation campaigns that may be state controlled. Moreover, some countries have used the misinformation narrative as justification for introducing disproportionate restrictions on fundamental rights and freedoms, e.g. Slovakia,[30] Hungary,[31] Russia,[32] Azerbaijan,[33] Romania,[34] Armenia[35] and Bosnia and Herzegovina.[36] The outbreak of COVID-19 unceasingly tests the capacity of the existing fact-checking systems to crack down on falsehood during a global emergency that is increasingly politicised.[37]

As a result, unreliable information or unverifiable data are spreading at unprecedented speed,[38] which, in the middle of a public health emergency, can create an environment of heightened uncertainty, fuel anxiety and racism (both in person and online),[39] prompt people to make bad choices

---

28 Associated Press, 'Iran Leader Refuses US Help, Citing Virus Conspiracy Theory', *VOA News*, 26 March 2020, https://www.voanews.com/science-health/coronavirus-outbreak/iran-leader-refuses-us-help-citing-virus-conspiracy-theory-0.

29 A. Allen, 'How the anti-vaccine movement crept into the GOP mainstream', *Politico*, 27 May 2019, https://www.politico.com/story/2019/05/27/anti-vaccine-republican-mainstream-1344955.

30 Sirotnikova, *supra* note 26.

31 Euronews & AP, 'Hungary's Viktor Orban handed sweeping new powers with COVID-19 law', 31 March 2020, https://www.euronews.com/2020/03/30/blank-cheque-hungary-expected-to-pass-controversial-covid-19-law.

32 J. Mankoff, 'Russia's Response to Covid-19', *Centre for Strategic & International Studies*, 10 April 2020, https://www.csis.org/analysis/russias-response-covid-19.

33 RadioFreeEurope/RadioLiberty, 'HRW Says Azerbaijan Abuses COVID-19 Restrictions To Crack Down On Critics', 16 April 2020, https://www.rferl.org/a/hrw-azerbaijan-abuses-covid-19-restrictions-to-crack-down-on-critics/30559657.html.

34 Romania Insider, 'Coronavirus in Romania: Authorities increase penalties for those who don't respect Covid-19 restrictions', 29 March 2020, https://www.romania-insider.com/coronavirus-romania-higher-sanctions.

35 Human Rights Watch, 'Armenia: Law Restricts Privacy Amid COVID-19 Fight', 3 April 2020, https://www.hrw.org/news/2020/04/03/armenia-law-restricts-privacy-amid-covid-19-fight.

36 Council of Europe, 'Press freedom must not be undermined by measures to counter disinformation about COVID-19', https://www.coe.int/en/web/commissioner/-/press-freedom-must-not-be-undermined-by-measures-to-counter-disinformation-about-covid-19.

37 G.M. Leung and K. Leung, 'Crowdsourcing data to mitigate epidemics', (2020) 2(4) *The Lancet* e201, https://www.thelancet.com/journals/landig/article/PIIS2589-7500(20)30055-8/fulltext.

38 Lytvynenko, *supra* note 18.

39 A. Kaplan, 'TikTok is hosting videos spreading misinformation about the coronavirus, despite the platform's new anti-misinformation policy', *Media Matters for America*,

(both in private and public life) and, in effect, hamper all efforts to tackle the pandemic.[40] However, mis- and disinformation disproportionally affects individuals with less access to information channels, who are thus more likely to ignore government health warnings.

All these factors together create the ideal conditions for, *inter alia*, distrust, bad-faith interpretations, political manipulation, fear, panic and anxiety, and diminishes the collective ability to find the best available information at the time. In turn, this brings to the fore profound negative ramifications not only for the health of individuals, but also for public health as well as, more broadly, for the functioning, and safeguarding, of a democracy. Given that the pandemic has, at the same time, become an information crisis, national governments, international and supranational organisations, and the largest social media platforms have been struggling to control the narrative about the origin of the virus, as well as the best way to curb it. This is a particularly challenging task due to its scale, i.e. roughly one in three people across the US, Spain, Germany, the UK, Argentina and South Korea claimed they had already seen false or misleading information on social media platforms linked to the coronavirus.[41] In addition, in a recent study about the spread of misinformation, it was revealed that information from both reliable and unreliable sources propagate in similar patterns.[42] All in all, assessing the impact of mis- and disinformation in the context of the COVID-19 pandemic is complicated, and once it is politicised it can also be overstated or understated.[43]

3. FIRST RESPONSES TO THE PROBLEM

3.1. INTERNATIONAL LEVEL: THE WORLD HEALTH ORGANIZATION

Along with other international organisations, national governments and social media platforms, the WHO has taken a series of initiatives to stop

28 January 2020, https://www.mediamatters.org/fake-news/tiktok-hosting-videos-spreading-misinformation-about-coronavirus-despite-platforms-new.

40 Y. Mejova and K. Kalimeri, 'Advertisers Jump on Coronavirus Bandwagon: Politics, News, and Business', *ISI Foundation*, 2 March 2020, https://arxiv.org/pdf/2003.00923.pdf.

41 M. Scott, 'One-third of people have seen misleading info on COVID-19 on social media: report', *Politico*, 15 April 2020, https://www.politico.eu/article/one-third-of-people-have-seen-misleading-info-on-covid-19-on-social-media-report/.

42 M. Cinelli, W. Quattrociocchi, A. Galeazzi, C.M. Valensise, E. Brugnoli, A.L. Schmidt, P. Zola, F. Zollo and A. Scala, 'The COVID-19 Social Media Infodemic', *Cornell University*, 10 March 2020, https://arxiv.org/abs/2003.05004.

43 J. Donovan, 'Here's how social media can combat the coronavirus "infodemic"', *MIT Technology Review*, 17 March 2020, https://www.technologyreview.com/2020/03/17/905279/facebook-twitter-social-media-infodemic-misinformation/.

the spread of falsehood concerning COVID-19[44] and has been particularly proactive in tackling the related 'infodemic'.[45] Current efforts to counter mis- and disinformation focus mainly on technological solutions (such as filtering software, artificial intelligence or modified algorithms aimed primarily at social media platforms) and tighter institutional oversight. First, the WHO has established the Information Network for Epidemics (EPI-WIN) that aims to ensure the veracity of the official information conveyed to the public.[46] This pilot programme brings together technical and social media teams working closely to disseminate and amplify the evidence-based information about COVID-19, and to track and respond to misinformation, myths and rumours.[47] The teams are currently developing an 'infodemic' response framework that includes reviewing and verifying evidence, interpreting and explaining the science to different audiences, as well as providing advice for action and recommending the reliable channels for information distribution.

The WHO has also defined a plan for Risk Communication and Community Engagement (RCCE) about COVID-19, which divides countries into the three categories, i.e. countries without any cases, countries with one or more cases, and countries with ongoing COVID-19 transmission.[48] Its technical risk communication and social media teams have also created an SOS Alert on COVID-19 for the six official United Nations (UN) languages. The WHO is also working with social media platforms and search engine companies to track the spread of specific rumours and to ensure that WHO content is displayed at the top of searches for terms related to the virus.[49] The WHO, numerous scientific journals and state health care organisations are regularly posting guidance across such platforms. In parallel, the United Nations Educational, Scientific, and Cultural Organization (UNESCO) has also created a 'resource centre' of selected responses to COVID-19. It includes a collection

44 WHO, 'Coronavirus disease (COVID-19) advice for the public: Myth busters', 2020, https://www.who.int/emergencies/diseases/novel-coronavirus-2019/advice-for-public/myth-busters.

45 United Nations, 'UN health agency warns against coronavirus COVID-19 criminal scams', 29 February 2020, https://news.un.org/en/story/2020/02/1058381.

46 https://www.who.int/teams/risk-communication.

47 W. Vota, 'Today: Help WHO Develop COVID-19 Infodemic Response Framework', *ICTworks*, 7 April 2020, https://www.ictworks.org/covid19-infodemic-response-framework/#.XpAtncgzbIU.

48 A. Vaezi and S.H. Javanmard, 'Infodemic and risk communication in the era of CoV-19', (2020) 9(10) *Advanced Biomedical Research*, http://www.advbiores.net/article.asp?issn=2277-9175;year=2020;volume=9;issue=1;spage=10;epage=10;aulast=Vaezi.

49 C. Newton, 'Google has been unusually proactive in fighting COVID-19 misinformation', *The Verge*, 11 March 2020, https://www.theverge.com/interface/2020/3/11/21173135/google-coronavirus-misinformation-youtube-covid-19-twitter-manipulated-media-bidenin.

of examples of actions related to communication and information made available for the purpose of sharing practices, identifying priorities, facilitating partnerships, providing advice and technical assistance to governments and relevant national stakeholders, and fostering North-South, South-South and triangular cooperation.[50]

The WHO has been working with Facebook to target specific populations and demographics with adverts that provide important health information.[51] The WHO has also cooperated with Google to boost the visibility of verified information and its efforts are directed toward screening relevant information in order to assist the community to respond in a logical and efficient way. Next, by partnering with all major media platforms such as Weibo, Twitter, Facebook, Instagram, LinkedIn, Pinterest and TikTok, the WHO has tried to take extensive measures to redefine online harms, to fight against them and to safeguard their users from phishing, conspiracy theories, malware and misinformation around COVID-19.[52]

3.2. INTERNATIONAL LEVEL: SOCIAL MEDIA PLATFORMS AND INDEPENDENT FACT-CHECKING ORGANISATIONS

Major social media platforms have too undertaken a series of initiatives on their own. The COVID-19 pandemic has led them to elevate authoritative content and remove medically-disproved claims. For example, Facebook, Microsoft, Twitter, LinkedIn, YouTube, Reddit and Google recently issued a joint statement,[53] promising that they were working together to combat misinformation, emphasising 'authoritative content' and sharing 'critical updates in coordination with government healthcare agencies'.[54]

In particular, Facebook is using the news feed function to direct users to the WHO website and websites of local health authorities.[55] Next, the Facebook

---

50 UNESCO, *Resource Center of Responses to COVID-19*, https://en.unesco.org/covid19/communicationinformationresponse/mediasupport.

51 Facebook, *Connecting people with resources. Facebook Health*, https://preventivehealth.facebook.com/.

52 K. Hao and T. Basu, 'The coronavirus is the first true social-media "infodemic"', *MIT Technology Review*, 12 February 2020, https://www.technologyreview.com/s/615184/the-coronavirus-is-the-first-true-social-media-infodemic/.

53 https://twitter.com/fbnewsroom/status/1239703497479614466.

54 N. Statt, 'Major tech platforms say they're "jointly combating fraud and misinformation" about COVID-19', *The Verge*, 16 March 2020, https://www.theverge.com/2020/3/16/21182726/coronaviruscovid-19-facebook-google-twitter-youtube-joint-effort-misinformation-fraud.

55 R.M. Merchant and N. Lurie, 'Social Media and Emergency Preparedness in Response to Novel Coronavirus', (2020) *JAMA*, doi:10.1001/jama.2020.4469.

Preventive Health tool provides individuals with vetted guidelines about preventive health recommendations (e.g. heart disease, cancer screening) and directs users to geotargeted locations where these services are available.[56] Facebook relies on third-party fact-checkers and health authorities flagging problematic content, and removes posts containing false claims. It also blocks or restricts hashtags that spread falsehood on its sister platform, Instagram, and bans content that could cause people harm, such as claims that discourage treatment or advise against taking appropriate precautions against the virus.[57] Posts and videos that shared conspiracy theories were clearly marked as falsehood, once they had been reviewed by fact-checkers. Facebook has also offered the WHO free advert space to point people towards accurate information on the virus.

However, Twitter and YouTube have taken less decisive positions. Twitter stated it had acted to protect against malicious behaviour, whereas YouTube stated it had removed videos claiming to prevent infections.[58] YouTube, meanwhile, is using its homepage to direct users to the WHO and other groups, for education and information, while working to remove videos suggesting alternative cures as soon as they go live. Google announced a new 24-hour incident response team dedicated to coronavirus and has committed to scrubbing falsehood from its search engine and YouTube while promoting accurate information from health agencies.[59]

The COVID-19 pandemic has been subjected to independent fact-checking too. The pace and size of the problem is unprecedented as, for example, the cybersecurity firm Check Point stated that more than 4,000 coronavirus-related websites that include words like 'corona' or 'covid' have been registered since the beginning of the year. Amongst the many initiatives undertaken, Full Fact – a UK-based fact-checking charity – has completed around 70 fact checks on 'popular myths, bad health advice and conspiracy theories' around COVID-19 and published a guide to fact-checking coronavirus claims for members of the general public.[60] Agence France Presse (AFP) has created its own verification hub and is working with the Trusted News Initiative, a shared

---

56 Facebook, *supra* note 51.

57 S. Frenkel, D. Alba and R. Zhong, 'Surge of Virus Misinformation Stumps Facebook and Twitter', *New York Time,* 8 March 2020, https://www.nytimes.com/2020/03/08/technology/coronavirus-misinformation-social-media.html.

58 B. Chakravorti, 'Social media companies are taking steps to tamp down coronavirus misinformation – but they can do more', *The Conversation,* 30 March 2020, https://theconversation.com/social-media-companies-are-taking-steps-to-tamp-down-coronavirus-misinformation-but-they-can-do-more-133335.

59 A. Hern, 'YouTube moves to limit spread of false coronavirus 5G theory', *The Guardian,* 5 April 2020, https://www.theguardian.com/world/2020/apr/05/youtube-to-suppress-content-spreading-coronavirus-5g-conspiracy-theory.

60 https://fullfact.org/.

alert system with partners from media organisations, whereas First Draft,[61] a project 'to fight mis- and disinformation online', launched a new online course on coronavirus in April 2020 with tools and advice on how to tackle disinformation.[62] Last but not least, an army of at least 48 fact-checking organisations from 30 countries in the form of a collaborative project, coordinated by the International Fact-Checking Network, has been working since early March 2020 to debunk falsehood about COVID-19.[63]

3.3. SUPRANATIONAL LEVEL: THE EUROPEAN UNION

The fight against mis- and disinformation, in the context of the COVID-19 pandemic and beyond, has been a joint effort of all European institutions. The EU institutions have repeatedly warned of the risks linked to disinformation attempts and scams.

The crisis has induced the EU to deploy its Rapid Alert System against disinformation for the first time, so as to counter disinformation efforts regarding the pandemic, enabling Member States to share knowledge on such disinformation efforts. The tool is a key element of the EU's 2018 Action Plan Against Disinformation and is meant to facilitate the exchange of information in the wake of fake news campaigns. It is based on open-source information and will also draw upon insights from academia, fact-checkers, social media platforms and some international partners.[64]

All EU Member States have designated a national contact point for the monitoring of fake news and have also agreed on a specific threshold for the system to be activated. The EU East StratCom[65] service and EUvsDisinfo[66] have been detecting disinformation campaigns and have produced an overview of currently trending false narratives.[67] The East StratCom Task Force reports on and analyses disinformation trends, and raises awareness about

---

61 https://firstdraftnews.org/.

62 J. Crowley, 'Tackling misinformation during Covid-19: a journalistic and ethical imperative', *Ethical Journalism Network,* 6 April 2020, https://ethicaljournalismnetwork.org/tackling-misinformation-during-covid-19-an-journalistic-and-ethical-imperative.

63 A. Abidi, 'Fact-checkers go into battle against coronavirus misinformation', *European Journalism Observatory*, 9 March 2020, https://en.ejo.ch/ethics-quality/fact-checkers-go-into-battle-against-coronavirus-misinformation.

64 EUvsDisinfo, 'Rapid Alert System: Strengthening Coordinated and Joint Responses to Disinformation', March 2019, https://eeas.europa.eu/sites/eeas/files/ras_factsheet_march_2019_0.pdf.

65 European Union External Action, 'Questions and Answers about the East StatCom Task Force', 5 December 2018, https://eeas.europa.eu/headquarters/headquarters-homepage/2116/-questions-and-answers-about-the-east-stratcom-task-force_en.

66 https://euvsdisinfo.eu/.

67 EUvsDisinfo, *supra* note 25.

manipulated news and narratives related to the pandemic. A joint EU page[68] about Europe's response to the virus has been set up in order to support factual and reliable information. It also busts the most common myths related to the pandemic. According to a report by the European External Action Service (EEAS) anti-disinformation taskforce EUvsDisinfo, some false claims come from actors close to the US 'alt' right, China and Russia. In these cases, the aim is political, to undermine the EU or to create political shifts.

Moreover, the European Commission is cooperating closely with social media platforms, encouraging them to promote authoritative sources, demote content that is verifiably false or misleading, and take down illegal content or content that could cause physical harm. Joseph Borrell, the Commission's Vice President and High Representative for Foreign Affairs and Security Policy, addressed the ongoing 'battle of narratives' on 23 March 2020, saying 'we must be aware there is a geopolitical component, including a struggle for influence through spinning and the "politics of generosity"'.[69] In a recent meeting with Věra Jourová, the Commission's Vice-President for Values and Transparency, these platforms assured her that they have started to actively promote coronavirus information coming from authoritative sources and have also pledged to demote or remove related forbidden or harmful content.[70]

3.4. DATA-SHARING INITIATIVES

During public health crises, such as outbreaks of disease, rapid data sharing may allow for a better understanding of the origins and spread of the infection, and can serve as a basis for effective prevention, treatment and care. The capacity of information and communications technologies (ICT) to allow for low-cost dissemination and collaboration of data has led to the establishment of a multitude of repositories. At least two types thereof can be observed: first, the data that are being processed concern statistics about the spread of the virus; second, these data concern research data and scientific publications (e.g. the genome of the virus) or open-source designs for the production of critical medical equipment (e.g. ventilators or face shields). Most of these data collection activities are coordinated by international

---

68 European Commission, *Fighting disinformation*, https://ec.europa.eu/info/live-work-travel-eu/health/coronavirus-response/fighting-disinformation_en.

69 J. Borell, 'EU HRVP Josep Borrell: The Coronavirus pandemic and the new world it is creating', *Delegation of the European Union to China*, 24 March 2020, https://eeas.europa.eu/delegations/china/76401/eu-hrvp-josep-borrell-coronavirus-pandemic-and-new-world-it-creating_en.

70 S. Stolton, 'Digital Brief: Europe's COVID-19 App Attack', *EURACTIV.com*, 2 April 2020, https://www.euractiv.com/section/digital/news/digital-brief-europes-covid-19-app-attack/.

organisations such as the WHO and the European Centre for Disease Prevention and Control (ECDC), an agency of the EU, and concern daily status reports on new cases. At the same time, an increasing number of bottom-up, open-data initiatives,[71] such as the Johns Hopkins University's COVID-19 Resource Center[72] are engaging in an increasing number of pandemic-related activities.

To complement these efforts, many open-source projects have surfaced,[73] facilitating access to research data, scientific publications and blueprints for the production of critical medical equipment. For instance, health authorities, universities and clinical laboratories are releasing genomic data from COVID-19 specimens at unprecedented speed. Major publishers, including Elsevier, Springer, Wiley, Emerald or Oxford University Press, have committed to making all of their COVID-19-related publications, and the available data supporting them, immediately accessible in public repositories.[74] In parallel, researchers have also been sharing new findings about the genomic profile of the virus through open-source publications and preprint sites such as bioRxiv[75] and ChinaXiv.[76] Open-source analytics tools for studying the COVID-19 outbreak have contributed to the immediate sharing of collective intelligence about the virus and the generation of bottom-up insights that inform decision-making in a collaborative and accessible manner, and have even helped to address the shortage of testing equipment and ventilators.

Data sharing can bring to the fore benefits such as accessibility of information, open standards that enable all stakeholders to contribute and rapid prototypes that can lead to rapid discoveries. Such initiatives can also help individuals exercise their freedoms – without necessarily involving data intermediaries – and become shapers of an expanding data ecosystem. However, there is a need to streamline and coordinate the main open-source activities of the same type so as to unlock the public interest value of the data collected and harness their potential so as to accelerate international action to fight the pandemic.

---

71 N.V. Patel, 'The best, and the worst, of the coronavirus dashboards', *MIT Technology Review*, 6 March 2020, https://www.technologyreview.com/2020/03/06/905436/best-worst-coronavirus-dashboards/.

72 https://coronavirus.jhu.edu.

73 T. Wu, X. Ge, G. Yu and E. Hu, 'Open-source analytics tools for studying the COVID-19 coronavirus outbreak', (2020) *medRxiv*, https://www.medrxiv.org/content/10.1101/2020.02.25.20027433v2.

74 Welcome, 'Publishers make coronavirus (COVID-19) content freely available and reusable', Press release, 16 March 2020, https://wellcome.ac.uk/press-release/publishers-make-coronavirus-covid-19-content-freely-available-and-reusable.

75 https://www.biorxiv.org/.

76 http://chinaxiv.org/.

Furthermore, most of the challenges in establishing a sustainable open-data ecosystem centre on data interoperability, their quality and integrity, that are necessary for the exploitation of their value and for the effective combination of data from different sources. Special attention then needs to be paid to whether (some of) these data are personal or breach the privacy of individuals and if that is the case, to introduce the necessary privacy and data protection safeguards.[77]

4. INFORMATIONAL CHALLENGES

Fighting mis- and disinformation in the context of COVID-19 appears to be a difficult technological and political exercise. First of all, the *novelty* of the coronavirus makes the challenge even greater, because viral speculation can easily overwhelm the limited and, largely, unverified information scientists and decision-makers do have about COVID-19.

Second, the WHO and national health agencies – like anybody else – operate with *incomplete information* at the moment.[78] Lack of reliable evidence on e.g. how many people have been infected, or how the pandemic is evolving constitutes a further challenge, given that the statistics collected so far may be unreliable.[79] Much of the data – from health statistics to economic indicators – are simply flawed or (still) evolving. In view of these structural limitations, the WHO and the ECDC have a difficult job in finding and interpreting incomplete, complex and sometimes contradictory evidence in real time.[80]

Given that every country's COVID-19 statistics (e.g. hospital admissions and deaths) are the result of a specific set of testing and accounting regimes, inconsistencies have been noted in the tracing and interpretation of the available data. For example, in the US, the surge in testing has exposed gaps in reporting, raising concerns about whether complete results and basic information about patients that test positive is communicated and classified

[77] G. González Fuster and M. Hildebrandt, 'Fundamental Rights More Important Than Ever', *VUB Today*, 9 April 2020, https://today.vub.be/en/article/fundamental-rights-more-important-than-ever.

[78] I. Lapowsky, 'Tech giants are navigating an "infodemic." Are they doing it right?', *protocol*, 1 April 2020, https://www.protocol.com/social-media-misinformation-infodemic-stanford.

[79] J.P.A. Ioannidis, 'A fiasco in the making? As the coronavirus pandemic takes hold, we are making decisions without reliable data', *STAT*, 17 March 2020, https://www.statnews.com/2020/03/17/a-fiasco-in-the-making-as-the-coronavirus-pandemic-takes-hold-we-are-making-decisions-without-reliable-data/.

[80] T. Haelle, 'Should Everyone Wear A Mask In Public? Maybe – But It's Complicated', *Forbes*, 1 April 2020, https://www.forbes.com/sites/tarahaelle/2020/04/01/should-everyone-wear-a-mask-in-public-maybe-but-its-complicated/#199d279fa02f.

properly. Countries also vary wildly in relation to how they report the numbers, which leads to publicised national tallies that are uneven and provide incomplete pictures that may not be all that comparable. The disparate character of these parallel data-collection procedures, the limited number of tests, and the variety of testing procedures and testing strategies followed may undermine trust in the official statistics, which in effect can further pave the way for the spread of additional falsehood. In an environment where even specialists struggle to find answers and the WHO is severely criticised,[81] anybody can offer their interpretation. Some experts are even referring to the data collection methods followed in the context of COVID-19 as a once-in-a-century evidence fiasco.[82]

Third, stakeholders operate with a plethora of *unverified information*, i.e. as the pandemic is ongoing, the veracity of information thereon has not yet been confirmed or rejected, but this information is already being used for making decisions. This uncertainty is exemplified by e.g. contradictory guidance and messaging from public authorities. The sheer avalanche of information regarding the most suitable types of protective equipment, the most effective containment measures and the possibilities of finding a successful antivirus vaccine complicate the efforts for deciding the truthful character of the claims made. The case in point concerns facial masks,[83] for which various guidance has been issued.[84] The shift in advice and the caveats that have come therewith not only confused people,[85] but also fuelled suspicions that public health guidelines were adopted out of pragmatic reasons rather than any scientific rationale.[86] Providing top-down guidance with such obvious contradictions may backfire exactly because the lack of trust is what not only fuels mis- and disinformation, but also undermines the work of fact-checkers that rely on the expertise of health authorities for flagging content

81 S. Buranyi, 'The WHO v coronavirus: why it can't handle the pandemic', *The Guardian*, 10 April 2020, https://www.theguardian.com/news/2020/apr/10/world-health-organization-who-v-coronavirus-why-it-cant-handle-pandemic.

82 Ioannidis, *supra* note 79.

83 C. Colizza, 'Why There's Still So Much Confusion About Wearing Masks to Combat the Coronavirus', *wirecutter*, 3 April 2020, https://thewirecutter.com/blog/coronavirus-masks-confusion/.

84 J. Geddie and J. Sipalan, 'To mask or not to mask: confusion spreads over coronavirus protection', *Reuters*, 1 January 2020, https://www.reuters.com/article/us-china-health-masks-safety/to-mask-or-not-to-mask-confusion-spreads-over-coronavirus-protection-idUSKBN1ZU0PH.

85 A. Lai-yam Chan, 'To wear or not to wear: WHO's confusing guidance on masks in the covid-19 pandemic', *thebmjopinion*, 11 March 2020, https://blogs.bmj.com/bmj/2020/03/11/whos-confusing-guidance-masks-covid-19-epidemic/.

86 C. Paun, A. Furlong, S. Mortkowitz and J. Mischke, 'Authorities' shifting advice on face masks adds to confusion in coronavirus crisis', *Politico*, 6 April 2020, https://www.politico.eu/article/eu-fissures-over-face-masks-coronavirus/.

to proactively remove falsehood. Uncertainty can lead to people to believe misinformation[87] as they are left confused about what they can do to help curb the spread of the virus. This can undermine the whole establishment of scientific advice given, and where there is an absence of verified facts, these gaps may be filled in by rumours and speculative claims.

In addition, preprint servers, namely openly accessible online repositories containing works or data associated with various scholarly papers that are not yet peer reviewed or accepted by traditional academic journals, have become a vital medium for the rapid sharing of scientific findings. This has been made clear by the speed with which researchers have developed new knowledge about the pandemic. However, this speed and openness has also contributed to the ability of low-quality preprints to derail public debate and feed conspiracy theories.[88]

Furthermore, this global outbreak has illustrated how social media posts can sometimes be magnified by engagement-hungry algorithms, and vetted by fact-checkers much later, if at all.[89] Algorithms cannot decipher complex human interactions whereas tweets, even if they are removed, can easily be edited and reposted to avoid algorithmic detection.[90] This was the case for certain videos that pushed dubious information about the origin of coronavirus and its means of transmission.[91] Facebook, for example, acknowledged that it incorrectly marked some posts linking to information and articles about COVID-19 as spam (though this was attributed to a software bug rather than artificial intelligence used specifically for the virus).[92] However, no social media platform has a transparent blocking policy founded on solid fact-checking. In fact, several scholars have stated that attributing falsehood without sufficient evidence, or with a restricted lens, can cause

87 M. De Witte, 'People's uncertainty about the novel coronavirus can lead them to believe misinformation, says Stanford scholar', *Stanford News*, 16 March 2020, https://news.stanford.edu/2020/03/16/fake-news-coronavirus-appealing-avoid/.

88 M. Heimstädt, 'Between fast science and fake news: Preprint servers are political', *London School of Economics*, 3 April 2020, https://blogs.lse.ac.uk/impactofsocialsciences/2020/04/03/between-fast-science-and-fake-news-preprint-servers-are-political/.

89 C. Newton, 'Misinformation about the coronavirus is threatening to overwhelm tech platforms', *The Verge*, 29 January 2020, https://www.theverge.com/interface/2020/1/29/21111849/coronavirus-misinformation-hoaxes-facebook-youtube-twitter-china.

90 T.R. Keller and R. Gillett, 'Why is it so hard to stop COVID-19 misinformation spreading on social media?', *The Conversation*, 13 April 2020, https://theconversation.com/why-is-it-so-hard-to-stop-covid-19-misinformation-spreading-on-social-media-134396.

91 Newton, *supra* note 89.

92 J. Peters, 'Facebook was marking legitimate news articles about the coronavirus as spam due to a software bug', *The Verge*, 17 March 2020, https://www.theverge.com/2020/3/17/21184445/facebook-marking-coronavirus-posts-spam-misinformation-covid-19.

more harm than good, and people should not be blinded by a blame game between countries and institutions.[93]

Moreover, the work of fact-checkers involves various selection biases due to the large volume of content to debunk and scarce resources. As a result, fact-checking a politician who says something extreme about COVID-19 is of lesser importance compared with a claim about a false cure.[94] Fact-checkers also have limited access to misinformation spreading in private channels; closed groups via messaging apps and offline conversations are out of scope.[95] Given that labelling something as 'false' requires expert verification, such annotated data that can train machine learning models on supervised learning solutions are missing in the case of COVID-19. Therefore, unsupervised, or semi-supervised solutions should be sought that may further accentuate the efforts for handling the imbalance in the distribution of misinformation versus legitimate information. As a result, fact-checking in such a dynamic environment where guidance and best practices are changing is a tricky exercise.

Fourth, misinformation is not just a problem of content; it is also one of *transmission*.[96] Although state officials can activate emergency alert systems across e.g. mobile phones and radio to reach the public, no such emergency protocols currently exist for social media.[97] Fifth and finally, the pandemic poses the risk of increased *cyberattacks* that are taking advantage of people's increased dependence on digital tools by exploiting the vulnerabilities in the security protections of medical facilities, homes and factories to attack hospitals' critical information systems.[98]

5. CONCLUDING REMARKS

Ensuring that the decision-makers and the public alike have the best possible (health) information during a public health emergency context is crucial for the functioning, and safeguarding, of a democracy and, at the same time,

93 G. Machado, 'Being cautious with attribution: Foreign interference & COVID-19 disinformation', *EU Disinfo Lab,* 10 April 2020, https://www.disinfo.eu/publications/being-cautious-with-attribution-foreign-interference-covid-19-disinformation.

94 Suárez, *supra* note 11.

95 Brennen, Simon, Howard and Nielsen, *supra* note 19.

96 Donovan, *supra* note 43.

97 J. Donovan, 'Here's how social media can combat the coronavirus "infodemic"', *Berkman Klein Center,* 17 March 2020, *https*://cyber.harvard.edu/story/2020-03/heres-how-social-media-can-combat-coronavirus-infodemic.

98 H. Fowler and C. Duncan, 'Hackers made their own coronavirus map to spread malware, feds warn', *The Miami Herald*, 13 March 2020, https://www.miamiherald.com/news/nation-world/national/article241171546.html.

constitutes an essential aspect of the ethics of public health in the context of emergencies, such as the COVID-19 pandemic. Mis- and/or disinformation, and similarly practices, run contrary to these principles. Such falsehood can lead to behaviour that increases disease transmission, countering the efforts to end the pandemic, and – at the same time – threatens a democracy. In this context, two aspects in particular merit further remarks, namely fact-checking and open-data practices.

The avalanche of falsehood in the media concerning the pandemic has triggered an immediate and a relatively well-coordinated reaction by the EU, the WHO and social media platforms alike. One of the most notable elements in their response so far is the formation of partnerships with international organisations and national governments, and the greater use of artificial intelligence and machine learning systems for content moderation.[99] Their responses are mostly focused on demoting or removing falsehood, but also on providing authoritative information about COVID-19. It also seems that the EU's approach is to allow social media platform operators to self-regulate and take down harmful content within a reasonable timeframe.

However, the outsourcing of content moderation to automated algorithms may not fit well with the scientific uncertainties about the origin, spread, containment and treatment of the virus. Given the uncertainty surrounding any ongoing public health crisis, it is extremely difficult to filter all information released on the topic and decide how truthful it is in a timely and credible manner. Such filtering that is not based on verifiable scientific evidence and does not acknowledge relevant uncertainties could undermine the legitimacy and credibility of democratic institutions that are, in principle, built on evidence-based policies. In any case, removing falsehood cannot justify the restriction of the freedom of speech where individuals post opinions that may differ from official narratives.[100]

In fact, combating the spread of alternative scientific accounts or statistical interpretations may become a threat to democracy. The gradual centralisation of the provision of authoritative scientific advice runs the risk of marginalising alternative interpretations of the available scientific data, as well as of the relevant uncertainties, and may lead to a situation where even scientific disagreements may be seen as possible sources of falsehood. Diverse viewpoints co-create pluralistic communities and information ecosystems. As a case in point, the UK government's initial discussions about herd

---

99 Public Knowledge, *Tracking Report: Digital Platform Responses to Misinformation During the Pandemic*, https://www.publicknowledge.org/tracking-report-covid19-misinformation/#_ftn6.

100 D. Gilbert, 'These 30 Regimes Are Using Coronavirus to Repress Their Citizens', *Vice*, 9 April 2020, https://www.vice.com/en_us/article/dygbxk/these-30-regimes-are-using-coronavirus-to-repress-their-citizens.

immunity were quickly challenged on various social media platforms, especially after the release of Neil Ferguson's report,[101] compelling a change of direction leading to the lockdown.[102] Indeed, independent media safeguard the provision of reliable information and strengthen democratic discourse by bolstering trust in independent fact-checkers and counterbalance authoritarian reactions to open and informed debate, which is vital for the proper functioning of a democracy. Trust in governments, public health institutions and international organisations does not only depend on how quickly falsehood is fought, but also on the political willingness to acknowledge the relevant scientific uncertainties, the medical unknowns and the knowledge limitations, among others.

In a state of emergency, a proportionate and evidence-based response to vague or subjective content-moderation is needed. Such an approach should be accompanied by safeguards that protect the freedom of expression and the right of access to information (in particular, freedom of the press). In fact, appeal and due process mechanisms should be in place to allow users to substantiate their claims, but also assess the legality of the content removal measures in a transparent manner. Especially with regard to scientific information, it is important to safeguard the integrity of information as an essential part of the credibility of the scientific advice system, but also make explicit the imperfect and dynamic nature of the process to acquire new knowledge about this novel virus. Indeed, ensuring a free, independent and diverse media environment is crucial to the safeguarding of free communication of information and the functioning of a democratic polity, especially in the context of a public health emergency. This includes establishing an ethical, industry-accepted framework for 'red-team' methods[103] to identify vulnerabilities,[104] which will enable individuals to be proactive rather than endlessly reactive.

The current 'infodemic' also raises the question about the need for the development and adoption of some further, dynamic fact-checking methods, particularly surrounding the dissemination of falsehood that work at scale and in all languages. Given that the most powerful spreaders of misinformation have been politicians, celebrities or other public figures,[105]

---

101 D. Adam, 'Special report: The simulations driving the world's response to COVID-19', *Nature*, 2 April 2020, https://www.nature.com/articles/d41586-020-01003-6.

102 C. Frost, 'Reporting the pandemic ethically', *Ethical Journalism Network*, https://ethicaljournalismnetwork.org/reporting-the-pandemic-ethically.

103 Synopsys, *What is Red Teaming*, https://www.synopsys.com/glossary/what-is-red-teaming.html.

104 R. DiResta and M. Godwin, 'The Seven Step Program for Fighting Disinformation', *Just Security*, 28 February 2019, https://www.justsecurity.org/62718/step-program-fighting-disinformation/.

105 P. Howard, R.K. Nielsen, N. Newman and J.S. Brennan, 'The COVID-19 "infodemic": what does the misinformation landscape look like and how can we respond?', *Oxford Internet*

independent fact-checkers, independent news agencies, citizen reporting and open public discourse should be employed to ensure some form of informational distancing. In practice, there is a need to identify new technical and non-technical ways to prevent the dissemination of false scientific information that is, currently, mostly driven by algorithms and conducted with unprecedented scale and efficiency. Yet, technological means such as automated content recognition systems should not be used to enforce censorship. Special attention should be paid to enhancing science education and digital literacy programmes, and empowering individuals to act as information filters in an uncertain and ever-evolving information environment. Last but not least, as it may take months or years – and many other studies – before experts understand the full picture of COVID-19, the information landscape may change and new sources of authoritative evidence may emerge that will shift the boundaries of fact-checking.

At the same time, a comprehensive and even a legally binding code of ethics on responsible information dissemination in the context of pandemics, to which social media platforms and their users are beholden, needs to be adopted.[106] Such a code should entail specific provisions on how science-related information should be treated and filtered in the context of a public health emergency and on transparent safeguards against falsehood. This requires a collaborative approach with governments and international institutions as well as with journalists and media professionals to ensure fair and consistent enforcement.

The combating of the pandemic has also bolstered open data and, more broadly, open-science practices. Many initiatives to monitor and, eventually, prevent the spread of the disease have been based precisely on an ever-growing ecosystem of open science, i.e. bottom-up, open data shared through open-source platforms, including dashboards, information and resources of vital importance for decision-makers and citizens. This development indicates the potential of open-source technologies and data-sharing structures to efficiently address the pandemic. However, within the 'infodemic', open-science initiatives and international cooperation on data-sharing need to be strengthened so as to bolster, and – sometimes – restore the credibility of health-related information and the sources that produce it. As there is a pressing need for an open-analytics environment that allows stakeholders to analyse, interpret, and share COVID-19 data, data-sharing and common fact-checking initiatives, at least at the EU level, could address the lack of comparable data sets and pools, and considerable analytical obfuscation.

Institute, 15 April 2020, https://www.oii.ox.ac.uk/blog/the-covid-19-infodemic-what-does-the-misinformation-landscape-look-like-and-how-can-we-respond/.

106 TELLME, *Deliverables*, https://www.tellmeproject.eu/documents/deliverable.

It could prevent the spreading of fake news regarding this pandemic disease. Digital platforms should be encouraged to share more comprehensive, real-time insight on issues directly related to public health, public safety, and national security.

More broadly, a well-coordinated data-sharing structure, possibly established at WHO level, could facilitate the breaking of the chain of misinformation and restore the currently fragmented nature of knowledge production in the context of the pandemic. It might also strengthen the normative and bottom-up features of science advice mechanisms and, in effect, enrich decision-making structures by allowing open-source initiatives to flourish and even ground public health policy interventions.

In any case, striving for efficiency in combating a pandemic, whether it be this pandemic or any other in the future, must not trump the respect for fundamental rights and freedoms, and for scientific and ethical plurality.

CPSIA information can be obtained
at www.ICGtesting.com
Printed in the USA
LVHW101253130721
692519LV00004B/35

9 781780 689753